Crete

Hania
p62

Rethymno
p118

Iraklio
p162

Lasithi
p216

Andrea Schulte-Peevers, Trent Holden, Kate Morgan, Kevin Raub

PLAN YOUR TRIP

STORAGE JARS, PALACE OF KNOSSOS P178

JON DAVISON/LONELY PLANET ©

ON THE ROAD

Contents

DOLMADHES P51

UNDERSTAND

SURVIVAL GUIDE

SPECIAL FEATURES

Welcome to Crete

Crete is a tapestry of splendid beaches, ancient treasures and landscapes, weaving in vibrant cities and dreamy villages, where locals share their traditions, wonderful cuisine and generous spirit.

Bewitching Scenery

There's something undeniably artistic in the way the Cretan landscape unfolds, from the sun-drenched beaches in the north to the rugged canyons spilling out at the cove-carved and cliff-lined southern coast. In between, valleys cradle moody villages, and round-shouldered hills are the overture to often snow-dabbed mountains. Take it all in on a driving tour, trek through Europe's longest gorge or hike to the cave where Zeus was born. Leave time to plant your footprints on a sandy beach or swim in crystalline waters.

Rich Historical Tapestry

Crete's natural beauty is equalled only by the richness of its history. The island is the birthplace of the first advanced society on European soil, the Minoans, who ruled some 4000 years ago. You'll find evocative vestiges all over, most famously at the Palace of Knossos. At the crossroads of three continents, Crete has been coveted and occupied by consecutive invaders. History imbues Hania and Rethymno, where labyrinthine lanes are lorded over by mighty fortresses, and where gorgeously restored Renaissance mansions rub rafters with mosques and Turkish bathhouses. The Byzantine influence stands in magnificent frescoed chapels, churches and monasteries.

Bountiful Cuisine

If you're a foodie, you will be in heaven in Crete, where 'locavore' is not a trend but a way of life. Rural tavernas often produce their own meat, cheese, olive oil, raki and wine, and catch their own seafood. Follow a gourmet trail across the landscape and you'll delight in distinctive herbs and greens gathered from each hillside, cheeses made fresh with unique village- or household-specific recipes, and honey flavoured by mountain herbs. Pair your meal with excellent local wine, and cap it off with a fiery shot of raki.

Village Culture

Untouched by mass tourism, villages are the backbone of Cretan culture and identity – especially those tucked in the hills and mountains. The island's people still champion many of their unique customs, and time-honoured traditions remain a dynamic part of daily life. Look for musicians striking up a free-form jam on local instruments, such as the stringed *lyra* (lyre), or wedding celebrants weaving their traditional regional dances. Meeting regular folk gossiping in *kafeneia* (coffee houses), preparing their Easter feast, tending to their sheep or celebrating during the island's many festivals is what makes a visit to Crete so special.

Why I Love Crete

By Andrea Schulte-Peevers, Writer

Wits its mysterious tales of Zeus, the Minoans and rebellious monks, Crete first captured my imagination when I was just a wee kid. When I finally set foot on the island, it instantly captured my heart. I fell in love with its kind and generous people, the spellbinding scenery, from pink beaches to snow-smothered peaks, and the incredible food that's so closely tied to the soil and the seasons. Crete feels big and intimate at once, letting me slow down while energising me anew every single day. It's a love story that continues to evolve with each visit.

For more about our writers, see p320

Above: Seitan Limania (p82), Akrotiri Peninsula

Crete

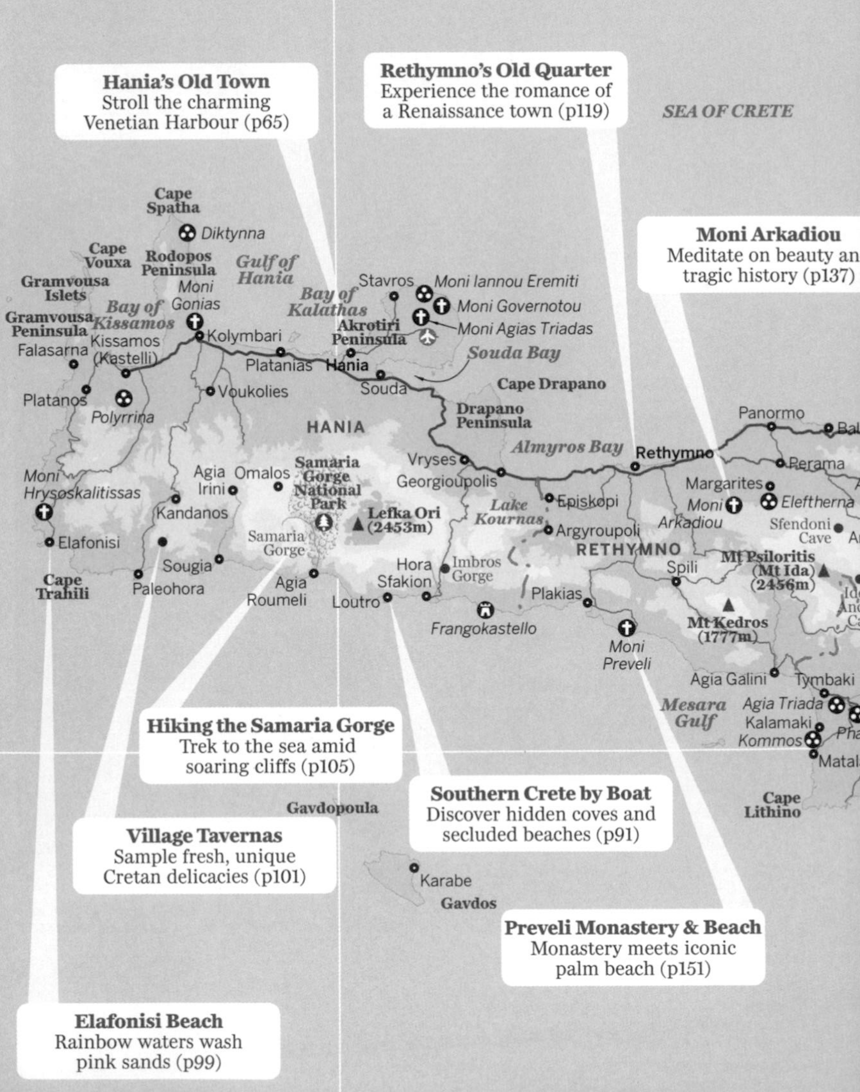

Hania's Old Town
Stroll the charming Venetian Harbour (p65)
Rethymno's Old Quarter
Experience the romance of a Renaissance town (p119)
SEA OF CRETE
Moni Arkadiou
Meditate on beauty and tragic history (p137)
Cape Spatha
Diktynna
Cape Vouxa
Rodopos Peninsula
Gulf of Hania
Gramvousa Islets
Moni Gonias
Bay of Kissamos
Bay of Kalathas
Stavros
Moni Iannou Eremiti
Moni Governotou
Moni Agias Triadas
Gramvousa Peninsula
Akrotiri Peninsula
Kissamos (Kastelli)
Kolymbari
Falasarna
Platanias
Hania
Souda Bay
Souda
Cape Drapano
Platanos
Polyrrina
Voukolies
HANIA
Drapano Peninsula
Panormo
Bali
Almyros Bay
Rethymno
Perama
Vryses
Samaria Gorge National Park
Agia Irini
Omalos
Georgioupolis
Margarites
Moni Hrysoskalitissas
Kandanos
Lefka Ori (2453m)
Lake Kournas
Episkopi
Moni Arkadiou
Eleftherna
Argyroupoli
Elafonisi
Samaria Gorge
Sfendoni Cave
RETHYMNO
Imbros Gorge
Hora Sfakion
Spili
Mt Psiloritis (Mt Ida) (2456m)
Sougia
Cape Trahili
Paleohora
Agia Roumeli
Loutro
Plakias
Frangokastello
Mt Kedros (1777m)
Moni Preveli
Agia Galini
Tymbaki
Mesara Gulf
Agia Triada
Kalamaki
Kommos
Matala
Cape Lithino
Hiking the Samaria Gorge
Trek to the sea amid soaring cliffs (p105)
Gavdopoula
Southern Crete by Boat
Discover hidden coves and secluded beaches (p91)
Village Tavernas
Sample fresh, unique Cretan delicacies (p101)
Karabe
Gavdos
Preveli Monastery & Beach
Monastery meets iconic palm beach (p151)
Elafonisi Beach
Rainbow waters wash pink sands (p99)
MEDITERRANEAN SEA
24° E

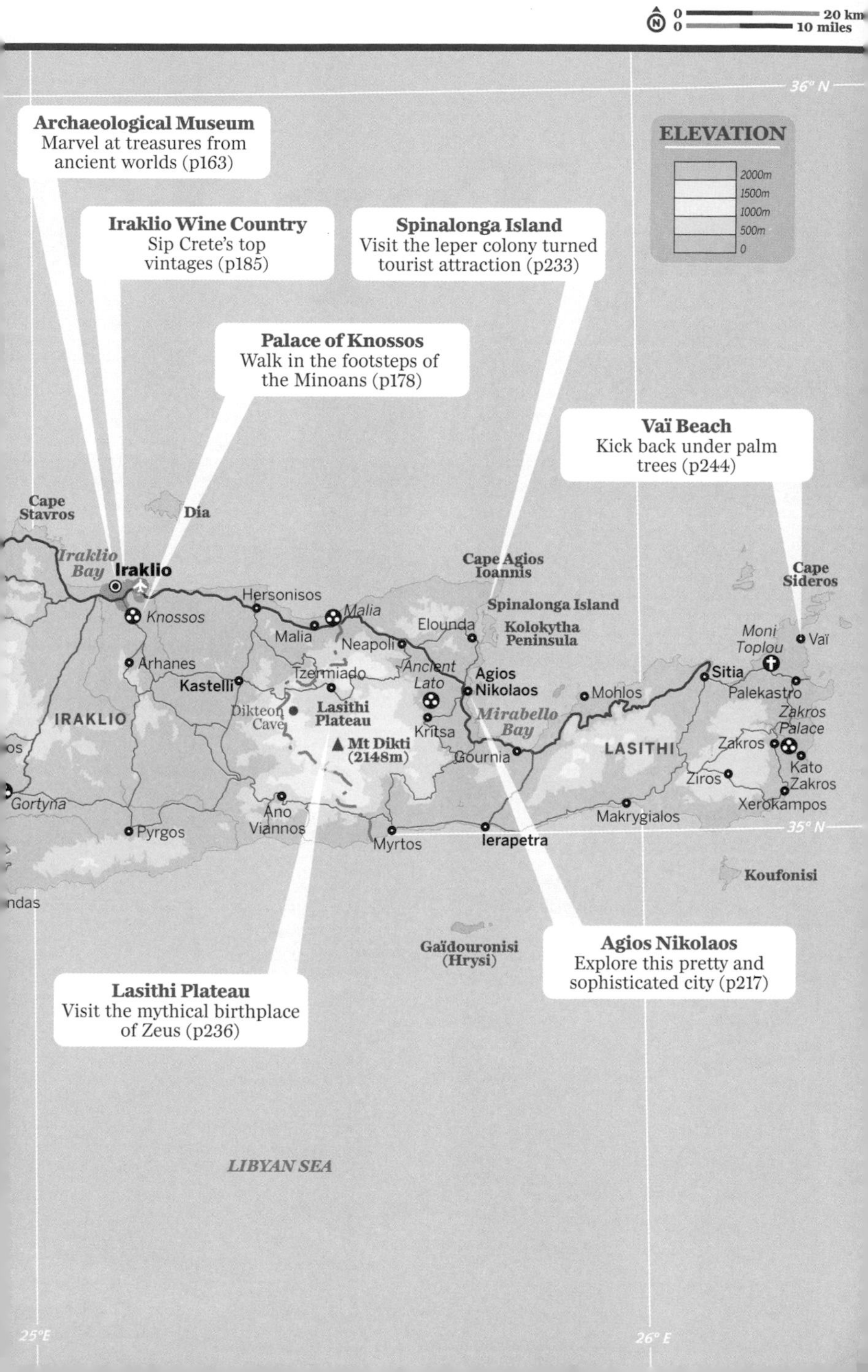

0 20 km
0 10 miles
36° N
ELEVATION
2000m
1500m
1000m
500m
0
Archaeological Museum
Marvel at treasures from ancient worlds (p163)
Iraklio Wine Country
Sip Crete's top vintages (p185)
Spinalonga Island
Visit the leper colony turned tourist attraction (p233)
Palace of Knossos
Walk in the footsteps of the Minoans (p178)
Vaï Beach
Kick back under palm trees (p244)
Cape Stavros
Dia
Iraklio Bay
Iraklio
Knossos
Hersonisos
Malia
Malia
Neapoli
Arhanes
Kastelli
Tzermiado
Dikteon Cave
Lasithi Plateau
Mt Dikti (2148m)
IRAKLIO
Gortyna
Pyrgos
Ano Viannos
Myrtos
Ierapetra
Cape Agios Ioannis
Spinalonga Island
Kolokytha Peninsula
Elounda
Ancient Lato
Agios Nikolaos
Kritsa
Mirabello Bay
Gournia
Mohlos
LASITHI
Makrygialos
Cape Sideros
Moni Toplou
Vaï
Sitia
Palekastro
Zakros Palace
Zakros
Kato Zakros
Ziros
Xerokampos
35° N
Koufonisi
Gaïdouronisi (Hrysi)
Agios Nikolaos
Explore this pretty and sophisticated city (p217)
Lasithi Plateau
Visit the mythical birthplace of Zeus (p236)
LIBYAN SEA
25°E
26° E

Crete's Top 15

1

Palace of Knossos

1 Rub shoulders with the ghosts of the Minoans, a Bronze Age people who attained an astonishingly high level of civilisation and ruled large parts of the Aegean from their capital in Knossos (p178) some 4000 years ago. Until the site's excavation in the early 20th century, an extraordinary wealth of frescoes, sculptures, jewellery, seals and other remnants lay buried under the Cretan soil. Despite a controversial partial reconstruction, Knossos remains one of the most important archaeological sites in the Mediterranean and is Crete's most-visited tourist attraction.

Rethymno's Old Quarter

2 Traffic fades to a quiet hum in the labyrinthine lanes of this historic old quarter (p119), with its charismatic Renaissance-era Venetian buildings sprinkled with exotic features from the Turkish period. Embark on an aimless wander and you'll find wonderful surprises: a romantic flower-filled courtyard, perhaps, or an idyllic plaza, a cafe in an Ottoman bathhouse or a Venetian mansion turned boutique hotel. Don't miss a spin around the massive fortress, and cap your old-quarter exploration with dinner in one of the many excellent restaurants.

CONSTANTINOS ILIOPOULOS/ALAMY STOCK PHOTO ©

2

JAN WLODARCZYK/ALAMY STOCK PHOTO ©

Agios Nikolaos

3 Agios Nikolaos (p217) is well established as one of the loveliest towns in Crete. The setting on the Gulf of Mirabello – the Venetians' 'beautiful view' – is a winner, and the town's pleasing layout around a small harbour and circular lake adds to the appeal. You can relax by day in the lakeside cafes and then enjoy the night-time scene, when an influx of visitors from nearby resorts mixes happily with modish young locals in the harbourside bars.

Spinalonga Island

4 One of Greece's most iconic sights, this one-time leper colony has shot to stardom, thanks to the bestselling romantic novel *The Island*, by British writer Victoria Hislop. The book was adapted as a Greek television series *(To Nisi)* that has won critical acclaim for its atmospheric take on Spinalonga's powerful history. You may have to share the experience with lots of fellow admirers, but Spinalonga (p233), with its ruins of Venetian fortifications and reconstructed buildings of the period described in the novel, is both moving and inspiring.

3

4

PECOLD/SHUTTERSTOCK ©

IMAGEBROKER/ALAMY STOCK PHOTO ©

raklio Wine Country

5 South of the urban sprawl of Iraklio lie iillsides quilted with olive groves and vineyards, and lotted with villages whose pride and joy is their lo-cal vintage. About 70% of Crete's excellent wine comes from the Iraklio Vine Country (p185). relatively relaxed and ld-world region, the wine country is based around he gateway villages of rhanes, also home to rumbling Minoan ruins, nd Dafne, which share wo dozen wineries be-ween them. The region ets particularly lively in he autumn, with the grape arvest.

Heraklion Archaeological Museum

6 A treasure trove spanning thousands of years, Iraklio's extraordinary museum (p163) opens a fascinating window onto the ancient world. Top billing goes to the world's largest and finest Minoan collection, and with its proudly renovated building and grounds, it's become a superbly curated and presented feast of priceless and unusual artefacts from other periods as well. A visit will deeply enrich your understanding of Knossos and the other famous archaeological sites on the island. If you see only one museum in Crete, make it this one.

Moni Preveli & Preveli Beach

7 Get high on the knock-out views from this 17th-century monastery (p151) in its lofty aerie above the Libyan Sea, then descend to Preveli Beach – its rare grove of palm trees makes it one of Crete's most celebrated sandy strips. There's fantastic swimming, but in peak season you won't be alone. The monastery itself has repeatedly entered the tomes of history, the last time during WWII, when the local abbot facilitated the evacuation of 5000 Allied soldiers trapped in Crete during the Nazi occupation.

Elafonisi Beach

8 It's the beach everyone promises to see while in Crete, though not everyone manages to fulfil the promise, hidden as it is deep in the wild southwest of the island, beyond the craggy mountains and little villages. Elafonisi (p99) is a long sandy stretch renowned for its sparkling, clear turquoise waters and pink-and-cream sands. It gets busy in high summer, but in autumn, when most visitors disappear, it is heavenly. Wade out to Elafonisi's tiny tidal island and feel the warm southern winds...bliss.

Lasithi Plateau & Dikteon Cave

9 Getting to the Lasithi Plateau (p236) can feel epic, as the main access routes climb relentlessly from sea level through ever-steepening bends on scenic roads. Lasithi bursts dramatically into view and you realise that the green expanse before you is more plain than plateau, surrounded as it is by soaring mountains. The drama continues at famous Dikteon Cave (p238), the mythical birthplace of Zeus and a cathedral-like space. Zeus may be long gone, but the Olympian spirit lingers on.

Hania's Old Town

10 You will be enthralled by Hania's old town (p65). At its romantic and cap-ivating Venetian harbour, pastel-coloured historic townhouses rim the waterfront promenade, where tourists and locals stroll, gossip and people-watch. The sea swirls between a peachy portside mosque, cream-stone lighthouse and the imposing Firkas Fortress. In the winding old streets radiating out from the quay, you'll find minarets, boutique hotels and some of the island's best dining options. The Splantzia quarter offers cool, leafy cafes and shops filled with handmade and hard-to-find traditional goods.

Hiking the Samaria Gorge

11 The gaping gorge of Samaria (p105), starting at Omalos and running down through an ancient riverbed to the Libyan Sea, is the most-trod canyon in Crete – and with good reason. The magnificent 16km trek presents you with varied wildlife, soaring birds of prey and a dazzling array of wildflowers in spring. It's a full day's walk (about six hours down), and you'll have to start early, but the scenery is worth it. To get more solitude, try lesser-known gorges such as Agia Irini, Imbros and Aradena, running roughly parallel to Samaria.

AN WLODARCZYK/ALAMY STOCK PHOTO ©

Vaï Beach

12 This remote beach (p244) in the far northeast is where Crete takes on the feel of the South Seas, with an exotic ribbon of white-gold sand backed by a deep forest of palm trees. Vaï means 'palm frond' in the local dialect and the palms are said to have sprouted from date stones cast off by Roman soldiers or pirates. Vaï is a popular place, but on the quieter edges of summer it's a pleasure; during busy times, just follow your nose to either end of the beach for less-crowded options.

Village Tavernas

13 A highlight of Cretan travel is the island's delicious and distinctive cuisine. Make time to stop at village tavernas, where you'll frequently find yourself presented with a wholesome feast at surprisingly reasonable prices, and with great pride. Don't be surprised if you're offered a complimentary sweet and raki (Cretan distilled spirit) at meal's end. One surefire spot for top Cretan treats is To Skolio (p101), in the hills near Paleohora, where local produce is crafted into inventive small dishes, and served with views of the Libyan Sea.

Southern Crete by Boat

14 This is for escapists, beach lovers and adventurers – and it's so easy! Large sections of southern Crete's mountainous coast are accessible only by boat (p40), and in season a regular ferry service allows you to reach remarkable sites, such as the glittering jewel of Loutro (pictured), tucked between secluded beaches and laid-back Sougia, with its friendly folk and fresh seafood. The beginning and end of the voyage – Paleohora and Hora Sfakion – are two of the most iconic (and affordable) towns in Crete, full of rugged individuals and live Cretan music.

Moni Arkadiou

15 Moni Arkadiou (p137) offers a particularly moving experience, combining beauty and tragedy. The 16th-century stone church and cloister, enclosed by stone walls on a rolling high plain, appear pastoral and lovely. But the monastery was also the site of one of Crete's great tragedies. In 1866 some 2000 Turkish soldiers surrounded hundreds of Cretan men, women and children here; rather than surrender, they set off their gunpowder, killing all but one small girl. The monastery remains a place of quiet and moving contemplation, and is particularly striking in soft evening light.

LEOKS/SHUTTERSTOCK ©

15

Need to Know

For more information, see Survival Guide (p289)

Currency
Euro (€)

Language
Greek

Visas
Generally not required for tourist stays up to 90 days (or at all for EU nationals). Some nationalities need a Schengen Visa – check with the Greek embassy or consulate.

Money
ATMs widely available in cities, towns and larger villages. Visa and MasterCard accepted in cities and tourist centres, rarely in villages.

Mobile Phones
Local SIM cards can be used in European and Australian phones. Most other phones can be set to roaming. US and Canadian phones need to have a dual- or tri-band system.

Time
Eastern European Time (GMT/UTC plus two hours)

When to Go

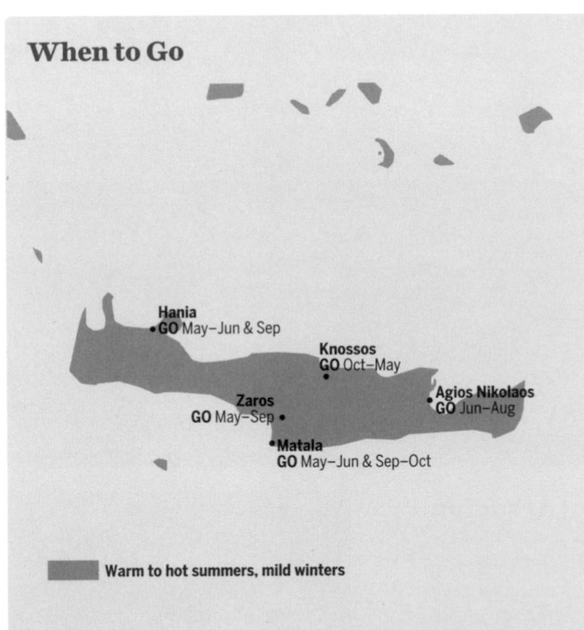

High Season (Jul & Aug)

- Queues at big sights, heavy traffic, busy beaches.
- Prices for lodgings at their peak.
- *Meltemi* winds can make sandy beaches unpleasant.
- Hot days, but balmy evenings and warm sea for swimming.

Shoulder (Apr–Jun & Sep–Oct)

- Best time for hiking and outdoor activities.
- Moderate temperatures, smaller crowds.
- Wildflowers in springtime, grape harvest in autumn.
- Lower rates and wide availability for lodgings.

Low Season (Nov–Mar)

- Sights, attractions and restaurants scale back their hours; beach resorts close.
- No crowds at major sights, some sights closed.
- Locals have the most time to sit and chat.
- Highest chance of rain.

Useful Websites

Cretan Beaches (www.cretanbeaches.com) Excellent site about beaches and more.

Crete Region (www.crete.gov.gr) Official government site.

Explore Crete (www.explorecrete.com) Good general travel site.

Interkriti (www.interkriti.org) Comprehensive guide to the island.

Lonely Planet (www.lonelyplanet.com/crete) Destination information, hotel bookings, traveller forum and more.

Visit Greece (www.visitgreece.gr) Greece's official tourism portal.

Important Numbers

To call any normal number in Greece, dial the full 10-digit number.

Greece country code	☎30
International access code	☎00
Ambulance	☎166
Police/ tourist police	☎100 / 171
Fire	☎199

Exchange Rates

Australia	A$1	€0.62
Canada	C$1	€0.66
Japan	¥100	€0.81
NZ	NZ$1	€0.58
UK	UK£1	€1.13
US	US$1	€0.89

For current exchange rates see www.xe.com.

Daily Costs

Budget: Less than €60

- Hostel, camping or simple room: €20–25
- Picnic or meal at basic taverna: €10–15
- Admission Heraklion Archaeological Museum: €10

Midrange: €60–150

- Apartment or double room in family hotel: €35–70
- Meal at nice taverna with wine: €25–30
- Hire car per day: €35
- Admission to Palace of Knossos & Heraklion Archaeological Museum: €16

Top End: More than €150

- Double room in boutique hotel or beach resort: from €120
- Meal in high-end tavernas and gourmet restaurants in prime locations: €35–70
- Activities like diving and boat hire: €80–150

Opening Hours

Opening hours vary throughout the year. The following are high-season opening hours.

Banks 8am–2.30pm Monday to Thursday, 8am–2pm Friday

Bars 8pm–late

Cafes 10am–midnight

Clubs 10pm–late

Post Offices 7.30am–3pm Monday to Friday (rural); 7.30am–8pm Monday to Friday, 7.30am–2pm Saturday (urban)

Restaurants 11am–4pm and 7–11pm

Shops 9am–2pm Monday to Saturday and 5.30–8.30pm or 9pm Tuesday, Thursday and Friday; all day in summer in resorts

Arriving in Crete

Nikos Kazantzakis International Airport (Iraklio) Buses serve the city centre, port and bus stations every 10 to 15 minutes between 6am and midnight (€1.20, or €2 if bought on board). Taxis into town cost a flat €15 (other destinations are metered).

Hania Airport Ioannis Daskalogiannis Buses serve central Hania between 5.30am and 11pm (€2.50, 30 minutes). Taxis cost €25.

Sitia Airport No airport bus; taxis cost €6 to €8.

Iraklio Ferry Port Walkable, 500m east of the old harbour. The main bus station is just opposite the main entrance to the port.

Hania Ferry Port Linked to town by bus (€2, or €2.50 if bought on board) and taxi (€10).

Kissamos Ferry Port In summer a bus (€1.50) meets ferries; taxis cost around €8.

Safe Travel

Crete is generally a safe, friendly and hospitable place. Still, as with anywhere, it pays to follow a few simple precautions.

- Keep track of your possessions in busy public places.
- Lock your car and hotel room, and put valuables in the room or hotel safe.
- Watch out for adulterated drinks made from cheap illegal imports, and drink spiking, especially at party resorts.
- File reports first with the tourist police, who have offices in the cities and popular tourist destinations.

For much more on **getting around**, see p298

First Time Crete

For more information, see Survival Guide (p289)

Checklist

- Ensure your passport is valid for at least six months after your arrival date.
- Make bookings for accommodation and travel, especially in high season.
- Check airline baggage restrictions, especially for regional flights.
- Inform your credit-card company of your travel plans.
- Organise travel insurance.
- Check if you'll be able to use your mobile (cell) phone.

What to Pack

- Hat, sunglasses, sunscreen
- Waterproof money belt
- Credit and debit cards
- Driving licence/ international driving licence
- Diving qualifications
- Spare phone for local SIM
- Mainland European power adapter
- Lock/padlock
- Seasickness remedies
- Mosquito repellent
- Lightweight raincoat
- Swimwear, snorkel and fins

Top Tips for Your Trip

- If at all possible, visit in the shoulder seasons – mid-May to June and September to October. The weather is less extreme and the crowds are slim.
- Be sure to visit a few out-of-the-way villages, where you can still find full-on, unselfconscious traditional culture. The best way to do this is to hire a car and explore. Stop for lunch, check out the local shops and test out your Greek.
- Visit at least one local *kafeneio* (coffee house), one seafood taverna on the waterfront, and one traditional live-music venue. This is where you'll experience Cretan culture at its most vibrant.

What to Wear

Crete is casual. Locals wear simple but respectfully covered-up clothes. Bring quick-drying tops and cool dresses. Bars or fashionable restaurants require more effort – the scene is stylish rather than dressy. Think tops and trousers rather than T-shirts and cut-offs. Don't wear swimsuits into shops and tavernas without a cover-up. Cretans will not go nude on beaches; you'll see some Europeans do it, but it pays to be respectful of locals and therefore discreet.

Sleeping

In high season it's essential to reserve, as hotels can be fully booked well in advance. Many hotels on the islands are closed during winter.

- **Apartment and villa rental** Ideal for space-cravers, families and self-caterers. Usually equipped with full kitchens.
- **Campgrounds** Found in the majority of regions and islands, and often include hot showers, communal kitchens, restaurants and swimming pools.
- **Domatia** The Greek equivalent of the British B&B, minus the breakfast. Often have a fridge and kettle.
- **Hotels** Run the gamut from simple family-run places with just a few rooms to full-service resorts with pools, water sports and restaurants.

Shopping

➡ Crete is famous for its local produce such as olive oil and thyme honey. You will typically find the best quality (and prices) at humble local shops in the villages, rather than at souvenir shops in the cities. Look beyond snazzy packaging with submerged twigs for big unmarked bottles, fresh from the farm.

➡ Although credit card use is slowly becoming more widespread, hard euros remain the preferred form of payment, especially in rural areas. Always carry some with you and plan to pay with bills and coins almost everywhere. Village ATMs sometimes run out of money on weekends.

➡ Making change can be quite a challenge for small-shop owners, so carry a stash of small bills and coins to pay for small purchases.

Bargaining

Gentle bargaining is acceptable in flea markets and other markets, but elsewhere you are expected to pay the stated price.

Tipping

➡ **Bellhops** Bellhops in hotels and stewards on ferries expect a small gratuity of €1 to €3.

➡ **Restaurants** Usually service is included, but a small tip is customary if service was good. Round up the bill or leave 10%.

➡ **Taxis** Round up the fare by a couple of euros. There's a small fee for handling bags; this is an official charge, not a tip.

LANGUAGE

Tourism is big business in Crete and, being good businesspeople, many Cretans have learned the tools of the trade – English. In cities and popular resorts, you can get by with less than a smattering of Greek; in smaller villages and out-of-the-way spots, a few phrases in Greek will go a long way. Wherever you are, Cretans will hugely appreciate your efforts to speak their language.

For more on language, see p302.

Etiquette

➡ **Body language** In Cretan body language, 'yes' is a swing of the head and 'no' is a curt raising of the head or eyebrows, often accompanied by a 'ts' click-of-the-tongue sound.

➡ **Eating & dining** Meals are commonly served family-style and shared. Always accept an offer of a drink as it's a show of goodwill (unless it's an unwanted advance). Don't insist on paying if invited out; it insults your hosts. In restaurants, dining is a drawn-out experience and it's impolite to rush waitstaff.

➡ **Places of worship** When visiting churches, carry a shawl or wear long sleeves and a long skirt or trousers to cover up in a show of respect.

➡ **Social visits** If you are invited to a Greek home, it's a nice gesture to bring a small gift such as flowers or a box of chocolates.

Eating

Like other southern Europeans, Cretans dine late and many restaurants don't open their doors for dinner until 7pm. Reservations are only needed for the most popular restaurants and can usually be made a day in advance.

➡ **Estiatorio** More formal restaurant serving similar fare to tavernas or international cuisine.

➡ **Mezedhopoleio** Serves mezedhes (small dishes, like tapas); an *ouzerie* is similar but serves a round of ouzo with a round of mezedhes.

➡ **Rakadiko** The Cretan equivalent of an *ouzerie* serves increasingly sophisticated mezedhes with each round of raki. Popular in Sitia, Ierapetra and Rethymno.

➡ **Taverna** Informal and often specialising in seafood, chargrilled meat and traditional homestyle oven-baked dishes.

What's New

Change comes slowly to tradition-minded Crete, but an increase in tourism, infrastructure improvements and sustainability initiatives are helping to fuel a more optimistic, post–fiscal-crisis outlook. Meanwhile, global trends like craft beer and hip coffee bars are making inroads without compromising Crete's unique character.

Museum of Ancient Eleutherna

This compact but excellent museum (p140) showcases treasures unearthed at the nearby settlement of Ancient Eleutherna over the past 30 years. Objects trace the entire history of the site from 3000 BC to 1300 AD and include jewellery, glass and earthenware, sculptures and figurines, and clay and bronze vases.

Cultural & Conference Center

With the 2019 opening of the Cultural and Conference Center (p175), Iraklio has a sleek new hub of culture and the arts. The five-building complex presents an eclectic program of theatre, musicals, ballets, classical and contemporary concerts, movie screenings and lectures.

Craft Beer

In keeping with global trends, Crete has started to spawn its own craft-beer scene. Look for Psaki IPA, Skotidi Imperial Stout and Askianos Porter from Iraklio-based Solo Brewery (p175) or a tasty Charma Lager, Charma Dunkel or Charma Pale Ale from Cretan Brewery (p102) in Hania. Also check out tiny Lafkas Brewery (p79) just outside Hania.

Indie Hostels

Much to the delight of budget-minded travellers, a crop of indie hostels has sprung up of late. With the Cocoon City Hostel (p73) and the Kumba Hostel (p73), Hania has two new contenders, while Iraklio added the So Young Hostel (p170) in 2018 and even Kissamos is fielding a small place called Hostel Stylianos (p109).

LOCAL KNOWLEDGE

WHAT'S HAPPENING IN CRETE

Andrea Schulte-Peevers, Lonely Planet writer

Things are looking up in Crete as the island, along with the rest of Greece, is slowly emerging from the economic crisis that held it in its grip over the last decade.

Growing tourism has played a key role in the recovery, even though the flip side of such popularity is, of course, early signs of overtourism. This is especially true of the population centres in the north and at such bucket-list sights as Knossos.

However, efforts to entice tourists off the well-worn 'sun and sea circuit' by developing alternative attractions are starting to pay off. Working farms offer a taste of a traditional way of life through such activities as cheesemaking workshops or cooking classes. Wine-lovers are increasingly intrigued by the Iraklio Wine Country which has become more visitor-friendly thanks to a slew of new tasting rooms and vineyard tours.

Meanwhile, a flurry of new third-wave coffee shops and craft breweries and pubs indicate that Crete can just as easily tap into contemporary trends.

Wine Tourism

Cretan winemaking is going from strength to strength with a new generation of vintners and a growing number of wineries offering tasting rooms and vineyard tours. Newcomer Digenakis Winery (p186) is among those worth keeping an eye on. See Wines of Crete (www.winesofcrete.gr) for details.

In Paleohora, the new Monika's Garden Wine Bar (p98) is an enchanting retreat to sample island wines by the glass.

Coffee Bars

Cold brew to classic Greek double, Crete has discovered the joys of good coffee and a growing roster of roasteries to show for it. Try Brew Your Mind (p129) in Rethymno, Monogram (p78) in Hania and Crop (p175) in Iraklio

Boutique Hotels

Crete's line-up of chic boutique hotels has grown a few new contenders, including Domus Renier (p76) and Monastery Estate (p75) in Hania, Hammam Oriental Suites (p125) in Rethymno and Sunshine Hotel (p211) in Malia

Public Art

A recent addition to Agios Nikolaos' public art scene, this stunning perspective mural (p217) by artist Manolis Anastasakos depicts a Minotaur on a zigzagging flight of stairs.

New Gavdos Ferry

Ferry operator Anendyk (www.anendyk.gr) has begun trialling a service linking Agia Galini with Gavdos Island in about two hours, four times weekly in the summer months.

LISTEN & WATCH

Tis Kritis Ta Politima (Various; 2009) A good overall introduction to Cretan music.

Dimotiki Anthologia (Nikos Xylouris; 1976) The album that shot Crete's legendary musical son to stardom.

Anastorimata (Psarantonis; 1982) Landmark album heralding Psarantonis' unique style.

Zorba the Greek (1964) Boasting three Academy Awards, this is still the quintessential Crete-filmed movie, based on Nikos Kazantzakis' famous novel of the same name.

Night Ambush (1957) Gripping retelling of the kidnapping of Nazi General Heinrich Kreipe by British forces in 1944.

El Greco (2007) Greek-made biopic telling the life story of the Cretan-born Renaissance painter.

FAST FACTS

Food Trend Local, organic, seasonal fare

Main Religion Greek Orthodox (95%)

Blue Flag beaches 112

Population 633,000

Accommodation

Find more accommodation reviews throughout the On the Road chapters (from p61)

Accommodation Types

Agritourism Rural tourism is booming in Crete. Traditional guesthouses, villas and apartments in tranquil villages away from the coastal hubbub are sometimes attached to organic farms.

All-inclusive resorts Almost 80% of visitors to Crete arrive on a package holiday. Big resorts are especially prevalent east of Iraklio and west of Hania along the northern coast.

Campgrounds Found in the majority of regions and islands, and often include hot showers, communal kitchens, restaurants and swimming pools.

Domatia The Greek equivalent of the British B&B, minus the breakfast. Rooms often come with a fridge and coffee- and tea-making tools .

Hostels Crete does not have any Hostelling International–affiliated hostels, but there are independent contenders in Rethymno, Plakias, Iraklio, Hania and Kissamos.

Hotels These run the gamut from simple family-run places with just a few rooms to full-service resorts with pools, water sports, bars and restaurants.

Self-catering apartment & villa rental Ideal for space-cravers, families and self-caterers. Cooking facilities vary widely from just a microwave, fridge and kettle to a full kitchen with stove-top and oven.

PRICE RANGES

The following price ranges refer to a double room in high season (July and August) with private bathroom facilities.

€	less than €60
€€	€60–€150
€€€	more than €150

Booking Your Accommodation

In most cases, booking ahead is only necessary in peak season, ie between June and August, although the most popular places may also get snapped up during the shoulder season. During busy periods, some properties, especially apartment and villa rentals, may impose a minimum stay, ranging from two days to one week. Outside the cities, and especially along the coasts, many places close from November to early May.

Airbnb (airbnb.com) Offers over 300 places to stay on the island, mostly in western Crete and along the northern coast. Averages around €100 for private apartments in peak season.

Bed & Breakfast Crete (www.bedandbreakfast.eu) Hundreds of indie vacation spots (not only B&Bs) ranging from €21 for a simple double to hundreds of euros for villas with private pool.

Crete Escapes (www.crete-escapes.com) Extensive inventory of larger villa rentals, many with private pool. Weekly rates from €650.

Great Small Hotels (www.greatsmallhotels.com) Worldwide site specialising in boutique hotels starting at €70.

I-escape (www.iescape.com) A curated list of design and boutique retreats with 24 contenders throughout Crete starting at €75.

Lonely Planet (lonelyplanet.com/hotels) Find independent reviews, as well as recommendations on the best places to stay – and then book them online.

Top Choices

Best on a Budget

Crete is an excellent destination for wallet-watchers. Family-run domatia (rooms in private homes), studios and apartments generally offer the best value-for-money and are plentiful throughout the island. Most are purpose-built, modern places with air-con, kitchenette, internet and balcony. There is also a growing number of indie youth hostels, especially in the cities. Rates are significantly lower outside the peak months of June to August.

Best budget choices:

Atelier Frosso Bora (p123), Rethymno

Cocoon City Hostel (p73), Hania

Katerina Apartments (p247), Kato Zakros

Plakias Youth Hostel (p148), Plakias

Captain's House (p156), Panormo

Best Rural Escapes

The countryside (especially in Hania and Rethymno) is peppered with traditional guesthouses, villas and villages. Many are old stone houses that have been given a 21st-century makeover while preserving such features as wooden-beamed ceiling and fireplaces. Some are solar-heated, those attached to organic farms often have tavernas that serve dishes prepared from home-grown bounty.

Rural retreats to love:

Milia (p115), Innahorion

Enagron Ecotourism Village (p142), Axos

Eleonas Country Village (p192), Zaros

Thalori Retreat (p202), Kapetaniana

Stella's Traditional Apartments (p248), Kato Zakros

Best for Beach Lovers

Crete has plenty of options for sand-and-sea worshippers who want to stay as close as possible to the blissful 'big blue'. Large resorts cluster in Bali, Hersonisos and Malia and offer watersports, bars and sunloungers on long sandy strands. Those seeking tranquility should point the compass to the villages on the southern shore.

PRISMA BY DUKAS PRESSEAGENTUR GMBH/ALAMY STOCK PHOTO ©

Thalori Retreat (p202)

Fabulous seaside abodes:

Minos Beach Art Hotel (p224), Agios Nikolaos

Karavostassi Apartments (p238), Agios Nikolaos

Pavlos' Place (p152), Triopetra

Sunrise Apartments (p159), Bali

Pension Girogiali (p152), Triopetra

Best Boutique Hotels

Getaways don't get any more stylish than in Crete's boutique hotels that often occupy sensitively restored 17th-century Venetian mansions. Typical design features include exposed stone walls, arched windows, antique furniture and four-poster beds. The old towns of Chania and Rethymno brim with these charismatic retreats, but even rural areas yield the occasional gem.

Top boutique hotel picks:

Hammam Oriental Suites (p125), Rethymno

Serenissima (p75), Hania

Casa Delfino (p75), Hania

Kouriton House (p137), Margarites

Arcus Villas (p135), Argyroupoli

Getting Around

For more information, see Transport (p296)

Travelling by Car

Nothing beats the freedom that travelling around Crete by car provides. You'll be able to access beautifully footprint-free beaches, trails to remote canyons and unspoiled villages that are impractical or impossible to reach otherwise.

Driving in Crete

When driving in Crete, it's worth being aware of a few peculiarities. Driving is on the right and (unless indicated otherwise) cars coming from the right have the right of way at intersections. In roundabouts drivers in the roundabout must yield to entering cars. On narow roads, if a car flashes its lights at you from behind, the driver intends to pass you. Where passing would require driving into the opposite lane, drivers are expected to move half onto the hard shoulder so that the vehicle can pass more safely. Do keep an eye out for parked cars, though! If there is no shoulder, keep driving until it is safe to pull over and let traffic pass.

Road Conditions

All major routes are sealed and well maintained, but in more remote, off-the-beaten-track areas you may still encounter dirt roads. Road conditions can change suddenly when a section of road has succumbed to subsidence or weathering, especially after heavy winter rains. Always watch out for potholes, gravel, fallen rocks and other hazards.

Car Hire

Hiring a car is essential for exploring Crete's many wonderful off-the-beaten

RESOURCES

Bus Schedules Timetables change seasonally. For the latest information, go to http://e-ktel.com for western Crete and www.ktelherlas.gr for central and eastern Crete.

Maps For those times when your GPS-based navigation system lets you down (eg in the mountains or remote corners of the island), an old-school road map, such as those published by Anavasi (www.anavasi.gr), will come in handy.

Emergencies If your car breaks down, call your car-hire company. In the case of an accident, dial ☎112 for emergency services (in several languages) to request an ambulance or police.

track places that are difficult or impossible to reach otherwise. It's easy to hire a car in the cities and most coastal towns, although not in the rural areas. Major international agencies have offices at the airports and in the big city centres, but local agencies may have more competitive rates. Most hire vehicles have manual transmission; automatic cars are more expensive.

Fuelling Up

Petrol (or 'fuel') is widely available but, outside the cities and major highways, petrol stations may close at 7pm and not open on weekends. Always top up before heading into the countryside. Self-service stations are not the norm. Tipping is not required but definitely appreciated. Few stations accept credit cards.

Parking

Parking is permitted on city streets, but finding an empty spot can be a nightmare. Few hotels have on-site parking but staff should be able to direct you to the nearest car park. Many villages with narrow roads have municipal car parks (often free) on the outskirts. A word to the wise: do use them (unless you have mobility issues).

No Car?

Bus

Crete has an extensive cross-island bus network. Not only does it link the four major cities (Hania, Rethymno, Iraklio, Agios Nikolaos) along the north coast but it also serves villages in the mountains and on the south coast, albeit on a more limited schedule. Many routes only operate on weekdays. Because of the mountainous terrain, there are no direct lines linking destinations in the south: you have to go back to the north coast city hubs and connect there.

Bicycle

Exploring Crete by bicycle is not for the faint hearted. Roads in the cities and along the north coast are reasonably flat, but erratic drivers don't make for a leisurely – or safe – ride. Prepare for major thigh-burn if you're heading south into the mountains.

Tour Companies

Many local tour operators and travel agencies run guided coach trips to major tourist attractions from Knossos to Samaria Gorge.

Walking

Walking around the island is an option for fit types with plenty of time. The E4 European Long-Distance Path traverses Crete. A few mountain huts provide shelter.

DRIVING FAST FACTS

- Drive on the right.
- All vehicle occupants must wear a seatbelt.
- Using a mobile phone while driving is illegal.
- Carry your licence at all times.
- Maximum speed 90km/h on highways, 50km/h in built-up areas unless signs indicate otherwise.
- Blood alcohol limit is 0.05%.

ROAD DISTANCES (KM)

	Hania	Iraklio	Ierapetra	Agios Nikolaos
Iraklio	130			
Ierapetra	220	90		
Agios Nikolaos	205	60	30	
Plakias	95	95	155	185

If You Like...

Bewitching Beaches

Balos Go tropical on this sultry and incredibly photogenic lagoon-like sandy beach. (p111)

Elafonisi Pink sands and warm waters extending across shallow isles make this Crete's most magical beach. (p99)

Vaï Watch out for falling dates as you revel in Europe's largest natural palm forest. (p244)

Preveli Beach Crete's 'other' famous palm beach, at the confluence of river and sea amid cave-combed cliffs. (p151)

Agios Pavlos For crowd-free tanning, head to the massive sand dunes spilling into this isolated southern-coast beach. (p160)

Xerokambos Find solitude and natural beauty along the dozen or so beaches stretching 4.5km in this remote southeastern region. (p249)

Chrissi Island Count shades of blue and green as you contemplate the shimmering waters lapping Chrissi (aka Gaïdouronisi Island). (p252)

Gavdos Island The southernmost spot in Europe exudes a sense of happy isolation outside busy August. (p100)

Falasarna Enjoy the waves, then watch the sun slip from pink to gold on this long, sandy ribbon. (p113)

Enchanting Villages

Kritsa Clinging to the Dikti mountains, Kritsa offers fine shopping, an atmospheric old town and a church with amazing Byzantine frescoes. (p234)

Hora Sfakion This whimsical southern port boasts larger-than-life characters and a long, colourful history. (p89)

Argyroupoli Devour trout while surrounded by rushing natural springs in this ancient mountain village. (p134)

Mohlos Minoan antiquity meets seashore vibes and some of Crete's best tavernas. (p239)

Myrthios On clear days you can spot Africa from this whitewashed village high above the Libyan Sea. (p150)

Amari In the heart of pastoral Amari Valley, this village has an enchanting medley of Venetian buildings and a square filled with cafes and overflowing flowerpots. (p138)

Theriso Recharge your batteries at this historically significant mountain village in thick forest south of Hania. (p104)

Food & Drink

Iraklio Wine Country Sample fine vintages on a tasting tour of Crete's largest wine-growing region. (p185)

Agreco Farm Visit a showcase of traditional, organic farming at this enchantingly located farm. (p135)

Maroulas Cretan hillsides are covered with sage, thyme and other herbs. Learn their medicinal purposes at a herb shop in Maroulas. (p132)

Thalassino Ageri Watch the sun set while dining on Crete's most expertly prepared seafood. (p77)

Taverna Iliomanolis The village taverna, one of the delights of travelling through Crete, is a must. (p150)

Ergospasio Savour meat slow-cooked in an *antikristo* grill at this elegant waterfront lair in a former carob factory. (p229)

Ancient Sites

Knossos Crete's marquee Minoan site is ideally paired with Heraklion Archaeological Museum. (p178)

Phaestos The most important Minoan complex after Knossos has awe-inspiring panoramas of Messara Plain and Mt Psiloritis. (p194)

Malia Excavations are still ongoing at this spectacular Minoan palace complex on the northern coast. (p209)

Top: Falasarna (p113).

Bottom: Kritsa (p234)

Ancient Lato This fortified Dorian hilltop city-state is one of the best preserved non-Minoan ancient sites and enjoys a stunning setting. (p236)

Kato Zakros Trek Zakros Gorge, past Minoan burial caves, to reach the ruins of the small coastal Zakros Palace. (p246)

Armeni This late Minoan cemetery is set in a beautiful oak forest with 231 tombs carved into the rock. (p145)

Polyrrinia This Dorian stronghold offers spectacular sea and mountain views from its acropolis. (p110)

Museums

Heraklion Archaeological Museum A must for every visitor to Crete, this is the island's top collection of Minoan and other artefacts. (p163)

Maritime Museum of Crete Sail into local nautical history from the Bronze Age to today, with major stops in Venetian times and WWII. (p65)

Lychnostatis Open Air Museum Time-travel to a traditional Cretan village. (p207)

Hania Archaeological Museum Minoan sarcophagi, a marble sculpture of Hadrian and miniature clay bulls are arranged against the backdrop of a gorgeous Venetian church. (p65)

Nikos Kazantzakis Museum Discover what the famous Cretan writer was up to when not writing *Zorba the Greek*. (p190)

Museum of Cretan Ethnology Become immersed in centuries of Cretan daily life. (p198)

Historical Museum of Crete Take an insightful whirlwind tour of Crete's often turbulent past. (p167)

Month by Month

TOP EVENTS

Orthodox Easter, March or April

Carnival, February

Iraklio Summer Festival, July to mid-September

Independence Day, March

Assumption Day, August

January

Winter is the time when Cretans have the island pretty much to themselves. Views of the snow-capped mountains are tremendous, but cold and windy weather makes this a good month for museums and churches.

New Year's (Feast of St Basil)

A day of gift-giving, singing, dancing, feasting and the slicing of the *vasilopita* (golden glazed cake). The person who gets the piece of cake with the hidden coin is promised a lucky year.

February

It's not as sweltering as Rio, but Cretan Carnival is still a good excuse for a big party. Blossoming almond trees hint at impending springtime.

Carnival

Pre-Lent is celebrated with three weeks of dancing, masquerade balls, games and treasure hunts, culminating in a grand street parade on the last Sunday. The biggest party is in Rethymno.

March

Winter will soon be a distant memory as days get longer and sunshine more frequent. No swimming yet, but a great time for avoiding crowds.

Independence Day

It's a double whammy on 25 March: military parades and dancing commemorate the beginning of the 1821 War of Independence, while the Feast of the Annunciation celebrates the day when Mary discovered she was pregnant.

April

A painter's palette of wildflowers blankets the island as locals prepare for the big Easter feast.

Easter

The most important religious holiday in Greece. Endeavour to attend some of the Orthodox Easter services, including a candlelit procession on Good Friday evening and fireworks at midnight on Easter Saturday. On Sunday, feast on roast lamb. It's often not the same date as Catholic Easter.

May

Sunny weather and moderate temperatures make May the perfect month for walking, cycling and island explorations. The scent of thyme, sage and other aromatic herbs pervades the countryside.

May Day

There's a mass exodus to the countryside on 1 May. During picnic excursions, wildflowers are gathered and made into wreaths to decorate houses and cars. Since this is also International Labour Day, the bigger cities stage demonstrations.

Battle of Crete Anniversary

This epic WWII battle and the Cretan resistance are commemorated during the last week of May with ceremonies, re-enactments, athletic events and folk dancing. The biggest celebrations take place in Hania and Rethymno. (p73)

June

The start of summer, and time to head for the beaches before they get crowded. Gourmands rejoice in the bounty of fresh local produce in the markets.

Navy Week

Navy Week honours Crete's relationship with the sea, with music, dancing, swimming and sailing. Held in late June, celebrations are especially big in Souda, near Hania.

July

Peak season starts, so you'd better be the gregarious type. Definitely prebook if you're coastbound or else escape the heat by heading for the hills and traditional villages. Strong winds are common.

Kornaria Festival

From early July to mid-August, this cultural festival with dancing, music, theatre and sports events erupts throughout Sitia in the far east. (p242)

Rethymno Renaissance Festival

Top international talent descends upon Rethymno on the northern coast for this two-week festival of theatre, dance and music from the Renaissance period. (p123)

Iraklio Summer Festival

Renowned local and international performers (from the Bolshoi Ballet to the Vienna State Opera) come to this high-calibre festival of dance, music, theatre and cinema, held from July to mid-September.

August

It's hot, hot, hot! The height of the festival season spills over from July, with the sea at its balmiest and markets jam-packed with ripe melons, figs, peaches and cherries. It's still windy.

Assumption Day

The day Mary ascended to heaven, 15 August, is a major celebration that sees everyone on the move back to their villages for family reunions. Expect curtailed services and heavy traffic.

September

The sun is high, though less and less blazing, as peak season wanes and the crowds begin to thin on beaches and at the big sights. Figs are in season.

October

Autumn is a fabulous time weather-wise, with warm seas and few crowds. Winds die down and the harvest of sun-plump grapes kicks into high gear. A good time for exploring Crete's natural beauty on foot.

Ohi Day

A simple 'no' (*ohi* in Greek) was Prime Minister Ioannis Metaxas' famous response when Mussolini demanded free passage through Greece for his troops on 28 October 1940. The date is now a national holiday with remembrance services, parades, feasting and dance.

November

Tourist resorts all but close in early November as the weather gets cooler and more unpredictable. The air is clear and mountains start receiving a dusting of snow.

Moni Arkadiou Anniversary

Patriotism kicks into high gear from 7 to 9 November during the anniversary of the explosion at Moni Arkadiou, a key holiday unique to Crete. (p137)

December

Days are short and quite cold, making this month a good time for indoor activities. The mountains receive their first sprinkling of snow.

Christmas

Although not as important as Easter, Christmas is still celebrated with religious services and feasting. Western European influences include trees, decorations and gift-giving.

GEORGIOS TSICHLIS/ALAMY STOCK PHOTO ©

Plan Your Trip
Itineraries

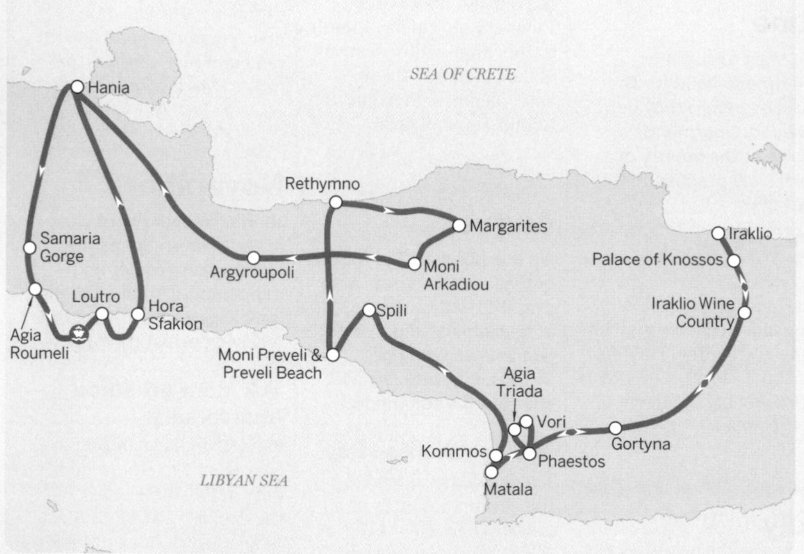

Essential Crete

Bookended by two of Crete's great cities, this route is a roller-coaster ride through the natural wonders of mountain and sea and the best of the island's historical treasures. You'll also get to soak up Venetian architecture, and feast on both mountain-village and seafront cuisine.

Start in **Iraklio**, checking out the superb museums before heading to the **Palace of Knossos** where the mysterious Minoans ruled about 4000 years ago. Spend a day enjoying the fruits of the **Iraklio Wine Country Country**, where 70% of Crete's wine is produced, and which is dotted with wineries.. Next, stake out a base near **Matala** to combine trips to **Gortyna**, the former capital of Roman Crete, as well as the Minoan palaces of **Phaestos** and **Agia Triada**. The outstanding Cretan cultural museum at **Vori** and swimming at wide, sandy **Kommos** and Matala beaches round out the area's offerings.

Travelling west, lunch in the quaint village of **Spili**, home to several excellent tavernas creating tradtional Cretan cuisine.

Loutro (p91)

Then drive to **Moni Preveli**, a working monastery on a hill with sweeping views of the Libyan Sea, and picture-postcard **Preveli Beach**, before steering north to **Rethymno** for a wander around its lovely maze of Venetian lanes. From here, venture into the countryside, folding the pottery village of **Margarites**, **Moni Arkadiou** or the mountain village of **Argyroupoli** into your route.

Zip west to **Hania**, a lively modern city wrapped around a romantic Venetian harbour and atmosphere-laden pedestrianised quarters, and also your next base. When you've had your fill of this historic beauty, take the early bus to **Samaria Gorge** and trek one of Europe's most famous canyons to the beachfront terminus at the small hamlet of **Agia Roumeli**. Stay over or catch a boat to **Loutro** to overnight in this quaint village accessible only on foot or by boat. Next morning, take the boat to **Hora Sfakion** where you can have a seafood lunch and the local cheese-stuffed-crêpe speciality, and then loop back to Hania.

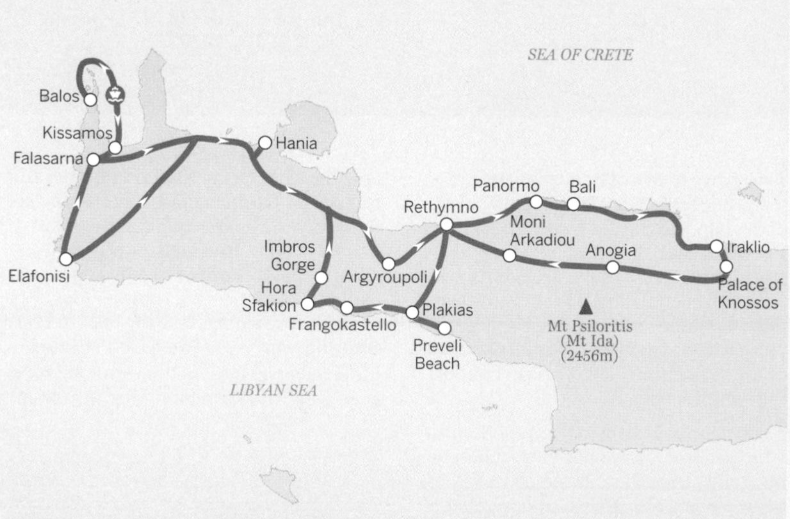
SEA OF CRETE
Balos
Kissamos
Falasarna
Hania
Elafonisi
Panormo
Bali
Rethymno
Moni
Arkadiou
Anogia
Iraklio
Palace of
Knossos
Imbros
Gorge
Hora
Sfakion
Argyroupoli
Frangokastello
Plakias
Preveli
Beach
Mt Psiloritis
(Mt Ida)
(2456m)
LIBYAN SEA

ARKANTO/SHUTTERSTOCK ©

MNF74/GETTY IMAGES ©

Top: Balos (p111)
Bottom: Imbros Gorge (p107)

Central to West Crete

This trip presents you with the mother lode of soul-stirring attractions, including the unspoiled southern coast, higgledy-piggledy mountain villages and some of Crete's best beaches, as well as spirit-lifting culture and gastro treats in Crete's two most attractive towns, Rethymno and Hania.

Kick off your trip in **Iraklio**, taking in the Heraklion Archaeological Museum and imposing fortress, and swing out to the **Palace of Knossos**, before steering west to quaint **Anogia**, where ancient traditions and Cretan music thrive at the foot of Mt Psiloritis. Continue west via the pottery village of Margarites to **Moni Arkadiou**, the site of one of the bloodiest moments in Crete's struggle for independence from the Turks. Spend the next day in **Rethymno**, taking your sweet time ambling around its bewitching mix of Turkish and Venetian buildings.

From Rethymno push on to the southern coast, where the lively beach town of **Plakias** makes an ideal base for exploring nearby secluded beaches, including **Preveli Beach**, stunningly located at the mouth of a rugged gorge.

Heading west, stop at the seaside fortress of **Frangokastello** before zipping over to **Hora Sfakion**, where you can hop on a boat to explore the remote villages along this beautiful stretch of coast. Continue north towards the Lefka Ori (White Mountains) and make time for a hike through spectacular **Imbros Gorge**. Continue to the northern coast and linger a night or two in **Hania**, with its beautiful harbour, grand fortress and ambience-packed old town.

From here you can easily zip over to the far western reaches of Crete. Take the circular route southwest via Kolymbari and the Innahorion villages to the westernmost tip of the island at **Elafonisi**, which beckons with pink-shimmering sandy beaches. Pushing back north via the coastal road, continue the beach theme at broad **Falasarna** with its rolling waves, or detour to the Gramvousa Peninsula. You'll most likely access the peninsula's spectacular lagoon-like beach at **Balos** by day-boat from Kissamos.

Returning to Iraklio via Hania, consider making a quick detour to the springs of **Argyroupoli**, before taking the coastal road east of Rethymno via peaceful **Panormo** and busy **Bali**.

1 WEEK Around Iraklio

Iraklio is a big, busy city, but it can be a useful base for visiting many of Crete's most famous sights. Since the bus network is decent in this province, it can even be done without your own vehicle. Alternatively, if you do have wheels and your budget allows, stay in more scenic Arhanes in the nearby Iraklio Wine Country, to make these looping day trips.

Crete's largest city, **Iraklio** offers top-notch museums, a Venetian fortress, a colourful street market, lively nightlife and excellent dining. While here, make sure you visit the expertly curated Heraklion Archaeological Museum so that you'll be prepared for Crete's grandest Minoan relic, the **Palace of Knossos**. Drive or hop on a bus for the quick ride to this mesmerising, and partially reconstructed, introduction to Minoan society.

On another day, apply what you've learned in Knossos on a visit to the **Palace of Malia**, another Minoan site, and some people's favourite, with sweeping sea views. You can then explore small mountain villages by zigzagging through tiny Krasí to **Kerá**, which is home to the revered Kerá Kardiotissas Monastery, with its 14th-century frescoes and holy icon. Nearby Sfendile was controversially inundated by the creation of a dam.

If you have your own wheels, designate a driver and spend a day sampling the local vintages of the **Iraklio Wine Country**, home to many wineries and tasting rooms. Plan to stop at the Nikos Kazantzakis Museum in **Myrtia** and the moody Minoan vestiges in **Arhanes**, which also has great traditional tavernas – perfect for a lunch break. Or sample the tipple around Dafnes, the other main hub of wine country.

Take a scenic drive to the rustic mountain village of **Zaros**, at the foot of Mt Psiloritis. Leave time to hike nearby trails, explore Byzantine churches and dine on fresh trout. If you're thirsty for a beach day instead of a hike, continue a bit further along to beautiful sands at **Kommos** or **Matala**. And if you have time to sleep over, the next day you can explore quaint villages such as Sivas, Minoan ruins at **Phaestos**, and Roman ones at **Gortyna**, before looping north again.

LUXERENDERING/SHUTTERSTOCK ©

ARTISTIQUE7/SHUTTERSTOCK ©

Top: Phaestos (p194)
Bottom: *Pithos* (storage jar), Palace of Malia (p209)

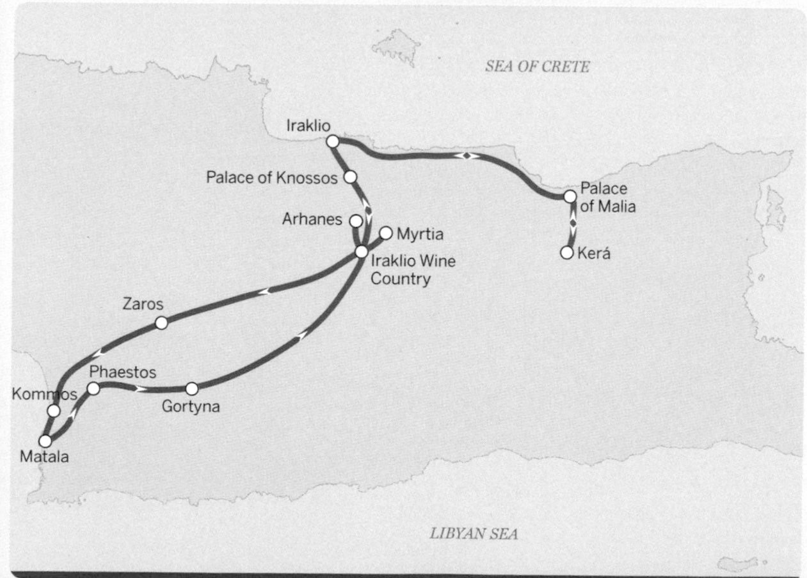
SEA OF CRETE
Iraklio
Palace of Knossos
Arhanes
Myrtia
Iraklio Wine Country
Palace of Malia
Kerá
Zaros
Phaestos
Kommos
Gortyna
Matala
LIBYAN SEA

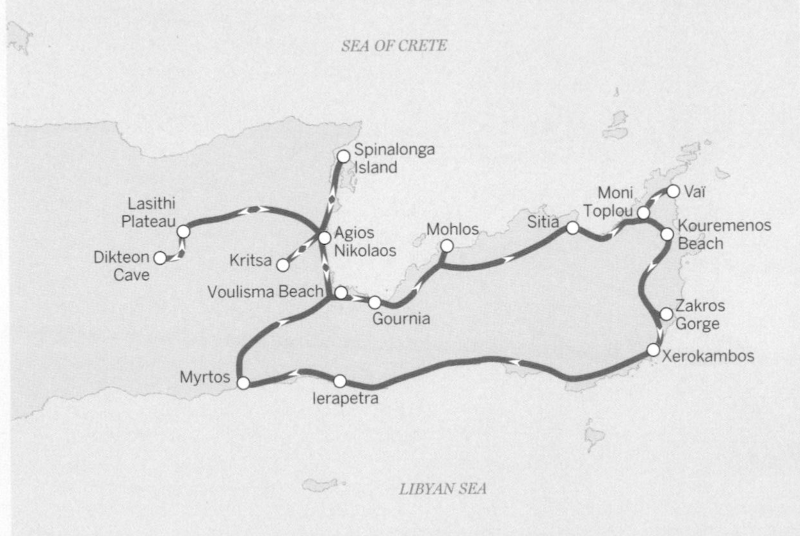
SEA OF CRETE
Spinalonga Island
Lasithi Plateau
Dikteon Cave
Agios Nikolaos
Kritsa
Mohlos
Sitia
Moni Toplou
Vaï
Kouremenos Beach
Voulisma Beach
Gournia
Zakros Gorge
Xerokambos
Myrtos
Ierapetra
LIBYAN SEA

JOE DANIEL PRICE/GETTY IMAGES ©

Eastern Crete

There's a world of discoveries awaiting in eastern Crete, from the cosmopolitan town of Agios Nikolaos to some of the island's most beautiful churches, moodily historic sights and pristine beaches. Arm yourself with some curiosity and a good map, and the week will fly by with no two days spent the same way.

Make your first base at charismatic **Agios Nikolaos**, where bustling cafes line the waterfront, the harbour and a dark and mysterious lake. Steer north to ritzy Elounda and the ferry ride to **Spinalonga Island**, a former leper colony turned sightseeing magnet thanks to Victoria Hislop's novel, *The Island*, and ensuing TV series.

Another delightful day-trip option from Agios Nikolaos takes you west to the **Lasithi Plateau**, high on the upper decks of the Dikti mountains, where wind power once drove the sails of thousands of windmills. The main attraction here is **Dikteon Cave**, where none other than Zeus himself was born.

South of Agios Nikolaos, **Kritsa** is one of Crete's most bewitching mountain villages, with a cool gorge, the island's oldest church frescoes and the ruins of the ancient city-state of Lato among its attractions. More ruins are in **Gournia**, reached by heading east along the coast, perhaps preceded by a swim at **Voulisma Beach** and followed by a fish lunch in **Mohlos**.

Sitia is a handy base in these eastern reaches for trips to **Moni Toplou**, a brooding fortified monastery, and the palm-lined beach at **Vaï**. More beaches await near Palekastro, including **Kouremenos Beach**, Crete's windsurfing mecca.

The mountains get bigger and more rugged as you head south to Zakros, the launch pad for the trek through **Zakros Gorge** down to the beach community of Kato Zakros with its Minoan palace ruins. For splendid solitude, brave the serpentine roads leading south to ultra-remote **Xerokambos**, with its gorgeous sandy beaches.

From here steer west, perhaps stopping in bustling **Ierapetra** or, better yet, in pretty nearby **Myrtos** where you can soak up bohemian beach living. The route north back to Agios Nikolaos is wonderful, taking you past bare mountains crowned with cockcombs of rock rising from woods.

HEMIS/ALAMY STOCK PHOTO ©

Top: Ierapetra (p249)
n: Fresco, Church of Panagia Kera in Kritsa (p234)

Plan Your Trip

Outdoor Activities

Crete's outdoor environments are nothing short of extraordinary – whether you're tackling mythical mountains where gods were born, sailing gem-coloured seas, hiking gorges where the Minoans buried their dead, or making finny friends on underwater expeditions. You'll find a wealth of tour specialists to show you the best of it all.

Best Outdoor Activities

Best Coastal Hike

Delve into the ancient past while trekking to Hellenistic, Roman and Byzantine ruins at Lissos on this 13km hike through lovely coastal scenery beween Paleohora and Sougia (p99).

Best Dive Site

At the Messerschmitt WWII wreck (p40), explore an intact and ghostly German aircraft that lies upside down near Malia and is patrolled by groupers and moray eels.

Best Birdwatching

The marshes, rivers and lakes of the northern coastal town of Georgioupoli (p85) throng with migrant birds such as kingfishers, egrets, herons, ducks and little grebes.

Best Off-Road Bike Trip

Get high pedalling along the mountain trails linking the Lasithi and Katharo Plateaus (www.cyclingcreta.gr/katharo).

Best Gorge Walk

Eastern Crete's Zakros Gorge (p246) packs in all that's best in gorge walking, without the crowds of the more famous Samaria Gorge.

Planning Your Trip

Get outdoors and active in Crete to experience the rewards of this stunning island, beyond the relaxed pleasures of sun and sand. Crete's rugged terrain, muscular mountains, dramatic gorges and untamed coastline beyond the resorts make for an adventurer's paradise. The relative ease of access to these splendid areas opens the door to enjoying just about every outdoor adventure you set your sights on.

If you're keen on sampling edgier or more strenuous or exhilarating outdoor sports, you'll find a growing number of specialist operators in Crete. Pursuits such as rock climbing, canyoning and sea kayaking are available with experienced guides and instructors.

When to Go

Spring (April to June) and autumn (September and October) are the best times for hiking and cycling, but July and August, when temperatures rise to around 40°C (104°F), are not much fun. Water enthusiasts will find the Med warm enough by mid-June to go swimming or windsurfing without trepidation.

Water Sports

Crete's long northern and southern coasts are bookended by short eastern and western shorelines, resulting in a range of sea conditions that lend themselves to all sorts of water sports.

What to Do

On Crete's northern coast, you'll find a water-sports centre attached to most luxury hotels, and they are usually open to non-guests. The gamut of 'fun sports' is on offer, including waterskiing, parasailing, jet-skiing, pedalos, banana boats and doughnut rides.

The more specialised water sports available in Crete include diving and snorkelling, windsurfing, kayaking and sailing. Numerous commercial operators organise trips and offer hire equipment.

Diving & Snorkelling

The sea off much of Crete's coastline is a paradise for snorkelling and diving. There is nothing quite like cruising gently through water that can be as clear as air, with visibility at times well over 30m.

Greek law insists that diving be done under the supervision of a diving school in order to protect the many antiquities in the depths of the Mediterranean and Aegean Seas. Until 2005, dive sites were severely restricted, but many more have been opened and diving schools have flourished.

The diving landscape of Crete is superb, with a fascinating mix of natural features, rocks, reefs, caverns, cliffs and shining sand. Sea life on view includes the beautiful 'wallpaper' of marine plants, red and green algae, corals, sea anemones and sponges that coat undersea rocks and reefs, while the often variegated volcanic rocks of Crete create a kaleidoscope of undersea colour. You stand a good chance of spotting a roll call of favourite fish and crustaceans, including octopus, cuttlefish, squid, sea horses, lobster, moray, scorpionfish, snapper, bream and even stingrays.

The most popular region for diving is Crete's north coast, where accessibility and sea conditions are more favourable. Many diving outfits also operate at south coast sites, where there is a distinct upping of the ante on diving's sense of adventure.

Some of the more interesting, easy snorkelling is around the sunken city of Olous near Elounda, which can be accessed from the shore. Bali and Panormo, Ammoudara and Malia, Plakias and Paleohora are popular diving sites.

Most dive centres offer courses ranging from beginners to PADI certification. In peak season, call at least a day in advance to book a dive.

DIVE OPERATORS

Crete has many reputable dive operators. The Professional Association of Diving Instructors (PADI; www.padi.com) has a list of all PADI-approved dive centres in Greece. A few favourites include the following:

Creta's Happy Divers (p221), Agios Nikolaos.

Pelagos Dive Centre (p221), Agios Nikolaos.

Blue Adventures Diving (p73), Hania.

Paradise Diving Center (p121), Rethymno.

WATER WISE

The sea can still be a hostile environment even when flat-calm and lapping a Greek beach, making all water sports potentially dangerous. The more specialised sports such as diving and kayaking are usually well regulated and clients are accompanied by qualified instructors. You should, however, always check your operators' certification. With beach sports such as parasailing, make sure that whoever is operating the facility has full certification and a good safety record. Ringo (inflatable ring) rides are best left to capable youngsters with good swimming abilities! Parents should also keep an eye on teenagers when jet skis are up for hire. By law, operators must exercise strict checks on age limits and ensure that the driver is not under the influence of alcohol.

POSEIDON'S SECRETS: CRETE'S BEST DIVE SITES

El Greco Cave Stunning stalactites and stalagmites in a 30m-long underwater cave with a depth of up to 40m, home to lobster, moray eel, grouper and tuna. Close to Agia Pelagia.

Messerschmitt WWII wreck An upended German WWII plane wreck lies 24m down in fragmented sections, though the cockpit is still intact. Groupers love to hang out here. Off Analipsi.

Mononaftis Rich in marine life: you'll meet octopus, barracuda, moray eel, scorpionfish and often dolphin and stingray in these reefs, canyons and grottoes. This dive is also suitable for beginners. Find it at Mononaftis Bay near Agia Pelagia.

Shrimps Cave More experienced divers can expect to see masses of shrimp in this stunning cave, which plunges to a depth of 40m. Close to Hersonisos.

Kalypso Walls This shore dive in Kalypso Bay enchants both novices and veterans with its whimsical rock formations and abundant critters from starfish to octopus.

Sea Kayaking

Crete's south coast has become increasingly popular for sea-kayaking excursions. Between Paleohora and Hora Sfakion, especially, the coast is dramatic and fascinating, with plenty of places to pull ashore at remote beaches and coves. However, there are not many kayaking operators in Crete and the tendency is for multiday expeditions catering to groups, with accommodation included along the way. It's worth enquiring about day trips, however, and you may even be able to hire a kayak for the day if you can demonstrate expertise. Some trips combine kayaking with hiking. We recommend the following companies:

Hania Alpine Travel (p73) offers canoeing holidays, for families, groups and individuals.

Petros Watersports (p233) in Plaka (near Elounda) offers hire kayaks by the hour and day.

UCPA Sports (p84) in Almyrida hires kayaks by the hour and day.

Skippers (p158) in Bali hires kayaks by the hour and day.

Windsurfing & Stand-Up Paddling

Windsurfing and kitesurfing are exhilarating water sports that require a lot of practice and much skill before you get anywhere near the spectacular freestyle and wave jumping of the experts. Still, even in the early stages of learning they are exciting sports, and enjoying them off the beautiful beaches of Crete is a bonus.

The best windsurfing in Crete is at Kouremenos Beach, north of Palekastro in Sitia, where Freak Surf Crete (p245) is a key local operator. Kouremenos is affected by the *meltemi,* the summer wind that can blow fiercely throughout the Aegean, and this wind, coupled with a local funnelling effect, creates some ideal windsurfing conditions. Windsurfing is also pretty good in Almyrida, Paleohora, Falasarna, Elounda and Hersonisos.

You'll find sailboards for hire almost everywhere. Hire charges range from €15 to €30, depending on the gear and the location. If you are a novice, most places where you can hire equipment also give lessons.

Stand-up paddling (SUP) is also growing in popularity, especially in the calmer northern seas around Hania, Iraklio, Elounda and Hersonisos. Hania-based SUP in Crete (p73) runs daily SUP tours around Crete, including one to Elafonisi.

Sailing & Boating

To sail round Crete on a well-found yacht is a glorious experience, but unless you are an experienced yachting fan with your own boat, the only way to get afloat is on a charter trip. Some companies in Crete do offer daily sailing excursions and most commercial tourist offices have information on sailing.

Amazing Sailing in Crete (p227), in Elounda, takes you to hidden coves and a traditional fishing village. From Agios Nikolaos, Sail Crete (p221) and Nostos Cruises (p221) will both take you to Spinalonga Island. In Ierapetra, Nautilos

Cruises (p252) delivers you to Chrissi Island in style, while Notos Sailing (p73) takes you to hidden places from Hania.

Hiking

Crete offers an enormous variety of options for keen hikers and trekkers of all skills and fitness levels, with the nicest trails passing through remote villages, across plains and into gorges. While popular routes are well walked and maintained, lesser-known paths are often overgrown and inadequately marked. Ask locally before setting out, especially after heavy rainfall.

Especially if you're venturing off the beaten track, a good map is essential. Most tourist maps are inadequate; the best hiking maps for the islands are produced by Anavasi (www.anavasi.gr) and Terrain (www.terrainmaps.gr), both Greece-based companies. Be realistic about your abilities, and always let somebody know where you're headed before setting out.

Spring (April to June) is the best time for hiking; the countryside is green and fresh from the winter rains, and carpeted with wildflowers. Autumn (September to October) is another good time to avoid the summer heat. Whatever the season, come equipped with a good pair of walking boots to handle the rough, rocky terrain, a wide-brimmed hat, a water bottle and a high-UV-factor sunscreen.

Walking the Gorges

Crete's numerous gorges attract hikers from all over the world. The walks can be a breathtaking and sometimes hard-going experience. The bonuses include the sheer pleasure of the spectacular surroundings, the aroma of wild herbs and flowers,

SAMARIA GORGE ALTERNATIVE: MT GINGILOS

The Samaria Gorge is considered a must-do for many visitors to Crete, even if 'wild walking' is not their thing. The result is an often less than solitary experience. If you're an experienced mountain walker and fancy an 'up' rather than a 'down' adventure, veer off to the right from Xyloskalo at the entrance to the gorge. This will take you towards the top of the 2080m Mt Gingilos, the mighty peak whose precipitous north face towers over Samaria. Head uphill past the cafe and on to where the surfaced road ends at a lodge-style building and a good path begins.

Tackling the Mountain

It will take about six hours to climb to the summit of Gingilos and back. This is a real mountain trek with some rocky sections. The path throughout the first part of the climb winds delightfully up steep slopes on well-laid stones and stepped sections dotted with shrubs and gnarled cypresses. The trail then levels off and winds south, passing beneath a photogenic rock arch. The ground for the next few hundred yards can be a touch loose, especially just after the springtime thaw. The path soon leads up to the spring of Linoseli and then zigzags up steep scree to a rocky saddle at 1700m, from where the Trypiti Gorge can be seen running to the south below.

From the saddle the route turns east and climbs steadily through a rocky landscape. There is no well-defined path and care should be taken at the start to stay clear of a steep-sided cavity. Red paint spots and arrows on boulders point the way to the summit. The descent is rocky at first, but should pose no problem for experienced hikers.

Preparation & Safety

Keep an eye on the weather reports: as late as the month of May, heavy rain can fall and hikers have become trapped in the past, when the river that flows through the gorge flooded its banks. Reliable mountain footwear and clothing are musts. Carry plenty of water and some food. You should also carry a compass or GPS and think twice about continuing if mist descends. From the saddle to the summit, there can be fierce winds and care should be taken. For more details visit www.west-crete.com/gingilos.htm. And remember: you don't have to go all the way...

E4 Walking Trail

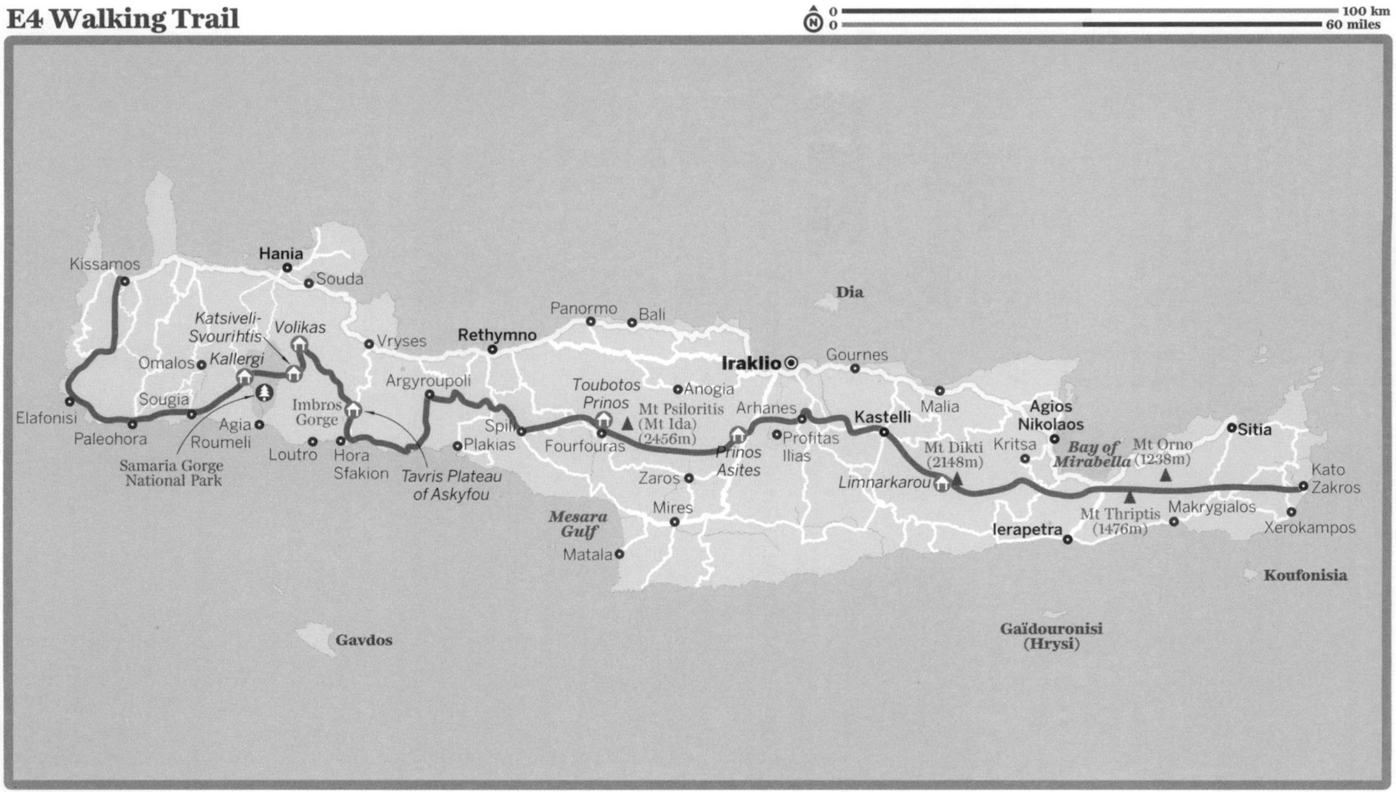

0 — 100 km
0 — 60 miles

Kissamos
Hania
Souda
Dia
Panormo
Bali
Katsiveli-Svourihtis
Volikas
Vryses
Rethymno
Omalos
Kallergi
Iraklio
Gournes
Argyroupoli
Toubotos Prinos
Anogia
Malia
Elafonisi
Sougia
Imbros Gorge
Mt Psiloritis (Mt Ida) (2456m)
Arhanes
Agios Nikolaos
Agia Roumeli
Spili
Kastelli
Sitia
Paleohora
Loutro
Plakias
Fourfouras
Profitas Ilias
Mt Dikti (2148m)
Kritsa
Bay of Mirabella
Mt Orno (1238m)
Samaria Gorge National Park
Hora Sfakion
Prinos Asites
Kato Zakros
Tavris Plateau of Askyfou
Zaros
Limnarkarou
Mesara Gulf
Mires
Mt Thriptis (1476m)
Makrygialos
Xerokampos
Ierapetra
Matala
Koufonisia
Gavdos
Gaïdouronisi (Hrysi)

shaded picnic spots and the potential for spotting wildlife.

Preparation

Most gorge walks require a decent level of fitness as well as sturdy footwear. Some involve only straightforward walking, while others demand some rock-scrambling experience and agility. The most extreme, such as the mighty Ha Gorge, require serious canyoning and rock-climbing abilities and the services of a competent guide. If you plan to set out just after the winter rains, there's a chance that river levels may still be high, making passage more difficult.

Getting Around

Gorge walking involves a bit of planning if you use your own transport. You will either have to backtrack to your vehicle, arrange for someone to collect you at the other end or take a taxi. Buses can sometimes get you to within striking distance of a gorge entrance.

Several companies run walking and hiking tours across Crete, including specialists Happy Walker (p122), Strata Walking Tours (p109) and Cretan Adventures (p170).

Nine Great Gorge Hikes

Samaria Gorge (p105) Crete's longest and most famous (and usually very crowded) gorge hike.

Agia Irini Gorge (p93) A full-day walk best tackled from the village of Agia Irini, north of Sougia. This is a fairly straightforward and rewarding hike with only a few steep sections. The last couple of kilometres to Sougia are along surfaced road.

Agiofarango Gorge (p205) An easy and popular 3.5km round-trip hike in south-central Crete, ending at a lovely pebble beach with crystal-clear water.

Kritsa Gorge (p235) This easy to moderate hike along a stony riverbed involves some bouldering and comes in a 5km and a 10km version.

Hohlakies Gorge Not as well known as its near neighbour Zakros Gorge, this short 3km walk runs from Hohlakies village to the coast. Hikers can continue 7km northwards to Palekastro.

Imbros Gorge (p94) Perhaps the most popular gorge walk after Samaria, and a reasonable outing for walkers. It runs from just south of the village of Imbros for 8km to Komitades, near Hora Sfakion.

Rouvas Gorge (p204) This short link hike runs from the village of Zaros on the southern slopes of Mt Psiloritis to meet up with the alpine route of the E4 European Path. It's a convenient way to get to and from the trans-Crete hike (E4).

Zakros Gorge (p246) A stunning two-hour hike in far-eastern Crete, past Minoan burial caves and palace to the turquoise waters at Kato Zakros.

Anydri Gorge (p101) An easy 3km trek from Anydri to gorgeous Gialiskari Beach.

Cycling & Mountain Biking

Get on your bike and take off for freewheeling Crete. Cycling, even for a day, is a rewarding way to explore Crete's country byways and off-road tracks. Traditional cycling has caught on in a big way on the island, despite the mountainous terrain. While it's possible to cycle from one end of Crete to the other and barely raise a sweat, north–south routes and the southern coast are likely to test your stamina and fortitude. In contrast, the escarpment villages and valleys of the northern coast, the Lasithi Plateau and the Mesara Plain of

THE E4 EUROPEAN PATH

The trans-European E4 walking trail starts in Portugal and passes through Crete before culminating in Cyprus. In Crete, it picks up at the port of Kissamos in the west and ends – after 320km – on the pebbly shore of Kato Zakros in southeastern Crete. Enthusiasts planning to tackle the Cretan leg should budget a minimum of three weeks, allowing for 15km per day; four weeks is more comfortable, allowing for stops and/or shorter hiking trips. You can, of course, tackle only sections of the route if your time is limited or if you just want to walk the most interesting parts. However, you will need to make important decisions early on, as the trail splits into two distinct sections through western Crete: the coastal and alpine routes.

MOUNTAINEERING CLUBS

To tackle Crete's mountains, the island has a number of established mountaineering clubs. Each prefecture has its own club, which maintains the E4 European Path and mountain refuges. They are all members of the association of Greek Mountaineering Clubs (EOS) and organise regular climbing, walking, speleology and skiing excursions around Crete, which visitors are welcome to join.

For decent info on Cretan climbs check out www.climbincrete.com.

Greek Mountaineering Association (p72) Visit the EOS branch in Hania or check its website to get the scoop on outdoor sports, including serious climbing in the Lefka Ori, mountain refuges and the E4 European Path.

Mountaineering Club of Iraklio (p169) The Iraklio chapter arranges hiking trips across the island most weekends (trip programs are published on its website). Anyone is welcome to join.

Mountaineering Club of Lasithi (☎28970 23230; www.fysi.gr) Maintains a refuge on Mt Dikti.

Mountaineering Club of Rethymno (p122) Offers advice on local hikes along with the possibility of joining excursions. It's best to make contact via the website.

the south do allow for some relatively flat cycling experiences on surfaced roads.

Be sure to carry puncture-repair and first-aid kits with you. Motorists are notoriously fast and not always travelling in the expected lane; extra caution on corners and narrow roads is well warranted. In July and August, most cyclists break between noon and 4pm to avoid sunstroke and dehydration.

Bike Touring

Plateau tours (especially around the Lasithi Plateau) are big business, with specialist companies transporting bikes up to the plateau to save you the gruelling Tour de France–type haul up from the coast.

Several companies and small specialist operators offer tours for all levels of experience and fitness. Rates usually include bike hire and transfers.

Martinbike Crete (☎28410 26622; www.martinbike.com; Hotel Sunlight, Elounda Rd, Ellinika; day trips €60-85; ⏲Mar-Nov) Small specialist operator going strong for over 20 years. Based near Agios Nikolaos, it runs mountain bike holidays as well as one-day trips in the surrounding areas.

Freak Mountain Bike Centre (p245) This Palekastro-based operator offers four-day escapes around eastern Crete and can customise private tours.

Hub MTB Adventures (p210) Operating out of Malia, Hub covers the whole of Crete with various tours, including a one-day exploration of the Lasitihi Plateau and two-day coast-to-coast tours.

Cretan Adventures (p170) This well-regarded Iraklio-based company organises mountain biking, hiking tours and extreme outdoor excursions.

Cycling Creta (www.cyclingcreta.gr) Guided one-day mountain bike tours for various skill and fitness levels from their base in Hersonisos.

Hellas Bikes (p73) Based near Hania, this outfit runs one- to seven-day mountain biking and bike trekking tours.

On Your Own

Independent cyclists coming to Crete with their own bikes are advised to bring sturdy touring bikes with multiple gears. You can hire mountain bikes from about €20 per day from a range of places on the island.

Canyoning

Canyoning is a developing sport in Crete and should not be confused with gorge walking. Most canyoning routes require serious rock climbing and/or caving experience, including the ability to abseil (rappel) under your own control. Most routes also require swimming ability and experience of constricted water flows. There is no shortage of wild and challenging canyons on the island, giving you the chance to experience areas that few ever get to see.

The well-organised **Cretan Canyoning Association** (☎6997090307; www.canyon.gr) has equipped about 45 gorges in southern Crete with abseil and belay bolt anchors and guide wires. One of the most awe-inspiring is the Ha Gorge, a savage cleft that splits apart the great curtain wall of the Thripti Mountains in eastern Crete. The gorge is over 1.5km in length and rises in a series of rocky steps between narrow walls over 300m high. Its name is said to derive, not surprisingly, from the Greek word 'to gape', which is what most of us do from a safe distance. A 1km hike to the exit starts near the village of Monastiraki, on the road between Ierapetra and the north coast.

The Association has useful information and a published guide to Crete's canyons on its website. It also organises regular excursions and runs beginners' courses. Canyoning is not a 'thrill-seeker's' day out and you should be certain of your capabilities before getting involved. If you're new to the sport, you should always be accompanied by an experienced canyoning guide.

See if you can get your hands on a copy of the multilingual *Canyoning in Crete,* by Yiannis Bromirakis (Road Editions 2007), which covers many of Crete's gorges in fine detail with maps and drawings. Check out Cretan Adventures (p170) for well-run, safety-conscious canyoning trips.

Rock Climbing

Southern Iraklio is one of the most popular areas for climbing, particularly the stunning cliffs around Kapetaniana and Mt Kofinas on the southern flanks of the Asteroussia mountains. The Agiofarango Gorge near Matala is another popular climbing spot and additional venues are being developed around Samaria, Plakias, Loutro and Malia.

Unless you are experienced, you are advised to contact local organisations, including mountaineering clubs (p44), before attempting any form of rock climbing. Visit Climb in Crete (www.climbincrete.com) for plenty of information and some entertaining articles, including an account of an early descent of the Ha Gorge.

Golf

Crete has a few nine-hole golf courses, but the island's only 18-hole pro course is the **Crete Golf Club** (☎28970 26000; www.cretegolfclub.com; Roussos Lakos; 9/18 holes €60/90; ⏲7am-3hr before sunset) in Hersonisos. This desert-style, par-72 course makes challenging use of the hillside setting and is definitely not for hackers. A new 25-room hotel and clubhouse opened in 2018. A nine-hole round costs €60 and an 18-hole round €90 (excluding clubs and buggies).

Horse Riding

Several places in Crete offer horse riding and guided trail rides through the countryside.

Arion Stables (p207) This sweet little horse farm in the hills between Hersonisos and Analipsi gets praise for its treatment of animals and its rides through the countryside and along the beach.

MOUNTAINEERING CLUB REFUGES

Call the respective EOS member club to book a space.

NAME	LOCATION	ALTITUDE	CAPACITY (BEDS)	EOS
Kallergi	Above Samaria Gorge	1680m	50	Hania (p72)
Katsiveli	Svourihtis, central Lefka Ori (White Mountains)	1980m	22	Hania
Limnakarou/Strovili	Lasithi Plateau	1530m	12	Lasithi
Prinos	Asites, East Psiloritis	1100m	30	Iraklio (p169)
Tavris	Plateau of Askyfou	1200m	45	Hania
Toumbotos Prinos	Western Mt Psiloritis	1600m	30	Rethymno (p122)
Volikas	Near Kambi, northern White Mountains	1450m	30	Hania

ALTERNATIVE ACTIVITIES

If you're tired of the beach or the hiking trail and keen on delving deeper into Cretan culture, check out the following activities.

Experience Traditional Farm Life

Working farms that also welcome visitors are scattered throughout Crete and offer an immersion in local pre-industrial life through a slew of traditional agricultural activities. Options include cheese- and bread-making, herb gathering, olive harvesting, raki distilling, grape squashing and sheep-shearing. Places to check out include Agreco Farm (p135), Enagron Ecotourism Village (p142), Stone Village (p158) and Dalabelos Estate (p156).

Become an Olive Oil Connoisseur

Learn how Crete's most famous export, olive oil, gets from tree to table on fragrant tours of such farms as Koronekes (p184) near Iraklio, Paraschakis Olive Oil Factory (p141) in eastern Rethymno and Cretelaio Olive Oil Mill (p88) near Frangokastello.

Get the Low-Down on Cretan Grapes

If Mandilari, Liatiko and Kotsifali sound like opera characters to you, it's time to take a tour of a Cretan winery and learn about indigenous grape varieties and the delicious wines they produce. Many estates in the Iraklio Wine Country (p185) and other parts of the island offer tours and tastings. See our self-guided driving tour (p188) for a suggested route or join a guided bus tour run by Made in Crete (p187).

Plug into Crete's Craft-Beer Scene

Local craft-beer pioneer Cretan Brewery (p102) in the hills near Hania runs tours of its facility (book ahead) followed by a sampling session and pub grub on the covered terrace.

Yoga by the Sea

Get into your downward-facing dog or mountain pose overlooking the shimmering Med. Options include Yoga on Crete (p89) in Hora Sfakion, which runs both week-long retreats and drop-in visits. Single sessions are also offered by Freak Surf Crete (p245) in Palekastro.

Learn about Traditional Cretan Village Life

Poke around a windmill, school and farmer's home at the engaging Lychnostatis Open Air Museum (p207) near Hersonisos, then gets hands-on in weaving workshops, ceramics and plant-dying demonstrations, tours of orchards and herb gardens, and other charmingly old-school activities.

Horseback Riding Plakias (p147) Family-run stables offering one- to four-hour rides on horses or donkeys along beaches and up into the surrounding mountains.

Melanouri Horse Farm (p199) Located in Pitsidia, near Matala. Runs one- and two-hour rides along the beach or into the mountains.

Odysseia Stables (☎28970 51080; www.horseriding.gr; Velani 46) These stables above Avdou, at the foot of Mt Dikti, have excellent facilities (including accommodation) and run anything from two-hour beginners' jaunts to three-day rides on the Lasithi Plateau and week-long trails through the Dikti mountains to the southern coast. Typical prices include €45 for a two-hour hack, €75 for a day trip and from €805 for eight-day courses including accommodation and meals. An eight-day trek up to the Lasithi Plateau area costs about €1245.

Zoraida's Horseriding (p85) Located near Georgioupoli, between Kavros village and Lake Kournas, Zoraida's offers guided beach and nature-trail horse riding, including trips to Lake Kournas.

Plan Your Trip

Eat & Drink Like a Local

Cretan food, which is distinct from Greek food in general, is some of the best to be found in the Mediterranean. This rustic but rich cuisine combines seasonal ingredients and balanced flavours that reflect the bounty of Crete's sun-blessed fertile land. Across the island, regional variations create a diverse gourmet trail.

Food Experiences

One of the delights of travelling through Crete is coming across a family-run taverna where traditional local dishes are made from ancient recipes using farm-fresh, homegrown produce; where the wild aromatic greens were picked in the mountains earlier that day; and where the oil and cheese are homemade, the tender lamb is from a local shepherd and the fish was caught by the owner. Really, that happens.

Meals of a Lifetime

➡ **To Maridaki** (p76) This mezedhes restaurant offers tender calamari, panna cotta to die for and friendly service to match, in Hania town's cool Splantzia quarter.

➡ **Peskesi** (p173) A top farm-to-table dining shrine in a stylish Venetian villa with dishes built from heirloom produce and organic meats.

➡ **Garden Arkoudenas** (p136) Set aside a few hours for a long, leisurely lunch of organic, modern Cretan cuisine in this delightful setting among fruit trees.

➡ **Avli** (p128) One of Rethymno's top tables, Avli never disappoints, perfectly melding the Venetian with the Cretan.

➡ **Hope** (p229) The lamb chops in this charismatic cliff-side taverna above Elounda are so succulent, you'll gnaw them right to the bone.

The Year in Food

Spring (March–May)

Easter feasts feature tender roasted lamb, *kreatotourta* (meat pies) and *kokoretsi* (grilled innards wrapped in intestines), and red-dyed boiled eggs decorate *tsoureki* (brioche-style bread). Spring brings edible wild plants, herbs and artichokes.

Summer (June–August)

Cheesemaking kicks into high gear. By July, watermelon, peaches and other fruit fill markets; mussel season peaks. August food festivals: Sitia pays homage to the sultana raisin, Tzermiado celebrates the potato, and Arhanes toasts the grape/wine.

Autumn (September–November)

Grape harvest begins. In October sample sweet chestnuts in Elos, with its quirky Chestnut Festival. Raki distilling hits its peak in November with raucous festivals all over, especially in mountain villages.

Winter (December–February)

Sugar-dusted *kourabiedes* (almond shortcake) and honey-dipped *melomakarona* are top Christmas cookies. The *vasilopita* (New Year's cake) comes with a hidden coin, which promises a year of good luck.

➡ **Milia** (p115) This farm retreat in the untamed western mountains wows palates with plates tied to nature and the seasons.

➡ **Hiona Taverna** (p246) It's a long way to this east-coast taverna, but one spoonful of the *kakavia* fish soup and you'll be hooked.

Cheap Treats

Food to go In a hurry but want a full meal? Tavernas with *mayirefta* (ready-cooked dishes such as *mousakas*) are the best bet.

Kalitsounia Cretan-style pies, usually filled with *myzithra* cheese and herbs or served sweet and drizzled with thyme honey.

Pies Bakeries make endless variations of *tyropita* (cheese pie) and spanakopita (spinach pie) and other pies.

Souvlaki Greece's favourite fast food, both the *gyros* and skewered-meat versions wrapped in pitta bread, with tomato, onion, french fries and lashings of tzatziki.

Street food Includes *koulouria* (fresh pretzel-style bread) and seasonal snacks such as roasted chestnuts or corn.

Dare to Try

Ameletita Literally, 'unspeakables'; fried sheep's testicles.

Gardhoumia Stomach and offal wrapped in intestines.

Kokoretsi Heart, lung, sweetbreads, kidneys and other innards wrapped in lamb or goat intestine and spit-grilled over charcoal; eaten at Orthodox Easter.

Cooking Classes

Culinary tours and cooking courses are becoming more popular in Crete, and some restaurant owners will give them upon request.

➡ **Crete's Culinary Sanctuaries** (www.cookingincrete.com) Greek-American chef and writer Nikki Rose focuses on organic agriculture and traditional approaches to Cretan cuisine, with hands-on classes and demonstrations in people's homes and visits to local farmers and producers. Courses are held island-wide.

➡ **Eco Events** (p122) Rethymno-based sustainable tour operator, which organises traditional Cretan cooking courses in a nearby village with a local woman, paired with unlimited laughs and raki.

➡ **Eleonas Country Village** (p192) Head to Zaros, in central Iraklio province, to stay in traditional and ecofriendly cottages while learning to cook with organic Cretan produce.

➡ **Enagron Ecotourism Village** (p142) Outside the village of Axos, Enagron runs cooking workshops and organises seasonal events around the production of cheese, wine and raki. The farm setting is lovely and there's accommodation on site.

➡ **Rodialos** (☎28340 51310; www.rodialos.gr; Vassilis Damvoglou) One- to seven-day cooking courses in a stunning villa in Panormo. Learn firsthand the principles of Cretan cooking and take the recipes away with you. Fees include sharing a meal of what you've created.

➡ **Vamos Traditional Village** (p85) Conducts Cretan cooking courses in an olive press and rents restored stone cottages, east of Hania.

OLIVE OIL: CRETAN 'GOLD'

The Minoans were among the first to grow wealthy on exporting the olive, and Crete remains an important olive-growing area, producing the largest quantity of extra virgin olive oil in Greece. Today, with an estimated 30 million olive trees in Crete, it works out to 62 olive trees for every man, woman and child. More and more organic oil is being produced and at least nine olive regions have gained the EU's Protected Appellation of Origin status.

Much of the olive oil made in Crete is for export and not always of high quality. Since 2014, an international panel of olive oil experts has ferreted out the top producers at the Cretan Olive Oil Competition (www.greekliquidgold.com), organised by the Agronutritional Cooperation of the Region of Crete. Recent winners have included Pamako, Critida Phenoil and Physis of Crete.

Top: Greek salad *(horiatiki)*

Bottom: Spanakopita

MUBUS7/SHUTTERSTOCK ©

Cook it at Home

Leave room in your baggage for local treats (customs and quarantine rules permitting) such as olives and extra virgin olive oil from small, organic producers; aromatic Greek thyme honey; dried oregano, sage, mountain tea or camomile flowers; and dried barley rusks. A jar of fruit preserves or 'spoon sweets' makes an easy dessert poured atop Greek yoghurt or ice cream. Check www.greek-recipe.com or these new and time-tested cookbooks if you want to replicate those feasts you had on the island.

➡ *Cretan Cuisine: Traditional Mediterranean Recipes For Eating Healthy and Living Well* (2018) by Aura Tatu is based on the cooking of Mama Katerina, the retired kitchen queen at a resort in Maleme.

➡ *Cooking With Katerina: Traditional Cretan Recipes* (2015) by Katerina Goniotaki presents family recipes handed down from generation to generation, with lots of images and easy-to-follow step-by-step instructions.

➡ *Cretan Cooking* (2003) by Maria and Nikos Psilakis is a well-translated version of their popular guide to Cretan cooking. It contains 265 mouth-watering recipes, some fascinating asides on the history of the dishes, and background to the Cretan dietary phenomenon.

➡ *The Glorious Foods of Greece* (2001) by award-winning Greek-American food writer Diane Kochilas is a must-have for any serious cook, with a regional exploration of Greek food and a 60-page chapter on Crete.

THE HEALTHY CRETAN DIET

Cretan cuisine gained legendary status for its health benefits following scientific studies of the Mediterranean diet in the 1960s that showed Cretans had the lowest levels of heart disease and other chronic illnesses. This was largely attributed to a balanced diet high in fruits, vegetables, pulses, whole grains, virgin olive oil and wine, and few processed foodstuffs. Another important factor may be the *horta* (wild greens) that Cretans gather in the hills (and survived on during wars), which may have protective properties that are not yet fully understood.

Local Specialities

The grand Cretan diet evolved from the abundance of local produce, coupled with enormous Cretan ingenuity. You'll find not only all the Greek staples but a wonderful array of Cretan specialities, as well as regional variations across the island. While the cuisine has its roots in antiquity, and has been influenced by all the visiting cultures over time, it essentially relies on organically grown, farm-fresh, unadulterated seasonal produce, aromatic herbs, free-range meats and locally caught seafood. Cretan olive oil, produced in vast quantities across the island, is among the world's best and is an integral part of cooking and meals.

Cheese & Dairy

Beyond the ubiquitous and delicious fresh feta (in stores, ask for the kind wet from the barrel, not mass-produced), Crete produces its wonderful cheeses primarily from goat's and sheep's milk, or a combination of the two. Many Cretan villages have their own signature cheese.

➡ **Anthotiro** Buttery white cheese that can be soft or hardened when dry.

➡ **Graviera** Nutty, mild Gruyère-like hard sheep's-milk cheese, often aged in special mountain caves and stone huts called *mitata*. Delicious eaten with thyme honey.

➡ **Myzithra** Soft, mild ricotta-like cheese produced from sheep's-milk whey, which can be eaten soft or hardened for grating; the hardened sour version is *xinomyzithra*. Hania's specialty is *galomyzithra*. Variations abound across the island.

➡ **Pichtogalo Chanion** Hania's thick yoghurt-like sheep's-milk or sheep's-and-goat's-milk cheese enjoys EU-designated Protected Designation of Origin (PDO) status. It is sometimes used in *bougatsa* (pastry stuffed with creamy custard or cheese and sprinkled with powdered sugar).

➡ **Xigala** Creamy cheese from Sitia in eastern Crete with a rich, slightly acidic flavour.

➡ **Yiaourti** This thick, tangy sheep's-milk yoghurt is something to savour, and best eaten with honey, walnuts or fruit.

MAGICAL MEZEDHES

Cretans love to share a range of mezedhes (small dishes), or mezes for short. Think tapas, Greek style! Eateries that serve only mezedhes are called *mezedhopoleio*, *ouzerie* or *rakadhiko*, and typically offer raki or ouzo along with the morsels. Have them as an appetizer or make a meal by ordering several.

Common mezedhes are dips such as *taramasalata* (fish roe), tzatziki (yoghurt, cucumber and garlic) and *fava* (split-pea purée). Hot mezedhes include *keftedhes* (small tasty rissoles, often made with minced lamb, pork or veal), *loukanika* (pork sausages), *saganaki* (skillet-fried cheese) and *apaki* (Cretan cured pork), as well as a full range of bite-sized seafood. Also look for rice-filled dolmadhes (vine leaves), deep-fried zucchini (courgette) or eggplant (aubergine) slices. If you can't make up your mind, often you can order a *pikilia* (mixed mezedhes plate).

Wild Greens, Vegetables & Salads

Part of the magic of Cretan cuisine are the ingredients gathered from hillsides and around villages. For centuries Cretans have been gathering extremely nutritious *horta* (wild greens) and boiling them for warm salads or cooking them in pies and stews. There are more than 100 edible *horta* on Crete, though even the most knowledgeable locals might not recognise more than a dozen. The *vlita* (amaranth) variety is the sweetest, while *stamnagathi*, found in the mountains, is considered a delicacy and served boiled as a salad or stewed with meat. Other common *horta* include wild radish, dandelion, nettles and sorrel.

Another Cretan hillside specialty is *askordoulakous* (mountain bulbs), the bulbs of a kind of wild greens. They usually come fresh as a salad, dressed with oil and vinegar or lemon, pickled, or stewed with olive oil, vinegar and flour. The plant's tender white blossoms are boiled or incorporated into recipes.

Cretan *paximadia* (rusks), a hangover from times of famine, are made from barley flour or whole wheat and double-baked to produce a hard, dry cracker that can keep, literally, for years. Don't miss the excellent and popular dish called *dakos* (also known as *koukouvagia* and *koulouk-opsomo*), in which the rusks are moistened with water or oil and topped with tomato, olive oil and creamy *myzithra*.

Cretan cuisine also shines in such vegetable dishes as *aginares* (artichokes) and tasty *anthoi* (zucchini flowers) stuffed with rice and herbs. Beans and pulses were the foundation of the winter diet, so you will find dishes such as delicious *gigantes* (lima beans in tomato and herb sauce). Also look for *fasolakia yiahni* (green bean stew), *yemista* (stuffed tomatoes) and *bamies* (okra). *Melitzana* (eggplants) are widely used, particularly in dishes such as *briam* (oven-baked vegetable casserole) or wonderful *melidzanosalata* (a smoky garlicky purée).

Seafood

Fish is usually sold by weight in restaurants. You will usually be asked to pick from the day's catch displayed on ice in a glass case or in the kitchen, or brought to your table. Make sure it's weighed (raw) so you don't get a shock when the bill arrives, as fresh fish is not cheap. Fish is often grilled whole and drizzled with *ladholemono* (lemon and oil dressing). Smaller fish such as *barbounia* (red mullet) and *maridha* (whitebait) are lightly fried. *Ohtapodi* (octopus) is grilled, marinated or stewed in wine sauce.

Although fish is healthy and delicious, the World Wide Fund for Nature (WWF) and other organisations report that 93% of Mediterranean fish stocks are overfished, in part because popular species such as tuna and swordfish are often caught as juveniles. Other menu staples such as sea bream and sea bass are also threatened. Check the Marine Conservation Society's Good Fish Guide (www.mcsuk.org/goodfishguide) for details.

Specialty Cretan Dishes

Cretan tavernas usually offer the full range of Greek one-pot stews, casseroles and *mayirefta* (ready-cooked meals), in addition to food cooked to order *(tis oras)* such as grilled meats. The most common *mayirefta* are *mousakas* (baked layers of eggplant or zucchini, minced meat and potatoes topped with cheese sauce), *pastitsio* (layers of buttery macaroni and seasoned minced lamb), *yemista* (stuffed vegetables), *youvetsi* (a hearty dish of baked meat or poultry in a fresh tomato sauce with *kritharaki,* rice-shaped pasta), *stifadho* (meat, game or seafood cooked with onions in a tomato puree), *soutzoukakia* (meat rissoles in tomato sauce) and *hohlioi* (snails). Meat is commonly baked with potatoes, with lemon and oregano, or braised in tomato-based stews or casseroles *(kokkinisto).*

And then there are the Cretan specialties that should not be missed. As you travel, you'll see the flocks of sheep and goats that figure so prominently in Cretan mountain cuisine, and Cretans have their own way of barbecuing called *ofto* or *antikristo,* in which big chunks of meat are slow-roasted upright around hot coals. In parts of Crete, meat is cooked *tsigariasto* (sautéed).

➡ **Arni (lamb) me stamnagathi** In this favourite Cretan specialty, local lamb is cooked to tenderness with a popular type of wild greens called *stamnagathi.* You may also find the dish with *katsiki* (young goat).

➡ **Boureki** Richly layered cheese and vegetable pie.

➡ **Gamopilafo** This rice dish is offered at traditional Cretan weddings (*gamos* means wedding) and some high-end restaurants. It's a sort of deluxe risotto prepared in a rich meat broth and *stakovoutiro* – a butter created from the creamy skin that forms on the top of boiled fresh goat's milk which is then made into a roux.

➡ **Hirina apakia** It takes an involved, multiday process to create this delicious smoked pork. The meat is first marinated in vinegar for several days, then smoked over a fire stoked with local herbs. It can also be served cold in thin slices.

➡ **Hohlioi (snails)** Collected after rainfall and prepared in dozens of interesting ways: try *hohlioi bourbouristoi*, simmered in wine or vinegar and rosemary, or snails stewed with *hondros* (cracked wheat). Cretans eat more snails than the French do and even export to France.

➡ **Kouneli (rabbit)** Local favourite stewed *(stifadho)* with rosemary and *rizmarato* (vinegar).

➡ **Psari (fish)** A staple along the coast and cooked with minimum fuss – usually grilled whole and drizzled with *ladholemono* (a lemon and oil dressing). Also look for *ohtapodi* (octopus), *lakerda* (cured fish), mussel or prawn *saganaki* (skillet-fried, usually with tomato sauce and cheese), crispy fried *kalamari* (calamari, squid), fried *maridha* (whitebait) and *gavros* (anchovy), either marinated, grilled or fried.

➡ **Soupies (cuttlefish)** Excellent stewed with wild Cretan fennel.

➡ **Staka** Rich, soft buttery roux somewhere between a cheese, yoghurt and sauce, usually found on menus with goat or pork. It's a rich but delicious dish, with the meat absorbing the flavours of the *staka*. It's also often added to rice *pilafi* (pilaf) to make it creamier.

➡ **Vrasto (mutton or goat stew)** Found in traditional mountain village tavernas.

Sweet Treats

As well as traditional Greek sweets such as baklava, *loukoumadhes* (ball-shaped doughnuts served with honey and cinnamon), *kataïfi* ('angel hair' pastry; chopped nuts inside shredded pastry soaked in honey), *ryzogalo* (rice pudding) and *galaktoboureko* (custard-filled pastry with syrup), Cretans have their own sweet specialities. Also, traditional syrupy fruit preserves (known as spoon sweets) are served as dessert, but are also delicious on yoghurt or ice cream. Some tavernas serve *halva* (wedge of semolina) after a meal.

➡ **Bougatsa** Traditional breakfast food, a pastry stuffed with creamy custard or cheese and sprinkled with powdered sugar.

➡ **Kalitsounia** Cretan stuffed cheese pies start with handmade pastry dough, often formed into tiny cups. Fillings vary by region and household, though they tend towards the sweet, using cheeses such as *myzithra* or *malaka* (but not feta) and honey or spices.

➡ **Sfakianes pites** From the Sfakia region of Hania, fine pancake-like sweets with a light *myzithra* cheese filling, served with honey. The dough incorporates a dash of raki.

➡ **Xerotigana** Deep-fried pastry twirls with honey and nuts.

Wine

Krasi (wine) has been produced in Crete since Minoan times, and Crete's farmers have long made wine for their own consumption. Commercial production, however, did not start until the 1930s and only in 1952 did Minos in Peza become the first winery to bottle wine on Crete.

Today, Crete produces about 20% of Greek wine, most of it through huge cooperatives that aim for higher yields rather than higher quality. Much of that type is blended and sold in bulk, and is usually what you get when you order 'house wine' in restaurants. An ever-growing number of boutique wineries are overseen by internationally trained winemakers, who produce excellent bottled wines. Minos-Miliarakis, Lyrarakis, Douloufakis and Rhous are among those producing Crete's top wines, some of which are exported. Wine tourism, too, is picking up, as some wineries have opened visitor centres with exhibits and tasting rooms.

Retsina, white wine flavoured with the resin of pine trees, has taken on an almost folkloric significance with foreigners. An acquired taste, it goes well with strongly flavoured mezedhes and seafood.

Beer

The global craft-beer craze has reached Crete with Iraklio-based Solo and the Cretan Brewery (p102) near Hania whipping up some fine ales and lagers. Another local brewery is Brinks, which makes organic lagers near Rethymno. In dedicated craft-beer pubs, you might also encounter Vergina and Hillas lagers from northern Greece, organic Piraiki made in Piraeus, Craft from Athens, and Yellow Donkey from Santorini. Major commercial Greek brands are Mythos, Fix and Alfa.

Coffee & Tea

➡ **Greek coffee** Traditionally brewed in a special copper *briki* (pot) and served in a small cup. Grounds sink to the bottom (don't drink them). It is drunk *glykos* (sweet), *metrios* (medium) and *sketo* (plain; without sugar).

➡ **Frappé** Iced instant-coffee concoction that you see everyone drinking.

➡ **Tsai (tea)** Try camomile or aromatic Cretan *tsai tou vounou* (mountain tea), both nutritious

CRETAN WINE VARIETALS

Crete has three wine-producing areas. The largest is the Iraklio Wine Country, which makes about 70% of Cretan wine. It produces mostly Kotsifali, Mandilaria and Vilana grapes in two centres; one around Peza/Arhanes south of Iraklio and the other around Dafnes, a bit further west. The smallest wine region is east of here in Lasithi. Vineyards cluster primarily around Sitia and specialise in Liatiko grapes. In western Crete, the main grape-growing region is west of Hania, where the main varietal cultivated is Romeiko.

Dafni Lively with subtle acidity and an aroma resembling laurel, this white grape is common in the Lasithi and Iraklio wine regions.

Kotsifali Indigenous red grape with high alcohol content and rich flavour, typical of Iraklio region and often blended with Mandilaria.

Liatiko Very old indigenous red variety with complex character, found mainly around Sitia.

Malvasia Original Cretan white variety; strong flower aroma with notes of muscat, and ages well if blended with Kotsifali.

Mandilaria Dark-coloured but light-bodied red wine, prevalent around Arhanes and Peza.

Romeiko Red grape mostly grown around Hania and turned into robust red, white and rosé wines.

Vidiano White indigenous grape with intensive and complex peach and apricot aromas; often blended with Vilana.

Vilana Main white grape of Iraklio growing area; fresh, low-alcohol wine with a delicate aroma evoking apples.

and delicious. Endemic *diktamo* (dittany) tea is known for its medicinal qualities.

How to Eat & Drink

Food and the ritual of dining together play an integral role in Cretan life, whether at home or eating out with family and friends. Cretans will travel far to get to a great restaurant or eat specific food, heading to the mountains for local meat and the sea for fresh fish. Some of the best tavernas are tucked away in unexpected places.

Given the long summers and mild winters, al fresco dining is central to the dining experience – with tables set up on pavements, roads, squares and beaches.

When to Eat

Most tavernas open all day, but some upmarket restaurants open for dinner only. Cafes do a roaring trade, particularly after the mid-afternoon siesta.

➡ **Breakfast** Greece doesn't have a big breakfast tradition, unless you count coffee and a cigarette, and maybe a *koulouria*, *tyropita* or *bougatsa* eaten on the run. You'll find Western-style breakfasts in hotels and tourist areas.

➡ **Lunch** While changes in working hours affect traditional meal patterns, lunch is still usually the biggest meal of the day, starting after 2pm.

➡ **Dinner** Cretans eat dinner late, after sunset in summer. This coincides with shop closing hours, so restaurants often don't fill until after 10pm. Arrive by 9pm to avoid crowds.

Where to Eat

Estiatorio Restaurant with upmarket international cuisine or Greek classics in a more formal setting.

Kafeneio Coffee house and cultural institution, largely the domain of men.

Mayirio Restaurant specialising in *mayirefta*, ready-cooked homestyle one-pot stews, casseroles and baked dishes.

Mezedhopoleio & ouzerie Serves lots of different mezedhes (shared small dishes), often with ouzo or raki.

Rakadhiko The Cretan equivalent of an *ouzerie* serves increasingly sophisticated mezedhes with each round of raki. Particularly popular in Sitia, Ierapetra and Rethymno.

Taverna Common, casual, family-run (and child-friendly) place. They usually have barrel wine, paper tablecloths and traditional menus. Specialist variations: *psarotaverna* (fish and seafood), and *hasapotaverna* or *psistaria* (chargrilled or spit-roasted meat).

Zaharoplasteio Cross between a patisserie and a cafe (some only do takeaway).

Menu Decoder

Cover Small compulsory charge (usually €1 or €2) for bread and butter.

Mezes or Mezedhes Hot or cold small plates such as tzatziki (sauce of grated cucumber, yoghurt

RAKI & OUZO

Raki (also known as *tsikoudia*), the Cretan pomace brandy, is an integral part of local culture. A shot of the fiery brew is offered as a welcome, at the end of a meal and pretty much at any time and on all occasions. Distilled from grape stems and pips left over from the grapes pressed for wine, it is similar to the *tsipouro* found in other parts of Greece, Middle Eastern arak, Italian grappa, Irish poteen or Turkish *rakı*.

Each October, the raki distilling season starts, with distilleries and private stills around the island producing massive quantities. Expect lots of drinking and feasting, and if you pass a village distilling raki, you may well get an invitation. Good raki has a smooth mellow taste with no noticeable after-burn and shouldn't cause a hangover. It does not incorporate herbs, and is drunk neat. Family-owned distilleries bottle the potent brew in plastic water bottles, sold in groceries, tavernas or by the roadside.

In winter, look for warm *rakomelo* – heated raki with honey and cloves.

Ouzo, the famous Greek aniseed spirit, has a more limited following in Crete. It is served neat, with ice and a separate glass of water for dilution (which makes it turn milky white).

ETIQUETTE & CUSTOMS

- Try to adapt to local eating times – a restaurant that was empty at 7pm might be heaving with locals at 11pm.
- Book for upmarket restaurants, but reservations are unnecessary in most tavernas.
- In tavernas, it's fine to browse the *mayirefta* behind the counter before ordering.
- Taverna dress code is generally casual, but in high-end restaurants dress nicely.
- There is a small charge for bread and nibbles served on arrival.
- Often you will be served complimentary fruit or dessert and/or raki at the end of a meal, usually after asking for the bill.
- Dining is a drawn-out ritual; if you eat with locals, pace yourself, as there will be plenty more to come.
- Tipping is not mandatory, but Greeks usually round up the bill or add around 10% for good service. To split the bill, it's best to work it out among your group rather than asking staff to do it.
- Cretans are generous hosts. Don't refuse a coffee or drink – it's a gesture of hospitality and goodwill. If you're invited out, the host normally pays.
- If you are invited to someone's home, take a small gift (flowers or sweets). Remember to pace yourself, as you'll be expected to eat everything on your plate.
- Smoking is banned in enclosed public spaces, including restaurants and cafes, but you'll see plenty of Cretans flouting the law. Smoking on terraces is permitted.

and garlic), *saganaki* (fried cheese), dolmadhes (stuffed vine leaves) and *dakos* (tomato-topped rusks), eaten as an appetizer and meant to be shared.

Salads May include grilled vegetables or boiled mountain herbs in addition to crisp classics such as Greek salad *(horiatiki)*.

From the Grill Grilled meats including souvlaki (pork skewer) or lamb chops, usually served without sides.

Traditional Greek dishes Typcially *mayirefta* such as *mousakas*, *stifadho* (stew) and *pastitsio* (baked pasta).

Fish Ideally the catch of the day, sold by weight, grilled and served whole.

Pasta May feature classics such as spaghetti bolognese as well as local variations.

Plan Your Trip

Family Travel

While Crete doesn't cater to kids the way that some destinations do, children will be welcomed and included wherever you go. Greeks generally make a fuss over children, who may find themselves receiving many gifts and treats. Teach them some Greek words and they'll feel even more appreciated.

Keeping Costs Down

Accommodation

Apartment or villa rentals generally offer the best value, more space, privacy and amenities, including cooking facilities. Larger hotels usually have extra-spacious family rooms with three or four beds or two adjoining rooms connected by a door. Others may be able to squeeze in a cot if space permits. In some places, small children stay for free in their parents' room.

Sightseeing

Most fun places, including beaches, caves and hiking trails, are totally free. Admission to Knossos and other ancient sites and museums is free for anyone under 18 (bring ID if your age is not obvious). At major family attractions, such as water parks, children under 12 score significant discounts, and pre-purchasing tickets online also yields savings.

Eating

Most restaurants are happy to serve smaller portions for children. Ordering lots of mezedhes (appetisers) lets little ones sample the local food and find their culinary favourites. Some dishes that kids might grow to love include *kalamari* (fried squid), *tiropitakia* (cheese parcels in filo pastry), dolmadhes (flavoured rice wrapped in vine leaves) and *saganaki* (fried cheese).

Children Will Love...

Awesome Beaches

➡ **Bali** (p158) A series of accessible coves with all services.

➡ **Elafonisi** (p99) Fun bathing in tiny lagoons amid beautiful surroundings.

➡ **Paleohora** (p95) Choice of two town beaches with safe bathing.

➡ **Vaï** (p244) Palm tree paradise; avoid in July and August.

➡ **Voulisma** (p238) Crystalline bay with shallow water and fine golden sand.

Interactive Attractions

➡ **Agora, Hania** (p79) Browse through Hania's lively daily market.

➡ **Dinosauria Park** (p207) Interact with dinos at this prehistoric adventure in Gournes

➡ **Fortezza, Rethymno** (p119) Dial back centuries while exploring Rethymno's Venetian fortress.

➡ **Natural History Museum, Iraklio** (p168) Nose around the engaging children's section in this imaginative museum.

➡ **Watercity, Anopolis** (p207) Enjoy this water fun park southeast of Iraklio.

Outdoor Adventures

- **Boat trips** Along Hania's south coast or around Elounda (p227) in Lasithi.
- **Caves** Dikteon Cave (p238) on the Lasithi Plateau or Skotino Cave (p211) near Hersonisos.
- **Hiking** Short sections of easier gorges such as Imbros (p94) or Agia Irini (p93).
- **Horse riding** At Avdou (p46), below the Lasithi Plateau.
- **Kite flying** On quiet beaches.

Tasty Treats

- **Bougatsa** Try a pastry filled with creamy custard and dusted with powered sugar at Bougatsa Iordanis (p76) in Hania or Phyllo Sophies (p173) in Iraklio.
- **Goat's-milk ice cream** At Meli (p127), Rethymno's best ice cream shop, classic and creative flavours are all made with goat's-milk from the owner's farm.
- **Kaïltsounia** Cretan-style cheese pies drizzled with local thyme honey. Some of the best are from Cretan Divine Family Bakery (p90) in Hora Sfakion or Bitzarakis Bakery (p173).
- **Mousakas** This meat-eggplant-potato casserole is comfort food at its best and a menu staple. Elia & Diosmos (p190) in the Iraklio Wine Country makes an especially delicious version.
- **Souvlaki/Gyros** Slivered grilled meat tucked into a pitta pocket and doused with tzatziki is the local fast food fave. Fine purveyors include Special (p251) in Ierapetra and Oasis (p76) in Hania.

Region by Region

Hania

Crystalline and gentle waters at Elafonisi (p99), Balos Lagoon (p111) and Paleohora (p96) are big draws, as are the ghost stories of Frangokastello (p87) castle, and the labyrinthine old quarters of Hania (p65) and Rethymno (p119). Take teens to tackle one of the many gorges, including Europe's longest, the fabled Samaria Gorge (p105). The giant water park at Limnoupolis (p72) is great for keeping tempers cool.

Rethymno

Youngsters love Rethymno's Venetian fortress (p119) and the playgrounds of the municipal park. Adventures outside the city include an olive oil factory (p141), a spooky ossuary in a rebellious monastery (p137) and cool caverns like the mighty Melidoni Cave (p141). Teens might like the challenge of hiking up Mt Psiloritis (p144). Preveli (p151) beach with its palm trees, and Plakias (p160), are favourite seaside frolicking grounds. The latter also offers horse riding (p147).

Iraklio

Crete's most family-friendly region, with big beach resorts, water sports of all sorts, high-octane water parks, Minotaur mysteries in Knossos (p178) and even a chance to mingle with dinosaurs (p207). The low-key south coast beaches around Matala (p196), with its intriguing caves, are tailor-made for family vacations. Another popular cooling-off destination is the Watercity (p207) water park. If your little ones are into horses, take them to Odysseia Stables (p46) in a lovely location at the foot of Mt Dikti or the Melanouri Horse Farm (p199) near Matala. Another place to make new friends is at the Agia Marina Donkey Sanctuary (p199).

Lasithi

This low-key region comes with an extra-dose of appeal for outdoor-loving kids. Clamber around fabulous canyons like the Kritsa Gorge (p235) or the epic Zakros Gorge (p244), visit the cave (p238) where Zeus was born, fancy yourself Robinson Crusoe on uninhabited Chrissi Island (p252), explore a spooky former leper colony (p233) or go swimming on palm-studded Vaï beach (p244). Just south of here, Kouremenos Beach (p245) is Crete's windsurfing mecca.

Good to Know

Look out for the icon for family-friendly suggestions throughout this guide.

Babies & Toddlers Cretans are generally quite relaxed about breastfeeding in public. Formula, fresh milk and heat-treated milk are widely available in large towns and tourist areas. Supermarkets are the best places to look.

Changing facilities Nappy-changing tables are extremely rare. Bring a portable mat and hand sanitiser.

Dining out Kids are welcome just about everywhere. High chairs are rare, though, so consider bringing a deflatable booster seat or a cloth one that attaches to the back of a chair.

Prams & strollers Cobbled streets and steep hills that are not particularly stroller-friendly are ubiquitous, so it's best to bring a baby sling or backpack.

Sightseeing Always watch youngsters at ancient sites where there may be loose masonry or no safety fences.

Swimming Be careful at isolated beaches and coves that may look peaceful but could have powerful and dangerous offshore currents.

Transport Seatbelts must be worn in front and back seats. Children under 11 or less than 1.35m tall must sit in a child restraint in the back. If hiring a car, check for agencies that have child seats available and fit the seats yourself.

Useful Resources

Adventures of Annie & Ben in Crete (www.youtube.com/watch?v=DpWI6paUacA) Short animated film aimed at pre-school kids on the HooplaKidz YouTube channel.

Kiddle (kids.kiddle.co/Minoan_civilization) All kids ever wanted to know about life in ancient Minoan times.

Kids Love Greece (www.kidslovegreece.com) Family-travel planning service with extensive online info on Crete.

Kids Love Knossos Free IOS app with audio stories in which a young Minoan boy introduces listeners to the secrets of the Palace of Knossos.

Lonely Planet Kids (www.lonelyplanetkids.com) Loads of activities and great family travel blog content.

Mamma Mia (https://play.google.com, Netflix, Amazon Prime) Romantic comedy set in Greece with songs by ABBA.

Mr Donn (greece.mrdonn.org) History, myths, games and quizzes for kids and teachers.

Kids' Corner

Say What?

Hello.	Γειά σας. *ya*·sas
Goodbye.	Αντίο. an·*di*·o
Thank you.	Ευχαριστώ. ef·ha·ri·*sto*
My name is ...	Με λένε ... me *le*·ne ...

Did You Know?

- Mighty Zeus, the king of gods, was born on Crete.
- Crete has more than 4500 mapped caves.

Have You Tried?

Hohlioi
Snails are a popular in Crete.

Regions at a Glance

The birthplace of Zeus, Crete is a vast and multifaceted island whose sun-blessed landscape is a quilt of soaring mountains, dramatic gorges and stunning beaches.

The northern coast, with its nearly uninterrupted strip of beach resorts, has built-up infrastructure and gets the most visitors.

The rugged interior, by contrast, is largely untouched by mass tourism. A dreamy mosaic of sleepy villages, terraced vineyards and fertile valleys, punctuated with Byzantine churches and historic monasteries, the interior invites exploration at a leisurely pace.

Those with a sense of adventure will be enchanted by the largely untamed south. Serpentine roads dead-end in isolated coves and the landscape is sliced by steep gorges, where rare plants and animals thrive.

Hania

History
Beaches
Activities

Venetian Chic

The splendid Venetian port of Hania is bursting with colour and the time-tested pomp appropriate to the former maritime empire of Venice. Trace your way down the massive stone walls, past the arsenals and shipyards, and along the historic mansions (now housing stylish hotels) to gaze over the waterfront, drink in hand.

Crystalline Seas

Embraced by the open Mediterranean (next stop, Spain or Africa!), western Crete has pristine, crystal-clear waters, heated to almost tropical temperatures at pink-sand beaches such as Elafonisi, Balos and Falasarna.

Ultimate Survival

The Lefka Ori (White Mountains) south of Hania comprise Crete's wildest terrain, interspersed with deep gorges, labyrinthine caves and raw cliffs. Whether you're after white-knuckle driving, gorge trekking, rock climbing or even (way) off-piste skiing in winter, this is the place to go.

p62

Rethymno

History
Beaches
Scenery

Historic Sites

All phases of Cretan history are represented in Rethymno, whose eponymous main town is itself a pretty pastiche of Venetian and Ottoman architecture. Monasteries that stood firm against the Turks, and remote mountain villages drenched in age-old traditions, will leave you wanting more.

Remote Shores

There's something otherworldly about Rethymno's corrugated southern coast, where craggy inlets embrace perfect little beaches that are often footprint-free. This is the place to dig your toes in the sand and indulge in island dreams.

Mesmerising Views

Lorded over by Crete's highest peak, the often snow-capped Mt Psiloritis, Rethymno delights shutterbugs with dazzling vistas of dramatic gorges, tranquil valleys and velvety hills blanketed with olive groves, vineyards and wildflowers.

p118

Iraklio

Ancient Sites
Beaches
Family Travel

Minoan Marvels

Endowed with the greatest concentration of Minoan ruins, Iraklio is a magnet for archaeology fans. Stand in awe of the achievements of Europe's oldest civilisation when surveying the palaces of Knossos, Malia, Phaestos and Zakros, plus scores of minor sites.

Life's a Beach

Whether you like your sandy strand infused with a party vibe or prefer a tranquil and remote setting, there's a beach waiting for you to spread your towel.

Childish Delights

Not only do Cretans love children, in Iraklio they have also come up with myriad ways to entertain them in grand style. Let the kids frolic by the sea or take them to enchanting aquariums, adrenaline-packed water parks, placid playgrounds and hands-on museums.

p162

Lasithi

Ancient Sites
Beaches
Hiking

Lesser-Known Minoans

Lasithi may not have the painted and polished Minoan ruins of Knossos, but Gournia and Kato Zakros evoke a sometimes deeper awareness. Their wild surroundings and the haunting sense of a lost world fire the imagination towards a more personal sense of place and of the past.

Isolated Beaches

Although famous venues such as palm-lined Vaï draw summer crowds, Lasithi's beaches are generally free of too much organised lounging. You'll find hidden coves and small sandy bays where you'll luxuriate in blissful isolation, such as Itanos and Xerokambos.

High Hiking

Some of Crete's finest mountains dominate the Lasithi skyline. Their airy summits and deep gorges offer superb hiking and trekking amid the heady scents of wildflowers and aromatic herbs. Hiking the spectacular Zakros Gorge to the sea is a prime option.

p216

On the Road

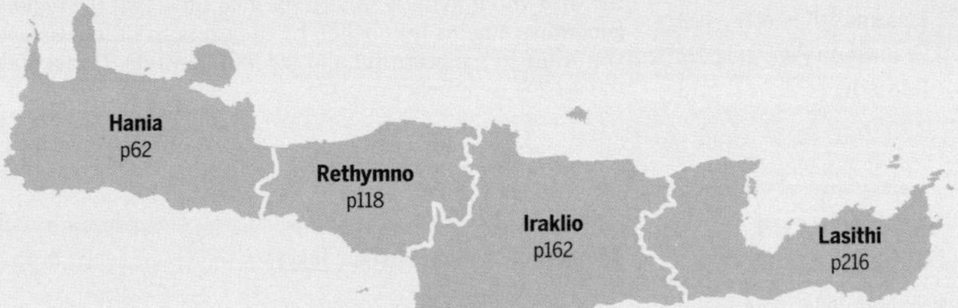

Hania
p62

Rethymno
p118

Iraklio
p162

Lasithi
p216

Hania

Includes ➡

Best Places to Eat

- ➡ To Maridaki (p76)
- ➡ Thalassino Ageri (p77)
- ➡ Gramboussa (p112)
- ➡ To Skolio (p101)

Best Places to Stay

- ➡ Serenissima (p75)
- ➡ Milia (p115)
- ➡ Casa Delfino (p75)
- ➡ Vamos Traditional Village (p85)

Why Go?

The west of Crete stands apart in so many ways. A land of giant mountains, grandiose legends and memorials to great battles past, it is presided over by the romantic port city of Hania, once Venice's jewel of a capital and now filled with boutique hotels, interesting shops and some of Greece's best restaurants. The region also has the grandest gorge in Europe, impressive west-coast beaches, Europe's southernmost possession (tranquil Gavdos, a remote island nearer to Africa than to Greece), and mountain villages that are like a step back in time. The steep mountains that ripple across the west and into the southern sea guarantee that the region generally remains untouched by the excesses of tourism. If you want to see beautiful and traditional Crete, Hania and the west is definitely the place.

Road Distances (km)

	Omalos	Hora Sfakion	Kissamos	Paleohora
Hora Sfakion	107			
Kissamos	59	106		
Paleohora	56	137	44	
Hania	38	73	38	72

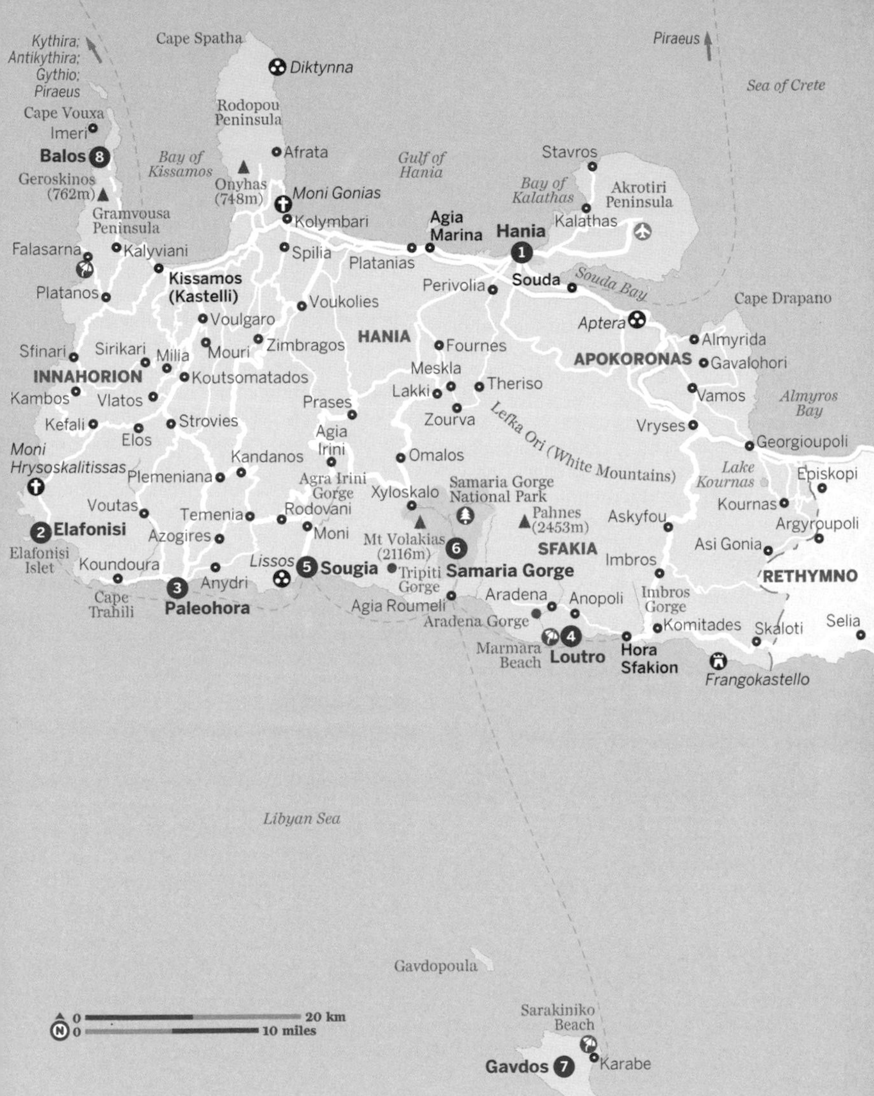

Hania Highlights

❶ **Venetian Harbour** (p65) Strolling along Hania's splendid Venetian harbour.

❷ **Elafonisi** (p99) Relaxing on the fine pink-cream sands of this southwestern beach.

❸ **Paleohora** (p95) Enjoying live Cretan music and the laid-back vibes of this coastal town.

❹ **Loutro** (p91) Travelling by boat to escape the masses in this sparkling southern hamlet.

❺ **Sougia** (p92) Taking to the nearby hiking trails before unwinding in this refreshingly undeveloped beach town.

❻ **Hiking** (p105) Tackling the grand Samaria Gorge.

❼ **Gavdos** (p100) Really getting away from it all on this remote island at the southernmost tip of Europe.

❽ **Balos** (p111) Swimming in the magical teal lagoons at the western edge of the remote Gramvousa Peninsula.

HANIA ΧΑΝΙΑ

POP 54,000

Hania (also spelled Chania) is Crete's most evocative city, with its pretty Venetian quarter criss-crossed by narrow lanes and culminating at a magnificent harbour. Remnants of Venetian and Turkish architecture abound, with old townhouses now transformed into atmospheric restaurants and boutique hotels.

Although all this beauty means the old town is deluged with tourists in summer, it's still a great place to unwind. The Venetian Harbour is ideal for a stroll and a coffee or cocktail. Thanks to an active modern centre, the city retains its charm in winter. Indie boutiques and an entire lane (Skrydlof) dedicated to leather products provide good shopping, and a multitude of creative restaurants means you'll eat very well here.

History

The important Minoan settlement of Kydonia was centred on the hill to the east of Hania's harbour, between Akti Tombazi and Karaoli Dimitriou. Kydonia was destroyed along with the rest of Crete's Minoan civilisation in 1450 BC, but it was rebuilt and later flourished as an ancient Greek city-state during Hellenistic times. It continued to prosper under Roman and Byzantine rule.

Hania, along with the rest of Crete, was claimed by the rising power of Venice following the Fourth Crusade (1204), and the city was renamed La Canea. After briefly losing the city to their Genoese rivals in 1266, the Venetians wrested it back in 1290. They constructed massive fortifications to protect the city from pirates, making it a key strategic hub in their Mediterranean trading empire for three and a half centuries.

In 1645 Hania was captured by the Ottoman Empire, after a two-month siege. The Turks made it the seat of the Turkish Pasha until they were forced out in 1898. During the Turkish occupation of Greece, the city's churches were converted into mosques and the architectural style received some Arabic flourishes, such as wooden walls, latticed windows and minarets (two survive today).

When Crete became independent of Turkish rule in 1898, Hania was declared the island's capital by Europe's Great Powers. It remained so until 1971, when the administration was transferred to Iraklio.

The WWII Battle of Crete largely took place along the coast to the west of Hania. The town itself was heavily bombed during WWII, particularly around Ancient Kydonia, but enough of the old town survives for it to be regarded as Crete's most beautiful city.

Sights

From Plateia 1866, the Venetian Harbour is a short walk north up Halidon. Zambeliou, once Hania's main thoroughfare, is lined with craft shops, small hotels and tavernas. The slightly bohemian Splantzia quarter, running from Plateia 1821 between Daskalogianni and Halidon, brims with atmospheric

HANIA IN...

Two Days

Take a morning stroll along Hania's wonderful Venetian harbour and out to the lighthouse (p69). Visit the fascinating Archaeological Museum or Maritime Museum by the Venetian Firkas Fortress before lunch at Kouzina EPE (p76). Spend the afternoon with a drive out to the botanical gardens (p103) or stop at Manousakis Winery (p77) for some wine tasting, or sample the beer at Cretan Brewery (p102).

On day two, drive out to superlative Elafonisi beach (p99) at the island's western edge for swimming and sunbathing. Head back to one of Hania's outstanding restaurants, such as Thalassino Ageri (p77), for dinner, or spend the night in Elafonisi and enjoy this magical place once the day visitors have gone home.

Three Days

Go for a full-day trek through Samaria Gorge (p105) or the shorter Agia Irini (p93) or Imbros (p94) Gorges. Along the way, look out for the elusive *kri-kri* (Crete's shy wild goat) up in the cliffs. When you emerge at the coast, you can ferry between remote hamlets Agia Roumeli and Sougia, staying the night on the Libyan sea, or boat all the way to Hora Sfakion for a dinner of fresh fish and *Sfakiani pita* (a crêpe-like pie filled with soft cheese) at Nikos (p90), the harbour-front taverna, or for the bus back to Hania.

restaurants and cafes, boutique hotels and traditional shopping. The headland near the lighthouse separates the Venetian Harbour from the crowded town beach in the modern Nea Hora quarter.

★Venetian Harbour HISTORIC SITE

FREE There are few places where Hania's historic charm and grandeur are more palpable than in the old Venetian Harbour. It's lined by pastel-coloured buildings that punctuate a maze of narrow lanes lined with shops and tavernas. The eastern side is dominated by the domed Mosque of Kioutsouk Hasan, now an exhibition hall, while a few steps further east the impressively restored Grand Arsenal (p68) houses the Centre of Mediterranean Architecture.

At sunset, join locals and tourists on a stroll out to the lighthouse (p69) that stands sentinel over the harbour entrance.

★Hania Archaeological Museum MUSEUM

(☎28210 90334; http://chaniamuseum.culture.gr; Halidon 28; adult/concession/child €4/2/free; ⏲8.30am-8pm Wed-Mon Apr-Oct, to 4pm Wed-Mon Nov-Mar) The setting alone in the beautifully restored 16th-century Venetian Church of San Francisco is reason to visit this fine collection of artefacts from Neolithic to Roman times. Late-Minoan clay baths used as coffins catch the eye, along with a large glass case with an entire herd of clay bulls (used to worship Poseidon). Other standouts include Roman floor mosaics, Hellenistic gold jewellery, clay tablets with Linear A and Linear B script, and a marble sculpture of the head of Roman emperor Hadrian.

Downstairs is a private collection of Minoan pottery, jewellery and clay models. Also particularly impressive are the statue of Diana and, in the pretty courtyard, a marble fountain decorated with lions' heads, a vestige of the Venetian tradition. A Turkish fountain is a relic from the building's days as a mosque.

The church itself was a mosque under the Turks, a movie theatre in 1913, and a munitions depot for the Germans during WWII. At the time of research there were plans to move the museum to a new location sometime in 2020; check ahead before visiting.

Firkas Fortress FORTRESS

(⏲8am-2pm Mon-Fri) The Firkas Fortress at the western tip of the harbour heads the best-preserved section of the massive fortifications that were built by the Venetians to protect the city from marauding pirates and invading Turks. The Turks invaded anyway, in 1645, and turned the fortress into a barracks and a prison. Today, parts of it house the Maritime Museum of Crete. There's a great view of the harbour from the top.

HANIA'S BEST BEACHES

Elafonisi (p100) Sublime southwestern beach famed for its pink sands.

Balos (p111) Stunningly clear lagoon of translucent blues and greens, on the Gramvousa Peninsula.

Falasarna (p113) The best waves in the west slam into this long, sandy beach.

★Maritime Museum of Crete MUSEUM

(☎28210 91875; www.mar-mus-crete.gr; Akti Koundourioti; adult/concession €3/2; ⏲9am-5pm May-Oct, to 3.30pm Nov-Apr) Part of the hulking Venetian-built Firkas Fortress at the western port entrance, this museum celebrates Crete's nautical tradition with model ships, naval instruments, paintings, photographs, maps and memorabilia. One room is dedicated to historical sea battles, while upstairs there's thorough documentation of the WWII-era Battle of Crete. You might be lucky enough to see artists working on new model ships in the ship workroom.

Venetian Fortifications FORTRESS

Part of a defensive system begun in 1538 by Michele Sanmichele, who also designed Iraklio's defences, Hania's massive fortifications remain impressive. Best preserved is the western wall, running from the Firkas Fortress to the **Siavo Bastion**. Entrance to the fortress is via the gates next to the Maritime Museum. The bastion offers good views of the old town.

Mosque of Kioutsouk Hasan MOSQUE

(Mosque of the Janissaries) One of the prettiest and most dominant vestiges of the Turkish era is this dusky-pink multidomed former mosque on the eastern side of the Venetian Harbour. It was built in 1645, making it the oldest Ottoman building in town. It's sometimes open for temporary art exhibits.

Byzantine & Post-Byzantine Collection MUSEUM

(☎28210 96046; Theotokopoulou 78; adult/concession/child €2/1/free; ⏲8am-4pm Wed-Mon) In the impressively restored Venetian Church of San Salvatore, this small but fascinating

Hania

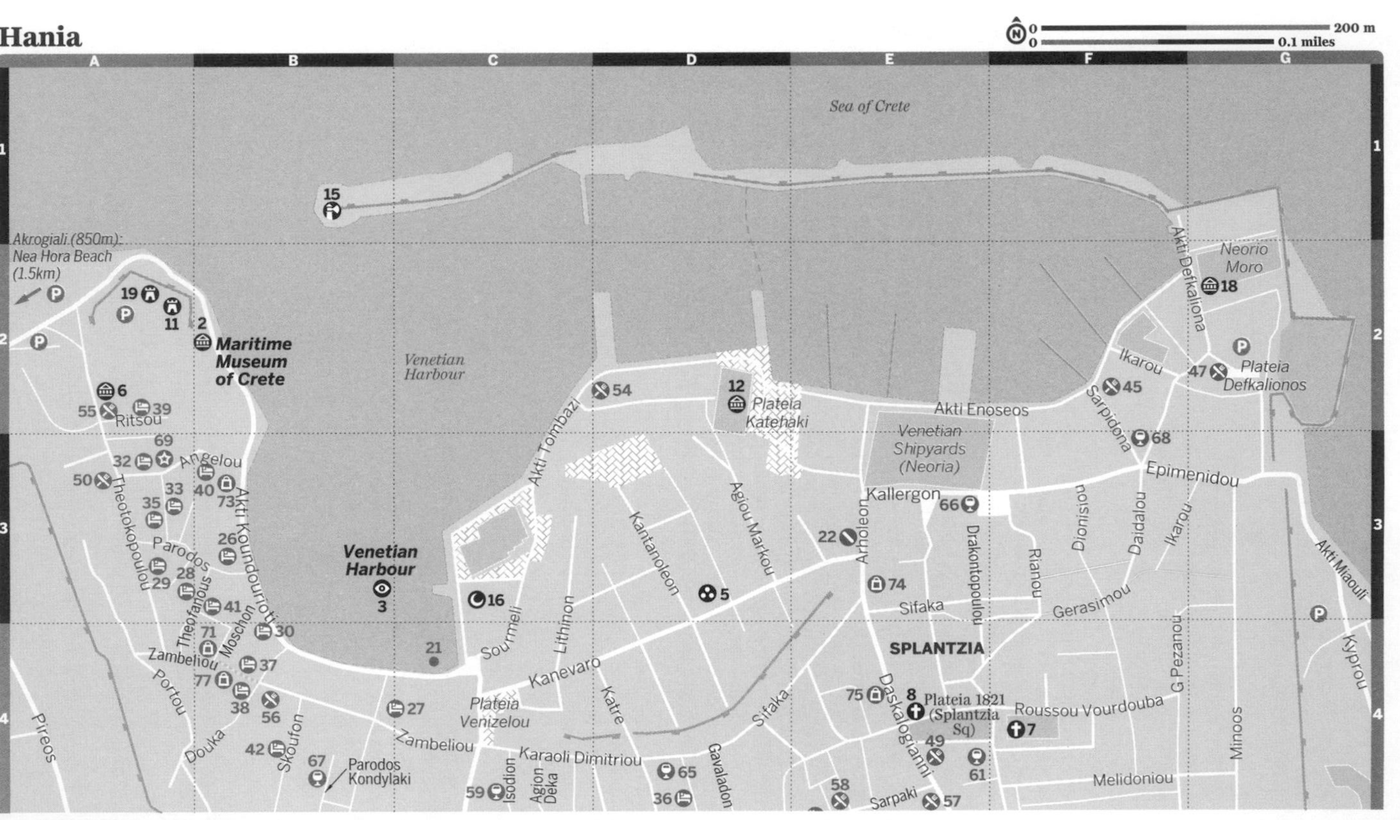
0 200 m
0 0.1 miles
Sea of Crete
Venetian Harbour
Akrogiali (850m); Nea Hora Beach (1.5km)
Maritime Museum of Crete
Venetian Harbour
Venetian Shipyards (Neoria)
Neorio Moro
Plateia Defkalionos
Plateia Katehaki
Plateia Venizelou
Plateia 1821 (Splantzia Sq)
SPLANTZIA
Akti Defkaliona
Akti Enoseos
Akti Tombazi
Akti Koundourioti
Akti Miaouli
Ikarou
Sarpidona
Epimenidou
Kallergon
Drakontopoulou
Rianou
Dionisiou
Daidalou
Gerasimou
G Pezanou
Roussou Vourdouba
Minoos
Melidoniou
Kyprou
Arholeon
Sifaka
Daskalogianni
Sarpaki
Agiou Markou
Kantanoleon
Lithinon
Sourmeli
Kanevaro
Katre
Gavaladon
Karaoli Dimitriou
Agion Deka
Isodion
Zambeliou
Parodos Kondylaki
Skoufon
Douka
Portou
Moschon
Theofanous
Parodos
Theotokopoulou
Angelou
Ritsou
Pireos

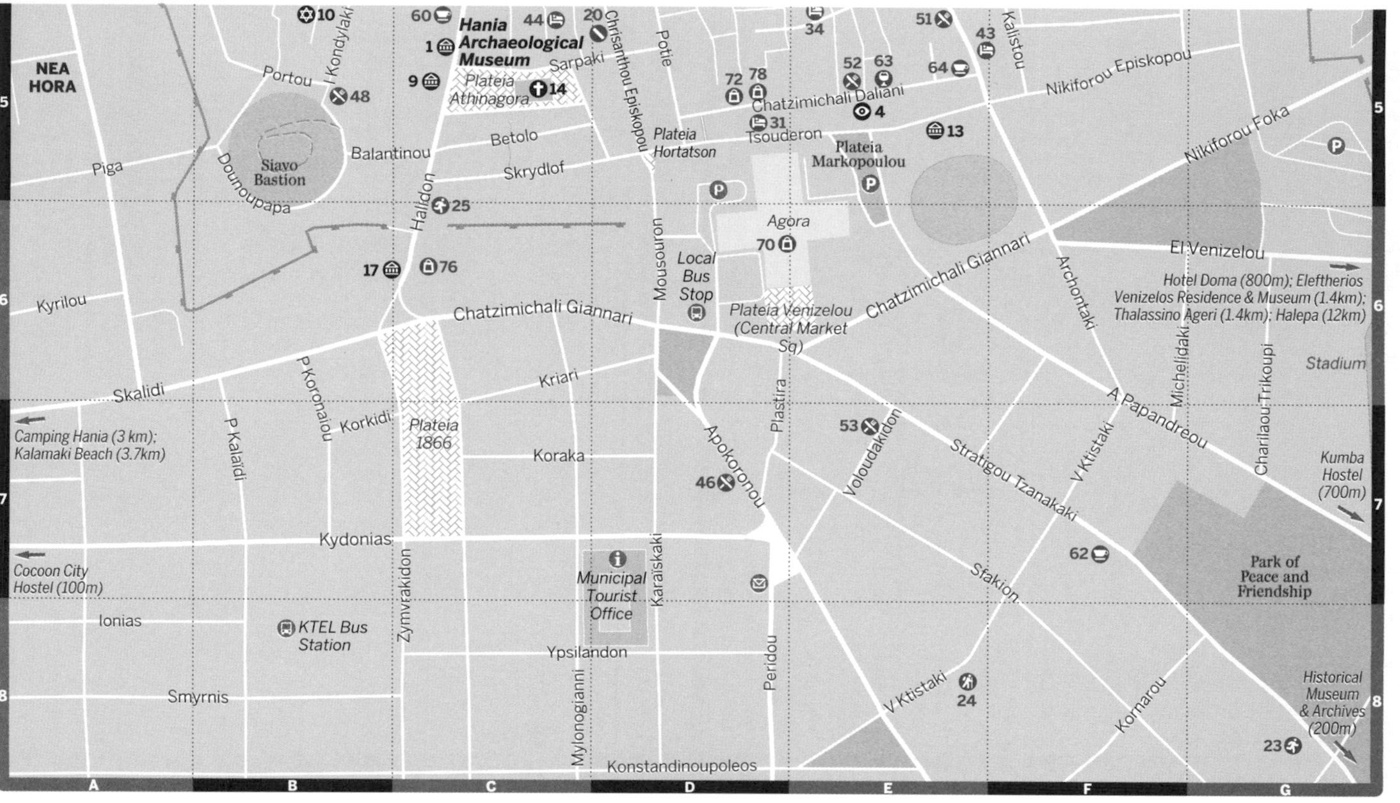
NEA HORA
10
I Kondylaki
60
44
20
1
Hania Archaeological Museum
9
Plateia Athinagora
14
Sarpaki
Chrisanthou Episkopou
Potie
34
51
43
Kalistou
72
78
52
63
64
Chatzimichali Daliani
4
31
Tsouderon
13
Nikiforou Episkopou
Nikiforou Foka
Portou
48
Siavo Bastion
Balantinou
Betolo
Skrydlof
Plateia Hortatson
Plateia Markopoulou
Piga
Dounoupapa
Halidon
25
Agora
70
El Venizelou
17
76
Mousouron
Local Bus Stop
Hotel Doma (800m); Eleftherios Venizelos Residence & Museum (1.4km); Thalassino Ageri (1.4km); Halepa (12km)
Kyrilou
Chatzimichali Giannari
Plateia Venizelou (Central Market Sq)
Archontaki
Stadium
Michelidaki
Charilaou Trikoupi
Skalidi
P Koronaiou
Kriari
A Papandreou
53
Korkidi
Plateia 1866
Plastira
Voloudakidon
Camping Hania (3 km); Kalamaki Beach (3.7km)
P Kalaïdi
Koraka
Apokoronou
Stratigou Tzanakaki
V Ktistaki
Kumba Hostel (700m)
46
Kydonias
62
Cocoon City Hostel (100m)
Municipal Tourist Office
Karaiskaki
Zymvrakidon
Sfakion
Park of Peace and Friendship
Ionias
KTEL Bus Station
Ypsilandon
Smyrnis
Mylonogianni
Peridou
V Ktistaki
24
Kornarou
Historical Museum & Archives (200m)
23
Konstandinoupoleos
A
B
C
D
E
F
G
5
6
7
8

Hania

Top Sights
1 Hania Archaeological Museum C5
2 Maritime Museum of Crete B2
3 Venetian Harbour B3

Sights
4 Ahmet Aga Minaret E5
5 Ancient Kydonia D3
6 Byzantine & Post-Byzantine Collection A2
7 Church of Agios Nikolaos F4
8 Church of San Rocco......................... E4
9 Cretan House Folklore Museum C5
10 Etz Hayyim Synagogue B5
11 Firkas Fortress A2
12 Grand Arsenal D2
13 Greek National Football Museum E5
14 Greek Orthodox Cathedral C5
15 Lighthouse B1
16 Mosque of Kioutsouk Hasan C3
17 Municipal Art Gallery B6
18 Permanent Collection of Ancient & Traditional Shipbuilding G2
19 Venetian Fortifications A2

Activities, Courses & Tours
20 Blue Adventures Diving D5
21 Captain Nick's Glass Bottom Boat C4
22 Chania Diving Center E3
23 Greek Mountaineering Association G8
24 Hania Alpine Travel E8
25 Trekking Plan C6

Sleeping
26 Amphora Hotel B3
27 Bellmondo C4
28 Casa Delfino A3
29 Casa Leone A3
30 Domus Renier B4
31 Elia Daliani Suites D5
32 Iason Studios A3
33 Ifigenia Rooms & Studios A3
34 Ionas Hotel E5
35 Madonna Studios A3
36 Monastery Estate D4
37 Nostos Hotel B4
38 Palazzo Duca B4
39 Pension Lena A2
40 Pension Theresa B3
41 Porto de Colombo B3
42 Serenissima B4
43 Splanzia Hotel E5
44 Vranas Studios C5

Eating
45 Apostolis I & II F2
46 Bougatsa Iordanis D7
47 Christostomos G2
48 Ela B5
49 Glymidakis E4
50 Kalderimi A3
51 Kouzina EPE E5
52 Mesogiako E5
53 Oasis E7
54 Pallas D2
55 Pulse A2
56 Tamam Restaurant B4
57 To Maridaki E4
58 Well of the Turk E4

Drinking & Nightlife
59 Ababa C4
60 Bohème C5
61 Kleidi E4
62 Kross Coffee F7
63 Monastery of Karolos E5
64 Monogram E5
65 Plaka D4
66 Rudi's Beerhouse E3
67 Sinagogi B4
68 Ta Duo Lux F3

Entertainment
69 Fagotto Jazz Bar A3

Shopping
70 Agora D6
71 Exantas Art Space B4
72 Georgina Skalidi D5
73 Mediterraneo Bookstore B3
74 Miden Agan E3
75 Mikro Karavi E4
76 Pelekanakis C6
77 Roka Carpets B4
78 Sifis Stavroulakis D5

collection of artefacts, icons, jewellery and coins spans the period from AD 62 to 1913. Highlights include a segment of a mosaic floor from an early-Christian basilica, an icon of St George slaying the dragon, and a panel recently attributed to El Greco.

The building has a mixed bag of interesting architectural features from its various occupiers. A combined ticket (€6) also gives you entry to the archaeological museums of Hania (p65) and Kissamos (p109).

Grand Arsenal HISTORIC BUILDING

(☎28210 34200; Plateia Katehaki; ⏲varies by exhibit) FREE Impressively restored from a roofless ruin, the 16th-century Venetian arsenal was the last of the 17 shipyard buildings in Hania's Venetian Harbour. After stints as school, hospital and city hall, it is now home to the KAM Centre of Mediterranean Architecture, which hosts regular events and exhibitions.

Lighthouse LIGHTHOUSE

FREE The lighthouse at the mouth of the Venetian Harbour is one of Hania's landmarks, sparkling at sunset and then illuminated after dark. The stone tower rises 21m above a stone base and was built in the 16th century by the Venetians, although it underwent various changes over the years. It's a lovely walk out here with photogenic views of the waterfront.

Permanent Collection of Ancient & Traditional Shipbuilding MUSEUM

(☎28210 91875; Neorio Moro, Akti Defkaliona; adult/child €2/free; ⏱9am-5pm Mon-Sat, 9.30am-5.30pm Sun May-Oct) The *Minoa*, a painstaking replica of a Minoan ship that sailed from Crete to Athens for the 2004 Olympic Games, now permanently docks in a converted Venetian shipyard *(neorio)*. Tools used in its making and photographs from the epic journey bring to life this amazing feat.

Historical Museum & Archives MUSEUM

(☎28210 52606; Ioannou Sfakianaki 20; ⏱9am-3pm Mon-Fri) FREE The Historical Museum & Archives of Hania, about a 1.5km walk southeast of the old harbour, traces Crete's wartorn history with a series of exhibits focusing on the struggle against the Turks. There is a section on WWII displaying an execution pole used by the German army and a *katsouna* (wooden crook) local Cretans used to kill German paratroopers. There are also belongings of national hero Eleftherios Venizelos (1864–1936), the Cretan leader and Greek prime minister, plus a folklore collection.

There's an English brochure and some English signs throughout.

Greek Orthodox Cathedral CATHEDRAL

(Church of the Trimartyri; ☎28210 27807; Plateia Athinagora; ⏱7am-noon & 2-7pm) This three-aisled basilica with its prominent bell tower is dedicated to the Virgin of the Three Martyrs, Hania's patron saint. The present structure was completed in 1860 and sits atop an older church dating to the 14th century that was demoted to soap factory during Turkish rule.

Etz Hayyim Synagogue SYNAGOGUE

(☎28210 86286; www.etz-hayyim-hania.org; Parodos Kondylaki; donation €2; ⏱10am-3pm Mon-Fri) Crete's only remaining synagogue (dating from the 15th century) was badly damaged in WWII and reopened only in 1999. It sports a *mikveh* (ritual bath), tombs of rabbis and a memorial to the local Jews killed by the Nazis. Today it serves a small congregation and is open to visitors. Find it on a small lane accessible only from Kondylaki.

Cretan House Folklore Museum MUSEUM

(☎28210 90816; Halidon 46b; adult/child €3/free; ⏱9am-3pm & 6-9pm Mon-Sat) Hania's interesting Folklore Museum contains a selection of crafts, including weavings with traditional designs; local paintings; and several rooms of a traditional Cretan house. Find the entrance inside the courtyard near the Catholic Church of Assumption and head upstairs.

Municipal Art Gallery GALLERY

(☎28210 92294; www.pinakothiki-chania.gr; Halidon 98-102; admission varies; ⏱10am-2pm & 6-9pm Mon-Sat) Hania's modern art gallery evokes the interior of a boat and presents temporary exhibitions of contemporary works by local and national artists on three elegant, well-lit floors. Shows are mostly free but sometimes ticketed at around €2 to €4.

Greek National Football Museum MUSEUM

(☎69743 31691; Tsouderon 40; by donation; ⏱10am-5pm, closed Sun Mar-Oct, reduced hours Nov-Mar) This tiny museum might look like a shop, but it's actually crammed with more than 2000 items of soccer memorabilia. Run by Nikos, the passionate president of the Greek Football Supporters Club, it houses signed shirts by legendary players such as David Beckham, Pelé and Zinedine Zidane, as well as the Euro 2004 cup won by Greece.

Ahmet Aga Minaret LANDMARK

(Chatzimichali Daliani) Soaring above the rooftops of the charismatic Splantzia quarter, the Ahmet Aga Minaret is one of Hania's two remaining minarets from the Ottoman era.

Church of San Rocco CHURCH

(Plateia 1821) This 17th-century Venetian church was probably built following an outbreak of plague and was turned into a military guardhouse under the Turks. Restored to all its late Renaissance glory, it is rarely open to the public.

Church of Agios Nikolaos CHURCH

(Plateia 1821; ⏱7am-noon & 2-7pm) One of Hania's most intriguing buildings is this Venetian-era church with both a bell tower and a double-balconied minaret – the latter replaced a second bell tower during its stint as a mosque under Turkish rule. Inside, the

ROAD TRIP > SOUTHWESTERN HANIA

This southwestern driving tour is a swerving mountain adventure into the wildest stretches of Crete – a DIY dream through bucolic villages, past stunning ravines where olive trees cling to precipitous cliffs, and to the island's most serene beaches. It's a full-day trip, so start early.

❶ Botanical Park

Head south from Hania towards Fournes. Make your first stop at the **Botanical Park** (p103), where you can have a quick jaunt among the interesting collection of tropical, medicinal and ornamental plants and trees, and then enjoy a coffee with sweeping views on the terrace.

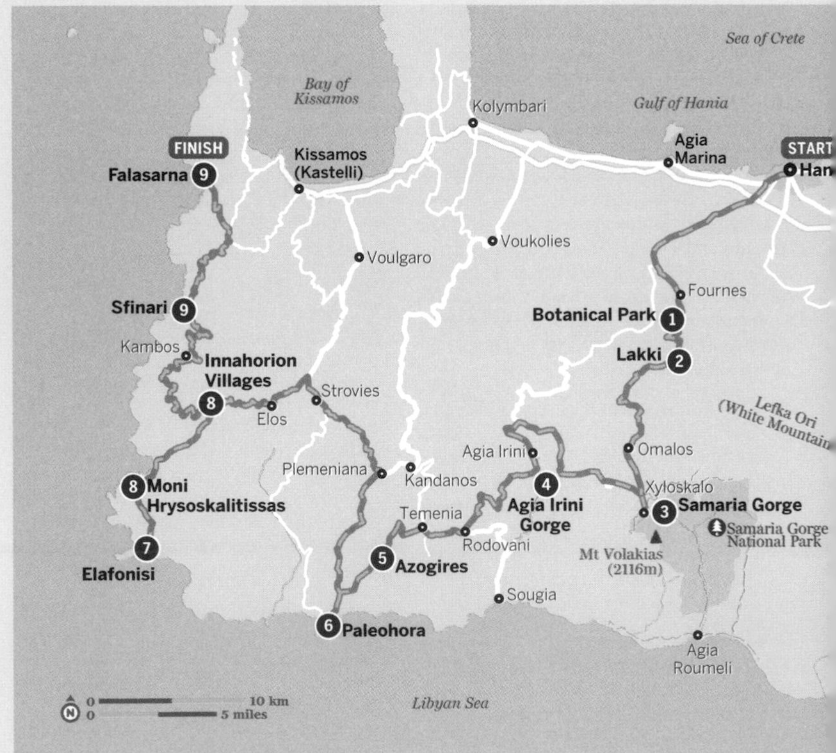

One Day 118 miles/190km

Great for... Outdoors, Food & Drink

Best Time to Go Late spring or early autumn

❷ Lakki

Continue on to the unspoilt mountain hamlet of **Lakki** (p103) and check out the stunning church here.

❸ Samaria Gorge

Next, head for mountain-shrouded Omalos and peek into the awe-inspiring **Samaria Gorge** (p105) at Xyloskalo. Turn back a few kilometres and go west across the Omalos Plateau to return to the jagged north–south road.

❹ Agia Irini Gorge

Going south you'll reach the top of **Agia Irini Gorge** (p93) for a quick look down into the gorge, as stupendous as Samaria. The zigzagging road south requires concentration and passes through several traditional villages.

❺ Azogires

Turning west at Rodovani, you will soon reach a junction near Temenia; if you're in need of cool refreshment, stop in at this tiny place, known for its juices. Keep heading west and then south to the lovely Azogires, a curious village of local legends. Stop for tourist info, a chat and a snack at **Alpha Restaurant** (p98); if no one is around, the community-run cafe works on an honour system, so just take what you like and leave your payment. Don't leave Azogires before checking out local art in the gallery across the road.

❻ Paleohora

Drop to the /.*o*coast at colourful, laid-back **Paleohora** (p95). Grab some lunch at the excellent vegetarian restaurant **Third Eye** (p98), have a quick dip at **Pahia Ammos** (p95) and enjoy a coffee at local favourite hang-out **Agios** (p98) before moving on.

❼ Elafonisi

Next up are the magnificent pink sands of **Elafonisi** (p99), Crete's most sublime beach. As the water swirls across the sands, rainbows shimmer across its surface. If the main beach is looking a little crowded, head around the islet for more secluded spots. This stop requires you to loop north again via Plemeniana and Elos; don't take the more direct-looking dirt road that appears on some maps, as it's suitable only for serious 4WDs.

❽ Moni Hrysoskalitissas & Innahorion Villages

After blissing out at Elafonisi, drive 4km north to visit ethereal **Moni Hrysoskalitissas** (p100). Continue along the coast through the **Innahorion villages**, with traditional architecture and delicious honey, cheese and olive oil.

❾ Sfinari & Falasarna

Stop at **Sfinari** (p114) for a seaside fresh-fish meal, then plan to spend the night at relaxing **Falasarna** (p113), a lovely rose-sand beach with plenty of good accommodation and magical sunsets.

massive bronze chandeliers dangling from a barrel-vaulted coffered ceiling will likely draw your attention.

The church was originally part of a Dominican monastery founded in 1320. The only section left from this era is the cross-vaulted arcade on the north side (off Vourdouba).

Eleftherios Venizelos Residence & Museum MUSEUM
(☎28210 56008; www.venizelos-foundation.gr; Plateia Helena Venizelou, Halepa; adult/child €4/2; ⊙11am-2pm & 6.30-9pm Mon-Fri, 11am-2pm Sat mid-Jun–Sep, shorter hours Oct–mid-Jun) Some 2km east of the old town, in the Halepa neighbourhood, the Eleftherios Venizelos Residence & Museum preserves the great statesman's home in splendid fashion, with original furnishings, maps and other information.

Ancient Kydonia RUINS
(cnr Kanevaro & Kantanoleon) The discovery of clay tablets with Linear B script during ongoing excavations on Kastelli Hill to the east of the Venetian Harbour has led archaeologists to conclude that present-day Hania sits atop an important Minoan city and palace site called Ancient Kydonia. The finest among the unearthed artefacts are displayed in Hania's Archaeological Museum (p65). There are information boards in English at the site of the ruins.

Beaches

The town beach 2km west of the Venetian Harbour at Nea Hora is crowded but convenient if you just want to cool off and get some rays. Koum Kapi is less used (and less clean). For better swimming, keep heading west to the beaches (in order) of Hrysi Akti, Agioi Apostoli and Kalamaki, which are all served by local buses heading towards Platanias.

Nea Hora Beach BEACH
(Akti Papanikoli) Hania's in-town beach is only a 10-minute walk west of the Venetian Harbour. The 500m-long yellow-sand strip is backed by tavernas and holiday-apartment rentals. Fairly shallow, it's good for kids and popular with locals at weekends.

Hrysi Akti Beach BEACH
(Nea Kydonia) Located 2.5km west of Hania, Hrysi Akti (which translates aptly as Golden Sands) is a lovely 500m arc of sandy beach; the shallow waters are suitable for families with young children.

Agioi Apostoli BEACH
Two small beaches make up the Agioi Apostoli (The Holy Apostles) area, around 3.5km west of Hania. These sheltered coves are perfect for families.

Kalamaki BEACH
The small, sandy beach of Kalamaki is 5km west of Hania and has calm, shallow waters, making it a good choice for families with young children.

HANIA FOR CHILDREN

If your youngster has lost interest in Venetian architecture, head to the Park of Peace and Friendship between Tzanakaki and A Papandreou, where there's a playground and a shady cafe. Eight kilometres south of town, the giant water park **Limnoupolis** (☎28210 33246; www.limnoupolis.gr; Varypetro; day pass adult/child 4-12yr €25/18, afternoon pass €17/14; ⊙10am-6pm mid-May–mid-Jun & Sep, to 7pm mid-Jun–Aug) has enough slides and pools to keep kids amused, and cafes and pool bars for adults. Buses leave regularly from the KTEL bus station.

Activities

Hania is a popular gateway for guided excursions to Samaria Gorge and other hiking trips; the Greek Mountaineering Association has information.

Diving outfits, including Blue Adventures and Chania Diving, offer boat dives and snorkelling trips in the area.

For something more sybaritic, you can opt for a private cruise to islands nearby for a spot of swimming and light snorkelling.

Greek Mountaineering Association OUTDOORS
(EOS; ☎28210 44647; www.eoshanion.gr; Tzanakaki 90; ⊙9-11pm Mon-Fri) For all your hiking and mountaineering needs on Crete, this is the go-to organisation. Check the website or swing by the local EOS chapter in Hania in the evening to get the full scoop, including climbing in the Lefka Ori (White Mountains), and info on mountain refuges and the E4 European Path.

Trekking Plan OUTDOORS
(☎28210 27040, 6932417040; www.cycling.gr; Halidon 85; ⊙9am-2pm & 6-8.30pm, closed Sun

Nov-Apr) Trekking Plan (operating out of the Attios travel agency) arranges hikes to Agia Irini, Samaria and Imbros Gorges; climbs of Mt Gingilos; canyoning, rappelling and rock climbing; and kayaking and mountain-biking tours. There are ski tours in winter.

Hania Alpine Travel HIKING
(☎28210 50939, 6932252890; www.alpine.gr; Boniali 11-19) Well-run outfit offering tailored trips, including hiking, climbing and sea-kayaking holidays, for families, groups and individuals.

Chania Diving Center DIVING
(☎28210 58939; www.chaniadiving.gr; Arholeon 1; 2 dives €90, snorkelling tour €55) Runs dives around Hania, including PADI courses (open-water certification €460), dive trips, beginner dives and snorkelling trips. Prices include transport to/from your accommodation.

Blue Adventures Diving DIVING
(☎28210 40608; www.blueadventures.gr; Chrysanthou Episkopou 39; 2 dives incl gear €90, snorkelling tour €50; ⏲9am-9pm Mon-Sat May-Oct) This established outfit offers a host of dive options, including discover courses (€85), PADI open-water certification (€460), and diving trips around Hania, including beginner dives in PADI training standards. There are also snorkelling trips.

SUP in Crete WATER SPORTS
(☎6936072730; www.supincrete.com; SUP & snorkelling tour adult/child €59/45) Runs daily stand-up paddleboard (SUP) tours around Crete, including at Elafonisi, and a SUP and snorkelling tour around Marathi and Loutraki. Free transfers included from accommodation in Hania.

Hellas Bikes CYCLING
(☎28210 60858; www.hellasbike.net; Agia Marina; bicycle per day from €13; ⏲9am-1pm & 5-8.30pm) In Agia Marina, 10km west of Hania, this group hires out bikes and leads half- and full-day bike tours around the region.

Tours

Notos Sailing BOATING
(☎69471 81990; www.notos-sailing.com; full-day trip for 3/8 people €550/880) Set off on a private cruise around Hania with your friendly and informative captain, Nikos. Full-day trips include stops at islands to swim and snorkel, and snacks and drinks on board. Shorter trips can also be arranged.

Captain Nick's Glass Bottom Boat BOATING
(☎6944156831; www.captainnickchania.com; Hania Harbour; 1/2½/3½hr trip €10/20/25) The best bet among Hania's lacklustre day-trip boats, friendly and fun Captain Nick cruises the nearby offshore islands, including a stop to see the wreckage of a WWII German plane through the boat's glass bottom. There's snorkelling equipment on board. The price includes a drink.

Festivals & Events

Battle of Crete CULTURAL
(⏲May) Hania commemorates the WWII Battle of Crete anniversary with athletics competitions, folk dancing and ceremonial events for a week at the end of May.

Summer Festival PERFORMING ARTS
(www.chaniatourism.com; ⏲Jun-Aug) From June to August the municipality hosts cultural events around the city, including in the public gardens and at the open-air theatre on the outskirts of the city walls (on Kyprou), which has regular music and theatrical performances.

Sleeping

Hania's old town brims with boutique hotels and atmospheric pensions in restored Venetian buildings. Tip: while rooms overlooking the harbour have views, noise from harbour-front restaurants and bars can be an issue. A couple of hip hostels have recently opened in the new city. Book ahead for accommodation in Hania in summer, when there may also be minimum-stay requirements. There's a campground on the beach 5km west of town.

★**Cocoon City Hostel** HOSTEL €
(☎28210 76100; www.cocooncityhostel.com; Kydonias 145; dm from €18, d with/without bathroom from €40/35; ❄📶) Within easy reach of the bus station and the old town, this modern, spick-and-span hostel has four- and six-bed mixed dorms that come with their own light, charging point and under-bed storage. Private rooms share a bathroom, except one that comes with its own (though its proximity to the lobby cafe-bar means some noise). Helpful staff can arrange excursions to Samaria Gorge.

Kumba Hostel HOSTEL €
(☎28210 08282; www.kumbahostel.com; Iroon Politechniou 37; dm from €18, d from €40; ❄📶) On

a main road a 15-minute walk from the old town, this beautifully restored whitewashed building has become a hip hostel. There's African art on the walls, decorative tiled flooring, a bright cafe-bar and young, friendly staff. Dorms are spacious and modern, each bed with light and charging point. Most dorms have sparkling bathrooms, while private rooms are quiet and comfortable.

Iason Studios APARTMENT **€**
(☎28210 87102; www.iasonstudios.gr; Angelou 32; d from €40; ❄📶) These simple, spacious studios in the old town are run by friendly and helpful English-speaking proprietress Despina. They have kitchenettes with everything you need, and some have town-facing balconies. The location is charming and convenient, close to Firkas Fortress (p65) and the harbour, yet quiet and peaceful.

Vranas Studios APARTMENT **€**
(☎28210 58618; www.vranas.gr; Agion Deka 10; studios €45-70; ❄📶) In the heart of the old town, this place is on a lively pedestrian street and has spacious studios with wooden floorboards, renovated sparkling bathrooms and kitchenettes. Service is warm and friendly. Some of the decor in a few rooms is a little worn.

Pension Theresa PENSION **€**
(☎28210 92798; www.pensiontheresa.gr; Angelou 8; s €25-30, d €40-70; ❄📶👪) This creaky old Venetian house with a long, steep, winding staircase and antique furniture delivers eight snug rooms with character aplenty. The location is excellent, the ambience is rustic and convivial, and there are fab views from the rooftop terrace, plus a communal kitchen stocked with basic breakfast items. There's an annexe nearby with apartments suitable for families.

★Ionas Hotel HOTEL **€€**
(☎28210 55090; www.ionashotel.com; cnr Sarpaki & Sorvolou; s/d/ste incl breakfast from €85/100/120; ❄📶) In the quieter Splantzia quarter, Ionas is housed in a historic building with contemporary interior design and friendly owners. The nine charming rooms are kitted out with all mod cons (including a spa bath in one) and share a rooftop terrace. Original features include a Venetian archway in the entrance and walls from the mid-16th century.

Elia Daliani Suites GUESTHOUSE **€€**
(☎28215 04684; www.eliahotels.com; Chatzimichali Daliani 57; d from €100; ❄📶👪) These four spacious, stylish suites fill a restored Venetian townhouse on pedestrianised Daliani, just behind the town market. The look is contemporary, with all-white furniture, and features wall-sized black-and-white photographs of scenes from rural Crete. A small balcony looks out over the quiet street. No on-site reception.

Palazzo Duca BOUTIQUE HOTEL **€€**
(☎28210 70460; www.palazzoduca.gr; Douka 27-29; d €100-180; ❄📶) In a backstreet off the harbour, this protected building with Byzantine origins has been meticulously restored and turned into a pint-sized luxury hotel offering eight elegantly furnished rooms with kitchenettes that are spread over three floors (there's a lift). The best is the vast top-floor suite with kitchenette and private patio with Jacuzzi.

Ifigenia Rooms & Studios GUESTHOUSE **€€**
(☎28210 94357; www.ifigeniastudios.gr; Gamba 23; r €50-130; ❄📶) This network of refurbished buildings around the Venetian Harbour has a bed for every budget, from basic rooms to luxurious bi-level suites with Jacuzzis and sea views. Most of the 25 units brim with such old-timey touches as wrought-iron canopy beds and beamed ceilings. The pricier ones have kitchens and can sleep up to four.

Management can also arrange car or bicycle hire, diving trips and excursions.

Bellmondo HOTEL **€€**
(☎28210 36217; www.belmondohotel.com; Zambeliou 10; s/d/tr incl breakfast from €73/90/105; ❄📶) With Turkish and Venetian features, including part of an old *hammam* (Turkish baths) in one room, the Bellmondo is furnished with simple wooden pieces and offers friendly service. The nicest rooms have balconies (for about €25 more than the standard rate) and harbour views.

Hotel Doma BOUTIQUE HOTEL **€€**
(☎28210 51772; www.hotel-doma.gr; Venizelos 124; d/ste incl buffet breakfast from €100/200; ⊙Apr-Oct; ❄📶) One could imagine Hercule Poirot peering down the curving stairway at Doma, a quiet, century-old classic overlooking the sea in the Halepa district. Decorated with period furnishings and scattered antiquities, this former Austro-Hungarian and British consulate features classy rooms and suites

(the top-floor suite comes with incredible views), a relaxing garden, extraordinarily kind service and a tasty buffet breakfast.

Splanzia Hotel BOUTIQUE HOTEL **€€**
(28210 45313; www.splanzia.com; Daskalogianni 20; d incl breakfast from €110;) This smartly renovated hotel in a Venetian mansion in the lively Splantzia quarter has eight stylish rooms, each different but all outfitted with custom-made wooden furniture, huge comfy beds – some of them canopied – and coffee machines. The back rooms overlook a bougainvillea-festooned courtyard with a Turkish well.

It's run by friendly folk with a knack for hospitality.

Casa Leone BOUTIQUE HOTEL **€€**
(28210 76762; www.casa-leone.com; Parodos Theotokopoulou 18; d/ste incl breakfast from €135/160;) This Venetian residence has been converted into a lovely romantic family-run boutique hotel. The rooms are spacious and well appointed, with drape-canopy beds and sumptuous curtains, though some show ever-so-slight signs of wear and bathrooms are small. Some have balconies overlooking the harbour. The central salon is delightful; it sits above the harbour.

Amphora Hotel HOTEL **€€**
(28210 93224; www.amphora.gr; Parodos Theotokopoulou 20; s/d/tr from €95/110/115;) Most of the elegantly decorated rooms at this restored Venetian mansion wrap around a courtyard, with a few more in a connected wing. Those on the top floors have harbour views, but front rooms can be very noisy in summer. Breakfast is served on the rooftop terrace looking out over the harbour.

Madonna Studios APARTMENT **€€**
(28210 94747; www.madonnastudios.gr; Gamba 33; studios €90-120;) This charming small hotel in a Venetian building has five attractive and well-appointed studios around a lovely flower-filled courtyard. Rooms are furnished in traditional style; the front top room has a superb balcony, while the courtyard room has the original stone wash trough.

Porto de Colombo HOTEL **€€**
(28210 70945; www.portodelcolombo.gr; cnr Theofanous & Moschon; d/apt incl breakfast from €90/100;) Once the French embassy and the office of Eleftherios Venizelos, this 600-year-old Venetian townhouse is now a charming hotel with 10 well-appointed rooms; the top suites have fine harbour views. The standard rooms can fit up to three (though it's a bit snug).

Nostos Hotel BOUTIQUE HOTEL **€€**
(28210 94743; www.nostos-hotel.com; Zambeliou 42-46; s/d/tr incl breakfast from €80/110/150;) Mixing Venetian style and modern fixtures, this hotel occupies a characterful 600-year-old building. There are 12 decent rooms with fridge and TV; studios have kitchens. Take in the views from the roof garden or balcony rooms with harbour views.

Pension Lena PENSION **€€**
(28210 86860; www.lenachania.gr; Ritsou 5; s/d €45/65;) This pension near Firkas Fortress has tastefully done rooms with an old-world feel and a scattering of antiques, though the front rooms are the most appealing. Lena also offers three independent houses in restored traditional buildings.

★ **Serenissima** BOUTIQUE HOTEL **€€€**
(28210 86386; www.serenissima.gr; Skoufon 4; d incl breakfast from €170;) This tranquil Venetian townhouse, renovated to impeccable standards, packs plenty of design cachet into its historic walls. The elegant rooms feature the gamut of mod cons, along with period touches such as stone walls, wooden beams and candlelit niches. Rates include an à la carte breakfast in the downstairs restaurant-bar.

★ **Casa Delfino** BOUTIQUE HOTEL **€€€**
(28210 87400; www.casadelfino.com; Theofanous 9; r/apt/ste incl breakfast from €190/245/265;) Luxury is taken very seriously at this elegant 17th-century mansion in the Venetian quarter. Choose from standard rooms, one-bedroom apartments and suites, which come in various sizes but are all richly fitted out with bespoke furniture, marble floors and romantic flourishes. Days start with breakfast in the pebble-mosaic courtyard, while the Turkish spa and the rooftop terrace are perfect end-of-day unwinding spots.

Monastery Estate Venetian Harbor BOUTIQUE HOTEL **€€€**
(28210 52184; www.monasteryestate.com; Kallinikou Sarpaki 40; d from €150;) This chic hotel is tucked away in a quiet alley and housed in a meticulously restored Venetian mansion (check out the ruins under the lobby's glass floor). Some rooms have their own

bathtub, while others have a retractable roof leading to a rooftop hot tub with old-town views (though they don't offer much privacy from neighbouring rooms' rooftops).

Service is faultless and extremely helpful. There's an on-site spa and restaurant.

Domus Renier LUXURY HOTEL €€€
(☎28210 88806; www.domusrenier.gr; cnr Akti Kountourioti & Moschon; r from €200; ❄📶) An impressive boutique hotel with just nine suites, Domus Reiner is housed in a stunning restored Venetian building right on the harbour. Rooms are elegantly fitted out yet comfortable; most come with fantastic sea views and some have an outdoor Jacuzzi. Service is impeccable: personable yet professional. Access from the harbour is through Zepos restaurant.

Eating

Hania has some of the finest restaurants in Crete, most of which are located in the old town. Many of the harbourside options are bland, overpriced tourist traps; the best of the bunch are on the eastern side, or head into the maze of the old town's backstreets for great dining.

★**Kouzina EPE** CRETAN €
(☎28210 42391; www.facebook.com/kouzinaepe; Daskalogianni 25; dishes €5-10; ⊙noon-7.30pm Mon-Sat; 📶🌿) This cheery lunch spot gets contemporary designer flair from the cement floor and hip lighting. It wins the area's 'local favourite' hands down, by serving a mix of modern à la carte options and great-value, delicious blackboard-listed *mayirefta* (ready-cooked meals); you can inspect what you're about to eat in the open kitchen. Good veg options, too.

Bougatsa Iordanis CRETAN €
(☎28210 88855; www.iordanis.gr; Apokoronou 24; bougatsa €3; ⊙6am-2pm) Locals start salivating at the mention of this bakery dedicated since 1924 to making the finest *bougatsa*. The flaky treat, filled with sweet or savoury cheese, is cooked fresh in enormous slabs, carved into bite-sized pieces and served on simple aluminium trays. Pair it with a double Greek coffee and you're set for the morning. There's nothing else on the menu!

Pulse VEGAN €
(Theotokopoulou 70; mains €9.50; ⊙noon-midnight daily May-Oct, noon-9pm Mon-Sat Nov-Mar; 🌿) Settle in at an outdoor table with sea views for some fantastic vegan dishes at meat-free Pulse, located at the western end of Firkas Fortress. The mezes boards are great for snacking on, as are the potato cakes with chilli jam; mains include a tasty cheeseburger and a beef-free red-wine casserole. The *mousakas* is an absolute highlight.

Oasis FAST FOOD €
(Vouloudakidon 2; souvlaki €2; ⊙9am-10pm) Locals swear by the undeniably tasty *gyros* (meat slivers cooked on a vertical rotisserie) and souvlaki at tiny, old-style Oasis. There are a few seats, but it's mostly a takeaway joint.

Glymidakis BAKERY €
(☎28210 61714; Plateia 1821; baked goods from €1; ⊙6am-9pm) Packed with fresh Cretan breads and sweets, this bakery gets jammed with locals, too, buying its wares or taking them out to the shaded plaza tables with coffee.

★**To Maridaki** SEAFOOD €€
(☎28210 08880; www.tomaridaki.gr; Daskalogianni 33; dishes €6-13; ⊙noon-midnight Mon-Sat) This modern seafood *mezedhopoleio* (restaurant specialising in mezedhes) is often packed to the gills with chatty locals and tourists. Dishes straddle the line between tradition and innovation with to-die-for mussels *saganaki,* charcoal-grilled fresh fish, and delicious house white wine. The complimentary panna cotta is a worthy finish.

Christostomos CRETAN €€
(☎28210 57035; www.chrisostomos.gr; cnr Akti Defkaliona & Ikarou; mains €7-12; ⊙6pm-late) A taverna tucked away from the crowds behind the harbour, Christostomos is popular with tourists and locals for its classic Cretan cuisine. Start with stuffed zucchini flowers before moving on to dishes cooked in the wood-fired oven or in the pot, such as lamb *ofto* with baked potatoes or beef *stifado* (stew cooked in tomato and onion sauce).

Kalderimi CRETAN €€
(☎28210 76741; Theotokopoulou 53; mains €9.80-12.50; ⊙noon-midnight) With its stone-arched interior, warm welcome and well-executed dishes, this is a great all-rounder in a quieter part of the old town, not far from Firkas Fortress. Start with deep-fried *saganaki* cheese with homemade sweet-tomato jam, then move on to lamb chops marinated with herbs and honey raki, paired with local mountain greens.

Pallas INTERNATIONAL €€
(☎28210 45688; www.pallaschania.gr; Akti Tombazi 15; mains €8-16; ⊙8am-4am; 📶) This hip, much-

buzzed-about cafe-bar has a sweet location in an impeccably renovated 1830 customs house right in the Venetian Harbour. Grab a high chair, sofa or table to linger over breakfast, a crisp salad for lunch or a juicy steak dinner – or pop by just for coffee or cocktails. Service can be slow and unenthused.

Mesogiako MEDITERRANEAN **€€**
(☎28210 57992; www.mesogiako.com; Chatzimichali Daliani 36; mezedhes €5-8, mains €8.50-13; ⏰7pm-midnight, shorter hours Nov-Mar; ❄📶) Opposite the minaret in the Splantzia quarter, this cosy restaurant with modern country-style furniture and an appealing flower-strewn terrace sits among a group of similarly popular spots. The menu is most creative when it comes to the mezedhes – salmon croquettes, mushrooms with balsamic vinegar, and zucchini balls with *manouri* and feta cheese are all winners.

Tamam Restaurant MEDITERRANEAN **€€**
(☎28210 96080; www.tamamrestaurant.com; Zambeliou 49; mains €7-14; ⏰noon-midnight; 📶🌱) This stylish, convivial taverna, part of which is in a converted Turkish bathhouse, has captured people's attention since 1982 with strong-flavoured Cretan dishes that often incorporate Middle Eastern spices and touches. The boneless lamb in tomato sauce and yoghurt is a winner. Tables spill onto the narrow alleyway.

Apostolis I & II SEAFOOD **€€**
(☎28210 43470; Akti Enoseos; mains €9-14, fish per kg from €50; ⏰noon-midnight May-Sep, shorter hours rest of year) In the quieter eastern harbour, these well-respected spots for fresh fish and Cretan dishes are in two separate buildings away from each other. Apostolis II is the more popular, as the owner reigns there, but the other has the same menu at marginally cheaper prices. A seafood platter for two, including salad, is €30.

Akrogiali SEAFOOD **€€**
(☎28210 71110; www.akrogiali-taverna.gr; Akti Papanikoli 20; mains €7-12; ⏰9am-midnight May-Oct; 📶) This airy white-and-blue space on Nea Hora beach, to the west of town, does fabulously fresh fish and seafood, including some inspired stuffed-squid varieties.

Well of the Turk MIDDLE EASTERN **€€**
(☎28210 54547; www.welloftheturk.gr; Sarpaki 1-3; mains €10-15; ⏰6pm-midnight Wed-Mon; ❄📶) In an age-old stone building that used to house a *hammam*, and flanking a quiet square, this romantic taverna serves richly textured dishes with a strong French and Moroccan identity, prepared with the finest Cretan ingredients. Specialities include the shish kebab, and slow-cooked lamb with preserved lemons and couscous. The cheesecake with orange blossom is an imaginative culinary coda.

> **LOCAL KNOWLEDGE**
>
> **FINE CRETAN FARE**
>
> About 10km west of Hania, **Leventis** (☎28210 68155; Ano Stalos; mains €6.50-14.50; ⏰5pm-midnight Mon-Fri, noon-late Sat, Sun & daily mid-Jul–Aug) is an award-winning taverna that attracts locals and visitors for its authentic and refined Cretan cuisine. Tables fill an elegant stone-and-wood-beam dining room and a terrace and have views of the lush hills all around. It's a super place to get the best sampling of Crete's top cuisine.

Ela CRETAN **€€**
(☎28210 74128; Kondylaki 47; mains €9-22; ⏰11.30am-midnight; 📶) Built as a soap factory in 1650, Ela has also seen incarnations as school, distillery and cheese-processing plant and is now a charismatic roofless lair serving upscale Cretan specialities. The multilingual menus arrayed in the street signal tourist trap, but it does solid meals.

★Thalassino Ageri SEAFOOD **€€€**
(☎28210 51136; www.thalasino-ageri.gr; Vivilaki 35; fish per kg €55-65; ⏰6.30pm-midnight Mon-Sat, 12.30pm-midnight Sun Apr & May, from 7pm daily Jun-Oct) This solitary fish taverna among the vestiges of Hania's old tanneries in Halepa, 2km east of the centre, is one of Crete's top restaurants. Take in the sunset from the superb waterside setting and peruse the changing menu, dictated by the day's catch, which is cooked over charcoal. The fried calamari melts in your mouth.

There's an indoor restaurant, but it's all about the tables plonked on the sand next to the water here, so bring a jacket on cooler nights.

🍷 Drinking & Nightlife

The cafe-bars around the Venetian Harbour are nice places to sit, but they charge top euro. For a more local vibe, head to Plateia 1821 in the Splantzia quarter, the interior

WORTH A TRIP

MANOUSAKIS WINERY

A family-run business for over 25 years, this pretty **winery** (☎28210 78787; www.manousakiswinery.com; Vatolakkos; wine tasting from €10; ⊙11am-5pm Apr, to 10pm May–mid-Nov, by appointment rest of year) in the village of Vatolakkos – 16km southwest of the centre of Hania – is well worth a visit. Taste the Nostos wines (the rosé is made blending the *Romeiko* grape, which is indigenous to Hania), take a free 15-minute tour of the winery production, or simply settle in for lunch or dinner with a bottle on the tree-shaded terrace set among olive groves and citrus trees.

A bus from Hania stops at the main square in Vatolakkos, an eight-minute walk from the winery.

streets near Potie, or to alt-flavoured Sarpidona at the eastern end of the harbour.

★Monogram COFFEE
(☎28215 07046; www.facebook.com/monogramchania; Daskalogianni 5; ⊙8am-9pm) Soak up the sun at a street-side table with music wafting from this hip corner coffee spot. Beans are sourced from around the globe, including Guatemala and Ethiopia, then roasted locally in Iraklio. It also has a large range of teas you'd be hard-pressed to find elsewhere in Greece, and a few tempting cakes.

★Sinagogi BAR
(☎28210 95242; Parodos Kondylaki 15; ⊙noon-5am May-Oct; 📶) Housed in a roofless Venetian building on a small lane next to the synagogue, this popular summer-only lounge bar with eclectic decor is a laid-back place to relax and take it all in. After dark it's bathed in a romantic glow while DJs play soft electro and bartenders whip up mojitos and daiquiris.

Bohème CAFE
(☎28210 95955; www.boheme-chania.gr; Halidon 26-28; ⊙8am-3am; 📶) Bohème's pretty, tree-shaded terrace and vine-covered pastel-pink stone building provide the perfect retreat. Sip coffee, craft beer or cocktails while relaxing on bright, cushioned wrought-iron chairs; it's especially atmospheric under fairy lights at night. Inside, the multi-space cafe-bar evokes modern Med vibes and does a menu of everything from brunch pancakes to bao (steamed buns) and burgers.

Ababa BAR
(www.facebook.com/ababa.bar; Isodion 12; ⊙10am-2am Sun-Thu, to 3am Fri & Sat) Friendly and relaxed cafe-bar tucked down an alley and decorated with colourful and eclectic art, from paintings of Lenin and Frida Kahlo to a horse's head hanging on the wall and legs dangling from the ceiling. Stop in for a fresh juice or decent cocktails.

Kross Coffee COFFEE
(☎28210 41087; Stratigou Tzanakaki 58; ⊙7.30am-9pm, to 4pm Sun) Locals in the know get their caffeine at this corner cafe, bedecked in pastel green and pink and plenty of greenery. It also has a small branch in the old town close to the central market at Tsouderon 73.

Kleidi BAR
(☎28210 52974; Plateia 1821; ⊙9am-late; 📶) By day locals fill the tree-shaded plaza tables at this modern, cool cafe and sip iced coffee, and by night the place buzzes with party life. There's no written sign, just the image of a keyhole (*kleidi* means key).

Koukouvagia BAR
(www.koukouvaya.gr; Venizelos Graves; ⊙10am-late) About 5km east and uphill from Hania town is the spot where great statesman Eleftherios Venizelos is buried. The site and its neighbouring owl-themed cafe-bar enjoy panoramic views of Hania. It's a popular hang-out for students from the nearby technical university and does delicious snacks and desserts. A taxi from/to Hania costs about €8.

Ta Duo Lux BAR
(☎28210 52519; Sarpidona 8; ⊙8am-2am; 📶) Hidden just off the eastern edge of the harbour, arty cafe-bar Ta Duo Lux is a perennial favourite among alternative types and is lively day and night. There's a short menu of baguettes and sandwiches, too (from €3).

Monastery of Karolos BAR
(☎6974556106; Chatzimichali Daliani 22; ⊙9pm-4am; 📶) Beautifully set in the courtyard of a 16th-century monastery turned art centre, this open-air bar has a vibrant ambience, attentive service, great cocktails and live music.

Rudi's Beerhouse BAR
(☎28210 20319; Kallergon 16; ⊙6pm-2am Mon-Thu, to 3am Fri & Sat) Austrian-born long-time Hania resident Rudi is a knowledgeable beer buff who runs the show at this pub a block

back from the harbour. There are Trappist beers on tap and a huge range of mostly Greek, German and Belgian bottled beers. It's also one of the few places apart from the brewery where you'll find Cretan Brewery pale ale on tap.

Lafkas Brewery MICROBREWERY
(☎06945430402; www.lafkasbrewery.com; Leoforos Kazantzaki 102) Michalis and his Belgian wife, Aurelie, run this nanobrewery 4.5km southwest of Hania. They brew two beers: a triple-hop pale ale and an annual special collaborating with local producers, which might be a stout using Kross cold brew. Buy a bottle (€2.50) to enjoy at the outdoor tables next to a wall-sized mural and with views of the Lefka Ori (White Mountains).

Plaka BAR
(Sifaka 8; ⏰10am-late) Look for the psychedelic decorated facade at this tiny bar with a bamboo-covered terrace. The owner spins vinyl from his collection of over 700 albums, and there's a great selection of Greek beers as well as bar snacks.

☆ Entertainment

★Fagotto Jazz Bar LIVE MUSIC
(☎28210 71877; Angelou 16; ⏰8.30am-2pm & 9pm-late) Established in 1978, this Hania institution in a Venetian building offers smooth jazz and blues, and occasionally live bands or DJs, in an intimate setting in a narrow lane close to the Maritime Museum. The action picks up after 10pm. It opens in the mornings as a cafe and does great breakfasts, too.

Shopping

Hania offers top shopping, especially in the backstreets. Theotokopoulou is lined with souvenir and handicraft shops. Skrydlof offers a vast array of local and imported sandals, belts and bags. Find some of the most authentic crafts in the Splantzia quarter, along Chatzimichali Daliani and Daskalogianni. The central *agora* (market hall) is touristy but still worth a wander.

★Sifis Stavroulakis JEWELLERY
(☎28210 50335; www.sifisjewellery.gr; Chatzimichali Daliani 54; ⏰10am-2pm Mon-Sat, plus 5.30-8.30pm Tue, Thu & Fri) Beautiful naturalistic jewellery made with semi-precious stones and metals takes on floral and human forms in this small shopfront and jeweller's workshop.

Mikro Karavi BOOKS
(Daskalogianni 59; ⏰9am-7pm Mon, Wed & Sat, to 9pm Tue, Thu & Fri, 11am-7pm Sun) Stocks travel guides and a range of books on Crete and Greece, along with a great selection of English-language novels and Greek music CDs.

Georgina Skalidi FASHION & ACCESSORIES
(☎28215 01705; www.georginaskalidi.com; Chatzimichali Daliani 58; ⏰11am-2.30pm & 6-11pm Mon-Sat, 7-11pm Sun) This local designer, whose work is distributed internationally, creates wonderful contemporary leather bags (from €100), jewellery and accessories.

Mediterraneo Bookstore BOOKS
(☎28210 86904; Akti Koundourioti 57; ⏰9am-11pm Apr-Oct, to 9pm Nov-Mar) On the waterfront, this bookshop sells a good range of travel guides, hiking guides to Samaria Gorge and books on Crete, as well as international press and a small selection of English-language novels.

Roka Carpets ARTS & CRAFTS
(☎28210 74736; Zambeliou 61; ⏰11am-9pm Mon-Sat) This is one of the few places in Crete where you can buy genuine, hand-woven goods (note, though, that they're not antiques). Amiable Mihalis Manousakis and his wife, Annie, weave wondrous rugs on a 400-year-old loom, using methods that have remained essentially unchanged since Minoan times.

Agora MARKET
(Covered Market; Chatzimichali Giannari; ⏰8am-5pm Mon, Wed & Sat, 8am-9pm Tue, Thu & Fri) Hania's cross-shaped market hall opened in 1913 and bustles mostly with souvenir-hunting tourists, though a few stands selling traditional Cretan produce and products (herbs, honey, baked goods, raki, cheese) – along with cafes – are still part of the mix.

Miden Agan FOOD & DRINKS
(☎28210 27068; www.midenaganshop.gr; Daskalogianni 70; ⏰10am-5pm Mon-Wed & Sat, to 9pm Thu & Fri) Food and wine lovers are spoilt for choice at this excellent shop, which stocks more than 800 Greek wines as well as its own wines and liquors, along with local gourmet deli foods, including its own line of spoon sweets (try the white pumpkin). Wine tastings are also available (by appointment; 15 minutes to one hour from €15 per person).

Pelekanakis BOOKS
(☎28210 92512; Halidon 89; ⏰8am-11pm Apr-Oct, 9am-2pm Nov-Mar) Sells driving and hiking

maps, guidebooks in several languages and otherwise hard-to-find books about Crete, along with a few mainstream English-language novels.

Exantas Art Space ARTS & CRAFTS
(☎28210 95920; cnr Zambeliou & Moschon; ⏲11am-9pm) This high-concept store has great postcards with old photos, a small selection of rare books, handmade arts and crafts by local artists, Cretan music, and a good range of travel, art and kids' books.

ℹ Information

EMERGENCY

Tourist Police (☎171, 28210 25931; ⏲24hr)

INTERNET ACCESS

Free wi-fi is widely available in public spaces, including the harbour, around the central market and at Plateia 1866, as well as at most hotels, restaurants, cafes and bars.

MEDICAL SERVICES

General Hospital St George (☎28210 22000; www.chaniahospital.gr; Mournies; ⏲24hr) Located 4.5km south of town – take a local bus, or a taxi (€8 to €10).

Private Hospital Tsepeti (☎28210 28828; www.chaniaclinic.com; Papanastasiou 9) Has a medical clinic with international English-speaking doctors and specialists. Call for appointments. Located just under 2km south-east of the old town.

MONEY

Banks cluster around Plateia Markopoulou in the new city, but there are also ATMs in the old town on Halidon.

Alpha Bank (cnr Halidon & Skalidi; ⏲8am-6pm Mon-Fri, 10am-5pm Sat, ATM 24hr)

National Bank of Greece (cnr Tzanakaki & Giannari; ⏲8am-2pm)

POST

Post Office (☎28210 28444; Peridou 10; ⏲7.30am-8.30pm Mon-Fri)

TOURIST INFORMATION

Municipal Tourist Office (☎28213 36155; Kydonias 29; ⏲9am-3pm Mon-Fri) Modest selection of brochures, maps and transport timetables.

TRAVEL AGENCIES

Diktynna Travel (☎28210 41458; www.diktynna-travel.gr; Archontaki 6; ⏲9am-9pm Mon-Fri, to 3pm Sat)

Tellus Travel (☎28210 91500; www.tellustravel.gr; Halidon 108; ⏲9am-9pm)

USEFUL WEBSITES

Chania Tourism (www.chaniatourism.com) The city's tourism portal.

Western Crete Information (www.west-crete.com) Tourism info for Hania province.

ℹ Getting There & Away

AIR

Hania's airport (p296) is 14km east of town on the Akrotiri Peninsula, and is served year-round from Athens and Thessaloniki and seasonally from throughout Europe. Carriers include Aegean Airlines, Olympic Air, easyJet and Ryanair. A taxi from the airport to anywhere in Hania costs €25. Public buses into town stop right outside the terminal (€2.50, 30 minutes) and run between 5.30am and 11pm daily.

BUSES FROM HANIA

DESTINATION	FARE (€)	DURATION	FREQUENCY
Elafonisi	11	2¼hr	1 daily
Falasarna	8.30	1¾hr	3 daily
Hora Sfakion	8.30	1¾hr	3-4 daily
Iraklio	15.10	2¾hr	hourly
Kissamos (Kastelli)	5.10	1hr	2 daily
Kolymbari	3.60	40min	frequent
Moni Agias Triadas	2.60	30min	1-2 daily
Omalos (for Samaria Gorge)	7.50	1hr	2 daily
Paleohora	8.30	1¾hr	2 daily
Rethymno	6.80	1¼hr	hourly
Sougia	7.80	1¾hr	1 daily
Stavros	2.30	40min	5 daily

BOAT

Hania's port is at Souda, 7km southeast of town (and the site of a NATO base). The port is linked to town by bus (€2, or €2.50 if paying onboard) and taxi (€10). Hania buses meet each boat, as do buses to Rethymno.

Anek Lines (www.anek.gr) runs an overnight ferry between Piraeus and Hania (from €38 per person, nine hours). Buy tickets online or at the port; reserve ahead for cars.

BUS

Hania's **KTEL bus station** (☎ info 28210 93052, tickets 28210 93306; www.e-ktel.com; Kelaidi 73-77; 📶) has an information kiosk with helpful staff and timetables, a cafeteria, a minimarket and a left-luggage service. Check the excellent website for the current schedule.

ℹ Getting Around

Hania town is best navigated on foot, since most of it is pedestrianised.

BUS

Local buses are operated by **Chania Urban Buses** (☎ 28210 98115; http://chaniabus.gr). Zone A/B tickets cost €1.20/1.70 if bought from a kiosk or vending machine and €2/2.50 from the driver.

A handily central **bus stop** for Souda port, Halepa, Nea Hora and other local destinations is on Giannari, near the *agora*.

CAR & MOTORCYCLE

Major car-hire outlets, including **Europrent** (☎ 28210 27810; www.europrent.gr; Halidon 87; ⏱ 8am-8.30pm), are at the airport and you'll find outlets on Halidon in the old town, including recommendable **Kriti Plus** (☎ 6947404801; www.kritiplus.gr; Halidon 99; ⏱ 8.30am-9pm).

There's free parking just west of Firkas Fortress and along the waterfront towards Nea Hora beach, or by the eastern edge of the harbour off Kyprou, but avoid areas marked residents only.

TAXI

Taxi (☎ 28210 98700; www.chaniataxi.gr)

EAST OF HANIA

The northeastern corner of Hania prefecture includes the rocky Akrotiri Peninsula with a couple of interesting monasteries, and the Apokoronas Peninsula (which is more like a promontory). The island's only natural freshwater lake, Lake Kournas (p86), is a highlight of the area. Beach resorts such as Kalyves, Almyrida and Georgioupoli are slightly less over-built than the resorts spread along the coast west of Hania, but they can't hold a candle to the beaches in the south and west. You'll find the most Cretan character at the restored village of Vamos, the ancient site of Aptera, and in traditional villages such as Gavalohori.

Akrotiri Peninsula
Χερσόνησος Ακρωτήρι

The Akrotiri (ak-roh-*tee*-ree) Peninsula, northeast of Hania town, is a barren, hilly stretch of rock covered with scrub. It has a few coastal resorts, Hania's airport, a massive NATO naval base and an Allied war memorial on Souda Bay, and a few interesting monasteries. There are few buses and the poorly signposted roads make it difficult to explore, but if you have a car (and GPS) you can make a day trip combining a swim and lunch with a visit to the monasteries. If you want to stay at the beach near Hania, Akrotiri's Kalathas and Stavros settlements are much quieter than the overblown package-tour strip west of Hania but, overall, southwestern Crete has much better beaches than Akrotiri.

The beach settlement of **Kalathas**, 10km north of Hania, has two sandy beaches lined by tamarisk trees. It's the preferred weekend haunt of Haniots, many of whom own summer and weekend houses nearby.

Stavros, 6km north of Kalathas, is little more than a dilapidated scattering of houses, but has an array of restaurants and a few good accommodation options, plus a famous cove (p82).

👁 Sights

★Moni Agias Triadas MONASTERY
(Agia Triada Tsagarolon; www.agiatriada-chania.gr; adult/child €2.50/free; ⏱ 7am-7pm Jun-Aug, 8am-6pm Sep-May) Akrotiri Peninsula's major cultural site, the impressive and beautiful 17th-century Moni Agias Triadas, is an active monastery with a rich library and is well worth a visit for its altarpiece, Venetian-influenced domed facade and Cretan School icon paintings. It was founded by Venetian monks Jeremiah and Laurentio Giancarolo, who were converts to the Orthodox faith. In the store you can do tastings of the monastery's fine wine, oil and raki before picking up a few bottles to take home.

The store also has a small folk museum displaying traditional tools and machinery used in the production of raki, olive oil, honey, butter and more.

Moni Ioannou Erimiti MONASTERY

(Moni Katholikou) From Moni Gouvernetou it's around a 2km (30-minute) walk (uphill on the way back) down to the coast to the ruins of Moni Ioannou Erimiti. In disuse for many centuries, the monastery is dedicated to St John the Hermit, who lived in the cave behind the ruins, at the bottom of a rock staircase. When St John died in the cave, his 98 disciples are said to have died with him.

Near the entrance to the cave there's a small pond believed to be holy.

Moni Gouvernetou MONASTERY

(Our Lady of the Angels; adult/child €2.50/free; ⌚9am-noon & 5-7pm Mon, Tue & Thu, 9am-noon & 5-8pm Sat, 5am-noon & 5-8pm Sun Apr-Oct, shorter hours Nov-Mar) The 16th-century Moni Gouvernetou, 4km north of Moni Agias Triadas (p81), may date as far back as the 11th century, from a time when an inland sanctuary was an attractive refuge from coastal pirates. The building itself is rather plain, but the church inside has an ornate sculptured Venetian facade. The grounds are usually open from 9am to 9pm and from here you can walk down the rocky path (2km, 30 minutes) to the coast, to the ruins of Moni Ioannou Erimiti.

About 1km down the hill towards Moni Ioannou Erimiti are a viewpoint and caves where the monks of the area were known to live. Continue down to the coast for the monastery. Swimming in the cove at the bottom is not permitted.

The monastery was attacked and burnt down during the War of Independence, but the monks were warned and managed to save the treasures (though not themselves) and shipped them off to Mt Athos in northern Greece. The monastery is now run by a handful of monks from the Holy Mountain.

Allied War Cemetery MEMORIAL

(Souda Bay; ⌚24hr) This striking war memorial with white crosses against a backdrop of Souda Bay holds the graves of 1500 Commonwealth soldiers who died during WWI and, in particular, WWII. Battle of Crete ceremonies take place here on the anniversary week in May each year.

Beaches

Marathi Beach BEACH

On the eastern side of Akrotiri Peninsula the pleasant beach of Marathi is a lovely spot beyond the NATO base with two sandy coves and turquoise waters on either side of a small pier. The ruins of Ancient Minoa are next to the car park. Marathi gets crowded with local families at weekends and has a couple of tavernas.

Further south along this coastline you'll find another nice swimming and snorkelling spot at the small white-stone cove of **Loutraki**.

Seitan Limania BEACH

While it might be a white-knuckle drive down hairpin bends to get here, the incredibly vivid turquoise waters of this secret cove are more than worth it. Take in the views from the top or brave the steep, rocky path that leads down to the remote, tiny, sandy beach to take a dip. It's located on the northeastern side of the Akrotiri Peninsula.

Stavros Cove BEACH

Near Akrotiri Peninsula's northern tip, Stavros' sandy beach is covered with umbrellas and lines a cove dominated by a mammoth rock. It famously served as the dramatic backdrop for the final dancing scene in the classic movie *Zorba the Greek*. The beach and its neighbouring clutch of cafes and tavernas can get crowded. Other thin, windswept beaches line Stavros' western shores.

Sleeping

The beach settlements of Stavros and Kalathas have some lovely accommodation, including comfortable apartment complexes with swimming pools.

Blue Beach APARTMENT €

(☎28210 39404; www.bluebeach.eu; Stavros; d €50-65, apt €100-130; P❄📶🏊) On a pretty promontory at the western edge of Stavros, Blue Beach is a low-key hotel complex with comfortable, self-contained rooms equipped with fridge, kitchenette and TV. There's also a restaurant, a bar and a swimming pool.

Artemis Apartments APARTMENT €€

(☎28210 39005; www.artemis-village.gr; Stavros; apt €60-145; ❄📶🏊👪) This well-kept, cream stone apartment complex, 1km back from the cove at Stavros, is a welcoming spot to while away your holiday. Fully equipped modern apartments are chic and comfortable and come with a terrace or balcony, most with sea views. The large pool beckons when you can't make it down to the beach, and there's a play area for kids.

OFF THE BEATEN TRACK

GAVALOHORI ΓΑΒΑΛΟΧΩΡΙ

The charming village of Gavalohori, 25km southeast of Hania, makes an interesting stop. The main attraction is the **Folklore Museum** (☎28250 23222; Gavalohori; adult/child €2/free; ⌚9am-8pm Mon-Fri, 9am-7pm Sat, 11am-6pm Sun), which is located in a renovated building that was constructed during Venetian rule and then extended by the Turks. The exhibits are well labelled in English and include examples of pottery, weaving, woodcarving, stonecutting and other Cretan crafts, including the fine *kapaneli* (intricately worked silk lace). A historical section documents Cretan struggles for independence. At the time of research there were plans to extend the museum into the neighbouring building.

The **Women's Cooperative** (Gavalohori; ⌚10am-10pm Apr-Oct), on the main square, sells a few rare pieces of *kapaneli* made by local women. You can normally see women hard at work on this painstakingly long process. Prices for quality lacework range from €15 to €1500, depending on the size of the piece.

Signs direct you to the Byzantine wells, Venetian arches and Roman tombs about 1.5km above the village. You can also poke you head in to see an olive-oil mill dating back to Venetian times. It's a short walk signposted from the main square.

Georgi's Blue Apartments APARTMENT €€
(☎28210 64080; www.blueapts.gr; Kalathas; apt incl breakfast €100-180; P❄@📶🏊👪) Georgi's is an immaculate complex of well-furnished studios and apartments with satellite TV, fridge and kitchen. Unwind at the pleasant lounge area near the pool, or swim off the rocks at a private little cove. The owner can advise on local outdoor activities and car hire. It occasionally gets booked out by NATO groups.

Lena Beach Hotel HOTEL €€
(☎28210 64750; www.lenabeach.gr; Kalathas; s/d/tr from €75/90/120; ❄📶🏊) Simple seafront rooms make this tidy hotel tops for a carefree holiday. Rooms have small TVs and fridges, plus there's a big pool.

Eating

Beachside seafood tavernas are the best bets on the peninsula.

Sunset Beach CAFE €
(Iliovasilema; ☎28210 39780; Stavros; dishes €5-9; ⌚11am-11pm Jun-Aug) On the beach at the southwestern edge of Stavros, have a drink or a light meal at the Sunset Beach cafe, tucked under a huge tree with a shady timber deck and thatched umbrellas evoking the tropics. The French and Greek proprietors serve a range of local dishes and fresh seafood.

Patrelantonis SEAFOOD €€
(☎28210 63337; Marathi; mains €8-15, fish per kg from €40; ⌚8am-11pm Easter-Oct) On Marathi beach, this dependable seafood taverna is well regarded by locals and visitors. Lunch under the shady beachside tamarisk trees on dishes like cuttlefish with fennel and olives or grouper fricassee. There's a good wine list, too.

Getting There & Away

From Hania there are at least a few **KTEL** (☎28210 93052; www.e-ktel.com) buses daily to Stavros beach (€2.30, 40 minutes) that stop at Kalathas and two buses daily to Moni Agias Triadas (€2.60, 30 minutes). If you're coming by car from Hania, follow signs to the airport and branch off at the turn-offs from there.

Aptera & Around Απτέρα

★Aptera RUINS
(adult/child €2/free; ⌚8.30am-6pm Wed-Mon) The ruins of the ancient city of Aptera, about 13.5km east of Hania, spread over two hills that lord grandly over Souda Bay. Founded in the 7th century BC, it was one of the most important city-states of western Crete and was continuously inhabited until an earthquake destroyed it in the 7th century AD. Aptera revived with the Byzantine reconquest of Crete in the 10th century, and became a bishopric. You'll need your own wheels to get here.

In the 12th century, the monastery of St John the Theologian was established; the reconstructed monastery is the centre of the site. Excavations have exposed the remains of a fortified tower, a city gate and a massive wall that surrounded the city. You can also see Roman cisterns, an amphitheatre and a 2nd-century-BC Greek temple. At the western end of the site, a Turkish fortress, built in 1872, enjoys a panoramic view of Souda Bay.

The fortress was built as part of a large Turkish fortress-building program during a period when the Cretans were in an almost constant state of insurrection. Notice the 'Wall of the Inscriptions' – this was probably part of an important public building and was excavated in 1862 by French archaeologists.

If you arrive outside the opening hours, the only section open to the public will be the ruins of a Roman house.

Eating

Tzitzikas CRETAN €

(28250 41144; www.tzitzikas.com; Armenoi; mains €4-9; 10am-late Wed-Sun May-Sep, Sat & Sun only Oct-Apr;) In the village of Armenoi, south of the ruins at Aptera, seek out Tzitzikas for a fresh Cretan meal or a coffee on the edge of a river, under lush, shading trees, with horses and goats grazing nearby. The focus is on all things organic, from sausage to salad.

Almyrida Αλμυρίδα

POP 56

The former fishing village of Almyrida, 21km east of Hania, is considerably less developed than its neighbour, Kalyves, although it's pretty built up, with ever more new hotels going in. It has a long, exposed beach and is popular for windsurfing. History buffs can find the remains of an early Christian basilica at the western end of the village.

Activities

Omega Divers DIVING

(28250 31412; www.omegadivers.com) Reputable outfit offering diving trips to Elephant Cave (€110) as well as Discover Scuba (€80), PADI courses, and three-hour boat and snorkelling trips (€60).

Flisvos Tours CYCLING

(28250 31100; www.flisvos.com; 3-day mountain-bike hire €30; 9am-9pm) Just off the main road; rents out mountain bikes, as well as cars and scooters.

UCPA Sports OUTDOORS

(28250 33100; www.almyridasummersports.com) French-run UCPA Sports offers windsurfing for beginners and experienced surfers (€15 per hour) outside high season, and rents out kayaks (one-person kayak €8 per hour), stand-up paddleboards (€12 per hour) and pedal boats (€12 per hour).

Dream Adventure Trips SNORKELLING

(6944357383; www.facebook.com/dreamadventuretrips; 2hr snorkelling trip €28) Offers snorkelling trips to nearby caves and islets.

Sleeping & Eating

There's no shortage of hotels in Almyrida, though many are generic affairs. Most have sea views.

Almyrida Studios APARTMENT €€

(28250 32075; www.almyridaresort.com; studios incl breakfast €80-100; May-Oct;) Studios perched at the water's edge are just the way to soak up the summer sun. Some are large enough for four, and all have kitchens (though they're fairly dated) and renovated bathrooms. Each studio has a sea-facing balcony, and there's a swimming pool.

Lagos TAVERNA €

(28250 31654; mains €6-12; noon-late May-Oct) Located at the entrance to Almyrida, this popular and atmospheric taverna serves good-value traditional cooking on a lovely shaded terrace or back covered patio.

Dimitri's TAVERNA €

(28250 31303; mains €7-14; 10am-late Apr-Oct) This beachside family tavern is recommended for its friendly service. It serves Greek staples as well as some Cretan specialities, such as rabbit *stifadho* (stew), using mainly local produce.

Getting There & Away

There are four to five KTEL (p83) buses a day from Almyrida to Hania (€3.20, 45 minutes) via Kalyves from May to October.

Vamos Βάμος

POP 706

The pretty 12th-century village of Vamos makes for a lovely day trip from Hania, only 26km away. Capital of the Sfakia province from 1867 to 1913, it was the scene of a revolt against Turkish rule in 1896. It is now the capital of the Apokoronas province and in 1995 a group of villagers banded together to preserve Vamos' traditional way of life. The residents got EU funding to showcase the crafts and products of the region, and restored the old stone buildings using traditional materials and crafts and turned them into guesthouses. In the town's main square you can buy local raki, herbs, organic oil and other Cretan products.

Sleeping & Eating

★Vamos Traditional Village VILLA €€
(28250 22190; www.vamosvillage.gr; villas €55-200; 9am-8pm Mon-Sat, 10am-6pm Sun;) This village organisation rents out Vamos' many restored homes. The lovely stone cottages have kitchens, fireplaces and TVs and are decorated in traditional style. The houses accommodate anywhere from two to nine people, and some of the larger cottages also have a pool. Also rents cars, books excursions and runs Cretan cooking lessons in a restored olive press.

★I Sterna tou Bloumosifi TAVERNA €€
(28250 83220; mains €9-14; 12.30pm-midnight;) The old stone taverna I Sterna tou Bloumosifi has a welcoming tree-shaded courtyard garden and is known far and wide for its excellent Cretan cuisine. For starters try the *gavros* (anchovy) wrapped in vine leaves or the cheese-and-herb mushrooms, and then move on to the *hilopites* (fettucine-style pasta) with rooster.

Getting There & Away

There are three to five KTEL buses (p83) to Vamos from Hania (€3.60, 55 minutes) from Monday to Saturday in high season.

Georgioupoli Γεωργιούπολη

POP 455

No longer the quiet getaway it once was, Georgioupoli has been swamped by coastal hotel development and is popular with holidaying foreign families.

Nature lovers look beyond to appreciate its setting at the junction of the Almyros River and the sea. It's a nesting area for the endangered loggerhead sea turtle. The marshes surrounding the riverbed are known for birdlife, especially egrets and kingfishers, which migrate into the area in April. The marshes also produce hordes of mosquitoes in summer.

Picturesque Agios Nikolaos chapel perches on a narrow, rocky jetty in the sea. The long, narrow stretch of hard-packed sand east of town, spliced by another river leading to the sea, becomes a beach that continues for about 10km towards Rethymno.

Activities

Zoraida's Horseriding HORSE RIDING
(28250 61745; www.zoraidas-horseriding.com; 1hr nature ride €25, 2hr ride to Lake Kournas €40) Located between Kavros village and Lake Kournas, Zoraida's offers guided beach and nature-trail horse riding, including trips to Lake Kournas, for all skill levels.

Adventure Bikes CYCLING
(28254 00661; www.adventurebikes.org; bicycles per day from €12) Hires bikes and runs bike tours around the region (€57). Can also arrange excursions to Samaria Gorge, Elafonisi and Balos (p111).

Talos Express Tourist Train RAIL
(www.facebook.com/TalosExpress; adult/child return €8/free) A small tourist train connects Georgioupoli to nearby Lake Kournas and Argiroupoli.

Sleeping

Large hotels and resorts on the beach are aimed at package tourists, but there are a few pensions and hotels in the backstreets.

Egeon PENSION €
(28250 61161; www.the-egeon-crete.com; studios €45-50;) Near the bridge at the entrance to Georgioupoli, but a fair walk to the beach, these 18 renovated and spacious rooms and studios are run by friendly Greek-American Polly and her fisherman husband. Some rooms have kitchenettes.

Zorba's HOTEL €
(28250 61381; studios/apt from €50/60; May-Oct;) Zorba's is set back from the beach near the town's main square. Studios and apartments are contemporary and come with kitchenettes, flat-screen TVs and balconies. There's a lap pool, too.

Porto Kalyvaki APARTMENT €
(28250 61316; www.kalivaki.com; studios €40-50; Apr-Oct;) Located behind a taverna on the more isolated northern beach, Kalyvaki has a mix of plain studios spread across two buildings in well-established gardens. Some rooms have sea or mountain views, and there's a playground for kids. Air conditioning is an extra €5.

Corissia Princess Hotel RESORT €€
(28250 83707; www.corissia.com; d/q incl breakfast from €140/220;) This large complex on the beachfront in Georgioupoli caters to package tourists and has bright modern rooms with balcony or terrace.

Eating

There's a range of options for eating out in Georgioupoli, from traditional Cretan to

WORTH A TRIP

LAKE KOURNAS ΛΙΜΝΗ ΚΟΥΡΝΑΣ

Lake Kournas, 4km inland from Georgioupoli, is a bit of a tourist trap but still a lovely place to have lunch or pass an afternoon. The island's only natural lake, it is about 1.5km in diameter, 45m deep and fed by underground springs. There's a narrow, sandy strip encircling the lake and you can walk two-thirds of the way around. The crystal-clear water is now off-limits for swimming (to protect the environment) and changes colour according to season and time of day. You can hire pedal boats (€7 per hour) and canoes (€5 per hour) and view the turtles, crabs, fish and snakes that make the lake their home.

Tourist buses crowd the lake in the peak of summer, and the basic tavernas on the shore fill up. To get away from the fray, head up the hill to stone-built, balconied **Ambrosia** (☎28250 83008; www.ambrosialakekournas.com; Lake Kournas; mains €7-20; ⏰10am-10pm May-Oct), where you can dine on traditional Cretan dishes like *gamopilafo* (lamb and stock-cooked rice) or faves like homemade pizza, or just grab an iced coffee and take in the excellent vista.

The lake sits below **Kournas village**, a steep 5km southeast up the hill. It's a simple village with pleasant countryside scenery and a couple of *kafeneia* (coffee houses). You can enjoy a delicious meal at **Kali Kardia Taverna** (☎28250 96278; Kournas; grills €5-7; ⏰12.30-10pm daily May-Nov, Fri-Sun only Dec-Apr) on the main street: owner Andreas is known for his award-winning sausages, excellent *apaki* (cured pork) and meats cooked on the grill outside. If you're lucky you might get to try his delicious *galaktoboureko* (custard pastry) while it's still warm.

A tourist mini-train (p85) runs from Georgioupoli to Lake Kournas in summer, but there's no public transport.

seafood joints. Don't miss a trip out to Kournas village to dine at Kali Kardia Taverna.

Lygaria TAVERNA €

(Lake Kournas; mains €4-11; ⏰9am-10pm or later Apr-Nov) Shady Lygaria, at the quieter end of Lake Kournas, makes decent traditional Greek dishes such as lamb *tsigariasto* (sautéed lamb).

Poseidon Taverna SEAFOOD €€

(☎28250 61026; www.poseidon.georgioupoli.eu; fish per kg €30-50; ⏰6pm-midnight, shorter hours Nov-Apr) Signposted down a narrow alley to the left as you come into Georgioupoli, this well-regarded taverna is run by a fishing family. You can choose from the day's fish and seafood laid out on the counter and enjoy an excellent meal in the lovely courtyard.

Arolithos TAVERNA €€

(☎28250 61406; www.arolithos-georgioupolis.gr; mains €7.50-15; ⏰noon-11pm May-Oct) Near Georgioupoli's central church, Arolithos has an extensive selection of appetisers and traditional Greek dishes such as *spetsofaï* (sausage-and-pepper stew).

Information

The main street from the highway leads to the town centre, where there are travel agencies and ATMs. Find basic info at www.georgioupoli.net.

Ballos Travel (☎28250 83073; www.ballos.gr; ⏰9am-2pm & 5.30-9pm Mon-Sat) organises boat tickets, and excursions to Balos, Samaria Gorge, Elafonisi and more. Also has car hire.

Getting There & Away

KTEL (p83) buses between Hania and Rethymno stop on the highway outside Georgioupoli (€4.50, 45 minutes, hourly).

Vryses Βρύσες

Vryses is a pleasant town 30km southeast of Hania – a centre for the region's agricultural products, so you'll find good produce and excellent yoghurt and honey, a town speciality. If you want to stop for a bite to eat, you'll be tempted by the lamb or other tasty meat grilling on the spit outside **Taverna Progoulis** (☎28250 51086; grills €6-9; ⏰9am-1am), which has tables under the trees next to a pebbly dry riverbed.

SOUTHWEST COAST & SFAKIA ΣΦΑΚΙΑ

The mountainous province of Sfakia extends from the Omalos Plateau down to the southern coast, and has some of the island's most spectacular landmarks, including Samaria (sa-ma-ria) Gorge, the Lefka Ori (White Mountains) and Mt Gingilos (2080m) in the rugged interior. The memorable drive from Hania to Hora Sfakion – descending through the mountains on numerous loop-back turns overlooking the sea – is one of the most stunning sights in Crete.

The stark, muscular Lefka Ori meet the Libyan Sea along Crete's corrugated south-western coast indented with a handful of laid-back beach communities, such as Frangokastello and Loutro. Hora Sfakion is Sfakia's main village, and a small outpost, perfect for relaxing and boat-hopping further down the coast. Sougia and the larger Paleohora, west of Sfakia proper, are also some of the best places in Crete to unwind.

This rocky southern coast is arguably the least changing place in Crete – thanks to the massive cliffs running to the sea. Some of the villages and beaches are accessible only by boat and therefore completely untouched by mass tourism. You can walk or boat-hop to perfectly isolated little coves or soak up the majestic scenery and fragrant air on a scramble through wildly romantic gorges. Summer winds blast through the gorges and across the Libyan Sea, which means there is often good windsurfing to be had, especially at Paleohora.

Askyfou Ασκύφου

POP 450

The road to Hora Sfakion takes you across the formerly war-torn plain of Askyfou, which in 1821 was the scene of one of the most furious battles of Crete's part in the War of Independence. Here the Sfakiot forces triumphed over the Turks in a bloody battle, which is still recounted in local songs. More than a century later the plain was the scene of more strife as Allied troops retreated towards their evacuation point in Hora Sfakion. The small War Museum is worth a stop for its interesting military collection.

The central town on the plateau is also called Askyfou, and stretches out on either side of a hill. The post office is at the top of the hill, along with a mini-market and several tavernas.

Sights

Askyfou War Museum MUSEUM

(☎6979149719; www.warmuseumaskifou.com; admission by donation; ⏰8am-7pm Mon-Sat) Signs along the way direct you to this small museum displaying the extensive gun and military odds-and-ends collection of the Hatzidakis family, who are happy to show you around. Displays include Nazi porcelain sets, German propaganda material, a German plane propeller, working telescopes, bombs, helmets and an English Norton motorcycle, all collected from across Crete.

Sleeping & Eating

You won't find much in the way of accommodation in this area, aside from a few tavernas in the town of Askyfou that have rooms for rent. Otherwise, Hora Sfakion is 30 minutes away and Hania is an hour away.

For a glimpse of traditional Sfakiot village life, seek out the small square in town flanked by *kafeneia* (coffee houses) and statues of local resistance heroes. You can normally get a simple meal of local sausage and *Sfakiani pita*, or at weekends traditional wild goat or lamb *tsigariasto* (sautéed) or *vrasto* (boiled), charged by the kilo – and lots of raki.

Getting There & Away

KTEL (p83) buses run from Hania to Askyfou (€6.30, one hour) and on to Hora Sfakion.

Frangokastello Φραγγοκαστέλλο

POP 148

Dominated by a mighty 14th-century Venetian fortress, Frangokastello is a low-key resort with a fabulous wide and sandy beach that slopes gradually into shallow warm water, making it ideal for kids. There's no actual village, just a smattering of tavernas, small markets, and low-rise holiday apartments and rooms scattered along the main street.

Sights

Orthi Ammos Beach BEACH

Adjoining the Frangokastello fortress is the stunning Orthi Ammos beach, a long stretch of fine sand with shallow, warm waters. It's blissful and child-friendly, unless (as is frequently the case) the wind whips up the sand and forces you to retreat into the nearby cafe.

Frangokastello FORTRESS

(Waterfront; adult/child €2/free; ⏰10am-6pm Apr-Oct) Frangokastello is a ruined 14th-century fortress, constructed soon after the Fourth

Crusade (1204) by the Venetians, who sought a stronghold against pirates and Sfakiot warriors. The legendary Ioannis Daskalogiannis, who led a disastrous rebellion against Ottoman oppression in 1770, was persuaded to surrender at the fortress but was later flayed alive by the Turks. On 17 May 1828, in one of the bloodiest battles of the Greek War of Independence, 385 Cretan rebels made a last stand here. About 800 Turks were killed along with the rebels.

Legend has it that at dawn each anniversary the rebels' ghosts, the *drosoulites*, can be seen marching along the beach. The name comes from the Greek word *drosia* meaning 'dew', which may refer to the dawn moisture during the hours when the ghosts are said to appear. The site is under construction until around 2022 but will remain open to the public.

Cretelaio Olive Oil Mill FACTORY

(☎6974581061; ⊙10am-6pm Mon-Sat) Drop by this factory to learn the process of olive-oil production from extraction to end product. Tours take 10 to 15 minutes, followed by a spot of olive-oil tasting to help you decide what you might like to stock up on to take home. It's located approximately 4km northeast of Frangokastello.

Sleeping

Accommodation consists mainly of apartments and is reasonably good value, especially a bit further from the beach across the east–west road. There's also the chance to stay in a renovated century-old stone windmill on the beach.

PROUD SFAKIOTS

The interior of Sfakia is known for being the only part of Crete never subdued by the Arabs, Venetians or Turks. It was the centre of resistance during the island's long centuries of domination by foreign powers, and its steep ravines and hills made effective hideaways for Cretan revolutionaries. The Sfakiot people are renowned for their proud fighting spirit and strong culture, and they have a colourfully tragic history of clan vendettas. Their local cuisine includes the delicious *Sfakiani pita* (a thin, flat cheese pie drizzled with honey)

Milos APARTMENT €

(☎28250 92162; www.milos-sfakia.com; cottages €35-50, windmills €50-70, apt from €70; P❄📶👪) An apartment in a renovated, century-old stone windmill (*mylos* in Greek) on a pretty spot on the beach is the most captivating of several atmospheric rooms and studios here. Four basic stone cottages sit under the tamarisk trees on the sand, and modern, well-equipped studios are nearby. Book ahead to stay in the mill in high season.

Stavris Studios APARTMENT €

(☎28250 92250; www.studios-stavris-frangokastello-crete.com; studios/2-bedroom apt from €35/60; ⊙Apr-Oct; P❄📶👪) This collection of 24 studios and two-bedroom apartments is decent value, especially considering its position smack on the beach, though the decor is a little old fashioned. All options come with kitchenettes, balconies and sea views. The owners can advise about local activities.

Fata Morgana APARTMENT €€

(☎28250 92077; www.fata-morgana.gr; studios & apt €40-90; P❄📶👪) Set amid an olive grove above Orthi Ammos beach, this simple complex has a range of fully equipped contemporary studios and larger apartments for families, as well as two cosy, but dated, mock castles. There's a playground to amuse the kids and a taverna overlooking the water. Service is friendly and helpful.

Eating & Drinking

There are a few good restaurants attached to hotels in Frangokastello serving home-cooked Cretan dishes and fresh seafood.

Your choices for nightlife are a drink at a taverna or heading to the beachside bar in front of Taverna Babis & Popi.

Oasis Taverna CRETAN €

(☎28250 83562; Frangokastello Beach; mains €5.50-12; ⊙8am-10pm or later Apr-Oct; P📶) Part of an excellent family-run studio and apartment complex at the western end of the beach, about 1km from the fortress (p87), this is the best place to eat not only for the well-executed Cretan home-cooked meals but also for the sea view from the flower-festooned stone-floor terrace.

Taverna Babis & Popi TAVERNA €

(☎28250 92093; www.babis-popi.com; mains €6.50-12; ⊙8am-10pm Apr-Nov) This taverna is known for its fresh fish and decent Cretan specialities, such as wild snails or goat in white-wine sauce. Enjoy your meal under a shady vine canopy tucked behind the family's rooms and mini-market. It's also a good spot for breakfast.

Getting There & Away

KTEL (p83) buses run along the main road; there's no official stop, but you can flag one down. In summer there are three daily buses from Hora Sfakion to Frangokastello (€2.30, 30 minutes).

Hora Sfakion
Χώρα Σφακίων

POP 212

The more bullet holes you see in the road signs along the way, the closer you are to Hora Sfakion, long renowned in Cretan history for its streak of rebellion against foreign occupiers. But don't worry: the tiny fishing village is today an amiable and somewhat scenic place that caters well to visitors, many of whom are Samaria Gorge hikers stumbling off the Agia Roumeli boat on their way back to Hania. Most pause just long enough to catch the next bus out, but there's sufficient appeal here to tempt you to stay, from boat trips to nearby isolated beaches to hiking the Aradena Gorge.

History

Under Venetian and Turkish rule Hora Sfakion was an important maritime centre and (with the upland regional capital of Anopoli) the nucleus of the Cretan struggle for independence. The Turks inflicted severe reprisals on the inhabitants for their rebelliousness in the 19th century, after which the town fell into an economic slump that lasted until the arrival of tourism several decades ago. Hora Sfakion played a prominent role during WWII when thousands of Allied troops were evacuated by sea from the town after the Battle of Crete. Today, a memorial to the last British, Australian and New Zealand soldiers evacuated after the battle stands on the town's eastern bluff.

Sights & Activities

Sweetwater Beach BEACH

(Glyka Nera) West of Hora Sfakion, lovely Sweetwater Beach is accessible by a small daily ferry (p91), by taxi boat (one way/return €25/50) or on foot via a stony and partly vertiginous 3.5km coastal path starting at the first hairpin turn of the Anopoli road. A small cafe rents umbrellas and sun chairs.

Vrissi Beach BEACH

Abutting the western edge of the village, this tiny grey-sand cove is the closest beach for unfolding your towel or a quick dip. There's a taverna (p90) on the bluff above for snacks and refreshments.

Notos Mare Marine Adventures DIVING

(28210 08536, 6947270106; www.notosmare.com; New Harbour; 1/2 dives €49/85; 8am-9pm Apr-Oct) In addition to PADI certification and dives for beginners and advanced divers, this long-running professional outfit also rents boats, organises charter boat and fishing trips, and operates taxi boats 24/7 to secluded beaches along the south coast, including Sweetwater Beach, Mareme and Loutro.

Yoga on Crete YOGA

(6937363890; www.yogaoncrete.gr; drop-in classes €15-20; May-Oct) Warm and welcoming Eugenia Sivitou and her husband run excellent all-inclusive week-long yoga retreats (from €560 including accommodation) in different disciplines, with teachers from all over the world. There's also a work-exchange option (€510), where you perform household duties for a few hours per day, or you can simply opt for drop-in classes.

Liquid Bungy BUNGEE JUMPING

(6937615191; www.bungy.gr; per jump €100; Sat & Sun Jul & Aug) Liquid Bungy offers jumps from 138m-high Vardinogiannis bridge into Aradena Gorge (p93); the package includes photos and a T-shirt.

Sleeping

Hora Sfakion has a number of basic hotels and pensions clustered around the waterfront, though none particularly stands out. However, at the time of research Xenia Hotel was undergoing a complete renovation, so expect modern, contemporary rooms by the time you're in town.

Xenia Hotel HOTEL €

(28250 91490; www.sfakia-xenia-hotel.gr; Old Harbour; d incl breakfast €58;) Well positioned overlooking the water, this hotel has been around since the early 1960s but has seen a number of upgrades, with another renovation underway at the time of writing. See in the evening by toasting the waves on your sea-facing balcony.

Lefka Ori HOTEL €

(28250 91209; www.chora-sfakion.com; s/d/ste from €28/40/80;) This long-established

WORTH A TRIP

ANOPOLI ΑΝΩΠΟΛΗ

A scenic, winding, hair-raisingly steep 12km road west from Hora Sfakion takes you to Anopoli, a quiet village in a fertile plateau at the base of the Lefka Ori (White Mountains), with a memorial to resistance fighters in the main square. It was one of the few areas that did not fall to the Venetians or the Turks. In earlier centuries Anopoli was the Sfakiot capital, presiding over the regional port of Loutro (still accessible, albeit on an extremely steep path, by hikers).

On the village's main roundabout, **Platanos** (☎28250 91169; www.anopoli-sfakia.com; Anopoli; mains €6.50-9; ⏲7.30am-10pm daily, Sat & Sun only Nov-Mar) serves hearty lunches, and is known for its roast lamb (available most weekends in summer) and other homemade local delicacies. The friendly English-speaking owner, Eva Kopasis, can advise about hikes to Loutro and local beaches, and has rooms (doubles €33).

Don't miss the delicious baked goods at **Cretan Divine Family Bakery** (☎28250 91524; Anopoli; ⏲6am-9pm), where friendly Angeliki serves up cookies, *kalitsounia* (Cretan cheese pies), homemade ice cream in summer, and hot Greek coffee at wonderful outdoor tables with views around the plateau. She also sells homemade raki and liqueurs to take with you.

little hotel at the western end of the port has a collection of rooms, studios and suites with kitchenettes, all clean and well kept though fairly basic. Avoid the sub-par taverna below.

Hotel Stavris HOTEL €
(☎28250 91220; www.hotel-stavris-sfakia-crete.com; s/d/tr/apt €35/39/44/55; ❄📶) At this hotel up the hill overlooking the old harbour, the Perrakis clan has welcomed guests since 1969, though these days don't expect an overly enthusiastic reception. Rooms and apartments vary by size, configuration and amenities, although all are spacious and have air-con, fridge and balcony. The nicer ones have kitchenettes and harbour-facing views. Cash only.

Eating

There are tavernas lined up along the harbour, but most are fairly touristy affairs. For stunning views, check out Three Brothers, set on a hill overlooking the sea backed by cliffs. Be sure to try the local *Sfakiani pita* – this thin, circular pancake filled with sweet *myzithra* (sheep's-milk cheese) and flecked with honey makes a great breakfast when served with a bit of Greek yoghurt on the side.

Taverna Nikos TAVERNA €€
(☎28250 91111; Old Harbour; mains €7-15; ⏲8am-midnight May-Oct) At the beginning of the gauntlet of harbour-front tavernas, family-run Nikos is a reliable spot for Greek staples, grilled fish and meat, and Cretan specialities such as smoked pork. Don't leave without sampling local dessert *Sfakiani pita*.

Three Brothers TAVERNA €€
(☎28250 91040; www.three-brothers-chorasfakion-crete.com; Vrissi Beach; mains €7.50-18; ⏲9am-midnight May-Oct; 📶) The extensive menu here features all the staples, but it's the location and the sensational views overlooking Vrissi Beach (p89) with a backdrop of cliffs that set this taverna apart from those in the harbour; it's particularly great at sunset. Things get especially crowded when Giannis fires up the barbecue. There are rooms for rent, too (doubles from €39).

Delfini SEAFOOD €€
(☎20250 91002; mains €6-15, fish per kg €38-50; ⏲9am-11pm) Among the row of seafront tavernas, Delfini is recommended for its fresh fish dishes and friendly service.

Information

Sfakia Tours (☎28250 91272; www.sfakia-tours.com; ⏲8am-midnight Apr-Oct) Has hire cars, can help with accommodation, and arranges tours to Imbros and Samaria Gorges. Located on the harbour.

Getting There & Away

BOAT

Hora Sfakion is the eastern terminus for the south-coast **Anendyk** (☎8am-4pm Mon-Fri ☎28250 91221; www.anendyk.gr; New Harbour) ferry route. Ferries run to Paleohora (€20.70), Loutro (€6, 20 minutes), Agia Roumeli (€12.50, one hour) and Sougia (€16.20). Boats make extended stops in Agia Roumeli to accommodate Samaria Gorge hikers. Ferries may be cancelled in bad weather, so be careful not to get stuck in Agia Roumeli or Loutro. There are also two to three boats per week to/from Gavdos Island via Loutro and Agia Roumeli (€21.20, four hours). Some ferries carry vehicles (to Sougia with car one way/return €29/50, to Paleohora €36.40, reservation required). There are also ferries direct to Gavdos Island from Hora Sfakion from July to early September (€21.20, 2½ hours).

Schedules vary seasonally, so always check ahead. Often boats only run as far as Agia Roumeli, where you must change for another ferry to Sougia and Paleohora.

Day trippers to Gavdos Island can take the **Gavdos Cruises** (6981920076; www.gavdos-cruises.jimdo.com; adult/child return €40/20) fast boat departing at 10.10am and returning from Gavdos at 5pm. The journey takes one hour.

There's a daily small **ferry** (6978645212; New Harbour) to Sweetwater Beach (May to October; per person return €8). A boat taxi for up to six people costs €25 to Sweetwater and €40 to Loutro.

BUS

KTEL buses (p83) leave from the square up the hill above the municipal car park. Schedules change seasonally; check online. In summer there are three daily services to/from Hania (€8.30, 1¾ hours) and to/from Frangokastello (€2.30, 30 minutes).

Loutro Λουτρό

POP 56

The pint-sized fishing village of Loutro is a tranquil crescent of flower-festooned white-and-blue buildings hugging a narrow pebbly beach between Agia Roumeli and Hora Sfakion. It's only accessible by boat and on foot and is the departure point for coastal walks to isolated beaches, such as Finix, Marmara and Sweetwater.

Activities

Loutro Canoes CANOEING
(28250 91433; Hotel Porto Loutro; canoe hire 1hr/half day/full day from €4/10/14) Hotel Porto Loutro hires out canoes and pedalos. Note: no children under 10 years old, except in August.

Sleeping

Practically all lodging options overlook Loutro's scenic little bay; many have their own taverna.

Blue House PENSION €
(28250 91035; www.thebluehouse.gr; d incl breakfast €50-65;) Midway along the white buildings lining the port, the Blue House has spacious, well-appointed rooms with big verandas overlooking the water. The nicest rooms are in the refurbished top-floor section. The taverna downstairs serves excellent *mayirefta* (ready-cooked meals; mains €6 to €9), including delicious *bourekia* baked with zucchini, potato and goat's cheese.

Villa Niki APARTMENT €
(6972299979; www.loutro-accommodation.com; studios/apt from €55/80;) These elegantly rustic studios with beamed ceilings and stone floors accommodate up to four people and come with a kitchenette with basic equipment. Since Niki is located just above the village, you get great views over the water from the balconies.

Rooms Sofia PENSION €
(28250 91354; www.sofiarooms-loutro.gr; d/tr €40/50; Apr-Oct;) Above the Sofia mini-market, one street back from the beach, these plain and clean rooms can be a bit cramped but have fridge and kettle. They share a veranda, which has sea and mountain views.

Hotel Porto Loutro HOTEL €€
(28250 91001, 28250 91433; www.hotelportoloutro.com; s/d incl breakfast from €75/85; Apr-Oct; @) The classiest hotel in the village has rooms and studios furnished in smartly contemporary island style and spread across two hotels, one on the beach and the other on the hill, all with spacious furnished balconies perfect for counting the waves or chilling with a beer. Days start with a lavish breakfast spread at the on-site restaurant.

Eating

Given the captive market, the tavernas that line the waterfront in Loutro are surprisingly good. Most offer the usual array of fresh fish, local grills and traditional *mayirefta* (ready-cooked meals).

Notos CRETAN €
(28250 91501; http://notos.loutro.gr; dishes €3.50-9.50; 7.30am-11.30pm Apr-Oct) Excellent mezedhes are on offer at this place set back from the beach. Order a range of small plates, like stuffed onions, and dig in.

Ilios SEAFOOD €€
(☎28250 91160; www.iliosloutro.gr; mains €5-15; ⏲8am-11pm mid-Apr–Oct; 📶) Ilios is the best spot in town for fish and seafood, though it offers a full range of Cretan classics and breakfast, too. Rooms are also available.

Pavlos TAVERNA €€
(☎28250 91336; www.pavlos.loutro.gr; mains €8-14; ⏲8am-midnight Apr-Oct) Sit by the harbour and feast on all manner of freshly grilled meat and fish.

Information

There's no bank, ATM or post office, and many places do not accept credit cards. Bring plenty of cash. The nearest ATM is in Hora Sfakion.

Getting There & Away

Loutro is on the Paleohora–Hora Sfakion boat route operated by Anendyk (p90). Ferries go to Paleohora (€19.70), Hora Sfakion (€6), Sougia (€15.20) and Agia Roumeli (€7.50, 45 minutes). Boats from Hora Sfakion to Gavdos Island also stop in Loutro.

Agia Roumeli Αγία Ρουμελή

POP 125

This coastal cluster of tavernas and pensions punctuates the southern end of Samaria Gorge and is only reachable on foot and by boat. While not spectacular in itself, its fine pebble beach and sparkling sea are inevitably welcome sights at the end of the trail. The village is also the launch pad for doing Samaria Gorge the 'lazy way': by hiking just a short distance north.

There are no tourist facilities or ATMs and not much to see other than the ruins of a Venetian castle (about 1km above the village) and the church, which has some remnants of a Roman mosaic floor.

Sleeping & Eating

There's a handful of beachfront pensions and apartments for hikers wanting to overnight here.

Beachfront tavernas attached to pensions serve home-cooked Cretan fare.

Calypso Hotel & Taverna HOTEL €
(☎28250 91314; www.calypso.agiaroumeli.gr; s/d/tr from €25/35/40; ❄📶) Beachfront and well established, Calypso offers tidy rooms with fridges, and ocean views from the balconies. Its spacious taverna-bar serves excellent mezedhes, slow-cooked meats and local wine (mains €5.50 to €12).

Artemis Studios APARTMENT €
(☎6936761303, 28250 91377; www.agiaroumeli.com; s/d/tr/q from €35/45/55/65; ⏲Apr-Oct; ❄📶👪) Fifty metres from Agia Roumeli's pebble beach, the family-run Artemis has 11 spacious self-catering studios with balconies; studios accommodate up to four people. It's a good bet if you want to be near the water and away from the crowds. The owners provide info on local hill walks, too, and there's a taverna 100m away.

Gigilos Taverna & Rooms PENSION €
(☎28250 91383; www.gigilos.gr; s/d/tr €30/35/45; ⏲May-Oct; ❄📶) Gigilos is right on the beach at the western end of the village. Its best rooms are at the front, on the beach road. They're clean and nicely furnished, with fridges and decent renovated bathrooms. The taverna, which serves home-cooked Cretan fare (mains €6 to €11), has a huge shady deck on the beach. Free beach chair and umbrella for guests.

Paralia Taverna & Rooms PENSION €
(☎28250 91408; r €35-40; ⏲Apr-Oct; ❄📶) Right by the ferry dock, this family-run taverna serves an array of home-cooked Cretan dishes and also rents nine simple and clean rooms, all with fridge, some with sea view.

Getting There & Away

Agia Roumeli can only be reached on foot, at the end of the Samaria Gorge hike, and by boat. It's a stop on the **Anendyk** (☎28250 91251; www.anendyk.gr) south-coast route, with boats coming in from Hora Sfakion (€12.50, one hour), Loutro (€7.50, 40 minutes), Sougia (€11, 40 minutes) and Paleohora (€17.20, 1½ hours). The ferry to Gavdos Island (€21.20) also stops at Agia Roumeli.

Sougia Σούγια

POP 136

Sougia, 67km south of Hania and on the Hora Sfakion–Paleohora ferry route, is one of the most chilled-out and refreshingly undeveloped southern beach resorts. Cafes, bars and tavernas line a tamarisk-shaded waterfront promenade along a grey pebble-and-sand beach. Most pensions and apartments enjoy a quieter inland setting roughly 100m to 200m from the beach. There is little to do other than relax or explore the local hiking trails, including the popular Agia Irini Gorge and Lissos beach and ruins.

OFF THE BEATEN TRACK

ARADENA GORGE

The virtually abandoned stone hamlet of Aradena, about 2km west of Anopoli, is famous for the **Vardinogiannis bridge** (named for the wealthy local businessman who endowed it), which crosses the Aradena Gorge. Look down into the depths in fascinated horror as the structure rattles under your wheels. At weekends you may see people jumping into the gorge from the bridge – at 138m, it's the highest bungee-jumping bridge in Greece. Contact Liquid Bungy (p89) to join in.

There's a *kantina* (small kiosk) next to the bridge serving coffee, tea, snacks and *Sfakiani pita* (Sfakian pie). You can also ask for information and directions here for the remote **Church of Agios Ioannis**, a whitewashed early-Byzantine structure around 5km away. It has frescoes inside, though the church is rarely open. From it, however, begins a forking path down to the sea: the western fork leads to Agia Roumeli via the Byzantine **Church of Agios Pavlos**, the eastern to **Marmara Beach** with its brilliant teal waters.

The more-often-used **Aradena Gorge hiking route** to Marmara Beach goes through the gorge and is a two-hour (3.5km) trek of moderate difficulty; ask for trailhead directions from the kiosk. From the beach, you can walk to the glittering nearby port of Loutro, with its creature comforts, and catch a ferry out.

Sights & Activities

Sougia has a pleasant 1km-long grey sand-and-pebble beach, but its drop-off is steep, so it's not ideal for families with small children.

Like most south-coast villages, Sougia is great hiking territory. The most popular **walk** is to the archaeological site of Lissos, some 3.5km away. It involves a rocky ascent and descent, but most of the way is relatively easy, with lovely views. It follows the coastal E4 path to Paleohora (though it's not on the actual coast). If you don't feel like hiking back to Sougia, a water taxi (p95) can pick you up.

A taxi to the Samaria Gorge trailhead is €60, but with a day or two's notice, staff at the taxi kiosk can put together a pool of hikers to share the cost. If you don't like the Samaria crowds, head for Agia Irini Gorge instead.

Lissos RUINS

The ruins of ancient Lissos are a pleasant 3.5km hike from Sougia on the coastal (though not waterfront) path to Paleohora, which starts at the far end of Sougia's small port. Lissos arose under the Dorians, flourished under the Byzantines and was destroyed by the Saracens in the 9th century. A port for inland Elyros (now gone), it was part of a league of city-states, led by ancient Gortyna, that minted its own gold coins inscribed with the word 'Lission'.

If you don't fancy a hike, the other option is take a water taxi (p95) to the nearby cove and walk up.

At one time there was a reservoir, a theatre and hot springs here, but these have not yet been excavated. Most of what you see dates from the 1st to the 3rd century BC, when Lissos was known for its curative springs. The 3rd-century-BC Temple of Asklepion was built next to one of the springs and named after the Greek god of healing, Asclepius.

Excavations here uncovered a headless statue of Asclepius along with 20 other statue fragments now in Hania's Archaeological Museum (p65). You can still see the marble altar base that supported the statue next to the pit in which sacrifices were placed. The other notable feature is the **mosaic floor** of multicoloured stones intricately arranged in beautiful geometric shapes and images of birds. On the way down to the sea there are traces of Roman ruins, and on the western slopes of the valley are unusual barrel-vaulted tombs.

Nearby are the ruins of two early Christian basilicas – **Agia Kyriakos** and **Agia Panagia** – dating from the 13th century.

Lissos has a beautiful pebbly beach to cool off at after the hike, and if you come on 15 July you'll stumble on the festival held in honour of Agios Kyriakos.

★**Agia Irini Gorge** HIKING

(€2; year-round) Pretty Agia Irini Gorge starts around 13km north of Sougia near the village of Agia Irini. The well-maintained, well-signposted and mostly shaded 7.5km trail (with a 500m elevation drop) follows the riverbed, is shaded by oleander, pines and other greenery, and passes caves hidden in the gorge walls. Allow around three hours to complete the hike.

LOCAL KNOWLEDGE

REMOTE GORGE HIKES

Samaria Gorge isn't western Crete's only canyon worth conquering. For the gorges below, which are more remote, it's always wise to go with a guide or with thorough pre-planning if you're an experienced trekker. Check in first with Hania's EOS (p72) for advice on local conditions, water sources and lodgings, and pick up the Anavasi hiking maps (available in Hania bookshops), marked with GPS coordinates, trails and other key details. Find additional info at www.west-crete.com.

Agia Irini Gorge (p93) More lush than most; ends 4.5km north of Sougia.

Imbros Gorge (€2; year-round) About half as long as Samaria and open year-round; ends at Komitades near Hora Sfakion. See Hiking in Hania (p106) to find out more.

Aradena Gorge (p93) Moderate-to-steep hike; ends at Marmara Bay, 5km west of Loutro.

Trypiti Gorge (p94) Tough and little visited; ends 12km east of Sougia. Guide essential.

Klados Gorge This gorge, marked by a sheer and unforgiving rock face, runs between and parallel to Samaria and Trypiti Gorges. This is the place to go for serious rock climbers; it offers great abseiling (rappelling), too. It lets out on the barren south coast. For experienced mountaineers only.

It makes for a lovely, less crowded alternative to Samaria Gorge. The trail includes a few steep sections but is mostly relatively easy, with a few river crossings. There are rest stops with benches and toilets along the way, but be sure to take plenty of drinking water with you. You'll emerge at a taverna where you can call a taxi (€15) or continue on foot for another 4.5km via a quiet and paved road to Sougia.

Trypiti Gorge HIKING

Little-visited Trypiti Gorge near Mt Gingilos is one of Crete's longest and most strenuous hikes, starting in Omalos and ending on the southern coast 12km east of Sougia at Cape Trypiti. You'll have blissfully little company on the 10-hour jaunt, making Trypiti great for those seeking unspoilt nature and solitude. You'll need a guide, as well as maps, water and food.

Sleeping

Sougia offers a handful of places to stay, most of which are comfortable and well run. There are a couple on the waterfront, while the rest are on the main strip about 100m to 200m from the water. A small settlement of campers and nudists sometimes crops up at the eastern end of the beach. Note, there is only one ATM in Sougia.

Aretousa Studios & Rooms APARTMENT €

(28230 51178; studios €55-65; Apr-Oct; P ❄ 📶) This lovely pension on the road to Hania, 200m from the sea, has bright and comfortably furnished studios with tile floors and balconies. There's a tranquil garden, friendly service and even a kids' playground out the back.

Rooms Ririka PENSION €

(28230 51167; www.sougia.info/hotels/ririka; d from €40; ❄ 📶) This cosy place consists of six double rooms (try for an upstairs room with balcony and sea views) and a leafy garden. Sweet elderly owner Ririka speaks a little bit of English. It's just up from the eastern side of the beach.

Syia Hotel HOTEL €€

(28230 51174; www.syiahotel.com; studios/apt from €60/80; P ❄ 📶) This professionally run family hotel is as fancy as things get in laid-back Sougia. Set in a quiet garden, units have plenty of elbow room, plus balcony and full kitchen.

Hotel Santa Irene APARTMENT €€

(28230 51342; www.santa-irene.gr; Beach Rd; apt €45-80; late Mar-early Nov; P ❄ 📶) In a traditional building set back from the beach in a lovely garden setting, Santa Irene has 15 roomy, bright and balconied studios sleeping two to five. Whip up breakfast or a small meal in the kitchenette or grab a snack at the attached beachside bar.

Eating & Drinking

For a such a small coastal town, Sougia offers some great dining. A few tavernas line the waterfront and the main strip.

Taverna Oasis TAVERNA €

(📞28230 51121; mains €6-10; 🕒11am-9pm Apr-Oct) Restore your energies with a cold beer and classic Greek snacks after you tackle lovely Agia Irini Gorge (p93). From here it's another 7km walk or a €15 taxi ride back to Sougia.

Polyfimos TAVERNA €

(📞28230 51343; www.polifimos.gr; Main Rd; mains €5-11; 🕒1pm-midnight Apr-Oct) Hidden in a pretty grapevine-shrouded courtyard off the Hania road, this charismatic restaurant specialises in traditional charcoal-grilled local meats, fresh fish of the day, hearty stews such as rabbit *stifadho* (cooked with onions in a tomato puree) and lamb *tsigariasto*. It's run by ex-hippie Yiannis, who also makes his own oil, wine and raki.

Taverna Rembetiko CRETAN €

(📞28230 51510; dishes €5-9; 🕒noon-late Apr-Oct; 🌿) On the road to Hania, this popular taverna serving mezedhes (small dishes) is a great place for a quick, well-priced snack or meal. The friendly owners offer an extensive menu of Cretan dishes, such as *bourekia* and stuffed zucchini flowers. Good vegetarian options, too.

★**Omikron** INTERNATIONAL €€

(📞28230 51492; Beach Rd; mains €7-12; 🕒8am-late Apr-Oct; 📶🌿) At this elegantly rustic beachfront spot with crushed pebbles underfoot, Jean-Luc Delfosse has forged his own culinary path in a refreshing change from taverna staples. From mushroom crêpes to *Flammekuche* (Alsatian-style pizza), seafood pasta to pepper steak – it's all fresh, creative and delicious.

Kyma SEAFOOD €€

(📞28230 51688; mains €5-16; 🕒noon-late Apr-Oct) You'll know Kyma by the fish tank out the front. It's known for its seafood, supplied by the owner's brother, and the restaurant raises its own meat. Try the goat *tsigariasto* (sautéed) in wine sauce, the rooster in wine sauce or the rabbit *stifadho*. Fried *kalamari* is a top seafood pick.

Fortuna CLUB

(📞6977423023; 🕒11pm-7am Jun-Sep) Fortuna, on the left before the entrance to the town, is a great open-air place for a late-night drink. Things really get going after midnight.

ℹ Getting There & Away

BOAT

Ferries on the **Anendyk** (📞28230 51230; www.anendyk.gr) Paleohora–Agia Roumeli route stop in Sougia. The trip to either Paleohora or Agia Roumeli takes about 40 minutes and costs €11.20 and €11, respectively. In Agia Roumeli you can continue east to Hora Sfakion via Loutro. There are also two or three weekly ferries to Gavdos Island via Agia Roumeli.

Captain George's Water Taxi (📞28230 51133, 6947605802; www.sougia.info/taxi-boats) has several boats for up to 15 passengers that serve remote south-coast beaches such as Lissos (€5 per person one way), Tripiti and Pefki, and also go out to Paleohora and Agia Roumeli.

BUS

At least one daily bus operates between Sougia and Hania (€7.80, 1¾ hours), with a stop in Agia Irini to drop off gorge hikers. The bus departing Sougia at 6.15pm waits for the Agia Roumeli boat. In summer there are also daily buses to Omalos (for Samaria Gorge; €5.30, one hour).

TAXI

Local taxi drivers, including **Selino Taxi** (📞6940859860; www.taxi-selino.com) and **Sougia Taxi** (📞6970344422; www.sougiataxi.com), have a central kiosk on the waterfront.

Paleohora Παλαιόχωρα

POP 1900

Appealing, laid-back and full of character, Paleohora lies on a narrow peninsula flanked by a long, curving, tamarisk-shaded sandy beach (Pahia Ammos) and a pebbly beach (Halikia). Shallow waters and general quietude make the village a good choice for families with small children. The most picturesque part of Paleohora is the maze of narrow streets below the castle. Tavernas spill out onto the pavement and occasional cultural happenings inject a lively ambience. In spring and autumn Paleohora attracts many walkers.

👁 Sights

Pahia Ammos BEACH

(Sandy Beach) Pahia Ammos, often simply called Sandy Beach, lives up to its name. When the winds kick up it's good for windsurfing, and it's got the best sunsets in town. You'll find it on the western side of Paleohora's peninsula. The drop-off is gradual, so it's great for kids.

Paleohora

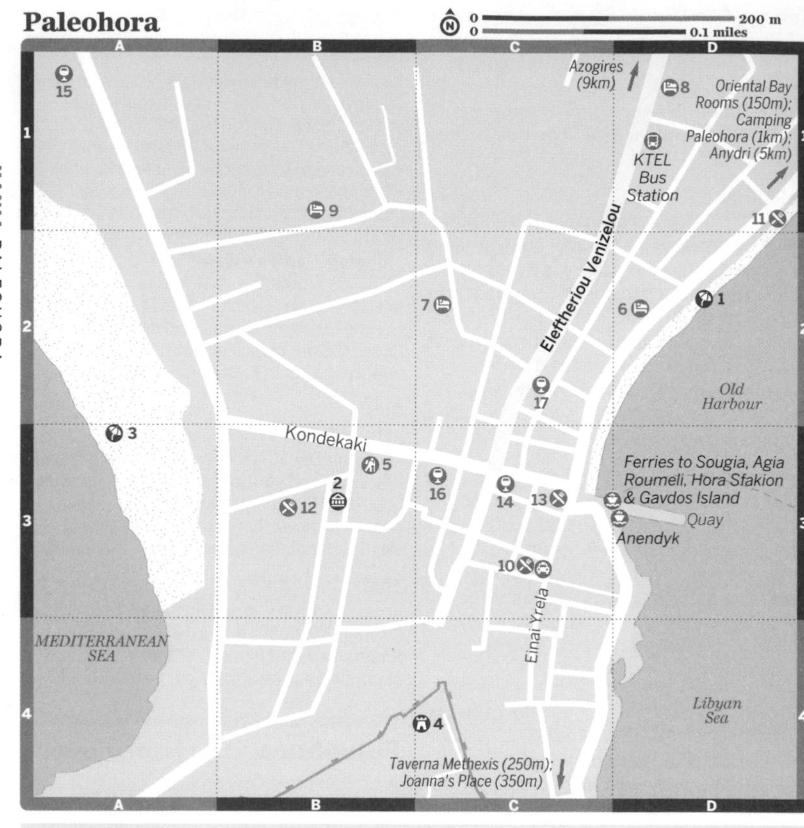

Paleohora

Sights
1 Halikia Beach D2
2 Museum of the Acritans of Europe B3
3 Pahia Ammos A3
4 Venetian Fort C4

Activities, Courses & Tours
5 Paleohora Nature B3

Sleeping
6 Corali D2
7 Homestay Anonymous C2
8 Libyan Princess D1
9 Villa Anna B1

Eating
10 Aristea C3
11 Christos Taverna D1
12 Third Eye B3
13 Vakakis Family Bakery C3

Drinking & Nightlife
14 Agios C3
15 La Jetee A1
16 Monika's Garden Wine Bar C3
17 Nostos Club C2

Museum of the Acritans of Europe MUSEUM
(6979228604; 10am-1pm Mon-Fri) FREE This little museum is dedicated to the border fighters and heroes of Europe's medieval and Byzantine times. It has a well-displayed historical exhibition, along with musical instruments, weapons and other items from the period.

Venetian Fort FORT
(Kastro Selino; 24hr) FREE There's not much left of the 13th-century Venetian castle looming above Paleohora, but it's worth climbing the stairs for the splendid views of the sea and mountains, especially at sunset.

Built in its commanding hilltop position to monitor the southwestern coast, it was destroyed in turn by Cretan rebels, the pirate Barbarossa and the Ottomans.

Halikia Beach BEACH
(Pebble Beach) Halikia Beach is Paleohora's pebble beach, on the eastern side of Paleohora's peninsula. It can occasionally be better protected from the wind than sandy Pahia Ammos.

Activities

There are several great **walking trails** nearby. From Paleohora, a six-hour walk along the scenic coastal path leads to Sougia, passing ancient Lissos. An easier inland loop goes to Anydri and then through small, lush Anydri Gorge to the sea. Contact **Paleohora Nature** (28230 43259; www.paleochoranature.com; Kondekaki; 9am-2pm & 6-9pm Mon-Sat) for walking tours in the area.

When a stiff summer breeze is blowing, **windsurfing** off Pahia Ammos is excellent.

Notos Car & Motorbike Rentals (6976436044; www.notoscar.gr; Eleftherios Venizelou 53; 8.30am-2pm & 5.30-9pm) and **Selino Travel** (28230 42272; Kondekaki; 8am-1.30pm & 6-9pm Mon-Sat Apr-Oct, shorter hours rest of year) can hook you up with guided hikes of Samaria and Agia Irini Gorges.

Sleeping

Paleohora packs plenty of sleeping options in, with everything from homely guesthouses and a high-end hotel to budget-friendly pensions and a campground.

Corali APARTMENT €
(6974361868; www.corali-studios.com; Halikia Beach; studios €45-55;) A friendly Greek-Italian family runs these three studios kitted out with kitchenettes, modern furniture, large bathrooms and waterfront balconies.

Joanna's Place APARTMENT €
(6978583503, 28230 41801; www.joanna-place.com; studios €50-60, 2-bed apt €100-110; Apr-Nov;) This modern beige building sits in a quiet spot across from a small stone beach at the southeastern tip of the peninsula. The 16 spacious and spotless studios are outfitted with functional locally made furniture, and there's a kitchenette for preparing breakfast to enjoy on your balcony. There's also a two-bedroom apartment that will suit families.

Homestay Anonymous PENSION €
(28230 42098; www.anonymoushomestay.com; s/d/apt from €25/30/55;) This simple but good-value pension with private bathrooms and shared cooking facilities in the courtyard garden is an excellent budget pick. Friendly, well-travelled owner Manolis cultivates a welcoming atmosphere and is a mine of information on local activities. The nine units are in two quaint stone buildings and furnished in charming country style.

Villa Anna PENSION €
(28103 46428; www.villaanna-paleochora.com; apt €50-75;) Run by the warm and welcoming Anna and set in a lovely shady garden bordered by tall poplars, these well-appointed, family-friendly apartments sleep up to five. There are cots, and swings and a sandpit in the garden, and the grounds are fenced.

Oriental Bay Rooms PENSION €
(28230 41076; www.orientalbay.gr; Halikia Beach; s/d/tr €30/35/50;) These immaculate rooms in a large modern building at the northern end of Halikia Beach have balconies with sea or mountain views and come with kettle and fridge. There's a downstairs taverna, too.

Alpha Hotel HOTEL €
(28230 41620; www.alfahotelazogires.blogspot.com; Azogires; r from €30;) Caters to yoga groups but has decent digs for independent travellers, too, in a relaxed wooded setting just above the village centre. It's run by friendly Lucky from Alpha Restaurant and information centre.

Camping Paleohora CAMPGROUND €
(28230 41120; www.campingpaleochora.gr; sites adult/child/tent €6/3.50/4;) This large campground is 1.5km northeast of town, about 500m east of stony Halikia beach. There's a taverna, kitchen facilities and a playground, and it's near the sea, but there's no mini-market, and facilities in general are a bit run down.

Libyan Princess HOTEL €€
(28230 42030; www.libyanprincess.gr; d incl breakfast from €115;) This full-service hotel is Paleohora's plushest option. Thirty-five rooms and one executive suite curl around a sparkling pool and boast all mod cons, from flat-screen TV and phone to safe and tea- and coffee-making facilities. There's a gym and massage service as well. Downside: it's on the busy main street.

WORTH A TRIP

AZOGIRES ΑΖΟΓΥΡΕΣ

An eccentric hill village 9km north of Paleohora, Azogires and its sylvan valley are the place of legends involving river Nereids in its waterfalls and medieval ascetics who inhabited cave dwellings. Both the waterfalls and the caves can be visited today. Stop in at Alpha Restaurant for information; owner Lucky leads walks in the area and to the caves.

Eating

The town has some decent Cretan restaurants, and in summer little tavernas spill onto the pedestrian-only central street and make for great ambience. In the Paleohora region, the excellent *myzithra* (sheep's-milk cheese) is generally unsweetened, unlike the usual sweetened version served elsewhere in Crete. The olive oil produced in this region is among the best in Greece.

Third Eye VEGETARIAN €
(☎6986793504, 28230 41234; https://thirdeye-paleochora.com; mains €6-9; ⌚1-10pm; 📶🌶) A local institution and community gathering spot since 1990, the Third Eye knew what to do with beetroot, quinoa and hummus long before meatless fare went mainstream. The globally inspired menu features delicious salads, rotating mains, and snacks such as a juicy portobello burger and caramelised-onion *fava* dip with bread. Sit on the streetside patio or in the tranquil garden.

Alpha Restaurant TAVERNA €
(Azogires; mains €3-7; ⌚9am-10pm) Breakfast, sandwiches and Cretan pies are served at Alpha, the community-run cafe and tourist-info office in Azogires village. It's usually staffed, but the door is always unlocked and the cafe operates on an honour system if no one's around.

Local guide Lakkis 'Lucky' Koukoutsakis leads tours of the village, Azogires Gorge and caves in the area. You can also check out local art in the gallery across the road.

Christos Taverna CRETAN €
(☎28230 41359; www.christospaleochora.com; mains €6-12; ⌚6pm-late May-Oct) Straightforward Cretan and Greek dishes are the order of the day at this long-standing taverna near stony Halikia Beach. Pick from what's fresh, arrayed in casserole dishes behind the glass.

Vakakis Family Bakery BAKERY €
(☎28230 41850; www.fournosvakaki.gr; baked goods from €1; ⌚6.45am-10.30pm, or later in summer) Load up on fresh bread and sweet treats paired with hot or iced coffees to go, or dine in on sweet and savoury crêpes or gelato at the attached cafe.

Taverna Methexis CRETAN €€
(☎28230 41431; www.facebook.com/MethexisTaverna; Waterfront; mains €7-12; ⌚12.30-11.30pm; P📶🌶) It's well worth the short saunter to the peninsula's southeastern tip to sample the authentic comfort food and warm hospitality at this taverna, popular with locals and tourists, across from a small beach. All the classics are accounted for, along with such tasty surprises as salt cod with garlic sauce and delicious pies filled with fennel or local *myzithra*.

Aristea CRETAN €€
(☎28230 43130; dishes €6-15; ⌚noon-late) In a traditional stone building with a tree-shaded courtyard, Aristea does a menu of grilled meats, seafood, and Cretan classics such as snails, rooster in wine sauce and *briam* (oven-baked vegetable casserole). It's set one block back from the promenade.

Drinking & Nightlife

There's a lively, laid-back atmosphere when the sun goes down in Paleohora and visitors are spoilt for choice with nightlife options, particularly in the central streets between the promenade and Pahia Ammos.

★Monika's Garden Wine Bar WINE BAR
(☎28230 41150; www.facebook.com/monikasgarden; Kondekaki; ⌚6pm-1am Apr-Oct) One of the best spots for a drink in town, this attractive, modern wine bar with a delightful garden courtyard features more than 40 top-quality wines by the glass, all from Crete. Drop in for a tipple paired with snacks such as cheese platters and traditional *kalitsounia* (filled pastries).

Agios BAR
(☎28230 41258; www.agiosbar.gr; ⌚7am-late) A hip, relaxed bar and music venue, Agios is one of Paleohora's best hang-outs any time of day. It's a great spot for breakfast, with good coffee, and perfect for an arvo drink or to party on into the night, with great cocktails and craft beer.

La Jetee BAR
(9am-2am May-Sep;) Plonked on the sand at Pahia Ammos (p95), this tourist haunt is known for its cocktails and sunset views. A menu of snacks (€4 to €8) is served all day to keep the hunger in check.

Nostos Club CLUB
(6.30pm-4am Apr-Oct) Nostos has a terrace bar and a small indoor club playing Greek and Western music.

Information

There's a couple of ATMs on the main drag, Eleftheriou Venizelou.

Getting There & Away

BOAT

Ferries depart from the quay at the far southern end of the Halikia pebble beach. Buy tickets at Selino Travel (p96).

Ferries (www.anendyk.gr) run to Sougia (€11.20, 40 minutes), Agia Roumeli (€17.20, 1½ hours) and Hora Sfakion (€20.70). Some boats can transport cars and scooters.

There are also two or three weekly ferries to Gavdos Island (€23.30, four hours) via Sougia and Agia Roumeli.

BUS

KTEL (28230 41914; www.e-ktel.com; Eleftherios Venizelos) runs four daily buses to Hania (€8.30, 1¾ hours) and one bus daily except Sunday at 6.15am to Omalos (€7, one hour) for Samaria Gorge. Buses also stop in Sougia and, on request, at the Agia Irini Gorge trailhead. There are also Elafonisi-bound buses (€5.50, one hour).

CAR & MOTORCYCLE

Notos Rentals (p96) has cars, motorcycles and bicycles for hire. There are two petrol stations in town. Fuel up before heading on longer drives in the region, where petrol stations are rare to nonexistent.

Getting Around

Paleochora Taxi (6979594667, 28230 41128; www.paleochora-taxi.com; 7.30am-10pm) This professional outfit runs shuttle buses to the trailheads for Agia Irini (€19 per person) and Samaria Gorges (€25 per person including the boat ticket for the return) three times a week, departing at 7.30am.

Elafonisi Ελαφονήσι

POP 15

Tucked into Crete's southwestern corner, **Elafonisi** (2 sunbeds & umbrella €9, umbrella only €3) is a symphony of fine pink-white sand, turquoise water and gentle rose dunes that looks like a magical dreamscape. As the water swirls across the sands, rainbows shimmer across its surface. Off Elafonisi's long, wide strand lies Elafonisi Islet, occasionally connected by a thin, sandy isthmus, which creates a lovely double beach; otherwise, it's easily reached by wading through 50m of knee-deep water. The islet is marked by low dunes and a string of semi-secluded coves that attract a sprinkling of naturists. Walk the length of the beach and up to its high point for mind-blowing views of the beaches, sea and raw mountainscape. The area is part of EU environmental-protection program Natura 2000.

LOCAL KNOWLEDGE

PALEOHORA–SOUGIA COASTAL WALK

Following a portion of the E4 European Path, this hike connects two charming coastal towns via a 13km path that runs mostly along the coast and then heads inland from Lissos to Sougia.

From Paleohora, follow signs to the camp sites to the northeast and turn right at the sign for Anydri. After a couple of kilometres the path climbs steeply for a beautiful view back to Paleohora. You'll pass **Anydri Beach** and several inviting **coves** where people may be getting an all-over tan. Take a dip, because the path soon turns inland to pass over **Cape Flomes**. You'll walk along a plateau carpeted with brush that leads towards the coast and some breathtaking views over the Libyan Sea. About 10km into the hike you'll reach the Dorian site of Lissos (p93), from where the path weaves through a pine forest before spilling out at Sougia.

Allow five to six hours for the nearly shadeless walk and take plenty of water, a hat and sunblock. From June to August it's best to start at sunrise in order to get to Sougia before the heat of the day. The boat back to Paleohora runs at around 6pm (check the schedule at www.anendyk.gr).

Alas, this natural gem is less than idyllic in high summer, when hundreds of umbrellas and sunbeds clog the sand (dash out to the island, where you can find peace). The invasion puts enormous pressure on this delicate ecosystem and on the minimal infrastructure, especially the toilets (€0.50). Come early or late in the day; better yet, stay overnight to truly sample Elafonisi's magic. Outside high season, when there's no public transport to the beach and very few tours, you may have it all to yourself. There are a few snack bars and stores at the beach entrance.

Sights

Kedrodasos Beach BEACH

If you'd like to get even more off the beaten track than gorgeous Elafonisi, head 1km east to similarly gorgeous Kedrodasos, a soft arc of sand favoured by nudists and backed by junipers. You can reach it via 2.5km of dirt lanes through the greenhouses behind the beaches and then a 10-minute walk down a rocky path, or by the E4 coastal trail.

Moni Hrysoskalitissas Monastery MONASTERY

(adult/child €2/free; ⌚9am-sunset Jun-Aug, from 10am Sep, Oct & Mar-May, 10am-1pm & 5-6pm Nov-Feb) Four kilometres north of Elafonisi is this beautiful monastery perched on a rock high above the sea. The church is recent, but the monastery is allegedly a thousand years old and may have been built on the site of a Minoan temple. The monastery has created two small rudimentary **museums** on-site: a folk museum with a selection of weavings and objects from rural life and an ecclesiastical museum with mostly icons and manuscripts.

Hrysoskalitissas means 'golden staircase'. Some accounts suggest that the topmost one of the 98 steps leading to the monastery was made of gold but could only be seen by the faithful. Another version says that one of the steps was hollow and used to hide the church's treasury. In any case, during the Turkish occupation the gold, along with much of the monastery's estate, was used to pay hefty taxes imposed by the Ottoman rulers.

Sleeping & Eating

In addition to the lodging near the beach, there are several pensions about 5km north near Hrysoskalitissas, including Glykeria with its modern rooms and attractive pool.

Elafonisi Resort HOTEL €

(☎6983516137, 28250 61274; www.elafonisi-resort.com; d/studios from €45/60; ⌚Apr-Oct; P❄📶👪) This cluster of low-rise whitewashed buildings dotted around a peaceful olive grove has a range of accommodation, from clean, basic rooms above the restaurant to spacious contemporary studios with balconies – perfect for relaxing with a drink and enjoying the mountain views. The affiliated **restaurant** serves the catch of the day and classic Greek fare (mains €8 to €15).

Elafonisi Village Rooms & Taverna HOTEL €

(☎6942254382, 28220 61548; www.elafonisi-village.gr; Beach Rd; d €40-60; ⌚Apr-Oct; P❄📶👪) Just 250m from Elafonisi Beach, these 12 spacious rooms have tiled floors and wooden furniture, and some have private terraces. They're strung across an arid courtyard with sea views for catching the sunset. Four units sleep up to four and have a kitchenette.

Glykeria HOTEL €€

(☎28220 61292; www.glykeria.com; Hrysoskalitissas; d/tr incl breakfast from €60/80; P❄🏊) Small, friendly family-run Glykeria has updated modern rooms with fridges and sea-facing balconies, as well as an inviting pool and a beloved taverna across the road. It's on the main road before Moni Hrysoskalitissas Monastery.

Glykeria Tavern TAVERNA €€

(mains €7.50-15; ⌚8.30am-11pm May-Oct) One of the best options for a feed in Elafonisi, family-run Glykeria offers a mix of Cretan classics, burgers, pasta and seafood, as well as sea views and friendly service. The family's hotel is across the road.

Getting There & Away

Elafonisi is about 75km southwest of Hania town – reckon on 1½ to two hours for the nonstop drive.

From Paleohora, one boat (€10, one hour) and one bus (€5.50, one hour) make a daily trip from June to September. There's also one daily bus from Hania (€11, 2¼ hours) via Kissamos (Kastelli; €6.90, 1¼ hours) from June to September.

Gavdos Island Γαύδος

POP 150

In the Libyan Sea, 65km from Paleohora and 45km from Hora Sfakion, Gavdos is Europe's most southerly point and as much a

WORTH A TRIP

ANYDRI ΑΝΥΔΡΟΙ

The village of Anydri, 5km northeast of Paleohora, is a popular destination for walkers and is reached via a picturesque drive or walk through the lush 3km-long **Anydri Gorge**, carved by a small stream. To get there from Paleohora, take the road that goes past the campground and follow the paved road (which is bordered by steep rocks) that forks to the left. As you enter Anydri village you'll see a sign directing you to the gorge. After a few hundred metres on a footpath you'll encounter an overgrown path on the left. Red markers direct you to the gorge.

After walking along the dried-out riverbed, signs direct you to wide **Gialiskari Beach** at the end of the gorge. The nicest stretch is the area with coarse sand at the eastern end, left of the *kantina* (beach bar). From here you can either backtrack to Anydri or head west to Paleohora following the E4 markers, which will take you along the coastal cliffs after about 4.5km. The beach is also accessible via a drivable dirt road, from where it's signposted to the right, well before the gorge.

The founding fathers of the village were two brothers from Hora Sfakion fleeing a murderous vendetta, which is why most villagers have the same surname. A path from the village leads to the **Church of Agios Georgios**, which has 14th-century frescoes.

Sleeping & Eating

Christos Place (☎28230 42200; www.christosplace.gr; cottages €80-130; P ❄ ☈) These six lovely small cottages in an olive grove above Anydri sleep three to five and have kitchenette, underfloor heating, private terrace and satellite TV. Note: showers are outdoors. Views sweep to the Libyan Sea.

To Skolio (☎28230 83001; dishes €5-13; ⊙coffee from 9am, food noon-11pm daily Easter-Oct; ☈) Whether gorge walker or hire-car driver, do not miss the chance to dine at wonderful To Skolio, about 5km east of Paleohora. The converted red-and-white schoolhouse has cheerily painted tables on a tree-shaded cliff-side terrace with views out to sea. The daily-changing chalkboard menu of mezedhes (small dishes) incorporates the best local produce.

state of mind as it is an island. It's a blissful spot with only a few rooms, tavernas and unspoilt beaches, some accessible only by foot or boat. There's little to do here except swim, walk and relax. Gavdos attracts campers, nudists and free spirits happy to trade the trappings of civilisation for an unsullied nature experience.

The island is surprisingly green, with almost 65% covered in low-lying pine and cedar trees and vegetation. Most of the electricity is supplied by generators, which are often turned off at night and in the middle of the day. Note that the Anendyk ferry schedule does not make it possible to visit Gavdos on a day trip, but you can arrange a day trip with Gavdos Cruises.

History

Archaeological excavations indicate that the island was inhabited as far back as the Neolithic period. In the Graeco-Roman era Gavdos, then known as Clauda, belonged to the city of Gortyna. There was a Roman settlement in the island's northwestern corner. Under the Byzantines, Gavdos was the seat of a bishopric, but when the Arabs conquered Crete in the 9th century the island became a pirates' nest. It is thought to be the island home of the legendary Calypso of Homer's *Odyssey*, where the nymph held Odysseus captive for many years.

Sights

There are no villages per se on the island, just hamlets and loose encampments.

Boats land at **Karave** on the island's eastern side, which has a couple of tavernas and a mini-market. The teeny capital, **Kastri**, is in the centre of the island and also has a couple of tavernas.

The biggest beach community is at **Sarakiniko**, just north of Karave, and has a wide swathe of sand, several tavernas, a minimarket and showers.

Agios Ioannis beach, in the north, has a ragtag summer settlement of nudists and campers and is a 15-minute walk to the nearest taverna or road.

WORTH A TRIP

CRETAN CRAFT BEER

Established in 2007, Charma was the first beer to be produced in Hania and you can sample the excellent brews at the **Cretan Brewery** (☎28240 31002; www.cretanbeer.gr; Zounaki; guided tour €3; ⏲10am-8pm Apr-Nov), set up by a local. There's a covered terrace where you can enjoy the range of beers, from a blond lager to an excellent pale ale, along with seasonal brews, or opt for a tasting flight of five beers (€5). There's good beer-soaking pub grub on the menu and you can join a guided tour of the brewery; book ahead.

It's located in Zounaki village, around 25km west of the centre of Hania. The attached shop is the only place in Crete where you can buy the beer to take away.

Lavrakas beach is a half-hour walk from Agios Ioannis and has one of the most remote beach encampments. There's a natural freshwater well, and tanned, naked campers with dreadlocks blend in with the surroundings.

Potamos and **Pyrgos** are even more remote but gorgeous beaches on the northern coast (there are no facilities). You can reach them on foot from Kastri along the path leading north to **Ambelos** and beyond. The restored 1880 **lighthouse** (Faros) on the road to the village of Ambelos has a cafe. Before it was bombed by the Germans in 1941 it was the world's second-brightest lighthouse after Tierra del Fuego in Argentina.

South of Karave, **Korfos** has a pebbly beach and a couple of tavernas with rooms. From here a 3.5km trail leads down via near-unpopulated **Vatsiana** to **Tripiti** – the southernmost tip of Europe. Three giant arches carved into the rocky headland at Tripiti are the island's best-known natural feature. It's also reachable by small boat.

Despite the meagre population, there are 20 small **churches** dotted around the island. Most local boat owners offer full- and half-day **cruises**, including trips to the remote, uninhabited island of Gavdopoula, although there are no good beaches there. Ask at the tavernas.

Sleeping & Eating

In addition to hotel rooms, people free camp around the island – but do find out about local water sources before setting out. Gavdos has a short season (June to August), and most tavernas and rooms start closing in early September. Many places are already booked out in April – plan ahead!

Fresh fish, of course, is the singular highlight of dining in Gavdos. Most pensions have attached tavernas.

Consolas Gavdos Studios APARTMENT €
(☎28230 42182, 210 324 0968; www.gavdostudios.gr; Sarakiniko Beach; d/tr studio incl breakfast €70/85; ❄📶) These comfortable studios perch right above Sarakiniko beach. Villas sleeping up to five (€110) are also available. Guests may use the satellite internet connection. Phone ahead for harbour pick-up.

Gavdos Princess APARTMENT €€
(☎28230 41181; www.gavdos-princess.com; Kastri; apt €70-105; ❄📶👪) Open year-round in the hamlet of Kastri, Gavdos Princess offers pretty stone cottages with one or two bedrooms sleeping four to six. Cottages are air-conditioned and have kitchenettes and terraces. There's wi-fi in the public areas and a restaurant.

Theophilos Cafe CAFE €
(☎69448 07411; mains €5-10; ⏲8am-1am May-Oct) About a 10-minute walk up from Agios Ioannis beach, this place caters to campers with coffee and snacks.

Taverna Sarakiniko SEAFOOD €€
(☎28230 41103; Sarakiniko Beach; mains €5-15; ⏲7am-1am Jun-Sep) Run by Manolis the fisherman and his wife, Gerti, this taverna serves Manolis' fresh catch daily. Try the tangy grilled octopus or red snapper braised with lemon and olive oil.

Information

There are no banks or ATMs on the island.

There's usually a doctor on the island in summer.

Mobile coverage is patchy. Most lodgings and tavernas have wi-fi, but strong winds can disrupt or slow down service.

Getting There & Away

Anendyk (☎28230 41222; www.anendyk.gr) ferries serve Gavdos from Hora Sfakion (€21.20, 3¼ hours) via Loutro and Agia Roumeli. From July to September the ferry is direct from Hora Sfakion to Gavdos (2½ hours). Ferries from Paleohora to Gavdos (€23.30, four hours) via Sougia and Agia Roumeli run three to four times per week. Bad weather can suspend service.

Gavdos Cruises (p91) fast boats depart at 10.10am from Hora Sfakion to Gavdos Island and return from Gavdos at 5pm. The trip takes one hour.

Getting Around

Bike, scooter and car hire are available in Karave and Sarakiniko. Enquire about boat taxis to take you to remote beaches. From Karave, it's about 2.5km to Sarakiniko, 2km to Korfos and 4km to Kastri.

LEFKA ORI & SAMARIA GORGE

ΛΕΥΚΑ ΟΡΗ & ΦΑΡΑΓΓΙ ΤΗΣ ΣΑΜΑΡΙΑΣ

Deep in central Hania province, the Omalos Plateau breaches the towering Lefka Ori (White Mountains) and marks the northern entry to the Samaria Gorge. Many will approach the region from Hania and start the gorge hike in little Omalos. But you can also reach Omalos easily from Paleohora and Sougia on the southern coast. The Samaria Gorge trail descends to Agia Roumeli, also on the southern coast.

Hania to Omalos

The road from Hania to the beginning of Samaria Gorge in Omalos is varied and, in places, spectacular. After heading through orange groves you'll get to the village of **Fournes**.

If you detour up a left fork in the road after Fournes, you'll twist and turn along a gorge offering beautiful views to **Meskla**. Although the bottom part of the town is not particularly attractive, the road becomes more scenic as it winds uphill to the modern, multicoloured **Church of the Panagia**. Next to it is a 14th-century chapel built on the foundations of a 6th-century basilica that might have been built on an even earlier temple of Aphrodite. At the entrance to the town a sign directs you to the **Chapel of the Metamorfosis Sotiros** (Chapel of the Transfiguration of the Saviour) that contains 14th-century frescoes. The fresco of the Transfiguration on the southern wall is particularly impressive.

On the main Hania–Omalos road south of Fournes, the excellent **Botanical Park** (☎6976860573; www.botanical-park.com; Km 17 Hania–Omalos Rd; adult/child €6/4; ⏰gardens 9am-8pm Apr-Oct, kitchen 9am-6pm daily Apr-Oct, plus Sat & Sun Nov-Mar) is well signposted about halfway between Fournes and Lakki. It was created by four brothers who transformed the family's 80 hectares of agricultural land into a hilly park of medicinal, tropical, ornamental and fruit trees, all well signed and beautifully arrayed from mountaintop to valley floor. The restaurant (mains €8 to €14.50) is a must for heaping regional dishes using locally sourced ingredients, some grown right in the park. Tables fill a hilltop terrace with sweeping views.

The main road continues to the unspoilt village of **Lakki**, 24km from Hania, which affords stunning views in all directions and has a striking **church**. The village was a centre of resistance both during the uprising against the Turks and in WWII against the Germans.

Rooms for Rent Nikolas (☎28210 67232; Lakki; d €30; 📶) has comfortable, simple rooms above a taverna, with magnificent views over the valley.

Omalos Ομαλός

POP 30

Most tourists hurry through Omalos, 36km south of Hania, on their way to Samaria Gorge 4km further on, but for those inclined towards solitude or the outdoors, this plateau settlement warrants a longer stay. During summer the air is bracingly cool compared with the steamy coast, and there are great mountain walks offering magnificent views, birding, caving and climbing. If you want to beat the crowds bussing in from Hania for Samaria, Omalos is a good base to overnight and wake up early to hit the trail.

Omalos itself is little more than a few hotels on either side of the main road cutting across the plateau. After the morning Samaria rush, there's hardly anyone on the plateau except goats and shepherds, and it's practically deserted in winter.

Sleeping & Eating

Some Omalos hotels are open only when the Samaria Gorge is open. Most have restaurants that do a bustling trade serving breakfast to hikers and are open at mealtimes the rest of the day. Many proprietors will drive you to the start of the gorge. As at other mountain locations, air-conditioning is not necessary.

Agriorodo COTTAGE €

(☎28210 67237; 2/3-bedroom cottages from €60/80; ⊙year-round; P 📶) These lovely modern stone cottages are a comfy base camp for expeditions to Samaria Gorge, whose entrance is a mere 500m away. Decorated in rustic style, each cottage sleeps four to five and is kitted out with satellite TV, wi-fi, kitchen, and living room with plush sofas and a fireplace.

Hotel Neos Omalos HOTEL €

(☎28210 67269; www.neos-omalos.gr; Chania-Omalos Rd; s/d/tr incl breakfast €38/49/59; P 📶) This rustic mountain hotel has welcomed generations of nature lovers since it opened in 1954. Convivial public areas lead to basic but comfortable rooms with balcony views that will get you in the mood for hiking. The owners are a fount of information on local hikes and other outdoor activities, and can shuttle you to Samaria Gorge, some 4km away.

Kallergi Hut HUT €

(☎28210 44647; www.kallergi.co; dm member/non-member €11/13; ⊙Apr-Oct) Located in the hills between Omalos and the Samaria Gorge, the bare-bones Kallergi Hut has five rooms with bunk beds and a shared bathroom and makes a good base for exploring Mt Gingilos and surrounding peaks. Reaching the hut from the Omalos plateau entails a 4.5km hike. The hut is maintained by Hania's EOS (p72).

Hotel Exari HOTEL €€

(☎28210 67180; www.exari.gr; s/d/tr €30/40/50; ⊙Apr-Oct; P 📶) This traditional-style stone-built hotel has 21 simply furnished rooms with TV and balconies, and there's an attached taverna with fireplace. The owner shuttles people to Samaria Gorge free of charge.

Omalos Village VILLA €€

(☎28210 67169; www.omalosvillage.gr; 2-bedroom villas €60-120; ⊙year-round; P 📶 👪) Omalos Village is a cluster of three well-equipped, spacious two-bedroom stone villas with large dining and kitchen areas. They have a fireplace and outdoor seating with great views, though the feel is a little marred by the fact that it's in an unattractive compound setting.

Getting There & Away

For hikers, early-morning buses serve Hania (€7.50, one hour). One bus daily (except Sunday) comes from Paleohora via Sougia (€7) in summer.

To hike Samaria Gorge and return to your room (and luggage) in Omalos, you can take the late-afternoon boat from the hike terminus at Agia Roumeli to Sougia (€11, 40 minutes), then taxi back to Omalos (about €50) or catch a bus from Sougia that departs after the boat has arrived and stops in Omalos (€5.30).

LOCAL KNOWLEDGE

SCENIC ROUTE FROM HANIA TO THERISO

For a day trip or an alternative route to Omalos, take the scenic road from Hania via the village of Perivolia to Theriso, 14km south. This spectacular drive follows a coursing stream through a green oasis and the 6km Theriso Gorge.

A steep and winding road takes you through rugged mountain terrain and around an ever-changing landscape of plane, olive, orange, eucalyptus and pine trees through the village of Zourva to Meskla and Lakki, where you can continue to Omalos or head back to Hania.

Theriso Θέρισο

At the foot of the Lefka Ori, at 500m above sea level, Theriso holds a special place in the hearts of Cretans as it was the site of historical battles against the Turks and is famous for its connection with statesman Eleftherios Venizelos and the late-19th-century revolutionary period in Crete. These days it's popular for its fine tavernas that host marathon Sunday lunches.

Sights

Museum of National Resistance MUSEUM

(☎28210 78780; €1; ⊙11am-3pm) Close to the village centre, this small museum chronicles Crete's resistance movement from 1941 to 1945. There's limited information in English. The millstone on display was used by Turkish occupiers in 1821 to crush resistance fighter Chrysi Tripiti to death in the local olive press.

Sleeping & Eating

A few villas and room-for-rent pensions are scattered around the area. Otherwise, Hania is a 30-minute drive away.

Tavernas in Theriso offer traditional Cretan cuisine and are well worth visiting on Sunday for long, leisurely lunches.

Leventogiannis Taverna CRETAN €
(☎28210 74095; https://sites.google.com/site/leventogiannistherisso; mains €5.50-10; ⊙12.30-6pm Tue-Sun) Leventogiannis Taverna has a lovely courtyard under a giant canopy of plane trees and does a menu of grilled meats, toasted sandwiches and sometimes a delicious and sizable *kreatotourta* (local meat pie).

Antartis CRETAN €
(☎28210 78833; mains €6-11; ⊙11am-6pm Wed-Mon) Antartis has excellent mezedhes and Cretan dishes such as *staka* (goat's-milk sauce over juicy cubes of goat meat).

Getting There & Away

The best way to reach Theriso is by car. It's a 30-minute drive from Hania, or there's a longer scenic route.

Samaria Gorge

Φαράγγι της Σαμαριάς

Hiking the 16km-long **Samaria Gorge** (☎28210 45570; www.samaria.gr; Omalos; adult/child €5/free; ⊙7.30am-4pm May–mid-Oct), one of Europe's longest canyons, is high on the list of must-dos for many visitors to Crete. There's an undeniable raw beauty to the canyon, with its soaring cliffs and needlenose passageways. The hike begins at an elevation of 1230m just south of Omalos at Xyloskalo and ends in the coastal village of Agia Roumeli. It's also possible to do it the 'lazy way': hiking a shorter distance by starting at Agia Roumeli. The only way out of Agia Roumeli is by taking the boat to Sougia or Hora Sfakion, which are served by bus and taxi back to Hania.

The best time for the Samaria trek is in April and May, when wildflowers brighten the trail. Keep your eyes peeled for the endemic *kri-kri*, a shy endangered wild goat.

Hiking the Gorge

For the low-down on what to expect once you hit the trail, see our Hiking in Hania (p106) feature.

Sleeping & Eating

It is forbidden to camp (or indeed spend the night) in the gorge. Stay at Omalos at the northern end, or Agia Roumeli in the south.

There are tavernas in Omalos, including one right by the gorge entrance. When the gorge is open, stands sell souvenirs, snacks, bottled water and the like. Agia Roumeli has several tavernas. There's also a snack stall at the national-park exit selling beer, coffee and other refreshments.

Xyloskalo CRETAN €
(☎28210 67237; mains €5-11; ⊙10am-6pm) Perched just over the spectacular drop of Samaria Gorge, with eagles occasionally circling outside its wraparound windows, this cosy restaurant dishes up classic Cretan and Greek meals, and offers the last chance to use indoor plumbing before you set off to hike the gorge. The owners also have a cafe (open 7am to 1pm) at the gorge entrance.

Getting There & Away

Most people hike Samaria one way, going north–south on a day trip that can be arranged from every sizeable town and resort in Crete. Confirm whether tour prices include gorge admission (€5) and the boat ride from Agia Roumeli to Sougia or Hora Sfakion.

With some planning, it's possible to do the trek on your own. There are early-morning public buses to Omalos from Hania (€7.50, one hour), Sougia (€5.30, one hour) and Paleohora (€7, one hour), once or twice daily in high season. Check www.e-ktel.com for the schedule, which changes seasonally. Taxis are another option.

At the end of the trail, in Agia Roumeli, ferries operated by Anendyk (p92) depart for Sougia (€11) and Hora Sfakion (€12.50) at 5.30pm and take 40 minutes. These are usually met by public buses back to Hania from Hora Sfakion at 6.30pm and Sougia at 6.15pm; some buses from Sougia go to Omalos.

NORTHWEST COAST

Far northwestern Crete is less affected by tourism than the city of Hania and its satellite resorts. Once you move past the overbuilt Platanias region west of Hania, the northern coast is defined by the virtually uninhabited Gramvousa and Rodopou Peninsulas. Kolymbari, at the foot of the Rodopou Peninsula, is the most developed tourist town (but more famous for its nationally distributed olive oil).

HIKING IN HANIA

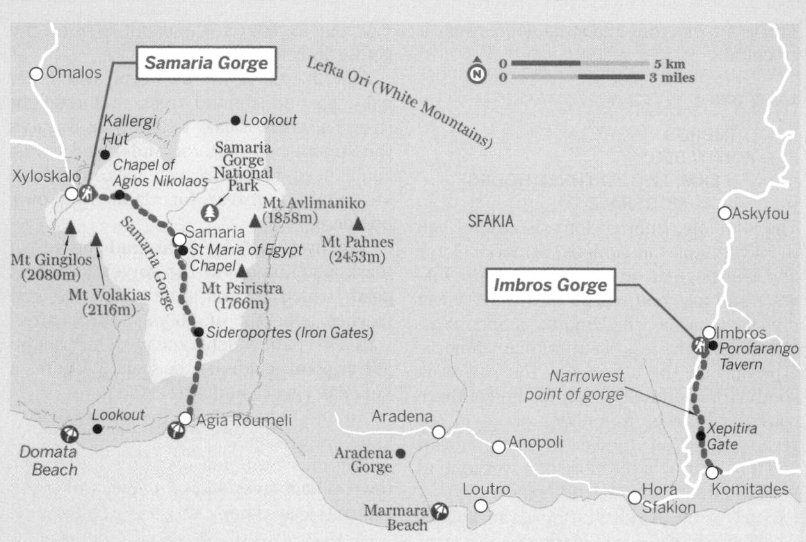

SAMARIA GORGE

START XYLOSKALO
END AGIA ROUMELI
LENGTH 16KM; FOUR TO SIX HOURS
DIFFICULTY MODERATE

The trail begins just south of Omalos at **Xyloskalo** (p105), where there's a tavern if you want to have a drink, eat breakfast and use the toilet before beginning. From the start of the trailhead a steep, serpentine stone path descends some 600m into the canyon. In under an hour you'll come to the first rest stop, with water and toilets. Continue on to arrive at the simple, cypress-framed **Chapel of Agios Nikolaos**.

Beyond here the gorge is wide and open and not particularly scenic for the next 6km until you reach the abandoned settlement of **Samaria**, whose inhabitants were relocated when the gorge became a national park. This is the main rest stop, with toilets, water and benches for taking a breather and having something to eat. Just south of the village is a 14th-century **chapel dedicated to St Maria of Egypt**, after whom the gorge is named.

Further on, the gorge narrows and becomes more dramatic, and you'll see warning signs for falling rocks between the 9km and 11km marks. It's advisable to walk as quickly as you can, though safely, through here. At 11km along the walls are only 3.5m apart and you'll find the famous **Sideroportes (Iron Gates)**, where a rickety wooden pathway leads hikers the 20m or so across the water.

The gorge in the national park ends at the **13km mark** just north of the almost abandoned village of Palea (Old) Agia Roumeli. From here it's a further 3km to the seaside village of **Agia Roumeli**, whose fine pebble beach and sparkling water are a most welcome sight. Few people miss taking a refreshing dip or at least bathing their aching feet before they fill up at one of the seaside tavernas.

The entire trek takes about four hours (for sprinters) to six hours (for strollers).

Like a fine wine, Crete's landscape wants to be sipped, not downed in one big gulp. So get out of the car and onto the trail for a slow-mo close-up of gorges chiselled by time and the elements.

This is a rocky trail and suitable footwear is essential.

IMBROS GORGE

START IMBROS
END KOMITADES
LENGTH 8KM; TWO TO THREE HOURS
DIFFICULTY MODERATE

The 8km-long Imbros Gorge is around half the length of the famous Samaria Gorge and is a popular alternative for many hikers – and for good reason. It attracts fewer crowds, is not as challenging, is open year-round and is no less beautiful than Samaria, especially in the afternoon. You can walk south from Imbros village to the southern coastal village of Komitades or go in the reverse direction, though the latter means you'll be getting a bit more of a workout, as you'll be walking up a gentle grade.

Start in the mountain village of **Imbros**, where there are a few cafes and tavernas, including family-run **Porofarango** (☎28250 95450; mains €6-11; ⏰7.30am-7pm), to fuel up and use the toilet before you start the hike. Pay your fee (€2) at the booth to begin the gentle descent.

The hike takes you past cypresses, holm oaks, fig and almond trees, and redolent sage. The track is easy to follow, as it traces the stream bed past rockslides and caves; you'll need to ensure you have appropriate sturdy footwear for clambering over boulders.

Just over halfway, at around the 4.5km mark, you'll come to the gorge's **narrowest point**, which is just under 2m wide and reaches a height of 300m. Shortly afterwards the path widens, and most hikers stop at this point to admire the scenery. There's a Venetian cistern and a rest stop here.

Around 6km along is the **Xepitira Gate**, a giant natural stone arch.

Continue until you reach the end in the town of **Komitades**. Plonk yourself down at a taverna to give your weary legs a rest and reward yourself with a meal of Cretan cuisine.

It's possible to take a taxi back to Imbros village (about €20 to €25) – this can usually be arranged by one of the tavernas.

The Kissamos province is a rugged region of scattered villages and towns sustained by agriculture. Its capital, Kissamos (Kastelli), is the port for boats from the Peloponnese. On the western coast you'll find two of Crete's finest beaches, which are surprisingly underdeveloped: Falasarna and the even more remote Balos (Gramvousa). The Selino province includes the Innahorion region of small mountain villages.

Rodopou Peninsula
Χερσόνησος Ροδοπού

POP 1088

Barren, rocky Rodopou Peninsula has a few villages clustered at its base, but the rest is uninhabited. A paved road goes as far as **Afrata**, which has a couple of great tavernas, but then becomes a dirt track that meanders through the peninsula. The Diktynna ruins at the end of the peninsula can be reached with a 4WD or by boat excursion, but make sure you've planned your journey and are well supplied with petrol, food and water. From Afrata a road winds down to gravelly **Afrata Beach**, with a small summer-only snack bar.

Kolymbari, at the eastern base of the peninsula, appeals to those seeking a low-key holiday. This former fishing hamlet has developed into a small tourist resort, taking advantage of the village's long pebbly beach. It has an interesting monastery and museum, Moni Gonias, and is known for its seafood tavernas.

Sights

Diktynna RUINS

At the eastern tip of Rodopou Peninsula are the remains of a temple to Diktynna, Cretan goddess of hunting, who was worshipped fervently in the west of the island. The most important religious sanctuary in the region under the Romans, the temple was desecrated after the collapse of the Roman Empire. Now you'll find foundations and a sacrificial altar at the site, as well as Roman cisterns. There's also a lovely sandy beach.

Legend has it that Diktynna's name derives from the word *diktyon,* meaning 'net': a fisherman's net saved her when she leapt into the sea to avoid the amorous desires of King Minos. The temple dates from the 2nd century AD, but it was probably built on the site of an earlier temple.

By car, Diktynna is accessible by dirt road from Kolymbari; a 4WD is best. Travel agencies in Hania also offer boat excursions.

Moni Gonias MONASTERY

(€3; 9am-7pm May-Oct, to 5pm Nov-Apr) Founded in 1618, Moni Gonias was damaged by the Turks in 1645 but rebuilt in 1662 and extended in the 19th century. The monastery houses a unique collection of icons dating from the 15th to the 19th century in its impressive, well-presented museum. The most valuable icon is that of Agios Nikolaos, painted in 1637 by Palaiokapas. It exemplifies the Cretan school of icon painting that flourished in the 17th century.

The museum also has interesting displays on the history of the monastery and ancient manuscripts, plus there's a small store selling raki and olive oil produced by the monks.

The monastery, which also incorporates Crete's Theological College, is easy to reach from Kolymbari. Take the beach road north from the town centre for about 500m.

Sleeping & Eating

Kolymbari has a load of uninspiring hotels catering to package tourists that book out well in advance, and a few generic apartment complexes that will do the job.

Most of the peninsula's eating options are also in Kolymbari, where you'll find waterfront seafood tavernas. Otherwise, Afrata has a couple of fine tavernas. No food is available further on.

Aeolos Apartments APARTMENT €

(28240 22203; Kolymbari; studios/apt from €45/50; P) Signposted up the hill from Kolymbari town, this dated but well-maintained complex has big balconies with sea views. Breezy studios and two-room apartments are spacious, with carved timber beds, TVs and kitchenettes.

Tis Litsas Ta Kamomata TAVERNA €

(6976228778; Afrata; mains €6-12; 10am-10pm daily Apr-Oct) Friendly proprietors welcome you to this tried and true Cretan taverna. The dishes take the form of outstanding country fare, and the views of the sea are to die for.

Argentina SEAFOOD €€

(28240 22243; Kolymbari harbour; fish per kg €46-65, mains €6-13; noon-late) Considered one of the best fish tavernas in the area, the classic Argentina has tables on the main road and across the street overlooking the harbour. It serves seafood dishes such as octopus with olives and top-quality fish.

Diktina SEAFOOD €€
(☎28240 22611; Kolymbari harbour; fish per kg €40-60, mains €8.50-14; ⏲noon-late) This modern fish taverna has harbour views and a range of reliable seafood dishes.

Drinking & Nightlife

Milos tou Tzerani CAFE
(☎28240 22210; Kolymbari harbour; ⏲8.30am-late) In a beautiful restored stone mill on the sea, this cafe-bar is a great place for a coffee or an evening drink and also serves light snacks, pizza, pasta and mezedhes.

Information

There's an ATM on the main street and a post office in the centre of Kolymbari.

Getting There & Away

Kolymbari is 23km west of Hania. Frequent buses from Hania to Kissamos (Kastelli) stop at Kolymbari (€3.60, 40 minutes) on the main road, from where it's a 500m walk down to the settlement.

Kissamos (Kastelli)
Κίσσαμος (Καστέλλι)

POP 4275

Kissamos is not a place given entirely over to tourism and exudes an unpolished, almost gritty, air compared to other north-coast towns. It's a good base for day-tripping to Balos in the Gramvousa Peninsula by cruise boat and it has an archaeological museum to keep history buffs interested. There are two beaches in town, separated by a waterfront promenade: the sandy Mavros Molos in the west and the pebbly Telonio to the east.

The largest town and capital of Kissamos province, it is referred to interchangeably as Kissamos and as Kastelli (though the official name is the former).

History

Kissamos was the harbour of important Dorian city-state Polyrrina, 7km inland, and reached its heyday during Roman times. Artefacts from that period are now displayed in the local museum and in archaeological museums in Hania and Iraklio. Most of the ancient city, however, lies beneath modern-day Kissamos and cannot be excavated.

The city gained independence in the 3rd century AD and then became a bishopric under the Byzantines. It was occupied by the Saracens in the 9th century and flourished under the Venetians, who built a castle here, at which point it became known as Kastelli. That name persisted until 1966, when authorities decided that too many people were confusing it with Crete's other Kastelli, near Iraklio. The official name reverted to Kissamos, though it's still often called Kastelli or Kissamos-Kastelli. Ruins of the castle wall survive to the west of Plateia Tzanakaki.

Sights

Archaeological Museum of Kissamos MUSEUM
(☎28220 83308; http://odysseus.culture.gr; Plateia Tzanakaki; adult/child €2/free; ⏲8.30am-6pm Wed-Mon) In an imposing two-level Venetian-Turkish building on the main square, this museum presents locally excavated treasure, including statues, jewellery, coins and a large mosaic floor from a Kissamos villa. Most items are from the Hellenistic and Roman eras, though there are also some Minoan objects. There are exhibits from Falasarna, Polyrrinia and Nopigia, too.

Tours

Strata Walking Tours HIKING
(☎6974092913, 28220 24249; www.stratatours.com) Based in Kissamos, Strata Tours offers anything from leisurely day trips to Elafonisi beach to guided walks in Samaria Gorge.

Sleeping

Kissamos offers a range of accommodation to suit most budgets, with a number of modern waterfront hotels, along with a hostel and a campground.

Thalassa APARTMENT €
(☎28220 31231; www.thalassa-apts.gr; Drapanias Beach; studios from €45; P❄@🛜≋👪) The isolated Thalassa complex, about 5km east of Kissamos at Drapanias beach, is ideal for a quiet retreat. The studios are airy and well appointed, and there's a barbecue on the lawn, a small playground and a saltwater swimming pool. It's helpful to have a car.

Hostel Stylianos HOSTEL €
(☎28220 23326; www.hostelstylianos.gr; Iroön Polytechniou 86-88; dm/d €14/30; ❄🛜) Hostel Stylianos offers basic female-only and male-only dorms with metal bunks and a few private rooms upstairs sharing a huge

balcony terrace. Dorm-room walls have a gap at the top, so noise travels; bring earplugs. The helpful owner is a good source of info on the area and provides free transport to the harbour.

Camping Mithymna CAMPGROUND €
(☎28220 31444; www.campingmithimna.gr; Paralia Drapania; camp sites adult/child/tent €7/3.50/5; P ☎ ♿) About 5km east of Kissamos, Camping Mithymna is a pleasant shady site near a great stretch of beach. There's a restaurant, a bar, a playground and a mini-market. Take a bus to the village of Drapanias, from where it's a pleasant 15-minute (800m) walk through olive groves to the campground.

Nautilus Bay Hotel APARTMENT €€
(☎28220 22250; www.nautilusbay.gr; Plaka Beach; apt from €110; P ❄ ☎ ≋ ♿) Well-proportioned and modern apartments with streamlined furniture and small kitchenettes fill this modern complex right on the sandy beach and in the centre of town. Balconies have sweeping water views, and there's a restaurant and bar and a large pool area.

Christina Beach Hotel APARTMENT €€
(☎28220 83333; www.christina-beach.gr; studios from €40; P ❄ @ ☎ ≋) This smart studio complex on the western side of Kissamos represents the upper end of accommodation in town. Right across from the water, the modern studios are large and airy, and the sandy beach is right nearby, or you can just lounge by the inviting pool.

Stavroula Palace HOTEL €€
(☎28220 23620; s/d/tr incl breakfast €50/65/80; ❄ ☎ ≋ ♿) Run by the warm and gracious Stavroula and her family, this cheery and good-value waterfront hotel has breezy, modern rooms with balconies fronting a large swimming pool and an immaculately kept garden where breakfast is served. Children's recreation area, too.

Eating & Drinking

For Kissamos' best eating, head to the waterfront, where a few taverns serving seafood and classic Greek dishes cluster.

Taverna Petra FAST FOOD €
(mains €6-12; ⏰9am-10pm) This unassuming place cornering the main square serves decent souvlaki (€8), along with a range of grilled meats and the usual Greek dishes.

Taverna Sunset TAVERNA €€
(☎28220 83478; Paraliaki; mains €7-14; ⏰noon-midnight) Locals mix with in-the-know visitors at this quintessential family taverna presided over by Giannis, who's usually ensconced behind the grill coaxing meat

OFF THE BEATEN TRACK

POLYRRINIA ΠΟΛΥΡΡΗΝΙΑ

The wonderful mountaintop ruins of the ancient city of Polyrrinia lie about 7km south of Kissamos (Kastelli), above the village of the same name. Sea, mountain and valley views from this defensible spire are stunning and the region is blanketed with wildflowers in spring. The site's most impressive feature is the **acropolis**, built by the Byzantines and Venetians. There's also a **church** built on the foundations of a Hellenistic temple from the 4th century BC.

When you arrive in town there's an information board; take the path to the right and follow the acropolis signs. There's a small information office–cafe staffed by volunteers before you head up. It's a 15-minute scramble up rocks and an overgrown path from town to the church, and from there another 20-minute climb to the acropolis.

Polyrrinia was founded by the Dorians in the 6th century BC and was constantly at war with the Kydonians from Hania. Coins from the period depict the warrior-goddess Athena, who was evidently revered by the warlike Polyrrinians.

Unlike their rivals the Kydonians, the Polyrrinians did not resist the Roman invasion and thus the city was spared destruction. It was the best-fortified town in Crete and the administrative centre of western Crete from the Roman through to the Byzantine period. The Venetians used it as a fortress. Many of the structures, including an **aqueduct** built by Hadrian, date from the Roman period. Near the aqueduct is a **cave** dedicated to the nymphs; it still contains the niches for nymph statuettes.

There is no public transport to the site.

and fish into succulent perfection. It's right on the waterfront, so you can feel the breezes coming from offshore.

Fish Tavern 1960 SEAFOOD €€
(☎28220 22340; Paraliaki; mains €7-17; ⌚noon-late May-Oct; 📶 🌱) This classic taverna on the central waterfront is known for fresh fish (which you can take a look at in the kitchen before ordering) but also has plenty of *mayirefta* (ready-cooked meals) and grills, plus a good range of vegetarian options.

★**Babel Cafe Bar** BAR
(☎28220 22045; ⌚8am-late; 📶) Not only a good choice for a quick breakfast or snack, this smart modern waterfront cafe-bar is a great place for coffee and gets lively at night with young locals. It has one of the most extensive beer and cocktail lists in town, and it's worth swinging by simply for the amazing bay views from its bustling patio.

ℹ Information

Chalkiadaki Travel (☎28220 22009; Skalidi 49; ⌚9am-2pm & 6-9.30pm)
Horeftakis Tours (☎28220 23250; Skalidi; ⌚9am-3pm & 6-9pm)

ℹ Getting There & Away

BOAT

From the port 3km west of town, **Triton** (☎28210 75444; www.tritonferries.gr) has three ferries to Kythira (€15, four hours) and one to Gythion (€25, seven hours). In summer a bus meets ferries; otherwise, taxis into town cost around €8. Schedules change seasonally.

BUS

Bus schedules change seasonally – check at **KTEL Bus Station** (☎28210 93052; www.e-ktel.com; Kampouri). There are frequent buses to Hania (€5.10, one hour); change in Hania for Paleohora, Rethymno and Iraklio. There's a daily bus to Falasarna (€3.80, 40 minutes) in summer only, and one daily to Elafonisi (€6.90, 1¼ hours) from May to October.

CAR

Kissamos is about 40km west of Hania. **Kissamos Rent a Car** (☎28220 23740; www.kissamosrentacar.com; Iroön Polytechniou 210; ⌚9am-9pm) is one of several car-hire agencies along Iroön Polytechniou, the main drag.

Gramvousa Peninsula
Χερσόνησος Γραμβούσα

Northwest of Kissamos (Kastelli) is the beautifully wild and remote Gramvousa Peninsula, whose main attraction is the stunning lagoon-like beach of Balos, on Cape Tigani on the western side of the peninsula's narrow tip. Kalyviani village is a good base for visiting the peninsula, where there are several lovely villas and guesthouses, plus atmospheric dining spots.

History

The offshore island of Imeri Gramvousa was of strategic importance to the Venetians, who built a fortress here to protect their trade routes from the Turks. Outfitted with a huge cache of armaments, the fortress was indeed not conquered by the Ottomans with the rest of Crete in 1645; it remained in Venetian hands until it became Turkish in 1691 (thanks to a turncoat captain). Next it fell into the hands of Cretan rebels, who took it over in 1821, resorting to piracy when cut off from the western part of the islands by the Turks during the War of Independence. Local legend has it that the pirates amassed a fabulous fortune that they hid in caves around the island.

👁 Sights

★**Balos** LAGOON
The rugged Gramvousa Peninsula cradles the lagoon-like sandy beach of Balos, whose shallow, shimmering turquoise waters draw huge crowds in summer. This remote stretch features on many tourist brochures for Crete, and when it's at its best it's a heavenly scene, with lapping waters shimmering with darting fish. If the tide is out, the wind is whipping up or it's overrun by visitors off the cruise ferry, it can be something of a letdown.

Balos can be accessed by a very rough, 12km dirt road, precarious at times, that begins at the end of the main street of Kalyviani village. While some cars do make the drive, a 4WD is really necessary (and note that most car-hire companies won't cover you for damage sustained on the drive to Balos). The views from the car park when you arrive are sensational. From here there's a 1km walking path down to the beach. The other option is to visit Balos on a cruise (p112) from Kissamos, which stops first for around 90 minutes at the peninsula's offshore island Imeri Gramvousa, overlooking Balos, where you can make the sweaty climb to the ruins of a humongous Venetian fortress built to keep pirates at bay.

Note: there's no shade at Balos, but you can hire a sun-lounger and an umbrella. Toilet facilities are basic.

Tours

Cretan Daily Cruises BOATING
(28220 24344; www.cretandailycruises.com; adult/child €27/13; late Apr-Oct) The easiest way to get to Gramvousa and Balos lagoon is by boat from Kissamos port. (The only other option is to drive on the very rocky road, for which you will need a 4WD.) There's one departure daily at 10am (more in summer), but check ahead to make sure the service hasn't been cancelled due to strong winds.

The ferry can get overcrowded in summer, so it's best to arrive early to try to claim a seat. It stops for about 90 minutes at Imeri island – where you can swim, or walk up to the Venetian castle for stunning views – before travelling a further 10 minutes to Balos. Reasonably priced food and drink are available on board. Summer-only KTEL buses from Hania are timed to boat departures. A €1 tax is payable on each ticket.

Sleeping

The best base for touring this region is the village of Kalyviani, 6km west of Kissamos (Kastelli). Kalyviani has decent accommodation choices, among them a charming guesthouse and a couple of luxury villas. There's no lodging at Balos.

Olive Tree Apartments APARTMENT €
(28220 24336; www.olivetree.reserve-online.net; Kalyviani; apt/maisonettes from €45/70; P) This attractive complex in an olive grove just east of Kalyviani village has spacious, comfortable and well-presented apartments and maisonettes suitable for families and longer stays, as well as an inviting pool and great sea views.

Kaliviani GUESTHOUSE €€
(28220 23204; www.kaliviani.com; Kalyviani; r €30-120; P) This welcoming stone-built guesthouse has comfortable, tastefully furnished rooms, with fridge and balcony, that sleep two to four. There's also an excellent modern Cretan restaurant and a kids' play area.

Patriko & Kotoi VILLA €€€
(6972299675; www.villapatriko.com; Kalyviani; villas per week from €1800; Apr-Oct;) The fully kitted-out luxury two-storey Patriko villa in the heart of Kalyviani village sleeps 10 and has everything from iPod docking stations to dishwasher, laundry, wood-stove oven, swimming pool and organic bath products. Next door there's a smaller villa called Kotoi that sleeps two.

Eating

There are some excellent restaurants in Kalyviani; you can dine on well-executed dishes in a stunning garden setting at Gramboussa or on the pretty terrace at Mama's Dinner. There are no eating options at Balos, so pack a picnic; if you're travelling there by ferry there are meals on board.

★ **Gramboussa** CRETAN €€
(28220 22707; http://gramvousarestaurant.com; Kalyviani; mains €8-17; 11am-11pm May-Oct; P) In Kalyviani village, about 6km west of central Kissamos, Gramboussa serves fine traditional Cretan cuisine in an elegantly rustic stone building set in a superb garden. It's a cut above other restaurants and offers the chance to sample the freshest regional cuisine Crete has to offer, as well as wood-oven specials like suckling pig or lamb with honey.

Mama's Dinner CRETAN €€
(28220 23204; www.mamasdinnerkaliviani.com; Kaliviani; mains €11-24; 6.30pm-midnight Jun-Sep) Dine on modern creative Cretan cuisine at this summer-only terrace restaurant at the Kaliviani guesthouse. Dishes are well presented and might feature delights such as grilled squid on tabbouleh, fried Gruyère cheese with mint pesto and bitter-orange jam, and lamb on mashed artichoke with honey-glazed onions. There's a great all-Greek wine list, too.

Getting There & Away

From May to October, day trippers arriving by cruise boat from Kissamos (Kastelli) – with a 90-minute stop at the peninsula's offshore island of Imeri Gramvousa – deluge Balos between 11am and 4pm. The only way to avoid the crowds is to get there by car before or after the boats arrive, but you'll need a 4WD. The approach is via a scenic corduroy road that picks up near the village of Kalyviani. It ends 12 axle-shaking kilometres later at a parking lot, from where a 1km trail leads down to the lagoon. Nondrivers could try hitching a ride or walking, although you'll be eating a lot of dust from passing vehicles.

Falasarna Φαλάσαρνα

POP 25

Some 16km west of Kissamos (Kastelli), Falasarna is little more than a blotch of habitations on a long, sandy beach – but what a beach. This broad sweep of pink-cream sand is considered among Crete's finest and is famous for its clear water, stunning sunsets and rolling waves. Spread your towel on the Big Beach (Megali Paralia) at the southern end or pick a spot in one of the coves separated by rocky spits further north.

Falasarna has no centre as such, although there are hotels and several tavernas, bars and small supermarkets.

History

The Falasarna area has been occupied at least since the 6th century BC, but it reached the height of its power as a city-state in the 4th century BC. Although ancient Falasarna was built next to the sea, its ruins are about 400m inland because the coast has risen over the centuries.

Falasarna owed its wealth to agricultural produce from the fertile valley to the south. It was the west-coast harbour for Polyrrinia but later became Polyrrinia's chief rival for dominance over western Crete. By the time of the Roman invasion of Crete in 67 BC, Falasarna had become a haven for pirates. Stone blocks excavated around the old harbour entrance may indicate that the Romans tried to keep the pirates out.

Sights

Ancient Falasarna RUINS
(9am-3pm Tue-Fri) FREE Wander among Falasarna's ancient ruins, reached via a 2km dirt road that starts where the paved road ends. The entrance is just past the 'stone throne'. Further on are the remains of the wall that once fortified the town and a small harbour. Notice the holes carved into the wall, which were used to tie up boats. At the top of the hill are the remains of the acropolis wall and a temple, as well as four clay baths.

★Falasarna BEACH
This broad sweep of beach has magical-looking pink-cream sands and teal waters and is known for its stunning sunsets. Along with superb water clarity, Falasarna has wonderfully big waves: long rollers coming from the open Mediterranean. It gets busy from mid-July to mid-August, primarily with day trippers from Hania and Kissamos.

Sleeping

There are plenty of accommodation options in Falasarna, from modern beachfront hotels to welcoming guesthouses, and most come with spectacular views of the sea.

Magnolia Apartments APARTMENT €
(28220 41407, 6945605438; www.magnolia-apartments.gr; studios from €45, apt €60-90; P) Just a five-minute walk from the beach, Magnolia is a quiet holiday retreat offering 12 well-equipped studios and apartments kitted out with pleasant decor and good-quality appliances. Enjoy a leisurely breakfast, or sunset drinks from your large sea-facing balcony or in the neatly groomed garden.

Falassarna Beach Hotel HOTEL €
(28220 41436; www.falassarnabeach.gr; studios/apt from €30/45; P) This well-kept modern hotel (situated right where the bus from Kissamos stops from June to August) is a good bet for those who want quick access to the beach: it's a two-minute downhill walk away. Rooms are simple and spacious, with wooden furniture and good views from most of the sea-facing rooms. There's a shady patio taverna, too.

Apartment Anastasia-Stathis PENSION €
(6986731677, 28220 41480; www.stathisanastasia.com; d/apt from €45/60;) Set back from the sea and the day crowds, the airy, attractively furnished rooms here, with fridges and large balconies, are perfect for stress relief, as friendly owner Anastasia puts it. Her enormous breakfasts are open to all comers and guests can pick veggies from the rose-rimmed garden.

Sunset Rooms & Apartments APARTMENT €
(28220 41204; www.sunset.com.gr; d/apt/villas €35/70/140; P) In an enviable location steps from one of Crete's finest sandy beaches, Sunset has 13 rooms and six apartments above a convivial taverna with fig trees and a natural spring. Rooms are snug, but they're tastefully decked out with wrought-iron beds, tile floors and sea-facing balconies. Families are catered for in the four nearby two-floor stone villas with full kitchens.

Eating & Drinking

Galasia Thea CRETAN €

(☎28220 41421; mains €5-12; ⏰9am-late mid-Apr–Oct; P 📶 👪) On the cliff overlooking the great expanse of Falasarna beach, this cafe has spectacular views from its huge lawn terrace. It offers a full range of Cretan *mayirefta*, such as *Sfakiano* lemon lamb. Service is friendly but can be very slow. There's a play area to keep the kids entertained.

Orange Blue BAR

(www.facebook.com/orangebluebar; ⏰9am-late mid-Apr–Oct) This is the perfect spot to witness Falasarna's famous sunsets, under a thatched umbrella on a hill overlooking the sea with cocktail in hand. It gets pretty lively as the night goes on. There are sandwiches, burgers and pizzas on the menu.

Getting There & Away

Bus schedules vary seasonally (check www.e-ktel.com). In summer at least three daily buses make the trip out to Falasarna from Hania (€8.30, 1¾ hours) via Kissamos (Kasteli; €3.80, 40 minutes).

Innahorion Villages
Ινναχωριών

Some of western Crete's most scenic and unvisited mountain villages, the Innahorion (derived from *Enneia Horia*, meaning 'nine villages') are spread across the far-western coastal region, along the route connecting Moni Hrysoskalitissas and Elafonisi beach in the south with Falasarna and Kissamos (Kastelli) in the north. This quiet area renowned for its chestnuts and olives is one of the lushest and most fertile parts of the island. The coastal road from Kefali to Sfinari is one of Crete's most beautiful: it winds around cliffs with magnificent coastal views unfolding after every bend.

For the area's best eating, as well as blissfully serene traditional lodgings, plan to visit the ecotourism settlement in Milia.

Sights

Topolia Gorge CANYON

Three kilometres south of Voulgaro, the main road towards Elafonisi reaches Topolia, a lovely village clustered with whitewashed houses overhung with plants and vines. Beyond it, the road skirts the edge of the 1.5km-long Topolia Gorge, bending and twisting and affording dramatic views. The gorge ends at tiny **Koutsomatados**, from where hikers can access the gorge.

Elos VILLAGE

Elos, near the south of the Innahorion region, is the area's largest town and the centre of the chestnut trade – hence the annual **chestnut festival**, usually held on the third Sunday of October. The plane, eucalyptus and chestnut trees around the main square make Elos a cool and relaxing place to stop. Behind the taverna on the main square stand the remains of an **aqueduct** that used to power the old mill.

Agia Sofia Cave CAVE

(⏰8am-8pm) Just south of the village Koutsomatados, and after a narrow tunnel on the way from Hania, the Agia Sofia cave contains evidence of settlement from as far back as the Neolithic era. The cave is often used for baptisms and celebrates the patron saint's day on 13 April. A third of the way up the 250 rock-cut steps to the cave, a taverna has great views over the ravine.

Voulgaro VILLAGE

Idyllic Voulgaro is located 9km southeast of Kissamos (Kastelli) on the inland road towards Elafonisi. Its name (by allusion, 'Bulgarian village') is said to descend from the identity of settlers brought to the place when Byzantine emperor Nikiforos Fokas recaptured Crete from Arab rule in the AD 961 expedition to Crete.

Sfinari VILLAGE

The Innahorian coastal road winds along by Sfinari, 9km north of Kambos and 9km south of Platanos. It's a languid, laid-back agricultural village with a long grey-stone beach. The northern end is backed by greenhouses and the cove has a basic campsite and several excellent beachside fish tavernas.

Pappadiana & Amygdalokefali VILLAGE

The western Innahorion villages that line the coastal road enjoy a stunning location between mountains and ravines. First is the hamlet of Pappadiana, about 2km west of Kefali, from where the road rises into the mountains before manifesting superlative sea views from a bluff at Amygdalokefali.

Perivolia & Kefali VILLAGE

Two and half kilometres west of Elos, atmospheric Perivolia leads to Kefali, with its 14th-century frescoed **church**. Kefali has a handful of tavernas taking advantage of the

WORTH A TRIP

MILIA ECO-VILLAGE

One of Crete's ecotourism trailblazers is the isolated **mountain resort village** (28210 46774; www.milia.gr; Vlatos; cottages incl breakfast from €85; year-round; P) of Milia, which makes a great base for those who wish to unwind and see the Innahorion region. Inspired by a back-to-nature philosophy, 16 abandoned stone farmhouses were transformed into ecocottages sleeping one to four, with only solar energy for basic needs. The cottages have antique beds, rustic furnishings, and fireplaces or wood-burning stoves. Since it's all solar powered, it's best to shelve the laptop and hairdryer.

Milia is one of the most peaceful places to stay in Crete, but it's also worth visiting just to dine at the superb organic **restaurant** (28210 46774; www.milia.gr; Vlatos; mains €9-13; 1-8pm; P). Its frequently changing seasonal menu incorporates organic produce cultivated on the farm, including its own oil, wine, milk, cheese and free-range chickens, goats and sheep. Try the homemade *kalitsounia*, the smoked-pork plate with tabbouleh and pitta, or orzo pasta with chestnut mushrooms, porcini powder and lemon.

To reach Milia, follow the signposted turn-off north of the village of Vlatos. The narrow access road becomes a drivable 3km dirt road.

lovely setting and view. From here you can travel south to Elafonisi beach or loop north along the coast.

Kambos VILLAGE

Good hiking, beach access and decent accommodation can be found at Kambos, a tiny village at the edge of a gorge along the Innahorian region's winding coastal road.

Sleeping

There's rough camping and rooms for rent in the coastal town of Sfinari, and many villages have some very basic rooms to let. Milia is the premier accommodation in the area.

Sunset Rooms PENSION €

(28220 41128; Kambos; s/d €30/40; P) In Kambos, Sunset has great views over the valley. Rooms are basic but pleasant enough. The attached taverna serves up good-value grills and salads.

Hartzoulakis Rent Rooms PENSION €

(28220 41445; manolis_hartzoulakis@yahoo.gr; Kambos; r €30-50; P) Small and basic but very clean, with large verandas, the rooms here make a good base for walkers. The taverna on the terrace serves good Cretan fare and excellent raki.

Eating

Sfinari is the place to head for excellent fresh seafood at seafront tavernas, while some of the inland villages have simple tavernas doing Greek classics and home-cooked meals. Don't miss dining at the organic restaurant with mountain views at Milia, and tasting the olives and chestnuts the region is renowned for.

Thalami SEAFOOD €

(6934893780, 28220 41170; www.thalami-kissamos.gr; Sfinari; mains €6-12; 11am-10pm May-Sep) One of Sfinari's excellent fish tavernas, Thalami offers the local catch in a seafront setting – perfect for taking a midday dip before your grilled fish and mountain greens.

Panorama Taverna & Rooms TAVERNA €

(Kefali; mains €6-9; 9am-9pm May-Oct;) This taverna with dramatic views down the valley in Kefali village certainly lives up to its name – and then some. It serves Greek classics and grilled meats and has a kids' menu. Rooms are available to rent (from €45).

Iliovasilema SEAFOOD €€

(Sunset; 28220 41627; Sfinari; mains €4-13, fish per kg €42-50; 10am-late May-Oct) Seafront in Sfinari, this simple taverna grills up the fresh catch of the day and locally grown (and some organic) produce, with tables lining the gravel beach and back under the shade trees. It does, indeed, have views of the sunset.

Getting There & Away

It's best to have your own wheels to explore the Innahorion Villages, as places are spread out. There's a KTEL (p83) bus from Kissamos to Sfinari in the afternoon (€3.80, 25 minutes).

DE AGOSTINI / ARCHIVIO J. LANGE/GETTY IMAGES ©

1. Agia Panagia (p93)
This stone basilica found in the village of Lissos dates back to the 13th century.

2. Lake Kournas (p86)
The colour of this beautiful lake changes according to the time of day and the season.

3. Hania's Old Town (p65)
There are few places where Hania's historic charm and grandeur are more palpable than around its historic Venetian Harbour.

4. Paleohora (p95)
The gorgeous town of Paleohora lies on a narrow peninsula.

FREEARTIST/GETTY IMAGES ©

GATSI/GETTY IMAGES ©

HERACLES KRITIKOS/SHUTTERSTOCK ©

Rethymno

Includes ➡

Best Places to Eat

- ➡ Garden Arkoudenas (p136)
- ➡ Taverna Sideratico (p146)
- ➡ George & Georgia's (p157)

Best Places to Stay

- ➡ Hammam Oriental Suites (p125)
- ➡ Dalabelos Estate (p156)
- ➡ Enagron Ecotourism Village (p142)

Why Go?

Wild beauty Rethymno is peppered with historic sites and natural wonders. Ribbons of mountain road wind through the timeless interior, passing fields of wildflowers and traditional hamlets cradled by olive groves. Descend into the spooky darkness of grotto-like caves; explore steep, lush gorges; and rest in the shade of lofty Mt Psiloritis, Crete's highest peak. Visit enduring monasteries, Minoan tombs and Venetian strongholds. Rethymno is also a magnet for artists, many practising age-old trades with modern twists.

The eponymous capital on the northern coast is a bustle of atmosphere-soaked cobbled lanes, laden with shops, restaurants and bars and flanked by a wide, sandy beach. The southern coast is graced with bewitching beaches in seductive isolation. Weave your way through this spellbinding land from shore to shore.

Road Distances (km)

	Agia Galini	Anogia	Plakias	Rethymno
Anogia	99			
Plakias	47	94		
Rethymno	53	56	39	
Argyroupoli	58	79	24	23

RETHYMNO ΡΕΘΥΜΝΟ

POP 35,000

Basking between the commanding bastions of its 15th-century fortress and the glittering azure waters of the Mediterranean, Rethymno is one of Crete's most enchanting settlements. Its Venetian-Ottoman quarter is a lyrical maze of lanes draped in floral canopies and punctuated with graceful wood-balconied houses, ornate monuments and the occasional minaret.

Crete's third-largest centre has lively nightlife thanks to its sizable student population, some excellent restaurants and a worthwhile sandy beach right in town. The busier beaches, with their requisite resorts, line up along a nearly uninterrupted stretch all the way to Panormo, some 22km away.

History

Archaeological findings suggest that the site of modern Rethymno has been occupied since Late Minoan times. Around the 4th century BC 'Rithymna' emerged as an autonomous state of sufficient stature to issue its own coinage. It waned in importance during Roman and Byzantine times but flourished again under Venetian rule (1210–1645), when it became an important commercial centre as well as a cultural and artistic hub.

The Venetians built a harbour and began fortifying the town in the 16th century against the growing threat from the Turks. Nevertheless, the massive hilltop fortress was captured by the Ottomans in 1646. Rethymno was an important seat of government under the Turks, but it was also a centre of resistance to Turkish rule, resulting in severe reprisals.

The Ottomans ruled until 1897, when Russia became overseer of Rethymno during the European Great Powers' occupation. The town's reputation as an artistic and intellectual centre grew from 1923, when the mandated population exchange between Greece and Turkey brought many refugees from Constantinople.

Sights

Rethymno is fairly compact, with most sights, accommodation and tavernas wedged within the largely pedestrianised **old quarter** off the Venetian Harbour. The long, sandy beach starts just east of the harbour.

★Fortezza — FORTRESS

(adult/concession/family €4/3/10; ⏲8am-8pm Apr-Oct, 10am-5pm Nov-Mar; P) Looming over Rethymno, the star-shaped Venetian fortress cuts an imposing figure with its massive walls and bastions but was nevertheless unable to stave off the Turks in 1646. Over time, an entire village took shape on the grounds, most of which was destroyed in WWII. Views over the town, the Mediterranean and mountains are fabulous up here and it's fun to poke around the ramparts, palm trees and remaining buildings, most notably the **Sultan Bin Ibrahim Mosque** with its huge dome.

Head inside the mosque to admire its impressive mosaic ceiling, with wonderful acoustics that are perfect for the occasional musical event held here. A few other buildings (like the twin buildings of the Bastion of Agios Nikolaos) are also used to showcase art exhibits. Pick up a free map from the ticket office, which offers useful info on the site. Last entry is 45 minutes before closing.

★Archaeological Museum of Rethymno — MUSEUM

(☎28310 27506; www.archmuseumreth.gr; Argiropoulon; adult/concession €2/1; ⏲10am-6pm Wed-Mon) Set inside the atmospheric Venetian-built Church of St Francis, this well-curated museum features a stunning collection of well-preserved relics unearthed from major archaeological digs around Rethymno Province. Its collection offers a comprehensive snapshot (without leaving you overwhelmed) that predominantly covers pieces from the Minoan, Byzantine and Venetian periods. Highlights include exquisite hand-painted Minoan ceramics, a 9000-year-old limestone deity statue and a bronze lamp from the Hellenistic period (1st century BC) depicting Dionysus riding a panther.

Venetian Harbour — LANDMARK

Rethymno's compact historic harbour is chock-a-block with tourist-geared fish tavernas and cafes. For a more atmospheric perspective, walk along the harbour walls, past the fishing boats to the prominent lighthouse (p121), built in the 19th century by the Egyptians.

Agios Spyridon Church — CHAPEL

(Kefalogiannidon) FREE Built right into the cliff beneath the Venetian fortress, tiny Agios Spyridon has enough atmosphere to fill a cathedral. This Byzantine chapel is filled

Rethymno Highlights

1. **Rethymno** (p119) Exploring the maze of the Venetian-Ottoman quarter.
2. **Argyroupoli** (p134) Taking a long lunch before wandering through Lappa's old town.
3. **Moni Arkadiou** (p137) Learning why this monastery is so important to the Cretan soul.
4. **Beaches** (p147) Hitting the strands along Rethymno's southern coast.
5. **Margarites** (p137) Watching potters work their magic in this artists' hamlet.
6. **Anogia** (p142) Feasting on charcoal-roasted lamb while being humbled by famed Cretan mountain hospitality.
7. **Amari Valley** (p138) Winding along cobbled roads among charming villages on a drive through the island's interior.
8. **Melidoni Cave** (p141) Descending into Cretan history in the stunning underworld of this monumental cave.

with richly painted icons, swinging bird candleholders and the sound of the nearby pounding surf. You'll see pairs of slippers, baby shoes and sandals in crevices in the rock wall, left as prayer offerings for the sick. Find the chapel at the top of a staircase on the fortress' western side. Opening hours are erratic.

Paleontological Museum MUSEUM
(☎28310 23083; cnr Satha & Markellou; adult/student/child €3/2/free; ⏲9am-3pm Mon-Sat May-Oct, 9am-3pm Tue, Thu & Sat Nov-Apr) The highlight of this dusty old museum are the displays of fossilised tusks and bones from the dwarf Cretan elephant and pygmy hippopotamus. Both were endemic to the Rethymno region before becoming extinct around 12,000 years ago. The museum is in the restored 17th-century Temple of Mastaba (aka Veli Pasha Mosque), with nine domes and the city's oldest minaret.

The complex, a branch of Athens' Goulandris Natural History Museum, often has touring exhibits from the capital and abroad.

Museum of Contemporary Art MUSEUM
(☎28310 52530; www.cca.gr; Mesologhiou 32; adult/concession/student €3/1.50/free, Thu free; ⏲9am-2pm & 7-9pm Tue-Fri, 10am-3pm Sat & Sun May-Oct, reduced hours Nov-Apr) The cornerstone of the permanent collection of this well-curated modern-art museum, founded in 1992, is the oils, drawings and watercolours of local lad Lefteris Kanakakis, but over time it has amassed enough works to present the arc of creative endeavour in Greece since the 1950s. Temporary exhibits keep things dynamic. Entrance is off Mesologhiou.

Municipal Park PARK
(Igoumenou Gavriil) Located between Iliakaki and Dimitrakaki, the trails and tree-shaded benches found here offer respite from the heat and crowds. Old men doze and chat while children romp around the playground.

Neratzes Mosque MOSQUE
(Vernardou) This triple-domed mosque began life as an Augustinian church and was converted by the Turks in 1657, although the recently restored minaret wasn't added until 1890. Today the building is a music conservatory and performance space, with events held most Friday and Saturday evenings.

Historical & Folk Art Museum MUSEUM
(☎28310 23398; Vernardou 28; adult/concession €4/2; ⏲10am-3pm Mon-Sat) In a lovely 17th-century Venetian mansion, the five-room permanent exhibit here documents traditional rural life on Crete with displays of clothing, baskets, weavings, pottery, weapons and farming tools. Labelling is also in English.

Lighthouse LIGHTHOUSE
(Venetian Harbour) Punctuating the old pier in the Venetian Harbour, the 9m-high lighthouse was built in the 1830s, when Egypt ruled Crete. (Britain forced Egypt to give Crete back to the Turks in 1840.)

Loggia HISTORIC BUILDING
(cnr Paleologou & Arkadiou) This nicely restored 16th-century landmark originally served as a meeting house for Venetian nobility to discuss politics and money, and morphed into a mosque during the Turkish era. Arcaded on three sides, it now houses a shop selling replicas of ancient statuary.

Head inside to pick up a brochure detailing the building's storied history.

Rimondi Fountain FOUNTAIN
Another vestige of Venetian rule is this small fountain where water spouts from three lions' heads into three basins flanked by Corinthian columns. Above the central basin you can make out the Rimondi family crest. It was built in 1626 by city rector Alvise Rimondi. Located off Paleologou.

Kara Musa Pasha Mosque HISTORIC SITE
(cnr Arkadiou & Hugo) This building began life as a monastery but was turned into a mosque by the Turks, who added the domes and a minaret, of which only bits remain. It is named after the Ottoman admiral instrumental in the capture of Rethymno. It is not open to the public.

Porta Guora HISTORIC SITE
(Great Gate; cnr Antistaseos & Dimakopoulou) At the southern edge of the old quarter, this arched stone gate is the only remnant of the Venetian city wall. It was built in the late 16th century and originally topped with the Venetian emblem – the Lion of St Mark.

Activities

Cretan Ski School SKIING
(www.facebook.com/skiincrete) Offers equipment hire, lessons and trips to Mt Psiloritis.

Paradise Dive Center DIVING
(☎28310 26317; www.diving-center.gr; Petres Geraniou; 2 dives incl equipment from €100, open-water certification €400) Runs diving trips for all

grades of diver from its base at Petres, 14km west of Rethymno. Its most popular dive is to the underwater Elephant Cave, where fossilised remains of elephants were discovered in 1999. Paradise also offers night dives and PADI courses for beginners. Book through travel agencies, by phone or via the website.

Popeye Watersports ADVENTURE SPORTS
(28310 52803; www.popeyewatersports.gr; Sofokli Venizelou; 10am-6pm May-Oct) At the western end of Rethymno's sandy beach, Popeye will take you parasailing (from €60), waterskiing (€40) or banana-boat riding (€15). It also offers 1½-hour jet-ski safaris (€130 for two people) that explore nearby caves only accessible from the water.

Mountaineering Club of Rethymno CLIMBING
(28310 57766; www.eosrethymnou.gr; Dimokratias 12; 9-11pm Tue) Offers advice on local hikes along with the possibility of joining excursions. It's best to make contact via the website. It's affiliated with the Cretan Ski School (p121), which runs ski excursions to Mt Psiloritis in winter.

Tours

★Happy Walker HIKING
(28310 52920; www.happywalker.com; Tombazi 56; guided day walks €32; 10am-2pm Apr-Oct) In operation for over a quarter of a century, this congenial Dutch-run outfit takes up to 16 global ramblers on day hikes to gorges, ancient shepherd trails and traditional villages. It's ideal for solo travellers. Rates include transport to and from trailheads and an English-speaking guide, but coffee and a vegetarian lunch with wine are an extra €12.

Multiday tours are also available.

Eco Events TOURS
(6946686857, 28310 50055; www.ecoevents.gr; Eleftheriou Venizelou 39; tours €18-70; 10am-9pm) This outfit specialises in small-group English-language tours that get you in touch with land, people and culture. Options include the Eco Tour, on which you'll meet a baker, a weaver and a woodcarver before sampling charcoal-grilled lamb in a traditional shepherd's shelter in the mountains. Cooking classes, wine and olive-oil tastings, and hiking trips are also part of the lineup.

Dolphin Cruises BOATING
(28310 57666; www.dolphin-cruises.com; Marina of Rethymno, Sofokli Venizelou 24; cruises €19-25) Runs 1½- to three-hour boat cruises to visit pirate caves, Panormo or Georgioupoulis.

Cretan Safari ADVENTURE
(28310 20815; www.cretansafari.gr; 4 Sofokli Venizelou; tour €75; 10am-8pm) Join an all-day off-road 4WD adventure to beaches, gorges and traditional villages.

RETHYMNO IN...

Two Days

Spend a half day exploring Rethymno's stunning Venetian fortress (p119), wandering the town's labyrinth-like historic quarter and strolling along the picturesque harbour. Enjoy a long lunch at classy Avli (p128).

Hit the beach at Panormo, enjoying a leisurely mid-afternoon dip and a spot of wine-tasting (p156). Take a short drive to moody Melidoni Cave (p141), site of a horrendous massacre under Turkish rule. Head back north to Bali for authentic Cretan cuisine at Taverna Karavostasi (p159) and a magical Mediterranean sunset.

Next day, get an early start and beat the bus crowds to Margarites (p137) to browse for handmade pottery. Next, visit the world-class Museum of Ancient Eleutherna (p140) and its surrounding Minoan tombs (p140), before continuing on to atmospheric, history-soaked Moni Arkadiou (p137).

Three Days

Glimpse traditional Cretan life by driving through the picturesque Amari Valley (p138), with cobblestone villages and Byzantine churches. Arrive in Spili for a well-earned lunch at Cafe Platia (p146), overlooking the town's Venetian fountain.

Don't miss Preveli Beach (p151), then head back uphill for a dose of Cretan history at Moni Preveli (p151). Otherwise, visit the fabulously secluded beaches further east. When you've finished splashing, head to fun-lovin' Plakias, stopping at nearby Myrthios to enjoy a modern Cretan country dinner at Vrisi (p151).

Festivals & Events

Carnival CARNIVAL
(Feb or Mar) The annual pre-Lent celebrations bring four weeks of dancing and masquerading, games and treasure hunts, and a grand street parade.

Rethymno Renaissance Festival MUSIC
(www.rfr.gr; Jul) For two weeks in July, Rethymno celebrates its Renaissance pedigree with top-flight concerts featuring international artists. Performances take place in the fortress's Erofili Theatre and in the Neratzes Mosque.

Sleeping

The old town has an ample supply of lovely restored mansions, boutique hotels, and friendly pensions and hostels to cater for all budgets. Many hotels are open year-round. Along the beach east of town is an uninterrupted stretch of mostly uninspired hotels and resorts.

★ **Rethymno Youth Hostel** HOSTEL €
(28310 22848; www.yhrethymno.com; Tombazi 41; dm €12-14; reception 8am-1pm & 5-11pm Sep-May, 8am-midnight Jun-Aug;) Centrally located in a quiet street, this cheerful and professionally run hostel sleeps six to 12 people in clean, well-presented dorms (one is for women only). Dorms have comfy mattresses, personalised power points and good-size lockers, and it's a nice place to relax, with a sociable patio, a bar and a flowering garden. Offers excellent travel info for Crete and beyond.

Facilities include a communal kitchen, free snorkelling and beach gear, a book exchange and Chromecast TV. Cheap drinks keep things social, and breakfast is available for €3.

★ **Atelier Frosso Bora** PENSION €
(28310 24440; www.frosso-bora.com; Chimaras 25; d €35-60; Mar-Nov;) Run by local artist Frosso Bora and located above her pottery studio, these four spotless, ambience-laden rooms with exposed stone walls, small flat-screen TVs, modern bathrooms and kitchenettes are a superb budget pick. Two units have small balconies facing the old town, while the other two sport Venetian architectural features and a beamed ceiling.

Rethymno House PENSION €
(28310 23924, 6955666625; www.rethymnohouse.com; Vitsentzou Kornarou 3-5; s/d €30/35;) Right in the heart of the old town, stumbling distance to the waterfront and nightlife action, is this cheapie housed within an attractive building that dates to Venetian times. While the exposed-stone walls show elements of its history, for the most part it's a no-frills affair, with basic amenities, but it remains an excellent budget choice.

RETHYMNO RESOURCES

Rethymno Guide (www.rethymno.guide) Official site with up-to-date listings of events and things to do.

Rethymno (www.rethymnon.gr) Local history, maps, festivals, accommodation and sights.

Crete Travel (www.cretetravel.com/guide/rethymno) Tourist-company site with links to hotels, ferry tickets and activities.

Lonely Planet (www.lonelyplanet.com) Destination information, hotel bookings, traveller forum and more.

Camping Elizabeth CAMPGROUND €
(28310 28694, 6983009259; www.camping-elizabeth.net; Ionias 84, Missiria; camp sites adult/child €8.50/5, tent €7, caravans €32-50, glamping incl breakfast €60-95; year-round;) Crete's oldest campground is only 4km east of the old city but feels far removed from Rethymno, on beautiful Missiria beach. Bamboo, palm and tamarisk trees provide plenty of shade. If you don't have your own gear, it rents out tents with bedding (singles/doubles €20/28), as well as caravans and air-conditioned glamping (sleeping four) on the dunes overlooking the beach.

Axos Hotel HOTEL €
(28310 54472; www.axos-hotel.gr; Maxis Kritis 167, Platanias; studios/apt incl breakfast from €35/40; Apr-Oct;) Those looking to stay a bit outside town can choose Axos in the small seaside community of Platanias, some 5km east of Rethymno. While the common areas are somewhat institutional, rooms are modern and well proportioned. There are no sea views, but the beach is only 300m away, plus there's a sparkling pool and an alluring terrace cafe. Minimum two-night stay.

Casa Moazzo BOUTIQUE HOTEL €€
(28310 36235; www.casamoazzo.gr; 57 Tombazi; r incl breakfast €85-180;) Occupying the former home of Venetian nobles, these 10 newly renovated rooms are elegant and

Rethymno

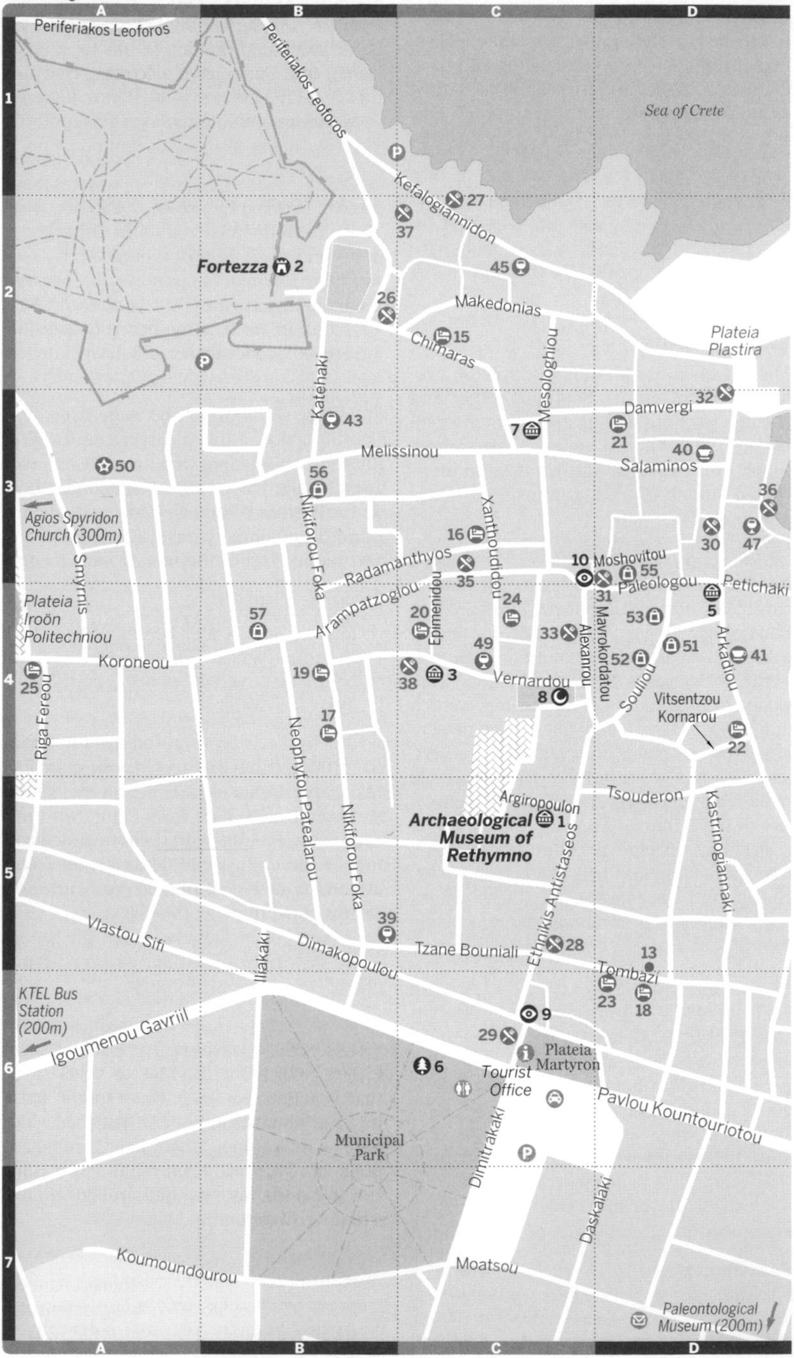

A B C D
1 2 3 4 5 6 7
Periferiakos Leoforos
Periferiakos Leoforos
Sea of Crete
Kefalogiannidon
27
37
Fortezza 2
45
26
Makedonias
15
Chimaras
Plateia Plastira
Katehaki
Mesologhiou
32
Damvergi
43
7
21
Melissinou
40
Salaminos
50
56
36
Agios Spyridon Church (300m)
Nikiforou Foka
Xanthoudidou
16
30
47
Smyrnis
Radamanthyos
10 Moshovitou
55
35
Paleologou
Petichaki
Plateia Iroön Politechniou
Arampatzoglou
Epimenidou
24
31
5
57
20
Mavrokordatou
53
Alexanrou
33
Arkadiou
49
51
41
Koroneou
52
25
19
38
3
Vernardou
Souliou
8
Riga Fereou
Vitsentzou Kornarou
17
22
Neophytou Patealarou
Tsouderon
Argiropoulon
Kastrinogiannaki
Archaeological Museum of Rethymno 1
Nikiforou Foka
Ethnikis Antistaseos
39
Vlastou Sifi
Dimakopoulou
Tzane Bouniali
28
Iliakaki
13
Tombazi
KTEL Bus Station (200m)
23
18
Igoumenou Gavriil
9
29
Plateia Martyron
6
Tourist Office
Pavlou Kountouriotou
Municipal Park
Dimitrakaki
Daskalaki
Koumoundourou
Moatsou
Paleontological Museum (200m)

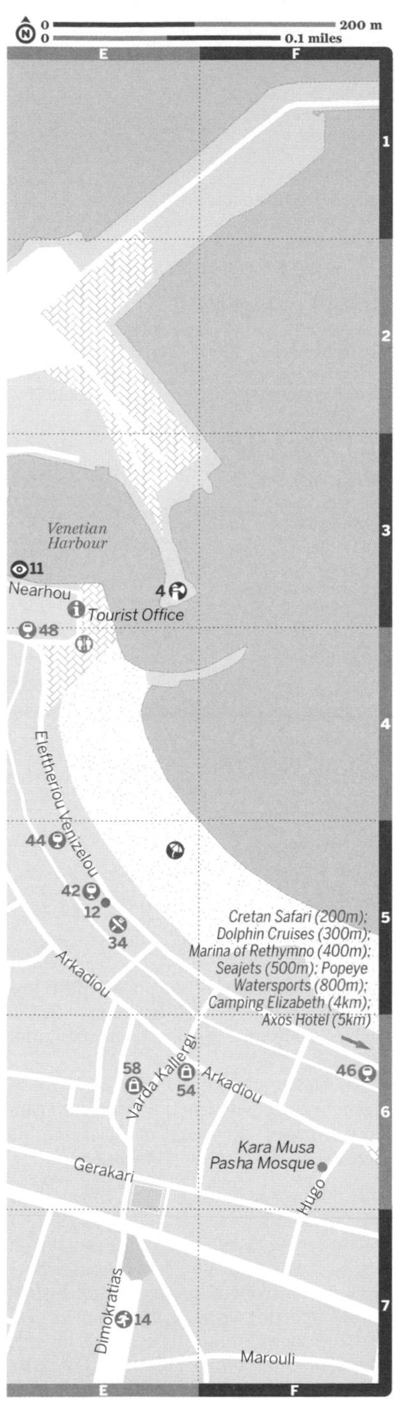

bright. Just a stone's throw from the harbour, they're nonetheless very private. Each room is unique, combining wallpaper, exposed stone and wooden beams for a classy Italian feel. Some have balconies, claw-foot tubs and kitchenettes, and all have king-size beds and an option for goose-down pillows.

Casa dei Delfini BOUTIQUE HOTEL **€€**
(☎28310 55120, 6937254857; www.casadeidelfini.com; Nikiforou Foka 66-68; r €95-110; ❄📶) The nine individual rooms in this elegant mansion exude historic character without skimping on modern comforts. In one room the bathroom used to be a *hammam* (Turkish bath), in another the bed is tucked into an arched stone alcove. All have kitchenettes. The two-storey maisonette comes with a large private terrace.

Sohora BOUTIQUE HOTEL **€€**
(☎28313 00913; www.sohora.net; Plateia Iroön Politechniou 11; studios €50-70, d €60-75, apt €100; ❄📶) Extremely comfortable and slightly quirky, the rooms with kitchenette in this 200-year-old home are named after the seasons and incorporate original architectural features alongside upcycled vintage furnishings. A solar water heater, organic bath products and a hearty, homemade breakfast (€6) provide eco-cred. Service is both friendly and professional.

Palazzino di Corina BOUTIQUE HOTEL **€€**
(☎28310 21205; www.corina.gr; Damvergi 9; d €70-170; ❄📶🏊) This regal Venetian mansion is an elegant place to unpack. Fine furniture, exposed stone walls and timber vaulted ceilings create a plush period ambience. You'll also find a good dose of mod cons, including Jacuzzi tubs. In the courtyard, a small, deep pool begs you to dive in, while the lounge is overflowing with antiques – from gramophones to sewing machines.

Hotel Veneto BOUTIQUE HOTEL **€€**
(☎28310 56634; www.veneto.gr; Epimenidou 4; s €70-95, d €95-130, ste €114-148; ❄📶) Soak up that Venetian vibe in these 12 rooms boasting traditional features like polished wood floors and ceilings, alongside a satisfying range of mod cons. Each room tells a story; stay in No 101, once a monk's cell, or No 106, a long-ago *hammam*.

★Hamam Oriental Suites BOUTIQUE HOTEL **€€€**
(☎28310 50378, 6981649377; www.hamamsuites.com; Nikiforou Foka 86; r incl breakfast €135-230) In

Rethymno

Top Sights
1 Archaeological Museum of Rethymno ... C5
2 Fortezza ... B2

Sights
3 Historical & Folk Art Museum ... C4
4 Lighthouse ... E3
5 Loggia ... D4
6 Municipal Park ... C6
7 Museum of Contemporary Art ... C3
8 Neratzes Mosque ... C4
9 Porta Guora ... C6
10 Rimondi Fountain ... C3
11 Venetian Harbour ... E3

Activities, Courses & Tours
12 Eco Events ... E5
13 Happy Walker ... D5
14 Mountaineering Club of Rethymno ... E7

Sleeping
15 Atelier Frosso Bora ... C2
16 Avli Lounge Apartments ... C3
17 Casa dei Delfini ... B4
18 Casa Moazzo ... D6
19 Hammam Oriental Suites ... B4
20 Hotel Veneto ... C4
21 Palazzino di Corina ... D3
22 Rethymno House ... D4
23 Rethymno Youth Hostel ... D6
24 Rimondi Boutique Hotel ... C4
25 Sohora ... A4

Eating
Avli ... (see 16)
26 Castelvecchio ... B2
27 En Plo ... C2
28 Gaias Gefseis ... C5
29 koo koo ... C6
30 Makan ... D3
31 Meli ... D3
32 Mojo Burgers ... D3
33 Othonas ... C4
34 Peperoncino ... E5
35 Raki Baraki ... C3
36 Taverna Knossos ... D3
37 Thalassographia ... C2
Veneto ... (see 20)
38 Yiorgos Hatziparaskos ... C4

Drinking & Nightlife
39 Ali Vafi's Garden ... B5
40 Arokaria ... D3
41 Brew Your Mind ... D4
42 Bricks Beerhouse ... E5
43 Chalikouti ... B3
44 Chaplin's ... E5
45 Inomena Voistasia ... C2
46 Livingroom ... F6
47 Metropolis ... D3
48 Minibar ... E4
49 Monitor ... C4

Entertainment
50 Asteria Cinema ... A3

Shopping
Avli Raw Materials ... (see 16)
51 Diskopoleion Music Store ... D4
Frosso Bora Pottery Studio & Shop ... (see 15)
52 Ilias Spondidakis ... D4
53 Leather Studio Kanakakis ... D4
54 Liranthos ... E6
55 Mediterraneo ... D3
56 Spanoioakis ... B3
57 Spantis ... B4
58 Wood Art ... E6
Xenos Typos ... (see 28)

a quiet alleyway in the old quarter is this former Venetian-Ottoman bathhouse that, after several reincarnations, has undergone an elegant refit to open as a boutique hotel. Each of its five atmospheric rooms is unique – some feature striking mosaics, domed ceilings, original stone walls and steam rooms or Jacuzzis – but all are lavishly decorated with period furnishings and antiques.

Rimondi Boutique Hotel BOUTIQUE HOTEL €€€
(☎28310 51001; www.hotelsrimondi.com; Xanthoudidou 21; ste incl breakfast €88-400;) Tucked in the heart of the old town, this luxurious Venetian mansion has historical ambience and cushy furnishings. The suites in the Estate building feature original domes and stone arches, while rooms in the Palazzo are equally plush but offer a little less atmosphere. There's a glittering pool in the relaxing courtyard and the breakfast buffet is a feast.

The on-site *hammam* is just the place to pamper yourself: bask in the hot-stone steam room or choose a massage or facial from its extensive menu of wellness treatments.

Avli Lounge Apartments BOUTIQUE HOTEL €€€
(☎28310 58250; www.avli.gr; Xanthoudidou 22; r incl breakfast €105-290;) Luxury is taken very seriously at this hushed retreat, where you'll be ensconced in warmly furnished studios sporting stone walls, beamed ceilings and Jacuzzi tubs. Retire to plush beds after a first-rate dinner downstairs in Avli's romantic courtyard restaurant.

Eating

Dining in Rethymno is rewarding, with the best eats found in the tiny side streets of the old quarter. Despite the magical setting, the tavernas in the Venetian Harbour are geared to tourists and mediocre at best. Better waterfront dining options are along Kefalogiannidon below the fortress.

★Raki Baraki CRETAN €

(☎28310 58250; www.facebook.com/1600raki baraki; Arampatzoglou 17; mezedhes €3.50-13; ⏲12.30pm-midnight; ❄📶🖋) Rustic, colourful and lively, this is a fantastic place to while away the evening over mezedhes (appetisers) like flavoursome grilled mushrooms with mountain herbs, warm homemade dolmadhes with yoghurt, or mussels steamed with sage. The fried filo-coated feta with marmalade is divine, as is the sheep's-milk ice cream. Comfort food at its finest.

All ingredients are sourced from small farms around Greece.

Meli ICE CREAM €

(☎28310 50847; www.melirethimno.com; Palеologou; ice cream from €1.80; ⏲10am-midnight mid-Feb–mid-Nov) Stop by Meli for its delicious array of fresh goat's-milk ice cream, in flavours ranging from ricotta and fig to yoghurt and pomegranate to its signature creamy vanilla. It also does more mainstream flavours, as well as sorbet. It's directly next to the Rimondi Fountain (p121).

There's also a branch along the waterfront on Sofokli Venizelou, opposite the marina.

koo koo CAFE €

(☎28310 26380; Plateia Martyron; dishes €4-6; ⏲7am-11pm; ❄📶🖋) The place to head if you need respite from traditional Greek food, this contemporary cafe does a menu of all-day brunch fare. Expect the likes of smashed avocado on toast, crispy chicken waffles, pizza by the slice and a heap of tasty burgers. There's a welcome choice of healthy and vegetarian options, too, along with top-notch coffees, smoothies and teas.

Otherwise, pop in for a pre-dinner Aperol spritz accompanied by a spot of people-watching in the main square.

Makan GREEK €

(☎28310 26001; https://makan.scaneat.gr; Arkadiou 230; gyros from €2.80; ⏲12.30pm-1am; ❄📶🖋) Not your average takeaway joint, Makan is more of a designer souvlaki bar, with a contemporary-chic interior yet old-school prices. Here you can build your own *gyros*, choosing from rye, 'Arabic thin' or 'giant' pitta, filling it with pork belly, grilled vegetables, halloumi or classic chicken, and finishing it with a handful of chips and a dab of tzatziki.

Mojo Burgers AMERICAN €

(☎28310 50550, 6987328252; www.facebook.com/mojoburgers; Damvergi 38; meals €2.40-11; ⏲noon-midnight daily Apr-Oct, Tue-Sun Nov-Mar) With a divey graffitied interior and a large menu, Mojo's delivers some of the best burgers and hot dogs this side of the Atlantic. Try the Alabama Mama, with crispy pork, coleslaw and pickles, or a classic flame-grilled cheeseburger. Slap on some extras like jalapeños or caramelised onions for good measure. Good selection of local beers, too, and it delivers.

Gaias Gefseis BAKERY €

(☎28311 00428; Ethnikis Antistaseos 15; pastries €0.50-2.50; ⏲7am-10pm) For *loukoumadhes* (doughnut-like concoctions drizzled with honey and cinnamon), follow your nose to Gaias Gefseis. This bakery creates some of the city's best traditional cakes and biscuits, as well as homemade sheep's-milk gelato. If your sweet tooth needs a break, there's a mammoth supply of savoury breads; try one stuffed with feta and olives.

Castelvecchio CRETAN €€

(☎28310 55163; Chimaras 29; mains €11-23; ⏲6-11pm Apr-Oct; ❄📶) In a Venetian-era building a bone toss from the fortress, chic yet chilled Castelvecchio is perfect for date night – especially if your date is a plate of tender boneless lamb, done up in numerous creative ways, including a foil-cooked version with creamy tomato and feta sauce.

Veneto CRETAN €€

(☎28310 56634; www.veneto.gr; Epimenidou 4; mains €15-20; ⏲6-11pm May-Oct; 📶) In a 14th-century manor house that doubles as a boutique hotel (p125), Veneto oozes historic charm from every nook and cranny. The kitchen adds a contemporary streak to traditional Cretan recipes, with results like fish with fennel and lime or meatballs with basil sauce. The owner is a wine buff and will happily help you pick a bottle to complement your meal.

Taverna Knossos TAVERNA €€

(☎28310 25582; Nearhou 40; mains €13-20; ⏲noon-midnight May-Oct; 📶👪) Most tout-fronted tavernas in the Venetian Harbour focus on

DON'T MISS

RETHYMNO'S LAST FILO MASTER

Established in 1948, **Yiorgos Hatziparaskos** (28310 29488; Vernardou 30; pastries €2-4; 8am-9.30pm) is one of the last traditional filo masters in all of Greece. Assisted by his wife, Katerina, and son, Paraskevas, today he still makes superfine pastry by hand in his workshop. Watch the spectacle and try some of the best baklava and *kataïfi* ('angel hair' pastry) you will ever eat.

The highlight is when they whirl the dough into a giant bubble before stretching it over a huge table.

folkloric ambience rather than food quality. Owned by the amiable Stavroulaki family for half a century, Knossos is a happy exception. When Mama Anna is in the kitchen you can be sure that the dishes will be loaded with flavour, the fish outstanding and the service swift and gracious.

Avli CRETAN €€
(28310 58250; www.avli.gr; Xanthoudidou 22; mains €12-20; 12.30-11pm;) This well-established Venetian villa serves creative Cretan food with a side of romance. Farm-fresh fare steers the menu, resulting in dishes with bold flavour pairings such as *creatotouria* (ravioli filled with lamb, cheese, mint and lime) or *fouriariko* (slow-cooked organic goat with honey and thyme). Be sure to reserve a table in the bewitching garden courtyard filled with flowers and palms.

Thalassographia GREEK €€
(28310 52569; Kefalogiannidon 33; mains €5-21; 10am-midnight May-Oct;) With cascading terraces from fortress to sea, this is where locals head for dinner and unbeatable coastal views. The eclectic Mediterranean menu offers up skilfully created dishes like stuffed mushrooms, Cretan cheese in filo with smoked pork and herbs, roasted sardines or steamed mussels in white wine. It's all best washed down with local Brink's beer. If it's windy, dress warmly.

En Plo GREEK €€
(28310 30950; Kefalogiannidon 28; mains €8-15; 11am-11pm Apr-Oct;) One of several tavernas right at the water's edge below the fortress, En Plo does dependable faves like shrimp spaghetti and grilled salmon but shows its most creative side when it comes to mezedhes such as as feta in pastry with caramelised figs.

Othonas CRETAN €€
(28310 55500; Mavrokordatou Alexanrou 27; mains €7-23; 11.30am-12.30pm) With its street-side 'host' and multilingual menus, Othonas may scream 'tourist trap', but it's actually well respected for its regional fare. Menu stars include the lamb with artichokes and the lip-smacking 'Chicken Dias' (with raki, feta, mustard and onions).

Peperoncino PIZZA €€
(28310 24776; www.facebook.com/peperoncinorethimno; Eleftheriou Venizelou 45; mains €6-20; noon-1am daily Apr-Oct, 6pm-midnight Fri, noon-midnight Sat & Sun Nov-Mar;) Come here for pizzas piled with fresh ingredients and baked in a stone oven even the Italians would approve of. Or fill up with fresh pasta, complemented by a decent wine list. Sit outside with a view of the beach or in the small, classy interior.

Drinking & Nightlife

Rethymno's young and restless are mostly drawn to the cafe-bars along Eleftheriou Venizelou. The area around the Rimondi Fountain and Plateia Petihaki is popular with tourists. Wander the side streets to find quieter places.

★ **Monitor** BAR
(6974130764; www.facebook.com/monitorartcafe; Vernardou 21-23; 10am-late) A gathering spot for Rethymno's slightly older indie crowd, this relaxed, unpretentious bar is decked out in arthouse-film posters and modern-art installations. Its atmospheric old-town setting makes it a wonderful spot for a relaxed coffee, beer or old-fashioned cocktail and a good burger. Check the Facebook page for upcoming bands, DJs and events.

Bricks Beerhouse CRAFT BEER
(6945297481; www.bricksbeerhouse.gr; Eleftheriou Venizelou 41; 10am-1am mid-Apr–Oct, from 6pm Nov–mid-Apr) While Cretans are still developing a thirst for craft beer, Bricks is doing its best to convert them with its selection of 30 ales produced by Greek microbreweries, including a few local ones. You can also try a gin distilled in Irakalio that uses Cretan botanicals.

Grab a tasting flight and enjoy it on the palm-lined promenade with a menu of beer-friendly food.

Chaplin's BAR
(☎28310 24566; Eleftheriou Venizelou 52; ⏰9am-4am) Rethymno's most raucous drinking spot is this smoke-filled rock bar that's been banging out tunes since the 1970s. It attracts a boozy crowd of black-clad students and older rockers propped at the bar sinking shots between beers. While the music is mainstream rock, the DJs (from 8pm) are pretty forthcoming with any requests.

Brew Your Mind COFFEE
(☎28313 01940; www.facebook.com/brewyourmind1; Arkadiou 251; ⏰8am-10pm; 📶) Wake up and smell the coffee at this hip microroaster that offers a pleasing array of speciality beans. Whether you're into V60, Aeropress, Chemex, syphon, cold brew, flat whites or your traditional Greek double, the baristas here have the full arsenal at their disposal to nail your next caffeine hit.

Arokaria CAFE
(☎28310 21442; www.facebook.com/arokaria; Salaminos 7; ⏰9.30am-midnight; 📶) A popular hang-out with locals is this vibrant cafe with a bohemian flavour that attracts a mixed crowd of students, fashionistas and artists. Join them on its enticing street-front patio for house-roasted coffees, Cretan beers and cheap carafes of house wine to go with plates of mezedhes and homemade cakes.

Inomena Voistasia BAR
(☎28310 54758; Kefalogiannidon 20; ⏰9am-1am) With an interior of tiles, wood and newsprint, this place has a cool, vintage vibe. The bar is well stocked, including a good selection of cocktails using the owner's homemade raki and infused with fruit picked from his garden. Come back the next day for healing Cretan mountain teas. When the sun's shining, soak it up on the waterside terrace.

Metropolis CLUB
(www.facebook.com/metropolisreth; Nearhou 12; ⏰9pm-dawn) Hobnob with fun-lovin' locals at this hot-and-heavy party palace. In summer DJs spin mostly international chart music for the tourist crowd, while Greek pop dominates in low season. Things don't start kicking till around 11pm.

Chalikouti BAR
(☎28310 42632; www.toxalikouti.org; Katehaki 3; ⏰9am-1am; 📶) In the alt-flavoured quarter below the Fortezza, this cooperative-run cafe draws chatty locals with coffee from Mexican Zapatistas, sugar from landless workers in Brazil, and organic raki and wines from Cretan producers. A selection of mezedhes and desserts provides sustenance.

Ali Vafi's Garden BAR
(☎28310 23238; www.facebook.com/pg/alivafis; Tzane Bouniali 65a; ⏰11am-late; 📶) In summer there are few locations more enchanting than this laid-back garden among the branches of orange, grapefruit and lemon trees. Occasional live music performances draw crowds here to sip wine and cocktails.

Minibar BAR
(☎6932349229; Petichaki 6; ⏰9pm-dawn May-Nov) A classic Rethymno hang-out, this place has been renamed and revamped but continues to house two bars and a dance floor filled nightly by tourists and local students.

Livingroom BAR
(☎28310 21386; www.livingroom.gr; Eleftheriou Venizelou 5; ⏰8am-3am; 📶) No matter where the hands are on the clock, the comfy lounge sofas of this popular hang-out are always packed with fashionable townsfolk. Mellow in the daytime, the vibe gets progressively more high octane after dark. Choose between the terrace-promenade bistro-cafe and the main bar with Euro-glam decor. A good place to ease into the nightlife scene.

☆ Entertainment

Asteria Cinema CINEMA
(☎28310 22830; www.cineapollonasteria.com; Melissinou 21; tickets €5-7; ⏰6pm-late May–Oct)

THE BIRTH OF THE ONE-EYED MONSTER

The Rethymno region seems to have more than its share of fossil-filled caves. In fact, it's the richest area in the Mediterranean for endemic fossils, including those of the dwarf elephant. Some scientists believe that when ancient Greeks entered the shore caves and discovered dwarf-elephant skulls, they were taken aback by what they saw. About twice the size of a human skull, a dwarf-elephant skull has a large, central nasal cavity for the trunk, which may well have been interpreted as a single enormous eye socket. The possible result? The birth of the Cyclops. Visit Rethymno's Paleontological Museum (p121) to see the skeletons for yourself.

1

ANDREI NEKRASSOV/SHUTTERSTOCK ©

ELLEPISTOCK/GETTY IMAGES ©

1. Kourtaliotiko Gorge (p151)
This stunning gorge leads to Preveli Beach.

2. Sultan Bin Ibrahim Mosque (p119)
This mosque sits inside the star-shaped Fortezza that looms over Rethymno.

3. Margarites (p137)
The village of Margarites is famous for its pottery, a tradition that can be traced back to Minoan times.

4. Venetian Harbour, Rethymno (p119)
Rethymno's Venetian Harbour features a lighthouse built in the 1830s by Egypt (which ruled Crete at the time).

LEOKS/SHUTTERSTOCK ©

WORTH A TRIP

MAROULAS

Make the 10km drive southeast of Rethymno to Maroulas, a pretty, higgledy-piggledy village with panoramic sea views. The protected town has a mix of nicely restored late Venetian and Turkish architecture, including 10 olive presses and a 44m tower jutting above the village.

Marianna's Workshop (☎28310 72432; www.mariannas-workshop.gr; Maroulas; ⊙10am-3pm & 5-7pm summer, call for winter hours) Just up from the main square you'll find this tiny shop run by Marianna Founti-Vassi, who collects aromatic medicinal herbs from the mountains to make her unique range of teas and oils from natural extracts using traditional methods. There are potions for all manner of ailments, including a tea made from 40 herbs once used by midwives.

Taverna Fantastiko (☎6988442728; www.facebook.com/tavernafantastiko; Maroulas; €7-12; ⊙11am-7.30pm) Head up the hill to this traditional taverna that lives up to its name with fantastic, all-encompassing views of the countryside from its expansive terrace. Most dishes are made from scratch, using produce sourced from its farm. Don't miss the charcoal-grilled meats, homemade cheeses (mixed plate €6.80) or sheep's-milk ice cream.

Katerina (☎28310 71627; Maroulas; mains €8-20; ⊙10am-11pm May-Oct) Report for a traditional lunch at Katerina, an outdoor taverna with sublime sea views, and an owner who's a bona fide character. It's located down a small lane beyond the Venetian tower.

Zamaros (☎6984085333; www.facebook.com/zamaros; Maroulas; ⊙9am-4pm Apr-Oct, to 3pm Nov-Mar) At the main square down from the Orthodox church is this small cheesemaker known mostly for its homemade halloumi and *graviera*. Everything's made on-site and available for tasting. In summer visit also for homemade ice cream and chocolate-filled cheeses.

This small open-air cinema near the fortress shows mostly new-release movies. It's lovely on a balmy evening, and has a bar for drinks.

Shopping

The narrow, cobbled pedestrian streets of the old quarter are packed with mainly tourist-geared stores and local retail outlets. There are also some gems worth searching for. Try the streets Mellissinou, Souliou and Arampatzoglou. The mainstream shopping strip is along Arkadiou.

Frosso Bora Pottery Studio & Shop CERAMICS
(☎28310 24440; www.frosso-bora.com; Chimaras 27; ⊙10am-9pm) Local artist Frosso Bora makes beautiful pots, vases, candlesticks, bowls and other vessels from local clay using the wheel or slabs. Prices are very reasonable.

Leather Studio Kanakakis ARTS & CRAFTS
(www.leatherstudio.gr; Souliou 23; ⊙9am-5pm & 7-9pm) At this small store-workshop you can watch the owner make quality handmade leather belts in all sorts of colours and designs. There's also a good assortment of leather handbags, wallets and accessories.

Diskopoleion Music Store MUSIC
(Souliou 38; ⊙10am-10pm) This pint-sized music store is run by a knowledgeable owner with good taste in Greek rock, punk, psychedelica and jazz, along with traditional Cretan music. Has both CDs and vinyl.

Liranthos MUSIC
(☎28310 29043, 6938993779; Arkadiou 66; ⊙9am-2pm & 5-8pm) This tiny store filled with musical instruments is the place to get that bouzouki or Cretan *lyra*. You can also pick up CDs of local Cretan music.

Avli Raw Materials FOOD & DRINKS
(Agora; ☎28310 58250; www.avli.gr; Arampatzoglou 40; ⊙10am-8pm) Foodies will love the store at Avli restaurant (p128), packed with a huge range of gourmet delights from around Greece, including great wines, olive oil, mountain tea and soaps.

Spanoioakis FOOD
(Nikiforou Foka 93; ⊙9am-9pm) Hidden away in Rethymno's labyrinth of alleys is this bakery that's been at it since 1958. As well as freshly baked spanakopita and pastries, it's most famous for its bread shaped like dinosaurs and flamingos, as well as *kouloures*, a lacquered, intricately decorated (but inedible)

embroidered bread that makes for a unique souvenir.

Found across Greece, the fading tradition of *kouloures* has its roots in Crete. In a practice passed down by his grandfather, baker Spanoioakis continues to create the decorated bread, including the wedding roll, the original Greek wedding cake. Each beautiful design is symbolic: pomegranates bring luck; trees, longevity; and rings, an eternal bond.

Spantis ARTS & CRAFTS

(www.leather-workshop.com; Koroneou 9; ⏲10am-10pm Apr-Nov, 10am-2pm & 5-9pm Nov-Mar) John Spantidakis works with raw leather – not pre-dyed or pre-cut – to create handmade bags, belts and wallets that will make you crave leatherware like never before. Paint strokes and unusual cuts lift this traditional art to a new level (wallets/belts/bags start at €20/55/130). Earthy greens, deep reds, Aegean blues and smoky blacks appear in varying degrees of vibrancy.

Wood Art ARTS & CRAFTS

(☎28310 23010; www.siragas.gr; Varda Kallergi 38; ⏲11am-6pm Mon-Sat) Many of the wooden ware you find in Greece has been imported from Tunisia. But Niko Siragas creates his own here using woodturning techniques dating back to the Minoans. An internationally acclaimed artist and teacher, his handcrafted bowls, vases and objects are each unique and silky smooth. His designs are intricate and often have a whimsical, organic feel. Niko also offers classes in woodturning. Check his website for details.

Ilias Spondidakis BOOKS

(☎28310 54307; Souliou 43; ⏲9am-10pm) Tiny bookstore tucked down a souk-like alley has novels in English, books on Crete, maps, CDs of Greek music and a small secondhand section.

Xenos Typos BOOKS

(☎28310 29405; Ethnikis Antistaseos 21; ⏲9am-9pm) This place sells foreign press, plus books on Crete and maps.

Mediterraneo BOOKS

(www.mediterraneo.gr; Paleologou 41; ⏲10am-8pm May-Nov) English-language books, travel guides, international periodicals and maps.

ℹ Information

EMERGENCY

Tourist Police (☎28310 28156, emergency 171; Sofokli Venizelou 37; ⏲on call 24hr)

INTERNET ACCESS

Hotels and restaurants offer wi-fi, but otherwise there are free public wi-fi hot spots at the town hall, Plateia Iroön Polytechniou, the Venetian Harbour and the Municipal Park, all within the old town.

Net Cafe (☎28310 20880; www.net.net.gr; cnr Kountouriotou & Daskalaki; per hour €2.50; ⏲24hr) Has computer terminals if you're travelling device free.

MEDICAL SERVICES

General Hospital of Rethymno (☎28313 42100; www.rethymnohospital.gr; Triandalydou 17; ⏲24hr)

BUSES FROM RETHYMNO

DESTINATION	FARE (€)	DURATION	FREQUENCY
Agia Galini (via Spili)	6.80	1½hr	up to 5 daily
Anogia	6	1¼hr	2 daily Mon-Fri
Argyroupoli	3.60	40min	2 daily
Hania	6.80	1hr	hourly
Hora Sfakion (via Vrysses)	8	2hr	1 daily
Iraklio	8.80	1½hr	hourly
Margarites	3.80	30min	2 daily Mon-Fri
Moni Arkadiou	3.10	40min	up to 3 daily
Omalos (for Samaria Gorge, via Hania)	14.30	1¾hr	2 daily
Plakias	5	1hr	2-5 daily
Preveli	5	1¼hr	2 daily

MONEY

National Bank (Kountouriotou 129-131; ⌚8am-2.30pm Mon-Thu, to 2pm Fri, ATM 24hr)

POST

Post Office (☎28310 22303; Moatsou 19; ⌚7.30am-8.30pm Mon-Fri) Accepts letters and parcels.

TOURIST INFORMATION

You'll find a **tourist information office** (www.rethymno.guide; Rethymno Old Port; ⌚9am-2.30pm Mon-Fri) at the Venetian Harbour, and a smaller **kiosk** (www.rethymno.guide; Plateia Martyron; ⌚9am-2.30pm Mon-Fri) just south of Porta Guora. Both offer local maps and regional information and their website is also useful.

TRAVEL AGENCIES

Cool Holidays (☎28310 35567; www.coolholidays.gr; Melissinou 2; ⌚9am-8pm) Helpful office that handles boat and plane tickets, hires out cars and motorcycles, and books excursions.

Getting There & Away

BOAT

Seajets (☎21041 21001; www.seajets.gr) runs a ferry from Rethymno's marina on Tuesday and Saturday at 8am to Santorini (€69, 2¼ hours), Ios (€70, 3½ hours), Naxos (€78, four hours) and Mykonos (€74, five hours). A car is an additional €60 to €65. A service to Piraeus was also due to be launched from mid-2019; check the website.

BUS

The **bus station** (☎28310 22785, 28310 22212; Kefalogiannidon; 📶) is at the western edge of the centre. Services are reduced at weekends and outside high season. Consult KTEL (www.e-ktel.com) for the latest schedule.

CAR & MOTORCYCLE

Auto Moto Sport (☎6945771933, 28310 24858; www.automotosport.com.gr; Sofokli Venizelou 48; bicycle/car per day from €8/32; ⌚7.30am-10pm) Hires out bikes, cars and motorbikes.

Getting Around

Rethymno's centre is wonderfully compact and best explored on foot. When visiting outlying areas, a **taxi** (Kountouriotou 12) or hire car is your best bet. For bicycle hire, head to Cool Holidays or Auto Moto Sport.

WEST OF RETHYMNO

The villages southwest of Rethymno, in the foothills of the Lefka Ori (White Mountains), make for a lovely afternoon drive. The main destination is the mountain village of Argyroupoli, built on an ancient settlement and famous for its springs and waterfalls. The road also passes through Episkopi, a pretty market town with winding lanes and traditional houses.

Argyroupoli Αργυρούπολη

POP 450

Located 25km southwest of Rethymno, Argyroupoli is built on the ruins of the ancient city of Lappa, one of the most important Roman cities in western Crete, though very few remnants of it survive. Argyroupoli's network of atmospheric cobblestone alleyways lined with Venetian-era stone houses and Byzantine churches makes it a lovely place to stroll. As it's in the foothills of the Lefka Ori, the town is a useful gateway to some fine hiking trails.

At the bottom of the town is a watery oasis formed by springs from the Lefka Ori that keep the temperature markedly cooler here than on the coast, making it a good place to escape the summer heat. Running through aqueducts, washing down walls, seeping from stones and pouring from spigots, the gushing springs supply water for the entire city of Rethymno.

Sights

Argyroupoli is divided into an upper town and a lower town. Most historical sights are near the main square at the top, while the springs and tavernas are at the bottom.

Necropolis HISTORIC SITE

Ancient Lappa's cemetery lies north of the town and is reached via a signed 1.5km footpath from the main square. Hundreds of tombs have been cut into the rock cliffs here, especially around the Chapel of the Five Virgins. The path leads on to a plane tree that is said to be 2000 years old.

Upper Town

Begin your exploration in the main square, dominated by the stately 17th-century Venetian church of **Agios Ionnis**. Carry on up the cobbled road, passing the crumbling remains of buildings set next to brightly painted homes. Exploring the riddle of alleyways, you'll find ancient Venetian columns and olive presses.

On your left, watch for a **Roman portal** with the inscription *Omnia Mundi Fumus*

WORTH A TRIP

A MODEL FARM

Embedded in rolling hills near the village of Adele, about 13km southeast of Rethymno, **Agreco Farm** (☎28310 72129; www.agreco.gr; Adelianos Kampos; tour & lunch or dinner from €38; ⏲11am-10pm May-Oct) is a replica of a 17th-century estate and a showcase of centuries-old, organic and ecofriendly farming methods. It uses mostly traditional machinery, including a donkey-driven olive press, a watermill and a wine press. Call ahead to make sure it's open.

You'll also find small shops selling local produce and artwork, plus a mini-zoo featuring *kri-kri* (Cretan goats), wild boar and bantam chickens.

The farm is usually open from May to October, but private events, such as weddings or baptisms, often keep it closed to the public. Normally, farm tours culminate in a 30-course **Cretan feast** in the taverna. Most of the dishes are prepared with produce, dairy and meat grown on the farm.

If you're more the hands-on type, enquire in advance for upcoming **farm days**, when visitors are invited to participate in traditional agricultural activities. Depending on the time of year, you could find yourself shearing a sheep, milking a goat, making cheese, pressing grapes with your feet or baking bread using hand-picked, freshly stoneground flour; see the website for the schedule. This is followed by a buffet-style Harvest Festival Lunch. Reservations are essential for the farm tour and the Sunday experience.

If you're just stopping by during the day, you can do an independent **tour** (€5) and enjoy a drink in the *kafeneio* (coffeehouse).

et Umbra (All things in this world are smoke and shadow).

At the T-junction, head right to the **Church of St Paraskevi**, where the lid of a baby's sarcophagus now serves as the entrance step to the courtyard. Then head left, looping past the atmospheric 13th-century **Church of Panagia Barotsiani**, to reach an impressive 7000-piece Roman **mosaic floor** from the 1st century BC. The road then returns you to the square.

A further 1.5km north of town is the enchanting necropolis of **Ancient Lappa**, with evocative ancient Roman cliff-carved tombs among the forest. It's easily accessed on foot or by car.

Lower Town

Heading downhill from the main square, then taking your first main left will get you to the tavernas clustered around the springs in the lower village. Towering chestnut and plane trees and luxuriant vegetation create a shady, restful spot for lunch among the waterfalls and fountains that have been incorporated into all the tavernas. It's especially lovely on a summer night. Aside from the tavernas, you'll find a 17th-century water-driven fulling machine, once used to thicken cloth by moistening and beating it, as well as the overgrown remains of a Roman bath and St Mary's Church, built atop a temple dedicated to Poseidon.

Sleeping & Eating

The upper town has a few cafes, but for something more memorable head down to the springs, where a series of tavernas sit among the shaded glen and water features. Local specialities here are farm-raised trout and sturgeon. Lamb and pork, spit-roasted over olive wood, are good non-piscine choices.

Foodies shouldn't miss Garden Arkoudenas (p136), 4.5km north of Argyroupoli.

★Arcus Villas BOUTIQUE HOTEL €€
(☎28312 00201; www.arcus.com.gr; ste €110-120, apt from €180; ❄@🛜🏊) In the heart of the upper town, this traditional 14th-century Venetian home has been given a plush new lease on life. Each of the five suites has kitchenette, Jacuzzi bathtub and stone fireplace; and some sleep up to six. Barbecue in the garden next to the pool and feel miles away from anywhere.

Shopping

Lappa Avocado Shop COSMETICS
(☎6936744528, 28310 81070; www.lappa-avocado.gr; ⏲10am-7.30pm mid-Apr–late Oct) Across the street from the remains of Ancient Lappa and under the stone archway, you'll find the Lappa Avocado Shop. It sells organic cold-pressed avocado oil and a range

WORTH A TRIP

GARDEN OF CULINARY BLISS

One of the most enjoyable places to experience traditional Cretan cuisine and hospitality is **Garden Arkoudenas** (O Kipos Tis Arkoudenas; 28310 61607; Episkopi; mains €10-18; 1pm-late), a vibrant taverna set among fruit trees and adjoining farmland. Gregarious host Georgios (who appears in Yotam Ottolenghi's *Mediterranean Feast* documentary) will take you through the day's specials, cooked by his mother using superb organic produce sourced from their farm and the mountains.

It's worth setting aside a few hours here for a long, leisurely meal. Many dishes are prepared in the wood oven and feature delightful creative, modern twists. The signature dish is the colourful, flower-decorated salad, loaded with glistening tomatoes, pomegranates, avocado, cashews, pumpkin seeds and raisins. The complimentary dessert of homemade ice cream and chocolate cake is the best you'll get on the island. Seating is in the lovely courtyard or the cosy interior, where inquisitive horses will poke their heads in to see what's going on. It's located at the outskirts of Episkopi village, 4.5km north of Argyroupoli.

of avocado-based facial creams and body lotions.

Getting There & Away

From Monday to Friday three daily buses ply the route from Rethymno to Argyroupoli. Before you head out, be sure to check that there is in fact a return bus to Rethymno (€3.60, 40 minutes); generally, the last bus back goes at 3.30pm.

THE HINTERLAND & MT PSILORITIS

Rethymno's mountainous hinterland offers lots of options for interesting routes and detours. In a single day, you could easily combine a visit to the historic Moni Arkadiou with a poke around the pottery village of Margarites while also taking in the ruins of Ancient Eleftherna. Further east, the foothills of Mt Psiloritis beckon with a couple of charismatic caves and traditional villages like Axos and Anogia; the latter is also the launch pad for the precipitous drive up to the Nida Plateau.

Mili Gorge

A popular hike from Rethymno is through this lush, leafy **gorge** (Myli) that spans 4km along a scenic stream. Along the route you'll encounter stone houses from the old, abandoned village and 16th-century watermills dating from Venetian times. Also here is an atmospheric church built into the cliff face, accessed via the path to the right as you take the stairs down from the gorge's entrance. In summer, several tavernas open up on the other side of the river.

Mili Gorge is located 7km south of Rethymno, approximately a five-hour return hike or a short drive or bus trip. A public bus departs Rethymno every two hours (€1.50, 30 minutes), from 8.15am till the late afternoon. A taxi charges around €10 one way.

Chromonastiri

Military Museum of Chromonastiri MUSEUM

(28310 75135; Chromonastiri; adult/child & student €3/free; 9am-3pm Tue-Fri, 10am-2pm Sun) Offering a sobering account of the Battle of Crete – one of WWII's most infamous battles, which was waged in 1941 in this very area – is this small war museum in the village of Chromonastiri, 10km south of Rethymno. It provides a day-by-day account of the conflict, mixed with graphic imagery and displays of the belongings of Allied and German soldiers. There's also video footage of the dramatic German paratrooper invasion.

It's run by the Greek military, so soldiers in uniform double as tour guides. The museum also covers the 1821 Hellenic revolution, and the building itself is of interest as the 17th-century residence of a Venetian nobleman.

To get here, take a public bus from Rethymno (€1.50, 30 minutes, every two hours from 8.15am); otherwise, Rethymno's hop-on, hop-off tourist bus passes by. A taxi costs €10 one way. Most visitors combine it with a trip to nearby Mili Gorge, 3km north of the museum.

Moni Arkadiou
Μονή Αρκαδίου

The 16th-century **Arkadi Monastery** (☎28310 83136; Arkadi; €3; ⏰9am-8pm Jun-Sep, to 7pm Apr, May & Oct, to 5pm Nov, to 4pm Dec-Mar), 23km southeast of Rethymno, has deep significance for Cretans. As the site where hundreds of cornered locals massacred both themselves and invading Turks, it's a stark and potent symbol of resistance and considered a spark plug in the island's struggle towards freedom from Turkish occupation.

Arkadiou's impressive Venetian church (1587) has a striking Renaissance facade topped by an ornate triple-belled tower. The grounds include a small museum and the old wine cellar where the gunpowder was stored.

In November 1866, massive Ottoman forces arrived to crush island-wide revolts. Hundreds of Cretan men, women and children fled their villages to find shelter at Arkadiou. However, far from being a safe haven, the monastery was soon besieged by 2000 Turkish soldiers. Rather than surrender, the entrapped locals blew up stored gunpowder kegs, killing everyone, Turks included. One small girl miraculously survived and lived to a ripe old age in a village nearby. A bust of this woman and another of the abbot who lit the gunpowder are outside the monastery not far from the old windmill – now an **ossuary** with skulls and bones of the 1866 victims neatly arranged in a glass cabinet.

Four to five buses arrive here each weekday (two to three at weekends) from Rethymno (€3.10, 40 minutes), leaving you about 90 minutes for your visit before returning.

Once a hamlet whose olives supplied nearby Moni Arkadiou, **Kapsaliana Village** (☎28310 83400; www.kapsalianavillage.gr; Kapsaliana; incl breakfast s from €105, d €180-288, ste €265-415; P❄📶🏊) has now been entirely converted into charming, stylish villas. The 12 original and 10 new rooms offer ultracomfy beds, fireplaces and view-filled verandas. The ambience is peaceful, there's a sparkling pool, and the restaurant serves expertly prepared organic meals.

The olive mill closed in 1955, leaving the village abandoned until its architect owner acquired the site in the 1970s to embark on this ambitious project. There's a museum inside the original factory with displays of olive presses and other agricultural items.

Margarites Μαργαρίτες
POP 300

Tiny Margarites, 26km southeast of Rethymno, is famous for its pottery, a tradition that can be traced back to Minoan times. The village has only one road, and no bank or post office, but it has more than 20 ceramics stores and studios. Most studios source their clay by hand (the area is known for its clay), and offer unique, bright and good-quality usable pieces. This is the perfect place to pick up a keepsake.

If possible, try to avoid mornings and lunchtime, when droves of tour buses flood the town. By afternoon all is calm, and you can explore the atmospheric alleyways, wander through the studios and enjoy wonderful valley views from the eucalyptus-lined taverna terraces on the main square.

Sleeping & Eating

★**Kouriton House** BOUTIQUE HOTEL €€
(☎6945722052, 28310 55828; www.kouritonhouse.gr; Tzanakiana; r incl breakfast €60-75; ❄@📶) Bunches of dried herbs and flowers dangling from the wood-beamed ceiling welcome you to this gem on the northern outskirts of Margarites in Tzanakiana. The beautifully restored stone manor was built in 1750 and each of its atmospheric rooms feels like something out of a folk museum, but with the modern comforts of a kitchenette, wi-fi, TV and air-con.

Owner Anastasia Friganaki has a wealth of local knowledge and demonstrates traditional methods of making honey, picking herbs and greens, and cooking Cretan and Minoan cuisine.

Mandalos CRETAN €
(☎28340 92294; mains €5-8; ⏰8.30am-late Mar-Oct) On the shady main square, Mandolos is a well-regarded taverna. Dig into big portions of local standards like slow-cooked

RETHYMNO'S TOP FIVE HISTORICAL SITES

- Moni Arkadiou (p137)
- Fortezza (p119)
- Moni Preveli (p151)
- Melidoni Cave (p141)
- Late Minoan Cemetery of Armeni (p145)

ROAD TRIP > TOURING THE AMARI VALLEY

The Amari Valley is a quilt of unspoilt villages punctuated by Byzantine churches and framed by olive groves and orchards. Mt Psiloritis looms grandly above the landscape. You'll need a good map to navigate around here; a map app on your phone or GPS will do the trick. Given that the villages here have tight, narrow, one-way lanes, hiring a small to medium-sized car will generally make life easier.

❶ Moni Arkadiou

Starting in Rethymno, begin with a visit to the ever-impressive **Moni Arkadiou** (p137). To reach it, head east from Rethymno, take the turn for Adele and follow the signs.

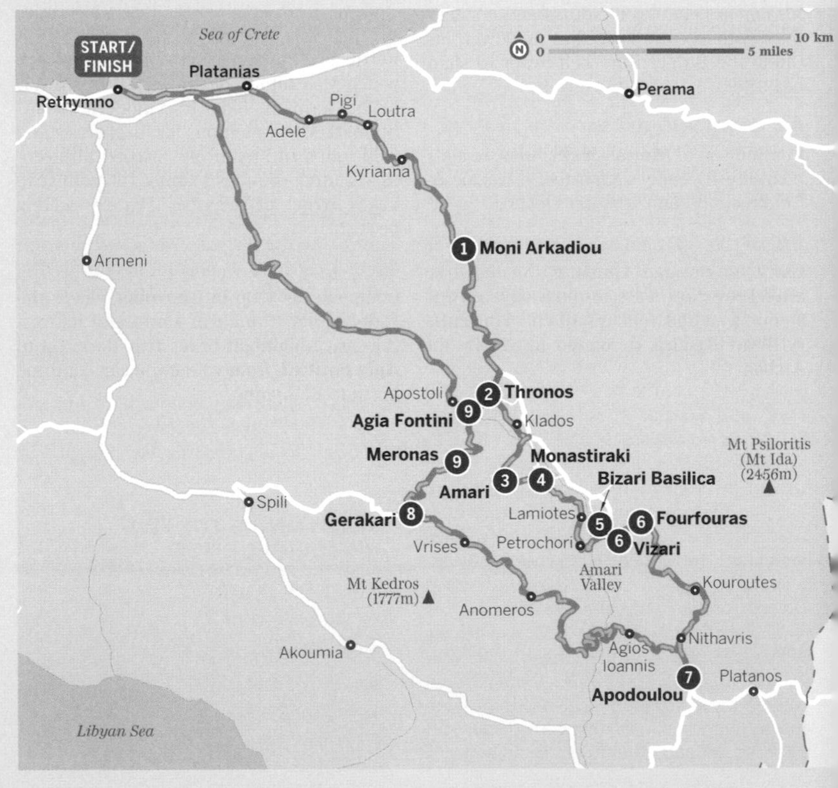

One day 93 miles / 150km

Great for... History & Culture

Best Time to Go Spring for cherry blossoms in Gerakari

❷ Thronos

Continue south to **Thronos**, whose Agia Panagia has extraordinary, if faded, 14th-century frescoes (the key is available at the cafe next door, whose owner will give you a quick rundown). The mosaics on its floor are even older, remnants of the 4th-century basilica that Agia Panagia was built upon. Drop by nearby Taverna Aravanes for wonderful valley views, good local info and traditional Cretan food that's cooked in a wood-fired oven; cooking classes (€6 per person) can also be arranged. From here, head downhill and turn left for Fourfouras.

❸ Amari

Follow the signs to **Amari**, an enchanting medley of Venetian buildings and a square filled with cafes and overflowing flowerpots. Climb the 19th-century bell tower to share beautiful views with the pigeons.

❹ Monastiraki

Continue on to **Monastiraki**, home to a Minoan site. It's badly signposted, so ask locally for directions, and keys if it's locked.

❺ Bizari Basilica

Carry on through Lamiotes, turning east after Petrochori. Pass through olive groves, stopping at the remains of the 7th-century Bizari Basilica, destroyed in 824 by the Arabs.

❻ Vizari & Fourfouras

In **Vizari**, visit olive-woodworking shops, then head east to pretty **Fourfouras**, where trails climb up Mt Psiloritis and you can refuel at the petrol station and bakery.

❼ Apodoulou

Head south to **Apodoulou**, for the ruins of the manor of Kalitsa Psaraki, named for a girl abducted by Turks and rescued by an English traveller (who then married her). Also here are more stone remains, of a Minoan settlement. Follow a dirt track west of town to Agios Georgios, with its still-colourful 17th-century frescoes.

❽ Gerakari

Return north, taking the turn for Agios Ioannis, through the western valley. Turn north for Anomeros and on to **Gerakari**, which was totally destroyed during WWII by the Germans. Today it's a modern, colourful market town famous for its cherries and wild tulips and its nicely frescoed 13th-century Church of Agios Ioannis. Its main strip has a string of tavernas if you're feeling peckish.

❾ Meronas & Agia Fontini

Complete the loop in **Meronas**, where the 14th-century Church of Maria and its frescoes are a highlight of the trip. Carry on to **Agia Fontini**, from where you can continue north to Rethymno.

goat while relaxing under the plane trees, drinking wine and taking in the countryside views.

Shopping

Keramion CERAMICS
(☎28340 92135, 6976332651; www.keramion.gr; ⊙9am-7pm Apr-Oct, by appointment Nov-Mar) Much of George and Marinki's pottery is created using Minoan techniques and designs and is fired in wood, resulting in a brown finish. (The red finish is achieved by using electricity.) The clay is of such fine quality that it needs only one firing and no glazing, the outside having been smoothed with a pebble.

Along with its signature Minoan-inspired ceramics, its whimsical hot-air balloons are a big seller.

Ilys CERAMICS
(☎28340 92440; ⊙10am-9pm Apr-Oct, to 6pm Nov-Mar) This gallery is an explosion of colour. Brightly glazed bowls, plates, light fixtures, raki cups and other small (and not so small) keepsakes line the shelves. Watch Manolis at work at his wheel, from where he's happy to share his local knowledge.

Gallios Ceramic Art CERAMICS
(☎28340 92304; https://galliosceramicart-potteryworkshop.business.site; ⊙9am-7pm) Down a side road at the top of the village (look for the sign 'Ceramic Art'), Konstantinos Gallios

WORTH A TRIP

ANCIENT ELEUTHERNA

About 7km east of Moni Arkadiou (p137), the archaeological site of **Ancient Eleutherna** (Αρχαία Ελεύθερνα; ☎28340 92501; http://en.mae.com.gr/archaeological-site; Eleutherna; necropolis adult/senior/student €4/2/free, with museum €6/3/free, acropolis free; ⊙necropolis 10am-6pm May-Oct, acropolis 24hr year-round) is a Dorian-built settlement that was among the most important in the 8th and 7th centuries BC, and also experienced heydays in Hellenistic and Roman times. Excavations have been ongoing since 1985 and archaeologists continue to make new finds all the time.

The 2010 discovery of the gold-adorned remains of a woman in a 2700-year-old double tomb made international news. The excavation of the tomb of a high priestess and three acolytes a year earlier prompted the Archaeological Institute of America to include Eleutherna in its Top 10 Discoveries of 2009.

The most easily accessible section of the site is the **acropolis**, with the remains of a tower atop a long, narrow ridge behind the Akropolis taverna. From here, an uneven, overgrown path leads down to vast and spooky **Roman cisterns** carved into the hills and, further along, to a **Hellenistic bridge**.

Down in the valleys flanking the ridge, active digs include the 2800-year-old **necropolis of Orthi Petra** to the west, where findings have produced evidence of human sacrifice. In summer you can enter the covered enclosure of the necropolis; follow the dirt road down a steep hill from the village of Eleutherna.

On the eastern slope, the remains of residential and public buildings from the Roman and Byzantine periods are being dug up. You can see these by following the main road east towards Margarites, turning off at the sign to the Church of the Sotiros and taking the dirt road just past this lovely Byzantine chapel.

Located 3km from the ruins, the accompanying modern **Museum of Ancient Eleutherna** (☎28340 92501; http://en.mae.com.gr/museum.html; Milopotamos; adult/senior/student €4/2/free, combined necropolis ticket €6/3/free, Sun free; ⊙10am-6pm Wed-Mon) contextualises the ancient city. Set over three rooms, the beautifully curated collection covers artefacts ranging from the early Iron Age and Minoan periods to Hellenic, Roman and Byzantine eras.

Its showpiece is the bronze shield with a protruding lion's head, unearthed from the Tomb of the Warriors and dating to the 8th century BC; it sits alongside a polished, gleaming replica of how it would have originally looked. Other artefacts excavated from the necropolis include beautiful ceramic vases and ornaments, detailed gold pendants and marble statuettes, all with exquisite workmanship and much that has retained its colour.

makes some beautiful pieces, displayed in his inviting gallery.

Getting There & Away

Two daily buses make the trip from Rethymno to Margarites (€3.80, 30 minutes) from Monday to Friday.

Perama to Anogia
Πέραμα Προς Ανώγεια

Melidoni Μελιδόνι

★**Melidoni Cave** CAVE
(Gerontospilios; www.melidoni.gr; adult/child under 12yr €4/free; 9am-8pm May-Sep, to 7pm Apr, Oct & Nov) About 2km outside the village of Melidoni is this stunning cathedral-like cave, an evocative underworld of stalactites and stalagmites. A place of worship since Neolithic times, it also carries heavy historical significance as the site of a massacre in 1824 during the Turkish occupation. Here 370 villagers and 30 soldiers sought refuge from the Ottoman army; after a three-month siege, the Turks lit a fire and asphyxiated the people inside, including 340 women and children.

Wear decent walking shoes, as the cave is poorly lit and the ground uneven and slippery in places. You'll need to descend 70 steps into the cave. Also bring a sweater: at 24m below ground, the temperature never gets above 18°C.

Episkopi Επισκοπή

This charming village, 9km southeast of Melidoni, served as a bishopric under Venetian rule and is a maze of lanes lined with well-preserved stone mansions. Stop to admire the faded frescoes gracing the crumbling ruins of the 15th-century **Church of Episkopi**. Also look for the Venetian **water fountain** next to the bridge at the end of the town.

Zoniana Ζωνιανά

Sfendoni Cave CAVE
(28340 61869; www.zoniana.gr; Zoniana; adult/child 10-18yr/under 10yr incl tour €5/4/free; 10am-5pm daily Apr-Oct, 10.30am-2.30pm Sat & Sun Nov-Mar) Here guided tours take you 270m below ground and through seven chambers with such fanciful names as Sanctuary of the Fairy and Zeus' Palace. All teem with illuminated stalagmites and stalactites shaped into drapery, organ pipes, domes, curtains, waves and other strange formations. The cave is home to more than 400 bats, who may greet you if you visit in the morning.

Tours run roughly every 45 minutes and take about 40 minutes. A 150m-long walkway makes the cave accessible to everyone.

There's a decent cafe to help pass the time if you need to wait for the next tour. From Monday to Friday two daily buses make the trip out from Rethymno (€6, one hour, 5.30am and 2pm).

WORTH A TRIP

OLIVE OIL FACTORY

If you're out this way for Melidoni Cave, tack on a visit to the nearby **Paraschakis Olive Oil Factory** (28340 22039, 6973863551; www.paraschakis.gr; Melidoni Geropotamou; 9am-6pm Mon-Sat Apr-Nov) for a lowdown on the olive oil production process. Its welcoming American-Greek owner, Joanna, will guide you through the evolution of olive-oil pressing, from donkey-driven methods to current-day machinery. The factory is part of a local co-op used by farmers to convert their yearly harvest into liquid gold. Local olive oil, raki and other goods are available for purchase.

Axos Αξός

The village of Axos has the kind of lazy Cretan ambience that has made it a popular stop for tour buses. During the day the village is quiet, but at night the tavernas with open-air terraces are hopping.

Museum of Wooden Sculptures MUSEUM
(6937691387; www.woodenmuseum.gr; Axos; adult/child €5/3; 9am-8pm) Fronted by a massive sculpture of Hercules killing the lion, this private museum in the village of Axos is essentially a showcase of the work of self-taught artist Georgios Koutantos. An enthusiastic and voluble man, he'll happily show visitors around his workshop and explain the stories and cultural references behind each of his sculptures. He has completed over 100, each carved from local trees. None of the pieces is for sale.

The large-scale works, including an eagle with a 6m wingspan, are the most impressive. Others depict family members, often in a highly personal fashion.

ANOGIA'S MUSICAL LEGACY

Anogia is known for its stirring music and is the birthplace of a large number of Crete's best-known musicians. The main instrument is the *lyra*, a three-sided, pear-shaped string instrument played sitting down and often accompanied by lutes and guitars. Local boy Nikos Xylouris (1936–80) took the world by storm with this instrument and his handlebar moustache, and is still considered Crete's best singer and *lyra* player.

Nikos' somewhat eccentric brother Psarantonis (b 1942) took over the reins and still has an international following for his haunting voice. A third brother, Giannis (Psarogiannis), is Greece's most accomplished lute player.

Psarantonis' charismatic son, Giorgos Xylouris (Psaragiorgis; b 1965), followed in his father's footsteps and is known for playing the lute as a solo instrument rather than in its traditional accompaniment role. Giorgos' sister, Niki, is one of the few female Cretan singers. Released in 2015, the Greek film *A Family Affair* is an intimate portrait of the Xylouris family and their strong connection with traditional Cretan music.

Other notable musicians from Anogia include the *lyra* players Manolis Manouras, Nikiforos Aerakis, Vasilis Skoulas and Giorgos Kalomiris.

The talented but capricious Giorgos Dramountanis, also known as Loudovikos ton Anogion (Ludwig from Anogia; b 1951), brings his brand of folksy, ballad-style Cretan compositions to audiences all over Greece. He's also the director of the annual **Yakinthia Festival** (www.yakinthia.gr), with open-air concerts held in an amphitheatre on a plateau at the foot of Mt Psiloritis about 11km from Anogia for a week in late July.

Sleeping & Eating

★Enagron Ecotourism Village RESORT €€
(☎28340 61611; www.enagron.gr; Axos Mylopotamou; studios/apt incl breakfast from €87/108; ⊙restaurant 2-4pm & 7-10pm; P ❄ ☜ ≋) This working farm offers an immersion in the traditional Cretan way of life. Its attractive villas, laid out like a small village, have elegantly rustic rooms featuring beamed ceilings, stone walls and fireplaces as well as kitchenettes. Three-night minimum stay. The restaurant serves Cretan dishes prepared with farm-foraged ingredients, and there's a delightful program of daily activities (included in rates).

Activities range from guided hikes to the mountains and villages, cooking classes and cheese- and bread-making workshops to birdwatching and botanical walks, plus donkey rides for the kids. The farm also provides excellent hiking maps if you want to go solo, and offers free bike hire and recommended cycling trails. Be sure to allow time to laze by the luxurious infinity pool.

Nonguests are welcome to visit the farm and its small museum, and its restaurant is highly recommended. Book ahead.

Anogia Ανώγεια

POP 2500

Perched beside Mt Psiloritis, 37km southwest of Iraklio, Anogia is a wonderful spot to slow things down and glimpse authentic rural Cretan life. It's the perfect base for excursions up to the Nida Plateau (1400m) and Zeus' cave.

Here locals cling to time-honoured traditions, and it's the norm to see men gossiping in the *kafeneia* (coffeehouses), flicking *komboloïa* (worry beads) in their hand, and dressed in traditional black shirts with *vraka* (baggy pants) tucked into black boots. Elderly women, meanwhile, keep busy selling traditional woven blankets and embroidered textiles. The town's turbulent history – in WWII and under Ottoman rule – has instilled a legacy of rebelliousness and a determination to express an undiluted Cretan character.

The town's also famous for its stirring music and has spawned many of Crete's best-known musicians, such as Nikos Xylouris.

Sights

Armi Square MEMORIAL
This peaceful square is anchored by a statue of an unknown solider that honours Anogia's role in WWII. As the main centre of resistance against Nazi occupation, the town was to pay a terrible price. In retaliation for the townspeople's aid in sheltering Allied troops and assistance in the kidnapping of a Nazi general, the Germans razed Anogia to the ground in 1944 and massacred its entire male population.

The monument is also dedicated to the struggle under Ottoman rule, during which Anogia was decimated in 1822 and again in 1867. In mid-August, public events take place to commemorate this sombre history, with a variety of traditional music and dance performances.

Also in the square is the 14th-century **Church of St John the Baptist**, notable for its original, though faded, Byzantine frescoes.

Museum of Grylios MUSEUM
(☎28340 31593; donations welcome) A short walk uphill from the lower village square, this humble museum presents the paintings and sculptures of Anogia-born folk artist Alkiviadis Skoulas (1900–97), aka Grylios. Many works depict local war scenes; there are few English explanations, but the paintings largely speak for themselves. It's now run by Grylios' son Yiorgos, who is known to hold impromptu *lyra* concerts. Opening hours are unpredictable; if the museum's not open, knock next door or ask at the square for Yiorgos.

Nikos Xylouris' Home NOTABLE BUILDING
(9.30am-9pm) FREE Crete's most famous musician, the *lyra* player and singer Nikos Xyouris, was born in this modest house on the lower village square, and today his family maintains an endearing collection of posters, letters and other memorabilia related to him.

There are also gig posters of his nephew Giorgos Xylouris, an accomplished current-day musician who tours the globe with his outfit Xylouris White.

Sleeping

Anogia has a handful of comfortable pensions, and there's a sizeable mountain resort a few klicks outside town on the road up to Mt Psiloritis.

Hotel Aristea HOTEL €
(☎6972410486, 28340 31459; www.hotelaristea.gr; Michaeli Stavrakaki; d/apt from €35/85; P) Run by the chatty and charming Aristea, this small inn offers sweeping valley views from balconies attached to five fairly basic but spotless and comfortable enough rooms. The four split-level apartments in a next-door annexe are more modern and have kitchen and a wood-burning fireplace for those chilly mountain nights. There's also a common kitchen with full cooking facilities.

Delina Mountain Resort RESORT €€
(☎28340 31701; www.delina.gr; d incl breakfast from €65;) About 1km outside Anogia, en route to the Nida Plateau, this sprawling resort with spacious, modern rooms exudes calm. If you're planning on hiking Mt Psiloritis it's a great place to unwind and relax your weary muscles in the sauna, pool or spa, or in your private in-room Jacuzzi. All rooms have verandas with views to the mountain.

The resort is owned by renowned local *lyra* player Vasilis Skoulas, who also gives the occasional concert; his gold records and memorabilia are displayed at Delina's traditional taverna. Also at the resort is a Venetian-era lake and a scenic chapel that offers wonderful mountain vistas.

Eating

This is a town for real food-lovers, with plenty of lively tavernas doing a roaring trade in traditional Cretan mountain food. It's most famous for *ofto* (a flame-cooked lamb or goat), which you'll see outside many tavernas – they're usually fired up from 2pm.

Taverna Aetos CRETAN €
(☎28340 31262; 13is Avgoustou 1944 17; grills €7-9; noon-11pm) This traditional taverna in the upper village has a giant charcoal grill out the front and fantastic mountain views out the back. On offer are such regional specialities as *ofto*, and spaghetti cooked in stock with cheese.

Arodamos CRETAN €
(☎28340 31100; www.arodamos.gr; Tylisos-Anogia Rd; mains €6-10.50; 10am-10pm;) This big restaurant in a modern stone house in the upper village is highly regarded for its hearty mountain fare and gracious hospitality. Local specialities include the flame-teased lamb or goat *(ofto)* and the deceptively simple but tasty dish of spaghetti cooked in stock and topped with *anthotiros* (white cheese). If you're ordering mezedhes, be sure to get the *dakos* (Cretan rusks).

Ta Skalomata CRETAN €
(☎28340 31316; 13is Avgoustou 1944; mains €5-12; 8am-midnight;) In the upper village, Skalomata has provided sustenance to locals and travellers for about 40 years. When you peel your eyes away from the view through panoramic windows, train your focus on the great grilled meats (the lamb is tops!), the homemade wine and bread, and the tasty meatless fare such as zucchini with cheese.

LOCAL KNOWLEDGE

PEAK-BAGGING MT PSILORITIS

The classic route to the summit of Mt Psiloritis follows the east–west E4 European Path from the Nida Plateau and in summer can be done in a round trip of about seven hours. While you don't need to be an alpine mountaineer, it's a long slog and the views from the summit may be marred by haze or cloud cover. En route, occasional *mitata* (round, stone shepherd's huts) provide shelter should the weather turn inclement, while at the summit there's a small, twin-domed chapel. The best map is the Anavasi 1:30,000 *Psiloritis (Mt Ida)*. For trekking conditions and general advice, get in touch with the visitor centre in Anogia prior to departure.

Backcountry skiing is possible at Mt Psiloritis from December to March; contact the Cretan Ski School (p121) for equipment hire, lessons and guided trips.

Staff offer a welcoming greeting, but given its popularity with tour buses there's not always time for the customary raki-and-dessert finish.

Information

An ATM and the post office are in the upper village.

Psiloritis Visitor Centre (AKOMM; 28340 31402; www.psiloritisgeopark.gr; 8am-4pm Mon-Fri) Anogia's well-run visitor centre offers maps, walking trails and general info on Mt Psiloritis. Its website has comprehensive coverage of the Nature Park of Psiloritis, including a PDF of its *Psiloritis Tourist Guide*.

Getting There & Away

From Monday to Saturday there are three daily buses from Iraklio (€4.10, one hour), and one on Sunday. From Rethymno (€6, 1¼ hours) two buses depart daily Monday to Friday.

Mt Psiloritis
Όρος Ψηλορείτης

At 2456m, Mt Psiloritis, also known as Mt Ida, is Crete's highest mountain. At its eastern base is the Nida Plateau (1400m), a wide, fertile expanse reached via a paved 21km-long road from Anogia. It passes several round stone *mitata* (traditional shepherds' huts used for cheesemaking and shelter) as well as the turnoff to the highly regarded (but rarely open) Skinakas Observatory.

From the Nida Plateau it's a short walk to the Ideon Cave (1538m) where, according to legend, the god Zeus was reared (although Dikteon Cave in Lasithi makes the same claim). Also on the plateau is Andartis, an impressive landscape sculpture honouring the WWII Cretan resistance.

If you're planning on tackling Psiloritis from a destination other than Anogia, visit www.psiloritisgeopark.gr for the comprehensive online *Psiloritis Tourist Guide*. Be sure to bring a warm jacket, even if the weather's fine, as conditions can change quickly.

Sights

★Ideon Cave CAVE

(P) FREE Although just a huge and fairly featureless hole in the ground, Ideon has sacred importance in mythology as the place where Zeus was reared by his mother, Rhea, to save him from the clutches of his child-devouring father, Cronos. (Some also believe it's where he died and is buried.) Ideon is on Mt Psiloritis about 15km from Anogia; it's a 1km uphill walk along a rocky path from the parking lot to the entrance.

Ideon was a place of worship from the late 4th millennium BC onward, and many artefacts, including gold jewellery and bronze shields, statuettes and other offerings to Zeus, have been unearthed here. The rail track used for these archaeological digs is still here.

In winter (and sometimes as late as May) the cave entrance can be blocked by snow, in which case it's easy enough to climb over the fence. However, for safety reasons, avoid clambering on the snow.

Skinakas Observatory OBSERVATORY

(in Iraklion 28103 94238; http://skinakas.physics.uoc.gr; 6-11pm around full moon May-Sep) FREE Near the top of Mt Psiloritis, at 1750m, Skinakas Observatory is operated by the University of Crete and is the country's most significant stargazing vantage point, with two powerful telescopes. From May to September the site opens to the public once a month around the full moon (see the website for exact dates). There are presentations and a chance to look through the telescope.

Note that the road here is in poor condition, and often not passable if there's snow on the mountain.

Andartis – Partisan of Peace MONUMENT

FREE Right on the Nida Plateau, high on Mt Psiloritis, you can make out this sprawling landscape sculpture created by German artist Karina Raeck in 1991 to commemorate the Cretan resistance in WWII. The monument itself is a pile of local rocks arranged in such a way that it looks like an angel when seen from above. It's a flat and easy 1.25km walk out here.

Sleeping & Eating

Anogia has by far the best choice of lodging. Otherwise, keep an eye out for a trekking hostel that, at research time, was expected to open on the Nida Plateau in 2020.

At the time of research there was nowhere to buy food or drink along the road to the Nida Plateau, so pack a picnic. A taverna was expected to open on the plateau in 2020.

Information

The visitor centre in Anogia is your best starting point for Mt Psiloritis. At the time of research an info centre, due for completion in 2020, was being constructed at the Nida Plateau car park.

Getting There & Away

To reach Mt Psiloritis, you really need your own wheels. The views en route are stunning.

Buses run from Rethymno to Anogia (€6, 1¼ hours, twice daily on weekdays).

COAST TO COAST

From Rethymno, the fastest and most direct route to the southern coast is via Armeni and Spili. For a more leisurely pace, travel via the almost ridiculously pastoral Amari Valley, a part of Crete that seems frozen in time.

Armeni Αρμένοι

Late Minoan Cemetery of Armeni ARCHAEOLOGICAL SITE

(28310 29975, 28210 44418; Rethymno-Agia Galini Rd; adult/concession/child €2/1/free; 8am-3pm Tue-Sun; P) Wandering around this leafy cemetery created by the Minoans between 1600 and 1150 BC, you can practically sense the presence of uncounted souls once buried in the more than 200 rock-cut tombs. Today, the tombs' *dromos* (long, sunken corridors) leading to damp chambers are open for exploration – tombs 159 and 200 are especially impressive. Some of the grave offerings unearthed at Armeni, including pottery, bronze ornaments, weapons, jewellery and a boar's-tusk helmet, are now at Rethymno's Archaeological Museum (p119).

The ticket office is rarely attended, so you can often just walk in. The site is a 15-minute drive south of Rethymno.

Alekos Kafeneio TAVERNA €

(28310 41185; Armeni; mains €5-10; noon-midnight) An excellent choice for lunch, this little taverna has a small but superb daily selection of traditional *mayirefta* (ready-cooked meals). There's no menu, but staff will take you downstairs to the kitchen and let you choose from simmering pots of mountain snails, slow-cooked meat, octopus and vegetable stews. The homemade sheep's-milk cheese and ice cream alone are worth visiting for.

Spili Σπήλι

POP 630

Spili is a pretty mountain village and shutterbug favourite thanks to its cobbled streets, big old plane trees and flower-festooned whitewashed houses. Most people just stop for lunch on a coast-to-coast trip, but it's well worth staying a day or two to explore the trails weaving through the local mountains. The rugged Kourtaliotiko Gorge, which culminates at the famous palm grove of Preveli Beach (p151), starts not far south of town.

Sights

Maravel Garden GARDENS

(28320 22056; www.maravelspili.gr; 8am-8pm Mar-Nov) FREE On the western outskirts of town are these botanical gardens filled with an aromatic variety of plant species from Crete and across the globe. You're free to wander and check out the herbs and medicinal plants staff use to distil essential oils and produce the organic products sold in the shop. The cafe has a deck overlooking the gardens and does a menu of light meals, homemade ice cream, herbal teas and superfood smoothies.

Call in advance for tours (€5), but usually they're for groups only. The garden's Maravel Shop (p146) in town has a larger stock of its products.

Folk Museum of Spili MUSEUM

(by donation; 10am-6pm Apr-Nov) Up a footpath at the northern end of town, this place is a treasure trove of local vintage artefacts. The giant loom or the coffee-bean roaster might catch your eye, or the shoemaker's room and the traditional kitchen from 220 years ago. Well maintained and run by the knowledgeable Manolis, this museum is worth hunting down.

Venetian Fountain FOUNTAIN

The main local attraction is this restored fountain that spurts water from 19 stone lion heads into a long trough. Fill up your own bottle with some of the island's best water. A walkway leads from the fountain uphill to the village's quiet and picturesque backstreets.

Monastery MONASTERY

(hours vary) Spili is a bishop's see (seat of a bishop), based at the massive modern monastery on the main road at the western end of town. You're free to walk around and admire the arched entryways, marble-floor courtyard, stunning valley views and opulently decorated church.

Sleeping

Spili has a couple of comfortable pensions and small hotels for those who wish to spend the night.

★Hotel Heracles PENSION €

(28320 22111, 6973667495; www.heracles-hotel.eu; s/d/tr/q €35/40/45/50;) These five balconied rooms are quiet, spotless and simply furnished, but it's the charming and softly spoken Heracles himself who makes the place so special. Intimately familiar with the area, he's happy to put you on to the right hiking trail, birdwatching site or hidden beach. Optional breakfasts (from €4.50) feature local eggs and an array of homemade marmalades.

Green Hotel HOTEL €

(28320 22225; www.maravelspili.gr; s/d/tr €30/35/40; Mar-Oct;) The 12 rooms here don't exactly fuel the imagination, but the hotel's centrally located on the main street and each room has a balcony. Optional breakfast is €5.

The owner also operates the Maravel Garden (p145).

Eating

You'll be spoilt for choice for places to eat in Spili, with a number of highly regarded tavernas doing traditional Cretan cuisine.

★Taverna Sideratico CRETAN €

(28320 22916; mains €8; noon-10pm Apr-Nov;) In an appealing location away from Spili's touristy centre, this delightful taverna sits on the main road 500m south of town. There's no menu, so you'll be guided through its mouthwatering array of *mayirefta* prepared by hard-working chef-owner-farmer Nico, who sources all ingredients from the immediate area. As well as slow-cooked meat dishes, its vegetarian meals are outstanding.

Cafe Platia CRETAN €

(697226668; www.spilicafeplatia.gr; mains €8-12; 9am-11pm Apr-Oct;) Perched above the Venetian fountain, this scenic taverna is run by a well-regarded husband-and-wife culinary team. It has a fairly basic menu, but its sunny terrace decorated with pot plants is a lovely setting in which to enjoy dishes such as homemade Cretan pie or grilled pork belly with fried potatoes.

Maria Kostas Taverna TAVERNA €

(28320 22436; https://taverna-maria-kostas.business.site; mains €6-9; 10am-10pm) Come here for the home cooking and dine on the patio hung with gourds and overflowing with flowers. You'll likely find Maria in the kitchen stuffing tomatoes and dishing up fantastic grills and casseroles. It's on the main road, at the northern end of town.

Yianni's CRETAN €

(28320 22707; mains €5.50-8; 11am-10pm) Just south of the Venetian fountain, this friendly place has a big roadside terrace, reliably good traditional cooking and a decent house red. Try the delicious rabbit in wine or the local mountain snails.

Shopping

Maravel Shop HEALTH & WELLNESS

(28320 22056; www.shop.maravelspili.gr; 9am-9pm) Along the main tourist drag is this store selling organic beauty products made using ingredients grown in its nearby garden (p145). There's an interesting assortment of herbal teas, essential oils, soaps (from donkey milk to watermelon), along with locally made wine and herb-infused raki, which are available for tastings.

Information

There are several ATMs and a post office on the main street. Most cafes and pensions offer free wi-fi.

Getting There & Away

Spili is on the Rethymno–Agia Galini bus route (€3.80, 30 minutes), which has up to five services daily.

SOUTHERN COAST

Rethymno's southern coast is bookended by the resort towns of Plakias and Agia Galini, which are linked by a string of marvellously isolated beaches, including the famous palm beach at Preveli. Massive summertime winds have spared the area from the tourism excesses that typify the northern coast. Approaching from the north, the scenery becomes increasingly dramatic and takes in marvellous views of the Libyan Sea. From the Rethymno–Agia Galini road, it's a fabulous drive through the rugged Kotsifou Gorge to Plakias. The road to Preveli travels via the equally spectacular Kourtaliotiko Gorge.

Plakias Πλακιάς

POP 300

Set beside a sweeping sandy crescent and accessed via two scenic gorges – Kotsifou and Kourtaliotiko – Plakias gets swarmed with package tourists in summer (when it can be very windy) but otherwise remains a laid-back indie travellers' favourite. While the village itself isn't particularly pretty, it's an excellent launch pad for regional excursions and hikes through olive groves, along seaside cliffs and to some sparkling hidden beaches.

Activities

Diving

Dive2gether DIVING

(☎28320 32313; www.dive2gether.com; dive packages incl gear from €120; ⏲8.30am-12.30pm & 2-7pm Apr-Oct;) A top-notch, Dutch-run operation in town with state-of-the-art equipment and super-high safety standards. Also runs one-on-one Discover Scuba Diving (€89) and Bubblemaker sessions for kids as young as eight. Snorkelling trips and hire are also available. Visit the website for full details.

Phoenix Diving Club DIVING

(☎28320 31335, 6932336525; www.phoenixdiveclub.com; 1 dive incl equipment from €53; ⏲9-11am & 5-8pm Mon-Sat) Crete's first PADI dive operator offers a heap of courses for all levels, and personalised trips to a multitude of dive sites. Also runs trips for snorkellers.

Plakias Boat Tours CRUISE

(☎28320 31229; www.plakiasboattours.gr; cruises from €15) When he's not cooking up seafood feasts at Tasomanolis (p149), Captain Tasos leads daily boat tours to Preveli and the beaches along Crete's southern coast. He also runs leisurely fishing trips or more full-scale deep-sea fishing, depending on your mood. For discounts, book directly through the taverna.

Kalypso Rock's Palace Dive Centre DIVING

(☎28310 74687; www.kalypsodivecenter.com; 1/2 dives incl gear from €42/80; ⏲9am-2pm & 5-8pm Apr-Oct) This PADI dive centre is based at spectacular Karavos Beach, about 5km south of town, but has an office in Plakias from where it offers free transfers. It runs open-water courses, night snorkelling trips and shore dives, among many ways of getting underwater.

Hiking

There are well-worn walking paths to the scenic villages of Selia, Moni Finika and Lefkogia, and a lovely walk along the Kourtaliotiko Gorge to Moni Preveli. An easy 30-minute uphill path to Myrthios begins just before the youth hostel.

Anso Travel HIKING

(☎6944755712, 28320 31444; www.ansotravel.com; ⏲9am-2pm & 6-10pm) For guided walks, including one to Preveli Beach that gets you back by boat. Also rents bikes (p150).

Horse Riding

Horseback Riding Plakias HORSE RIDING

(☎28320 32033; www.cretehorseriding.com; Damnoni; adult €30-100, child €15-25; ⏲8am-2pm & 4-8pm Apr-Oct) Set within olive groves outside Plakias, these family-run stables offer horse-riding tours along beaches and up into the surrounding mountains. With more than 30 horses and 11 routes, there's plenty to choose from, plus donkeys if you want to do it the Cretan way. Tours last one to four hours, and there's a whole string of ponies for children to ride.

Tours

Elena Tours TOURS
(☎6936371451, 28320 20465; tours from €45; ⏲9.30am-1.30pm & 6-9pm) Hop in Elena's minibus for an excursion into the less touristy side of the area. Hike through gorges, take boats to unheard-of beaches, visit ancient churches and meet locals in quaint villages. Each tour includes a maximum of eight people. The office is located in the centre of Plakias, just over the bridge.

Captain Lefteris Boat Cruises BOATING
(☎28320 31971, 6936806635; www.lbferries.gr; tours €15-39) In summer Baradakis Lefteris (owner-chef of the Smerna Bar) and his son Nikos run entertaining boat trips to nearby beaches such as Preveli (adult/child €15/8), Loutro (€39/20), and Agios Pavlos and Triopetra (€30/15). They also offer boat hire (€120 per day, excluding fuel).

Sleeping

Much of Plakias' accommodation is spread along its seafront promenade, ensuring that most folk get a sea view. Backpackers are looked after, too, with a pleasant hostel and a campground to choose from. Otherwise, there are plenty of good-value pensions as well as small hotel-resorts with swimming pools and restaurants.

★ **Plakias Youth Hostel** HOSTEL €
(☎28320 32118; www.yhplakias.com; dm €10-12; ⏲mid-Mar–Nov; P@🛜) This charismatic pad and 'Hoscar' winner for best Greek hostel is set in an olive grove about 500m from the beach. Serene and laid-back, it fosters an atmosphere of inclusiveness and good cheer that appeals to people of all ages and nationalities. There are six eight-bed dorms with fans, communal facilities, an outdoor kitchen and an honour-system fridge with cheap beers.

Friendly manager Uli is popular with guests and offers a heap of excellent local info and ideas for hikes. There are free beach towels and snorkels, a book exchange, and guitars that wait to be strummed. The hostel earns green points for recycling initiatives, composting and a herb garden that guests are free to pick from.

Its stamp-free postal service is based on an 18th-century system: postcards are put in a barrel and then hand-delivered by travellers if they're heading to that destination.

LOCAL KNOWLEDGE

BOOKWORM'S DELIGHT

In an unlikely location amid an olive grove is Plakias' multilingual **Lending Library** (⏲9.30am-12.30pm Sun-Fri). Staffed by expat volunteers, it operates on a subscription basis (€2 per month) that gives you access to its well-stocked selection of books and DVDs. It stays open later in summer, when alcoholic beverages are available. It's 300m beyond the youth hostel.

Gio-Ma PENSION €
(☎28320 31942, 694737793; www.gioma.gr; r from €40; ❄🛜) Located at the quiet end of town and fronted by a flower-filled balcony, the spacious self-contained rooms here are clean and comfortable, and feature fabulous sea views. Snag one of the upper units for postcard-perfect photos. The owners also run the waterfront taverna across the street.

Hotel Livikon HOTEL €
(☎28320 31216; www.hotel-livikon-plakias.com; d/tr €40/50; P❄🛜) This family-run affair was one of the first hotels in Plakias back in the 1970s, but the 10 impeccably kept, spotless and comfortable rooms barely reveal their age. All have a small kitchen and a balcony (get a beach-facing one). It's upstairs from an all-day cafe that also serves breakfast (items €5 to €9).

Plakias Suites APARTMENT €€
(☎28320 31680, 6975811559; www.plakiassuites.com; d €75-140; ⏲Mar–mid-Nov; P❄🛜👪) This stylish outpost has six two- and three-room apartments with contemporary aesthetics and zeitgeist-compatible touches such as large flat-screen TVs, supremely comfortable mattresses, a chic kitchen and a private balcony or patio. Staying here puts you within a whisker of the best stretch of local beach, albeit about 1km from the village centre.

Camping Apollonia CAMPGROUND €
(☎28320 31318, 28320 31507; camp sites adult/tent/caravan €6/4/5; ⏲May-Oct; 🛜🏊) You won't find much privacy here, but you can settle in under some olive and eucalyptus trees. Sites have cafeteria-style picnic tables, there's a big pool and pool bar, and the beach is your neighbour. It's on the main road into town.

LOCAL KNOWLEDGE

BEACHES IN & AROUND PLAKIAS

Though Plakias features 1.5km of beachfront, keep your expectations in check. For the best patch, head 200m south of the main drag, where you'll find a handful of bars, sunbeds and umbrellas. While the beach here is more crushed shell than powdery sand, its azure water is exquisite.

Between Plakias and Preveli Beach there are several secluded coves popular with freelance campers and nudists. **Damnoni Beach** is pleasant out of high season, despite being dominated by the giant Hapimag tourist complex.

To the west is **Souda**, a quiet beach with a couple of tavernas offering rooms. Continuing west, there are the low-key beach resorts of **Polyrizos-Koraka** (also known as Rodakino), with a handful of tavernas and a few small hotels scattered along a pleasant stretch of beach. The area is ideal if you want a quiet retreat at which to chill for a few days.

Alianthos Garden Hotel HOTEL €€
(28320 31280; www.alianthos.gr; s/d incl breakfast from €75/95;) Rooms at this modern hotel complex sparkle in breezy turquoise and come with high-end mattresses and flower-filled balconies, many with sea views. Common areas include a stylish bar, a pool, a library and a snooker table. A children's pool, games and a playground give it an edge with families.

Eating

There are plenty of tavernas and cafes catering to the tourist crowd, many with prime locations on the beach. Foodies will want to visit nearby Myrthios (p150), which has a renowned culinary scene.

Corner Souvlaki Creations GREEK €
(skewer/gyros €1.80/2.80; noon-late) Normally with *gyros* you're given the same ol' choice: chicken or pork, but here you can fill your pitta with anything from grilled lamb and prawns to mushroom to halloumi. There's even a dessert souvlaki, if that takes your fancy. Enjoy with a cold beer on the seafront terrace.

To Xehoristo GREEK €€
(28320 31214; sandwiches €2.80, mains €6-15; 11.30am-late) If the picture menu doesn't get you salivating, then the aroma emanating from the charcoal grill will likely do the trick. No matter whether you grab a quick *gyros* during a beach session or tuck into a full platter of grilled meat sliced off the rotisserie for dinner, you're in for a simple but tasty treat.

Tasomanolis SEAFOOD €€
(6979887749, 28320 31229; www.tasomanolis.gr; mains €7-16; noon-11pm;) Tasos and his Belgian wife, Lisa, preside over this nautical-themed family taverna towards the far end of town. Park yourself on the colourful patio to tuck into classic Greek grills and inspired daily specials like anchovy bruschetta, ouzo shrimp or the daily catch with wild greens. Children's menu available.

Enquire about their boat tours (p147).

Taverna Christos CRETAN €€
(28320 31472; mains €6-17; noon-late;) This established taverna has a romantic tamarisk-shaded terrace right next to the crashing waves, and lots of interesting dishes that you won't find everywhere, including home-smoked sea bass, black spaghetti with calamari, and lamb *avgolemono* with fresh pasta. Finish off with the orange pie.

Lysseos INTERNATIONAL €€
(28320 31479; dishes €8-18; 7-11pm May-Oct) This unfussy restaurant by the bridge has excellent homestyle cooking; try the pork in lemon sauce with almonds. It also does its bit for the international crowd, serving up goulash, shrimp cocktail and a fabulous chocolate cake.

Drinking & Nightlife

Cozy Backyard BAR
(5pm-late Apr-Oct) Down a side street off the main drag is this much-loved drinking hole with an intimate bar fronted by a patio under a palm tree. Jovial staff sling drinks – including the signature Cretan Cocktail, a fruity amaretto number topped with a mini Greek flag – to a tipsy crowd of holidaymakers.

Mes Tin Ammo Beach Bar BAR
(www.mes-tin-ammo-beach-bar.business.site; 10am-8pm Apr-Oct) Less is more is often the winning formula for a beach bar, and here at

DON'T MISS

SCENIC DRIVE: KOTSIFOU GORGE

Narrow and lush, this gorge makes for a jaw-droppingly beautiful drive. Blanketed in wildflowers in spring, the road north from Plakias twists its way from the coast like a piece of yarn. Heading north, stop at pretty **Agios Nikolas**, a small chapel built directly into the side of a mountain.

At the top of the gorge, mountainside **Taverna Iliomanolis** (☎28320 51053; Kanevos; mains €5-8; ⏰noon-9pm daily May-Oct, Tue-Sun Dec-Apr, closed Nov) in itself makes the trip worthwhile. The hearty homestyle Cretan food is superb and, while there's no menu, you'll be invited into the kitchen to peruse the tempting array of stews, casseroles, soups and local specialities prepared daily. Meat, wine, olive oil, cheese and raki all come from the family farm. You can also buy bags of local herbs and mountain teas.

If you have a map and plenty of time, head north from here. The roads are narrow, winding and badly signposted, but the scenery – mountaintop farms and forested ravines – is worth getting lost in. You can eventually wend your way right through to Rethymno.

Mes Tin Ammo they do simplicity at its best: a bamboo shack, chairs in the sand and a menu of cold drinks. A mojito here at sunset is bliss.

Ostraco Bar BAR
(☎28320 32249; www.plakias-ostraco.gr; ⏰8am-late; 📶) This downstairs waterfront cafe is a handy place to hang for breakfast, a cold beer or a snack any time of day, while the balconied upstairs bar kicks into gear after 9pm and keeps going until even the hardiest night owls are ready to roost.

ℹ Information

Plakias has numerous ATMs along the waterfront and about town.

Most accommodation and restaurants offer free wi-fi.

ℹ Getting There & Away

There are up to five buses daily to Rethymno (€5, one hour) and four to Preveli (€1.80, 30 minutes).

Anendyk (www.anendyk.gr) launched a new ferry in 2019 that heads to Gavdos Island (1½ hours, one way/return €30/55), departing at 9.30am on Friday and Sunday, and returning at 5pm the same days.

ℹ Getting Around

Anso Travel (☎28320 31444, 6944755712; www.ansotravel.com; per day from €10; ⏰9am-2pm & 6-10pm) Rents out mountain bikes, speed bikes and even electric bikes for taking to the mountains around town. Multiday rates available.

Alianthos Cars (☎28320 32033; www.alianthos-group.com; per day car/scooter from €36/23; ⏰8am-10pm) Reliable car-hire outlet.

Myrthios Μύρθιος

POP 100

The postcard-pretty village of Myrthios, draped across the hillside above Plakias, makes for a quieter and more traditional alternative to staying beachside. You might also be lured by great food and good deals on boutique accommodation.

Sleeping

Myrthios has several midrange pensions and a boutique hotel.

★ Stefanos Village Hotel BOUTIQUE HOTEL €€
(☎28320 32252; www.stefanosvillage.gr; d €95-100, apt €150-250; ⏰mid-Apr–Nov; ❄@🏊) On the northern outskirts of the village, this sprawling hillside hotel has spotless and tastefully decorated rooms. Each features fireplace, kitchenette and balcony with views, and the main infinity pool is one of Crete's finest, with amazing views over Plakias and the Libyan Sea. Or go for one of the newer luxurious apartments that come with private plunge pool.

AnnaView Apartments PENSION €€
(☎6973324775; www.annaview.com; d €85, apt €50-75; ❄📶) Run by a welcoming family, these attractive, roomy units have cranked up the comfort and hominess. Recently renovated, they're clean and modern, with full kitchens and satellite TV. Balconies are

a quiet kick-back zone, especially at sunset. Homemade biscuits and complimentary wine make for an agreeable first impression.

Eating

Despite its minuscule size, Myrthios has an outstanding selection of quality tavernas that specialise in traditional Cretan cuisine. Also be sure to check out Taverna Iliomanolis in Kanevos, 4.5km north of the village.

★Taverna Panorama CRETAN €€
(☎28320 31450; mains €6-16; ⏲11am-11pm Apr-mid-Nov; 📶) One of the oldest restaurants in the area, Panorama could not be more aptly named: on the shaded terrace, intoxicating views stretch towards the Libyan Sea. Women from the village prepare Cretan soul food here with passion and know-how, using impeccably fresh ingredients from the owner's farm. If there's freshly baked apple pie, don't miss it!

Vrisi CRETAN €€
(mains €8-12; ⏲1-10.30pm May-Oct; 📶) Set below the main road, this stylish restaurant creates delicious Cretan cuisine with panache. Dishes like chicken with honey and mustard, fig and chicken salad, and smoked pork with bulgur wheat are all served on a secluded patio. Service is first rate. If you're lucky, Fidel, the resident African grey parrot, might speak (or bark) at you.

The restaurant is named after a neighbouring traditional fountain, once a major water source for the village.

Plateia GREEK €€
(mains €6.50-12.50; ⏲11am-10pm Apr-Oct) With a view over Plakias, the fairly fashionable Plateia gives Greek standards a creative twist. Try chicken with okra, rabbit *stifadho* or one of the other tempting stews.

Getting There & Away

Myrthios is a short drive (about 4km) or a 30-minute walk (about 2km) from Plakias.

Preveli Πρέβελη

A smooth, curving ribbon of road winds from the bottom of Kourtaliotiko Gorge towards the southern coast, soaring up to the historic Moni Preveli and plunging down to palm-studded Preveli Beach. Although home to two of the region's biggest draws and receiving a lot of visitors, Preveli retains a feeling of remoteness.

Sights

Preveli Beach BEACH
(Παραλία Πρεβέλης) Also known as Palm Beach, dazzling Preveli is one of Crete's most celebrated strands. At the mouth of the Kourtaliotiko Gorge, where the river Megalopotamos empties into the Libyan Sea, the palm-lined riverbanks have freshwater pools good for a dip. The beach is backed by rugged cliffs and punctuated by a heart-shaped boulder at the water's edge.

A steep path leads down to the beach (10 minutes) from a car park (€2), 1km before Moni Preveli.

There's some natural shade, and umbrellas and loungers can be hired from a couple of seasonal snack bars. Once on the beach, you'll have to cross the ankle-deep river to reach the sandiest stretch.

Moni Preveli MONASTERY
(Μονή Πρεβέλης; ☎28320 31246; www.preveli.org; Koxaron-Moni Preveli Rd; €3; ⏲9am-6.30pm Apr, May, Sep & Oct, 9am-1.30pm & 3.30-7pm Jun-Aug; 🅿) Historic Moni Preveli cuts an imposing silhouette high above the Libyan Sea. Like most Cretan monasteries, it was a centre of resistance during the Turkish occupation and also played a key role in WWII, hiding trapped Allied soldiers from the Nazis until they could escape to Egypt by submarine. A small **museum** features exquisite icons, richly embroidered vestments and two silver candelabra presented by grateful soldiers after the war.

On the road to the monastery, a **memorial** showing a gun-toting abbot and an Allied British soldier also commemorates the site's wartime role, as does a **fountain** on the right as you enter the monastery complex.

Also at the monastery is an animal enclosure featuring *kri-kri* (Cretan goats), deer, emus and peacocks.

Sleeping & Eating

Most people visit Preveli on a day trip, but if you're keen to hang around a few of the tavernas offer rooms. Otherwise, Plakias, with plenty of accommodation choices, is a 15-minute drive away.

You'll find a few traditional tavernas for lunch in Preveli, including one right by the beach and another further inland along the river.

Taverna Rousolakos TAVERNA €
(mains €3-12; ⏲10am-7pm May-Oct) Just up from the car park at Preveli Beach, this

friendly taverna is perfect for a post-beach feed. It's within a centuries-old stone building and does a menu of mezedhes, grilled meats and *gyros* – including a fantastic veggie version with zucchini. Also lovely for a sunset beer or wine, with views out to the Libyan Sea.

Taverna Gefyra TAVERNA €
(☎6944986740; www.tavernagefyrapreveli.gr; mains €5.50-10; ⊙9am-8pm Apr-Nov) Cool off at tree-shaded tables, with a view to the river and a stone bridge built by local monks. The food here is fresh and traditional, and the service is friendly.

Getting There & Away

Moni Preveli is about 33km south of Rethymno and 9km east of Plakias.

In summer, two daily buses come in from Rethymno (€5, 1¼ hours) and four to six buses from Plakias (€1.80, 30 minutes).

Beaches Between Plakias & Agia Galini

Ligres Λίγκρες

Serene Ligres is a long sweep of greyish sand with some good swimming. Access to Ligres is via a tiny, winding road. Get off the main highway at Akoumia and follow the signs.

If you want to be in the thick of things, best not stay at **Villa Maria** (☎28320 22675, 6973232793; www.ligres.eu; d €30-45, studios from €60; ⊙Apr-Oct; ❄📶). With only the waves and a rushing creek for entertainment, this friendly, family-run property on an isolated beach is great for quiet relaxation. Rooms are comfortable without being fancy and come with balcony and kitchenette. The excellent **taverna** specialises in grilled meats and just-caught fish (mains €5 to €10).

Triopetra Τριόπετρα

Triopetra is one for those who want to avoid the package-tourist beach-resort scene and instead keep their holiday blissfully simple. Separated by a headland, Triopetra is divided into two beaches: 'Big Triopetra' and 'Little Triopetra'. The latter is low-key, but submerged sand shelves mean it's not ideal for swimming. Big Triopetra is the main attraction and its long wild beach with brownish sand is a real crowd-pleaser, featuring magnificent crystal-clear waters that are good for swimming. However, it's often blighted by winds – the only thing keeping it from appearing in any top-100 lists. Instead, the attraction here is more about the unhurried, mellow pace of life.

Triopetra is named after the three giant rocks jutting out of the sea. Other than a few tavernas and pensions scattered about, there's not much else out this way.

Sleeping & Eating

Most accommodation here comprises low-key pensions and hidden-away villas.

Pavlos' Place PENSION €
(☎6945998101; www.triopetra.com.gr; d €40-45; ⊙taverna 8am-4pm & 6-10pm Apr-Oct; ❄📶) Right above Little Triopetra Beach, dreamy Pavlos is the perfect chill spot and a popular yoga retreat. Rooms are down to earth (no TV), with kitchenettes, and balconies that catch the sea breeze. The attached taverna does homegrown fare (mains €8 to €12). Wi-fi is intermittent and available in public areas only – great for that digital detox.

Pension Girogiali PENSION €
(☎6976430145; r €40; ⊙Apr-Oct; ❄📶) Right on Triopetra's long beach, this friendly pension has clean, basic rooms with marble floors and balconies. The mattresses are on the thin side, however. Its laid-back taverna offers fresh seafood to enjoy while gazing out over the water. Free sunloungers and umbrellas for guests.

Getting There & Away

Triopetra can be reached via a winding, 12km asphalt road from the village of Akoumia on the Rethymno–Agia Galini road. It's also linked to Agios Pavlos (about 300m of the route between the two is drivable dirt road). Ask about road conditions locally before setting out on the latter.

Agios Pavlos Άγιος Παύλος

Cradled by cliffs, Agios Pavlos is little more than a couple of small tavernas with rooms and a beach bar set around a picture-perfect crescent with dark, coarse sand and the distinctive silhouette of Paximadia Island looming offshore. Its beauty and tranquillity have made it a popular destination for yoga retreats. A steep staircase at the bay's western end leads up Cape Melissa to some intricately pleated multihued rock formations.

Agios Pavlos' main beach comprises a brown arc of sand that's topped by steep dunes, and a rocky bluff that resembles a recumbent dragon. When the sun's out the aquamarine colours of the Libyan Sea are stunning. The bay gets busy in summer, when excursion boats arrive from Agia Galini, but it's possible to escape the crowds by heading to the beaches behind Cape Melissa.

For the beaches west of Agios Pavlos, be aware that getting there involves a scramble down (and up) a steep sand dune; bring water and snacks, since there are no facilities. The furthest cove is the least busy and is popular with nudists.

Sleeping

You'll find some decent accommodation out this way, with cosy pension rooms, self-contained apartments and luxurious villas scattered over the hillside above the beach.

Agios Pavlos Hotel HOTEL €
(28320 71104; www.agiospavloshotel.gr; s €25-30, d €35-45, apt €45-60; Apr-Oct; P ❄) Hugging a rugged and remote sandy bay, this place offers small but updated rooms, some with gorgeous bay views, below a traditional taverna. Alternatively, there are larger apartments with kitchens and balconies in a modern building about 1km uphill. At research time luxurious villas built into the natural landscape were under construction; these will have sea views and saltwater plunge pools.

Eating & Drinking

Sleepy Dragon CAFE €
(mains €4-7.50; 8am-midnight Apr-Oct) Named after Agios Pavlos' rocky peninsula that resembles a reclining dragon, this contemporary open-air cafe is all about its clifftop patio with views overlooking the bay. It's best known for its breakfasts and burgers but is also perfect for sunset beers, wines and smoothies. It's accessed via the Agios Pavlos Hotel.

The stairs from here lead down to the seasonal Cave bar.

Agios Pavlos Taverna TAVERNA €
(28320 71104; mains €6-13; 8am-late Apr-Oct;) Attached to the Agios Pavlos Hotel, this picturesque taverna dishes up fresh fish and Cretan standards to enjoy with stellar views of the Libyan Sea.

Cave BAR
(www.agiospavloshotel.gr/bar; 10pm-late Jul-Sep) If you're here in summer, head underground to rock out at the Cave bar. Built into a natural cave, it's one of Crete's more unique drinking spots, and live bands and DJs ensure a fun night out. It doesn't get going till later in the evening, and is accessed via steps down from the Sleepy Dragon cafe.

Getting There & Away

There's no public transport to Agios Pavlos. Drivers need to look for the turn-off to Saktouria on the Rethymno–Agia Galini road and follow the winding road 13km down to the sea.

Agia Galini Αγία Γαλήνη

POP 630

One of southern Crete's most touristy seaside towns, the picturesque erstwhile fishing village of Agia Galini serves as a handy base for exploring miles of remote beaches, mountain villages and nearby Minoan sights. Despite the sparkling Libyan Sea setting, the town itself is blighted by package tourism and overdevelopment, which has diluted much of its original charm.

With ageing hotels and restaurants clinging densely to a steep hillside and hemmed in by cliffs, small beaches and a fishing harbour, the town can feel claustrophobic in high season. However, with its concentration of lively tavernas and pubs, the evenings bring a fun holiday atmosphere. While the town's pebbly beach is nothing special, the remote beaches west of here are lovely. Agia Galini all but shuts down in winter.

Sights & Activities

Icarus & Daedalus Statues PUBLIC ART
Agia Gallini has its place in the annals of Greek mythology as the site where Icarus and Daedalus are believed to have taken their ill-fated flight from Crete. The moment is marked at the far-western end of the harbour, where you'll find statues depicting the two preparing for the journey at the hilltop amphitheatre. Here also is a small folk-art museum built into a cave.

Mare Sud Diving Centre DIVING
(6955909020; www.maresud.gr; dives from €60) This SSI dive centre caters to all levels, offering discovery dives, open-water courses and technical dives. Boat trips head to nearby sites at caves, remote beaches and uninhabited islands – including wall dives at the Paximadia Islands, the legendary birthplace

of Apollo and Artemis. It's on the main road leading to the port.

It also has a main dive shop in Kokkinos Pirgos, 11km east along the coast.

Tours

Galini Express CRUISE

(☎6936923848; www.galiniexpress.com; ⊙8.30am-2pm & 5-10pm mid-May–Oct) This operator arranges a number of day excursions to nearby attractions like Matali (€20 per person), Preveli Beach (€30) and Rethymno/Margarites (€25), and river trekking through Kourtaliotiko Gorge (€25). It also hires out mountain bikes (€18 per day) and e-bikes (€40), and runs airport transfers.

Elizabeth Boat FISHING

(☎6936848445; http://gogalini.com/elizabeth-fishing-trip; tour incl lunch €35) Cruise the Libyan Sea on this little boat. Tour local caves and coves, try your luck at prime fishing sites, and then stop at a remote beach for a barbecue lunch. Trips depart the harbour at 10.30am and return around 3.30pm.

Sactoris Cruises BOATING

(☎6976693729; http://gogalini.com/sactourisdc; boat trip €35; ⊙9.30-10.30am & 6-10pm) This modern, well-equipped motorboat will take you to Preveli Beach (p151) for a four-hour play on the sand. It departs at 10.30am and returns at 4.30pm. To book, visit the stand at the harbour during opening hours.

Sleeping

There's no shortage of places to stay in Agia Galini, but a large percentage of the accommodation is bland and prebooked by tour operators in peak season.

Hotel Aketon PENSION €

(☎28320 91208; www.akteonhotel.com; s/d/apt incl breakfast €40/50/85;) A glimpse of how life was before things took off in Agia Galini is this simple family-run pension in a prime spot overlooking the harbour. Its 10 basic rooms are brightly furnished, and there's a communal terrace for kicking back and enjoying the fantastic sea views. The top-floor two-bedroom self-contained apartment has more modern touches and is perfect for families.

Camping No Problem CAMPGROUND €

(☎28320 91386; camp site per person/tent/car/caravan €6/4/3/4; ⊙year-round;) With shady spots to pitch a tent, this well-maintained campground is about 100m from a pebbly beach and a 10-minute walk from the port and town centre. A minimarket meets basic needs, but there's also an excellent taverna overlooking a big swimming pool. The turn-off is on the main road near the Shell petrol station.

Glaros Hotel HOTEL €€

(☎28320 91151; www.glaros-agiagalini.com; incl breakfast d €50-85, tr/q €91/101;) These well-maintained rooms have a modern edge in a town full of ho-hum hotels. Some rooms have balconies overlooking the pool, and there's a stylish common area and a decent buffet breakfast. Excellent, friendly service seals the deal. It's at the back of town, straight up from the harbour.

Irini Mare RESORT €€

(☎28320 91488; www.irinimare.com; d/f incl breakfast €110/150; ⊙May-Oct;) Great for families, this beautifully landscaped resort sits a short walk from the main beach. Its 130 bright, modern rooms come in a variety of configurations (including villas with private pools), but all have terraces and sea or mountain views. Diversions include a gym, sauna and tennis court, while kids have their own pool and playground.

Palazzo Greco BOUTIQUE HOTEL €€

(☎28320 91187; www.palazzogreco.com; d incl breakfast €50-225; ⊙Mar-Nov;) A passion for design is reflected in the stylish details at this breezy hotel overlooking the sea. Match your mood to the wall colours – pale green, blue or red – in tranquil modern rooms with view-filled decks, flat-screen TVs, fridges and fabulous showers. Cheaper rooms don't have sea views, so go for the upgrade. Breakfast on the beautiful patio above the pool.

It's right on the main road before it descends into the village. If you're looking for something more exclusive, it also has luxury villas outside town, each with its own private pool.

Eating

Agia Galini's lower section near the harbour is crammed with tavernas catering to European holidaymakers. Most feature lovely sea views and fresh catch.

Taverna Kipos TAVERNA €

(☎28320 91239; www.tavernakipos.com; Camping No Problem; mains €7-13; ⊙9am-midnight Apr-Oct;) The tree-shaded and flower-filled patio here offers a peaceful setting for both classic taverna fare and international cuisine. It shares space with Camping No Problem about 750m from town. Bring a swimsuit to cool off in the big pool.

Platia CAFE **€€**
(☎28320 91185; mains €7-19; ⊙8am-2pm & 6pm-1am; 📶) Set in a square just up from the harbour, this cafe-bistro-bar is popular with locals. Excellent breakfasts (€6 to €10) offer everything from yoghurt and museli to ham and eggs, while dinner sees spaghetti with leeks and goat's cheese or garlic king-prawn salad. When the sun goes down, the long list of cocktails comes out.

Onar GREEK **€€**
(Food St; mains €6-21; ⊙noon-11pm Apr–mid-Nov; 📶👪) Even after 30-plus years in business, Onar still hasn't lost its grip on the crowd. There are plenty of other tavernas with romantic views over the port, but Onar's tasty mezedhes and finger-lickin' charcoal grills make it a standout option. There's a kids' menu, too.

Faros Fish Tavern SEAFOOD **€€**
(☎6944773702; mains €7-13; ⊙6-11pm) This no-frills family-run fish taverna is usually packed to the gills, and for good reason: the owner himself drops his nets into the Med, so you know that what's on the plate tonight was still swimming in the sea that morning. It's in the first lane coming from the port.

Squid cooked in its own ink, lobster spaghetti and fish soup are specialities (available on request only).

Drinking & Nightlife

The harbour isn't too shy to party, with countless bars booming out the beat. Most places are indistinguishable. Follow the crowd.

La Mar CAFE
(☎28320 91018; ⊙8.30am-late Apr-Oct) Classy La Mar is the standout among the port-side terrace cafes, with tasteful decor and an interesting menu of original cocktails. Here you can opt for a Martini shaken with a local twist, infused with *malotira* (mountain tea) or olive oil, or a G&T with local gin. Otherwise, pop in for a vegan burger or other Western fare.

Blue Bar BAR
(⊙7pm-1am Apr-Oct) This been-there-forever pub has a reputation for playing the best music in town. Owner Heinz is a singer-songwriter with eclectic tastes, which is why the turntables get a workout with everything from R&B to rock and soul to pop. It's tucked down the first alley, 100m from the port.

Information

A small tourist-information office sits beneath the amphitheatre at the far-western end of the port.

Otherwise www.gogalini.com and www.agia-galini.com offer up-to-date listings.

Getting There & Away

In high season there are up to seven buses daily to Iraklio (€8.70, two hours), up to five buses to Rethymno (€6.80, 1½ hours) and to Phaestos (€2.30, 30 to 45 minutes), and around five buses to Matala (€3.60, 45 minutes), with a change in Tymbaki. Buses stop down in the village near the port.

If enough people have booked, **Galini Express** (☎6936923848; www.galiniexpress.com) offers direct buses to the airport in Iraklio (from €20) and Hania (from €25).

In 2019 Anendyk (www.anendyk.gr) began trialling a ferry service linking Agia Galini with Gavdos Island (two hours, one way/return €30/55) departing on Tuesday, Friday, Saturday and Sunday; check the website for the latest.

Getting Around

Galini Express hires out mountain bikes (€18 per day) and e-bikes (€40).

Several car-hire agencies are located just behind the harbour, including **Auto Galini** (☎28320 91241; www.autogalini.com; ⊙9am-2pm & 5-8pm) and **Ostria** (☎6976619988, 28320 91555; www.ostria-agiagalini.com; ⊙9am-1pm & 5-9pm), which both offer small cars and 4WDs.

NORTHEASTERN COAST

Panormo Πάνορμο

POP 880

Panormo, about 22km east of Rethymno, is one of the few relatively unspoilt beach towns on the northern coast. Despite a couple of big hotel complexes, it retains an unhurried, authentic village feel and makes for a quieter alternative to the overcrowded scene immediately east of Rethymno and at nearby Bali. In summer, concerts and other events are held in a carob mill turned cultural centre.

Sights & Activities

Klados Winery WINERY

(☎28340 51589, 6973654840; www.kladoswinery.gr; tasting 5/7 wines €3/4; ⊙10am-6pm Mon-Fri, to 3pm Sat Apr-Oct, other times by appointment) While Iraklio gets all the plaudits as Crete's main wine producer, Rethymno has the honour of being the first place in Greece to be named a 'European City of Wine', in 2018. It's fitting recognition for this hard-working family, who've run their winery since 1997 and are known primarily for Vidiano, a dry white produced from a grape grown only in the immediate area.

You'll get a 30-minute tour of the small production site before tasting the range of organic reds, whites and rosés. With notice they can arrange mezedhes (€8) to enjoy overlooking the vines and olive groves. Bottles to take away are well priced (from €6). The winery is 2km east of Panormo, a 30-minute walk or short drive away.

Panormo Beach BEACH

There's no one main beach in Panormo but a series of small, attractive coves with brown sand and a brilliant turquoise sea. The tiny swoop of sand at the harbour with its calm waters is perfect for families.

Castel Milopotamo VIEWPOINT

For wonderful views overlooking Panormo's port, head up the hill to a *tiny* segment of stone wall that remains from a 13th-century fortress. It's believed to have been built by the Genoese during their fleeting rule in 1206 before the Venetians took over.

Basilica of Aghia Sophia RUINS

Coins unearthed in Panormo indicate that a village flourished here between the 1st and 9th centuries AD, but the only in situ evidence from this period are the crumbling bits and pieces of this 6th-century church. It's built on the slopes above the village but gated off. Look for signs directing you to the site.

Church of Agios Yiorgos CHURCH

Ecclesiastic-art fans should stop in town at Panormo's parish church, which has some stunning modern frescoes.

Atlantis Diving Centre DIVING

(☎6977506093, 28310 71640; www.atlantis-creta.com; Grecotel Club Marine Palace; 2 dives incl gear €110, snorkelling gear per day €15; ⊙9am-2pm & 5-8pm) Based at the beach at Grecotel Club Marine Palace is this five-star PADI outfit that offers both shore and boat dives as well as a range of courses from beginner to instructor level. There are dozens of sites to visit, where you'll encounter plenty of marine life and colourful fish, and you can explore underwater caves on night dives.

WORTH A TRIP

DALABELOS ESTATE

Hemmed in by vines, olives and fruit trees, the 10 traditional-style houses of **Dalabelos Estate** (☎28340 22155; www.dalabelos.gr; Aggeliana; d/ste from €80/100;) have a view over rolling hills to the sea. The modern rooms have stone fireplaces, private terraces, outdoor hot tubs and beautiful bathrooms. The infinity pool and restaurant are first class, plus there are seasonal activities from olive harvesting to raki distilling, as well as hands-on Cretan cooking classes.

It's located inland, 5km south of Panormo, so it helps to have your own transport, but otherwise there are free mountain bikes. The husband-and-wife owners are exceptionally hospitable and proud Cretans, with unsurpassed passion for local food and culture. In high season there's a minimum three-night stay.

Tours

Aitidis Travel TOURS

(☎28340 52040; www.aitidistravel.com; ⊙10am-10pm) Offers a whole gamut of tours, including excursions to Samaria Gorge (€35), to the island of Gramvousa and to Preveli Beach.

Tourist Train RAIL

(☎28340 20222; ⊙in town 3-11pm, to Margarites & Melidoni 9am-2.15pm Apr-Oct) In summer a cute little train chugs around Panormo (adult/child €5/3) and out to the pottery village of Margarites and the Melidoni Cave (adult/child €17.50/7.50). You'll find it on the western side of town, across from the carob factory.

Sleeping

Captain's House GUESTHOUSE €

(☎28103 80833; www.captainshouse.gr; apt €40-60; ⊙Apr-Oct;) In a prime waterfront location, the Captain's modern and spacious split-level apartments are an excellent choice – all are different, but each is spacious and comfortable, and catches the sea breeze.

They're equipped with satellite TV, fast wi-fi and kitchenette, and some feature sea views. Staff members are friendly, and a welcoming gift of fruit and wine is a lovely touch.

Its taverna opposite is a scenic spot for a meal overlooking pristine turquoise waters.

Christina APARTMENT €
(☎28340 51277, 6976861859; www.apartments-christina.gr; studios from €45, apt from €55; ⌚Apr-Oct; ❄📶) At this meticulously kept and efficiently run place, rooms are a little dated but spotless. All have a seafront balcony or terrace, but the studios are snug. The enclosed hydromassage showers are an unexpected bonus in the apartments.

★Idili GUESTHOUSE €€
(☎6970994408, 28340 20240; www.idili.gr; apt €65-95; ❄📶) If cookie-cutter rooms don't do it for you, you'll love the three traditionally furnished apartments in this protected stone house, which has seen incarnations as courthouse, carpenter's workshop and residence. Arches, wooden ceilings and sleeping lofts endow each unit with charm and uniqueness, while the fireplace and veranda are delightful places to unwind. The flowering garden offers a shady retreat.

Kastro PENSION €€
(☎28340 51362, 6937097757; www.kastroapartments.gr; studios €40-70, apt €40-90; ❄📶) Back from the seafront on the road out of town, these rooms are older but have nice touches like four-poster beds. Homely apartments sleep four and have private entrances, while some studios have sea views. It also has a classy taverna.

Eating

The touristy harbour tavernas serve standard Greek and international dishes as well as fresh fish. More traditional places can be found a block or two inland. If you have a car, try to make it out to Dalabelos Estate for lunch, a wonderful culinary experience.

★George & Georgia's CRETAN €
(To Steki tou Sifaki; ☎28340 51230; mains €7-12; ⌚12.30-4pm & 7pm-late; 🖉) Husband-and-wife team George and Georgia serve up satisfying homestyle Cretan food at this cheerful, hopping place. Expect scrumptious oven-roasted dishes and flavoursome grilled fish, along with a great selection of veggie options. Find it between the waterfront and the main road, near the post office.

Porto Parasiris CRETAN €€
(mains €7-20; ⌚9am-late) This upbeat, colourful harbourside patio is a great place to relax. Meals have a creative edge – try pork with dried fruit or chicken with lavender yoghurt. The Cretan spaghetti with smoked pork and *myzithra* (soft white cheese) and the homemade pasta are sure hits.

Taverna Kastro CRETAN €€
(☎28340 51362; www.kastro.restaurant; mains €7-22; ⌚noon-midnight May-Oct; 📶) The flower-festooned courtyard is a great place to sit, but it's what's on the plate that will truly wow you. Classic Cretan recipes get a modern makeover here, which translates into such palate teasers as lentils with *apaki* (cured pork), cod with garlic potatoes, or grilled pork belly. It's on the eastern side of town, back from the seafront.

Angira SEAFOOD €€
(mains €7-15; ⌚noon-11pm Apr-Oct) Seafood doesn't get any fresher than at this place right at the harbour. Choose from marinated anchovies, shrimp salad or grilled fish, along with a wonderful slow-cooked lamb in wine sauce.

Drinking & Nightlife

Panormo isn't known as a party town, but if you're after a drink the tavernas overlooking the picturesque waterfront are hard to beat.

Kharas To Kafeneio CAFE
(coffee €1.50; ⌚9am-9pm) Near the post office, this friendly *kafeneio* (coffee house) gives you a glimpse of village life. This is where local men come to drink coffee, eat snacks, sip raki and play cards. Tables spill into the big windowed room across the street.

Getting There & Away

In high season, hourly buses go from Rethymno to Panormo (€2.60, 25 minutes). Buses stop on the main road just outside town. For car hire, try **Rent-A-Car** (www.bestcars-rental.gr; ⌚9am-2pm & 5-8pm), with branches opposite the carob factory and the Grecotel Club Marine Palace.

A **taxi** (☎28340 23000) is available for drop-offs at Rethymno (€28) or Bali (€20).

Bali Μπαλί

POP 330

Bali, 38km east of Rethymno and 51km west of Iraklio, has one of the most stunning settings on the northern coast, with a series of little coves strung along the indented shore, marked by hills, promontories and narrow sandy beaches. But helter-skelter development has significantly marred the natural beauty and the former fishing hamlet has all but disappeared under the weight of package tourism. While the brown-sand beaches won't blow your mind, Bali's a fun place to come and enjoy the dramatic scenery and take advantage of lodging bargains. Be warned, though, that the beaches can get crammed with sun worshippers in summer.

In antiquity Bali was known as Astali, but no traces of ancient Astali now remain. For the record, the name Bali has nothing to do with the Indonesian island.

Beaches

Bali is rather spread out and it's a long and undulating walk from one end to the other – 25 minutes or more. The town has four brown-sand beaches, all of them reasonably kid-friendly.

Karavostasi BEACH
Karavostasi, the northernmost of Bali's string of beaches, is also the smallest and quietest. Its tanned-sandy beach is family friendly, with sunloungers and umbrellas available for hire from the tavernas tucked beneath the rocky cliffs. A coastal footpath leads here from the port, and the Bali Express tourist train goes out here as well.

Varkotopo BEACH
Bali's most central beach – between Livadi and Limani – is this pretty strip of sand flanked by young palm trees. There are some quite classy bars here that are a good spot for sunset cocktails.

Livadi BEACH
Brown-sand Livadi is Bali's biggest and widest beach, with bit of a party vibe. It's packed with chairs and umbrellas, and bars, tavernas and cafes run its entire length.

Limani BEACH
The old port of Limani has a narrow crescent of attractive beach with greyish-brown sand lined with sunloungers, plenty of cafes and water-sport operators.

Activities

Skippers WATER SPORTS
(☎28340 94102; https://catamaran-cruises-watersports-lefteris.business.site; ⏲9am-6pm Apr-Nov) At Limani's port, Skippers hires kayaks (€10/12 per hour single/double), motorboats (€40 per hour) and stand-up paddle boards (€10). Hop on a three-hour sunset catamaran trip (€35) for swimming and snorkelling, or take a day cruise (eight hours; €85 including lunch and alcoholic drinks) to check out some local caves and beaches.

Hippocampos Dive Centre DIVING
(☎28340 94193; www.hippocampos.com; 1 dive incl gear €56, snorkelling gear per day €15; ⏲9am-1pm & 5-9pm Mon & Wed-Sat, 5-9pm Tue) This well-run outfit near Limani Beach does shore and boat dives as well as the gamut of courses, including one-week open-water certifications (€460).

Bali Travel TOUR
(☎28340 94410, 6972505760; www.balitravel.gr; ⏲9am-2pm & 5-9pm) Whether you're yearning to visit Preveli (€32), Hania/Elafonisi beach (€37), Knossos (€32), or Samaria (€35) or Imbros (€32) Gorges, Bali Travel has a tour for you. It also runs overnight trips to Santorini. Note that prices exclude entrance fees. Located near Varkotopo Beach.

Mellisi Travel TOUR
(☎6932872897, 28340 94500; www.mellisitravel.gr/en; ⏲9am-2pm & 5-9pm May-Oct) This outfit near Limani Beach organises day excursions to well-known beaches and sites across the region, throwing in some more off-the-beaten-track stops to offer a genuine glimpse of local life.

Sleeping

There's no shortage of accommodation in Bali, and most places have sea views. Choose from holiday apartments, midrange hotels and beachfront resorts. There's a lack of budget choices, however.

★**Stone Village** RESORT €
(Petrino Horio; ☎6984378368, 28340 20140; www.stone-village.gr; Vlihada; d incl half board €45-70; ⏲Mar-Oct; ❄@🛜🏊) In the quiet hills above Bali, the traditional rooms here feel like your own small Cretan house. The village features 38 carefully crafted apartments with terraces or balconies, kitchens and fireplaces, set amid flowering trees and potted plants. It's a 10-minute walk to the beach and close to the Bali Express tourist train stop.

Three pools, a petting zoo (including free horse rides), a sauna and seasonal hands-on activities, such as cheesemaking, provide distractions. There's a good restaurant using organic ingredients from its farm, and very friendly service.

Sunrise Apartments APARTMENT €
(☎28340 94267; d €30-45, apt €45-65; ⊙Apr-Oct; ❄📶) Right on Karavostasi beach, these spacious, well-kept studios with kitchenette are great value for money and perfect for escaping the frenzy of Bali while still staying near the sand. The patios overlooking the cove are perfect for sunset drinks. This place is very popular, so book ahead.

Bali Blue Bay HOTEL €€
(☎28340 20111; www.balibluebay.gr; d incl breakfast €50-75; ❄📶🏊) Modern and comfortable, but not fancy, rooms here are spacious and have great sea views. Common areas are welcoming and open to the sea, and the service is top notch. The inviting rooftop pool is another reason to stay. Near Limani beach.

Hotel Lisa Mari HOTEL €
(☎28340 94072; lizamary.hotel@hotmail.gr; s/d/tr incl breakfast €50/60/70; P❄📶🏊👪) Popular with package tourists, Lisa Mari is a small-scale budget resort with clean, comfortable rooms and modern furnishings. Some rooms have sea views, but wi-fi can be patchy beyond the common areas. The real bonus, however, is the lovely private pool with bar and garden. The staff is ultra-friendly and there's an on-site restaurant. Near Livadi beach.

Eating

Most of Bali's tavernas are found along the beach, and offer fresh seafood, grilled meats and traditional Cretan cuisine.

★**Taverna Nest** CRETAN €€
(☎28340 94280; mains €7-15; ⊙9am-midnight May-Oct) For honest-to-goodness farm-to-table fare, report to this upstairs terrace where home-cooked meals are served in ample portions and with big smiles. Regulars crave the barbecue-spit lamb or piglet, and the grilled fish, nicely paired with the homemade *kolokythoanthi* (zucchini flowers stuffed with rice and herbs) and hand-cut fried potatoes. It's a few steps inland from the port. Satisfying breakfasts, too.

★**Taverna Karavostasi** TAVERNA €€
(☎28340 94267; mains €7-19; ⊙9am-5pm Mon, to 10pm Tue-Sun Apr-Oct; 👪) With veggies straight from its garden and local wine from the barrel, this taverna on pint-sized Karavostasi beach offers homemade dishes that are bursting with flavour. The speciality is stuffed aubergines, or try the lentil soup or the baked chicken with lemon. There's an awesome view, a kids' menu and friendly service.

Psaropoula TAVERNA €€
(mains €6-18; ⊙9am-11pm Apr-Oct, 11am-9pm Nov-Mar) The steep climb up to this family-run taverna is worth the effort for the outstanding views alone: there's a commanding outlook over the translucent waters of Varkotopo beach and its mountainous backdrop. In business since 1975, Psaropoula does Greek and Cretan standards, but it's the grilled-seafood banquets (€18 to €28 for two people) that attract most folk here.

Panorama CRETAN €€
(mains €4.50-17; ⊙9.30am-midnight Apr-Oct) Watch the boats bob in the port while enjoying excellent fish and homestyle food high on the terrace of this former carob warehouse. In business since 1968, it's one of the oldest and most respected eateries in town.

Drinking & Nightlife

While Bali isn't renowned as a party destination, most tavernas and beachfront cafes stay open late. In summer you'll find some lively bars at Livadi and Varkotopo beaches.

Mambo Beach Bar BAR
(⊙9am-midnight) Catch the sea breeze and a sunset with a pina colada in hand at this laid-back beach bar in a prime spot overlooking Varkotopo.

Alquimico CAFE
(☎28340 94259; ⊙9am-late) Just metres from the sands of Limani is this popular bistro that's good for Western breakfasts, sandwiches and burgers. It's also a top spot for drinks, serving icy mugs of beer and a long menu of classic cocktails.

Getting There & Away

From Rethymno there are regular buses to Bali (€3.80, 30 minutes) en route to Iraklio. Buses drop you at the main road, from where it's a 2km walk to the port of Bali.

Getting Around

A good way to get around is by the **Bali Express** (1 way/return €3/5; ⊙9am-11pm May-Sep), a tourist train that makes 11 stops in town and at the beaches.

Auto Bali (☎28340 94504; ⊙9am-2pm & 5-9pm) will bring a hire car to you at the airport. You can also hire cars through the tour agencies.

LAZY DAYS

From bar-backed busy strips to romantic palm-fringed strands and footprint-free crescents where solitude reigns, Crete has a beach with your name on it.

A TOUCH OF THE TROPICS

Powdery pink-white sand lapped by dazzling azure waters is the ammo of **Elafonisi** (p99), while **Vaï** (p244) has you spreading your towel against a huge grove of swaying palm trees. Just as exotic are the beaches in the shallow turquoise waters of the **Balos lagoon** (p111). More palm trees await at famous **Preveli Beach** (p151).

FAMILY FUN

Even away from the big resorts, Crete has plenty of family-friendly beaches. Places to steer towards include **Varkotopo Beach** (p158) and the other coves at Bali, **Voulisma Beach** (p238) near Agios Nikolaos, palm-fringed **Vaï** (p244) and **Preveli** (p151), the expansive beaches in **Plakias** (p149), and ethereal **Elafonisi** (p99).

WATER ACTION

Jump headlong into the high, long waves rolling in from the open sea on **Falasarna Beach** (p113), a tiara of coves separated by rocky spits in the northeast, or head across the island to Crete's windsurf capital at pebbly **Kouremenos Beach** (p245) near Palekastro. Fans of jet-skiing, banana-boat rides and the like get their fill at the busy north coast beaches flanking Iraklio.

ESCAPIST SPLENDOUR

For the ultimate trifecta of tranquillity, scenic splendour and rustic authenticity, point the compass to **Agios Pavlos** (p152) and **Triopetra** (p152) or to mountain-backed **Xerokambos** (p249), all on the south coast.

1. Vaï (p244)
2. The pink sand of Elafonisi (p99)
3. Preveli Beach (p151)

GATSI/GETTY IMAGES ©

ALEXANDROS PETRAKIS/SHUTTERSTOCK ©

Iraklio

Includes ➡

Best Places to Eat

- ➡ Peskesi (p173)
- ➡ George's Yard (p197)
- ➡ Elia & Diosmos (p190)
- ➡ Taverna Niki (p209)

Best Places to Stay

- ➡ Eleonas Country Village (p192)
- ➡ Thalori Retreat (p202)
- ➡ Villa Kerasia (p187)
- ➡ Villa Ippocampi (p208)

Why Go?

Iraklio is Crete's most dynamic region, home to almost half the island's population and its top-rated tourist site, the Minoan Palace of Knossos. Priceless treasures unearthed here, and at the many other Minoan sites around Crete, have catapulted the archaeological museum in the capital city of Iraklio onto the world stage.

Admittedly, the coastal stretch east of Iraklio is one continuous band of hotels and resorts. But a few kilometres inland, villages sweetly lost in time provide pleasing contrast. Taste the increasingly sophisticated tipple produced in the Iraklio Wine Country, walk in the footsteps of painter El Greco and writer Nikos Kazantzakis, and revel in the rustic grandeur of remote mountain villages such as Zaros.

On the quieter southern coast, the ex-hippie hangout of Matala is the only developed resort, while in the charming villages the laid-back life unfolds much the way it has since time immemorial.

Road Distances (km)

	Iraklio	Malia	Matala	Peza
Malia	37			
Matala	69	106		
Peza	17	48	70	
Phaestos	57	90	10	61

IRAKLIO ΗΡΑΚΛΕΙΟ

POP 140,730

Crete's capital, Iraklio (also called Heraklion), is Greece's fifth-largest city and the island's economic and administrative hub. It's also home to Crete's blockbuster sights: the must-see Heraklion Archaeological Museum and the nearby Palace of Knossos, which both provide fascinating windows into Crete's ancient past.

Though not pretty in a conventional way, Iraklio definitely grows on you if you take the time to explore its layers and wander its backstreets. You'll discover a low-key urban sophistication with a thriving cafe and restaurant scene, good shopping and bustling nightlife. A revitalised waterfront invites strolling, and the pedestrianised historic centre is punctuated by bustling squares flanked by buildings from the time when Christopher Columbus first set sail.

History

Settled since Neolithic times, Iraklio was conquered by the Saracens in AD 824 and reputedly evolved into the slave-trade capital of the eastern Mediterranean and the launching pad for the region's notorious pirates. Byzantine troops ousted the Arabs after a long siege in 961 and the city became known as Handakas. This was changed to Candia in 1204 when Crete was sold to the Venetians.

Under the Venetians the city became a centre for the arts and home to painters such as Damaskinos and El Greco. The magnificent fortress and many of the great public buildings and lofty churches date to this period. The Candians fought tooth and nail to keep the Ottomans at bay, even extending the fortress walls. But the Turks overran Crete in 1645, and began besieging Candia in 1648.

Under the Turks the city became known as Megalo Kastro (Big Castle). Artistic life withered and many Cretans fled or were killed. In August 1898 a Turkish mob massacred hundreds of Cretans, 17 British soldiers and the British consul. Within weeks, a squadron of British ships steamed into Iraklio's harbour and ended Turkish rule.

Iraklio got its current name in 1922. At the time Hania was the capital of independent Crete, but Iraklio's central location soon saw it emerge as the island's commercial centre. The city suffered badly in WWII, when bombs levelled much of the old Venetian and Turkish town. It resumed its position as Crete's capital in 1971.

Sights

Iraklio's main sights are wedged within the historic town, hemmed in by the waterfront and the old city walls. Many of the finest buildings line up along the main thoroughfare, 25 Avgoustou, which skirts the lovely central square, Plateia Venizelou (also called Lion Sq after its fountain). East of here the hub of Iraklio's cafe scene, Korai, leads towards the vast Plateia Eleftherias, with the Heraklion Archaeological Museum nearby.

★Heraklion Archaeological Museum MUSEUM

(www.heraklionmuseum.gr; Xanthoudidou 2; adult/concession/child €10/5/free, combined ticket with Palace of Knossos adult/concession €16/8; ⏲8am-8pm Mon & Wed-Sun, 10am-8pm Tue mid-Apr–Oct, 8am-4pm Nov–mid-Apr) This state-of-the-art museum is one of the largest and most important in Greece. The two-storey revamped 1930s Bauhaus building makes a gleaming showcase for artefacts spanning 5500 years from Neolithic to Roman times, including a Minoan collection of unparalleled richness. The rooms are colour coded and displays are arranged both chronologically and thematically, and presented with descriptions in English. A visit here will greatly enhance your understanding of Crete's rich history. Don't skip it.

The museum's treasure trove includes pottery, jewellery and sarcophagi, plus famous frescoes from the sites of Knossos, Tylissos, Amnissos and Agia Triada. The pieces are grouped into comprehensive themes such as settlements, trade, death, religion and administration. Along with clear descriptions, these bring to life both the day-to-day functioning and the long-term progression of societies in Crete and beyond. Allow at least two hours for this extraordinary collection. See our self-guided tour on p170.

★Koules Fortress FORTRESS

(Rocca al Mare; http://koules.efah.gr; Venetian Harbour; adult/concession €2/1; ⏲8am-8pm May-Sep, to 4pm Oct-Apr) After six years of restoration, Iraklio's symbol, the 16th-century fortress called Rocca al Mare by the Venetians, reopened in August 2016 with a brand-new exhibition. It tells the story of the building, zeroes in on milestones in city history, and displays ancient amphorae, Venetian cannons and other finds recovered from shipwrecks around Dia Island by Jacques Cousteau in 1976.

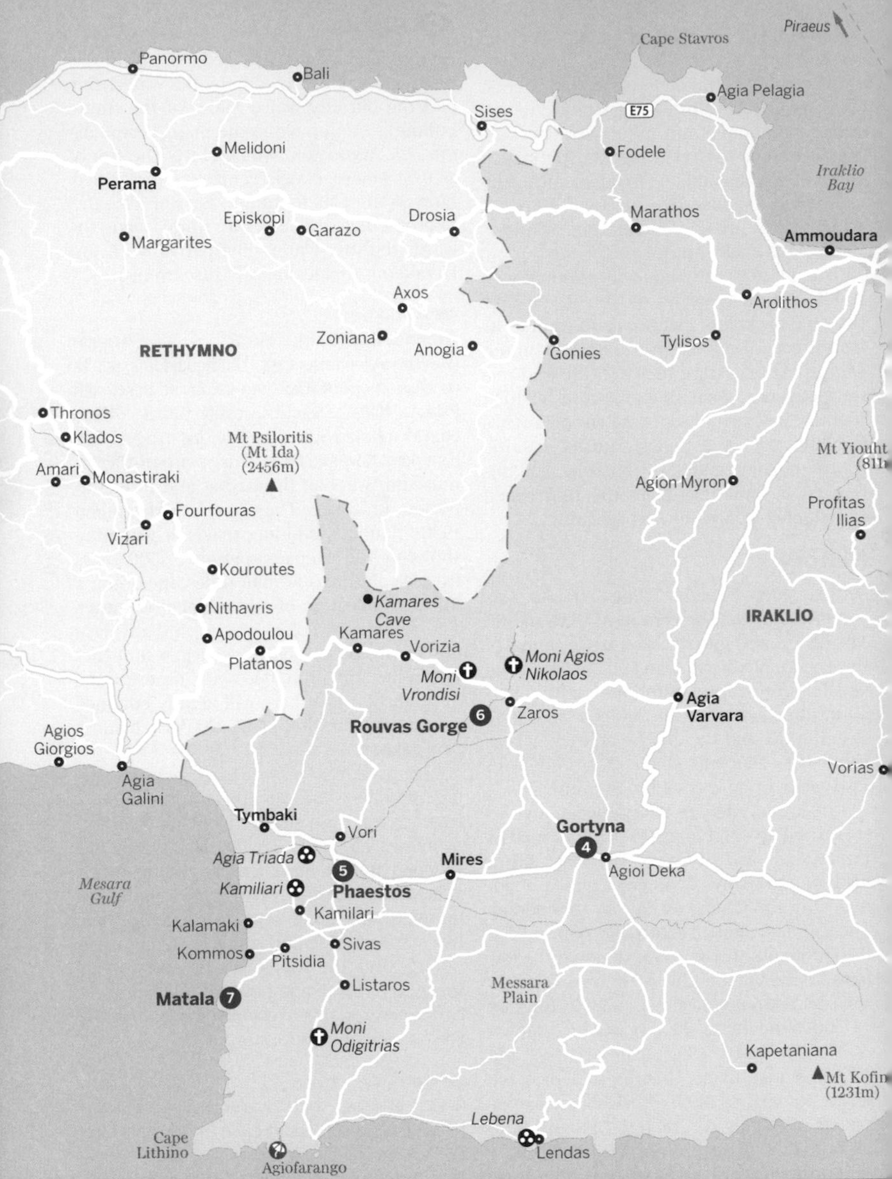

Iraklio Highlights

1 Heraklion Archaeological Museum (p163) Standing in awe of Minoan artistry at one of Greece's most incredible museums.

2 Iraklio Wine Country (p185) Discovering resurrected varietals on a wine-tasting excursion.

3 Palace of Knossos (p178) Making a date with King Minos at the cradle of Minoan civilisation.

4 Gortyna (p193) Squinting at 6th-century-BC law codes at this Roman Crete stronghold.

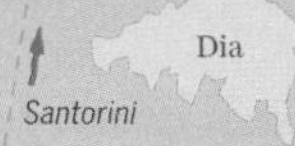

5 **Phaestos** (p194) Visiting the island's second-most-important Minoan palace-city.

6 **Rouvas Gorge** (p204) Ogling nature's creativity while hiking to Europe's largest Kermes oak–tree habitat.

7 **Matala** (p196) Gazing at the sunset cast across the cave-carved headlands of this mystical hippie hideaway.

8 **Nikos Kazantzakis Museum** (p190) Immersing yourself in the genius of Cretan-born author Nikos Kazantzakis in his ancestral village of Myrtia.

Iraklio

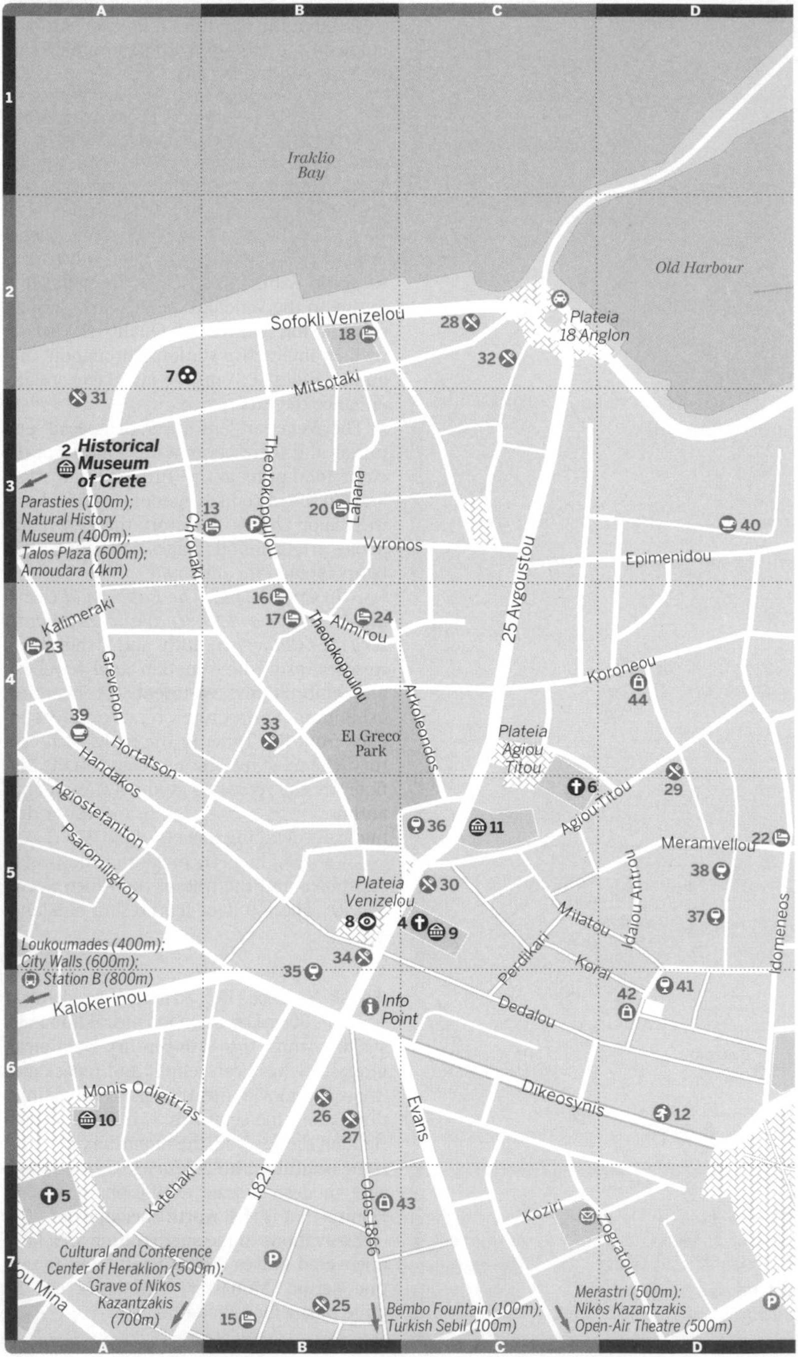

A B C D

1 2 3 4 5 6 7

Iraklio Bay

Old Harbour

Plateia 18 Anglon

Sofokli Venizelou

Mitsotaki

2 Historical Museum of Crete

Parasties (100m); Natural History Museum (400m); Talos Plaza (600m); Amoudara (4km)

Theotokopoulou

Lahana

Chronaki

Vyronos

Epimenidou

25 Avgoustou

Kalimeraki

Almirou

Theotokopoulou

Grevenon

Koroneou

Arkoleondos

El Greco Park

Plateia Agiou Titou

Hortatson

Handakos

Agiostefaniton

Psaromiligkon

Agiou Titou

Meramvellou

Plateia Venizelou

Milatou

Idaiou Antrou

Idomeneos

Perdikari

Korai

Loukoumades (400m); City Walls (600m); Station B (800m)

Kalokerinou

Info Point

Dedalou

Monis Odigitrias

Dikeosynis

Evans

Katehaki

1821

Odos 1866

Koziri

Zogratou

ou Mina

Cultural and Conference Center of Heraklion (500m); Grave of Nikos Kazantzakis (700m)

Bembo Fountain (100m); Turkish Sebil (100m)

Merastri (500m); Nikos Kazantzakis Open-Air Theatre (500m)

2 4 5 6 7 8 9 10 11 12 13 15 16 17 18 20 22 23 24 25 26 27 28 29 30 31 32 33 34 35 36 37 38 39 40 41 42 43 44

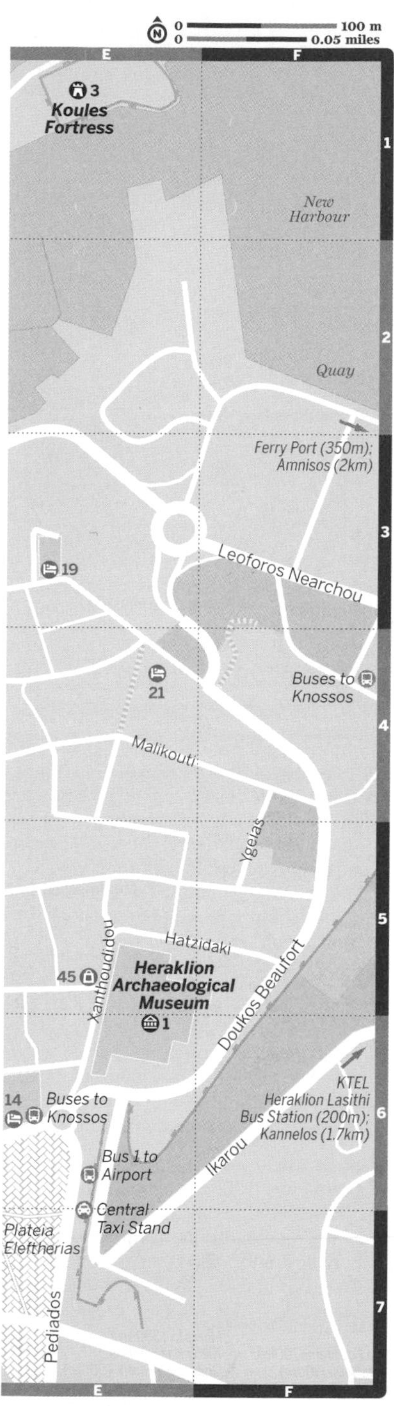

The presentation is insightful and atmospheric thanks to muted light filtering in through the old cannon holes. Visits conclude on the rooftop, with panoramic views over the sea and the city.

★**Historical Museum of Crete** MUSEUM
(www.historical-museum.gr; Sofokli Venizelou 27; adult/concession €5/3; ⏲9am-5pm Mon-Sat, 10.30am-3pm Sun Apr-Oct, to 3.30pm daily Nov-Mar) If you're wondering what Crete's been up to for the past, say, 1700 years, a spin around this engagingly curated museum is in order. Exhibits hopscotch from the Byzantine to the Venetian and Turkish periods, culminating with WWII. Quality English labelling, interactive stations throughout and audio guides (€3) in five languages greatly enhance the experience.

The Venetian era receives special emphasis and there's even a huge model of the city c 1650 prior to the Turkish occupation. Start in the introductory room, which charts the major phases of history through maps, books, artefacts and images. First-floor highlights include the only two **El Greco paintings** in Crete (1569's *The Baptism of Christ* and 1570's *View of Mt Sinai and the Monastery of St Catherine*), 13th- and 14th-century frescoes, exquisite Venetian gold jewellery, and embroidered vestments. A historical exhibition charts Crete's road to independence from the Turks in the early 20th century. The most interesting rooms on the 2nd floor are the recreated study of Cretan-born author **Nikos Kazantzakis** and those dramatically detailing aspects of the WWII **Battle of Crete** in 1941, including the Cretan resistance and the role of the Allied Secret Service. The top floor features an outstanding **folklore collection**.

Monastery of St Peter & St Paul RUINS
(Sofokli Venizelou 19; admission by donation; ⏲10am-2.30pm May-Sep) One of Iraklio's most striking ruins, this 13th-century Dominican monastery has been rebuilt and repackaged (mosque, movie theatre) numerous times throughout the centuries. Unusually located right on the sea wall, the monastery contains some beautiful 15th-century frescoes, as well as a modern mosaic exhibition by Loukas Peiniris that is well worth checking out.

Excavations in the surrounding area have uncovered graves dating to the 2nd Byzantine period. Monastery caretakers can be quite pushy for a donation.

Iraklio

Top Sights

1 Heraklion Archaeological Museum ... E6
2 Historical Museum of Crete ... A3
3 Koules Fortress ... E1

Sights

4 Agios Markos Basilica ... C5
5 Agios Minas Cathedral ... A7
6 Church of Agios Titos ... C5
7 Monastery of St Peter & St Paul ... A2
8 Morosini Fountain ... B5
9 Municipal Art Gallery ... C5
10 Museum of Christian Art ... A6
11 Venetian Loggia ... C5

Activities, Courses & Tours

12 Mountaineering Club of Iraklio ... D6

Sleeping

13 Atrion Hotel ... B3
14 Capsis Astoria ... E6
15 Crops Suites ... B7
16 Hotel Mirabello ... B4
17 Kastro Hotel ... B4
18 Kronos Hotel ... B2
19 Lato Boutique Hotel ... E3
20 Lena Hotel ... B3
21 Marin Dream Hotel ... E4
22 Olive Green Hotel ... D5
23 Rea Hotel ... A4
24 So Young Hostel ... B4

Eating

25 Athali ... B7
26 Bitzarakis Bakery ... B6
Brillant/Herbs' Garden ... (see 19)
27 Giakoumis ... B6
28 Ippokambos ... C2
29 Kouzeineri ... D4
30 Kritikos Fournos ... C5
31 Mare Cafe ... A3
32 O Vrakas ... C2
33 Peskesi ... B4
34 Phyllo Sofies ... B5

Drinking & Nightlife

35 Bitters Bar ... B6
36 Central Park ... C5
37 Crop ... D5
38 Fix ... D5
39 Utopia ... A4
40 Veneto ... D3
41 Xalavro ... D6

Shopping

42 Aerakis Music ... D6
43 Iraklio Central Market ... B7
44 Ora Gentleman ... D4
45 Zalo ... E5

Museum of Christian Art MUSEUM
(St Catherine of Sinai; St Catherine's Sq; adult/concession €4/2; 9.30am-7.30pm Apr-Oct, to 5pm Nov-Mar;) Housed in a 13th-century monastery that was later a mosque, this tiny but fascinating museum features well-displayed historic religious artworks from monasteries around Crete. Paintings, woodcraft, manuscripts and stone carvings are presented in a clear manner with English descriptions. Star exhibits include works by 15th-century icon hagiographer Angelos Akotantos and post-Byzantine painter Michael Damaskinos.

It's opposite Agios Minas Cathedral.

Agios Minas Cathedral CATHEDRAL
(Plateia Agias Ekaterinis; hours vary) One of Greece's largest cathedrals, with space for 8000 worshippers, Agios Minas was constructed between 1862 and 1895 and dedicated to the patron saint of Iraklio.

Highlights in the imposing interior include the wall frescoes, the trio of giant chandeliers dangling down the centre aisle and the white-marble iconostasis (the screen that separates the sanctuary from the main nave).

Morosini Fountain FOUNTAIN
(Lion Fountain; Plateia Venizelou) Four water-spouting lions make up this charming fountain, the town's most beloved Venetian vestige. Built in 1628 by Francesco Morosini, it once supplied Iraklio with fresh water.

Flanked by bustling cafes and fast-food joints, it's a fun spot to spend an hour resting and people-watching.

Municipal Art Gallery GALLERY
(cnr 25 Avgoustou & Plateia Venizelou; 9am-3pm) FREE The three-aisled 13th-century Agios Markos Basilica was reconstructed many times and turned into a mosque by the Turks. Today it's an exhibit space showcasing the work of Greek and foreign artists.

Turkish Sebil HISTORIC BUILDING
(Plateia Kornarou) FREE Iraklio's only remaining Turkish-era pump house once supplied drinking water to the local population. It was undergoing renovation at research time, with plans to turn it into a small cafe in the future.

Natural History Museum MUSEUM
(www.nhmc.uoc.gr; Sofokli Venizelou; adult/concession €7.50/4.50; 9am-9pm Mon-Sat, 10am-6pm

Sun Jun-Sep, 9am-3pm Mon-Fri, 10am-6pm Sat Nov-Apr, to 6pm daily May & Oct) In an imaginatively recycled power station, a 10-minute walk west from 25 Avgoustou along the waterfront, this museum uses huge dioramas and a terrarium wing to introduce you to the flora and fauna of Crete and the Mediterranean.

Stars of the show include the life-size (5m by 7m) representation of the elephant-like *Deinotherium gigantum*, the world's third-largest land mammal, and the shivering and shaking classroom earthquake simulator.

Grave of Nikos Kazantzakis HISTORIC SITE
(Martinengo Bastion) FREE A simple tomb in the well-preserved Martinengo Bastion south of the city centre honours Nikos Kazantzakis (1883–1957), Crete's most acclaimed 20th-century writer and the author of *Zorba the Greek*. The famous epitaph on his grave reads: 'I hope for nothing, I fear nothing, I am free'.

Kazantzakis was buried in the former fortifications because the Greek Orthodox Church, which had threatened him with excommunication because of his critical and controversial writings about the church and religion, denied him a burial in a cemetery.

Church of Agios Titos CHURCH
(www.agiostitos.gr; Plateia Agiou Titou; hours vary) This majestic church dominates the eponymous, palm-studded square. It had Byzantine origins in AD 961, was converted to a Catholic church by the Venetians and turned into a mosque by the Ottomans, who used the bell tower as a minaret. It has been an Orthodox church since 1925.

Its most revered possession is once again the skull relic of St Titus, returned here in 1966 after being spirited to Venice for safekeeping during the Turkish occupation.

City Walls FORTRESS
Iraklio burst out of its walls long ago, but these massive fortifications, with seven bastions and four gates, are still very conspicuous, dwarfing the concrete 20th-century structures around them. The Venetians built the defences between 1462 and 1562. You can follow the walls around the heart of the city, though it's not a particularly scenic trip.

Venetian Loggia HISTORIC BUILDING
(25 Avgoustou) FREE The attractively reconstructed 17th-century loggia by Francesco Morosini was the Venetian version of a gentlemen's club, where the male aristocracy gathered for drinks and gossip.

On the north side of the building, note the partly preserved relief that once adorned the town's Sagredo Fountain and was incorporated into the loggia during its 1962 reconstruction.

Agios Markos Basilica CHURCH
(cnr 25 Avgostou & Plateia Venizelou; 9am-3pm) FREE Located opposite Morosini Fountain and dedicated to St Mark, the patron saint of Venice, Agios Markos Basilica was built at the beginning of Venetian rule in 1239. Today it houses the changing exhibitions of the Municipal Art Gallery.

Bembo Fountain FOUNTAIN
(Plateia Kornarou) Iraklio's first fountain was cobbled together in the 1550s from antique materials, including Venetian coats of arms and a statue of a Roman official found near Ierapetra, and it channelled fresh water into town via an aqueduct running 13km south to Mt Yiouhtas.

The adjacent hexagonal building was originally a pump house added by the Turks.

Beaches

Ammoudara, about 4km west of Iraklio, and Amnisos, 2km to the east, are the closest beaches; the latter is just past the airport and gets quite a bit of noise. The strands in Agia Pelagia, some 20km west of town, are nicer.

Activities

Mountaineering Club of Iraklio OUTDOORS
(2810 227609; www.eos-her.gr; Dikeosynis 53; 8.30-10.30pm Mon-Fri) The club arranges hiking trips across Crete most weekends (trip programs are published on the website). Anyone is welcome to join in.

IRAKLIO RESOURCES

Heraklion History (http://history.heraklion.gr) Provides an excellent overview of the history of the city and its monuments through the ages.

Historical Museum of Crete (www.historical-museum.gr) The official museum website has an excellent overview of Crete since Byzantine times.

Municipality of Heraklion (www.heraklion-city.gr) The municipality website has brief general information on the city.

Tours

Cretan Adventures OUTDOORS
(☎6944790771; www.cretanadventures.gr) This well-regarded local company, run by friendly and knowledgeable English-speaking Fondas, organises hiking tours, mountain biking and extreme outdoor excursions.

It also coordinates fabulous week-long guided and self-guided hiking tours (from around €800), including detailed hiking instructions, luggage transfer and accommodation with breakfast. Fondas' office is up on the 3rd floor and easy to miss.

Sleeping

Iraklio is a big city and Crete's major point of entry, so it's well supplied with all manner of accommodation. Most options fall into the midrange price bracket, and there are a few smarter, boutique-style and business hotels peppered about. This is more a port than a resort, so beach retreats aren't a feature. The tourist tax ranges from €0.50 to €4 per room per night.

So Young Hostel HOSTEL €
(☎6978871355; www.facebook.com/soyoung heraklion; Almirou 22; dm/d from €21/40; ❄📶) One of Iraklio's best central hostels, So Young, opened in 2018, earns high marks for its wonderful guest kitchen and even better rooftop terrace. Dorms come in both female and mixed varieties, with four-to-six- and eight-bed configurations, good mattresses and particle-board lockers. Interestingly, showers are co-ed.

Lena Hotel HOTEL €
(☎28102 23280; www.lena-hotel.gr; Lahana 10; s with/without bathroom €40/35, d with/without bathroom €50/40, tr €70; ❄📶) Everything's a bit long in the tooth, but this no-nonsense 16-room hotel is still a good budget pick. Amenities vary, but each room has its own bathroom and solo travellers score double beds in the single rooms. Communal areas are nicely maintained and the staff is particularly friendly. Breakfast costs €8.

Rea Hotel HOTEL €
(☎2810 223638; www.hotelrea.gr; Kalimeraki 1; d/tr €46/54, d without bathroom €38; ⏰Mar-Nov; ❄📶) Family-run Rea has an easy, friendly atmosphere and 15 compact but neat-as-a-pin rooms dressed in shades from vanilla to chocolate. There's a book exchange, too. Optional continental breakfast costs €3.

Museum Tour
Heraklion Archaeological Museum

LENGTH: TWO HOURS

Start on the ❶ **ground floor**, where rooms I to III focus on the Neolithic period to the Middle Bronze Age (7000 BC to 1700 BC), showing life in the first settlements in Crete and around Knossos. In room II, don't miss the ❷ **golden pendant with bees** from Malia, a sophisticated jeweller's masterpiece depicting two bees depositing a drop of honey into a honeycomb; the finial sceptre handle in the shape of panther; and the extensive jewellery collection. The standout in room III is the elaborately embellished ❸ **Kamares tableware** of red, black and white clay, including a 'royal dinner service' from Phaestos.

Rooms IV to VI illustrate life in the Late Bronze Age (1700 BC to 1450 BC). This is when Minoan culture reached its zenith. Not surprisingly, these are among the most visited rooms and the collection here is vast. Highlights include the ❹ **small clay house from Arhanes**, a stunning ❺ **ivory-and-crystal inlaid draughts board** and a scale model of Knossos. Most visitors home in on the ❻ **Phaistos disc**, a stunning clay piece embossed with 45 signs that has never been deciphered. Nearby, the massive ❼ **copper ingots** from Agia Triada and Zakros Palace demonstrate important units of economic exchange. Other gems include the ❽ **bull-leaping fresco** and the incredible ❾ **bull-leaper sculpture** (room VI) that show daring sporting practices of the time.

Rooms VII and VIII reveal the importance of Minoan religion and ideology, with cult objects and figurines. Don't miss the stone bull's head and the gorgeous limestone lioness vessels. Room VII houses the ❿ **chieftain's cup** from Agia Triada, which portrays two men, one holding a staff, the other a sword. In room VIII, the ⓫ **snake goddesses** and ⓬ **stone bull's head** are two stunning ceremonial items from Knossos.

Rooms IX and X are dedicated to the Palace of Knossos and its emergence as a centralised state (after the administra-

HERAKLION ARCHAEOLOGICAL MUSEUM

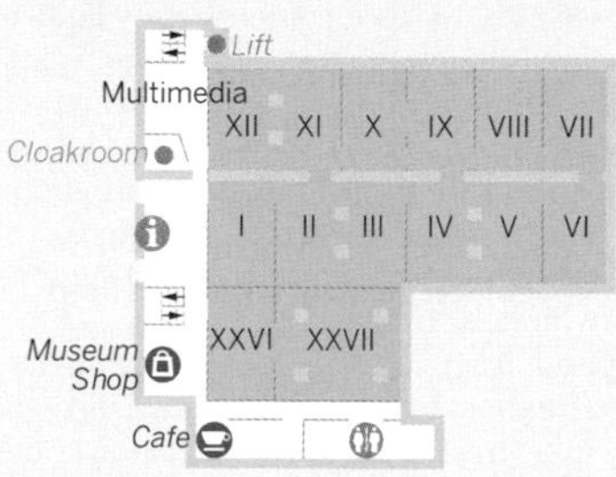

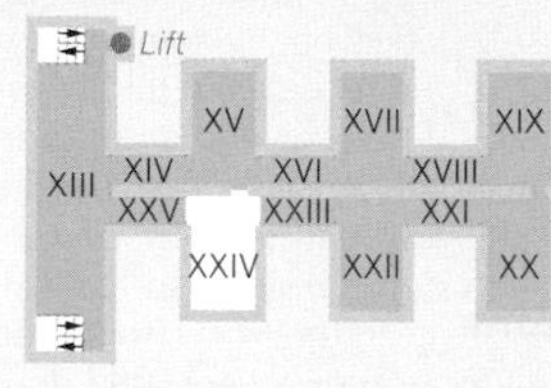

tive collapse of other palaces) along with evidence of the Mycenaeans. ⓭ **Linear B clay tablets** reveal the first 'Greek' script and indicate Knossos' complex administrative system and bureaucratic processes. In room X, look for the extraordinary ⓮ **boar's-tusk helmet** (complete with cheek guards) and the ⓯ **gold-handled swords**, displaying the importance of the aristocratic warrior status.

Rooms XI and XII feature settlements, sanctuaries and graves of the Late Bronze Age, including fascinating representations of death. The extraordinary ⓰ **sarcophagus** from Agia Triada (room XII) is presumed to be that of a ruler, given its detailed, honorific fresco-style scenes, including the sacrifice of a bull (you can just make out the horror in his eyes).

On the ⓱ **1st floor**, room XIII showcases Minoan frescoes (1800 BC to 1350 BC), including re-creations by archaeologist ⓲ **Sir Arthur Evans** (p182). The paintings, including the ⓳ **Prince of the Lilies**, the ⓴ **Ladies in Blue**, the ㉑ **Cupbearer**, ㉒ **La Parisienne** and the ㉓ **Dolphin Fresco**, reflect the interest in art and nature at the time.

Rooms XV to XIX focus on the Geometric and Archaic periods (10th to 6th century BC), the transition to the Iron Age and the formation of the first Greek cities (the terracotta rainwater channels from Palaikastro will highlight the reverse evolution of gutters!). The ㉔ **Apollonian Triad**, bronze statues from Deros, are the earliest known Greek hammered-bronze statues, while the ㉕ **bronze shields of the Ideon Cave** are extravagant votive offerings to Zeus.

Rooms XX to XXII move to the Classical, Hellenistic and Roman periods (5th to 4th century BC), where utensils, figurines and stunning mosaic floors and amphorae set the scene for the foundation of the autonomous Greek city states, followed by civil wars and, finally, the Roman period. The huge ㉖ **Phalagari hoard of silver coins** (room XXI) is thought to be a military or state fund. The cemetery finds of these periods are especially fascinating: look out for the bronze skull with the gilded clay wreath (room XXII).

Room XXIII exhibits two private collections donated to the museum.

Back on the ㉗ **ground floor (part II)**, rooms XXVI and XXVII (7th to 4th century BC) house the museum's sculpture collection. Architectural reliefs from Gortyna demonstrate the role of Crete in the development of monumental sculpture, while Roman sculptures and copies of heroes and gods of the preceding Classical era showcase art during the Roman period.

Hotel Mirabello HOTEL €
(☎2810 285052; www.mirabello-hotel.gr; Theotokopoulou 20; s/d from €40/50; ❄@📶) Despite its dated, plain-Jane looks, this friendly and low-key hotel offers excellent value for money. Assets include squeaky-clean rooms with modern bathrooms, beds with individual reading lamps, a fridge and a kettle, plus a location close to, well, everything. The nicest units have a balcony.

There's no breakfast, but coffee and a few assorted pastries are offered.

Kronos Hotel HOTEL €
(☎2810 282240; www.kronoshotel.gr; Sofokli Venizelou 2; s/d €55/62; ❄@📶) In a good, if noisy, position near the waterfront, the no-frills but pleasant rooms here have double-glazed windows to block out noise, as well as balcony, phone, fridge and tiny TV. Some doubles have sea views.

The distinctly average breakfast costs €6.

★Crops Suites APARTMENT €€
(☎6974320857; www.cropssuites.com; Thiseos 3; apt incl breakfast €65; ❄📶) Smack in the town centre, these stylish one-bedroom apartments will leave you feeling like a local hipster. Featuring canary-yellow cabinetry, plush grey sofas and light hardwoods throughout, they come with full kitchens stocked with coffee, olive oil, raki and more. Spacious balconies with city views are perfect for a glass of crisp white wine at sunset and/or a cuppa at daybreak.

Provocative signage keeps things fun. Yiannis and Anthi are fabulous and friendly as well.

IRAKLIO WITH CHILDREN

Numerous kid-friendly activities are concentrated on the northern coast east of Iraklio, in Gournes and Hersonisos and surrounds. You can get as wet and wild as you like at water theme parks, including Water City (p207), Acqua Plus (p208) and Star Beach. Or, in Gournes, get in touch with your inner brontosaurus at Dinosauria (p207). Horsey folk can canter about with Arion Stables (p207). For something more cultural but equally fun, the Lychnostatis Open Air Museum (p207) will appeal to young minds not so keen on archaeological ruins.

Further south, don't miss visiting the rescued donkeys at Agia Marina Donkey Sanctuary (p199) and head off on some sandy rides with Melanouri Horse Farm (p199).

★Olive Green Hotel HOTEL €€
(☎2810 302900; www.olivegreenhotel.com; cnr Idomeneos & Meramvellou; d incl breakfast €109-126; ❄📶) This chic, contemporary hotel is probably Iraklio's hippest digs. Clean rooms feature minimalistic white and olive-green decor, with separate shower and toilet (as opposed to the usual Greek-style all-in-one bathroom), and feature large, impressive photographs of tempting travel destinations within an hour of the city.

Guests are given a tablet to control electronic room features, and the bread, olive-oil and raki treatment from check-in. Club rooms are especially spacious, with espresso machines and larger terraces. Solar panels and low-impact building materials give the place an eco edge, and there's a cool cafe that spills out into the plaza.

★Lato Boutique Hotel BOUTIQUE HOTEL €€
(☎2810 228103; www.lato.gr; Epimenidou 15; d incl breakfast from €80; ❄@📶) Iraklio goes Hollywood – with all the sass but sans the attitude – at this mod boutique hotel overlooking the old harbour, recognisable by its jazzy facade. With 79 rooms, it's hardly boutique, but smallish rooms are styled with rich woods and warm reds and have pillow-top mattresses and a playful lighting scheme. A newer annexe across the street is even more modern.

Capsis Astoria HOTEL €€
(☎2810 343080; www.capsishotel.gr; Plateia Eleftherias 11; s/d incl breakfast from €60/90; P❄@📶) Though the building itself is not of the latest vintage, small but fantastic newer rooms beckon at the Capsis Astoria. With splendid oak hardwoods, contemporary art, new TVs, small desks and ceiling fans, they make older rooms accented with historic black-and-white photographs look downright drab. About 30% of the 131-room inventory was finished at research time, with the renovation ongoing.

The hotel's in a handy location next to the Archaeological Museum and the bus stop to Knossos, and there's a summer rooftop pool.

Kastro Hotel HOTEL €€
(☎2810 284185; www.kastro-hotel.gr; Theotokopoulou 22; s/d/tr incl breakfast from

€50/80/95; ❄ 📶) Clearly, plenty of thought has gone into the design of the smartly renovated Kastro, with rooms accented in airy, seafaring colours like turquoise and aqua. Good-quality mattresses, strong hot showers, a good breakfast buffet and the rooftop terrace are all welcome aspects of this central city hotel.

Atrion Hotel HOTEL €€
(☎ 28102 46000; www.atrion.gr; Chronaki 9; s/d incl breakfast from €67/80; ❄ 📶) Although this modern, streamlined 60-room hotel was designed with the business brigade in mind, it's also a handy launch pad for city explorers. The carpeted rooms in shades of white and cinnamon come with a balcony (ask for a sea-facing one) and squeaky-clean bathrooms. Breakfast is served in the light-filled central atrium.

Marin Dream Hotel HOTEL €€
(☎ 2810 300018; www.marinhotel.gr; Epimenidou 46; s/d incl breakfast from €70/95; ❄ @ 📶) The Marin Dream is primarily a business hotel, but it also scores with leisure travellers thanks to its great location overlooking the harbour and the fortress (be sure to get a front room with balcony). Rooms are decked out in palatable chocolate and cherry colour schemes, with plain, no-nonsense furniture.

Eating

Iraklio has restaurants to suit all tastes and budgets, from excellent fish tavernas to cosmopolitan cuisine and top-quality Cretan fare.

Kritikos Fournos CAFE €
(www.kritikosfournosgeuseis.gr; Plateia Kallergon 3; snacks €1-5; ⏲ 6am-midnight; 📶 ✍) This fun cafe-bakery is a Cretan chain, and it's a dependable stop for good espresso (it opens at 6am!), baked goods, pastries and sandwiches (including tasty vegan focaccia options) and even a craft beer or two. Perch yourself in a choice people-watching spot overlooking Lion Sq and banter with the hip, friendly staff. Signed in Greek only.

Loukoumades BAKERY €
(Kalokerinou 243; 6 pieces €2.50; ⏲ 6am-midnight) Come here for delicious, fluffy *loukoumadhes* (massive ball-shaped doughnuts drizzled with honey, sesame seeds and cinnamon). One serving easily feeds two.

Phyllo Sophies CAFE €
(www.phyllosophies.gr; Plateia Venizelou 33; mains €3.50-12.50; ⏲ 6am-midnight; 📶) With tables sprawling towards the Morosini Fountain, this is a great place to sample *bougatsa* (creamy semolina pudding wrapped in a pastry envelope and sprinkled with cinnamon and sugar). The less-sweet version is made with *myzithra* (sheep's-milk cheese).

They're traditionally eaten for breakfast but, quite frankly, taste good any time of day. If you can't decide whether to go sweet or savoury, ask for a combination of the two.

Bitzarakis Bakery BAKERY €
(7 Odos 1821; snacks from €0.50; ⏲ 7am-3pm Mon, Thu & Sat, 5-9pm Tue, Wed & Fri) Sells excellent freshly baked *kalitsounia* (lightly fried filled pastries) along with other traditional sweets made by a women's cooperative.

★ **Peskesi** CRETAN €€
(☎ 2810 288887; www.peskesicrete.gr; Kapetan Haralampi 6-8; mains €9-14; ⏲ 1pm-2am; 📶 ✍) 🌿 It's almost impossible to overstate how good Peskesi's resurrected, slow-cooked Cretan dishes are, nor the beauty of the revamped Venetian villa in which you'll partake of them: this is Crete's finest culinary moment. Nearly everything is forged from heirloom produce and organic meats and olive oils from the restaurant's own farm.

You need look no further than *kreokakavos,* a Minoan roast pork you'll be dreaming about for years afterwards, though everything on the menu will leave you satisfied. The all-Cretan wine list is tops, too. Peskesi oozes rustic sophistication from every nook and cranny of its maze of stone rooms lidded by wood-beam ceilings. It's located in a tiny lane off the northwestern corner of El Greco Park. Book ahead.

★ **Merastri** CRETAN €€
(☎ 2810 221910; www.facebook.com/merastri; Chrisostomou 17; mains €5-13; ⏲ 6pm-midnight Tue-Sun Jun-Aug, 6pm-midnight Tue-Sat, noon-midnight Sun Sep-May; 📶) Enjoying one of the most authentic Cretan meals in town, served in this stunning home (a former music building), is a highlight of dining in Iraklio. The family of owners is passionate about its products (including oil and wine), and will conjure up everything from slow-cooked lamb to porterhouse steak with wine and sage.

Parasties GREEK €€
(☎ 2810 225009; www.parastiescrete.gr; Handakos 81; mains €9-43; ⏲ noon-1am; 📶) Parasties' owner, Haris, is genuine about serving great-quality local produce and top Cretan

wines. And his passion shows in his gourmet menu of inventively updated traditional fare, including a daily special. Grab a seat under an annexe with a bar, in the roomy dining area or on the patio with sea views.

Kannelos SEAFOOD €€

(www.kanelos.gr; Ikarou 32; fish per kg €5-30; ⏲7am-3pm Mon-Sat) Escape the touristy seafood restaurants for this speciality shop, which has nabbed its own wares with proprietary fishing boats since 1926. With around 40 fish and shrimp varieties on ice, you'll be spoilt for choice. Pick your fish, and it'll be grilled or fried up on the spot (€3) and served with an olive-oil and lemon sauce.

Athali CRETAN €€

(☎2815 200012; www.athali.gr; Karterou 20; mains €8.50-15.50; ⏲noon-midnight; 📶) This colourful, crowd-pleasing restaurant is a true family affair: Dad oversees a massive central open fire, roasting spits of succulent lamb and pork for hours, while Mum handles traditional hearty stews such as rustic chicken, rooster and *youvetsi* (baked lamb with tomatoes and *kritharaki* pasta served with *anthotiro* cheese) in the kitchen and their three personable daughters serve.

Kouzeineri INTERNATIONAL €€

(☎2810 346452; www.facebook.com/kouzeineri; Agiou Titou 30; mains €10-49; ⏲noon-midnight Mon-Sat, to 11pm Sun; 📶) Those seeking a traditional Greek meal might be disappointed here, but diners looking for an ultra-contemporary experience will be happy with the modern music, cutting-edge design, and steaks- and chops-focused menu, which also dabbles in more global dishes (spicy buffalo wings, for example). Burgers, if you're in need, are perfectly charred and surprisingly rich – a welcome change of pace. Great wine list, too.

O Vrakas SEAFOOD €€

(Marinelli 1; mains €7-16; ⏲noon-2am; 📶) Along the waterfront on the tourist strip, this spot is neither grand nor out of the pages of a gourmet magazine, but it was started by the owner's grandfather and has morphed from *ouzerie* grilling fish on the pavement (no longer permitted) to a reliable, value-for-money place, with a Canadian-Greek chef dishing up Greek favourites.

Ippokambos SEAFOOD €€

(☎2810 280240; Sofokli Venizelou 3; mains €7-17; ⏲12.30am-midnight Mon-Sat; 📶) This long-running *ouzerie* just a stone's throw from the fish market specialises in fish – usually freshly caught (if not, they let you know it's frozen, as is the case with the seafood), simply but expertly prepared and sold at fair prices. In summer, park yourself on the covered waterfront terrace.

Mare Cafe CAFE €€

(☎28102 41946; www.mare-cafe.gr; Sofokli Venizelou; mains €4.50-22; ⏲8am-2am; 📶) In an enviable location on the beautified waterfront promenade opposite the Historical Museum (p167), trendy Mare is great for seaside munchies (burgers, salads, pasta and more sophisticated staples) and even better for post-culture java and sunset drinks.

Brillant/Herbs' Garden CRETAN €€

(☎28102 28103; www.brillantrestaurant.gr; Lato Boutique Hotel, Epimenidou 15; mains €8-18.50; ⏲1pm-midnight) The avant-garde decor at Brillant, the fashionable culinary outpost at Lato Boutique Hotel (p172), may almost distract you from the creatively composed, feistily flavoured Cretan cuisine. The menu changes seasonally, and from May to October it's also served on the Herbs' Garden rooftop, for alfresco dining with sea views.

Giakoumis TAVERNA €€

(www.facebook.com/giakoumisestiatorio; Theodosaki 8; mains €6-13; ⏲7am-11pm) The oldest among the row of tavernas vying for business in a quiet passageway off Odos 1866, Giakoumis offers myriad *mayirefta* (ready-cooked meals) and grills. Don't go past the lamb chops: the cook has been grilling them for over 40 years and has perfected the seasoning and method.

Drinking & Nightlife

In Iraklio it always seems to be 6pm (the official 'drinking' time in some countries). The hip crowd congregates around Korai and Perdikari, while El Greco Park has a more mainstream feel. West of here, Handakos, Agiostefaniton and Psaromiligkon are more alternative-flavoured hangouts. Nearby, there's a lively cafe scene in the tiny lanes of Zampeliou and Kagiampi.

★ **Xalavro** COCKTAIL BAR

(www.facebook.com/xalavro; Milatou 10; ⏲10am-3am; 📶) This rather idyllic open-air bar gets a whole lot right, with charming servers slinging creative cocktails to a diverse crowd of holidaymakers and locals in the ruins of an archaeologically protected roofless stone house. It exudes *Ef Zin* – the Greek art of living well.

Bitters Bar COCKTAIL BAR
(www.thebittersbar.com; Plateia Venizelou; ⌚8pm-3am Mon-Thu, to 5am Fri-Sun; 📶) The indisputable frontrunner of Iraklio's mixology scene is this den of Prohibition-inspired decadence centred on a retail alcove just off Lion Sq. Throwback cocktails dominate the classics on the list, but let the bartenders shine with creations such as Bitters House (gin, ginger syrup, pink-grapefruit and lemon juice, cardamom bitters) and Attaboy (vodka, mango puree, lemon juice, aromatic bitters).

Crop CRAFT BEER
(www.crop.coffee; Aretousas 4; ⌚7am-1am; 📶) Crop divides its focus equally between two vices: caffeine and craft beer. At the time of writing it was Iraklio's only craft-focused bar, with five independent taps (including Crete's own Solo Brewing and Brewdog, and 25 or so bottled; beers cost €4 to €6). It's also a highly recommended roastery specialising in Third Wave coffee preparations such as V60 and Chemex.

Fix BAR
(www.facebook.com/fix.heraklion; Aretousas 2; ⌚9am-3am Mon-Thu, to 11pm Fri & Sat; 📶) If the trendy cafes along this pedestrian strip don't do it for you, grab a table at down-to-earth Fix, which is sought out by an older crowd of conversationalists.

Central Park LOUNGE
(www.central-park.gr; Arkoleontos 19; ⌚8am-1am; 📶) Grab an outdoor table, guzzle a cold one (a brew or a Freddo espresso) and watch the world on parade at this buzzy cafe.

Utopia CAFE
(www.facebook.com/outopiacafebeeroutopia; Handakos 51; ⌚9am-2am; 📶) If you worship at the cocoa altar, make a beeline to this been-here-forever cafe for the best hot chocolate in town (14 varieties, none of which is translated; hazelnut praline is especially recommended). Go all out with a side order of ice cream or a delectable pastry, or skip the sweet stuff altogether and choose from the extensive beer menu.

Veneto CAFE
(www.facebook.com/Venetorestaurantira; Epimenidou 9; ⌚10am-1am; 📶) For a swanky night out, head towards this stylish outpost above the Venetian harbour for coffee, cocktails or a light meal. It's a lofty space with exposed wooden rafters and clubby leather chairs hemmed in by a long bar, panoramic windows and a naive mural of Venice.

WORTH A TRIP

NORWEGIAN BREW

Norwegian brewer Kjetil Jikiun started Norway's first craft brewery (Nøgne Ø) before he founded Crete's first craft brewery (he's clearly a man of firsts), **Solo Brewery** (www.solobeer.gr; Kointoirioti 35; ⌚noon-5pm; 📶). There's no taproom per se, but drinking here is a worthwhile excursion for beer connoisseurs. A wealth of IPAs, stouts and porters, and hoppy saisons across five taps and numerous bottles await for makeshift front-patio consumption.

It's 6km southeast of Lion Sq, in the industrial settlement of Kalithea. Bus 14 from Plateia Eleftherias (airport bus stop) drops you within 50m of the taps, but it only heads out six or so times per day. A taxi (€7 to €9) makes more sense.

☆ Entertainment

Cultural and Conference Center of Heraklion ARTS CENTRE
(☎2810 229618; Plastira 10) This new and modern five-building complex, opened in 2019, is Crete's most important cultural and events venue. It includes the gorgeous 800-seat Andreas and Maria Kalokairinou Hall, designed for theatre, opera and classical-music performances.

Shopping

Iraklio has some good shopping along 25 Avgoustou, Dedalou and Handakos. Institution the Iraklio Central Market has some worthwhile buys alongside lots of tourist tat.

★Zalo GIFTS & SOUVENIRS
(www.zalo.gr; Papa Aleksandrou 2; ⌚9am-9pm Mon-Sat, to 4pm Sun) This recommended shop specialises in the kinds of souvenirs that won't embarrass you a year down the track: designer art prints, jewellery, notebooks, frameable postcards, funky handbags and the like, all 100% made in Greece from a network of cutting-edge, contemporary artists and designers.

Ora Gentleman CLOTHING
(☎2810 331164; www.oragentleman.com; Koroneou 18; ⌚10am-2pm & 5.30-9.30pm Mon-Sat)

Cretan pursuer of finer things Nikos Makridakas designs his own top-shelf clothing for men (including made-to-measure options), combining the best of British and Italian-inspired design with his own epicurean Greek ethos. His popular pocket squares (from €25) are fashioned from Soufli silk, but the linen shirts, colourful polos and restrained T-shirts (all perfect upscale island wear) are enticing, too.

Aerakis Music MUSIC
(☎2810 225758; www.aerakis.net; Korai 14; ⊙9am-9pm Mon-Fri, to 5pm Sat) An Iraklio landmark since 1974, this little shop stocks an expertly curated selection of Cretan and Greek music, from old and rare recordings to the latest releases, many on its own record labels, Cretan Musical Workshop and Seistron.

Iraklio Central Market MARKET
(Odus 1866; ⊙hours vary) An Iraklio institution, if slightly touristy these days, this busy, narrow *agora* (market), along Odos 1866 between the Meidani crossroads and Plateia Kornarou, is one of the best in Crete and has everything you need to put together a delicious picnic.

Information

EMERGENCY

Tourist Police (☎28104 409500, emergency 171; Dikeosynis 10; ⊙7am-10pm) In the suburb of Halikarnassos, near the airport.

INTERNET ACCESS

Wi-fi is ubiquitous in hotels, restaurants and cafes, and there's also the free 'municipality_of_heraklion' wi-fi network. You'll see wireless charging benches scattered around town.

MEDICAL SERVICES

University Hospital of Heraklion (☎28103 92111; www.pagni.gr; Stavrakia; ⊙24hr)

Venizelio General Hospital (☎28134 08000; www.venizeleio.gr; Knossos Rd; ⊙24hr emergency)

MONEY

Banks with ATMs are plentiful, especially along 25 Avgoustou.

POST

ELTA (Hellenic Post; www.elta.gr; Plateia Daskalogianni; ⊙7.30am-8pm Mon-Fri, to 2pm Sat)

TOURIST INFORMATION

Tourist Info Point (☎28134 09777; www.heraklion.gr; Plateia Venizelou; ⊙8.30am-2.30pm Mon-Fri)

TRAVEL AGENCIES

Paleologos (☎28103 46185; www.paleologos.gr; 25 Avgoustou 5; ⊙9am-8pm Mon-Fri, to 3pm Sat)

Getting There & Away

AIR

About 5km east of Iraklio city centre, the Nikos Kazantzakis Heraklion International Airport (p296) has an ATM, a duty-free shop and a few cafe-bars. It receives numerous daily flights from throughout Greece and Europe as well as Tel Aviv with Bluebird Airways (www.bluebirdair.com).

BOAT

The **ferry port** (☎28103 38000; www.portheraklion.gr) is 500m east of Koules Fortress and the old harbour. Iraklio is a major port for access to many of the Greek islands, though services are spotty outside high season. Tickets can be purchased online or through travel agencies, including central Paleologos. Daily ferries from

FERRIES FROM IRAKLIO

DESTINATION	FARE (€)	DURATION (HR)	FREQUENCY
Halki	22.00	12	two weekly
Ios	69.00 to 71.00	2½	one to six weekly
Karpathos	19.00	8	two weekly
Kasos	20.00	6	two weekly
Mykonos	55.00 to 84.00	4½	daily to five weekly
Naxos	77.80	3½	daily
Paros	64.70	3¾	daily
Piraeus	29.00 to 46.00	8½	daily
Rhodes	29.00	14½	two weekly
Santorini (Thira)	42.00 to 68.80	1¾	daily to five weekly

Ferries to **Thessaloniki** are on again, off again seasonally – it's best to fly.

Iraklio's port include services to Piraeus and faster catamarans to Santorini and other Cycladic islands. Ferries sail east to Rhodes via Sitia, Kasos, Karpathos and Halki.

Popular services from Iraklio include the following. Price and duration vary by ferry company; frequency reflects the summer high season (June to September).

BUS

Iraklio's long-distance **bus station** (☎28102 46530; www.ktelherlas.gr; Leoforos Ikarou 9;) opened to fanfare in 2018 on the site of a revamped soap and olive-oil factory east of the centre on Ikarou. This highly organised depot serves major destinations in eastern and western Crete, including Hania, Rethymno, Agios Nikolaos, Sitia and the Lassithi Plateau.

City bus 2 to **Knossos** (€1.70, every 10 to 30 minutes) leaves from its own **stop** (Efessou) on the site of the old long-distance bus station at the rear of the GDM Megaron Hotel, 200m or so northwest of the new long-distance station. Perhaps more conveniently, you can also catch it at **Plateia Eleftherias** (Plateia Eleftherias).

Little more than a parking lot just beyond Hania Gate west of the centre, the now-decommissioned **Bus Station B** (Chanioporta Station; ☎28102 55965; Machis Kritis 3;) serves the traditional village of Anogia (€4.10, 1½ hours, 9am, noon and 2pm). There's a ticket office inside Restaurant Chanioporta across the street.

LONG-DISTANCE TAXI

For destinations around Crete, you can order a cab from **Crete Taxi Services** (☎6970021970; www.crete-taxi.gr; 24hr) or **Crete Cab** (☎6955171473; www.crete.cab). There are also long-distance cabs waiting at the airport, at Plateia Eleftherias (outside the Capsis Astoria hotel) and at KTEL Heraklion Lassithi Bus Station. Sample fares for up to four people include Agios Nikolaos €84, Hersonisos €40, Malia €50, Matala €86 and Rethymno €101.

Getting Around

TO/FROM THE AIRPORT

The airport is just off the E75, about 5km east of the city centre. Buses run to points in the city, including the port, the regional (and local) bus stations and Plateia Eleftherias, from 6am to midnight (€1.20, every 10 to 15 minutes) from a stop about 50m in front of the departures door. Buy tickets at the bus-stop machine or with the attendant (on board the fare is €2).

Taxis wait outside the arrivals terminal. The fare into town is a fixed rate €15 (outlying destinations are by meter).

BUSES FROM IRAKLIO

The following services leave from the main bus station on the waterfront east of Koules Fortress.

DESTINATION	FARE (€)	DURATION (HR)	*FREQUENCY
Agia Galini	8.70	2	5 daily
Agia Pelagia	2.70	¾	hourly 8.30am-9.30pm
Agios Nikolaos	7.70	1½	half-hourly 6.30am-8.45pm
Arhanes	2.00	½	14 daily
Hania	15.10	3	half-hourly 5.30am-9.30pm
Hersonisos	3.30	¾	20 daily
Ierapetra	12.00	2½	7 daily
Kastelli	4.00	1½	6 daily
Knossos**	1.70	½	frequent
Malia	4.10	1	18 daily
Matala	8.50	2	7.30am & 12.45pm
Mires	6.00	1¼	11 daily
Phaestos	7.10	1½	every 2hr
Rethymno	8.30	1½	hourly 5.30am-9.30pm
Sitia	16.00	3	4 daily

*Frequency reflects the summer high season (June to September).

** Leaves from stop adjacent to KTEL Heraklion Lassithi Bus Station.

BUS

KTEL (www.ktelherlas.gr) runs Iraklio's blue-and-white city buses. Fares are €1.20 (€2 if purchased on board). Two lines are free. The blue line runs hourly from 9.30am to 4.30pm, starting at Hotel Apollonia and stopping at the Heraklion Archaeological Museum, the Historical Museum of Crete, Koules Fortress and Knossos, while the red line runs hourly from 9.15am to 4.15pm from the port, making more or less the same stops. (These buses are not to be confused with the pay hop-on, hop-off blue-and-red buses.)

A daily bus pass is €5.

For the airport, catch **bus 1** (Plateia Eleftherias).

CAR & MOTORCYCLE

Iraklio's streets are narrow and chaotic, so it's best to drop your vehicle in a car park (between €5 and €12 per day), and explore on foot; though not the cheapest option, it doesn't get much more central than **Theseus Parking** (www.facebook.com/theseusparking; Thiseos 18; 1st hour €4.80, per additional hour €.80, overnight €12). All the international car-hire companies have branches at the airport. Local outlets line the northern end of 25 Avgoustou and include:

Caravel (28103 00150; www.caravel.gr; 25 Avgoustou 39; 8am-11pm)
Hertz (28103 00744; www.hertz.gr; 25 Avgoustou 17; 7am-9pm)
Motor Club (28102 22408; www.motorclub.gr; Plateia 18 Anglon 1; car per day/week incl insurance from €35/180, scooter from €25/100; 8am-10pm)
Loggetta Cars (28102 89462; www.loggetta.gr; 25 Avgoustou 20; 9am-1.30pm & 4.30-8.30pm)
Sun Rise (28102 21609; www.sunrise-cars.com; 25 Avgoustou 46; 8am-9pm May-Oct, 8am-2pm & 5-9pm Mon-Sat Nov-Apr)

TAXI

There are small taxi stands all over town, but the main ones are at the Regional Bus Station, on **Plateia Eleftherias** (Plateia Eleftherias) and at the northern end of **25 Avgoustou** (Venizelou). You can also phone for one on 28140 03084.

Useful taxi apps include Aegean Taxi (www.aegeantaxi.com).

AROUND IRAKLIO

Knossos Κνωσσός

Crete's must-see historical attraction is the Palace of Knossos, 5km south of Iraklio, and the capital of Minoan Crete. Combining a visit here with a spin around Iraklio's excellent Archaeological Museum is highly recommended.

To beat the crowds and avoid the heat, get to Knossos either bang on 8am – and stay a few steps ahead of the arriving tour buses – or later in the afternoon, when it's cooler and the light is good for photographs. Reckon on a couple of hours to do the place justice.

History

Knossos' first palace (1900 BC) was destroyed by an earthquake around 1700 BC and rebuilt to a grander and more sophisticated design. It was partially destroyed again between 1500 and 1450 BC, and inhabited for another 50 years before finally burning down.

The complex comprised domestic quarters, public reception rooms, shrines, workshops, treasuries and storerooms, all flanking a paved central courtyard.

After initial excavation of part of the palace by Cretan archaeologist Minos Kalokerinos, the ruins of Knossos were fully unearthed in 1900 by British archaeologist Sir Arthur Evans (1851–1941). Evans was so enthralled by the site that he spent 35 years and £250,000 of his own money excavating and reconstructing sections of the palace. Although controversial in expert circles, his reconstructions help casual visitors conceive of what the palace might have looked like in its heyday.

The first treasure to be unearthed in the flat-topped mound called Kefala was a fresco of a Minoan man, followed by the discovery of the Throne Room. The archaeological world was stunned that a civilisation of this maturity and sophistication had existed in Europe at the same time as the great pharaohs of Egypt.

Sights

★Palace of Knossos ARCHAEOLOGICAL SITE
(http://odysseus.culture.gr; Knossos; adult/concession €15/8, incl Heraklion Archaeological Museum €16/8; 8am-8pm Apr-Sep, to 7pm Oct, to 3pm Nov-Mar; P; 2) The setting of Crete's most famous historical attraction is evocative and the ruins and recreations impressive, incorporating an immense palace, courtyards, private apartments, baths, lively frescoes and more. Excavation of the site started in 1878 with Cretan archaeologist Minos Kalokerinos, and continued from 1900 to 1930 with British archaeologist Sir Arthur Evans, who controversially restored parts of the site.

Palace of Knossos

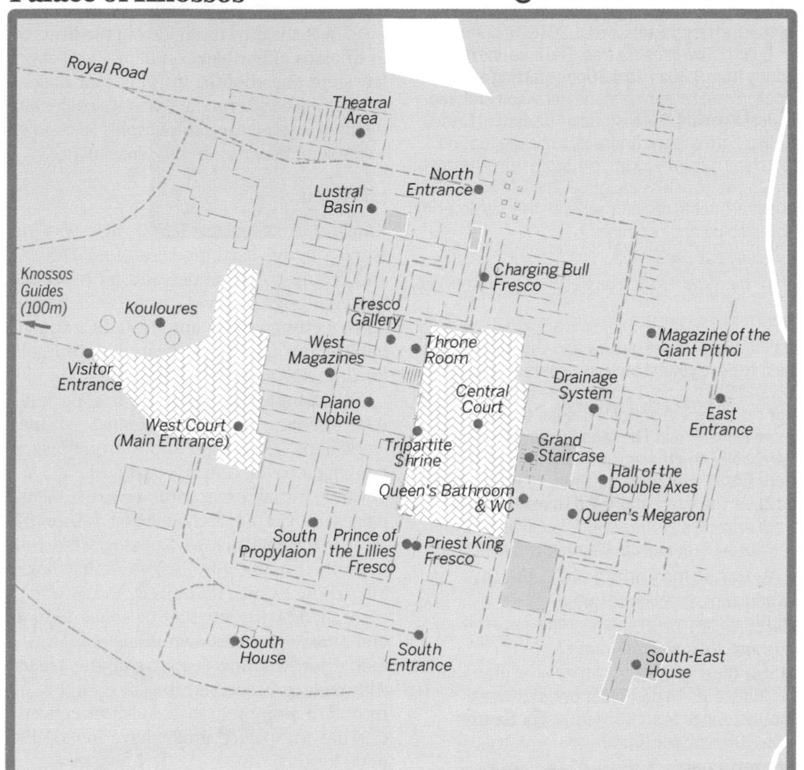

Evans' reconstructions bring to life the palace's most significant parts, including the columns, which are painted deep brown-red with gold-trimmed black capitals and taper gracefully at the bottom. Vibrant frescoes add dramatic flourishes. The advanced drainage system and a clever floor plan that kept rooms cool in summer and warm in winter are further evidence of Minoan society's sophistication.

There is no prescribed route for exploring the palace, but the following one takes in all the highlights. Entering from the **West Court**, which may have been a marketplace or the site of public gatherings, you'll note a trio of circular pits on your left. Called *kouloures*, they were used for grain storage. From here, continue counterclockwise, starting with a walk along the **Processional Walkway** that leads to the **South Propylaion**, where you can admire the **Cup Bearer Fresco**. From here, a staircase leads past giant storage jars to an upper floor that Evans called the **Piano Nobile** because it reminded him of Italian Renaissance palazzi and where he supposed the reception and staterooms were located. On your left, you can see the **west magazines** (storage rooms), where giant *pithoi* (clay jars) once held oil, wine and other staples.

The restored room at the northern end of the Piano Nobile houses the **Fresco Gallery**, with replicas of Knossos' most famous frescoes, including the *Bull Leaper*, the *Ladies in Blue* and the *Blue Bird*. The originals are now in the Heraklion Archaeological Museum (p163). From the balcony, a great view unfolds of the **Central Court**, which was hemmed in by high walls during Minoan times. Rooms facing the western side of the courtyard had official and religious purposes, while the residential quarters were on the opposite side.

Follow the stairs down to the courtyard and then turn left to peek inside the beautifully proportioned **Throne Room**, with its

Palace of Knossos

THE HIGHLIGHTS IN TWO HOURS

The Palace of Knossos is Crete's busiest tourist attraction, and for good reason. A spin around the partially and imaginatively reconstructed complex (shown here as it was thought to be at its peak) delivers an eye-opening glimpse into the remarkably sophisticated society of the Minoans, who dominated southern Europe some 4000 years ago.

From the ticket booth, follow the marked trail to the ❶ **North Entrance** where the Charging Bull fresco gives you a first taste of Minoan artistry. Continue to the Central Court and join the queue waiting to glimpse the mystical ❷ **Throne Room**, which probably hosted religious rituals. Turn right as you exit and follow the stairs up to the so-called Piano Nobile, where replicas of the palace's most famous artworks conveniently cluster in the ❸ **Fresco Room**. Walk the length of the Piano Nobile, pausing to look at the clay storage vessels in the West Magazine. Circle back and descend to the ❹ **South Portico**, beautifully decorated with the Cup Bearer fresco. Make your way back to the Central Court and head to the palace's eastern wing to admire the architecture of the ❺ **Grand Staircase** that led to what Sir Arthur Evans imagined to be the royal family's private quarters. For a closer look at some rooms, walk to the south end of the courtyard, stopping for a peek at the ❻ **Prince of the Lilies Fresco**, and head down to the lower floor. A highlight here is the ❼ **Queen's Megaron** (Evans imagined this was the Queen's chambers), playfully adorned with a fresco of frolicking dolphins. Stay on the lower level and make your way to the ❽ **Giant Pithoi**, huge clay jars used for storage.

PLANNING

To beat the crowds and avoid the heat, arrive bang on opening or two hours before closing. Budget one or two hours to explore the site thoroughly.

JOHN COPLAND/SHUTTERSTOCK ©

Fresco Room
Take in sweeping views of the palace grounds from the west wing's upper floor, the Piano Nobile, before studying copies of the palace's most famous artworks in its Fresco Room.

South Portico
Fine frescoes, most famously the Cup Bearer, embellish this palace entrance anchored by a massive open staircase leading to the Piano Nobile. The Horns of Consecration recreated nearby once topped the entire south facade.

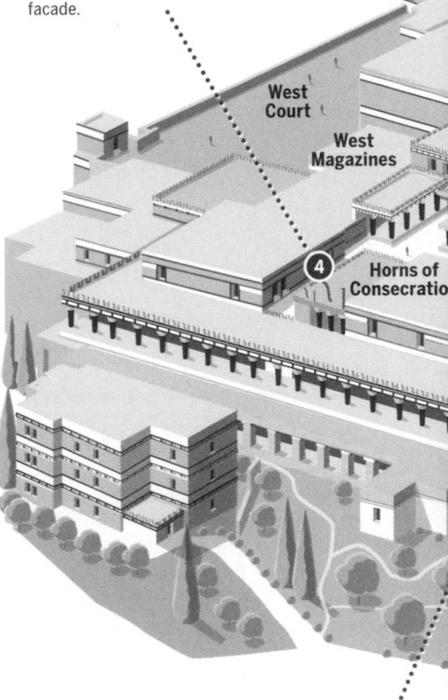

MICHAEL RUNKEL/GETTY IMAGES ©

Prince of the Lilies Fresco
One of Knossos' most beloved frescoes was controversially cobbled together from various fragments and shows a young man adorned in lilies and peacock feathers.

FOOD TIP

Save your appetite for a meal in the nearby Iraklio Wine Country, amid sunbaked slopes and lush valleys. It's just south of Knossos.

ANTON CHYGAREVI/SHUTTERSTOCK ©

Throne Room

Sir Arthur Evans, who began excavating the Palace of Knossos in 1900, imagined the mythical King Minos himself holding court seated on the alabaster throne of this beautifully proportioned room. However, the lustral basin and griffin frescoes suggest a religious purpose, possibly under a priestess.

BRUNO MORANDI/GETTY IMAGES ©

North Entrance

Bulls held a special status in Minoan society, as evidenced by the famous relief fresco of a charging beast gracing the columned west bastion of the north palace, which harboured workshops and storage rooms.

Grand Staircase

The royal apartments in the eastern wing were accessed via this monumental staircase sporting four flights of gypsum steps supported by columns. The lower two flights are original. It's closed to the public.

3

1

Piano Nobile

2

5

Central Court

Royal Apartments

8

6

7

Giant Pithoi

These massive clay jars are rare remnants from the Old Palace period and were used to store wine, oil and grain. The jars were transported by slinging ropes through a series of handles.

ANDREI NEKRASSOV/SHUTTERSTOCK ©

Queen's Megaron

The queen's room is among the prettiest in the residential eastern wing thanks to the playful Dolphin Fresco. The adjacent bathroom (with clay tub) and toilet are evidence of a sophisticated drainage system.

simple alabaster seat and walls decorated with frescoes of griffins (mythical beasts regarded by the Minoans as sacred). To the right of the stairs is a three-sectioned room that Evans called the **Tripartite Shrine**. Areas behind it yielded many precious finds, including the famous *Snake Goddess* statue.

Crossing the Central Court takes you to the east wing, where the **Grand Staircase** drops down to the royal apartments. Get there via the ramp off the southeastern corner, but not without first popping by the south entrance to admire a replica of the **Prince of the Lilies fresco**. Down below you can peek inside the **queen's megaron** (bedroom), with a copy of the *Dolphin* fresco, one of the most exquisite Minoan artworks. The small adjacent chamber (behind plexiglass) may have been the **queen's bathroom**, with some sort of toilet. Continue to the king's quarters in the **Hall of the Double Axes**; the latter takes its name from the double axe marks *(labrys)* on its light well, a sacred symbol to the Minoans and the origin of the word 'labyrinth'.

Beyond, you can admire the Minoans' surprisingly sophisticated **water and drainage system**, pop by a stonemason's workshop and check out more giant storage jars before jogging around to the palace's north side for a good view of the partly reconstructed north entrance, easily recognised by the Charging Bull fresco. Walking towards the exit, you pass the **theatral area**, a series of shallow steps whose function remains unknown. It could have been a theatre where spectators watched acrobatic and dance performances, or the place where people gathered to welcome important visitors arriving by the **Royal Road**, which leads off to the west and was flanked by workshops and the houses of ordinary people.

Unlike at other ruins around Iraklio, visitors make their way through the site on platform walkways, which can get very crowded. This makes it all the more important to time your visit for outside the tour-bus onslaught. Avoid ticket lines by buying in advance through the Archaeological Resources Fund e-Ticketing System (www.etickets.tap.gr).

Tours

Knossos Guides TOURS

(Palace of Knossos) Optional guided tours last about 1½ hours and are arranged from a little kiosk 30m before the ticket booth. Most tours are in English, though other languages are available, too. Prices vary according to group numbers (€10 per person in a group with an eight-person minimum). Private tours cost €100 with a maximum of six people.

Sleeping & Eating

Knossos is visited as a day trip from Iraklio or any number of charming wine-region hamlets (p185) nearby. There's plenty of choice regardless of where you choose to base yourself.

The on-site cafe and touristy tavernas across the street from the site are mediocre at best, so bring a picnic or save your appetite for a meal in the nearby Iraklio Wine Country – for instance at the excellent Elia & Diosmos (p190) in Skalani. Alternatively, eat in Iraklio.

SIR ARTHUR EVANS: EXCAVATOR OF KNOSSOS

British archaeologist Sir Arthur Evans was an avid amateur journalist and adventurer, as well as curator of the Ashmolean Museum in Oxford from 1884 to 1908. His special interest in ancient coins and the writing on stone seals from Crete brought him to the island for the first time in 1894. He had a hunch that the mainland Mycenaean civilisation derived originally from Crete. With the help of the newly formed Cretan Archaeological Society, he began negotiating the purchase of the land, originally excavated in 1878 by Cretan archaeologist Minos Kalokerinos, eventually securing it in 1900 after Greek laws changed in his favour. Digging began and the palace quickly revealed itself.

Over the course of 35 years of excavations, Evans unearthed the remains of a Neolithic civilisation beneath the remains of the Bronze Age Minoan palace. He also discovered some 3000 clay tablets containing Linear A and Linear B script and wrote his own definitive description of his work at Knossos in a four-volume opus called *The Palace of Minos*. Evans received many honours for his work and was knighted in 1911.

Evans' reconstruction methods continue to be controversial. Many archaeologist believe that he sacrificed accuracy to his overly vivid imagination.

Getting There & Away

Getting to Knossos is easy. City bus 2 runs from Iraklio's city centre – from the bus station or from Plateia Eleftherias – every 15 minutes. Tickets cost €1.70 if purchased from a kiosk or vending machine and €2.50 from the bus driver. If driving, from Iraklio or the coastal road there are signs directing you to Knossos. There's free parking across from the souvenir shops (spaces fill quickly).

WEST OF IRAKLIO

Agia Pelagia Αγία Πελαγία

POP 430

There's no denying that the beach resort of Agia Pelagia, some 20km west of Iraklio, occupies privileged seaside real estate - the whole area is spectacular. But the town lines a long, sandy beach that's rather built up with shops and development; far prettier is Mononaftis Beach, a few klicks north, which hugs a small, tranquil bay.

Achlada-Mourtzanakis Residence APARTMENT €€

(☎6970709525, 2810 812096; www.ecotourismgreece.com; Achlada; studios/apt from €115/163; ⊙Apr-Nov; P ❄ ☎ ≋ ⚲) A 10-minute drive (or a winding 3km) from Agia Pelagia, but seemingly a world away, this cluster of seven modern loft-style guesthouses offers plenty of elbow room and thoughtfully equipped kitchens. Enjoy a dip in the smallish pool, take in the grand sea vistas from your balcony or stroll to the nearby historic village of Achlada.

Taverna Vasilis SEAFOOD €€

(☎2810 811376; Mononaftis Beach; mains €4.50-17; ⊙11am-9.30pm Apr-Sep; ☎) In 1982 Taverna Vasilis was the first restaurant on this beach, and the impossibly polite and generous grandsons of the original owner show you the same hospitality today. Simple but fresh and well-prepared seafood and accoutrements from the farms and gardens of friends and family are what's on the menu. Service is outstanding and astonishingly humble.

Getting There & Away

From Iraklio's bus station, buses depart hourly between 8.30am and 9.30pm for Agia Pelagia (€2.70, 45 minutes).

DON'T MISS

IRAKLIO'S BEST ANCIENT SITES

➡ Knossos (p178)
➡ Malia (p209)
➡ Gortyna (p193)
➡ Phaestos (p194)

Fodele Φόδελε

Experts dispute that the tiny village of Fodele is El Greco's birthplace, and those expecting the real thing on all fronts may be disappointed, but the quaint little stone **El Greco museum** (adult/child €2.50/free; ⊙9am-7pm May-Sep, to 5pm Oct) has 24 backlit replica slides of the artist's works. The museum's prettily located about 1km from the village and has an idyllic shaded cafe.

Located 25km west of Iraklio, Fodele snuggles into a fertile valley fed by the diminutive Pantomantris River. There are several Byzantine chapels, like the beautiful small **Church of the Panayia** (open at weekends between 9.30am and 5pm), built on the ruins of an 8th-century basilica and opposite the El Greco museum.

CENTRAL IRAKLIO

South of Iraklio, past Knossos, the urban sprawl segues into an unhurried landscape of undulating hills, olive groves and rows of vineyards clambering up hillsides. It's all lorded over by the proud silhouette of Mt Yiouhtas (811m). Several Minoan sites are scattered on and around the mountain. These were once affiliated with ancient Arhanes, the main town in the area and the gateway to the Iraklio Wine Country, where you can sample the local product at several estates. Also of interest is the Nikos Kazantzakis Museum in Myrtia and the pottery town of Thrapsano.

Wine also grows near Dafnes and Venerato southwest of Iraklio, along the main road to Matala and the south coast. A wonderful detour takes you west to the southern slopes of Mt Psiloritis, where Zaros is a charismatic mountain village known for its spring water and trout. You'll need your own wheels to explore this region properly.

Arhanes & Around Αρχάνες

POP 4500

Arhanes, 14km south of Iraklio, is an agricultural town with a long history, important archaeological sites, interesting museums and excellent eateries. Considered a model of rural town redevelopment, it comprises a maze of narrow, flower-filled lanes, meticulously restored houses and tree-shaded squares. Wine has been produced in Arhanes since Minoan times.

The modern town sits atop a Minoan palace, of which only a tiny section has been excavated. It's believed that this may have been the Summer Palace of Knossos. During WWII, Arhanes was the hub of the German military command under General Heinrich Kreipe. On the road from Iraklio, at the turn-off to Kato Arhanes, a modern monument by local artist Manolis Tsompanakis commemorates Kreipe's famed 1944 kidnapping.

Sights

Arhanes is divided into upper and lower sections, with most sights of interest clustered in the latter. Getting around the one-way streets and narrow alleys can be confusing, so it's best to park your car and explore on foot. Fans of Minoan ruins can indulge their passion by visiting several sites within a short drive of Arhanes.

★Mt Yiouhtas Peak Sanctuary HISTORIC SITE

(Mt Yiouhtas; 24hr) FREE Driving south from Arhanes, look for the turn-off for Giourtas. The narrow (but drivable) road leads to the top of Mt Yiouhtas. After a bone-rattling 5km, you'll be rewarded with incredible panoramic views over to Mt Psiloritis and Iraklio. On the hill near the visible radar station are the fenced-in ruins of a Minoan peak sanctuary (sacred place located near a summit), dating from around 2100 BC, that is believed to have served the inhabitants of Knossos. At the top of Mt Yiouhtas is Afentis Christos Chapel.

Forgot about using your GPS to get here – it will take you all manner of ill-fated ways!

Fourni HISTORIC SITE

(2810 752712; by appointment) FREE On a hill west of town and reached via a steep footpath, Fourni is the most extensive Minoan necropolis in Crete. Burials took place here over a period of 1000 years, the oldest going back to 2500 BC. One of the tombs contained the remains of a Minoan noblewoman whose jewellery is on display in Iraklio town's Heraklion Archaeological Museum (p163). To visit, you must make arrangements in advance with the Archeological Collection of Archanes.

Vathypetro HISTORIC SITE

(8.30am-4pm Wed-Mon) FREE About 5km south of Arhanes, and well signposted, Vathypetro was built around 1600 BC, probably as the villa of a prosperous Minoan noble. Archaeologists discovered wine and oil presses, a weaving loom and a kiln in storerooms. The wine press can still be seen; archaeologists believe Vathypetro to house one of the oldest wineries in the world, and still today its surrounded by beautiful vineyards.

Archaeological Museum of Arhanes MUSEUM

(8.30am-3.30pm Wed-Mon) FREE This small museum displays many important finds from regional excavations, especially from Minoan times. Among the highlights are clay *larnakes* (coffins) for children, sarcophagi and replicas of musical instruments from Fourni, and a copy of the dagger presumably used for human sacrifice from the Anemospilia temple. The museum is in a side street just north of Arhanes' main square.

Anemospilia HISTORIC SITE

(Wind Caves; Oros Giouchta; 24hr) FREE Anemospilia packs major importance into its small frame. Excavation of this middle-Minoan three-room temple yielded evidence that human sacrifice played at least some role in Minoan society. The site is closed to the public, but you can peek through the fence and enjoy the sweeping views over Ar-

DON'T MISS

KORONEKES

This excellent 19-hectare **olive estate** (28107 31722; http://koronekes.gr; Kapnistou Metochi, Spilia; tour & tasting €5; 9am-3pm), located in Spilia, northeast of Arhanes, is one of only two left in Crete pressing the island's nectar of the gods (olive oil) the old-fashioned way. Tours, which must be booked in advance, focus on cultivation and explain the differences between the modern and traditional methods. A tasting of various oils and condiments follows.

hanes and surrounds. Anemospilia is about 1.5km northwest of Arhanes.

Sleeping

Arhanes offers good value for money, with most accommodation in historic stone villas of substantial size compared to elsewhere.

★Troullos Traditional Houses APARTMENT €€
(☎28107 53153; www.troullos.gr; Nikolaou Panagiotaki 10, Arhanes; s/d/tr/q €50/65/90/100;) This laid-back place is set around an attractive stone courtyard. Each of the four apartments and one maisonette features period furniture and paraphernalia. It's not high-end luxury but charming nonetheless. Delightful owner Athina serves up a great breakfast (€12 per person).

Arhontiko APARTMENT €€
(☎2810 752985; www.arhontikoarhanes.gr; Bogiatzaki 11, Arhanes; d/tr incl breakfast €60/75;) An air of rustic sophistication pervades this old-timey, charming 1893 garden villa that also saw incarnations as a military barracks and an elementary school. No hint of either survives in the three fully renovated apartments with traditional decor and furnishings. All have a fairly dark beamed-ceiling bedroom and bathroom downstairs and a kitchen and sitting room upstairs.

Eliathos Residence Houses APARTMENT €€€
(☎28107 51818, 6951804929; www.eliathos.gr; Ano Arhanes; studios/apt from €140/170;) Tucked into the hillside south of Arhanes and with grand views of Mt Yiouhtas, this cluster of four villas is a haven of peace wrapped around a swimming pool. Each villa is divided into breezy apartments and lofts sleeping up to six and sporting a design that is sleek and contemporary but also replete with nods to the setting.

The owners can help you get immersed in the local culture through cooking classes, excursions, and olive-oil, raki or winemaking workshops.

Eating

Practically all the tavernas in town have a good reputation, including those on the main square. A couple of attractive *kafeneia* (coffee houses) are in the surrounding laneways. If you're a foodie, Arhanes has you covered.

★Bakaliko CRETAN €
(www.bakalikocrete.com; Plateia Eleftheriou Venizelou, Arhanes; mains €7.50-9.50; 10am-11pm Apr-Oct, 5-10pm Fri, 10am-10pm Sat & Sun Nov-Mar;) *Bakaliko* means meeting point; traditionally, that meant *kafeneio* (coffee shop) and grocery shop in one. The concept has been revitalised in this lilac-accented restaurant where excellent cuisine (using organic produce where possible) and wine – an impressive choice of 70 by the glass, most from Crete – complements local products such as olive oils and marmalades. Although it's gourmet, prices are reasonable.

★Kritamon CRETAN €€
(☎2810 753092; www.kritamon.gr; Politechniou 78, Arhanes; mains €8-15; 5pm-1am Tue-Sat, noon-1am Sun;) Send your taste buds on a wild ride at this foodie outpost in a street off Arhanes' main square and set attractively around a garden courtyard with walnut trees. Ancient Cretan and creative modern recipes – including many veg dishes – result in a small but soulful menu with such signature choices as sea-bass fricassee with beans, fennel, spinach and lemon.

Ingredients come mostly from the organic family farm.

To Spitiko TAVERNA €€
(☎2810 751591; Plateia Eleftheriou Venizelou, Arhanes; mains €6.50-15; 9am-midnight Apr-Oct, shorter hours rest of year;) Locals will tell you To Spitiko is the best in town, but at research time it managed to run out of roast lamb *and* pork by 7.30pm in early May (blaming high season!). Nonetheless, the food at this one-room taverna overlooking the main square does satiate your desires for an authentic Cretan evening out.

Getting There & Away

Drivers coming from Iraklio should take the scenic Knossos road. On weekdays there's an hourly bus from Iraklio (€2, 30 minutes); weekend service dwindles to just two departures. Buses stop at the top of the village and close to the **main square** (Plateia Eleftherias).

If you're heading to Mt Yiouhtas, take the signposted **turn-off for Giourtas** south of Arhanes.

Iraklio Wine Country

Winemaking in the Iraklio Wine Country dates back to Minoan times, some 4000 years ago, as evidenced by the oldest stomping vat in the world, found at the ruins of Vathypetro. Unfortunately, today's vineyards are a lot younger, as a mighty bout of phylloxera (plant louse) in the 1970s nearly wiped out everything. But Cretan wine rebounded and today about 70% of the wine produced on the island comes from this region. Almost two dozen wineries are embedded in a harmonious landscape of round-shouldered hills, sunbaked slopes and lush valleys. Winemakers cultivate many indigenous, nearly extinct Cretan grape varietals – be sure to introduce your nose and taste buds to Kotsifali, Mandilari, Malvasia and Liatiko, among others – while many estates offer tours, wine museums and wine tastings.

Activities

Numerous wineries have tasting rooms where you can sample the local product, usually for a small fee. Some estates also have mini-museums showcasing historic tools and machinery. It's always a good idea to phone ahead, as some wineries are not staffed to the point that they can handle multiple walk-ins at the same time.

★Diamantakis Winery WINE

(☎6949198350; www.diamantakiswines.gr; Kato Asites; tastings €3-5; ⊙by appointment 9am-4pm Mon-Fri) This winery's Petali Liatiko red has a great story: it was produced as a table wine, but then experts tasted it and said, 'Whoa! Bottle this right now!' Diamantakis is one of a mere handful who make a Liatiko today, and tasting it on the extraordinary property between olive trees (there's no tasting room), surrounded by vineyards, is a remarkable experience.

★Lyrarakis WINE

(☎6981050681; www.lyrarakis.gr; Alagni; tastings €10-60; ⊙11am-7pm Mon-Sat Apr-Oct, by appointment rest of year) One of Crete's most visitor-friendly wineries, Lyrarakis should be your go-to if you must pick only one. It rakes in awards and is known for reviving three nearly extinct white varietals (Dafni, Plyto and Melissaki). It was also the first to produce a single-vineyard Mandilari red (a move ridiculed as 'absurd' – but it went on to become one of its bestsellers).

Stilianou Winery WINE

(☎69364 30368; www.stilianouwines.gr; Kounavi; tastings €5, with tour €7; ⊙11am-7pm Apr-Oct, 10am-5pm Mon-Sat Nov-Mar) Rustic, down-to-earth, boutique Stilianou sits above Kounavi (your GPS will never get you there, but it will get you to the signs, which are then easy to follow). Ioannis just about runs a one-man show, specialising in Minoan-strength organic wines with local varietals only, such as his Theon Dora blend (Vidiano, Vilana, Thrapsathiri; alcohol 13%!), and small-batch olive oils.

Visitors appreciate the lack of commercialism and tour buses. It's best to call ahead: walk-ins may have to wait for a tour to finish before they can be served. Be sure to try the unique Kotsifali dessert wine, too.

Digenakis Winery WINE

(☎28103 22846; www.digenakis.gr; Katakouzinon 7, Kaloni; tastings €7; ⊙by appointment 10am-5pm) Opened in 2017, this modern winery marches to a different drum, both in its design and in its winemaking. The striking edifice features poured concrete and glass, offset by colourful tapestry art. Its 2017 single-vineyard Kotsifali was produced from the fruit of 35-year-old vines – some of the few to escape the 1970s phylloxera outbreak that devastated Crete's vineyards.

Idaia Winery WINE

(☎2810 792156; www.idaiawine.gr; Kiparissou 90, Venerato; tasting €5; ⊙11am-4pm Mon-Fri, to 2pm Sat) This tiny boutique winery is hyper-focused on local varietals. Be on the lookout for its Ocean Thrapsathiri white (one of the island's best for pairing with seafood), its barrel-matured Liatiko and its sun-dried Liatiko dessert wine. The modern tasting room is small but one of the nicest.

Douloufakis Winery WINE

(☎28107 92017; www.cretanwines.gr; Dafnes; tours & tastings €5-12; ⊙by appointment 10am-3.30pm Mon-Fri) The highly recommended Douloufakis Winery grows Cretan grape varieties and also uses the grapes of surrounding smallholdings. Renowned for its Aspros Lagos (White Rabbit) line (the Vidiano white and the Cabernet Sauvignon red), Iraklio's first sparkling Vidiano, and its series fermented in traditional *amphorae* (clay storage vessels), it's also known for its colourful and quirky wine labels.

Silva Wines WINE

(☎2810 792021; www.silvawines.gr; Siva; tours & tastings €5-18; ⊙by appointment 9am-5pm Mon-Sat) A mother and daughter are among the extraordinary team at this biodynamic winery in Siva. They cultivate and harvest according to the agricultural calendar, which is based on such considerations as the solar and lunar cycles. The result is ongoing award-winning wines, especially the whites. Reserve tours a day ahead.

Domaine Gavalas WINE
(☎28940 51060, 6974642006; www.gavalascretewines.gr; Vorias; tastings €7-10; ⏰10am-5pm Mon-Fri) The Gavalas family has been making wine since 1906. It went fully organic in 2001 and today is one of the largest organic wineries in Crete. There's a pleasant private tasting room among the barrels. Top award-winning wines to seek out here include the Fragospito Syrah/Cabernet Sauvignon, the Vilana (100% Vilana) and the Monahikos Cabernet Sauvignon. It's in Vorias, about 20km south of Peza.

Domaine Gavalas WINE
(www.zacharioudakis.com; Plouti; tastings & tour €15-30; ⏰10am-4pm Mon-Sat Apr-Sep) Striking architecture and steeply terraced vineyards on the slopes of the Orthi Petra hill characterise this state-of-the-art boutique winery in Plouti, about 7km south of Zaros. The tasting room with views out to sea is a nice spot for sampling its fine wines, including the award-winning white Vidiano and red Orthi Petra Syrah-Kotsifali. Guided tours are also available.

Rhous Winery WINE
(Tamiolakis; ☎2810 742083; www.rhouswinery.gr; Houdetsi; tastings from €7; ⏰by appointment) This organic winery is in a dazzling hilltop location above the village of Houdetsi, 4km south of Peza. It's one of Crete's excellent new-generation wineries, with Bordeaux-trained winemakers, state-of-the-art equipment and visitor-friendly facilities.

Boutari Winery WINE
(☎28107 31617; www.boutari.gr; Skalani; tours & tasting €6-45; ⏰9am-5pm) Founded in 1879, Boutari is one of Greece's biggest wine producers. Visits to its Crete winery (one of six in the country) start with a short tour to learn about local grapes and winemaking, followed by an optional 15-minute video on the island and/or the company and the chance to sample the product in the vast, airy tasting room overlooking the vineyard.

The on-site accommodation (three suites; €120 to €150) is some of the wine country's best. Boutari is near Skalani, about 8km from Iraklio.

Minos-Miliarakis Winery WINE
(☎2810 741213; www.minoswines.gr; Main St, Peza; tasting €3; ⏰10am-6pm Mon-Fri May-Oct & by appointment) This massive enterprise was the first modern producer to bottle wine in Crete – in 1952. It makes very respectable vintages, especially under its Miliarakis label, including a full-bodied single-vineyard organic red and a fragrant Blanc de Noirs. The tasting room is vast and doubles as a museum featuring historical winemaking equipment. The shop also sells local olive oil and raki.

Tours

Made in Crete WINE
(☎6975626830; www.tours.madeincrete.com; €100) This Belgian-run agency leads the most highly recommended wine-tasting tours around Iraklio Wine Country. Tours take in two wineries as well as lunch at Bakaliko (p185) in Arhanes. The price includes transport, tastings (olive oil in addition to wine) and lunch paired with four wines. Pierre, a former journalist and chef, leads tours in French or English.

Groups top out at eight, so it's small and intimate.

Sleeping

Arhanes, with its high concentration of recommended accommodations and fine restaurants, is probably the best base for oenophiles, all things considered, but bear in mind that you will need to drive the long way round via Iraklio for wineries on the western side of the mountain. There are scattered gems elsewhere; at Boutari Winery you can sleep among the vineyards.

★Earino VILLA €€
(☎2810 861528; www.earino.gr; Kato Asites; studio s/d from €45/65, ste from €75; P ❄ 📶) This delightful family-run wood-and-stone place sits in one of wine country's most scenic spots, with expansive views from the highly recommended on-site taverna (p190) across vineyard and olive groves all the way to the sea. The three rooms – one studio, two mezzanine suites – feature tasteful, family-made woodwork (tree-limb–supported lighting, carved TV stands) and Cretan ceramics and textiles. Breakfast is wonderful.

Fireplaces, kitchens and the hospitality of Nikos are further pluses at this one-stop eat, drink and sleep destination.

★Villa Kerasia PENSION €€
(☎2810 791021; www.villa-kerasia.gr; Vlahiana; d/ste incl breakfast from €75/80; ⏰Apr-Oct; P ❄ 📶 🏊) In a gorgeous location in tiny Vlahiana, at the western edge of the wine region, this converted 18th-century farmhouse has five rooms and two suites that

ROAD TRIP > TOURING IRAKLIO'S WINE COUNTRY

There's something undeniably painterly in the way Iraklio's suburban sprawl rolls itself into luscious wine country, with snug villages, sun-dappled vineyards, and Mt Yiouhtas (811m) looming in the distance. Winemaking in the region dates back 4000 years and today a dozen or so wineries turn out some 70% of Crete's wine.

1 Patsides

Coming from Iraklio, follow the Knossos road south. A couple of kilometres beyond the palace ruins, the road skirts an impressive double-arched aqueduct from the early 1800s that once supplied Iraklio with water from Arhanes. Continue to **Patsides**, where a brutalist monument at the turn-off to Kato

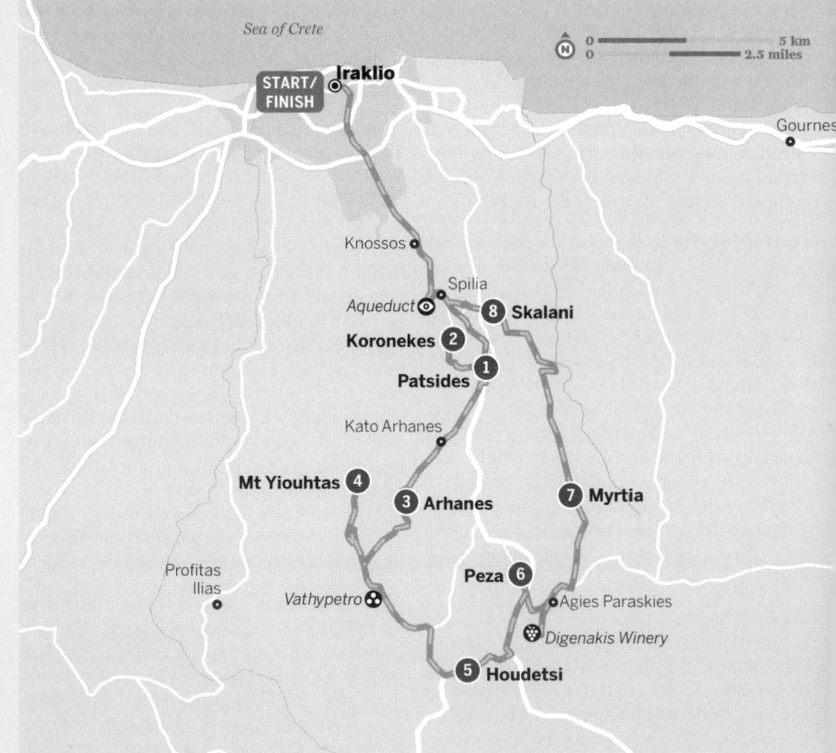

One Day 45km

Great For... Food & Drink, History & Culture

Best Time to Go Visit during spring or late summer

Arhanes marks the spot where General Heinrich Kreipe was kidnapped in 1944.

2 Koronekes

Make arrangements in advance for a tour and tasting at **Koronekes** (p184), a wonderful olive estate corralling over 2000 trees clocking in at 200 to 300 years old. It's a great spot for stocking up on olive oil pressed in the traditional way (don't miss its Fleur d'Huile) and other Cretan products.

3 Arhanes

Arhanes itself is a wine-country hub with Minoan roots. After visiting the village's small museum, soak up the atmosphere on the leafy plaza over a glass of wine at **Bakaliko** (p185), where Cretan wine enthusiast Giorgos offers some 45 island options by the glass.

4 Mt Yiouhtas

Afterwards, detour up **Mt Yiouhtas** for spellbinding wine-country views and a look at a Minoan peak sanctuary.

5 Houdetsi

Back in Arhanes, head south towards Houdetsi, stopping at **Vathypetro** (p184) to see what a Minoan stomping vat looked like (the one discovered here is the oldest known wine press in existence). A pretty hamlet wedged into a valley, **Houdetsi** is home to a wonderful museum of traditional musical instruments, **Labyrinth** (p190).

6 Peza

From here it's a quick drive north to Peza, the centre of wine production in Crete, with several wineries offering tastings and tours. Don't miss the modern **Digenakis Winery** (p186), 1.7km south of the village, with an art-driven tasting room.

7 Myrtia

From here, follow signs to **Myrtia** to pay your respects to Nikos Kazantzakis, the Cretan-born author of Zorba the Greek, at the excellent **museum** (p190) right on the town square.

8 Skalani

Conclude the day by indulging in a gourmet Cretan dinner paired with excellent local wines at the delightful **Elia & Diosmos** (p190) in **Skalani**, before you drive back to Iraklio.

are tranquil, intimate retreats, with stone walls, beamed ceilings and hardwood floors. Days start with an opulent breakfast entirely composed of local products that will easily tide you over till the afternoon.

Eating

The relationship between the wine and the food isn't as symbiotic as in the world's more famous wine regions, but that hardly matters: it's hard to go wrong stumbling into any taverna around these parts. Arhanes has the best concentration of excellent eateries, including Bakaliko (p185), one of the few offering a very serious local wine program.

Earino CRETAN €
(2810 861528; www.earino.gr; Kato Asites; mains €7.50-9.50; noon-10.30pm, closed Tue Dec-Mar;) Vying for wine country's top table views, this beautifully set taverna at Earino villa (p187) is worth a detour if you're not staying there, offering sweeping views across the vineyard- and olive-strewn landscape to Iraklio Bay. It concentrates on simple but well-prepared classic Cretan *mezedhes* (appetisers) – excellent *dolmadhes* (stuffed vine leaves) – clay oven–cooked meats and hearty specials such as lamb stew with artichokes.

Roussos Taverna CRETAN €
(6936156835; Houdetsi; mains €4.50-9.50; 7am-4pm & 5pm-2am Apr-Oct, Fri-Sun only Nov-Mar;) Toothsome and original is this simple spot's cooking style. Clued-in gourmets make the trip to Houdetsi from afar to dine on Roussos' Cretan cooking, including fantastic lamb chops and local *horta* (wild greens), which the staff collect. It's on the main square across from Ross Daly's Labyrinth, whose musicians sometimes give concerts here.

★**Elia & Diosmos** CRETAN €€
(2810 731283; www.olivemint.gr; Dimokratias 263, Skalani; mains €8-15; 11am-midnight Tue-Sun;) At this foodie destination, market-fresh ingredients shine in flavour-intense and progressive Cretan dishes from chef Argyro Barda. The menu chases the seasons, but classic choices from the stylish open kitchen include *mousakas* (baked layers of eggplant or zucchini, minced meat and potatoes topped with cheese sauce), fluffy fennel pie, and pork shank paired with wine, honey and citrus.

It's only a short drive from Iraklio and an excellent post-Knossos recuperation stop.

Entertainment

Labyrinth TRADITIONAL MUSIC
(28107 41027; www.labyrinthmusic.gr; Houdetsi; concerts Fri late Jun-Sep) FREE Established in 1982, Labyrinth is the brainchild of renowned Irish musician Ross Daly, one of the leading exponents of the Cretan *lyra* (lyre). This beautiful stone manor runs highly reputable summer-long musical workshops that draw top talent from around the world, and the lovely grounds become an atmospheric backdrop for free concerts in which both teachers and students participate. Call or check the website for the schedule.

Daly is also a master of the modal non-harmonic music of Greece, the Balkans, Turkey, the Middle East, North Africa and North India, and has released more than 35 albums. Check him out at www.rossdaly.gr. Houdetsi is about 4km south of Peza.

Information

Check Wines of Crete (www.winesofcrete.gr) for tourist info. Look for the burgundy-red road signs directing you to local wineries.

Getting There & Away

The majority of wineries are within 20km of Iraklio, beginning just south of Knossos (the industry is headquartered in Peza). Besides an organised tour (p187), having your own wheels is definitely a necessity to fully partake in a proper day of wine tasting: the wineries are spread out and not otherwise served directly by any public transport.

Myrtia Μυρτιά

Nikos Kazantzakis Museum MUSEUM
(2810 741689; www.kazantzaki.gr; Myrtia; adult/concessions €5/3; 9am-5pm daily Apr-Oct, 10am-3pm Mon-Fri & Sun Nov-Mar) In a modern building overlooking the *kafeneia*-flanked central plaza of author Nikos Kazantzakis' ancestral village, this well-curated museum zeroes in on the life, philosophy and accomplishments of Crete's most famous writer. Watch a short documentary, then use one of the wireless audio guides (€1) to add more meaning to the exhibits, which include movie posters, letters, photographs and various personal effects. Upstairs rooms present an overview of Kazantzakis' best-known works, including, of course, *Zorba the Greek*.

Don't miss the interesting 20-minute video (in 10 languages); ask staff to turn it on if it's not playing.

Myrtia is some 15km southeast of Iraklio.

OFF THE BEATEN TRACK

THRAPSANO

All those huge Minoan-style *pithoi* (storage jars) that grace hotel lobbies, restaurants and homes across Crete most likely hail from Thrapsano, 32km southeast of Iraklio. Today's designs and even methods have clearly been influenced by those of ancient times. The town's wares are fascinating to see if you have appreciated the ancient pots at archaeological sites and museums. Pottery workshops are scattered all around Thrapsano.

Koutrakis Art (☎28910 41000, 6945536145; www.cretan-pottery.gr; Thrapsano; ⏰8am-5pm) is a favourite is for its friendliness and accessibility, but there are many from which to choose, including **Nikos Doxastakis Workshop** (☎28910 41160; Thrapsano; ⏰hours vary). Note: these aren't touristy shops but factories preparing pieces for export around Greece and elsewhere, but they're normally welcoming to visitors. An annual pottery festival takes place in the town in mid-July.

In the middle of Thrapsano, the twin-aisled 15th-century **Timios Stavros church** houses well-preserved frescoes. You might have to ask around for the key.

From Iraklio, Thrapsano is best reached via the Knossos road, turning east at the village of Agios Paraskies, near Peza.

Zaros Ζαρός

POP 2120

At the foot of Mt Psiloritis, Zaros is famous for its natural spring water, which is bottled here and sold all over Crete. But Zaros also has some fine Byzantine monasteries, excellent walking and delicious farm-raised trout, served up in tavernas around town and on emerald-green Lake Votomos (actually a reservoir). The lake is also the kick-off point for the 5km trail through the mighty Rouvas Gorge, a major lure for hikers, birders and naturalists.

Sights

Moni Vrondisi MONASTERY

(⏰8am-1pm & 4pm-sunset Mon-Sat) FREE Situated 4km northwest of Zaros, this monastery is noted for its 15th-century Venetian fountain with a relief of Adam and Eve, and early-14th-century frescoes from the Cretan School, including one depicting the Last Supper.

Folklore Museum of Zaros MUSEUM

(adult/child €3/2; ⏰10am-2pm & 4-6pm) Opened in 2015, this tiny museum, housed within a traditional stone cottage, is one of those things you feel you should go to just to support them. It houses a quaint selection of donated items from the past, recreating life as it was until the advent of electricity. The 2nd floor houses a quirky geological collection.

The most interesting exhibition shows minerals in their pure state next to products they are used in (plastic bottles, batteries and the like). If it's closed, which is often, knock on the white door 20m down the street towards the church; the proprietor will open it up for you.

Lake Votomos LAKE

Emerald green and tree fringed, this small reservoir just northeast of Zaros was created in 1987 to store the town's natural spring water. It attracts scores of birds and is great for chilling in the shady park or enjoying a meal in the excellent taverna-cafe.

The trailhead for the Rouvas Gorge hike (p204) is also here.

Moni Agios Nikolaos MONASTERY

(⏰sunrise-sunset, closed 1-4pm) Just west of Zaros, a sign directs you to this monastery at the mouth of the Rouvas Gorge, about 2km up the valley. The church has some fine 14th-century frescoes. Don't confuse it with the new church under construction in front (with blue domes; quite striking in its own right!); the older church is behind this.

Sleeping

Zaros is home to one of Crete's most atmospheric places to stay, Eleonas Country Village, and a few simpler accommodation options, but the choice is not widespread by any means.

Studios Keramos PENSION €

(☎28940 31352; www.studiokeramos-zaros.gr; s/d/tr incl breakfast €35/50/65; ❄📶) Close to the village centre, this old-style pension is run by the friendly Katerina and is decorated with Cretan crafts, weaving and family heirlooms. Many of the rooms and studios pair antique beds and furniture with TV and kitchenette (the more modern four-room annexe is fine but lacks character). Katerina is up early preparing an absolutely fantastic traditional breakfast.

★Eleonas Country Village COTTAGE **€€**
(☎28940 31238, 6976670002; www.eleonas.gr; cottages/villas incl breakfast from €120/220; daily May-Oct, Sat & Sun Nov-Apr;) Owner Manolis has poured his heart and soul into this charming retreat of 22 stone cottages and two modern villas cradled by olive groves and built into a stunning terraced garden. It's a '*this* is Crete' kind of place, such is the fresh air and tranquil feel.

Fuel up for a day of hiking, exploring, biking or poolside chilling with a sumptuous breakfast of homemade Cretan treats. The public, on-site **taverna** (mains €9.50-19; 1-4pm & 6-10pm May-Oct, 1-10pm Sat & Sun Nov-Apr;) is also a delight, crafting Mediterranean specialities with its own olive oil. It's about 1.5km northwest of Zaros – just follow the signs. Three-night minimum stay.

Eating & Drinking

Trout farming drives most of the cuisine in Zaros, but Cretan-leaning and Greek tavernas are fairly plentiful, too. Besides the restaurants around Lake Votomos, most places to eat are along the short little main street through the village.

★Vegera CRETAN **€**
(all-you-can-eat buffet €12; 11am-11pm Apr–mid-Nov;) The vivacious Vivi has a knack for turning farm-fresh local produce into flavourful and creative dishes based on traditional recipes. Her philosophy is to 'cook the way we cook in our house' and indeed her cute place quickly feels like home. Allow ample time to savour the generous buffet of salads, cheese and olives, cooked mains, pastries and freshly baked bread.

Votomos Taverna TAVERNA **€€**
(☎6974867233; www.facebook.com/taverna.votomos; trout per kilogram €30, mains €7.50-12; 11am-11pm 25 Mar-Nov, Sat & Sun Dec-24 Mar;) Although you're in the mountains, you can be certain that the fish is fresh at this family-run taverna, where you can see trout splashing in large tanks before they end up on your dinner plate. Note: it's the second 'Taverna Votomos' as you follow signs to the lake, not the first taverna next to Idi hotel.

Za Rous CAFE
(snacks €2 to €6; 7am-midnight Mon-Sat, from 8am Sun;) Trendy Za Rous feels a little too cool for Zaros, but the town's best espresso is good reason to buck the traditional *kafeneio* template. Locals pack in for ridiculously tempting waffles, crepes and ice cream – the kitchen is quite generous with the Nutella!

Information

Most businesses are clumped together at the southern end of town. The post office and a supermarket are across the street from the police station. There's an ATM on the main street.

Getting There & Away

Zaros is about 46km southwest of Iraklio. The most scenic approach is by turning west off the main road at Agia Varvara. There's also a smaller road heading north from Kapariana just east of Mires (turn north at the small road between a bakery and Kafeneio i Zariani Strofi; look for the little sign). One daily bus heading from Iraklio's KTEL Heraklion Lassithi Bus Station to Kamares passes through Zaros (€5.20, one hour, 1.30pm). Alternatively, take one of the more frequent buses to Mires (€6, 75 minutes) and cab it to Zaros from there (around €16).

SOUTHERN IRAKLIO

The south-central region of Crete is blessed with a trifecta of archaeological treasures – Phaestos, Agia Triada and Gortyna – and a cluster of minor sites spanning Cretan history from the Minoans to the Romans. Touring them you'll be weaving your way right through the Messara Plain, one of Crete's most fertile regions, framed by Mt Psiloritis to the north, the Dhiktean mountains to the east and the Asterousia hills to the south.

A major highway links the busy commercial centres of Tymbaki, Mires, Agii Deka and Pyrgos, although they hold little interest for visitors. The nearby coastal towns are another matter. Matala, Kamilari and Kalamaki beckon with long stretches of sandy beach and smaller inland villages such as Sivas make excellent bases for exploring the region's ample charms. There are diversions aplenty: hiking through gorges, visiting ancient monasteries, poking around flower-festooned villages, chilling with locals on

Gortyna

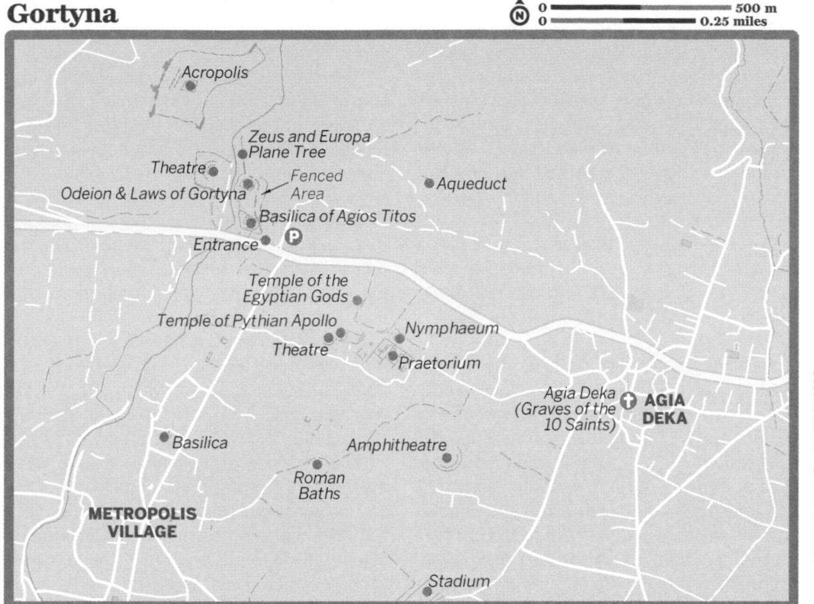

the village square or simply getting lost on the winding country roads.

Gortyna Γόρτυνα

Inhabited since Neolithic times, **Gortyna** (Iraklio-Phaestos Rd; adult/concession €6/3; 8am-8pm Apr-Oct, to 4pm Nov-Mar) – also called Gortyn or Gortys – reached its pinnacle after becoming the capital of Roman Crete from around 67 BC until the Saracens raided the island in AD 824. At its peak, as many as 100,000 people may have milled around in Gortyna's streets.

There are two sections, bisected by the highway. Most people only stop long enough to investigate the fenced area on the north side of the road past the entrance. However, several more important temples, baths and other buildings are scattered south of the road.

Fenced Area

The first major monument visible within the fenced area is the 6th-century Byzantine **Basilica of Agios Titos**, the finest early-Christian church in Crete. Probably built atop an even older church, its only major surviving feature is the soaring apse flanked by two side chapels. It reopened after a long-haul restoration in 2019.

A few steps away is the **Odeion**, a Roman theatre from the 1st century BC, which was levelled by an earthquake and rebuilt by Trajan in the 2nd century AD. The covered, arched structure on the far side of the theatre shelters Gortyna's star attraction: the massive stone tablets inscribed with the 6th-century-BC **Laws of Gortyna**. The 600 lines written in a Dorian dialect represent the oldest law code in the Greek world and provide a fascinating insight into the social structure of pre-Roman Crete. It turns out that ancient Cretans were preoccupied with the same issues that drive people into court today – marriage, divorce, property transfers, inheritance and adoption, as well as criminal offences. Behind the Odeion is an evergreen **plane tree** that, according to mythology, was Zeus and Europa's 'love nest'.

South of the Highway

Excavations are still in full swing in the area south of the highway and all the sites can only be seen through a chain-link fence. Still, it's fun to wander aimlessly and just stumble upon the ruins. If you prefer to explore in a more organised fashion, walk 300m east along the highway from the car parking to a double sign pointing to the **Temple of Apollo** and the **Temple of the Egyptian Gods**, dedicated to Isis, Serapis and Anubis. A narrow stone path leads to the latter after about 70m; there actually isn't much to see today. The same cannot be said of the **Temple of Pythian Apollo**, reached by continuing on the path past the sign pointing left to the Praetorium, the main sanctuary of pre-Roman Gortyna. It was built in the 7th century BC, expanded in the 3rd century BC and converted into a Christian basilica in the 2nd century AD. You can still make out its rectangular outline and the base of the main altar.

Backtrack and turn right at the sign to shortly reach the **Praetorium**. The palace of the Roman governor of Crete, it served as an administrative building, a church and a private residence. Most of the ruins date from the 2nd century AD and were repaired in the 4th century. To the north is the 2nd-century **Nymphaeum**, a public bath supplied by an aqueduct bringing water from Zaros. It was originally adorned with statues of nymphs.

Acropolis

For a bird's-eye view of Gortyna, climb to the hilltop **Acropolis**, which also features impressive sections of the pre-Roman ramparts. The trailhead is on the north side of the highway, about 100m west of the entrance; it takes about 20 to 30 minutes to get up here.

Getting There & Away

Gortyna is near Agia Deka, about 46km southwest of Iraklio. It's a stop on the Iraklio–Matala and Iraklio–Agia Galini bus routes. In Iraklio, buses leave from KTEL Heraklion Lassithi Bus Station.

Phaestos Φαιστός

The second-most-important Minoan palace-city after Knossos, **Phaestos** (http://odysseus.culture.gr; Iraklio-Phaestos Rd; adult/concession €8/4; 8am-8pm May-Aug, shorter hours rest of year; P) enjoys an awe-inspiring setting with panoramic views of the Messara Plain and Mt Psiloritis. It was built around 1700 BC atop an older, previously destroyed palace, and laid out around a central court. In contrast to Knossos, it had fewer frescoes, as its walls were likely covered with white gypsum. Phaestos was defeated by Gortyna in the 2nd century BC. Good English panelling and graphics stationed in key spots help demystify the ruins.

Past the entrance, the first stop is the **Upper Court**, which was flanked by a colonnade and overlooked the **West Court**, to which it is connected by a long staircase. Since the court is bounded by eight wide steps that may have served as bleachers, it may have been used as a **theatral area** – a staging ground for performances. On the side opposite the seats are four round, cistern-like structures called *kouloures* that may have been used to store grain.

East of the West Court, a 15m-wide **grand stairway** once led to the Propylaeum, the main palace entrance, of which only the pillar bases survive. Continue past the stairway and turn left to walk past a corridor lined with a series of storerooms – called **west magazines** – where *pithoi* held oil, wine and other staples of the Minoan diet. The walkway culminates in an antechamber, below which another room – the so-called **archive** – held records of the goods in the magazines.

The corridor spills out into the vast rectangular **Central Court**, the social heart of the palace, which was once flanked by colonnades and gives a sense of the structure's size and magnificence. Turning right takes you into an area believed to have contained several **shrines**, including a 'bench shrine' whose walls were lined with low benches, and a **'lustral basin'** with a sunken cistern that was perhaps used in purification rituals.

On the opposite side is the east wing, which contained royal apartments, although the main residential area was actually in the north wing, most of which is under cover. This is where you'll come across the **queen's megaron** (bedroom), which centred on twin pillars and featured gypsum-paved floors and benches. Immediately behind it is the **king's megaron**. The celebrated Phaestos Disk, now in the Heraklion Archaeological Museum (p163), was found in a building to the northeast of the king's chambers. Before exiting, swing by the columned **Peristyle Court**, the most elegant inner courtyard in the north wing.

Getting There & Away

Phaestos is 63km southwest of Iraklio and served by KTEL buses twice daily from Iraklio's bus station (7.30am and 12.45pm, €7.10, 1½

Phaestos

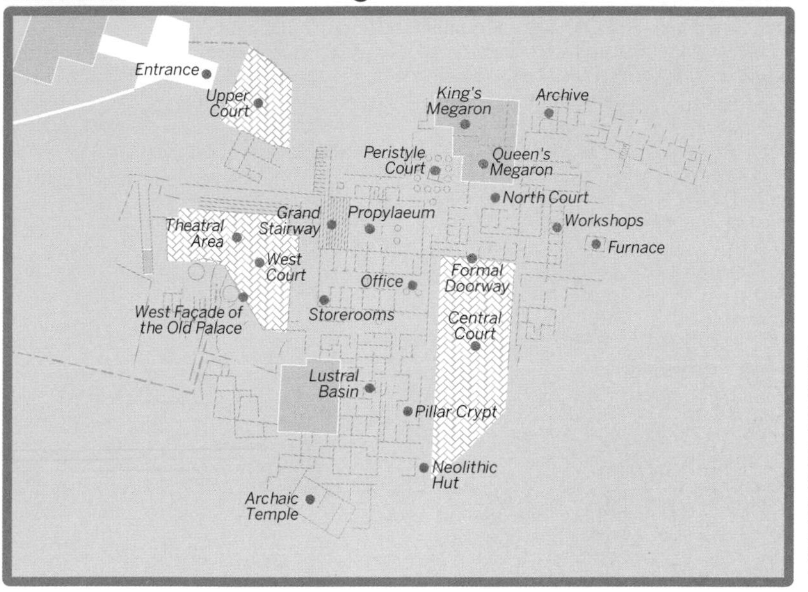

hours), three times daily from Matala (€2, 30 minutes) and six times daily from Agia Galini (€2.30, 35 to 45 minutes).

Agia Triada Αγία Τριάδα

In an enchanting spot 3km west of Phaestos, **Agia Triada** (adult/concession €4/2; 8.30am-4pm; P) encompasses vestiges of an L-shaped royal villa, a ramp once leading out to sea, and a village with residences and stores. Built around 1550 BC, Agia Triada succumbed to fire around 1400 BC but was never looted. This accounts for the many Minoan masterpieces found here, most famously the Agia Triada Sarcophagus, now a star exhibit at the Heraklion Archaeological Museum.

Unfortunately, the site is not very visitor friendly, as there's no labelling to be found. On the plus side, it drips with historic ambience and rarely sees crowds.

Past the entrance, the ruins in front of you are those of the palace, with structures arranged along two sides of a central courtyard. The Byzantine **chapel of Agios Georgios**, on the left, has some beautiful frescoes (ask at the ticket booth for the key). To the right of the palace is the village area, with the cemetery (closed to visitors) beyond the fence.

To your left, as you go down the stairs, are the ruins of a **Minoan house**, with a shrine dating from the early 14th century BC just behind it. It once featured a frescoed floor painted with octopuses and dolphins, also now at the archaeological museum in Iraklio. Beyond here is the paved **central courtyard** with the residential wing on the right beneath a protective canopy. The west wing, at the far end of the courtyard, is a maze of **storage rooms and workshops**; the 'Chieftain Cup' was found in one of them. One of the most beautiful rooms is in the northwestern corner: called the **fresco room**, and lidded with a modern cement ceiling, it has fitted benches, alabaster walls and gypsum floors.

A ramp running along the northern side of the palace is thought to have led all the way to the sea (which was at a much higher level then), hence the name given to it by archaeologists – **Rampa al Mare**. It leads up to the **village** area, with the marketplace and residential buildings. Of special interest here is the row of **stores** that were once fronted by a portico.

On the other side of the fence, beyond the stores, is the **cemetery**, dating from around 2000 BC, with two *tholoi* (beehive-shaped tombs). The famous sarcophagus decorated with funereal scenes was found here.

Agia Triada

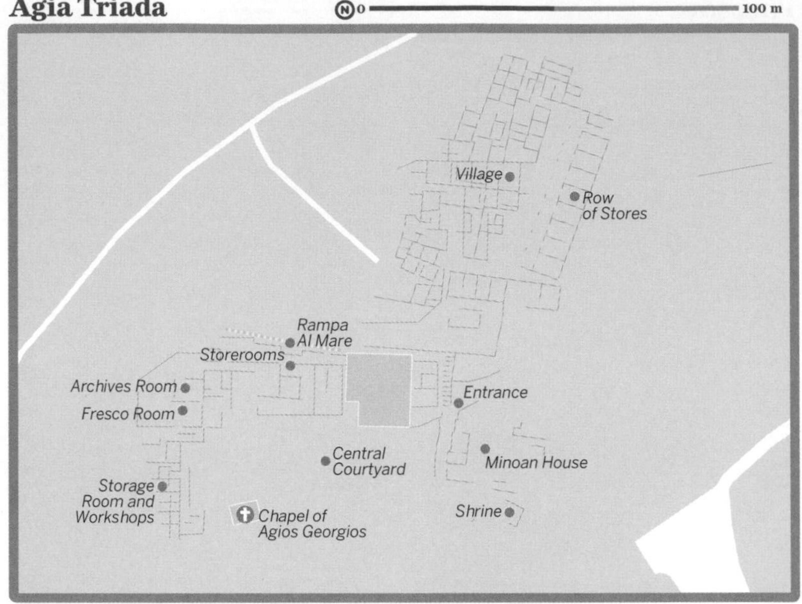

Getting There & Away

The signposted turn-off to Agia Triada is about 500m past Phaestos on the Matala road. There's no direct public transport to the site, so either walk 3.5km or try hitching a ride from Phaestos.

Matala Μάταλα

POP 70

In mythology, Matala is the place where Zeus swam ashore with the kidnapped Europa on his back before dragging her off to Gortyna and getting her pregnant with the future King Minos. The Minoans used Matala as their harbour for Phaestos and under the Romans it became the port for Gortyna (p193).

In more recent times, Matala became legendary thanks to the scores of hippies flocking here in the late 1960s to take up rent-free residence in cliffside caves once used as tombs by the Romans.

On summer days the village feels anything but peaceful, thanks to coachloads of day trippers. Stay overnight or visit in the low season, though, and it's still possible to discern the Matala magic: the setting along a crescent-shaped bay flanked by headlands is simply spectacular, especially at sunset.

Sights

Church of Our Lady CHURCH

(Church of Panagia; hours vary) Easily overlooked, this pint-sized chapel was carved straight out of a cliff, apparently during Venetian times. It contains some lovely icons and a carved iconostasis. Follow the signs (enter from opposite Petra and Votsalo Restaurant); note that it's not the small church in the centre of the village.

Red Beach BEACH

Matala's main beach below the caves is a lovely crescent but often gets uncomfortably crammed. To escape the crowds, follow signs to Red Beach, reached in a 30-minute scramble over the rocks. It's hardly a secret, but it does get fewer people, including a smattering of nudists. Bring water and snacks.

Matala Caves CAVE

(Roman Cemetery; €2; 10am-7pm Mar-Oct, 8am-3pm Nov-Apr) Matala's sightseeing credentials are limited to these famous caves where hippies camped out in the 1960s and 1970s (Joni Mitchell immortalised the scene in her 1971 song 'Carey'). Hewn into the porous sandstone cliffs in prehistoric times, they were used as tombs by the Romans.

Sleeping

Villas and hotels dominate Matala's landscape wherever there isn't a restaurant, bar-cafe or souvenir shop. If that's not your scene, there are more charming options in outlying villages Sivas, Pitsidia, Kalamaki and Kamilari.

Hotel Fantastic Matala HOTEL €
(☎28920 45262; www.fantastic-matala.com; s/d/tr €45/50/60; P ❄ 📶) Quirky host Natasa (and father) woos guests with her mystical Matala magic at this budget-friendly hotel, be it via motherly doting, morning *tiropites* (cheese pies) or Greek coffee. Whatever the method, you'll feel like one of the family. Rooms, across two traditional, partly stone buildings, are smallish, with frustrating showers (those pesky curtains!), but the hospitality trumps the grumps.

There's even a secret backdoor short cut straight to the main square.

Pension Antonios PENSION €
(☎28920 45123, 6932760145; s/d/tr/f from €45/50/60/90, 1-/2-bedroom apt €120/150; ⊙Mar-Oct; P ❄ 📶) This comfortable pension has a variety of furnished rooms, all refurbished in light and airy decor with glass shower doors (a Crete rarity!) and spacious balconies. Three new villas on higher ground are especially stylish (check out Selini with its stone arch) and afford expansive views.

Hotel Nikos HOTEL €€
(www.matala-nikos.com; s/d/q €55/65/110; P ❄ 📶) A standout on hotel row, family-run Nikos has 17 modernised rooms, many with small kitchens, a terrace and snazzy bathrooms, on two floors flanking a flower-filled courtyard. The nicest is the top-floor room 24, with cave views. Breakfast is €7.50.

Eating & Drinking

Eating in Matala is hardly an experience in haute cuisine, and there's little to distinguish any of the tourist joints on the bay, but there's no denying their dramatic setting overlooking the sea. Self-caterers can stock up at the good-size supermarket next to the beach-side car park.

Nearly anywhere in Matala is good for a tipple and a bit of people-watching, but most proper bars are along the southern side of the beach and stay open until dawn.

Mama's Bakery BAKERY €
(snacks €0.50-8.50; ⊙7am-midnight Apr-Oct; 📶) Early risers will appreciate the 7am opening of this alleyway patisserie steps from the main square. Good espresso pairs with all manner of pastries, cakes and baked fusion goods, such as baklava croissants, for breakfast. More savoury items like focaccia sandwiches filled with combinations of feta and *myzithra* or sausages and bell peppers highlight lunch and dinner.

Giannis Family Grill House GRILL €
(☎28920 45719; www.giannisfamily.com; mains €6-13.50; ⊙noon-4pm & 6pm-midnight Apr–mid-Nov; 👪) A refreshing change from the run-of-the-mill waterfront tavernas, this been-here-forever family place just past the central square exudes cheer with its turquoise furniture, potted flowers and no-nonsense homemade Greek food, including excellent takes on octopus and mixed grills.

★George's Yard GREEK €€
(☎69488 78600; mains €7.50-24.50; ⊙5-11.30pm May-Oct; 📶) George (Giorgos) was the lone local who dug in with the invading hippies in the 1970s, coining Matala's motto: 'Today is life. Tomorrow never comes.' George is no longer with us, but his home is occupied by Greek-German couple Manolis and Yvonne, who along with their Athenian chef are aces of hospitality at Matala's best restaurant. Service and culinary creativity are next level.

Innovative, impossibly fresh and tasty salads and *mezedhes,* as well as elaborate fish, beef and pork dishes (with Cretan cheese, sun-dried tomatoes and rosemary, or lemon, mustard and pickles) create a memorable meal on the aqua-accented patio, especially when accompanied by lovely wines and even a craft beer or two from the mainland. Reserve.

★Scala Fish Tavern SEAFOOD €€
(☎69813 88135; mains €7-19; ⊙10am-11pm Apr-Oct; 📶) Past all the bars at the easternmost end of the beach, this dramatically perched, multitiered pit stop is Matala's best seafood restaurant. It's been in the family for over 30 years, so it's doing something right. Top marks for its fresh fish, superior service and fabulous desserts – try the *tzizkeik* (cheesecake). The cave views are especially nice at sunset. Reservations recommended.

DON'T MISS

RURAL LIFE IN TIMES PAST

Well worth a detour to Vori, the non-profit **Museum of Cretan Ethnology** (www.cretanethnologymuseum.gr; Voroi Pirgiotissis, Vori; adult/concession €3/1.50; 11am-5pm Apr-Oct) lifts the curtain on how rural people lived on the island until well into the 20th century. The English-labelled exhibits are organised around such themes as food production, war, customs, architecture and music. Save for the extraordinary coppersmith's bellows, most items are rather ordinary – hoes, olive presses, baskets, clothing, instruments – but they're engagingly displayed in darkened rooms accented with spotlights. It's clearly signposted off the main Mires–Tymbaki road.

Shopping

Mooz Art ARTS & CRAFTS
(www.moozart.gr; 10am-midnight Jun-Aug, shorter hours Apr, May, Sep & Oct) This isn't your average souvenir shop. Local artists Katerina and Vasilis flip driftwood into rustic 3D wood art as well as clever hand-painted signage with thoughtful slogans. You'll see their work around town – they've designed signs and furniture for many of Matala's bars and restaurants. The shop also features like-minded works from artists all over Greece.

Information

Matala's main drag has a couple of ATMs.

Getting There & Away

Two KTEL buses daily leave Iraklio's KTEL Heraklion Lassithi Bus Station for Matala (€8.50, two hours, 7.30am and 12.45pm). Buses to Iraklio from Matala leave from a **stop** 800m east of the main village.

There's free roadside parking and a beach car park that charges €2.

Around Matala

If you find Matala too busy, there are several quieter and more authentic bases nearby from which to explore this southwestern pocket of Iraklio. Fine beaches beckon in Kommos and Kalamaki, while inland villages like Pitsidia, Sivas and Kamilari still preserve an unhurried, traditional feel along their impossibly narrow streets. Archaeology fiends can get their fix in Kommos and Kamilari.

The villages and ruins surrounding Matala are best reached in your own vehicle.

Kommos Κομμός

Kommos has a pedigree as a Minoan settlement, of which remnants can still be seen, but today it's most famous for its long sandy beach.

Kommos ARCHAEOLOGICAL SITE
(24hr; P) FREE The Minoan site of Kommos, 3km north of Matala above a fantastic wide and sandy beach, is believed to have been the port of the mighty palace-city Phaestos (p194), some 6km northwest of here. Although it's fenced off, it's still possible to discern the ancient town's streets and courtyards as well as the remains of workshops, dwellings and temples. Find the limestone-paved road leading towards Phaestos; look closely for the ruts from Minoan carts and a sewer running from the northern side.

Kommos Beach BEACH
(Pitsidia) Located 2km north of Matala near Pitsidia and reached by a steep and winding road, the sun-kissed sands of Kommos hug Messara Bay in one of the region's most idyllic settings (especially when viewed from above). Significant remnants of Minoan settlement, though off limits, can be seen here from various vantage points. The municipality hires out beach chairs and umbrellas (€2 each) in front of the two tavernas by the towering sandstone cliffs at the far southern end.

Some beach sections further north are popular with nudists. You'll pass through them if you're walking to the laid-back beach resort of Kalamaki.

Bunga Bunga CAFE €
(Kommos Beach; mains €6-12; 10am-10pm May-Oct; P) One of two tavernas at Kommos Beach, the Caribbean-style Bunga Bunga is a funky hang-out that serves tasty, fresh organic fare and makes for an ideal sunset spot. It's named after the WWII bunker in the towering ochre cliffs above.

Mystical View TAVERNA €€
(6972294084; Timpaki; mains €7-19.50, fish per kilogram €45-55; 11am-11pm mid-Apr–Oct;) Head to this appealing taverna for its

million-dollar sunset views over Kommos Beach and its fish and meat dishes. It's 1.2km before/after Matala on the Matala–Pitsidia road (at the entry/exit roundabout).

Pitsidia Πιτσίδια

Quiet and unspoilt, Pitsidia is only 5km northeast of Matala but could not be more different in look and feel. Its unhurried vibe, nicely restored stone buildings and maze of narrow lanes decorated with potted flowers give it charm and artistic flair. At night, locals mix with visitors for chat and sustenance in one of the low-key tavernas or *kafeneia* (coffee shops) around the square. Buses en route to Matala stop on the main road.

Activities

Melanouri Horse Farm HORSE RIDING
(☎28920 45040; www.melanouri.com; rides 1/2hr from €25/50; ⏲8am-6pm) Organises one- to two-hour horse rides along the beach or into the mountains.

Sleeping & Eating

Pension Aretoussa PENSION €
(☎28920 45555; www.pensionaretoussa.com; Main Rd; s/d incl breakfast from €34/40; P 📶 👪) This old stone house with lots of trees, flowers and herbs welcomes guests to 17 spiffed-up rooms with mosquito nets over the beds. Some have access to a private garden, making them ideal for families. Light sleepers should avoid the rooms facing the main road (though these are slightly cheaper). Breakfast is served on the cosy veranda. Lovely English-speaking owners.

Raftis MEDITERRANEAN €€
(www.facebook.com/raftisrestaurant; mains €6.50-23.50; ⏲6-11pm May & Oct, 6-11pm Wed-Mon Jun-Sep; 📶) This small place adds a touch of modern Mediterranean class to Pitsidia, serving up not only a lovely outdoor setting with citrus trees and its own veg garden but high-quality organic treats you don't see elsewhere (walnut-and-black-pepper-crusted beef tenderloin, for example; and vegan options).

Mike's Taverna CRETAN €€
(☎28920 45007; mains €7.50-16; ⏲6-11.30pm Mar–mid-Nov; 📶) Near Pitsidia's main square, low-key Mike's is a great place to hang out in the evening and reflect on the events of the day over wine and simple but delicious local fare.

Sivas Σίβας

North of Pitsidia, about 2km inland from the main road, the pretty village of Sivas has a homey feel, many heritage-protected stone buildings and a pretty, taverna-lined main square.

Sights

Agia Marina Donkey Sanctuary ANIMAL SANCTUARY
(☎28929 42556; www.agia-marina-donkeyrescue.com; Petrokefali; ⏲10am-1.45pm & 5-7pm Tue-Fri, 10am-2pm Sat) FREE This place is for animal lovers. The passionate folk at Kiwi-run Agia Marina Donkey Sanctuary feed and care for abandoned donkeys. At research time, 22 donkeys were in their care, along with a gaggle of geese, goats, dogs and at least one peacock. You'll learn the story of each donkey and be able to shower them with all manner of love and comfort. Note that hours are strict: as many of the donkeys are aged, they too need their siesta.

Visits are free, but the sanctuary accepts donations and sells donkey-related souvenirs and donkey sponsorships. Look for the sign on the Matala–Mires road. It's signposted 1km on the Matala side of Petrokefali.

Moni Odigitrias MONASTERY
(www.imodigitrias.gr; Phaestos; ⏲6am-6.30pm) FREE About 6km south of Sivas, Moni Odigitrias is a historic monastery with a tower from which the monks fought off the Turks, the Germans and the odd pirate. A rickety ladder leads to the top for superb views. Afterwards, take a quick spin around the small museum, with its wine and olive presses, and check out the 15th-century frescoes and icons in the church up the hill.

Sleeping & Eating

Sigelakis Studios APARTMENT €
(☎6974810905; www.sigelakis-studios.gr; studios/apt/cottages from €45/50/70; P ❄ 📶) Attractive one-bedroom apartments decked out in traditional Cretan style, on the outskirts of Sivas, framing fantastic hillside views from each terrace. Owner Giorgos has also built four new studios with kitchenettes and a handful of attractive stone cottages. He runs the taverna of the same name.

Horiatiki Spiti APARTMENT €€
(☎28920 42004; www.horiatiko-spiti.de; studios €45, apt €75; P 📶) Run by delightful owners Maria and Mihales, this converted home

1

PECOLD/SHUTTERSTOCK ©

2

4

YIANNISSCHEIDT/SHUTTERSTOCK ©

. Heraklion Archaeological Auseum (p163)
his stunning museum features the world's largest nd finest Minoan collection.

. Wine Country (p185)
he winemaking tradition in Iraklio dates back ɔme 4000 years to Minoan times.

. Matala (p196)
legendary hippie hang-out since the 1960s, ese days Matala is a popular spot for day ippers.

. Throne Room, Palace of Cnossos (p178)
ne former capital of Minoan Crete is the island's ust-see historical sight.

ALBERT NOWICKI/SHUTTERSTOCK ©

(where Maria grew up) has maintained touches of its history, including an old well and a wood-fired oven in the lovely courtyard garden. The house now comprises four simple but homey studios and one larger apartment (with a steep staircase). The upstairs studios with terraces are particularly appealing.

Taverna Sofia TAVERNA €
(☎6932242900; www.sactouris-sivas.com; mains €6.50-12.50; ⏲noon-1am; 📶) Formerly known as Taverna Sactouris, this is the most traditional-looking spot on the plaza. It makes good salads and vegetable dishes, sometimes featuring wild herbs gathered by the chef. With notice, Sofia also makes a fragrant fish soup.

Taverna Sigelakis TAVERNA €
(mains €6-9; ⏲5-11pm; 📶) Sigelakis, slightly north of Sivas' main plaza, has a less pretty setting than some of the town's central tavernas, but it has a fabulous range of traditional food, including delicious goat in tomato sauce.

Kamilari Καμηλάρι

Straddling three hills about 8km from Matala, Kamilari is a beautiful little village in a wonderful location on a hillside, with access to the beaches around nearby Kalimaki. It's particularly popular among Germans; many have homes here. It's the kind of place where the longer you stay the more you understand its appeal. Excellent tavernas and a quaint *kafeneio* provide excellent nosh. It's home to a well-preserved (but fenced-in) Minoan tomb.

Sights

Minoan Tomb ARCHAEOLOGICAL SITE
(⏲24hr) FREE Amid fields just outside Kamilari stands a fenced-in, extraordinarily well-preserved circular Minoan tomb with 2m-high stone walls. Side rooms were used for ritual purposes. Follow signs to Tympaki and, just after the small white church, look for signs to the right and then, about 500m on, to the left. You can drive through the olive groves on a dirt road for about 1.2km. This is also a pleasant walk.

Sleeping & Eating

★**Aloni Apartments** APARTMENT €
(☎6934404574; www.aloni-kamilari.net; studios €40; P❄@📶) These four casual and compact studio apartments with blue-and-white decor are simple but feature wonderfully tasteful beds, modern bathrooms, grapevine-draped patio canopies and a kitchen area for preparing a picnic or three. Each is enhanced with unique paintings from the owner's Argentine wife. There's a great little sundeck, too, with chairs for soaking up the rays.

OFF THE BEATEN TRACK

KAPETANIANA ΚΑΠΕΤΑΝΙΑΝΑ

In the heart of the Asteroussia mountain range that runs along the entire southern coast of Iraklio, and clinging to the slopes of the highest peak, Kapetaniana is a remote hamlet that's a mecca for rock climbers and hikers. A gorgeous 14th-century Byzantine church graces Kato ('lower') Kapetaniana. The last 8km of road corkscrews up into the mountains, making it one of the most exciting drives in Crete.

Despite its petite size (it has only about 80 residents), Kapetaniana is blessed with one of Crete's most interesting sleeping options, **Thalori Retreat** (☎28930 41762; www.thalori.com; Kapetaniana; studios/apt from €70/85; ❄📶🏊👪). Owners Marcos and Popi have rehabilitated the 'dying' village, renovating 22 original stone cottages to offer an atmospheric, old-style experience with modern comforts. There are 15 traditional cottages and seven purpose-built, more design-forward studios (from Nos 2 and 3 you have Mt Kofinas views from your bed). Horse riding (€25 per hour), off-road jeep tours, guided hikes to the summit of Mt Kofinas (€35 per person), boat trips (€350 for up to four people) and cooking classes (€25) can all be arranged from here. Its on-site restaurant (mains €8.50 to 12.50) serves hearty Cretan cuisine and is the only game in town for food.

The closest public transport comes to Kapetaniana is 18km north at Agioi Deka, so you'll need your own set of wheels to get here. Use extra caution ascending and descending the 8km of road closest to the town, which amounts to a lane and some change, and unravels like a discarded ball of yarn across the mountainside.

Asterousia APARTMENT €
(☎28920 42832; www.asterousia.com; studios/apt from €40/50; ❄📶) Feel your stresses melt away at this enchanting place run by Monica and Giorgos, who seek to impart their love for nature and the simple things in life to their guests. In line with their philosophy, the ageing studios and apartments have no frills, but this is one place where the hosts make the experience. French, English and German are spoken.

★**Pizza Ariadni** ITALIAN €
(☎28920 42439; pizza €7.50-11; ⏰7pm-1am May-Oct; 📶) For over 20 years Manolis has been kneading dough for the hundreds of loyal clients who head here not only for the lush setting on a candlelit garden terrace but also for the excellent brick-oven pizza. Manolis was originally trained by an Italian.

Things hot up into party mode later in the evening.

Kentrikon CAFE €
(www.facebook.com/pg/kentrikonkafeneio; ⏰4pm-1am Mon-Sat; 📶) Kentriko is a beautiful, congenial stone *kafeneio* (established 1922) on the narrow main drag. Decorated with old photos of village families, it's great for breakfast, a nightcap or anything in between. As friendly owner Irini explains, it runs to a rhythm: tourists, then regular elderly men who chat over a coffee, then local youths into the wee hours.

Taverna Acropolis TAVERNA €€
(mains €6-13; ⏰3pm-midnight Apr-Oct; 📶) This relaxing taverna, housed in a historic building, is delightful for a pre- or post-dinner nip. The walls are lined with eclectic artworks and the interiors reflect effortless good taste. That extends to the good, wholesome Greek cuisine, which comes highly recommended. Head to the kitchen to choose from a selection of daily offerings. The bonus is the terrace overlooking the village.

Kalamaki Καλαμάκι

With its long sandy beach and attractive setting, 7km from Matala, Kalamaki has all the trappings of an alluring resort town. Despite the presence of several skeletal half-finished buildings, it's a pleasant, low-key spot with good-value lodging and relaxed locals. The taverna- and lounge-lined beach promenade makes for fine strolling and you can walk to Kommos Beach along the shore. Many places close from December to February.

OFF THE BEATEN TRACK

SPICE OF LIFE

Southern Iraklio Province's one must-stop shop, **Botano** (www.botano.gr; ⏰10am-7pm Apr-Oct, 10am-2pm & 5-7pm Tue, Thu & Fri, 10am-2pm Mon, Wed & Sat Nov-Mar) is a family-run business in the tiny village of Kouses that will woo you with Cretan spices and teas from its own organic gardens, and fair trade hot-pepper sauces, flavoured sea salts, natural cosmetics and essential oils, in addition to like-minded products from throughout Greece (red saffron from Kozani, for example).

Sleeping & Eating

★**Arsinoi Studios** APARTMENT €
(☎28920 45475, 6986858923; www.arsinoi-studios.gr; studios €36-40, apt €35-85; P❄📶) Arsinoi would be just another apartment building near the beach were it not for the friendly Papadospiridaki family, who will fall over backwards for you – they epitomise Greek *filoxenia* (hospitality). You'll instantly feel at home when big-hearted Noi ushers you to your squeaky-clean and roomy digs and proffers up fruit and goodies from the family farm.

★**Yiannis** CRETAN €
(multicourse menu €10-17; ⏰noon-1am Apr-Nov) For something with a genuine bygone local flair, head one block inland from the Kalamaki beach to Yiannis, a bare-bones eatery that has been running for over 30 years. It enjoys cult status with locals and loyal visitors for its scrumptious mezedhes and lovably eccentric proprietor.

Italiana ITALIAN €
(☎28920 29236; www.facebook.com/italianakalamaki; pizza €7-10.50; ⏰9am-11.30pm Tue-Sun Apr-Oct, 9am-11.30pm Fri-Sun Nov-Mar; 📶) Jean-Marc is a half-French, half-Italian restaurateur who learned English in Spain – and that gives him top pizza and pasta cred in these parts. Real-deal uncut pizzas are cooked on a wood-fired rotating pizza stone imported from Italy; pasta, risotto, gnocchi and mains such as Roman-style saltimbocca and lemon or Marsala scaloppini are on the menu, too.

HIKING IN IRAKLIO

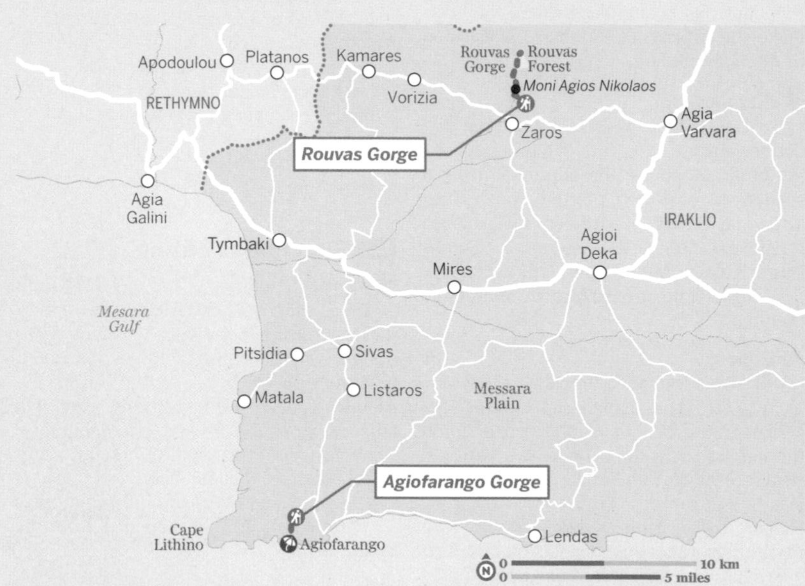

ROUVAS GORGE

START LAKE VOTOMOS
END LAKE VOTOMOS
LENGTH 10KM
DIFFICULTY DIFFICULT

Part of the E4 European Path, the Rouvas Gorge hike leads to a protected swath of forest home to some of the oldest oak trees in Crete. It's an especially lovely walk in springtime, when hooded helleborine orchids, poppies, irises and other wildflowers give the landscape the vibrancy of an impressionist painting, but is recommended any time from April to November. It's a 10km up-and-back trek from the main trailhead at Lake Votomos north of Zaros village. The trail is mostly signed in Greek (and mostly referring to the churches), but small red and white circles painted onto the rocks and trees lead the way.

The **trailhead** is at a steep staircase on the property of Limni Taverna on the shores of Lake Votomos. The route hugs the mountainside until it enters the gorge about 1km later, just past **Moni Agios Nikolaos** (p191), a modern monastery that wraps around a historic church replete with icons and fresco fragments. Alternatively, you can start the hike from the monastery and shave 2km off the round-trip route – follow the zigzagging gravel road to the left of the newly constructed blue-domed church until the two paths merge.

From here you enter the gorge, as the vegetation becomes increasingly lush with oak trees, lilies, orchids, sage and other mountain flora, and pass a few natural freshwater pools that will surely be appreciated in warmer months. The elevation change along the route clocks in at about 700m. Along the way, you'll cross first one **wooden bridge**, then another (and navigate a third quite shifty-looking one that has collapsed and been reinforced with steel girders), and encounter several uncleared rock falls that require a bit of clambering. Eventually, a gorgeous clearing emerges, home to the little **Chapel of Agios Ioannis** and several benches and tables that invite a leisurely picnic (camping here, surrounded by the Rouvas Forest, is allowed).

Wear sneakers or hiking boots, take at least 2L of water per person and pack some snacks (or a bit more, for the aforementioned picnic). Cold beers await lakeside at Limni Taverna once you descend.

AGIOFARANGO GORGE

START AGIOFARANGO GORGE CAR PARK
END AGIOFARANGO BEACH
LENGTH 1.8KM
DIFFICULTY EASY

Agiofarango Gorge is one of Crete's most gorgeous and accessible hikes, leading fleet-footed adventurers to one of the island's most isolated and wonderful beaches. There are caves, makeshift chapels and hermitages in the cliffs as well as a Byzantine chapel en route. The gorge emerges at a lovely pebble beach with crystal-clear water. Despite its remoteness, it can get busy.

From Moni Odigitrias, 12.5km southeast of Matala, drive on the dirt road signposted to Kali Limenes for approximately 3.5km, where you'll turn right at a sharp fork. Continue on this rough dirt road for around 2.5km until the road ends (at the Agiofarango Gorge car park). From here you'll walk for approximately 1.8km to the sea. A Cretan warning: don't park your car under trees for shade, as goats sometimes jump on the roofs to reach tree leaves. A small cafe here serves refreshments.

The trail begins cutting through meandering walls of stratified red rock (wrong turns are nearly impossible, as the gorge closes in on you, so simply continue forward along the riverbed through the canyon walls). The gorge is awash in oleander; birdsong and the clackity-clank of goat bells provide the only soundtrack.

Around 250m before the beach, the 14th-century **Byzantine Church of Agios Antonios** (St Anthony) sits in splendid isolation. It was once a monastery and the centre of asceticism among the 300 hermits that dwelt in total isolation from one another in the canyon. A well sits alongside it – the hermits' sole water source. Another 50m to the left as you walk towards the sea, **Goumenospilios Cave** can be seen. Despite its low and small entrance, it opens up into a 9m-high and 7m-wide conical dome. It was here that St Anthony once lived, and legend has it that hermits met here just once a year, learning only then whom had died during the previous 12 months. A lone icon sits inside. After another 200m the sea emerges at pretty **Agiofarango Beach**.

Lendas Λέντας

POP 80

Lendas appeals to those in search of a remote, laid-back beach retreat. Reached via a long, winding road that culminates in a dramatic plunge, the town clings to the cliff overlooking the beach. It attracts mostly long-standing return guests and independent travellers looking for a budget-focused experience. Aside from the sun, and a few beach bars and tavernas, there isn't much to do besides zone out to the sounds of the crashing waves.

Sights

Sanctuary of Asklepios ARCHAEOLOGICAL SITE
(8.30am-3.30pm Tue-Sun) FREE Under the Romans, Lebena (today's Lendas) was a health spa cherished for its therapeutic springs. The ancient settlement stood right above the beach, but only two granite columns of a 4th-century-BC temple remain (along with a few discarded columns strewn about). Next to the temple was a treasury with a mosaic floor that is still visible. Very little else is decipherable, and the springs have been closed since the 1960s. Nearby, the Byzantine church of St John also remains.

Beaches

The beach in town is narrow and pebbly and not particularly attractive, but there are better options not too far away.

Loutra BEACH
The pretty, if rocky, Loutro beach is the launching pad for a scenic 6km hike to Kronos via the Trakhoula Gorge. It's about 5km east of Lendas. Its setting, sandwiched between two hillsides spilling to the sea and next to a small marina, is probably Lendas' most dramatic.

Diskos BEACH
About 1km west of town, over the headland, there's a nice long stretch of sand called Diskos (or Dytikos), a naturists' favourite.

Sleeping

If Lendas has anything, it has places to stay. There are plenty of choices – apartments, villas, rooms – and the prices are lower than in other parts of Iraklio Province.

Villa Tsapakis APARTMENT €
(6947571900, 28920 95378; www.villa-tsapakis.gr; s/d/tr €25/35/45, studios/1-bedroom apt from €40/50; P ❄ ᯤ) Over the headland from town, on lovely sandy Diskos beach, which is mostly nudist, this flower-filled spot has good-value, no-nonsense studios with kitchens and balconies set around an oddly shaped central courtyard.

There's also a cafe, a yoga studio and an oceanside restaurant serving traditional dishes (mains €6 to €19).

Casa Doria HOTEL €€
(6972648013; www.casadoria.net; d/tr incl breakfast €85/100; Apr-Oct; P ❄ ᯤ) There's remote and then there's Casa Doria. The self-proclaimed 'slow-life hotel' has seven rooms, all individually and slightly quirkily decorated with Zenlike simplicity, perched dramatically overlooking the cerulean sea and the 'crocodile' cape. Its main draws are the charismatic Italian owners and a restaurant that delivers Mediterranean flavour explosions (cooking lessons, too; €30). Half-board is an extra €15.

Prices decrease significantly outside high season. With easy access to the Trakhoula Gorge, this is a great base for hikers, climbers and mountain bikers. It's about 3km from Lendas and is signposted to the east at the first turn-off out of town (the Loutra–Trakhoulas road).

Eating

As you'd expect, seafood rules the menus in the tavernas and cafes clustered around the beach, but international dishes, including some organic options, also make an appearance.

★ Taverna
Casa Doria ITALIAN €€
(6972648013; www.casadoria.net; Loutra; mains €7-14; 1-2.30pm & 7.30-9pm; ᯤ) Given that the owners are Italian, it's little surprise that your taste buds will receive a touch of Milanese flair here, three kilometres from town. Isabella's homemade pasta is to die for, but so are her main courses, such as *vitello tonnato* (using pork loin instead of veal, with tuna and capers). But leave room for dessert, especially the panna cotta or tiramisu (€4).

Porto Lentas SEAFOOD €€
(6982379199; mains €7-14; 8am-1am; ᯤ) So close to the sea that the ocean sometimes spills into the restaurant, this simple seafooder at the western end of Lendas Beach won't win any James Beard awards, but it hits the spot for those seeking a beachfront meal with a view.

Information

The town has a few of small markets and one ATM.

Getting There & Away

To get here you must change buses in Mires. There's one daily bus from Monday to Saturday plying the route between Mires and Lendas (€4, one hour). Alternatively, a taxi from Mires costs around €40 (€80 to €100 from Iraklio).

It's best to leave your car in the car park on entry to the village; the right fork heads to the main square. The bus stops outside the car park. The town has no petrol station.

NORTHEASTERN COAST

Ever since the national road along the northern coast opened in 1972, the coast between Iraklio and Malia has seen a frenzy of unbridled development, particularly in the seaside towns of Hersonisos and Malia. Hotels deal almost exclusively with package-tour operators who block-book hotel rooms months in advance. For independent travellers, the chain of villages above Hersonisos (Koutouloufari, Piskopiano and Old Hersonisos) are the most appealing places to stay in this area.

While Hersonisos has some family-friendly attractions, including fun water parks, Malia is primarily a party town. A bit incongruously, it's also home to the area's only significant historical site, the wonderful Minoan palace.

Buses link all the coastal towns along the Old National Rd at least every 30 minutes. If you want to avoid this area altogether, whoosh right past it on the E75 highway.

Gournes & Around

Gournes, about 15km east of Iraklio, was dominated by a huge US air force base until it closed in 1994.

Sights & Activities

Dinosauria Park AMUSEMENT PARK

(☎2810 332089; www.dinosauriapark.com; International Exhibit Centre, Gournes; adult/child €10/8; ⏲10am-6pm) Get in touch with your inner Tyrannosaurus rex at this fun and educational theme park. You enter a time tunnel (with explanations on the way) and exit into a Jurassic universe complete with moving, roaring, life-size animatronic beasts.

Watercity WATER PARK

(☎28150 00200; www.watercity.gr; Anopolis; adult/child under 140cm/child under 90cm €27/18.50/free; ⏲10am-6pm May & Sep, to 6.30pm Jun-Aug, to 5.30pm Oct) This compact water park is in Anopolis, about 12km east of Iraklio. While it's certainly seen better days, it still offers plenty of fun on a hot summer day. Most attractions are geared to the preteen set, but a few (like the Kamikaze dark tunnel and the Hydro Tubes & Free Fall) provide even grown-ups with proper thrills.

Hersonisos Χερσόνησος

POP 26,700

Hersonisos, about 25km east of Iraklio, has grown from a small fishing village into one of Crete's largest and busiest tourist towns and is deluged in summer. The main thoroughfare is lined with sprawling hotels, apartment buildings and a cacophonous strip of bars, cafes, tourist shops, clubs, fast-food eateries, travel agencies and quad-hire places. Its most decent stretch of sand is the quaint Sarandaris Beach.

To escape the bustle, base yourself uphill in one of three adjoining villages: Koutouloufari, Piskopiano or Old Hersonisos. Although touristy, these are nonetheless appealing and have some excellent tavernas and accommodation options.

Sights & Activities

★Lychnostatis Open Air Museum MUSEUM

(www.lychnostatis.gr; adult/child €6/2; ⏲9am-2pm Sun-Fri Apr-Oct) In a lovely seaside setting at Hersonisos' eastern edge, this family-operated, open-air folklore museum recreates a traditional Cretan village with commendable authenticity. The various buildings, including windmill, schoolhouse and farmer's home, were rescued around Crete and moved here. Elsewhere there are weaving workshops, ceramics and plant-dying demonstrations, olive-oil pressing and raki distilling, orchards and herb gardens, and a theatre that hosts music and dance performances. Guided tours and audio guides (€2) are available, as is a cafe.

Arion Stables HORSE RIDING

(☎6973733825; www.arionstables.com; Archangelou Michail Chersoniso; per hr €40; ⏲8am-8pm

Tue-Sun;) Run by the affable Zara and Georgio, this sweet little horse farm in the hills between Hersonisos and Analipsi gets praise for its treatment of animals and its rides through the countryside and along the beach. Lots of other animals, many of them rescued, live on the farm, which also has a playground and a tavern.

Acqua Plus WATER PARK
(28970 24950; www.acquaplus.gr; Hersonisos-Kastelli Rd; adult/child €27/17; 10am-6pm May, Jun, Sep & Oct, to 7pm Jul & Aug;) Greece's oldest water park is showing its age despite an expansion and upgrade but is still good for a few hours of fun. It's divided into an adult section, where wicked slides with names like Tsunami and Kamikaze should give adrenaline junkies a kick, and another for kids, with pools, playgrounds, an inflatable castle and gentler thrills like the 270m-long Lazy River.

Sleeping

Koutouloufari, Piskopiano and Old Hersonisos, uphill from Hersonisos, offer more charming villas and fewer resorts and condominiums.

Villa Iokasti APARTMENT €€
(28970 22607; www.iokasti.gr; Varnali 10, Koutouloufari; studios €75, 1-/2-bedroom apt €98/145;) Iokasti's 20 modern and bright studios, junior suites and apartments with balconies and cheerful aqua and ochre accents are set off the main drag towards the end of Koutouloufari and exude a village-within-a-village feel.

Balsamico Suites APARTMENT €€
(28970 23323; www.balsamico-suites.gr; Old Hersonisos; ste incl breakfast from €89;) This stone complex fuses old-world charm with such mod cons as smart TVs and hairdryers. Seventeen well-proportioned suites are decked out in rich, dark wood and come with balconies.

★ **Villa Ippocampi** APARTMENT €€€
(28970 22316; www.ippocampi.com; 4g Seferi, Koutouloufari; apt €150-190;) This relaxing Dutch-Greek retreat exudes style and will mesmerise you from the moment you step past its lavender bushes and pool. Once you're ensconced in your apartment (all are decorated in a strong blue-and-white theme), it'll be hard to go past two choices – laze by the pool or chat to the charming owners, Lydia and Nikos.

Eating

Skip the identikit tourist tavernas in Hersonisos proper and opt for a more authentic culinary experience uphill in Koutouloufari and Piskopiano. A table full of traditional mezedhes is what's for dinner.

★ **David Vegera** CRETAN €
(Piskopiano; mezedhes €4.50-10; 5pm-midnight Mon-Sat;) A fabulous spot housed in a former *kafeneio*, this place has a buzzy vibe due to the scores of Greeks and tourists who descend on it from opening time. David Vegera started this gig in 1954, and his great-grandson helps run the show today. It serves old-time mezedhes, efficiently and without fuss.

Taverna Areston TAVERNA €€
(28970 23453; Eleftherias 60; mezedhes €2.50-5.50, mains €7-15; noon-midnight;) Well away from the tourist track, sandwiched on a road between Piskopiano and Hersonisos proper, and catering to gaggles of locals – often celebrating a baptism or other family-oriented event – this is one of the few authentic tavernas in the area.

Kostas Tavern Meze CRETAN €€
(28970 237125; Gianni Ritsou 3, Piskopiano; mezedhes €3-5, mains €5.50-13.50; 1pm-1am mid-Apr–Oct;) It's easy to be distracted by the street-facing eateries in Piskopiano and Koutouloufari, so you might walk right past this gem, at the edge of the church plaza above the main thoroughfare. Kostas and family specialise in traditional mezedhes – baked feta, fava dip, impossibly soft stuffed vine leaves, fantastic *dakos* (rusks) – which go down a thrill chased with wine or ouzo.

Drinking & Nightlife

Hersonisos is a proper resort and you'll find all manner of nocturnal diversions – the main drag along the sea is lined with cafes, bars, pubs, clubs and even a cabaret! More atmospherically, you'll find a proper pub or two in Koutouloufari and Piskopiano.

Shopping

Maria Sanoudaki Ceramic Studio CERAMICS
(www.facebook.com/sanoudaki; Isiodou, Old Hersonisos; 11am-8pm) The antidote to mass-produced souvenirs in Old Hersonisos, Maria's creative pottery designs, often in soothing Greek blues, are a beautiful local craft that'll ensure you never forget Greece's

WORTH A TRIP

TOWARDS THE LASITHI PLATEAU

From Malia, the road climbs quickly to the Lasithi Plateau, passing through the charming village of Krasi and the monastery of Kerá along the way. Krasi's main claim to fame is a 2000-year-old plane tree with a mind-boggling 16m girth. It is fed by the adjacent spring spurting from an arcaded stone basin and provides shades for the taverna tables set up beneath its massive canopy.

Aposelemis Dam En route to/from the village of Krasí you will pass the controversial Aposelemis Dam, the construction of which was completed in 2012. Formerly wedged between the villages of Potamies and Advou, the village of Sfendile was flooded to allow for the damming of the Aposelemis Creek. The dam provides drinking water to the greater Iraklio and Agios Nikolaos areas. Depending on the dam levels, you may still see house roofs, including that of Sfendiles village church, plus a tattered Greek flag fluttering.

Kerá Kardiotissas Monastery (Panagía Kerá Pediádos; 9am-6pm) Continuing on from the Aposelemis Dam takes you to Kerá, home to one of Crete's most cherished monasteries, the Panagia Kardiotissa. Its teensy chapel is embellished with 14th-century frescoes depicting scenes from the life of Christ and the Virgin, but locals especially venerate an 18th-century icon of the Virgin and Child. Legend has it that the Turks spirited it three times to Constantinople, but it miraculously returned each time, despite being chained to a marble pillar.

Taverna Niki (28970 51204; www.nikitaverna.gr; Ano Kerá, Kerá; mains €5.50-12; 9am-10pm;) After visiting the nearby Kerá Kardiotissas, stop for the view and a bite at this traditional taverna perched on a hillside corner 850m from the monastery. The family's wood-fired oven is jam-packed with trays of pork, chicken, lamb and potatoes submerged in Cretan olive oil and slow-roasted for a few hours behind a door sealed with moistened chicken feed.

largest isle. Choose from decorative plates, fridge magnets, vases and ceramic flowers.

Getting There & Away

Buses from KTEL Heraklion Lassithi Bus Station (p177) run at least every 30 minutes to Hersonisos (€3.30, 40 minutes). Heading back, catch buses at **stop 19 (west)** (Palio EO Iraklio-Agios Nikolaos) heading west along the main road. Buses heading east to Malia and Agios Nikolas stop at **stop 19 (east)** (Palio EO Iraklio-Agios Nikolaos) on the opposite side of the road.

There's a **taxi stand** (Sanoudaki) on Sanoudaki just off the main drag. Parking uphill in Old Hersonisos, Koutouloufari and Piskopiano is mayhem, but there's a free **car park** just behind the main thoroughfare in Hersonisos proper.

Malia Μάλια

POP 5400

You won't need to look hard to find the party in Malia, 34km east of Iraklio: the party will find you. The small town is well known for its festive atmosphere (maybe you've seen it in 2011 British comedy *The Inbetweeners Movie*). For more charm and a quieter ambience, head to Old Town Malia, with its classic maze of narrow lanes. Outside town, the ruins of the Minoan Palace of Malia are among the area's more cerebral attractions. Potamos Beach is a lovely and less crowded swatch of sand near the palace.

Sights

★ **Palace of Malia** ARCHAEOLOGICAL SITE

(adult/concession/child €6/3/free; 8am-8pm Tue-Sun May-Nov, to 3pm Tue-Sun Dec-Apr) The Palace of Malia, 3km east of Malia, was built at about the same time as the great Minoan palaces of Phaestos and Knossos. The First Palace dates back to around 1900 BC and was rebuilt after the earthquake of 1700 BC, only to be levelled again by another tremor around 1450 BC. Most of what you see today are the remains of the Second Palace, where many exquisite Minoan artefacts, including the famous **gold bee pendant** (p170), were found.

Malia is a relatively easy site to comprehend thanks to a free map, labelling throughout and an **exhibition hall** where photographs and scale models of the ruined and reconstructed complex help you visualise the main palace and surrounding sites. There is no fixed route to follow and you're

Palace of Malia

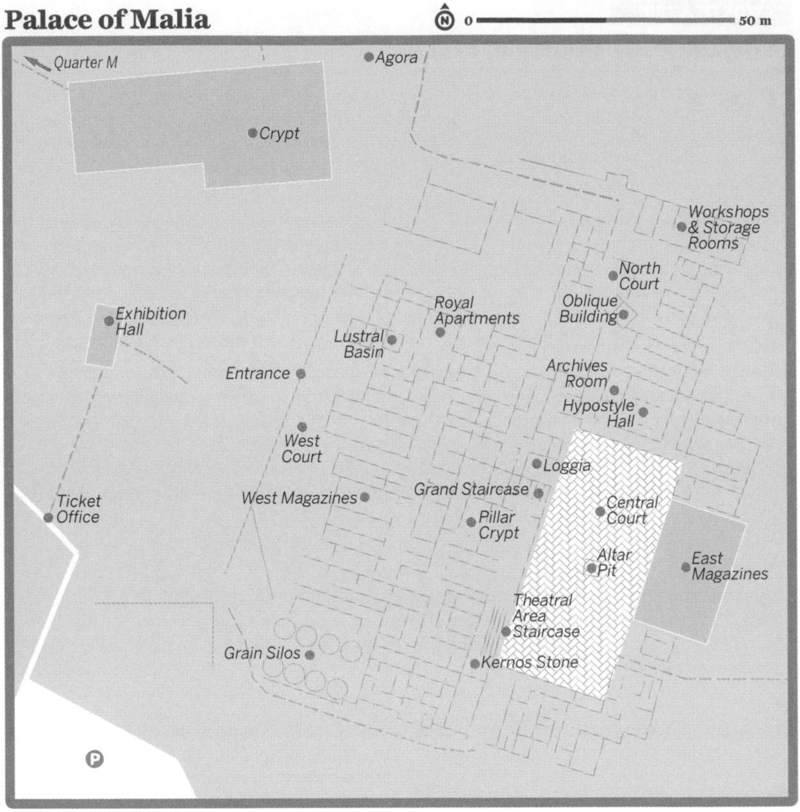

0 — 50 m

Quarter M
Agora
Crypt
Workshops & Storage Rooms
North Court
Oblique Building
Royal Apartments
Exhibition Hall
Lustral Basin
Entrance
Archives Room
Hypostyle Hall
West Court
Loggia
Ticket Office
West Magazines
Grand Staircase
Central Court
Pillar Crypt
Altar Pit
East Magazines
Theatral Area Staircase
Grain Silos
Kernos Stone
P

free to explore as you like. The following is merely a suggested approach.

Enter from the **West Court**, turn right and walk south along the **grain silos**, a series of storage rooms for eight *kouloures* (circular pits) that are believed to have stored grain. Continue past the silos and enter the palace's **Central Court**, which was once framed by arcades. On your left, in the ground, is the **Kernos Stone**, a disc with 34 impressions around its edge that may have had a religious function.

Walk to the sunken **altar pit** in the centre of the courtyard and take in its impressive dimensions: 48m long and 22m wide. Beneath a canopy on your right are the **east magazines**, where liquids were stored in giant *pithoi*. The south wing contained apartments and a small shrine, while the north wing had workshops, storerooms and a ceremonial banquet hall. The most important rooms of the palace were in the west wing. The structure furthest to the north, the **loggia**, was linked to the court by four steps and probably used for ceremonial purposes. Next are the 11 remaining steps of the **grand staircase**, which may have led to a shrine. A bit set back, behind a stone-paved vestibule, two remaining stumps mark the location of the **pillar crypt**.

Buses from Iraklio stop at bus stop 36 on the main road, 250m from the site.

Tours

Hub MTB Adventures CYCLING

(☎6936244588; www.mtbhub.gr; Cretan Malia Park; 4hr ride from €65; ⊙9am-2pm Mon-Sat) This respected operator covers the whole of Crete, with a range of tours including a one-day trip to Lasitihi Plateau and a two-day coast-to-coast trip.

Sleeping & Eating

Head to Old Town Malia or Potamos Beach near the Palace of Malia for better quality and more authentic ambience.

Sunshine Hotel BOUTIQUE HOTEL €€
(28970 31090; www.sunshine-malia.gr; Zoodoxou Pigis; d/q incl breakfast from €70/120;) This newish boutique hotel is the domain of friendly Danai, who flipped her mother's old hotel into one of Iraklio Province's most stylish abodes. Playing with colourful minimalism, there are cherry wood-lined hallways and a light and airy, mid-century modern aesthetic. Rooms (and showers) are noticeably spacious and value is palpable: in-room Nespresso machines, spa services and a pool.

Taverna Kalyva TAVERNA €€
(www.facebook.com/KalyvaMalia; Potamos Beach; mains €5.50-15; 8am-midnight Jun-Aug, shorter hours rest of year;) West of the Malia archaeological site and just before you hit Potamos Beach, Kalyva is a bare-bones, no-nonsense beachside taverna that's been serving locals and visitors since 1964, especially on Sunday, when Greeks pour in for extended lunches.

Milos TAVERNA €€
(28970 33150; Giorgio Lapidi 9; mains €9-15; 6-11.30pm May-Oct;) This is as near to an oasis as you can get in Malia – garlic strings hang from the walls, and flowers and leaves drip from the garden's lush trees. But what mainly draw the crowds are the *psito* dishes (roasted oven meats) cooked in the outdoor wood-fired oven, lit every afternoon. Reserve. Located at the eastern edge of Old Malia.

Stablos & Elisabeth TAVERNA €€
(28970 31320; Agios Dimitrios; mains €5.50-24; 6pm-midnight, closed Nov;) The best taverna on Old Malia's main square goes for the Crete-meets-English-B&B look, with plenty of knick-knacks and lace curtains. The nicely prepared Greek and international foods are best enjoyed in the rooftop garden. Presentation, from house wine poured from copper jugs to rice delivered in colourful metal tins, and service are a step up from the usual.

Drinking & Nightlife

The main strip, Dimokratias, goes from the east–west main drag, Eleftheriou Venizelou, north all the way to the beach and is chock-a-block with boisterous bars, pubs and high-energy clubs filled with carousing package tourists from June to September.

Getting There & Away

Buses from Iraklio's bus station (p177) near the port go to Malia at least half-hourly (€4.10, one hour). Heading to Iraklio from Malia, go to **bus stop 33 (west)** (Eleftheriou Venizelou). If you're moving on to Agios Nikolas and Sitia, you'll need to cross Eleftheriou Venizelou and head a few hundred metres down the road to **bus stop 33 (east)** (Eleftheriou Venizelou).

OFF THE BEATEN TRACK

SPOOKY CAVE

Also known as Agia Paraskevi Cave, after the chapel built above it, **Skotino Cave** (Gouves; hours vary) is one of the largest caves in Crete and deliciously spooky to boot. A gaping arch gives way to a dark chamber as lofty as a Gothic cathedral and teeming with stalactites, stalagmites and massive limestone formations. Let your mind wander and you'll make out all sorts of shapes (a bear, a dragon, a head) in the dim light.

Unless you have some spelunking experience and a flashlight, you probably shouldn't venture beyond here, because the chamber drops another 15m and it gets eerily dark.

Skotino was first explored by Arthur Evans in 1933. Later excavations have unearthed vases, bone needles and figurines dating as far back as Minoan times, suggesting that the cave has had religious significance. To this day, pilgrims leave votives and offerings.

There's no admission fee, no guard and few (if any) visitors. In fact, the site has a long-abandoned feel. Wear sturdy shoes and mind your footing at all times.

The cave is near the village of Skotino, some 8km inland from Kato Gouves. About 1km past Skotino, look for the turn-off to the 'Cave of Agia Paraskevi' sign and drive another 2.3km to the cave entrance.

LAZY DAYS

Cretan food and wine are feisty rather than fancy, usually made with freshly gathered ingredients and prepared in time-tested ways.

GRAPE DELIGHTS

If Kotsifali, Mandilari, Malvasia and Liatiko are music to your ears, they will please your taste buds even more. These grape varietals, all indigenous to Crete, blanket the rolling hills of **Iraklio Wine Country** (p185), which begins just past Knossos. Many estates offer tastings and tours.

TASTY TROUT

You'll see bottled natural spring water from **Zaros** (p191) all over Crete, but only in the village itself can you taste the famous local trout, ideally in a taverna overlooking deep-green Lake Votomos.

FANCIFUL FILO

A rare treat awaits in Rethymno at **Yiorgos Hatziparaskos** (p128), one of the last traditional filo masters in all of Greece. Watch the head-spinning process and sample the sublime baklava and *kataïfi* ('angel hair' pastry).

FISH VILLAGE

Fish lovers hit the jackpot in **Mohlos** (p239). Its quartet of harbour-fronting tavernas are all good places to devour the catch of the day with a view of Minoan ruins on an offshore island.

CRETAN GOLD

With over 1.5 million trees, olive oil is the lifeblood of Crete. You see, smell and taste it wherever you go. One place to peel back the curtain of mystery on how it is actually made is the **Paraschakis Olive Oil Factory** (p141), near Rethymno's Melidoni Cave.

1. Mohlos (p239)
2. *Kataïfi* ('angel hair' pastry; p52)
3. Dining in Zaros (p191)

GEORGIOS TSICHLIS/SHUTTERSTOCK ©

IMAGEBROKER/ALAMY STOCK PHOTO ©

DZIEWUL/SHUTTERSTOCK ©

1. Moni Arkadiou (p137) **2.** Laws of Gortyna (p193) **3.** *Lord Thou Art Great* icon, Moni Toplou (p244) **4.** Frangokastello (p87)

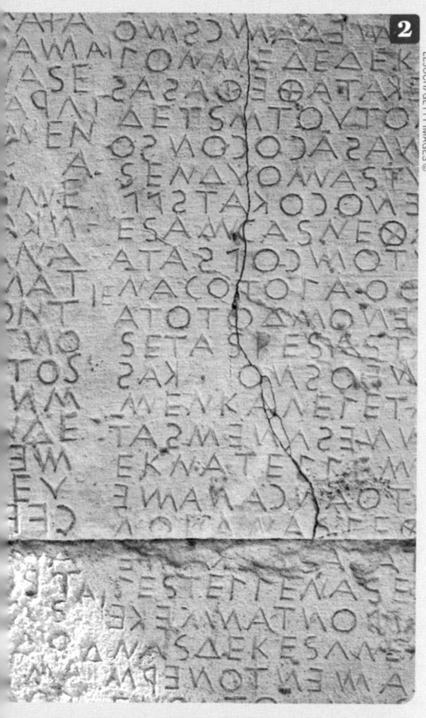

LEJOCH/GETTY IMAGES ©

Witnesses to History

At the crossroads of three continents, Crete's turbulent history has been shaped by many players. Hear whispers of the past as you visit grand Minoan palaces, remnants of a Roman city, showcases of Venetian architecture and monasteries with military pedigrees. If only stones could talk...

Magic Malia

Smaller than Knossos, and without the reconstructions and embellishments, the Palace of Malia (p209) is Crete's most accessible and easily understood Minoan site. Its sophisticated layout and infrastructure attest to this ancient society's advanced level of civilisation. Excavations are still ongoing.

Glorious Gortyna

Get lost amid the moody ruins of Gortyna (p193), Roman Crete's capital. Stop to admire what's left of a beautiful early-Christian church and marvel at 2600-year-old stone tablets engraved with a surprisingly modern legal code.

Fortified Monastery

Despite its fortifications, 15th-century Moni Toplou (p244) was sacked by pirates, looted by the Knights of Malta and finally captured by Turks in 1821. Its church shelters a precious icon by Ioannis Kornaros.

Mighty Fortresses

The most impressive vestiges of Venetian rule are the many stalwart fortresses built to keep pirates and Turks at bay. Visit those in Hania (p65), Rethymno (p119), Iraklio (p163) and Frangokastello (p87).

Monastery Siege

The hauntingly beautiful Moni Arkadiou (p137) is a window into the Cretan soul. During the revolt of 1866, local Cretans trapped within opted to blow up their gunpowder supplies rather than surrender to the Turks, killing nearly everyone, Turks included.

Lasithi

Includes ➡

Best Places to Eat

- ➡ Hiona Taverna (p246)
- ➡ Ta Kochilia (p239)
- ➡ Ergospasio (p229)
- ➡ Hope (p229)

Best Places to Stay

- ➡ Elounda Heights (p228)
- ➡ Karavostassi Apartments (p238)
- ➡ Villa Olga (p224)
- ➡ Nereids Apartments (p242)

Why Go?

Crete's easternmost region is home to the island's top resorts: Agios Nikolaos smoulders with cosmopolitan cool, while just around the bay, Elounda tiptoes between luxe and relaxed. Paradoxically, this is also the wildest region, with the richest biodiversity and the least trampled ranges; it's so rugged in places that you half expect Pan to emerge, pipes in hand, from the meadows.

For the wanderer in search of adventure and gastro delights, Lasithi ticks all the boxes: cyclists head up to misty Lasithi Plateau, trekkers tackle dramatic canyons such as the famous Zakros Gorge, and foodies enjoy some of Crete's finest tavernas and restaurants. Then there are attractions like the historic monastery of Toplou, Vaï's beguiling palm-lined beach, and scores of towns and villages that maintain a rich undertow of Cretan history and spirit. And let's not forget Lasithi's rich ancient history, with Minoan and Dorian sites to explore in numerous places.

Road Distances (km)

	Ierapetra	Agios Nikolaos	Elounda	Sitia
Agios Nikolaos	36			
Elounda	45	10		
Sitia	62	73	70	
Kato Zakros	98	106	116	36

NORTHERN COAST

Agios Nikolaos
Άγιος Νικόλαος

POP 12,000

Lasithi's capital, Agios Nikolaos has an enviable location on hilly terrain overlooking the sensuously curving Bay of Mirabello. There's a strong local character to Agios Nikolaos that imbues it with charismatic, low-key flair. A narrow channel separates the small harbour from the circular Voulismeni Lake, whose shore is lined with cafes and restaurants.

In the daytime the city beaches, while not particularly large or pretty, lend themselves to a few hours of relaxing and taking a dip in the sea. There's also some decent shopping in the pedestrianised lane above the lake.

Agios Nikolaos truly comes into its own at night, when a lively ambience descends on the lake, harbour and beaches, and lounge-bars fill with stylish young Greeks and holidaymakers from the nearby resorts.

Sights

Abduction of Europa Statue STATUE

The myth of the Phoenician princess Europa being abducted by Zeus in the guise of a bull finds expression in a monumental statue at the end of a ho-hum car park near the port, off Akti Themistokleous.

Designed by the late film director – and local boy – Nikos Koundouros, it shows a buxom beauty perched atop the beast while cradling an orb in one hand and a dove in the other.

Minotaur Mural PUBLIC ART

(cnr Akti Koundourou & Perikleous) Walking along the waterfront on Akti Koundourou, keep an eye out for a superb perspective mural depicting the Minotaur on a zigzagging staircase (next to Manolis bike hire). It's a 2018 work by Athens-born artist Manolis Anastasakos, whose fascination with mythology often finds expression in his work.

Folk Museum MUSEUM

(28410 25093; Konstantinou Paleologou 1; €3; 2-6.30pm Tue-Sun) This modest museum near the lake houses a well-curated collection of traditional handicrafts (especially textiles, costumes and embroidery), alongside photographs, rugs, books, manuscripts and other bits and bobs from the past.

Agia Triada Church CHURCH

(cnr Sofokli Venizelou & Kiprou; Mass) Right in the town centre, Agios Nikolaos' main church is a three-aisled Byzantine construction dedicated to the Holy Trinity. The mosaic above the main portal was added in 2001.

Beaches

Almyros Beach BEACH

The largest and best of the in-town beaches, sandy Almyros is about 2.5km south of the city centre, right where the eponymous river flows into the sea. With fine sand and

LASITHI IN...

Two Days

Start your Lasithi exploration in Agios Nikolaos with a short drive south to the delightful village of Kritsa (p234). Just before getting there, build in a stop at the Church of Panagia Kera (p234) with its feast of 13th-century frescoes. Have lunch in Kritsa, perhaps followed by some shopping, before travelling back 2000 years at the nearby Hellenistic-Dorian site of Ancient Lato (p236). Wrap up the day with a walk and dinner in Agios Nikolaos.

On day two, head up the coast to lovely Elounda and hop on a boat to the compelling island of Spinalonga (p233), a one-time leper colony. Finish the day at Elounda's Ergospasio restaurant (p229) for Cretan cuisine right by the sea.

Three Days

Head out early for the drive to Moni Toplou (p244), one of Crete's outstanding monasteries. Refresh yourself with a swim against the backdrop of swaying palm trees at Vaï beach (p244) before pointing the compass south for the winding drive through muscular mountains to Zakros. Embark on a trek through the stunning Zakros Gorge (p246), emerging at a Minoan palace (p246) and the delightful beachfront tavernas of Kato Zakros. Have an early dinner here before getting a taxi uphill to your car in Zakros and the drive back to your base.

Lasithi Highlights

❶ **Kritsa** (p234) Exploring Byzantine frescoes, a rugged canyon and an ancient city-state in this charming village.

❷ **Kato Zakros** (p246) Trekking through a dry riverbed flanked by cliffs where the Minoans buried their dead.

❸ **Vaï** (p244) Settling in for a chill session among the palms on one of Crete's most famous beaches.

❹ **Spinalonga Island** (p233) Connecting with the ghosts of the past on a tour of a former leper colony.

❺ **Dikteon Cave** (p238) Braving the damp darkness of

this otherworldly cave where Zeus was born.

6 Chrissi Island (p252)
Playing Robinson Crusoe on an uninhabited island with beaches straight out of paradise.

7 Moni Toplou (p244)
Pondering the chequered past of this fortified monastery that's a beacon of Greek resistance and bravery.

8 Xerokambos (p249)
Escaping to Crete's lonesome southeastern corner for sublime beaches.

Agios Nikolaos

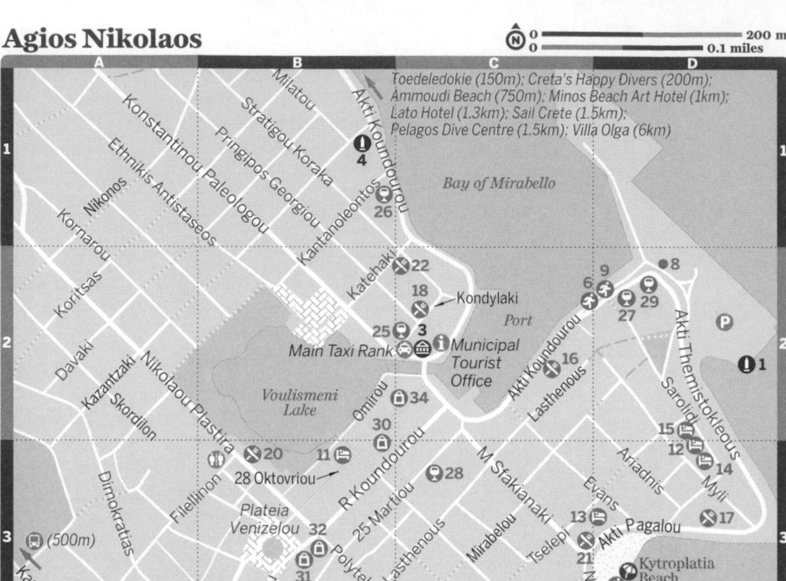

Agios Nikolaos

Sights
1 Abduction of Europa Statue D2
2 Agia Triada Church B3
3 Folk Museum C2
4 Minotaur Mural B1

Activities, Courses & Tours
5 Ammos Beach A4
6 Creta Semi-Submarine C2
7 Kytroplatia Beach D3
8 Little Train Tours D2
9 Nostos Cruises D2

Sleeping
10 Doxa Hotel A4
11 Du Lac Hotel B3
12 Hotel Creta D3
13 Hotel Delta D3
14 Pension Mylos D3
15 Pergola Hotel D2

Eating
16 Ble Katsarolakia C2
17 Chrisofyllis D3
18 Creta Embassy C2
19 Faros C3
20 Migomis Restaurant B3
21 Palazzo Cafe Bar C3
22 Pelagos C2
23 Portes A4
24 Sarris B4

Drinking & Nightlife
25 Alexandros Roof Garden C2
26 Arodo Cafe B1
27 Bajamar D2
28 Ellinadiko C3
29 Yanni's Rock Bar D2

Shopping
30 Ambrosia & Nectar B3
31 Aroma Coffee Shop B3
32 Jane's Fish Market B3
33 Kerazoza B3
34 Marieli C2

tranquil waters, it's popular with families, although active types can choose from the gamut of water sports. Umbrella hire and cafeterias are also part of the infrastructure.

Ammoudi Beach BEACH
This small but busy ribbon of sand in the northern part of town is backed by plenty of amenities, including bars, restaurants and water-sports facilities.

Kytroplatia Beach BEACH
This compact but central course-sand and small-pebble beach is backed by local tavernas and is mostly good for a quick dip rather than extended sun-worshipping.

Ammos Beach BEACH
This central sandy beach with calm and shallow waters starts at the marina and extends south as far as the stadium. It's quite small, so expect plenty of company in summer.

Gargadoros Beach BEACH
Popular with locals, this pebbly strip just over 1km south of the city centre is lapped by incredibly clear water and overlooked by a congenial cafe-bar but otherwise has no infrastructure.

Activities

Sail Crete BOATING
(6937605600, 28410 24376; www.sailcrete.com; Minos Beach Art Hotel, Agios Nikolaos-Vrouchas Rd; half/full day incl snacks & drinks €900/1300) This sailing-charter outfit arranges private half- and full-day cruises to Spinalonga Island and beyond aboard the *General*, a handsome 14m catamaran, and the 12m *Jaquelina* yacht. Boats depart from the Pelagos Dive Centre at Minos Beach Art Hotel. Bring a swimsuit and towels for a cooling dip during the cruise.

Nostos Cruises BOATING
(28410 22819; www.nostoscruises.com; Rousou Koundourou 30; trips to Spinalonga with/without barbecue €25/16; 8am-9pm) Nostos Cruises runs 4½-hour boat trips to Spinalonga Island (p233), including a swim at Kolokytha Beach, from the harbour in Agios Nikolaos on large vessels with two bars and a restaurant. Another version of this trip includes a barbecue on the beach. Fishing trips are also possible.

Creta Semi-Submarine BOATING
(28410 24822, 6936051186; www.semi-submarine.gr; adult/child €16/10; 11am, 1pm & 3pm;) Go diving without getting wet on 90-minute trips in the yellow submarine called *Nautilus*. Kids especially get a kick out of counting the fish swimming by the submerged viewing cabin.

Creta's Happy Divers DIVING
(28410 82546; www.happydivers.gr; Akti Koundourou 23; boat dive €50) In business since 1989, Happy Divers has a wealth of experience and knows local sites inside out. Rates include all equipment. Also offers PADI certification courses from open water to dive master.

Pelagos Dive Centre DIVING
(28410 24376, 6937605600; http://divecrete.com; Minos Beach Art Hotel, Agios Nikolaos-Vrouchas Rd; dives incl equipment from €60, night dives €80; Apr-Nov) Just north of town, this well-established PADI centre offers dives at all levels as well as PADI courses and introductory dives for kids. It's part of the Minos Beach Art Hotel but has its own entrance in the northern section of the compound. Boat hire is also available.

Tours

Travel agencies offer bus tours to Crete's top attractions, and boats along the harbour advertise their excursions to Spinalonga Island and other destinations.

Little Train Tours TOURS
(28140 25420; www.littletraintours.gr; Akti Themistokleous 12; adult/child 35min ride €9/3, 4hr trip €20/14;) These tours aboard a cute little tourist train are handy for those short on time, families and the mobility impaired. Choose from a 35-minute spin around town, a 70-minute tour towards Elounda or a four-hour trip into the mountains and to Kritsa.

Festivals & Events

Lato Cultural Festival CULTURAL
(Jul & Aug) The Lato Cultural Festival features concerts by local and international musicians, folk dancing, theatre and art exhibitions. Ask at the tourist office for details.

Sleeping

Except during July and August, finding a room in Agios Nikolaos shouldn't be a problem. Value-priced guesthouses cluster above Kytroplatia Beach. For fancier or more characterful lodgings, you'll need to travel a few kilometres outside town.

DRIVING TOUR > LASITHI MOUNTAIN MEANDER

A network of winding roads links tiny villages on the southeastern flank of the Dikteon Mountains within a landscape of rocky pinnacles and escarpments clothed in dense woodland and scrub.

1 Kalamafka

The route from Agios Nikolaos takes you south on the E75 Sitia road. After about 10km, turn right, following signs to Kalo Horio, from where the road climbs steadily into the mountains. Follow signs for the picturesque village of **Kalamafka**, which is dotted with limestone pinnacles. The road conveniently skirts the most important of

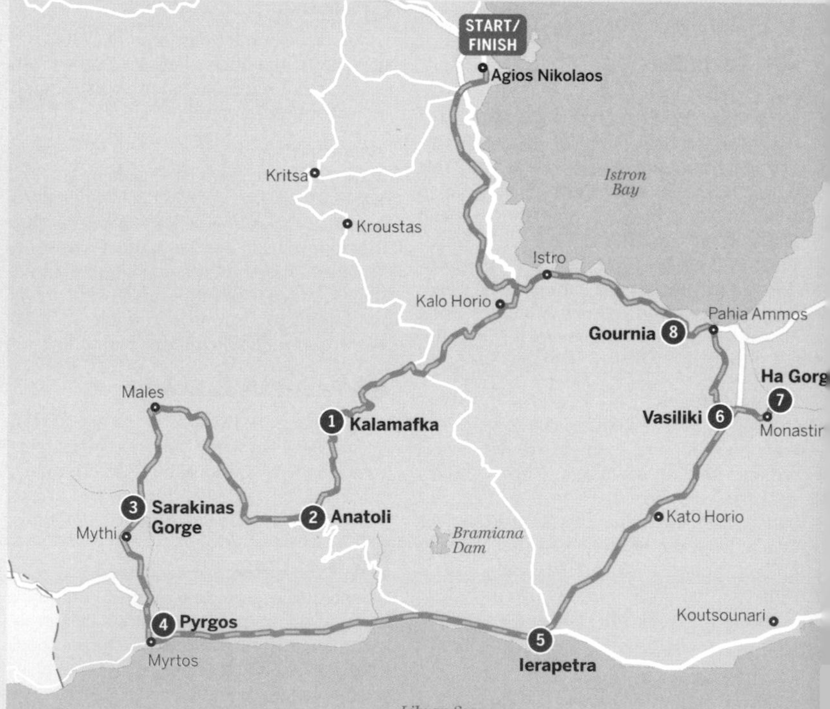

One Day 115km

Great For... Outdoors, History & Culture

Best Time to Go Summer, escape the heat in the hills

them, called Kastellos, which is topped by the cave chapel of Timios Stavros. The 220 steps will get your thighs burning, but it's well worth the effort for a look inside the tiny, whitewashed and icon-filled hole-in-the-mountain church and the sweeping views across the village and surrounding peaks.

2 Anatoli

Continue south from Kalamafka for a stroll around the Venetian-era village of **Anatoli**, whose descent into oblivion has been arrested by cashed-up and conservation-minded folks from Ierapetra and beyond. One by one, dilapidated shopfronts are being restored and ruins renovated into luxury vacation homes.

3 Sarakinas Gorge

Northwest from Anatoli you pass through wild and rocky countryside until the great valley of Sarakinas opens out. Follow the road south through the valley to Mythi, where signs direct you to the **Sarakinas Gorge** if you fancy stretching your legs even for a short stroll.

4 Pyrgos

Reach the coast at Myrtos, a lovely year-round holiday village with a strong communal spirit, excellent restaurants and a boho vibe. While here, cast your eye on what's left of **Pyrgos** (p254), a Minoan country house, just east of the village.

5 Ierapetra

Continue east to **Ierapetra** (p249) through less-than-scenic plastic-greenhouse country. Stop for a short exploration of Ierapetra's pleasant seafront and town centre and then point the compass north.

6 Vasiliki

With the escarpment of the Thrypti Mountains on your right, you'll see the turn-off to the small Prepalatial Minoan settlement of **Vasiliki** after about 12km. Park by the side of the road and follow the path through a carob and olive grove for about 100m to a fenced area. You can see quite a bit through the fence, or just walk along its perimeter and you might find a way in. The site is famous for the mottled pottery unearthed here – see it at Iraklio's Archaeological Museum.

7 Ha Gorge

Vasiliki's setting itself is stunning, with the gash of the **Ha Gorge** dramatically opening up across the valley. To see the mouth of the canyon up close, follow signs to Monastiraki, park on the road next to the trailhead and walk for about 1km. Monastiraki itself is a lovely village with three churches and atmospheric tavernas.

8 Gournia

Reach the E75 at Pahia Ammos, where a left turn leads back towards Agios Nikolaos past the splendid Minoan site of **Gournia** (p239).

Pension Mylos PENSION €
(☎28410 23783; http://pensionmylos.com; Sarolidi 24; s/d/tr €47/55/67;) At these prices, you know you're not getting the Ritz, but behind the faded facade lie surprisingly welcoming, though wee, rooms with bedside lamps, shiny en suites, seaward balconies and quality mattresses. The charming owner truly delivers on her tagline of 'home from home'. Fridge, TV and coffee-making service, too. Wi-fi in public areas only.

It's few minutes' walk up from the harbour. There's limited parking on the street.

Pergola Hotel HOTEL €
(☎28410 28152; http://pergola-hotel.agios-nikolaos-crete.hotel-crete.net; Sarolidi 20; s/d/apt €32/38/65; ⏲Apr-Oct;) Though not of recent vintage, this low-key guesthouse is an excellent base of operation whose owners get an A+ for charm. Lovingly spruced-up units range from singles to family apartments with kitchen; the nicest sport four-poster beds and balconies from where you can wave at passing ships. Optional breakfast is €5.

Doxa Hotel HOTEL €
(☎28410 24214; http://doxa-hotel.agios-nikolaos-crete.hotel-crete.net; Idomeneos 7; s/d/tr incl breakfast €50/60/73; ⏲May-Oct;) This 24-room old-school hotel within a stone's throw of Ammos Beach (p221) is well cared for, albeit a bit long in the tooth. Rooms are twee and come with chocolate-brown quilts and basic bathrooms. Most rooms have a balcony. Rates include a small breakfast.

Hotel Delta APARTMENT €
(☎28410 28893; www.agiosnikolaos-hotels.gr; Tselepi 22; r €50; ⏲year-round;) Budget-conscious space-cravers with cooking ambitions should thrive in these eight bright, basic but modern balconied units, four of which face Kytroplatia Beach (p221).

★Villa Olga APARTMENT €€
(☎28410 25913, 6948382121; www.villa-olga.gr; Anapafseos 18, Ellinika; studios €50-75, villas €55-155; ⏲Apr–mid-Nov; P) These seven charismatic self-catering studios and villas (sleeping up to six) with private patios enjoy serene views of the Bay of Mirabello and cling to terraced gardens bedecked with jasmine and gardenia. Scattered throughout the grounds are stone urns, terracotta pots and curios of yesteryear collected by owner Michalis. There's a fabulous pool. It's 6km north of central Agios Nikolaos.

Hotel Creta APARTMENT €€
(☎28410 28893; www.agiosnikolaos-hotels.gr; Sarolidi 22; apt €70-90; ⏲late Apr-Sep;) These 23 breezy and good-value self-catering studios and apartments sleeping two to four are in a quiet location, yet just a few minutes' walk from the harbour. All have balconies, but only units on the upper floors face the sparkling bay. There's a lift, as well as limited parking in the surrounding streets. Optional breakfast is €8.

Lato Hotel HOTEL €€
(☎28410 24581; www.lato-hotel.com.gr; Agios Nikolaos-Vrouchas Rd; r incl breakfast €75-140; ⏲May-Sep; P) On the busy road to Elounda, about 1.5km north of the city centre, this hotel is popular for its cleanliness, hot and homemade buffet breakfast, good-size pool and personable staff. Rooms are cosy, with fridge and spotless en suite. The upper ones have a sea view, but those at the back are quieter. The nearest beach is about 300m away.

The same management runs the charming Karavostassi Apartments (p238) on an isolated cove about 8km east from the Lato.

Du Lac Hotel HOTEL €€
(☎28410 22711; www.dulachotel.gr; 28 Oktovriou 17; d €50-70;) Smack dab in the town centre, this city hotel has fine views over Voulismeni Lake from generic but comfortable rooms decked out in shades from vanilla to chocolate. It's well worth the extra money for a more generously proportioned studio with kitchenette and lake-facing balcony.

The downstairs cafe serves breakfast, snacks and drinks all day and gets quite buzzy.

Minos Beach Art Hotel RESORT €€€
(☎28410 22345; www.minosbeach.com; Agios Nikolaos-Vrouchas Rd; r incl breakfast from €500; ⏲Apr-Oct; P) Privacy, luxury and tranquillity are taken very seriously in this sprawling resort in a superb waterfront location just north of town. Gardens dotted with conversation-sparking art lead to white-cube bungalows and villas kitted out in comfy but minimalist style. Some have private pools; the most coveted front the sea. Four restaurants, three bars, a gym and a spa invite lingering.

Eating

Agios Nikolaos has many excellent restaurants, even though the tourist-geared lakeside and waterfront tavernas often pair fine views with mediocre food. Enjoy the vibe here over a drink or snack and save your appetite for one of the quieter, more authentic places tucked away in the side streets.

Palazzo Cafe Bar CAFE €
(☎28410 27451; www.facebook.com/palazzocafebar; Akti Pagalou 8, Kytroplatia Beach; snacks €4-7; ⏲8am-late; ❄📶) Salads, toasties, ice creams, sandwiches, juices, cocktails – the menu reads like those of your average day-to-night cafe-bar, but in this upscale charmer facing Kytroplatia Beach (p221), drinks and snacks are delivered quickly and with a side of smiles. The interior is minimalist chic, with faux-marble walls and wood-topped tables.

Creta Embassy GREEK €
(☎28410 83153; www.cretaembassy.com; Kondylaki; mains €7-10; ⏲noon-late; ❄) Eclectic curios, wooden furniture and a fairy-tale garden make this traditional restaurant a few steps from the lake as welcoming as a hug from an old friend. Lamb *kleftiko* (slow oven-baked), veal with lemon, casseroles, and calamari with mouthwatering olives are among the menu stars.

Sarris CRETAN €
(☎28410 28059; Kyprou 15; mains €6-10; ⏲9am-3pm & 6pm-midnight Apr-Oct) This tiny, been-here-forever taverna in a quiet residential area has a dozen or so cheerfully painted tables across the street beneath a shady pergola and serves up honest-to-goodness Cretan home cooking in belt-loosening portions. Order zucchini fritters, lemony lamb with eggplant and a carafe of wine, and chill.

★Pelagos SEAFOOD €€
(☎28410 25737; Stratigou Koraka 11; mains €9-25; ⏲noon-midnight Apr-Oct; 📶) Pelagos is not for the indecisive. First you must choose whether to sit in the elegantly rustic historic house or in the romantic garden with colourful furniture and wall fountain. Tough one – but perhaps not as tough as deciding whether to feast on fresh fish, grilled meats, inventive salads or homemade pastas. If in doubt, go for the seafood pasta.

Portes CRETAN €€
(☎28410 28489; Anapafseos 2; mezedhes €2.50-7.50; ⏲12.30pm-1am; ❄) Conversation flows as freely as the excellent house wine at this garage-sized taverna, where wooden doors, all evocatively weathered and cheerfully painted, form part of the charming backdrop to home-cooked mezedhes (appetisers or small plates). Menu stars include a soulful rabbit *stifadho* (stew cooked with onions in a tomato puree) with plums and figs, and chicken with peppers and feta.

Faros GREEK €€
(☎28410 83168; Akti Pagalou; mains €6-20; ⏲noon-midnight; 📶) One of several tavernas fringing tiny Kytroplatia Beach, family-run Faros (which means lighthouse) sends signals to empty stomachs with aromas wafting from the brazier out the front. Sit at linen-draped tables under a blue-and-white awning next to the sand or soak up the old-school atmosphere inside. Meals are usually capped with free baklava and raki.

Ble Katsarolakia GREEK €€
(☎28410 21955; www.blekatsarolakia.gr; Akti Koundourou 8; mains €7-16; ⏲noon-1am; ❄📶🖉) Enjoying great views of the harbour, this effervescent restaurant, with its modern decor of exposed stone, turquoise walls and white-wood floors, offers a contemporary take on Greek cuisine, serving up tzatziki, halloumi, souvlaki, octopus and much more. It's packed with young Greeks and deservedly so. Take the lift to the top floor.

Chrisofyllis CRETAN €€
(☎28410 22705; Akti Pagalou; mezedhes €4-8, mains €7.50-13; ⏲12.30pm-12.30am; 📶) This colourful haunt has fed its feistily flavoured mezedhes menu to friends, couples and families since 2002. Rather than resting on its laurels, its kitchen creates contemporary spins on classic mezedhes, salads and mains without losing touch with tradition.

Migomis Restaurant MEDITERRANEAN €€€
(☎28410 24353; www.migomis.gr; Nikolaou Plastira 20; mains €3-38; ⏲noon-midnight Apr-Oct; ❄📶) Commanding Olympian views of Voulismeni Lake, this cliffside eyrie in a historic building exudes romance, with exposed stone walls, linen tablecloths and the soothing sounds of live piano on summer evenings. The kitchen wizards get creative with Greek and Med classics that appeal to both lunchtime collars and dinnertime heels. For the same views with a more casual vibe, head to the adjacent Migomis Cafe (open 8am to 2am).

Drinking & Nightlife

The buzziest party strip is along car-free Akti Koundourou east of the harbour, whose see-and-be-seen lounge bars are busy from midmorning until the wee hours. Akti

Koundourou continues north of the harbour, where a few grittier watering holes lure more low-key punters.

Toedeledokie BAR

(☎28410 25537; www.toedeledokiecafe-bar.com; Akti Koundourou 19; ⏲9am-late; 📶) Dutch for 'cheerio', Toedeledokie is the brainchild of Dutch artist Lucia, who supplies killer coffee, creamy milkshakes and creative toasties all day long below cheerful umbrellas on the waterfront terrace. At night, make new friends over cold beers and finely crafted cocktails and see if you can coax Lucia into divulging tips on the area's 'secret' destinations.

Votsalo Cafe-Bar CAFE

(☎28410 28048; Anapafseos 131; ⏲8am-late; 📶) Rub shoulders with gregarious locals at this contemporary cafe-bar sprawling over several tiers above pebbly Gargadoros Beach (p221), about 1km south of the town centre. It's a feel-good spot no matter where the hands of the clock are – breakfast to nightcap – with instaworthy sea and mountain views.

Bajamar BAR

(☎6973366035; Sarolidi 1; ⏲9am-2am or later) The most stylish among the harbour-front bars, Bajamar is a mellow daytime port of call for coffee, juices and snacks but is buzziest after 11pm, when the cocktails are flowing and a DJ showers shiny happy people with a high-energy mix of Latin, funk and house.

Arodo Cafe BAR

(☎28410 89895; www.facebook.com/pg/arodocoffeebeerwine; Akti Koundourou 6; ⏲11am-2am; 📶) This alt-flavoured lair buzzes with the conversation of earnest boho locals and offers a cocktail of cool tunes, a sea-facing terrace, and an eclectic selection of beer and wine. Located at the corner of Kantanoleontos. The entrance is up the steep stairs. Also serves breakfast and snacks.

Yanni's Rock Bar BAR

(Akti Koundourou 1; ⏲10pm-5am) The clientele is chatty, the rock music thunderous and the beer ice cold at this funky haunt that's rocked the waterfront since 1983, making it the town's oldest music bar. Its walls peppered with old Brando and Stallone photos, Yanni's oozes atmosphere from every nook and cranny and is a night owl's delight.

Alexandros Roof Garden BAR

(☎28410 24309; www.facebook.com/alexandrosroofgarden; Kondylaki 1; ⏲8pm-4am; 📶) Mark your turf amid hanging plants, shrubs and funky decor in this high-in-the-sky bar overlooking lake and harbour. Wallet-watchers invade before 10.30pm for €3 drinks that'll have you happy in no time.

Ellinadiko CLUB

(25 Martiou 8; ⏲noon-late) This casual haunt popular with locals and visitors prides itself on being the only place in town to play *only* Greek music. A low-key drinking den by day, it kicks into high gear after 1am at weekends.

Shopping

Ambrosia & Nectar ARTS & CRAFTS

(☎28410 21732; www.facebook.com/pg/ambrosiaandnectarcrete; 28 Oktovriou 24; ⏲9am-9pm Apr-Nov) Although unequivocally tourist geared, Pepi's little shop is crammed with Cretan-made quality souvenirs you're likely still to enjoy back home. Things to look out for include sharp-edged Cretan Knives, super-soft hammam towels by Aria Inspirations and perforated ceramic candle holders by Manolis Chalkiadakis.

Kerazoza ARTS & CRAFTS

(☎28410 22562; www.facebook.com/kerazoza; Metaxaki 4; ⏲9.30am-2pm & 5.30-9pm) This gem of a shop sells eye-catching necklaces, bracelets and rings, and masks and marionettes derived from ancient Greek theatre, along with some good-quality sculptures and ceramics. Everything is made by Greek artisans and artists.

Aroma Coffee Shop FOOD & DRINKS

(☎28410 21220; Plateia Venizelou 24; ⏲8am-2.30pm & 5.30-9.30pm) If you're a stickler for quality coffee, stock up on freshly roasted beans at this shoe-box-size shop that also sells biscuits, sweets and nuts as well as beautiful handmade copper *briki* (Greek coffee pots).

Jane's Fish Market FOOD

(☎28410 22859; Plateia Venizelou 2; ⏲7am-2.30pm Mon-Sat) In business since 1925, Jane's is a handy spot for self-caterers to pick up whatever the sea has yielded that night – from shrimp to octopus, snapper to sea bream.

Marieli CLOTHING

(28 Oktovriou 33; ⏲10am-11pm) This quirky little boutique sells stylish ladies' tees, dresses, shoes and beachwear.

Information

EMERGENCY

Tourist Police (☎28410 91409, emergency 171; Erythrou Stavrou 49)

INTERNET ACCESS

There's free wi-fi in the harbour area and its surrounds.

MEDICAL SERVICES

General Hospital (☎28413 43000; cnr Knosou & Paleologou; ⊙24hr) OK for broken bones and X-rays, but for anything more serious you'll need to head to Iraklio.

MONEY

There are numerous bank branches with ATMs in the commercial centre south of the lake and harbour.

Alpha Bank ATM (28 Oktovriou)

Eurobank ATM (Akti Koundourou)

National Bank of Greece (Nikolaou Plastira 2)

POST

Post Office (Karamanli Konstantinou 22; ⊙7.30am-2.45pm Mon-Fri)

TOURIST INFORMATION

Municipal Tourist Office (☎28410 22357; www.agiosnikolaoscrete.com; Akti Koundourou 21; ⊙9am-5pm Mon-Sat Apr-Nov, extended hours Jul & Aug;) One of the few remaining tourist offices on Crete, this small outfit has helpful staff, a city map, free bike hire and a few brochures.

TRAVEL AGENCIES

Several travel agencies have offices on Akti Koundourou, including **Byron Travel** (☎28410 24452; www.byrontravel.com; Akti Koundourou 4; ⊙8am-9pm). Many also rent cars.

Getting There & Away

BUS

The main **bus station** (☎28410 22234; Epimenidou 59) is about 1.5km north of the city centre. Buses serve Elounda, Kritsa, Iraklio and other destinations several times daily. Some buses also make stops around town, including on Akti Koundourou opposite the tourist office.

Check www.ktelherlas.gr for the current schedule or to book tickets.

CAR

Car-hire agencies, including **Club Cars** (☎28410 25868; www.clubcars.net; Agios Nikolaos-Vrouchas Rd; per day/week from €50/220; ⊙8am-9pm), cluster along Akti Koundorou north of the harbour.

TAXI

The most central **taxi rank** (Paleologou) is behind the tourist office down by the lake. Typical fares are €14 for Elounda, €21 for Plaka, €14 for Kritsa and €20 for Ancient Lato. There are additional ranks on Plateia Venizelou and at the main bus station.

Getting Around

Agios Nikolaos is best explored on foot. Free bicycles can be hired in the marina and at the tourist office. The main taxi rank is near Voulismeni Lake.

Elounda Ελούντα

POP 2200

Although surrounded by some of Crete's most luxurious resorts, Elounda retains a charming down-to-earth feel. Salty fishing craft bob in its little harbour, where you can board a boat to Spinalonga, a former leper colony and the area's biggest tourist attraction. Attractive shops, bars and tavernas wrap around the harbour and continue north along the sandy municipal beach and south along a paved waterfront promenade. Offshore lies the rugged Spinalonga Peninsula, linked to the mainland by a narrow causeway and home to ancient ruins, beaches and hiking trails.

Activities

Amazing Sailing in Crete BOATING
(☎6944586475; www.amazingsailingincrete.com; 3hr sunset cruise/4hr half-day cruise/full-day cruise €650/750/1100) Charter your private sailboat

BUSES FROM AGIOS NIKOLAOS

DESTINATION	FARE (€)	DURATION	FREQUENCY
Elounda	1.90	20min	up to 14 daily
Ierapetra	4.10	45min-1hr	up to 9 daily
Iraklio	7.70	1½hr	up to 22 daily
Kritsa	1.80	30min	up to 6 daily
Sitia	8.30	1½-2hr	up to 6 daily

(piloted by friendly Captain Yiannis) to explore isolated coves inaccessible by road, swim at hidden beaches and enjoy lunch in a traditional fishing village. Rates include drinks and fruit and swimming. Directions to the boat will be provided upon booking.

Blue Dolphin Diving Centre DIVING
(☎6955897711, 28410 41802; www.dive-bluedolphin.com; Ellinika; dive incl equipment €55, open-water course €390) The crystalline sea around Elounda offers excellent diving, with around 20 sites ready to be explored. Make finny friends on expeditions run by this professional and experienced PADI centre based at the Hotel Aquila Elounda Village in Ellinika, about 3.5km south of Elounda.

Sleeping

Luxury hotels and resorts are off the coastal road linking Elounda and Agios Nikolaos, while family-run pensions and apartment buildings can be found in the town and surrounding hills.

Corali Studios & Portobello Apartments APARTMENT €
(☎28410 41712; www.coralistudios.com; Akti Poseidonos; apt €45-75; P❄📶🏊) Immaculately kept Corali and Portobello sit side by side amid flower-festooned gardens and overlooking the town beach. The 35 stucco-walled studios and apartments come with balcony, kitchenette and wooden furniture painted cheerful shades of blue. All except the economy units have a sea view. Catch some rays by the good-size pool with snack bar.

Dolphins Apartments APARTMENT €
(☎28410 41641; http://dolphins.elounda-crete.hotel-crete.net; Papandreou 51; apt €50; P❄📶) These six one-bedroom apartments with pleasingly rustic furniture and tile floors pack a lot of features into a compact frame, including a kitchenette with microwave and a furnished balcony (with neat dolphin motif) overlooking the sea. It's a five-minute stroll into town along the waterfront promenade.

Kalypso Hotel HOTEL €
(☎28410 41197; www.kalypsoelounda.gr; Akti Vritomartidos 3; s/d €30/60; ❄📶) The 16 bright, spotless rooms above the Elo cafe are retro without even trying but will put you smack in the centre with easy access to beach, dining and the Spinalonga ferry. Most won't fit a ton of luggage but are comfy enough for a short stay. All have balconies, some facing the harbour, others the mountain or the church dome.

Marin APARTMENT €
(☎6972314067; Akti Poseidonos 49; r €40-55; P❄📶) Set back from the road paralleling the town beach en route to Plaka, these 18 whitewashed rooms and apartments are in no danger of appearing in the pages of *Architectural Digest*, but assets such as air-con, kitchenettes and patios make Marin a great value-for-money option in central Elounda.

Hotel Aristea HOTEL €
(☎28410 41300; www.aristeahotel.gr; Papandreou 3; s/d incl breakfast €35/45; ❄📶) Elounda's oldest hotel is getting a bit long in the tooth but still provides decent bang for your euro. Rooms come with a fridge, and the nicest have sea-facing balconies above a row of tavernas. Light sleepers should avoid units facing the busy main street.

★**Elounda Heights** HOTEL €€
(☎6932385337; www.eloundaheights.com; Emmanouil Pouli; apt €85-115; ⏲late Apr-Oct; P❄📶🏊) This hilltop hideaway run by a charming family is a class act all around. Swoon-worthy bay views unfold from your sunny studio or apartment with terrace, thoughtfully equipped kitchenette and crisp decor picking up the shades of the sea. A garden bursting with roses and oleander wraps around the units and the pool, where days start with a lavish breakfast.

Home-cooked dinners are available in the main house. No children permitted.

Elounda Island Villas APARTMENT €€
(☎28410 41274; www.eloundaisland.gr; Spinalonga Peninsula; 1-/2-bedroom apt €95/160; ⏲mid-May–mid-Oct; P❄📶) This serene hideaway is the only lodging option on the Spinalonga Peninsula, reached via a narrow causeway. Set amid sprawling gardens, the nine split-level apartments with well-equipped kitchens sleep two to five and feature traditional furnishings. Wind down the day with cocktails on your terrace overlooking Elounda and the mountains. There's an on-site cafe.

Eating

Elounda has a clutch of tourist-oriented but mostly good-quality tavernas flanking the main square by the little fishing harbour, and a few upscale restaurants in the side streets and at the southern end of the waterfront promenade. For trad fare with local ambience, it's also worth heading into the hills above the town.

Fresco Eatery MEDITERRANEAN €
(Eparchiaki Odos Agios Nikolaos-Vrouchas 30; gyros €5.50-8.50, pizza €9-12; 6am-late) This quick-feed stop on the main square has a lively al fresco area beside the clock tower and dishes up huge salads, pizza, *gyros* (meat slivers cooked on a vertical rotisserie), souvlaki and burgers.

★**Hope** CRETAN €€
(To Rakadiko Tou Kamari; 6972295150; Mavrikiano; mains €6-18; noon-11.30pm) Clinging to a steep hillside in the ancient hamlet of Mavrikiano above Elounda, Hope has been a local fixture since 1938. The terrace where fishermen once gathered nightly to suss out the next day's weather is now packed with people getting giddy on wine, raki, homemade mezedhes, succulent lamb chops and the stupendous bay view.

It's run by a charismatic couple, Dimitris and Amalia, with respect for the past *and* modern nutritional needs. If you're driving, the turnoff is about 600m north of Elounda's main square.

★**Okeanis** MEDITERRANEAN €€
(28410 44404; Akti Poseidonos 7; mains €8.50-14; 11.30am-4pm & 6-11pm Apr-Oct) At Okeanis, the decor, menu and service blend as perfectly as the rich oven-baked lamb with garlic and sweet wine that's a top menu pick, alongside chef Adonis' handmade stuffed ravioli and tortellini. It's all served in an elegant yet relaxed loft-style al fresco space with white furniture and leafy plants.

Despina Taverna SEAFOOD €€
(28410 41350; www.facebook.com/despinataverna; Akti Poseidonos, Mavrikiano; mains €8-21; 1-11.30pm May-Oct;) Book ahead for a table with front-row vistas of Mirabello bay to complement the fresh-off-the-boat snapper, lobster, sea bream or whatever else the fisherfolk have hauled in that day. The kitchen of this feel-good taverna is equally adept at adding clever twists to native dishes, perhaps infusing seafood pasta with lemongrass or having octopus cuddle up to black lentils.

Marilena GREEK €€
(28410 41322; Akti Poseidonos; mains €10-21; noon-11pm;) One of Elounda's oldest and most traditional tavernas, Marilena enchants with checked-cloth tables, decorative handicrafts and a lively atmosphere alongside convivial service and fine food. It has a stellar reputation for its mezedhes platter (€12.50), a smorgasbord of eight mouthwatering dishes that easily feeds two, but it also does a fall-off-the bone lamb *kleftiko*.

★**Ergospasio** GREEK €€€
(28410 42082; www.facebook.com/pg/ergospasio; Akti Olountos 5; mains €15-23; noon-midnight Apr-Oct) A design feast in a converted carob factory with rave-worthy food to match. Count the fish in the sea from tables lined up along – and above – the waterfront while savouring market-fresh and skilfully executed Greek faves. If you're here at dinner time, try lamb or chicken slow-roasted in the custom-designed *antikristo* spit grill. Also a great anytime spot for coffee or cocktails.

Drinking & Nightlife

Several cheerful bars and clubs line the harbour, some of which keep going until the wee hours in season and at weekends.

★**Beeraki** PUB
(28410 42785; Mavrikiano; 11am-midnight or later May-Oct) Well worth the uphill walk to the ancient village of Mavrikiano, this adorable drinking den does a roaring trade in bottled craft beers, quality local wines and expertly prepared cocktails. There's a small menu of elevated pub grub to keep your brain balanced so that you can enjoy the panoramic sea views just a little longer.

Alyggos Bar BAR
(28410 41365; Plateia Elountas; 9am-late) This day-to-night stalwart has been getting mobbed by tourists, expats and locals for nearly 30 years – and for good reason. The drinks are cold and strong, the vibe friendly and the prices reasonable. DJs heat up the action after 10pm at weekends. Also a good spot to watch football (soccer).

Babel Bar BAR
(28410 42336; Akti Vritomartidos; 9am-3am;) On the western side of the main square and overlooking the little harbour, this convivial bar is as busy as a beehive from morning till late at night. It's a good place to cheer on your team on the big screen or catch up on your social media over a coffee.

GVL/GETTY IMAGES ©

4

ANKARB/GETTY IMAGES ©

PETER MAERKY/SHUTTERSTOCK ©

ATYPEEK/GETTY IMAGES ©

1. Windmill, Lasithi Plateau (p236)
Surrounded by mountains, Lasithi Plateau is a windswept expanse of green fields interspersed with orchards.

2. Xerokambos (p249)
There's little to do here but relax on the beach, feast in the tavernas, and explore local caves and gorges.

3. Spinalonga Island (p233)
This one-time leper colony shot to fame due to the best-selling romantic novel *The Island*.

4. Gournia (p239)
The Late Minoan settlement of Gournia was last occupied around 1200 BC.

Shopping

Eklektos Bookshop BOOKS
(28415 01270; www.bookshopincrete.com; Papandreou 40; 10.30am-7pm Mon-Sat Apr-Oct) Friendly little Eklektos caters to summer reading needs in many languages, including English, German and French, and stocks covetable souvenirs and knick-knacks. The lovely English owner is often around to offer a wealth of tips and information about the town and area.

Information

There's free, albeit glacial, municipal wi-fi in the main square. Many cafes and tavernas also offer free access for their guests.

Olous Travel (28410 41324; www.olous-travel.gr; Plateia Elountas; 9am-11pm) Full-service agency handles air and boat tickets, finds accommodation, and organises car hire and excursions.

Getting There & Away

Up to 14 buses daily shuttle between Agios Nikolaos and Elounda (€1.90, 20 minutes). The **bus stop** (Plateia Elountas) is on the main square, where you can buy tickets at the kiosk next to Nikos Taverna.

The **taxi stand** (28410 41151; Plateia Elounda) is also on the square. The fare to Agios Nikolaos is €14 and to Plaka €8.

Cars, motorcycles and scooters can be hired at Olous Travel and **Elounda Travel** (28410 41800; www.eloundatravel.gr; Sfakianaki 3; car per day/week from €45/160; 8am-9pm), both with offices on, you guessed it, the main square, which also serves as a (fee-based) car park.

Local **ferries** (6974385854; www.eloundaboat.gr; Elounda harbour; return €12; 9am-5pm) travel to Spinalonga Island every half hour from Elounda's harbour.

Spinalonga Peninsula

The Spinalonga Peninsula is connected to Elounda by a narrow causeway, originally the isthmus of Poros. In order to distinguish it from the former leper colony on tiny Spinalonga Island just to the north, it is sometimes called Big Spinalonga. To get there, make a sharp turn off the Elounda main road at the Ergospasio restaurant (p229) and head downhill.

The ancient Greek settlement of **Olous** once stood on and around the isthmus, but what little is left today lies submerged on either side of the causeway. The area is popular with snorkellers, although, aside from some house foundations and the remnants of a harbour wall, there's not much to see.

To the right of the causeway you can still spot the shallow **salt pans** built by the Venetians in the 15th century and in use until 1972. Just beyond are three ruined **windmills** as well as the remains of an early Christian **basilica**, most notably bits and pieces of a mosaic portraying fish, birds and garlands. Find it after a short stroll to your right after the windmills.

A circular 7km **hiking route** follows the peninsula's ancient trails. Drivers can continue past the isthmus on a graded dirt road for about 1.5km to a parking area below the chapel of Agios Loukas. From here, it's about a half-kilometre walk down to the lovely **Kolokytha beach**, which does, however, get busy around 12.30pm when Spinalonga Island excursion boats drop their passengers here for swimming and barbecues. In the cove just north of Kolokytha beach you can spot the ruins of another early Christian basilica.

Plaka Πλάκα

POP 100

Wind-pounded Plaka, 5km north of Elounda, is a bijou village of attractive boutiques, a narrow pebble beach and a string of cosy tavernas hugging the waterfront. It's also the best jumping-off point for the famous former leper colony of Spinalonga Island.

Sights & Activities

Plaka Town Beach BEACH
You don't come to Plaka for the beach, but if you need your tan-and-swim fix, head towards the northern end of the village. There, next to a big car park and steps from cafes and tavernas, is the town's long, narrow and pebbly strand, whose distinctive asset is its priceless view of Spinalonga Island.

Boats to Spinalonga BOATING
(6977446229; https://plakaboat.gr; return €10) The local cooperative operates 19 boats to Spinalonga, with departures every 30 to 45 minutes. Boats leave from this spot at Plaka Marina as well as from another **location** 350m north. You can stay on the island for as long as you want and take any boat back to Plaka. The journey takes about 10 minutes.

DON'T MISS

CELEBRATED LEPER COLONY

Tiny **Spinalonga Island** (Νήσος Σπιναλόγκα; 28410 22462; adult/concession €8/4; 9am-6pm) became a leper colony in 1903 and catapulted into pop-cultural consciousness thanks to Victoria Hislop's 2005 bestselling novel *The Island* and the subsequent Greek TV series spin-off *To Nisi*. Boats departing from Elounda, Plaka and Agios Nikolaos drop visitors at Dante's Gate, the 20m-long tunnel through which patients arrived. From here, a 1km trail takes you past such 'sights' (mostly ruined) as a church, the disinfection room, the hospital and the cemetery.

Before it became a leper colony the island was a stronghold of the Venetians, who built a massive fortress in 1579 to protect the bays of Elounda and Mirabello. In 1715 the island fell under Ottoman control. Spinalonga's isolated location off the northern tip of the Spinalonga Peninsula made it a good leprosy quarantine zone. Also known as Hansen's Disease, the condition causes skin lesions, nerve damage and muscle weakness and has been around since ancient times. As many as 1000 Greeks were quarantined on Spinalonga, initially in squalid and miserable conditions. This changed in 1936 with the arrival of Epaminondas Remoundakis, a law student who contracted leprosy at the age of 21, and who fought passionately for better medical care and infrastructure on the island. A cure for leprosy was finally discovered in 1948 and the last person left Spinalonga in 1957.

Thanks to Hislop's tale about her own family's connection to the island, interest in Spinalonga has skyrocketed and you're unlikely to feel lonely during your visit.

Ferries operated by local boat cooperatives depart half-hourly from Elounda (€12) and Plaka (€8), giving you as much time on the island as you need. From Agios Nikolaos, Nostos Cruises (p221) runs one daily excursion boat.

Petros Watersports & Boat Rental WATER SPORTS
(6945891487; www.spinalonga-windsurf.com; Agia Paraskevi Beach, Elounda-Plaka Rd; 10am-7.30pm Apr-Oct) Feel the freedom of tooling around on the water in your own boat, which you can hire from €70 per hour (€360 for two hours on a speedboat), no licence needed. The affiliated water-sports centre offers sea kayaks (one/two hours €15/20), and waterskiing and wake-boarding (each €40), among other activities. Look for the Royal Marmim Bay Boutique & Art Hotel.

Sleeping & Eating

Overnight options are mostly limited to luxury villas and a superfancy resort just to the south. Stay in Elounda or Agios Nikolaos for better choice and value for money. Plaka has a surfeit of excellent, though fairly pricey, fish tavernas along the pedestrianised seaside promenade. Views of Spinalonga are free, though.

Stella Mare Studios APARTMENT €
(28410 41814; studios/apt €45/55;) Set back from the main road, about 300m from the pebbly town beach, Stella has charming hosts who run a tight ship and are full of good advice. Flowery gardens cradle the property, with its comfy, balconied apartments sleeping up to four. All are traditionally but tastefully furnished and accented by colourful art.

★ **Taverna Giorgos** SEAFOOD €€
(28410 41353; www.giorgos-plaka.gr; mains €8-20; 11am-midnight;) Favoured by the cast of hit TV series *To Nisi* (look for the fading photos inside), this wood-beamed hobbit hole on the seaside promenade has a welcoming terrace and additional seating below on a cliff with romantic views of Spinalonga. It's great for piscine treats, hauled in daily by its own team, and also scores high for its wine selection.

Captain Nikolas SEAFOOD €€
(28410 41838; mains €8-20; noon-midnight;) A welcoming family vibe pervades this attractive stone taverna on the waterfront that excels in its execution of dishes featuring fish and seafood, all caught by their own boats. The amazing views of the sea and Spinalonga Island are a nice bonus, especially from the tables on the rocky cliffs.

Ostria GREEK €€
(28410 41530; www.facebook.com/ostria.plaka; mains €9-23; noon-11pm;) Aptly named Ostria ('south wind') sits on the sea, buffeted

OFF THE BEATEN TRACK

MILATOS ΜΥΛΑΤΟΣ

Milatos is a low-key place just 13km east of Malia and the heavily touristed coastal strip further west. The village itself is 2km inland from Milatos Beach, which is hemmed in by a narrow, pebbly strand and a straggle of excellent fish tavernas with rooms.

Most people make the short detour from the E75 highway to visit the intriguing **Milatos Cave**, about 3km east of the village and well signposted. Park roadside, then follow a rough but flat 200m trail above a steep and picturesque gorge to the cave's main entrance. Bring a torch (flashlight) to explore its maze of chambers, including one containing a little chapel and an ossuary with bones of Cretans killed by the Turks in 1823. Some 2500 locals had taken refuge in the cave from the invaders but were discovered, besieged and eventually massacred. Admission is free.

Panorama (28410 81213; Paralia Milatos; mains €8-18; 9am-midnight Apr-Nov;) Both local and visiting fish fanciers flock to this charismatic taverna overlooking the petite harbour for dock-fresh piscine treats, although the big selection of mezedhes, grills and other Greek menu staples will also get you salivating.

Taverna Meltemi (28410 81286; Paralia Milatos; mains €6-12; 9am-midnight;) Right on the beach, this fish taverna is run by the lovely Anastasia and her fisherman husband. Come for great sunsets accompanied by well-prepared staples of Greek cuisine, although you can't go wrong ordering the catch of the day tickled to perfection on a charcoal grill.

by the breeze and blessed with unblemished views of Spinalonga. The menu yields few surprises, but consistent quality has vaulted this contempo-vibe spot to the top of many a local's and visitor's fave list. It's on the main street.

Drinking & Nightlife

Aside from the tavernas and a couple of cafe-bars, there's no nightlife to speak of in Plaka. Head to Elounda or, better yet, Agios Nikolaos for the full spectrum of after-dark fun.

Isla Bistrot & Cocktail Bar BAR
(6974335904; 9am-late;) On the main street at the beach end of town, Isla adds a dash of sophistication to Plaka with its lounge-style vibe and smart, grown-up menu of craft beers, good cocktails, fresh juices and whatever today's hipster heart desires. You can even smoke shisha here.

To Pefko CAFE
(28410 44032; 9am-midnight or later) In a lovely stone house in the pedestrian zone near the village entrance, just off the main street, this cosy cafe has sidewalk tables and is a good pit stop at any time of day.

Getting There & Away

Buses from Elounda shuttle back and forth up to six times daily (10 minutes). A taxi ride costs €8.

Kritsa Κριτσά

POP 2000

Clinging to the craggy foothills of the Dikti range, Kritsa is one of the oldest and prettiest mountain villages in eastern Crete. The upper village with its web of narrow, car-free lanes is especially atmospheric. Along the main strip, Kritsotopoulas, you'll find charming cafes, shops slinging local products and surprisingly sophisticated boutiques. Away from the village, rugged Kritsa Gorge, the romantic ruins of Ancient Lato and the church of Panagia Kera, with its stunning Byzantine frescoes, are all worth your attention.

Note that in season Kritsa is often clogged with tour buses and day trippers, so come early or late in the day to avoid the worst crowds.

Sights & Activities

★ **Church of Panagia Kera** CHURCH
(28410 51806; Eparchiotiki Odos Agios Nikolaos-Prinas; adult/concession €2/1; 8.30am-4pm Wed-Mon; P) This tiny triple-aisled church on the main road shelters Crete's best-preserved Byzantine frescoes. The oldest in the central nave (13th century) depict scenes surrounding the life of Christ, including the Ascension in the apse, the four Gospel scenes (Presentation, Baptism, Raising of Lazarus and Entry into Jerusalem) in the dome and a superb Last Supper. The south aisle is ded-

icated to St Anne, mother of Mary, with depictions including her marriage and Mary's birth. The north aisle focuses on St Anthony.

The church is about 1km south of Krista – look for the parking area opposite the Paradise restaurant. After your visit, you can sit in the garden cafe and ponder it all.

★Kritsa Gorge HIKING

Kritsa Gorge, signposted off the road to Ancient Lato, is one of eastern Crete's most enchanting canyons. Flanked by steep cliffs, it follows a riverbed dotted with oak and olive trees and resplendent with spring wildflowers. Sturdy shoes and reasonable fitness are essential, since the trail is stony and requires occasional bouldering and the handling of metal rails and a rope.

There are two routes. The shorter one (about 5km) follows the canyon for about 2km before heading uphill; turn right and follow the trail paralleling the gorge below back to the parking area. The longer one (about 11km) continues to the village of Tapes. Along the way you will encounter fences put there by shepherds to keep the goat herd together. Be sure to close their gates again after passing through.

The hike can be done year-round except after heavy rain. Check in Kritsa before setting out.

Sleeping

Most people visit Kritsa on a day trip, but there's a handful of small hotels and apartments catering to those who wish to spend the night.

Rooms Argyro PENSION €

(☎28410 51174; www.argyrorooms.com; d €38-45; ❄📶) Run by a sweet host, this delightful pension has compact, modern rooms with white furniture and tiled floors, and touches of colour on walls, curtains and bedspreads. Many rooms have balconies, though the triple has the best mountain view.

It's on the left-hand side as you enter the village from Agios Nikolaos.

Eating & Drinking

Taverna Platanos CRETAN €

(☎28410 51230; Kritsotopoulas; mains €6.50-9.50; ⏰10am-9pm) A taverna-*kafeneio* (coffeehouse) halfway along Kritzotopoula, Platanos has a pleasant setting under a giant 200-year-old plane tree and vine canopy. The tasty menu revolves around grills, *mousakas* and *stifadho*.

Cafe Bar Massaros CAFE €

(☎28410 51146; Olof Palme; snacks €3-6.50; ⏰7am-1am or later; 📶) Serving toasties, crêpes, salads and pizza mainly to tourists in the daytime, this simple, congenial cafe-bar turns into a locals' spot for chat and shots after the buses have left town.

Saridakis Kafeneio CAFE

(Kritsotopoulas; juice €3; ⏰8am-midnight) An excellent little cafe, this place makes for a cool stop in the shade to grab some homemade honey and yoghurt or a fresh orange juice.

KRITSOTOPOULA: THE CRETAN HEROINE

The rousing tale of the beautiful and heroic Cretan girl Kritsotopoula (child of Kritsa) tells the story of Rhodanthe (her real name), who lived in Kritsa in the early years of the 19th century during the Ottoman occupation of Crete. She was said to have a beautiful singing voice and it was her singing that one day caught the attention of a drunken Turkish officer, who attempted to push his way into her house. Rhodanthe's mother resisted his attempts and was stabbed to death. The soldier then abducted Rhodanthe, but later that night, while he slept, Rhodanthe slit his throat, cut off her long hair and took off for the mountains disguised as a man to join the Cretan freedom fighters.

In 1823 Rhodanthe distinguished herself in a fierce battle against the Turks near Ancient Lato. She was shot in the chest and died. Initial efforts to staunch the wounds revealed her sex and thereafter she became the revered Kritsotopoula, a classic symbol of Cretan resistance.

Kritsa's main village road is named in Kritsotopoula's honour, and in summer a lovingly cared-for small **museum** (at the far end of the main road) commemorates her deeds. Also look for the large **stone relief** depicting the dying heroine in the arms of her father, a local priest. Created by local sculptor Nigel Ratcliffe-Springall, it's in an enclosure on the way to Lato.

Shopping

Nostimon GIFTS & SOUVENIRS

(☎28410 52092; www.physisofcrete.gr; Kritsotopoulas; ⏰9am-7pm) This is the older of two factory outlets for Physis of Crete, a local brand and family business producing not only award-winning olive oil but also its own honey, herbs, pastes, dips, cosmetics and other traditional Cretan products.

Latia Hora SPICES

(☎28410 51805; Ethnikis Antistaseos 5; ⏰9am-9pm Mon-Sat) If you're into organic spices, herbs, teas, oils, dried fruit and other pantry stockers, you'll feel like a kid in a candy shop in this doll's-house-size emporium. It's fun just to browse for gifts, but if you need help, the charming owner will happily dispense advice and cooking tips in fluent English.

Anna's Heart FASHION & ACCESSORIES

(☎6945245528; Kritsotopoulas; ⏰10am-8pm) Only clothing, jewellery, bags, hats and other accessories crafted by Greek designers will make it into Anna's carefully edited and sophisticated boutique, which wouldn't be out of place in Athens. Look for cork bags, wooden sunglasses or fashion by Ioanna Kourbela.

Getting There & Away

Up to four buses on weekdays and three at weekends travel from Agios Nikolaos to Kritsa (€1.80). The **bus stop** (Olouf Palme) is in the centre of town. A taxi costs €14.

Around Kritsa

★Ancient Lato ARCHAEOLOGICAL SITE

(Λατώ; ☎28410 22462; http://odysseus.culture.gr; adult/concession €2/1; ⏰8.30am-4pm Wed-Mon) The fortified hilltop city state of Lato is one of Crete's best-preserved non-Minoan ancient sites and worth the trip for the rural serenity and stunning views down to the Bay of Mirabello alone. Founded by the Dorians in the 7th century BC, Lato reached its heyday in the 3rd century BC but was gradually abandoned. By the 2nd century AD its administrative centre had moved to its port in present-day Agios Nikolaos.

About 100m past the ticket gate, you enter the site via the **city gate**, from where a long, stepped street leads up to the **agora** (marketplace) past a wall with two towers, residences, and buildings that housed shops and workshops. At the top of the steps, as you approach the *agora*, you'll first come upon vestiges of a **stoa** (colonnaded portico). Immediately behind it is a rectangular temple where numerous 6th-century-BC figurines were unearthed. The deep hole to the left of the temple was Lato's public **cistern**. Behind it, a monumental staircase leads up to the **prytaneion** (administrative centre). At its centre, a hearth that burnt 24/7 was surrounded by stepped benches where the city leaders held their meetings.

South of the *agora*, climb up the slope to a terrace with another **sanctuary** fronted by a three-stepped **altar**. Views of the entire site are fabulous from here. Down below to your right (east) you can spot a **theatral area** that could seat about 350 spectators on stone benches cut into the rock and on an **exedra** (open portico with seats).

Lato's name derives from the goddess Leto. Legend has it that Leto's union with Zeus produced Artemis and Apollo.

There are no buses to Lato. The nearest stop is in Kritsa, from where it's a 3km walk north. The site is off the Kritsa–Lakonion road.

LASITHI PLATEAU

ΟΡΟΠΕΔΙΟ ΛΑΣΙΘΙΟΥ

The tranquil Lasithi Plateau, 900m above sea level (bring a sweater even in summer), is a windswept expanse of green fields interspersed with almond trees and orchards. Offering a sense of secluded rural Crete, it's really more a plain than a plateau, sitting as it does in a huge depression amid the rock-studded mountains of the Dikti range. It's sparsely inhabited, with just a few villages dotted along the periphery. Most people visit on a day trip to Psyhro, the gateway to the Dikteon Cave, where – so the myth goes – Zeus was born and hidden as an infant to protect him from his voracious father.

Lasithi must have been a stunning sight in the 17th century, when it was dotted with some 20,000 windmills with white-canvas sails, put up by the Venetians for irrigation purposes. The skeletal few that remain are an iconic (and much-photographed) sight.

The plateau is popular biking territory, utilising the intersecting tracks across the central plain.

OFF THE BEATEN TRACK

KATHARO PLATEAU & KROUSTAS

From Kritsa it's a scenic 16km climb to the spectacular **Katharo Plateau**, which is cultivated by people from Kritsa, some of whom have summer homes here. Sitting at an altitude of 1200m, this beautiful wildflower plateau is often under deep snow in winter, and home to only 500 inhabitants. There are a couple of seasonal tavernas here.

Just 4km south of Kritsa is the village of **Kroustas**, where locals go for very traditional local cuisine. The Cretan food on offer at popular **O Kroustas** (28410 51362; Kroustas; mains €5-10; noon-midnight;) includes a superb *lazania* (twisted handmade pasta, also called *stroufikta*) cooked in stock with *anthotiro* (a dry, white cheese) and rusks made in the wood oven.

Two buses daily except Sunday make the slog up from Kritsa to Kroustas. Walking takes about an hour.

Tzermiado Τζερμιάδο

At the northern edge of the plateau, Tzermiado is the largest of Lasithi's 20 villages and has managed to preserve some of its bucolic charm. It's also the gateway to the ho-hum Kronios Cave. There's only one main road running through town, plus an ATM and a post office on the main square.

Approaching Tzermiado from the south, look for the sign pointing to the **Kronios Cave** (Trapeza Cave) FREE, reached via a path leading to a series of stairs. Excavations have yielded objects going back to Neolithic times, when the cave likely served as a shelter. The Minoans used it as a burial site. Bring a torch and watch your footing when exploring the two chambers with their stalagmites and stalactites, many of which have been tampered with.

Sleeping & Eating

Argoulias APARTMENT €€
(6972234275, 28440 22754; www.argoulias.gr; apt €50-80;) Built into the hillside above the main village and constructed of exposed local stone, these 11 self-catering apartments sleep up to five and have sweeping views across the Lasithi Plateau to the mountains. Traditional decor and furnishings exude comfort, and a fireplace keeps things cosy in winter. Optional breakfast is €6 per person.

The owners also run an excellent restaurant across the road. Ask about use of bicycles. Look for signs to Argoulias at the entrance to Tzermiado coming from the east.

Taverna Kourites GREEK €
(28440 22054; mains €6.50-11; 9am-11pm Apr-Oct) This spacious taverna on the outskirts of Tzermiado does a brisk lunchtime trade with coaches full of day trippers. At other times it's a peaceful spot where menu options include lamb and suckling pig roasted in a wood-fired oven.

The same family rents simple **rooms** above the taverna and in a nearby hotel for €40 per double, including breakfast.

Agios Georgios Άγιος Γεώργιος

Agios Georgios is a tiny village at the south-eastern edge of the Lasithi Plateau and one of the more pleasant places to visit, out of a fairly colourless bunch. If you have your own bicycle, you can base yourself here and explore the plateau at leisure.

The endearing **Cretan Folk Museum** (6948501457; www.elsolas.gr; adult/concession €3/2; 10.30am-5pm Mon-Sat May–mid-Oct) opens a window on Crete's rural past, with exhibits spread over a 19th-century stone farmhouse and a slightly younger neoclassical building. Aside from the expected array of farming tools, wooden furniture, textiles, faded black-and-white photographs and WWII relics, also note the neat wine press cleverly upcycled into a bed. A nearby building has great valley views and an exhibit commemorating political legend Eleftherios Venizelos.

Sleeping & Eating

Hotel Maria HOTEL €
(28440 31774; http://mariahotelagiosgeorgios.blogspot.de; d incl breakfast €40; May-Oct;) These 15 pleasantly quirky rooms on the northern side of the village are in a building fronted by a leafy garden. The traditional mountain beds are rather narrow and are on stone bases. Local furnishings and

DON'T MISS

EASTERN CRETE'S BEST ANCIENT SITES

- Zakros Palace (p246)
- Ancient Lato (p236)
- Gournia (p239)

woven wall hangings add to the authentic atmosphere.

★**Taverna Rea** CRETAN €
(☎28440 31209; mains €6-8; ⏰10am-9pm) This cheerful little restaurant on the village's main street has stone walls decorated with Cretan artefacts. The soul of the kitchen is Maria Spanaki, who does a mean souvlaki, and if there's lamb on offer it'll likely be excellent as well. Upstairs are four **rooms** (doubles €30) with twin beds and bathroom.

Psyhro Ψυχρό

Psyhro is the launch pad for the Dikteon Cave, the mythological birthplace of Zeus, and is often clogged with tour buses. It has one main street, a sword-waving memorial statue, a few tourist tavernas and plenty of tacky souvenir shops. It's about a 1km uphill walk to the cave.

Sights

Dikteon Cave CAVE
(Cave of Psyhro; ☎28410 22462; http://odysseus.culture.gr; adult/concession €6/3; ⏰8am-8pm Apr-Oct, to 3pm Nov-Mar) According to legend, Rhea hid in this cave to give birth to Zeus, far from the clutches of his offspring-gobbling father, Cronos. A slick and vertiginous staircase corkscrews into the damp dark, passing overhanging stalactites, ethereal formations and a lake. From Psyhro it's a steep 800m walk to the cave entrance, via a rocky but shaded natural trail or the sunny paved path starting near the car park.

The most famous formation is a stalactite nicknamed 'the mantle of Zeus' in a chamber on the right-hand side off the larger hall. Offerings found in the cave, including daggers, arrowheads, figures and double axes, indicate that it was a place of cult worship from Minoan to Roman times. Key items are now on display at the Archaeological Museum (p163) in Iraklio.

Eating

Tavern Taksiarhos CRETAN €
(☎6978368992; mains €5-10; ⏰10am-11pm Apr-Oct; ❄📶) One of the better among the tourist-deluged pit stops below the Dikteon Cave, Taksiarhos offers the gamut of trad fare but is known for its succulent grilled pork.

Taverna Stavros CRETAN €
(☎28440 31453; grills €7-9; ⏰10am-10pm May-Oct) Long-established Stavros, eye-catchingly flanked by geranium pots, and propped up by old-timers, offers al fresco seating and a menu spanning salads, pasta, souvlaki and locally sourced veg.

Petros Taverna GREEK €
(☎6947022216; mains €6-8.50; ⏰9am-5pm) Average Greek fare is on offer at this long-standing tourist taverna at the foot of the Dikteon Cave.

Getting There & Away

The Lasithi Plateau is not served by public buses. A taxi to Tzermiado or Psyhro costs about €60 from Iraklio and €50 from Agios Nikolaos. To cut costs, take a bus to Malia and a taxi from there (about €25).

NORTHEASTERN COAST

Istro & Around

Wedged into a crescent bay about 12km east of Agios Nikolaos, **Voulisma Beach** (Golden Beach; Istro; 👪) is a ribbon of fine golden sand is lapped by shallow and usually calm, Caribbean-clear water shimmering in myriad shades of blue. There's a small restaurant by the stairs leading down from the parking area and water sports in high season.

★**Karavostassi Apartments** APARTMENT €€
(☎28410 24581; www.karavostassi.gr; apt from €120; P⊖❄📶🐾) Fall asleep to the sound of the waves in this trio of stylish-rustic bi-level apartments in a secluded stone house that feels much like your rich aunt's private villa. It sits at the northern end of Kavarostasi Beach, near Istro, some 10km south of central Agios Nikolaos, and has private patios from which you can jump right into the sea. Minimum three-night stay.

Gournia Γουρνιά

The Late Minoan settlement of **Gournia** (☎28420 93028; adult/concession €2/1; ⏲8.30am-4pm Wed-Mon; P) lies 19km southeast of Agios Nikolaos. Comprising a small palace and residential areas, it was built between 1600 and 1500 BC, destroyed in 1450 BC and reoccupied from 1375 to 1200 BC. There are streets, stairways and houses with walls up to 2m high. Domestic, trade and agricultural implements discovered here suggest that Gournia might have been fairly prosperous. Agios Nikolaos buses bound for Sitia and Ierapetra can drop you at the site.

Snap a picture of the overview map just past the entrance, then follow a narrow ancient road as it curves uphill to the palace ruins, skirting **workshops and storage rooms**, including one where a clay wine press was found. The trail ends at the palace's **central courtyard**, with steps on your right indicating the main entrance. On the opposite (western) side of the courtyard, smaller stairs lead down to an upright slab considered to have been a 'sacred stone'. Basic explanatory panels scattered around the site provide additional information.

Mohlos Μόχλος

POP 100

At the end of a narrow road winding past massive open-cast quarries, tranquil Mohlos is an off-the-radar gem along Crete's northern shore. In this pint-sized fishing village time moves as gently as the waves lapping the pebble-and-grey-sand beach. There's little to do but relax, soak up the peacefulness and enjoy a leisurely meal in one of the excellent waterfront cafes and tavernas.

In ancient times Mohlos was a thriving Early Minoan community, traces of which have been excavated on the small island that's now 200m offshore. If you want to visit, ask around in the village for someone to take you there in a boat. Swimmers should be wary of strong currents.

Sleeping

There's a full resort about 2km east of the village, but otherwise Mohlos is all about private rooms, apartment and villa rentals. Supply is limited and often booked solid in peak season.

To Kyma APARTMENT €
(☎28430 94177; soik@in.gr; studios €30-50; ⏲Apr-Oct; 🚭❄📶) These well-kept, modern studios are a reasonable deal if you don't need a lot of elbow room. All come with a balcony with sea views and a basic kitchenette for making breakfast or snacks. Check in at the mini-market Anna. Three-night minimum stay may be required.

Hotel Sofia PENSION €
(☎28430 94554; sofia-mochlos@hotmail.com; d/tr €35/45; ❄📶) Right by the sea, this amiably old-school taverna has small, low-frills rooms upstairs with wine-coloured bedspreads, traditional furniture, modern bathrooms and a fridge. You pay a little extra for a sea view. The owners also have spacious **apartments** (€40 to €55) 200m east of the harbour, where longer stays are preferred.

Petra Nova Villas VILLA €€
(☎6984365277, 28430 94080; www.petranovavillas.gr; 1-/2-bedroom villas €110/140; P❄📶) These five bi-level stone villas blend into the hillside and are just a few minutes' walk up the road from the waterfront. Each comes with plenty of privacy, a chic interior and a patio with stunning views of the sea – all ingredients for a soothing and mindful getaway. Minimum-stay requirement during peak season.

Mohlos Mare APARTMENT €€
(☎28430 94005; www.mochlos-mare.com; 1-/2-bedroom apt from €50/60; P❄📶🐾) In a sugar-white building exploding with coral-pink bougainvillea, these four apartments with basic kitchenettes are just steps from the village. All come with spacious balconies opening towards the sea, although the biggest assets are the hosts, who will often ply you with fruit or veg from the garden.

Eating

With not much else to do, eating well is a major pastime here, and the tavernas on the waterfront and side streets dish up some of the best meals in eastern Crete.

★Ta Kochilia CRETAN €€
(☎28430 94432; mains €5.50-17; ⏲10.30am-midnight; 📶) The oldest among several waterfront tavernas, Ta Kochilia has cooked up a storm for nearly a century and is still an excellent port of call for fanciers of fish and traditional Cretan dishes like spinach pies, lamb with artichokes, and oven-baked feta. Well-curated wine list, to boot.

Tavernaki Dimitris MEDITERRANEAN €€
(☎6945367035; mains €8.50-15; ⏰noon-4pm & 6pm-late; ❄📶) No direct sea view but Greek food with a dollop of French *je ne sais quoi* is what awaits at this little taverna where you can make your taste buds dance all day long. All the classics are accounted for, along with fish soup (weekends only), shrimp flambéed with Metaxa, and a selection of carpaccio and tartare.

To Bogazi CRETAN €€
(☎28430 94200; mezedhes €3-7, mains €7-15; ⏰10am-late Apr-Oct; ❄📶✎) Run by a lovely Greek-Swiss couple, this seafront tavern has a capacious terrace with cheerful purple-and-white furniture and a menu loaded with dishes prepared with the local harvest from land and sea. The quality is exceptional and there's live music on some nights in summer.

Getting There & Away

There's no public transport to Mohlos. Buses between Sitia and Agios Nikolaos can drop you at the Mohlos turnoff, from where you'll need to hitch or walk the 6km down to the village.

Getting Around

Mohlos Boat Service (per person €5) If you see the little boat grandly emblazoned 'Mohlos Boat Service' bobbing in the tiny harbour, you know that there's a skipper around to motor you to the offshore islet, where you can poke around the Minoan ruins. Just ask at any taverna and they will find him.

Sitia Σητεία

POP 9900

Though not conventionally pretty, Sitia exudes an attractive vibe that stems from not having sold its soul to mass tourism. It's a slow-paced, friendly place where agriculture is the mainstay of the local economy.

In the tranquil old town above the fishing harbour, whitewashed buildings tumble down a hillside laced by steep staircases and accented by a ruined Venetian castle. Down below, tavernas and cafes line the bustling waterfront and wide promenade along Karamanli. A long, sandy beach skirts the bay to the east.

Many visitors use Sitia as launch pad for explorations of Vaï, Moni Toplou, Zakros and other remote destinations further east, although it's well worth spending a day or two in town.

History

Excavations indicate that there were Neolithic settlements around Sitia and an important Minoan settlement at nearby Petras. In the Graeco-Roman era there was a town called Iteia in or around modern Sitia, although its exact site has not yet been located. In Byzantine times Sitia became a bishopric, which was then eliminated by the Saracens in the 9th century. Under the Venetians Sitia became the most important port in eastern Crete, and their name for the port, La Sitia, is said to have given the Lasithi area its name.

Sitia was hit by a disastrous earthquake in 1508 – a blow from which it never really recovered. The Turkish blockade of Sitia in 1648 marked its death knell. The remaining inhabitants fled and the town languished until the Turks made Sitia an administrative centre in the late 19th century.

Crete's most famous poet, Vitsentzos Kornaros, writer of the epic love poem 'Erotokritos', was born in Sitia in 1614.

Sights

Sitia Archaeological Museum MUSEUM
(☎28430 23917; Piskokefalou; adult/concession €2/1; ⏰8.30am-4pm Wed-Mon) This is a compact showcase of archaeological finds from eastern Crete spanning the arc from Neolithic to Roman times, with an emphasis on Minoan artefacts. Pride of place goes to the *Palekastro Kouros* – a statue carved from hippopotamus tusks that was once fully covered in gold leaf. Standout finds from the palace at Zakros include a wine press, a bronze saw and cult objects scorched by the fire that destroyed the palace.

Other notable finds are fragments of Linear A tablets found at Petras and Zakros as well as Minoan *larnakes* (clay coffins).

Sitia City Beach BEACH
(Sitia-Palekastro Rd) Sitia's city beach has mostly greyish sand and is lapped by crystalline, kid-friendly waters. Since it extends a couple of kilometres south of the town centre, it rarely gets crowded, although it lacks shade and is paralleled by a road, which temper its blissfulness.

Petras Archaeological Site HISTORIC SITE
(€2) About 2km southeast of Sitia on a low hill overlooking the sea is the site of an important Minoan settlement. You can see the remains of two houses from the Neopalatial

Sitia

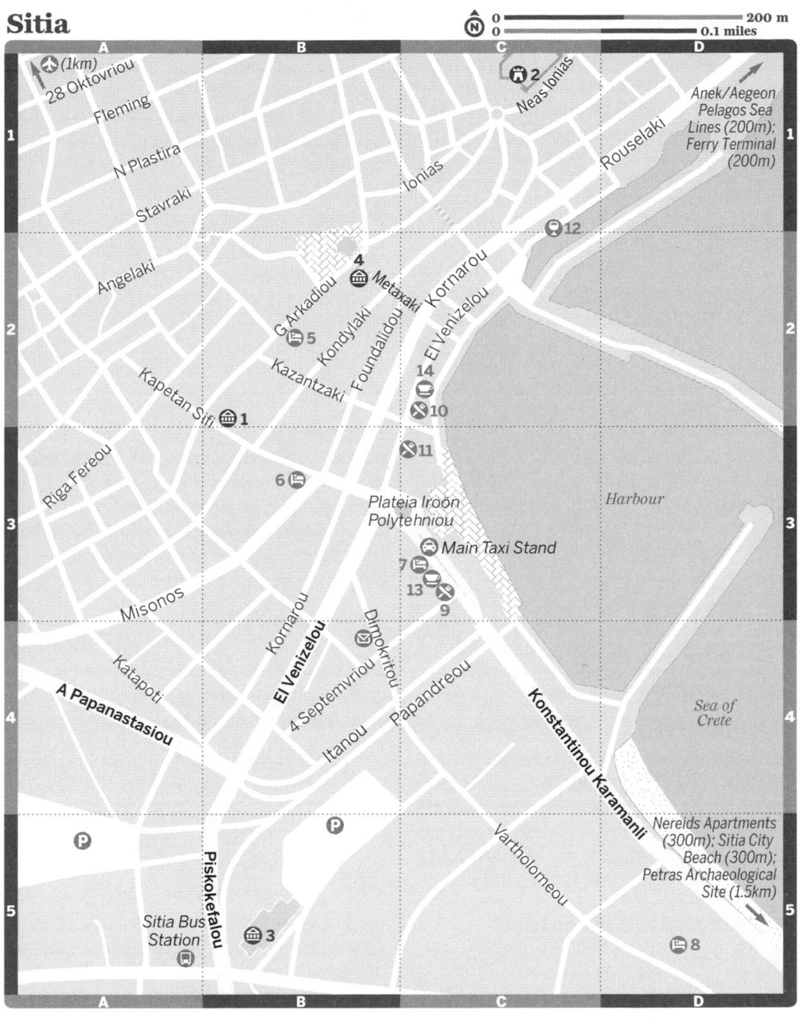

Sitia

Sights

1 Folklore Museum ... B2
2 Kazarma Fortress ... C1
3 Sitia Archaeological Museum ... B5
4 Venetian Building ... B2

Sleeping

5 Hotel El Greco ... B2
6 Hotel Krystal ... B3
7 Itanos Hotel ... C3
8 Sitia Bay Hotel ... D5

Eating

9 Mitsakakis ... C3
10 Rakadiko Oinodeion ... C2
11 Zorbas Taverna ... C3

Drinking & Nightlife

12 Black Hole ... C1
13 Kafe ... C3
14 Nouvelle Boutique ... C2

period as well as the palace itself, which is centred, as at Knossos and other Minoan sites, on a courtyard. Formal opening hours are erratic. For the latest details, check with Sitia's Archaeological Museum, which also displays many objects unearthed at Petras.

Folklore Museum MUSEUM
(☎28430 28300; Kapetan Sifi 28; €2; ⏰10am-2pm Mon-Fri) Anybody curious about traditional life in Sitia should spend half an hour or so nosing around this two-storey museum in a handsome 19th-century building. Displays include the predictable: costumes, embroidery, weaving, ceramics, tools, but it's all smartly laid out by theme and, if you wish, brought to life by the friendly guide.

Kazarma Fortress FORT
(☎28430 27140; Neas Ionias; ⏰8.30am-7.30pm Tue-Sun Apr-Oct, to 3pm Nov-Mar) FREE Looming high on the hillside above the port, Kazarma (derived from the Italian Casa di Arma) was built by the Venetians in the 13th century but destroyed (by earthquakes, pirates and marauders) and rebuilt multiple times. Pretty much gutted today, it's found new purpose as an atmospheric outdoor backdrop for summer cultural events. Views are tops from here year-round.

Venetian Building HISTORIC BUILDING
(cnr Arkadiou & Metaxaki; ⏰closed to the public) Just below Agia Ekaterini, the main church, look for a Venetian building that was once the administrative base of a French garrison based in Sitia during the transition from Ottoman power in the late 19th century.

Festivals & Events

Kornaria Festival PERFORMING ARTS
(⏰Jul–mid-Aug) This traditional summer festival enlivens Sitia with concerts, folk dancing, art exhibits, sporting events and theatre productions. Many events are staged in the Kazarma fortress. Posters around town announce the events, some of which are free.

Sitia Sultanina Festival CULTURAL
(⏰mid-Aug) Celebrating local grapes and raisins, this three-day festival kicks off the grape harvest with music, dancing and rivers of wine. Look for dishes featuring sultaninas, a special kind of grape and a famous export.

Nautical Week SPORTS
(⏰Jun) Held every other year, Sitia hosts a week-long festival featuring sailing races, traditional dances and a feast of local specialities.

Sleeping

With a few notable exceptions, hotels in Sitia are characterless and haven't caught up on 21st-century comforts. On the plus side, prices are pretty low and you're more likely to find peak-season vacancies here than elsewhere.

Hotel El Greco HOTEL €
(☎28430 23133; www.elgreco-sitia.gr; Arkadiou 13; d €50;) This old-school hotel has smart and impeccably clean rooms with tiled floors, nice but dated furniture, plasma TV, fridge and balcony (most with sea views). It's a good city hotel and a convenient base for short stays. A quality breakfast costs €5 per person.

Hotel Krystal HOTEL €
(☎28430 22284; www.ekaterinidis-hotels.com; Kapetan Sifi 17; d incl breakfast €55;) This city hotel is a handy bargain base. It has clean, functional rooms varying in size with tiled floors and dark-wood furniture. There's a nice eating area for breakfast.

★ **Nereids Apartments** APARTMENT €€
(☎6944909834, 28430 26027; https://nereids.gr; Sitia-Palekastro Rd; studios €70-90; ⏰May-Oct;) One of the nicest properties in Sitia, this bungalow complex with studios and family apartments sits right across from the beach in a colourful garden brimming with jasmine and geranium. The nicest units have verandas facing the sea, although those at the back are quieter. The stylish lounge-bar serves breakfast, a mean burger, crisp salads and good cocktails.

Sitia Bay Hotel HOTEL €€
(☎28430 24800; www.sitiabay.com; Vartholomeou 27; d from €100; ⏰reception 8am-8pm;) This modern beachfront hotel has friendly service and comfortable and tastefully done-up studios and family apartments, all with kitchens and sea views. If the sand with loungers doesn't beckon, perhaps the pool does. There is also a children's play area. At sunset, grab a drink at the bar and chill on the rooftop terrace.

Itanos Hotel HOTEL €€
(☎28430 22900; www.itanoshotel.com; Konstantinou Karamanli 4; d incl breakfast €46-65;) This central businesslike seafront hotel is clean and well kept, albeit of older vintage. Rooms pack fridge, desk and small TV into a compact frame and come with a balcony offering full or partial sea view. Breakfast is a

nice buffet spread, and there's a cafe-restaurant on the promenade and a summertime rooftop bar.

Eating

Locals still dominate the cafes and tavernas, all with air-conditioned indoor and sea-facing outdoor tables, that line Karamanli and its wide promenade as well as pedestrianised El Venizelou.

★Mitsakakis CAFE €

(28430 20200; Karamanli 6; galaktoboureko €2.70; 8am-midnight;) This cafe and pastry shop is a Sitian institution (open since 1965) and famous for its sugar-rush-inducing *galaktoboureko* (custard-filled pastry), *loukoumadhes* (ball-shaped doughnuts) and *kataïfi* (angel-hair pastry).

Sit on the seaside terrace or in the old-school cafe.

★Rakadiko Oinodeion CRETAN €

(28430 26166; El Venizelou 157; mezedhes €3.50-8, mains €7.50-13; 6pm-1am;) Tops among the waterfront tavernas, this rustic family place offers a recognisable array of Greek dishes, but it's the local seasonal specials that truly shine. Among these, anything with rabbit or goat gets top marks and is best paired with the local wine. Many ingredients, including the oil, bread and raki, are produced by the Garefalakis family itself.

Zorbas Taverna GREEK €€

(Kazantzaki 3; mains €7-15; noon-late;) Gregarious owner Zorba, with his sailor's roll, sea captain's cap and bushy moustache, lays on the Greek clichés with a trowel and a wink. Bouzouki music accompanies the rich aromas of home-cooked food and grilled meats served at blue tables and chairs in his waterfront lair. Good for kids.

Drinking & Nightlife

El Venizelou, the pedestrian strip paralleling the seaside, is chock-a-block with lively tavernas, cafes and bars that pull in an all-ages crowd until the wee hours.

Black Hole BAR

(28430 20422; El Venizelou; 10am-late;) This alt-flavoured lair plays it cool with head-bopping rock and an outdoor lounge area overlooking the promenade leading to the ferry terminal.

Kafe CAFE

(28430 25131; Karamanli 6; 6am-midnight;) With its sofas, old-fashioned lamps and quirky art on stone walls, this is a welcome slice of boho charm in Sitia. Fruit salads, club sandwiches, fresh juices and coffee make Kafe a characterful pit stop for breakfast, an afternoon pick-me-up (snacks €5) or a post-dinner drink.

Nouvelle Boutique CAFE

(6972825942; El Venizelou 161; 9am-late;) This comfy-chic local fave with huge backlit bar and stone-walled interior is a top after-dark spot, when a youthful crowd invades for funky sounds, sweet and strong drinks, dancing and the occasional band. Also a nice place for a daytime chill session, with some of the best cappuccino in town.

Information

EMERGENCY

Police (28430 22259, tourist police 171; Therisou 31) Has a special tourist police unit during the summer months.

INTERNET ACCESS

Many cafes and restaurants and practically all hotels offer free wi-fi, although reception can be spotty.

MONEY

There are lots of ATMs in the side streets behind the waterfront.

National Bank of Greece (Plateia Ethnikis Antistaseos; 8am-2pm Mon-Fri)

POST

Post Office (28430 22283; Dimokritou 10; 7.30am-2.45pm Mon-Fri)

TRAVEL AGENCIES

Tzortzakis Travel (28430 29211; www.tzortzakistravel.com; Papanastasiou 7; 8.30am-9pm Mon-Fri, 9am-3pm Sat, 10am-2pm Sun)

Getting There & Away

AIR

Small Sitia Municipal Airport (p296) is about 1km north of the town centre and handles domestic flights to Athens, Alexandroupoli, Iraklio, Kassos and Rhodes as well as seasonal charter flights from Germany and Scandinavia. A taxi into town costs €6 to €8.

BOAT

Ferries dock about 1km north of the town centre. **Anek/Aegeon Pelagos Sea Lines** (Hania 28210 24000; www.anek.gr) has service to Anafi (€20, eight hours), Chalki (€20, 8½ hours),

Diafani (€18, six hours), Iraklio (€16, three hours), Karpathos (€19, 4½ hours), Kasos (€12, 2¾ hours), Milos (€26, 14¼ hours), Piraeus (€44, 21½ hours), Rhodes (€28, 10½ hours) and Santorini (€28, 10 hours) on a seasonally changing schedule. Prices quoted are for deckchair seating.

BUS

Connections from Sitia's **bus station** (☎28430 22272, 28102 46530; http://ktelherlas.gr; Sitia-Palekastro Rd; 📶) include four buses daily to Ierapetra (€6.90, 1¾ hours), five buses to Iraklio (€16, three hours), and six to Agios Nikolaos (€8.30, 1¾ hours). Two buses leave for Zakros on Monday, Tuesday and Friday (€4.50, one hour). No services on Sunday.

TAXI

From the **main taxi stand** (☎28430 20420, 28430 22700), sample fares are €22 to Moni Toplou, €35 to Vaï, €50 to Zakros, €57 to Kato Zakros and €170 to Iraklio.

An easy way to hike **Zakros Gorge** on a day trip from Sitia is by hiring a private driver like **Yiannis** (☎6995900900; www.sitiataxi.com), who can pick you up in Sitia, take you to the trailhead, pick you back up post-hike in Kato Zakros and drive you back to Sitia for €60.

Moni Toplou Μονή Τοπλού

In splendid isolation on a windswept plateau, 15th-century fortified **Moni Toplou** (☎28430 61226; Toplou; €3; ⏱8am-6pm Apr-Oct) is one of the most historically significant monasteries in Crete. Its defences were tested by everyone from pirates to crusading knights to the Turks. The church brims with superb icons, although the main magnet is the intricate *Lord Thou Art Great* icon by celebrated Cretan artist Ioannis Kornaros. It depicts scenes from the Old and New Testaments, including Noah's Ark, Jonah and the Whale, and Moses parting the Red Sea.

The name Toplou is derived from the Turkish word for cannon, which is what the monks used to defend themselves against pirates during Venetian times. The monastery was also repeatedly active in the cause of Cretan independence. Under the Turkish occupation a secret school operated on the premises, while during WWII resistance leaders ran an underground radio transmitter here. A small exhibition in the museum recalls this period with rifles, helmets and a field telephone. The adjacent main room displays engravings and icons.

Today the monastery is not only an attraction for fans of history, religion, art and architecture but also the largest landowner in the area and an active producer of award-winning wine and olive oil, which you can sample in a nearby tasting room (open 10.30am to 5pm Monday to Saturday).

Moni Toplou is about 15km east of Sitia. Buses can drop you at the junction of the Sitia–Palekastro road, from where you'll need to hitch or walk for 3.5km.

EASTERN COAST

Vaï Βάϊ

The **beach** (parking €2.50) at Vaï, 24km northeast of Sitia, is famous for its large grove of *Phoenix theophrasti* (Cretan date) palms. With calm, clear waters, it is one of Crete's most popular strands and its rows of umbrellas and sunbeds often fill by 10am in July and August. Jet skis kick into gear shortly thereafter. Come early in the morning or late in the afternoon to avoid the crowds.

Alternatively, for a quieter beach (albeit without the palms), take the 1km scramble south over the rocky headland. The trail starts just past the gazebo lookout reached via stone steps leading up from the reasonably priced taverna at the southern end of Vaï beach. A 30-minute walk on another trail heading north leads to a trio of small beaches at Itanos that are overlooked by Hellenic and Roman ruins.

There are two daily buses to Vaï from Sitia (€3.30, one hour) from May to October.

Vaï Restaurant & Cafe CRETAN **€€**
(☎28430 61129; www.vai-restaurant.gr; Vaï Beach; mains €9-25; ⏱9am-late Apr-Oct; 📶) Enjoy lovely views of the palms, the gleaming sand and the cobalt sea from the covered terrace of this waterfront restaurant serving classic Greek fare, including fish and grilled meats, alongside such local specialities as Cretan couscous *hondros* (with snails). The cafe below has cold drinks, coffee, snacks and ice cream.

Itanos Ίτανος

About 3km north of Vaï, vestiges of the Graeco-Roman port of Itanos overlook a trio of beaches. **Ancient Itanos** was once an important settlement in eastern Crete and a key trading post with the Middle East by the 7th century BC. A few centuries later, it was at odds with local rivals such as Praisos and later with Ierapetra before being occupied by the Romans. Poke around to locate the remains of two early Christian basilicas, a Hellenistic watchtower and wall foundations.

The basilica ruin, on high ground towards the sea, is littered with toppled columns. Look for one stone base marked with circular motifs. To get there, follow the road from Vaï beach and at the first crossroads head right (north) for about 2.5km.

Itanos Beaches BEACH
(Ermoupoli) North of Vaï and reached on foot or by car, Itanos is a trio of small, pretty beaches watched over by the ruins of the ancient Graeco-Roman town of Itanos. Aside from a taverna a bit inland, there's no infrastructure, and the beaches rarely get crowded.

Palekastro Παλαίκαστρο

POP 1100

Palekastro (pah-leh-kas-tro) is an unpretentious farming village underpinned by low-key tourism. It lies in a rocky landscape interspersed with fields close to the beaches at Kouremenos (with Crete's best windsurfing), Hiona and Vaï. In the village you'll find an ATM, a petrol station and small markets.

About 1km east of town, about 150m south of Hiona Beach, is the archaeological site of Roussolakkos, where archaeologists are digging up a Minoan town and hoping for evidence of a major Minoan palace. This is where the *Palekastro Kouros* ivory figurine – now residing in the Archaeological Museum (p240) in Sitia – was found.

Sights & Activities

Kouremenos Beach BEACH
Kouremenos, about 7km south of Vaï and 3km northeast of Palekastro, is a long, grey sand-and-pebble beach with good shallow-water swimming, although it's best known for having some of the island's best wind- and kitesurfing conditions. There's no hotel but lots of apartments, a taverna for sustenance and a windsurfing centre.

Hiona Beach BEACH
Hiona Beach, 2.5km east of Palekastro, is a quiet sweep of of coarse sand and pebbles backed by clumps of tamarisk trees. It's overlooked by two excellent fish tavernas and also home to a coastal wetland that's a rest stop for migratory birds in winter and spring. Further on, archaeologists are unearthing what may well be a Minoan settlement.

Folk Museum of Palekastro MUSEUM
(☎69743 50180; Evropis 52; €2; ⏰10am-1pm & 5-8pm Tue-Sun May–mid-Oct) Tucked away in a backstreet and signposted from the main road, this compact and well-presented museum occupies a traditional Cretan manor house, with displays in the old stables and bakery. It displays crafts, tools, costumes and everyday items from the Turkish occupation period until 1960.

Freak Surf Crete WINDSURFING
(☎6979253861; www.freak-surf.com; Kouremenos Beach; ⏰10am-7pm May-Nov) This well-established windsurfing operator, located at Kouremenos Beach, rents the latest boards and sails (€265 per week) and offers windsurfing lessons (two hours for €60) as well as yoga sessions (€10) and mountain biking.

Freak Mountain Bike Centre MOUNTAIN BIKING
(☎6979253861; www.freak-mountainbike.com; ⏰10am-6pm Jun-Oct) Dutch-owned outfit offers guided four-day mountain-bike tours around eastern Crete (€850) and can also customise private tours.

Sleeping

The town itself has a few simple hotels, but the nicer and newer places, many of them self-catering, are towards Hiona Beach and up by Kouremenos Beach.

Hiona Holiday Hotel HOTEL €
(☎28430 29623; www.hionaholiday.gr; Elias; s/d incl breakfast €50/65; ⏰May-Sep; P ❄ ☎) The plain facade of this hotel belies its comfy rooms with balcony and decent facilities, including a well-stocked bar and pleasant public areas. It's a few minutes' walk down the hill from the centre of Palekastro and 2km from Hiona Beach.

Esperides Stone Houses APARTMENT €€
(☎6945255243, 28430 61433; www.palaikastro.com/esperides; apt €75-120; P ❄ ≋ 🐾) Although newly built, this stone retreat does a solid job of evoking traditional Cretan flair through its architecture and furnishings. It's in a placid spot surrounded by olive trees some 300m from Kouremenos Beach and 2km from the village. The five units sleep up to four and have terraces with nice sea views.

Grandes Apartments APARTMENT €€

(☎6946503909, 6972835843; www.grandes.gr; Kouremenos Beach; apt €70-100; P ❄) Overlooking Kouremenos Beach (p245), these five self-catering apartments are set among olive trees and a flower-filled garden. Sleeping up to five, they're spacious and comfortable, with well-equipped kitchens and rustic, slightly dated furniture. The owners also run the adjacent beachfront taverna.

Eating

There are a number of earthy tavernas around the town square as well as two excellent fish restaurants overlooking Hiona Beach.

Mythos CRETAN €

(☎28430 61243; www.mythos-restaurant.gr; mains €5-11; ⏲10am-1am Apr-Oct;) Attractively decorated, with its rock walls accented with colourful murals, this friendly family taverna on the main square cooks only with olive oil and has some lovely dishes, such as chicken with lemon sauce and tasty mezedhes with plenty of veggie options. Romantic by night.

To Finistrini MEZEDHES €

(☎28430 61117; mezedhes €5-6; ⏲10am-late) This easy-going *rakadhiko* (Cretan *ouzerie* – place that serves ouzo and light snacks) on the main square dishes up tasty mezedhes and simple fast-food-style dishes (*gyros*, souvlaki, pasta) that go down well with a shot or three of raki.

★**Hiona Taverna** SEAFOOD €€

(☎28430 61228; Hiona Beach; mains €15-25; ⏲noon-11pm Apr-Oct;) One of two top-ranked tavernas at the northern end of Hiona Beach (p245), this more upscale contender in a stone house is usually filled with patrons lusting after the fresh fish and seafood, including a rich bouillabaisse-style soup called *kakavia*. Book ahead for a romantic table on the cliffs.

Getting There & Away

There are four buses per day from Sitia to Palekastro (€2.80, one hour). Buses stop in the central square.

Zakros & Kato Zakros
Ζάκρος & Κάτω Ζάκρος

POP 800

Zakros, 45km southeast of Sitia, is the starting point for the trail through **Zakros Gorge** (Gorge of the Dead), also known as the Valley of the Dead because of the Minoan burial caves that honeycomb the canyon cliffs. The small town has lodging, mini-markets, an ATM and a petrol station but is otherwise a mere prelude to the coastal village of Kato Zakros. The 7km drive down a winding road is spectacular and delivers mesmerising views after every bend.

Shortly before reaching the village, you can see the huge jaw of Zakros Gorge breaching the cliffs in the distance. Look closely and you might also spot the ruins of the Minoan palace just up from Kato Zakros' pebbly, narrow beach and row of tavernas. Add to all this the isolated tranquillity and sense of peace, and you have the perfect recipe for escapism.

Sights & Activities

★**Zakros Palace** ARCHAEOLOGICAL SITE

(☎28410 22462; Kato Zakros; adult/concession €6/3; ⏲8am-8pm May-Sep, to 3pm Oct-Apr) Ancient Zakros, the smallest of Crete's four Minoan palatial complexes, sat next to a harbour and was likely engaged in sea trade with the Middle East, as suggested by excavated elephant tusks and oxhide ingots. Like Knossos, Phaestos and Malia, Zakros centred on a courtyard flanked by royal apartments, shrines, ceremonial halls, storerooms and workshops. While the ruins are sparse, the remote setting makes it an attractive site to nose around. Information panels help spur your imagination.

In Minoan times the main palace entrance would have been in the northeastern corner facing the sea, but today's visitors enter from the south, first passing vestiges of **workshops** that may have been used to produce pottery and perfume. This path leads to the **Central Court**, which measures 30m by 12m and was the focal point of the entire palace.

Flanking the western side of the courtyard were two fancy halls, dubbed the **Banquet Hall** and the **Hall of Ceremonies**; the bull's-head rhyton (ceremonial drinking vessel), now a star exhibit at Iraklio's Archaeological Museum (p163), was discovered in the latter. The cluster of small rooms west of the halls includes the **archive room**, where Linear A record tablets were found, as well as a **shrine** and a **lustral basin**. Also here is the **treasury**, so called because it yielded dozens of imported jars, rhyta and other objects.

The north wing contained the **kitchen** and an upstairs **dining hall** – you can still spot the column bases that supported the two-storey building. As in the other palaces, it is believed that the royal apartments were located in the east wing, which was fronted by a portico. A covered section shelters a **lustral basin**, which was once decorated with frescoes and abutted the queen's bedroom. These types of rooms probably served as a ritual cleaning space for those entering a shrine. Note the ledge and a niche in the southern wall that may have held ceremonial idols.

Unlike the other Minoan palaces, the east wing had three water features. The largest is the **Cistern Hall**, which featured a round basin surrounded by a colonnaded balustrade. Seven steps lead to the floor of the cistern, which may have been a pool, a bath or even an aquarium. The two **wells** located just south of the cistern may have supplied the workshops with water.

Zakros Natural History Museum MUSEUM
(☎28433 40540; Zakros; ⊙10am-1pm & 5-8pm Mon-Sat mid-Jun–mid-Oct) FREE A short distance past the village square en route to Kato Zakros, this little museum shines a spotlight on local flora and fauna through modest displays of fossils, minerals and stuffed animals.

Pelekita Cave HIKING
(www.sitia-geopark.gr/en/activities/geotourism/hiking-trails/georoute-12.aspx) A 3.5km trail along the rocky coast leads to this extraordinary 310m-long cave with magnificent views of the sea below and signs of Neolithic habitation within its stalactite- and stalagmite-rich interior. To explore it bring a torch (flashlight) and wear suitable shoes.

Near the cave is a quarry that was mined for building material for the Minoan palace at Kato Zakros. About 2km past the cave is the isolated, small-pebbled **Karoumes Beach**, which can also be accessed on a 3.5km trek via the Chochlakies Gorge.

Sleeping

Zakros is but a footnote to Kato Zakros and you should head to the latter for a spectrum of accommodation, from simple rooms to downright beautiful villas with panoramic views. Rooms in Kato Zakros fill up fast in high season, so it's best to book.

Katerina Apartments APARTMENT €
(☎6974656617, 28430 26893; www.kato-zakros.gr/_en/katerina.php; Kato Zakros; apt €50-70; ⊙Apr-Sep; P✻☜) These four stone-built studios and maisonettes sleep up to four and enjoy a lovely garden setting in the hillside at Kato Zakros. The 800m walk to the beach takes you past the trailhead for Zakros Gorge and the Minoan palace ruins. Units welcome you with family-style hominess, accented by the occasional lace doily, and a small jug of homemade raki.

Athena & Coral Rooms PENSION €
(☎6974656617, 28431 10710; www.kato-zakros.gr; Kato Zakros; r €60; ⊙Apr-Oct; ✻) Above the beach and within stumbling distance of the Akrogiali Taverna (p248) (same owner), these good-size rooms have attractive stone-effect walls and wood-beamed ceilings and count a fridge and TV among their amenities. Simple and romantic, they're just steps from the lulling waves.

Zakros Palace

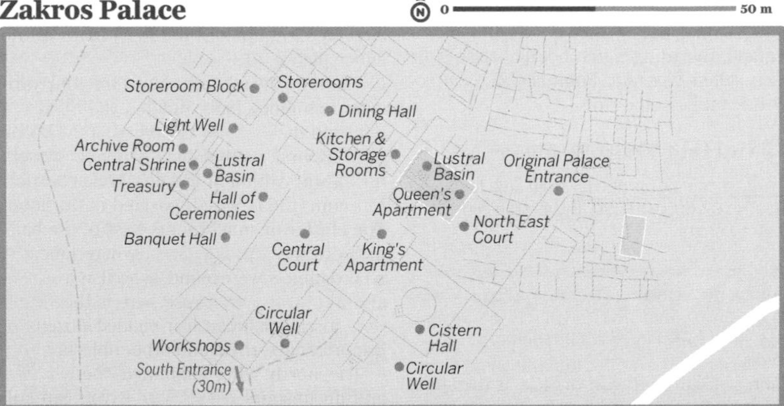

DON'T MISS

HIKING ZAKROS GORGE

One of loveliest hikes in eastern Crete is the easy-to-moderate trek through **Zakros Gorge**, also known as the Gorge of the Dead (or the Valley of the Dead) because the Minoans used to bury their dead in caves on the rugged cliffs.

There are two trailheads off the road from Zakros to Kato Zakros. For **Entrance A**, turn left at the sign and follow the tarmac for about 500m to a parking area to pick up the trail down into the canyon. You'll be in Kato Zakros in about 1½ to two hours.

The way's a bit shorter if you start at **Entrance B**, about 1km further down. Parking is by the side of the road. Note that the trailhead is to the left of the bus shelter and water fountain and *not* via the dirt track misleadingly indicated by the sign! Staying above the canyon (nice views), this latter easy route takes you down to Kato Zakros in about an hour.

The gorge hike itself follows the riverbed, which is dry in summer but may still run water as late as May. Prepare to ford the river several times by negotiating the slippery rocks or wading through the water.

At the gorge exit (turn left), a cold beer in one of Kato Zakros' beachfront tavernas is only a 10-minute walk past the Minoan palace ruins away. A taxi back uphill is €12.

Kato Zakros Palace Apartments APARTMENT €
(☎28430 29550, 6974888269; www.katozakros-apts.gr; Kato Zakros; r/studios €60/70; P ❄ 📶) Above Kato Zakros beach and beside the approach road, these immaculate studios with white interiors are well equipped, with safety-deposit boxes, spotless bathrooms, kitchenettes, satellite TV, mosquito screens and hairdryers. Free laundry facilities.

★ **Stella's Traditional Apartments** APARTMENT €€
(☎6976719461, 28430 23739; www.stelapts.com; Kato Zakros; studios €80-90; ⏲mid-Mar–mid-Nov; P ❄ 📶) Close to the mouth of Zakros Gorge (p246), these charming self-contained studios are in a lovely garden setting and decorated with distinctive wooden furniture and other artefacts made by joint owner Elias Pagianidis. Perks range from hammocks under the trees to barbecues and an external kitchen with an honesty system for supplies. Rates include free breakfast provisions.

Elias and his wife, Stella, have excellent knowledge of hiking trails in the area.

Terra Minoika Villas APARTMENT €€
(☎28430 23739; www.terraminoika.com; Kato Zakros; villas €100-150; ⏲mid-Jan–20 Dec; P ❄ 📶) On the hillside high above the surf, these arty cube houses built of local stone are architectural symphonies of wood-beamed ceilings, widescreen views from balconies, chic rustic furniture, urns mounted on walls, and stone floors. Every villa is individual and has a fully equipped kitchenette.

There's even a well-kitted-out gym. Owner Elias Pagianidis is a former Mr Greece bodybuilder and the driving force behind marking the walking trails in the area. He and his wife, Stella, are experts on trekking and local ecology.

Eating

A clutch of beachside tavernas compete for custom with some vigour.

Kato Zakros Bay CRETAN €
(☎28430 26687; Kato Zakros; mains €7-10; ⏲8am-midnight; 📶 ✍) With its stone floors, open range and tables topped with Cretan rugs, this is an atmospheric spot for dinner. Local vegetables are grown next door, and occasionally the owner plays live music. The menu features mussels, dolmadhes, and other Greek staples including rabbit *stifadho*.

Akrogiali Taverna CRETAN €€
(☎28430 26893; Kato Zakros; mains €6-19; ⏲8am-midnight; 📶) The food gods have been smiling upon Kato Zakros' oldest taverna, which does a brisk trade in fresh-off-the-boat fish and Cretan classics, all prepared with locally sourced ingredients, including oil made from the owner's trees. The cheerful blue-and-white furniture and the beachfront setting add two more notches to its appeal.

Getting There & Away

Buses from a central **stop** (☎28102 45020; http://ktelherlas.gr; Eleftherias) link Zakros and Sitia twice on Monday, Tuesday and Friday (€4.50, one hour), continuing down to Kato Zakros in summer (June to September). A taxi from Sitia to Zakros costs about €50, while the fare between Zakros and Kato Zakros is €12.

In summer there's usually one afternoon bus leaving Kato Zakros for Sitia Monday to Friday. Check the latest details at www.ktelherlas.gr.

SOUTHERN COAST

Ierapetra Ιεράπετρα

POP 16,150

Ierapetra is a laid-back seafront town and the commercial centre of southeastern Crete's substantial greenhouse-based agribusiness. Hot and dusty in summer, it offers a low-key, authentic Cretan experience and is also the jumping-off point for the semitropical Chrissi Island (p252) (also called Gaïdouronisi or Hrysi).

The city's grey-sand beaches are backed by tavernas and cafes where the nightlife is busy in summer. Though few visible signs remain, Ierapetra has an impressive history, with interludes as a Roman port and as a Venetian stronghold, as attested to by the harbour fortress. The narrow alleyways of the old quarter (Kato Mera) flash back to the Ottoman period.

Sights & Activities

There are no doubt better beaches on Crete, but if you want to spread your towel in the centre of town, head to the main beach, with coarse grey sand. Many waterfront cafes rent sunloungers and umbrellas or let you use them for free if you consume something.

Old Quarter AREA
(Kato Mera) Inland from the fortress is the labyrinthine old quarter, where you'll see a Turkish fountain, the restored mosque with its minaret, Napoleon's house and several churches, including **Agios Ioannis** (Katsanevaki) and **Agios Georgios** (Agiou Georgiou).

Mosque & Turkish Fountain MOSQUE
(Plateia Tzami) Dominating a triangular plaza at the northern edge of the old quarter, this yellow-sandstone mosque was built by the Turks in the late 19th century and still sports a finely wrought minaret. Together with the octagonal domed Ottoman fountain down in the square, it's a tangible reminder of the Turkish era.

Kales Fortress FORTRESS
(Stratigou Samouil 10; ⌚8am-3pm Tue-Sun) FREE
Overlooking the fishing harbour, the crenellated Venetian fort dates from the 17th century but was built atop an older defensive structure reputedly built by Genoese pirates in the 13th century and destroyed by an earthquake and the Turks. There's not much to see inside, but it's fun to climb up to the ramparts and the single tower for grand views of the bay and the mountains.

Napoleon's House NOTABLE BUILDING
This is where Napoleon Bonaparte is said to have stayed incognito with a local family when his ship anchored in Crete for one night in 1798 en route to his Egyptian campaign. He apparently left a note revealing his identity. The unidentified two-storey corner building (under renovation at research

OFF THE BEATEN TRACK

XEROKAMBOS ΞΕΡΟΚΑΜΠΟΣ

Tucked into the far southeastern corner of Crete, Xerokambos is an indie traveller's dream. There's little to do here but relax on the beach, feast in the tavernas, explore local caves and gorges, and scan the skies for the falcons that breed on the offshore Kavalli Islands.

The village itself has no real centre, as homes, apartments and a clutch of mini-markets and restaurants lie scattered over a sprawling area. The big attraction is the beaches, 14 in all, strung like pearls across 4.5km. Take your pick from sandy ribbons to snug coves, some backed by cliffs, sand dunes or wetlands. Outside July and August, many of them are often footprint free.

Next to the 'central beach', such as it is, are a couple of tavernas with sunloungers (free if you consume something), but that's pretty much it for seaside infrastructure.

Getting to Xerokambos is half the fun. Coming from Zakros, the road corkscrews for about 9km through a muscular mountainscape occasionally scarred by rugged gorges until it opens up to the showstopping panorama of the big, blue Libyan Sea. Another road serpentines down from Ziros in about 18km, delivering brake-worthy views after every hairpin turn.

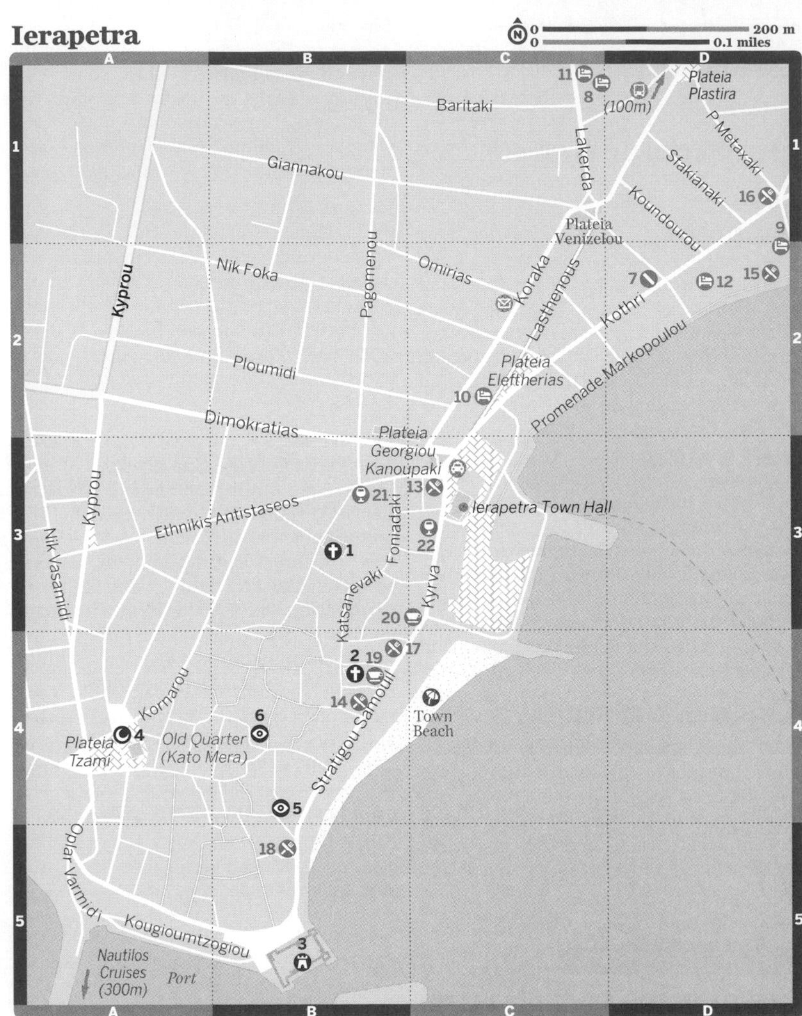

time) has the number 9 on its door. It's in the old quarter (Kato Mera).

Ierapetra Diving Centre DIVING
(☎6944534212, 28420 26703; www.ierapetradivingcentre.com; cnr Kothri 23 & Giannakou 5; dives from €55, open-water course €550; ⏰8am-2pm & 5-10pm) Run by Lefteris, this PADI-certified outfit offers cave and wreck dives and open-water courses. Dive sites include Koutsounari beach, the Peristeras reef and Agia Fotia island.

Festivals & Events

Kyrvia Festival CULTURAL
(⏰mid-Jul–Aug) Ierapetra's Kyrvia Festival features a program of cultural activities including singing and dancing nights by local folk and popular groups, special concerts by famous artists, film screenings, theatre performances, and much singing and dancing in the streets of the old town.

Sleeping

Many of Ierapetra's properties have a knack for infusing a city hotel with relaxed resort flair. You'll find the gamut from cheap guest-

Ierapetra

Sights

1 Agios Georgios ... B3
2 Agios Ioannis Church ... B4
3 Kales Fortress ... B5
4 Mosque & Turkish Fountain ... A4
5 Napoleon's House ... B4
6 Old Quarter ... B4

Activities, Courses & Tours

7 Ierapetra Diving Centre ... D2

Sleeping

8 Akrolithos Apartments ... C1
9 Astron Hotel ... D2
10 Coral Boutique Hotel ... C2
11 Cretan Villa Hotel ... C1
12 El Greco Hotel ... D2

Eating

13 Ariston Cafe ... C3
14 Napoleon ... B4
15 Pizzeria Ristorante Siciliana ... D2
16 Special ... D1
17 Taverna Gorgona ... B4
18 Vira Potzi ... B5

Drinking & Nightlife

19 Chocolicious ... B4
20 Island Cafe ... C3
21 Ntoukiani ... B3
22 Saxo Bar ... C3

houses to stylish boutique hotels and charming self-catering apartments.

★ Cretan Villa Hotel HOTEL €

(28420 28522, 6973037671; www.cretan-villa.com; Lakerda 16; d €45-56;) A heavy wooden door gives way to a vine-shaded courtyard at this restful, friendly space that's a happy coupling of historic touches and mod cons. Beautiful rooms havestone walls, elegantly rustic furniture, stone-tiled showers, wood-beamed ceilings, small fridges and satellite TV. A central city hotel with country flair.

Akrolithos Apartments APARTMENT €€

(6973037671, 28420 28522; www.ierapetra-apartments.net; Lakerda 16; apt €56-70;) Oozing ambience and comfort, these cosy apartments orbit a central courtyard and have such lovely traditional touches as exposed stone walls, wrought-iron beds, tasteful art, well-equipped kitchens and loads of space. It's all in a great central location. Note that there's usually a three-night minimum stay. Keys must be picked up at the adjacent Cretan Villa Hotel.

Astron Hotel HOTEL €€

(28420 25114; www.hotelastron.com; Papaioannou 1; r incl breakfast €70-120;) In a prime location at the eastern end of the waterfront promenade, this rejuvenated classic strikes a smooth balance between city and holiday hotel. Drift off to dreamland in a spruced-up room, preferably one with sea-facing balcony. Days start with an above-average breakfast buffet served in the art deco–accented lobby.

El Greco Hotel BOUTIQUE HOTEL €€

(28420 28471; www.elgreco-ierapetra.gr; Kothri 42; incl breakfast r €73-102, ste €140-180; @) The natural hues in the 21 rooms of this family-run hotel form a soothing contrast to the blinding blue of the sea right out the front. The attention to detail shows, from the free wine and water in your room on arrival to the big breakfast buffet. Romantic types should book the Jacuzzi suite.

Coral Boutique Hotel HOTEL €€

(28420 20444, 6977232766; www.coralhotelcrete.gr; Plateia Eleftherias 19; d €57-86) A recent facelift has turned this breezy city hotel into a cocoon of relaxed sophistication, with ultracomfy mattresses, an easy-on-the-eye palette of white and aqua tones, and accommodating staff. Breakfast is €7.50 extra but worth it.

Eating

Special FAST FOOD €

(28420 27835; cnr Metaxaki 1 & Kothri; dishes €3.50-8; 10.30am-12.30am;) Special jazzes up Ierapetra's dining scene with quality fast food served in an upbeat, contemporary setting. The menu is a reminder of the simple goodness of charcoal-grilled souvlakia or well-prepared rotisserie *gyros* (chicken or pork), although the burgers, salads and sausages hold their own. Portions are big enough to share, and there's a kids' menu to boot.

Ariston Cafe CAFE €

(28420 26120; www.facebook.com/aristonsnackandcoffee; Stratigou Samouil 14; snacks €4; 5am-10.30pm Sun-Thu, 4.30am-10.30pm Fri & Sat;) This modern cafe is known for its good coffee and gooey *loukoumadhes* along with generously stuffed fresh sandwiches, cakes and cheese pies. Also a handy spot to pick up picnic supplies for a day tour to Chrissi Island.

Napoleon GREEK €

(☎28420 22410; Stratigou Samouil 26; mains €6-12; ⌚noon-midnight; ❄📶🌶) This capacious traditional place looks just like any of Ierapetra's tourist-geared waterfront tavernas, but the quality of the home cooking and the service are a cut above. Sit on the covered terrace flanked by palm trees while picking from the tasty line-up of fresh fish and Cretan specialities.

★ **Vira Potzi** CRETAN €€

(☎28420 28254; www.facebook.com/virapotzi; Stratigou Samouil 82; mains €7-14; ⌚noon-midnight Tue-Sun; ❄📶🐾) Next to the Kales Fortress (p249), this next-gen Cretan seaside tavern has an enticing menu packed with culinary twists such as grilled calamari with zucchini sticks and *fava* (bean dip) or the crowd-pleasing shrimp orzo-pasta pilaf. A classy place with nary a plastic picture menu in sight.

Pizzeria Ristorante Siciliana ITALIAN €€

(☎28420 24185; www.facebook.com/ristorante.siciliana; Promenade Markopoulou 1; pizza & pasta €5.50-10, mains €7-19; ⌚1pm-midnight; ❄🌶) This *ristorante* with peach interior and linen-bedecked tables overlooks the big blue and offers a choice of classic Greek starters followed by wood-fired pizzas, soulful pastas and grilled-meat dishes, plus crêpes and local wines.

Taverna Gorgona GREEK €€

(☎28420 26619; Stratigou Samouil 12; mains €7-18; ⌚noon-late; ❄) All the expected Greek staples are accounted for on the multi-language picture menu of this classic taverna. Enjoy fetching views of the sea on the terrace, with its wooden tables shaded by a thatched roof.

🍷 Drinking & Nightlife

Saxo Bar BAR

(☎6944790652; Kyrva 14; ⌚10.30pm-late) Generations of locals have bopped their heads to rock of all stripes at this classic party den since it opened in 1990. Redone in 2015, it now flaunts a swish backlit bar, sexy lighting and excellent cocktails.

Chocolicious CAFE

(Stratigou Samouil 18; ⌚7.30am-late) Carb heaven for the sweet toothed. In this locally adored cafe cocoa, milk, nuts, fruit and other delicious morsels find their destiny in chocolates, cakes, biscuits, ice cream, pies and crêpes. A fun place to take a coffee break by the sea and watch the world on parade.

Ntoukiani BAR

(☎6939072810; Ethnikis Antistaseos 19; ⌚9pm-late; 📶) This tiny bar with petrol walls, flea-market finds and complexion-friendly lighting from basket lamps is a great backdrop for getting lost in conversation over expert cocktails until the wee hours. Boho flair, local crowd, best on cold nights.

Island Cafe CAFE

(☎28420 23615; www.facebook.com/islandcafebar; Stratigou Samouil 6; ⌚8am-late) With its mint-blue-and-white interior, modern tunes, and mixed crowd of young students and old boys flicking worry beads, this cafe-bar is a

WORTH A TRIP

CHRISSI ISLAND

Ierapetra is the launch pad for boat trips to uninhabited **Chrissi Island** (☎28420 20008; boat trip adult/child €25/12; ⌚mid-May–Oct) – also known as Gaïdouronisi or Hrysi Island –. It is famous for its golden beaches, clear water shimmering in myriad shades of blue, cedar forest, traces of Minoan ruins, and Belegrina, a beach covered with a mountain of shells. There are usually a couple of morning boat departures that give you 4½ hours on the island. Tickets are sold online and by agents around town. Bring a picnic or buy refreshments on board. One company that will take you there is **Cretan Daily Cruises** (☎28420 20008, www.cretandailycruises.com boat trip adult/child €25/12, mid-May–Oct); its vessels carry 200-400 passengers.

Travel to Chrissi Island in style – and arrive before the bigger boats – aboard **Nautilos Cruises'** (☎6972894279; www.nautiloscruises.com; cruises from €27.50; ⌚May-Oct) fancy motor yacht that will whisk you and up to 16 others there in about 30 minutes. It also runs semi-private tours that include lunch and an additional stop in a secluded bay (€65 per person) as well as customised private charters (€950).

good spot no matter where the hands are on the clock. In season it practically never closes.

Information

MONEY

There are ATMs throughout the town centre, including in Plateia Kanoupaki and along Koraka and Kothri.

POST

Post Office (Koraka 25; 8am-2pm Mon-Fri)

TRAVEL AGENCIES

Travel agencies near the harbour sell tickets for day trips to Chrissi Island and other excursions.

Getting There & Away

KTEL operates eight buses per day from **Ierapetra bus station** (28420 28237; www.ktelherlas.gr; Lasthenous 28) to Iraklio (€12, 2½ hours) via Agios Nikolaos (€4.10, one hour), four to Sitia (€6.90, 1½ hours) and five to Myrtos (€2.40, 30 minutes).

The **central taxi stand** (28420 26600; cnr Kothri & Plateia Kanoupaki) with fixed fares posted on a board is outside the town hall. Sample fares: Iraklio €128, Agios Nikolaos €50, Sitia €83 and Myrtos €20.

East of Ierapetra

Much of the coastline east and west of Ierapetra sits enveloped by plastic-covered greenhouses and haphazard tourism development, but there are still appealing places. Only 7km east of Ierapetra, **Koutsounari Beach** is one of the longest in Crete (4.5km) and ideal for walking and escaping the crowds. Keep going for another 8km or so for a dip at lovely **Agia Fotia Beach**. Around 10km further on, a new stretch of road bypasses **Koutsouras**, but turn off the main road for **Taverna Robinson** (28430 51026; www.robinsontaverna.gr; Koutsouras; dishes €5-10; noon-midnight;), housed in an attractively renovated Venetian-style building. The pink interior is hung with an installation of light bulbs, while the menu features innovative dishes and the owners' own organic wine.

Just beyond, the fine white sandy beach at the eastern end of **Makrygialos** is one of the best on the southeastern coast. It gets very busy in summer, but the beachside promenade is cheerful and there are plenty of cafes and eating places.

Near Makrygialos, just above Analipsi on the road to Pefki, is **Aspros Potamos** (28430 51694; www.asprospotamos.com; apt €50-100) . Here 300-year-old stone cottages have been lovingly restored as guesthouses by owner Aleka Halkia. Potamos uses a solar system to generate electricity for lights and hot water. Rooms have no electrical sockets, but you can plug in (and access the internet) in the reception area. Stone floors, traditional furnishings and winter fireplaces add to the warm ambience. It's the perfect spot for nature buffs and walkers, since you're close to the **Pefki Gorge** – a particularly appealing two-hour hike.

Sleeping & Eating

Koutsounari Camping CAMPGROUND €
(28420 61213; www.camping-koutsounari.gr; Koutsounari; campsites adult/child/tent from €6.50/3/4.50, cabins/studios from €22/32; May-Oct;) About 8km east of Ierapetra at Koutsounari, beachfront Koutsounari Camping counts a pool with snack bar, a restaurant and a mini-market among its assets. As well as pitches there are simple wooden cabins (bring your own linen or sleeping bag) and studios. Ierapetra–Sitia buses pass the site.

Myrtos Μύρτος

POP 600

Tiny Myrtos, 14km west of Ierapetra, is a positively delightful lived-in community: cheerful, trim and fringed by an apron of grey pebble-and-sand beach and bright-blue water. It's also an excellent base for mountain and canyon hikes and even has a couple of minor Minoan sites. All these assets attract a devoted clientele that also cherishes its slow boho pulse, flower-festooned guesthouses, and cluster of tavernas in the village and along its languid seafront. In short, it's a traveller's jewel, the perfect antidote to noise, haste and mass tourism.

Sights & Activities

Myrtos Museum MUSEUM
(28420 51065) FREE Next to the church, this small museum houses the private collection of a late teacher who sparked the area's archaeological digs after stumbling upon Minoan artefacts on field trips with students. The collection includes Vasiliki pottery from the nearby Minoan sites of **Fournou-Korifi**

and **Pyrgos**, as well as an impressive scale model of the Fournou-Korifi site, painstakingly assembled by museum director John Atkinson.

Paradise Scuba Diving Centre DIVING
(☎28420 51554; https://scuba.paradisemirtos.com; dives from €75, open-water course €500; ⏰10am-8pm) Run by Nikos, Paradise is right on the waterfront. It can take you cave and wreck diving and offers PADI certification courses. It also does boat and speedboat rentals and can arrange private charters with crew.

Sleeping

Staying in Myrtos means unpacking your suitcase in small hotels, studios or apartments, most of them run by local families with plenty of personal care and attention.

★**Big Blue** APARTMENT €€
(☎28420 51094; www.big-blue.gr; studios €56-98; ❄📶) Modern amenities meet traditional Greece in these breezy sea-facing and self-catering studios decorated with plenty of style and imagination. Apartment 'Blue Eye', for instance, has a neat display of evil eyes (for good luck); in fact, every room is different. Private decks have expansive views, and the fragrant front garden is a good spot for sundowners.

It's on the western side of the village, past the church.

Villa Mertiza APARTMENT €€
(☎28420 51208, 6932735224; www.mertiza.com; studios/apt from €53/74; ⏰Apr-Oct; ❄📶) Dutch owned, these boho-chic and good-size studios and apartments with kitchenettes and box-spring beds are an excellent launch pad for days on the beach or in the mountains. Swap experiences with fellow travellers in the lush garden or pick up new mind candy at the book exchange.

It's on the main street about 250m inland.

Eating

Myrtos has some excellent tavernas, both along the beach and dotted around the village.

Taverna Myrtos CRETAN €
(mains €7-12; ⏰6.30am-midnight; 📶🖉) Attached to the Myrtos Hotel, this high-ceilinged main-street joint offers excellent homemade food: souvlaki, *mousaka*, red mullet and pork chops. It's unpretentiously old school and popular with locals. In high season the cheerfully decorated terrace is the place to be.

La Sera MEDITERRANEAN €€
(☎28420 51261; mains €8-16; ⏰5pm-midnight Apr-Oct; 📶) Soft lighting, fine wine and delicious food are the hallmarks of a romantic night out in this al fresco–only lair wedged into an alley off the main drag. The compact menu includes farm-fresh salads, grilled seafood, and tender lamb chops from the local butcher, alongside wine from the renowned Lyrarakis winery (p186) in Alagni.

Thalassa Taverna SEAFOOD €€
(☎28420 51301; www.facebook.com/tavernathalassa; mains €8-16; ⏰9am-midnight Apr-Oct; ❄📶) This powder-blue, hole-in-the-wall waterfront restaurant has an interior festooned with coral and shells, and a few tables outside for tucking into mussels, calamari, cuttlefish, shrimp, octopus... There's enough seafood to keep a shoal of mermaids quiet.

O Platanos CRETAN €€
(mains €7-13.50; ⏰11am-late Apr-Oct; 📶🖉) Beneath a giant plane tree on the main street, Platanos is a focus of village social life and has live music on many summer evenings. Feast on reliable Cretan staples such as rabbit *stifadho*, or try such homey specials as the 'pita pizza' or grandma's meatballs with yoghurt sauce.

Information

MONEY

There's an ATM next to the Myrtos Hotel, but it's only in operation from April to October. The next nearest one is in Ierapetra.

TRAVEL AGENCY

Prima Tours (☎28420 51530, 28420 51035; www.sunbudget.net) Local agency can help with finding rooms, renting a car or any other travel-related needs. It's off the main street, near the Myrtos Hotel.

Getting There & Away

There are five buses daily from Ierapetra (€2.40, 30 minutes). A taxi costs about €20.

Understand Crete

History

Crete's colourful history goes back 5000 years and is evident across the island, from ancient palaces and Roman cities to spectacular Byzantine churches, Venetian fortresses and Ottoman buildings. Crete's prominent place in world history dates back to the illustrious Minoans, who were lording over lavish palaces at a time when other Europeans were huddled in primitive huts. Ever since, Crete's strategic location in the middle of the Mediterranean has involved it in a parade of momentous world events.

Myth & the Minoans

Crete's early history is largely shrouded in myth, making it all the more fascinating. It is clear from both legends and physical remains, however, that it was home to Europe's first advanced civilisation: the Minoans.

This enigmatic culture emerged in the Bronze Age, predating the great Mycenaean civilisation on the Greek mainland. Minoan society interacted with, and was inspired by, two great Middle Eastern civilisations: the Mesopotamians and Egyptians. Immigrants arriving from Anatolia around 3000 BC brought with them the skills necessary for making bronze, a technological quantum leap that enabled the emerging Minoans to flourish almost uninterrupted for over one-and-a-half millennia.

While many aspects of the less-attested Neolithic life endured during the Early Minoan period, the advent of bronze allowed the Minoans to build better boats and thus expand their trade in the Near East. Pottery and goldsmithing became more sophisticated, foreshadowing the subsequent great achievements of Minoan art, and the island prospered from trade.

The chronology of the Minoan age is debated. But most archaeologists generally split the Minoan period into three phases: Protopalatial (3400–2100 BC), Neopalatial (2100–1450 BC) and Postpalatial (1450–1200 BC). These periods roughly correspond, with some overlap, to the older divisions of Early Minoan (some parts also called Prepalatial), Middle Minoan and Late Minoan; the terms are used interchangeably throughout.

The Minoan civilisation reached its peak during the Protopalatial period, also called the Old Palace or Middle Minoan period. Around 2000 BC,

TIMELINE

6500 BC

Crete's earliest-known inhabitants are hunter-gathers. Neolithic people live in caves or wooden houses, worship female fertility goddesses, farm, raise livestock and make primitive pottery.

3000 BC

Bronze-making North African or Levantine immigrants arrive, and the Bronze Age begins. Society changes, with these early Cretans beginning to trade. Pottery and jewellery making develops.

2000 BC

Minoan civilisation reaches its peak: architectural advances lead to the first palaces in Knossos, Phaestos, Malia and Zakros, while pottery making improves and Crete's first script emerges.

the large palace complexes of Knossos, Phaestos, Malia and Zakros were built, marking a sharp break with Neolithic village life.

During this period, Crete was probably governed by local rulers, with power and wealth concentrated at Knossos. Society was organised along hierarchical lines, with a large population of slaves, and great architectural advances were made. The first Cretan script also emerged during this period. At first highly pictorial, the writing gradually changed from the representations of natural objects to more abstract figures that resembled Egyptian hieroglyphics.

In 1700 BC the palaces were suddenly destroyed by what most archaeologists believe was an earthquake. But soon after came the Minoan golden age, and the rebuilding of the palaces at Knossos, Phaestos, Malia and Zakros; their new and more complex design was remarkably advanced. There were multiple storeys, sumptuous royal apartments, grand reception halls, storerooms, workshops, living quarters for staff, and an advanced drainage system. The design later gave rise to the myth of the Cretan labyrinth and the Minotaur.

During the Neopalatial period, the Minoan state developed into a powerful *thalassocracy* (state known for prosperous maritime trade), purportedly ruled by King Minos, with the capital at Knossos. Trade with the eastern Mediterranean, Asia Minor and Egypt boomed, helped by Minoan colonies in the Aegean. Minoan pottery, textiles and agricultural produce such as olive oil and livestock subsequently found ready markets throughout the Aegean, Egypt, Syria and possibly Sicily.

Minoan civilisation came to an abrupt and mysterious halt around 1450 BC after the palaces (except for Knossos) and numerous smaller settlements were smashed to bits. Scientific evidence suggests the Minoans were weakened by a massive tsunami and ash fallout from a cataclysmic volcano that erupted on nearby Santorini. But there is much debate about both the timing and explanation for the ultimate demise

Minoan civilisation may have been destroyed by a tsunami. Minoan artefacts mixed with pebbles, shells and marine life have been found at sites 7m above sea level, and dated to 1450 BC, when Santorini's volcano erupted, sending a 23m-high wave spanning 15km into Crete's northern coast.

CRETE'S FIRST SEAFARERS

During excavations carried out in 2008 and 2009 near Plakias and Preveli, archaeologists were astonished to discover chiselled stone tools dating back at least 130,000 years. The tools were the first evidence that humankind had engaged in sea travel so long ago. (The earliest known sea voyage previous to the Crete finds was a mere 60,000 years ago.)

The idea that the first Cretans arrived by boat much earlier than anyone had ever thought has revolutionary implications for the entire anthropological conventional wisdom, which had it that the first humans migrated to Europe from Africa by land alone. Since experts believe the Cretan tools may in fact date back up to 700,000 years, it's clear that there are more revelations ahead. The digging continues.

1700 BC

The Minoan palaces are destroyed, probably by an earthquake. However, they are rebuilt bigger and better, with multiple storeys, storerooms, workshops, living quarters and advanced drainage systems.

1450 BC

Minoan culture comes to an abrupt and unexplained halt. The palaces (except Knossos) are destroyed by what some archaeologists believe was a massive tsunami following a volcanic eruption on Santorini.

1400 BC

The Mycenaeans colonise Crete. Weapons manufacture flourishes; fine arts fall into decline. Greek gods replace worship of the Mother Goddess.

1100 BC

The Dorians overrun the Mycenaean cities and become Crete's new masters; they reorganise the political system. A rudimentary democracy replaces monarchical government.

Ladies in Blue fresco, Palace of Knossos (p178)

of the Minoans. Some argue it was caused by a second, powerful earthquake a century later. Other archaeologists blame the invading Mycenaeans. Whether the Mycenaeans caused the fall or merely profited from a separate catastrophe, it is clear that their presence on the island closely coincided with the destruction of the palaces and Minoan civilisation.

The Rise & Fall of the Mycenaeans

The Mycenaean civilisation, which reached its peak between 1500 and 1200 BC, was the first great civilisation on the Greek mainland. Named after the ancient city of Mycenae, it is also known as the Achaean civilisation after the Indo-European branch of migrants who had settled on mainland Greece.

Unlike Minoan society, where the lack of city walls seems to indicate relative peace under some form of central authority, Mycenaean civilisa-

431–386 BC

While Greece is embroiled in the Peloponnesian War, Crete also sees internal strife: Knossos against Lyttos, Phaestos against Gortyna, Kydonia against Apollonia, and Itanos against Ierapitna.

67 BC

The Romans finally conquer Crete after invading two years earlier at Kydonia. Gortyna becomes the capital and most powerful city. The Pax Romana ends internal wars.

27 BC

Crete is united with eastern Libya to form the Roman province of Creta et Cyrenaica, reorganising population centres and ushering in a new era of prosperity.

AD 63

Christianity emerges after St Paul visits Crete and leaves his disciple, Titus, to convert the island. St Titus becomes Crete's first bishop.

tion was characterised by independent city-states, the most powerful of them all being Mycenae, ruled by kings who inhabited palaces enclosed within massive walls on easily defensible hill tops.

The Mycenaeans wrote in Linear B script. Clay tablets inscribed with the script found at the Palace of Knossos are evidence of Mycenaean occupation of the island. Their colonisation of Crete lasted from 1400 to 1100 BC. Knossos probably retained its position as capital of the island, but its rulers were subject to the mainland Mycenaeans. The Minoan Cretans either left the island or hid in its interior while the Mycenaeans founded new cities such as Lappa (Argyroupoli).

The economy of the island stayed more or less the same, still based upon the export of local products, but the fine arts fell into decline. Only the manufacture of weapons flourished, reflecting the new militaristic spirit that the Mycenaeans brought to Crete. The Mycenaeans also replaced worship of the Mother Goddess with new Greek gods such as Zeus, Hera and Athena.

Mycenaean influence stretched far and wide, but was eventually weakened by internal strife; they were no match for the warlike Dorians.

Classical Crete

Despite fierce resistance, Dorians conquered Crete around 1100 BC, and many inhabitants fled to Asia Minor. Those who remained, known as Eteo-Cretans or 'true Cretans', retreated to the hills and thus preserved their culture.

The Dorians heralded a traumatic break with the past. The next 400 years are often referred to as Greece's 'dark age', though they brought iron with them and developed a new style of pottery, decorated with striking geometrical designs. The Dorians worshipped male gods instead of fertility goddesses and adopted the Mycenaean gods of Poseidon, Zeus and Apollo, paving the way for the later Greek religious pantheon.

The Dorians reorganised Crete's political system and divided society into three classes: free citizens who owned property and enjoyed political liberty (including land-owning peasants); merchants and seamen; and slaves. The monarchical system was replaced by a rudimentary democracy. Free citizens elected a ruling committee that was guided by a council of elders and answered to an assembly of free citizens. Unlike in Minoan times, women were subordinate.

By about 800 BC, local agriculture and animal husbandry had become sufficiently productive to trigger renewed maritime trading. As new Greek colonies were established throughout the Mediterranean basin, Crete took on a prominent role in regional trade.

Greece's various city-states started to become more unified by the development of a Greek alphabet, the verses of Homer and the founding

Crete occupies a prominent spot in Ancient Greek mythology. It's where Rhea gave birth to Zeus and hid him from his child-gobbling father, and where Zeus' own son, Minos, had his legendary reign. Icarus and Daedalus launched their ill-fated flight here, and Theseus slayed the Minotaur in the famous labyrinth.

250

The first Christian martyrs, the so-called Agii Deka (Ten Saints) are killed in the village of the same name, as Roman officials begin major Christian persecutions.

395

The Roman Empire splits and Crete is ruled by Byzantium. Crete becomes a self-governing province; Gortyna is its administrative and religious centre. Trade flourishes; many churches are built.

824

Arab Saracens conquer Crete and establish a fortress called Chandax in Iraklio to store their pirated treasure. The island sinks into a century-and-a-half gloom and cultural life dwindles.

960

Byzantine General Nikiforos Fokas launches the Expedition to Crete, liberating the island. Coastal defences are fortified, and Chandax becomes capital and archdiocese seat.

of the Olympic Games. The establishment of central sanctuaries, such as Delphi, began to give Cretans a sense of national identity as Greeks.

Rethymno, Polyrrinia, Falasarna, Gortyna and Lato were built according to the new defensive style of Dorian city-states, with a fortified acropolis at the highest point, above an *agora* (market), the bustling commercial quarter, and beyond that residential areas.

As the rest of Greece entered its golden age from the 6th to 4th centuries BC, Crete remained a backwater. Constant warfare between large commercial centres and smaller traditional communities left the island increasingly impoverished. Although Crete did not participate in the Persian Wars or the Peloponnesian Wars, economic circumstances forced many Cretans to sign up as mercenaries in foreign armies or turn to piracy.

During this time, Crete's role as the birthplace of Greek culture drew the attention of philosophers such as Plato and Aristotle, who wrote extensively about Crete's political institutions. Knossos, Gortyna, Lyttos and Kydonia (Hania) continued to vie for supremacy, causing ongoing turmoil. Egypt, Rhodes and Sparta got involved in the Cretan squabbles and piracy flourished.

The 6th century BC *Laws of Gortyna*, discovered in the late 19th century AD at Gortyna, reveals the societal structure of Dorian Crete. Inscribed on 12 large stone tablets, the laws cover civil and criminal matters, with clear distinctions drawn among the classes of free citizens and between citizens and slaves.

The Roman Empire

In order to turn the Mediterranean into a 'Roman lake', the Roman Empire needed to curtail piracy and control shipping routes. As the most strategic island in the central Mediterranean, Crete had been on Rome's to-do list since the 3rd century BC. But it wasn't until the third Mithridatic War (73–63 BC) that it was able to intervene, playing the piracy card. When Mark Antony's father, Marcus Antonius, unsuccessfully attacked, the Cretans sent envoys to Rome, but were rebuffed. An army of 26,000 men was hastily established to defend the island. Roman consul Metellus launched the decisive invasion in 69 BC near Kydonia (Hania), and within two years had taken Crete, despite valiant local resistance.

Roman rule and reorganisation brought a new era of peace to Crete, and land and towns were given as favours to various Roman allies. In 27 BC, Crete was united with eastern Libya to form the Roman province of Creta et Cyrenaica. By this time, the Romans had spent decades building up their new possession, with Gortyna becoming the capital and most powerful city under Roman rule (c 67 BC). Roman amphitheatres, temples and public baths livened things up, and the population increased. Knossos fell into disuse, but Kydonia (Hania) in the west became an important centre. Roman towns were linked by roads, bridges and aqueducts, parts of which are still visible in places. Under the Romans, the Cretans continued to worship Zeus in the Dikteon and Ideon Caves, and also incorporated Roman and Egyptian deities into their rituals.

1204

After Crusaders sack Constantinople, Boniface of Montferrat sells Crete to Venice. Venice rapidly colonises Crete, importing settlers and building towns and defences in Rethymno, Hania, Iraklio and elsewhere.

1363

Venice quells a joint uprising by Crete's Venetian leaders and Greeks in the Revolt of St Titus, though fighting continues for several years against Greek nobles like the Kallergis clan.

1453

Constantinople falls to the Turks. Byzantine scholars and intellectuals flee to Crete, sparking a renaissance of Byzantine art. The Cretan School of icon painting emerges.

1541

Domenikos Theotokopoulos, later known as El Greco, is born in Candia; his subsequent creations in Italy and Spain are marked by both Cretan School influence and bold personal innovation.

Christianity Comes to Crete

In AD 63, Christianity was brought to Crete by St Paul himself. His disciple, St Titus (who died in AD 107 at the age of 94), remained to convert the island and became its first bishop. Although the early years of Cretan Christianity seem to have been quiet, the 3rd century brought large-scale persecution, as elsewhere in the Roman Empire. The first Christian martyrs, the so-called Agii Deka (Ten Saints), were killed in the eponymous village in 250.

In 324, Emperor Constantine I (also known as Constantine the Great), a Christian convert, transferred the capital of the empire from Rome to Byzantium, which was renamed Constantinople (now İstanbul). By the end of the 4th century, the Roman Empire was formally divided into western and eastern sections; Crete, along with the rest of Greece, was in the eastern half, also known as the Byzantine Empire.

Although the doctrinal differences that would later separate Catholicism from Orthodox Christianity were centuries from realisation, the division of the empire geographically also expedited divergences in practice, custom and allegiances that would come to define the Orthodox Church, presided over by the patriarch in Constantinople.

In the early Byzantine Empire, Crete was a self-governing province, with Gortyna as its administrative and religious centre. Piracy decreased and trade flourished, leaving the island wealthy enough to build many churches.

Crete's attachment to the worship of icons provoked a revolt in 727 when Emperor Leo III banned their worship as part of the iconoclastic movement, which broke out in different periods of the 8th and 9th centuries and had complex theological, economic and political roots, but was partly influenced by questions provoked by the rise of Islam. The uprising was smashed and the Byzantine emperor unleashed a fierce wave of retribution against Crete's iconophiles. However, the policy became officially overturned for good by decree of Empress Theodora in 843, an event still celebrated as the 'Triumph of Orthodoxy' on the first Sunday of Lent.

At Gortyna, the remnants of the 6th century AD Basilica of Agios Titus attest to this disciple of St Paul. St Titus' relics, recovered in 1966 from Venice, where they had been taken for safekeeping during the Ottoman period, are today found in the cathedral named after him in Iraklio.

Between Pirates & the Pope

The peaceful period of Byzantine rule came to an end around 824 with the arrival of Arabs from Spain, who gradually conquered Crete and used it as a base for raids around the Aegean. The Arabs established a fortress called Chandax in what is now Iraklio, essentially to store their seized treasure. As the island's criminal reputation grew, its economy dwindled and its cultural life ground to a halt. There are few records for this period, considered Crete's 'dark age'. While some of the population seems to

1587

Vitsentzos Kornaros of Sitia writes the 'Erotokritos', a voluminous verse epic that becomes Crete's greatest literary achievement – and remains one of the most important works of all Greek literature.

1645

A huge Turkish force lands in Hania, establishing the Turks' first foothold on the island. After Rethymno is defeated, they secure the western part of the island.

1669

Iraklio (Candia) finally falls to the Turks, 24 years after the capture of the rest of the island. Ottoman rule sees construction of mosques and heavy taxation of Christians.

1770

Under Ioannis Daskalogiannis, 2000 Sfakiots revolt in Sfakia, but are defeated. Daskalogiannis is skinned alive in Iraklio.

have been forcibly converted to Islam, these switches of faith would not outlive the occupation.

Byzantine armies sought to rescue Crete several times, in 842 and again in 911 and 949, but were not successful until Nikiforos Fokas launched the legendary Expedition to Crete in 960. After a bitter siege of Chandax, Crete was liberated in 961, and the Byzantines quickly started fortifying the Cretan coast and consolidating their power. Chandax emerged as the new capital of the theme (a Byzantine term for province) of Crete, and was the seat of the restored Cretan archdiocese. The church undertook efforts to bring errant sheep back to the Christian flock.

The following two-and-a-half centuries were relatively peaceful, save for a short-lived revolt by the governor, Karykes, in 1092. A few years later it was brought, with southern Greece and the Peloponnese, under the control of the Byzantine navy's main commander.

This happy existence was shattered by the infamous Fourth Crusade of 1204, which saw Venetian-bankrolled Western crusaders opt to attack

REBELLION & A SHORT-LIVED REPUBLIC

Some interesting twists in Crete's many revolts against the Venetian government indicate a complex and interesting reality. One example is the August 1363 Revolt of St Titus, which saw oppressed Cretans join forces with Venetian settlers exasperated at a new tax. Despite attempts at an amicable settlement, top officials proved deaf and the call to arms was raised. Aside from the commercial grievances that motivated rebels, the events showed that after only a couple of generations living in Crete, the settlers seemed to view their Greek neighbours as fellow countrymen (rather than those in far-off Venice).

The rebellion quickly resulted in the overthrow of the local government and the pronunciation of equality for Greeks and Orthodoxy. The island's patron saint, Titus, became the official emblem for this, the new 'Commune of Crete'. Venetian diplomats dissuaded other great powers, particularly the Genoese, from aiding the rebels, though, and by spring 1364 a Venetian military force had retaken Candia. After the leaders of the uprising were executed, the Venetian overlords celebrated. But it was not the end by any means.

Indeed, most fighters had already escaped into Crete's rugged mountains, where Greek noble families such as the Kallergis clan in the west sought to overthrow Latin rule completely, and reunite with Byzantium. This was all too much for the Venetian doge, who convinced the Pope to declare a crusade against the Kallergis. But all of western Crete joined the rebellion, under the banner of a battle for the salvation of Orthodoxy, and it would take the Venetians almost five years to restore order.

Although Venice kept ultimate control, these rebellions were not in vain, as they forced the colonisers to make concessions. And so, by the 15th century, Cretans of both Greek and Italian background had made a sort of truce – one that allowed a remarkable and unique cultural flowering that would help shape the Italian Renaissance.

1821

The Greek War of Independence is declared. The insurgency spreads to Crete but Turkish-Egyptian forces outnumber the rebellion. Continued resistance provokes massacres of Cretans.

1828

In one of the bloodiest battles in the War of Independence, 385 rebels make a heroic last stand at Frangokastello. About 800 Turks are killed along with the rebels.

1830–40

Crete is given to Egypt. The Turks defeat Egypt in Syria and reclaim Crete. Repeated violations spark more uprisings and demands for union with Greece.

1866

About 2000 Turkish soldiers attack Moni Arkadiou, where over 900 rebels and their families shelter. Refusing to surrender, the Cretans light a store of gunpowder, killing all but one.

Christian Constantinople rather than the 'infidels' down in Egypt. While Crete was originally granted to Crusade leader Boniface of Montferrat, he soon sold it to the Venetians. However, the latter's Genoese arch-rivals seized it first, and it took until 1212 for Venice to establish control. Their colonial rule would last until 1669. Today, Venice's former influence is evident throughout Crete's major towns, in former mansions and massive fortresses that guarded the port towns and harbours.

Venice colonised Crete with noble and military families, many of whom settled in Iraklio (Candia). About 10,000 settlers came during the 13th century alone, to be rewarded with the island's best and most fertile land. Formerly landowners, the Cretans now worked as serfs for their Venetian masters. Cretan peasants were ruthlessly exploited, and taxes were oppressive. Further, the all-powerful influence of the papacy meant that Venetian rulers sought to impose Catholicism over Orthodoxy. Unsurprisingly, revolts were frequent.

Sophistication & Spirit

Over time, the wealth and stability that the Venetian empire could provide for Crete would pay cultural dividends; an environment developed in which the cosmopolitan ideas and goods that came with a maritime trade power combined with local creative talent and tradition. While Western Europe, the Balkans and Byzantium were being decimated by civil wars, dynastic disputes and Islamic invasions, Crete was usually a tranquil isle in the sun (despite occasional revolts) where thinkers could take refuge and where first-rate educations were available, generally through the Church. Venetian Crete was also known for its intellectual centres, such as the Accademia degli Stravaganti in Candia (Iraklio), where rhetoricians sparred and philosophers pored over ancient texts.

This cultural flowering was greatly expedited by two factors: the renewed Western curiosity about ancient Greek and Latin thought, and the fall of Constantinople in 1453. After the capture of Trebizond, and of Mystras in the Peloponnese a few years later, Crete became the last major remaining bastion of Hellenism, and Byzantine scholars and intellectuals relocated to the island. They brought their manuscripts, icons and experience, and established schools, libraries and printing presses.

The cross-pollination between Byzantine traditions and the flourishing Italian Renaissance is particularly famous for its Cretan School of icon painting, which became most highly developed in the 16th and 17th centuries, combining Byzantine and Venetian elements. Already, from the 13th to the early 16th centuries, churches around Crete had been adorned with frescoes – many of which can still be seen today. The 14th century's greatest icon painter was Ioannis Pagomenos, while the world's best-known such artist is Domenikos Theotokopoulos (1541–1614), who

Cretan author Nikos Psilakis' 1998 book *Byzantine Churches and Monasteries of Crete* is a very useful and well-illustrated portable guide to hundreds of Crete's spiritual sites.

1877–78

The Russo-Turkish War prompts another Cretan uprising but, despite gains, the Treaty of Berlin rejects union with Greece. Crete becomes a semi-autonomous, discontented Ottoman province.

1883

Greece's most famous writer, Nikos Kazantzakis, is born in Iraklio. He becomes famous for works like *Zorba the Greek* and *The Last Temptation of Christ* in the mid-20th century.

1898

Turks slaughter hundreds of Christian civilians, 17 British soldiers and the British consul in Iraklio. Britain orders the Turks out; Crete is placed under international administration, with Hania as capital.

1900

Arthur Evans begins excavations at Knossos, quickly unearthing the palace and stunning the archaeological world with the discovery of the advanced Minoan civilisation.

studied in Italy before moving to Spain, where he became known as El Greco (The Greek).

At the same time, Crete enjoyed a tremendous literary flowering, in which the traditional Cretan folk verse style influenced – and was influenced by – poetic and musical trends popular in France, Italy and Constantinople. Indeed, the island's literary masterpiece, the epic 'Erotokritos', was penned in Greek by the Venetian-descended Vitsentzos Kornaros of Sitia in the late 16th century. A vernacular epic of more than 10,000 lines, it has a verse structure based on *mantinadhes* (traditional Cretan rhyming couplets), but its subjects of courtly love and bravery resemble 15th-century French predecessors, themselves influenced by earlier Byzantine Greek epics.

Venetian Vintage

- ➡ Harbour fortresses, Iraklio, Rethymno and Hania
- ➡ Morosini Fountain, Iraklio
- ➡ Spinalonga Island
- ➡ Moni Arkadiou

Resistance & the Tourkokratia

By the 17th century, the expanding Ottoman Empire was finally able to take on Venice on the high seas, with Cyprus and Crete the two most strategic Venetian possessions sought by the sultans. Following a two-month Turkish siege, Hania fell to the Turks in 1645, followed soon by Rethymno. However, Candia's massive walls kept the besieging Ottomans out until 1669. Only the fortresses of Gramvousa, Spinalonga and Souda remained in Venetian hands, the latter two until 1715. Thus began the *Tourkokratia* (Turkish rule).

Cretans who managed to escape the Turks took to the mountains, where they could enjoy freedom and attack the Turks, especially in the rugged southwestern Sfakia region. In 1770, Sfakiot leader Ioannis Daskalogiannis led 2000 fighters into battle, after Russia promised assistance. However, help never came, and the Turks publicly skinned Daskalogiannis alive in Iraklio.

The 1821 Greek War of Independence fuelled another fruitless uprising, and the Ottomans massacred Cretan civilians and priests, who they identified as ideological agitators behind Greek nationalism. Nevertheless, the Cretan resistance, combined with the Peloponnesian and mainland Greek insurrections, forced the sultan to ask Egypt's rulers to attack the Christians, which they did with gusto, massacring many thousands across the Aegean. Crete's rebels fought furiously, but lost to the numerically superior Turkish-Egyptian forces.

In 1830 Greece became independent, but Crete was given to Egypt. The Turks and the Egyptians then went to war in Syria, and the Egyptians were defeated, so in 1840 Crete reverted to Ottoman rule. Meanwhile, *Enosis i Thanatos* (Union or Death) became a slogan for continuing rebellions in western Crete.

The Turks and Egyptians brought more massacres to the Cretans, whose struggle attained international notoriety in 1866 when 900 res-

1905

A revolutionary assembly in Theriso declares unity with Greece. Eleftherios Venizelos sets up a rival government to administer the island. The Great Powers appoint a new governor of Crete.

1908

The Cretan assembly declares unity with Greece, but Cretan deputies are not allowed to sit in the Greek parliament until 1912.

1913

Turkey, angered by the Cretan assembly's declaration of unity, seeks revenge but is defeated in the Balkan Wars by Greece, Bulgaria, Serbia and Montenegro. The postwar Bucharest Treaty officially unites Greece with Crete.

1921

The Greek–Turkish population exchange sees 30,000 Cretan Muslims replaced by Anatolian Greeks. Ottoman structures languish.

olute rebels and their families holed up in Moni Arkadiou ignited their entire gunpowder stock, killing themselves and 2000 besieging Turkish soldiers. The event shocked the world, fuelling sympathy for the heroic Cretans. Yet Great Britain and France maintained a pro-Turkish stance, and prevented Greece from aiding the Cretan rebels.

Freedom & Union

Even the Great Powers (France, Britain, Italy, Austria-Hungary, and Russia) could not stop the wave of revolutionary nationalism sweeping southeastern Europe. The 1877 Russo-Turkish War, which liberated Bulgaria and almost toppled the Ottoman government, encouraged both Cretan rebels and the Greek government. Despite significant gains by the Cretan rebels, the controversial Treaty of Berlin in 1878 rejected the idea of *enosis* (unification); instead, Crete gained semi-autonomous status, with Greek becoming the official language, though the island was still under Turkish rule.

Following parliamentary infighting in 1889 another rebellion against Turkish rule prompted another Turkish crackdown. In Sfakia, Manousos Koundouros' secret fraternity, which sought to secure autonomy and eventual unification, besieged the Turkish garrison at Vamos, leading to violent reprisals and eventual intervention by the Great Powers, who forced a new constitution on the Ottomans.

When violence erupted again in 1896, the Greek government sent troops, declaring unification with Crete. However, the Great Powers blockaded the coast, preventing both Turks and Greeks from reinforcing their positions, and Greece withdrew. The unpopular Prince George, son of King George of Greece, was appointed as high commissioner of Crete by the Great Powers.

Violent outrage soon accomplished what decades of high international diplomacy hadn't: the expulsion of the Turks. In 1898 a group of Turks stormed through Iraklio slaughtering hundreds of Christian civilians – along with 17 British soldiers and the British consul. The main leaders were found and hanged, and a British squadron of ships arrived. Ottoman rule over Crete was finally over.

The charismatic Eleftherios Venizelos, a young politician from Hania and Prince George's minister of justice, broke with the regent, who refused to consider *enosis*. Venizelos convened a revolutionary assembly in the village of Theriso near Hania, in 1905, raising the Greek flag and declaring unity with Greece.

Venizelos' upstart government was given teeth by armed support from local Cretans. The Great Powers asked King George to appoint a new governor. In 1908 the Cretan assembly declared unity with Greece, but even with Venizelos now prime minister, the Greek government refused to

Iraklio's Museum of Christian Art has an important collection of icons from artists including the great Michael Damaskinos, who introduced a distinctive painting style to Cretan art in the 16th century.

1939

The first aeroplane, a Junkers 52 carrying 14 passengers, lands at what is today's Nikos Kazantzakis Heraklion International Airport in Iraklio. Commercial flights start operating in 1948.

1941

Germany invades Greece. Allied troops arrive to defend Crete. Germany launches an airborne invasion to capture the airport at Maleme, in the famous Battle of Crete. Allied soldiers are evacuated from Hora Sfakion.

1944

The Cretan Resistance kidnaps German commander General Kreipe and, aided by the Allies, sends him to Egypt, sparking fierce German reprisals. Cities are bombed, villages annihilated and civilians shot.

1946–49

Greek civil war breaks out between communists and right-wing royalists. Crete is largely spared the bloodshed and bitterness that engulfs Greece.

allow Cretan deputies into parliament, fearing it would antagonise both Turkey and the Great Powers. Not until the First Balkan War (1912) did Cretans finally enter parliament in Athens. The 1913 Treaty of Bucharest formally recognised Crete as part of the Greek state.

After the disastrous Greek invasion of Smyrna, the 1923 Treaty of Lausanne mandated a population exchange between Greece and Turkey. Crete's Muslim population of 30,000 people was swapped for incoming Greek refugees from Anatolia.

WWII & the Battle of Crete

As in innumerable conflicts of yore, Crete's strategic geographical position made it highly enticing to foreign invaders in WWII. Hitler sought to dominate the Mediterranean and have a base from which to challenge British Egypt and forces in the eastern Mediterranean. On 6 April 1941, mainland Greece was rapidly overrun from the north, as the Royalist Yugoslav government was defeated, and Greek leader Emmanouil Tsouderos (1882–1956) set up a government in exile in his native Crete.

With all available Greek troops fighting the Italians in Albania, Greece asked Britain to help defend Crete. Churchill obliged, as he recognised the strategic significance of the island and was determined to block Germany's advance through southeastern Europe. More than 30,000 British, Australian and New Zealand troops poured into the last remaining part of free Greece, two-thirds of them having first been evacuated from mainland Greece.

From the start, the defenders were faced with difficult challenges. Commitments in the Middle East were already draining military resources. There were few fighter planes, and military preparation was

BATTLE OF CRETE

The Battle of Crete had a monumental impact on the outcome of WWII, and the massive casualties on all sides make it a significant war memorial pilgrimage. Every May, war veterans from Great Britain, Australia, New Zealand and Greece attend commemoration celebrations held throughout Crete. Major anniversaries include a re-enactment of the airborne invasion at Maleme.

More than 1500 Allied soldiers are buried at the Souda Bay War Cemetery near Hania. War monuments overlook the cliffs at Moni Preveli and mark Stravromenos on the north coast, as well as Hora Sfakion, the southern port from where Allied troops were evacuated.

Ironically, one of the caretakers of the German war cemetery at Maleme, where 4500 soldiers are buried, was the late George Psychoundakis (1920–2006), the former shepherd boy whose memoir of being a dispatch runner during the German occupation was published as *The Cretan Runner* (1955).

1951

Greece joins NATO, together with Turkey. Both become key Western allies during the cold war. Military bases, used still (in 2011, against Libya's Colonel Gaddafi), are established at Souda Bay.

1955

The Cretan Runner, George Psychoundakis' memoir of being a dispatch runner during the German occupation, is published.

1967–74

Army colonels stage a coup and impose martial law across Greece. The junta is toppled seven years later following the Turkish invasion of northern Cyprus.

1970s

Tourism emerges as an important economic player, with large hotels and resorts developed along the north coast. Between 1971 and 2000, annual tourist arrivals grow from 150,000 to 2.5 million.

hampered by six changes of command in the first six months of 1941. Crete's difficult terrain also meant the only viable ports were on the exposed northern coast, while inadequate roads precluded resupplying from the more protected southern ports.

After a week-long aerial bombardment, Hitler launched the world's first full-bore paratrooper invasion on 20 May 1941, starting what became known as the Battle of Crete, one of the war's most deeply pitched battles. Aiming to capture the airport at Maleme 17km west of Hania, thousands of German paratroopers floated down over Hania, Rethymno and Iraklio.

Cretan civilians of all ages grabbed rifles, sickles and whatever they could find to join the soldiers in defending the island. German casualties were appalling, but they managed to rally and capture the Maleme airfield by the second day and, despite the valiant and fierce defence, the Allies and Cretans lost the brutal battle after about 10 days.

After the battle of Crete, the Cretans risked German reprisals by hiding thousands of Allied soldiers and helping them escape across the Libyan Sea. Allied undercover agents coordinated the guerrilla warfare waged by Cretan fighters, known as *andartes*. Allied soldiers and Cretans alike were under constant threat from the Nazis while they lived in caves, sheltered in monasteries such as Preveli, trekked across peaks or unloaded cargo on the southern coast. Among them was celebrated author Patrick Leigh Fermor (1915–2011), who lived in the mountains for two years with the Cretan Resistance and was involved in the daring kidnapping of German commander General Kreipe in 1944.

German troops responded with fierce reprisals against the civilian population. Cities were bombed, villages burnt down, and men, women and children lined up and shot. When the Germans finally surrendered in 1945 they insisted on surrendering to the British, fearing that the Cretans would inflict upon them some of the same punishment they had suffered for four years.

Intrepid and dedicated shoppers will occasionally still find (especially in village shops) late-19th-century flags emblazoned with the famous *Enosis i Thanatos* (Union or Death) slogan under which Cretan rebels fought against the Turks.

Greek Civil War & Reconstruction

Although the German occupation of Greece had ended, the strife was hardly over. The postwar scenario of a capitalist West trying to contain a communist East would play out violently in Greece, where the mainland resistance had been dominated by communists. When WWII ended, the communists boycotted the 1946 election that saw King George II reinstated, with the backing of Winstwon Churchill and other Western leaders. Fortunately for Crete, the island was largely spared the bloodshed of the Greek Civil War (1946–49). When all was said and done, Greece was in the Western camp and joined NATO in 1951. Souda Bay air and sea

1981

Greece becomes the 10th member of the EEC (now EU), giving Cretan farmers new access to EU funds. The islanders strongly back the first PASOK socialist government, led by Andreas Papandreou.

2002

Greece becomes a full member of the European Monetary Union and the drachma is replaced by the euro. Prices rise steeply across the country.

2008

Excavations near Plakias and Preveli unearth chiselled stone tools dating back at least 130,000 years.

2009

Eurozone countries approve a US$146 billion (€110 billion) rescue package for the country's economic crisis in exchange for implementing austerity policies. It's the first in a series of three bailouts.

base is the most important NATO base in Crete, and it was heavily used in the 2011 air campaign against Libya's Colonel Gaddafi.

For Crete as for Greece, the major challenge following the wars was reconstruction and the need to rebuild a shattered economy, while adjusting to a rapidly modernising world. In Crete, rural traditions play a strong social role, yet changes came in the 1960s and '70s with the arrival of foreign tourists who launched one of the island's major modern industries.

The branches given to athletes during the 2004 Athens Olympic Games were cut from a 3250-year-old olive tree – one of the world's oldest – which grows near Kavousi in northeast Crete.

The Junta & Modern Crete

In 1967, four Greek army colonels staged a coup, establishing a military junta that imposed martial law, abolished all political parties, banned trade unions, imposed censorship, and imprisoned, tortured and exiled thousands of citizens. In Crete, resentment intensified when the colonels muscled through major tourist development projects rife with favouritism. When the junta was toppled there was a resurgence of support for left-wing causes and a new democratic constitution. A 1975 referendum officially deposed the king, Konstantinos II, ending the last vestiges of Greek royalism, and previously exiled politician George Papandreou returned to Greece. A towering figure in modern Greek history, Papandreou founded the socialist PASOK party, winning elections in 1981.

Greece joined the EU (then known as the EEC) in 1981, and Cretan farmers have garnered EU agricultural subsidies, while the island's infrastructure has been modernised thanks to EU support. Tourism boomed with direct charter flights to Crete, almost tripling tourist arrivals between 1981 and 1991, and tourism numbers doubled again with the advent of package tourism and budget airlines during the next decade.

The major challenge affecting all Greece, however, has been the country's recent financial woes and the government's controversial austerity measures. Crete's relative abundance of natural resources and geographical isolation from the more urbanised mainland shield it to a degree from some problems, such as violent protests, but the island cannot be protected from pension cuts, bank instability and unemployment.

The 21st Century & the Fiscal Crisis

As with anywhere in Greece, Crete was not immune to the country's severe debt crisis. Between 2010 and 2012, the 'troika' (European Commission, European Central Bank and International Monetary Fund) approved two bailout loan packages totalling €240 billion (not all of which was disbursed) to prevent Greece from defaulting on its debt (equal to 150% of its GDP). The deals required the government to impose strict austerity measures, including public spending and pension cuts, reduction of red tape, crackdowns on tax evasion and across-the-board tax

2011-12

Tens of thousands march on Parliament in Athens to oppose government austerity policies. Nevertheless, a second, €130-billion bailout is approved.

2012

Parliament passes a €13.5-billion austerity plan to secure a second, €130-billion EU and IMF bailout, expiring on 30 June 2015. Cuts include 22% off minimum wage, 15% off pensions and 15,000 public-sector jobs.

2013

Unemployment rises to 26.8% – the highest rate in the EU. Youth unemployment climbs to almost 60%.

2015

Disillusionment with ruling parties New Democracy and PASOK rises. Left-wing Syriza comes to power in 2015, while fringe parties such as the neo-Nazi Golden Dawn find support.

Kavousi, in northeast Crete, is home to the world's oldest known olive tree

increases, as well as to raise billions through the privatisation of state-controlled assets. As a result, Greece overall plunged into a depression: GDP shrunk by about 20% and, by 2014, unemployment had climbed to 28%, with youth unemployment at a staggering 60%.

Throughout these machinations, tumultuous social and political repercussions rocked Greece, including mass protests and widespread strikes. Disillusionment with the long-ruling PASOK and New Democracy parties ultimately yielded parliamentary elections in January 2015, which saw Alexis Tsipras of the leftist anti-austerity party Syriza become prime minister, the first-ever such victory for the radical left-wing party. To reach a majority, Syriza established a coalition with right-wing Independent Greeks (ANEL), unlikely bedfellows united by their mutual condemnation of the bailout program.

2015

Greece defaults on its bailout loan repayments and is threatened with 'Grexit' – in other words, removal from the eurozone.

2016

A deal between the EU and Turkey closes European borders to refugees arriving in Greece, effectively trapping them in Greece or returning them to Turkey.

2018

Crete takes in some 50,000 refugees and migrants, mostly from Afghanistan, Syria and Iraq. Many benefit from an EU-funded accommodation program run by the UN Refugee Agency.

2019

After Prime Minister Alexis Tsipras' Syriza party is routed in European and local elections, a general election is called. Kyriakos Mitsotakis and his centre-right opposition party New Democracy regain power.

The Cretan Way of Life

Cretans are a very distinctive clan of Greeks, with their own spirited music and dances, remarkable cuisine and traditions. Proud, patriotic and fierce yet famously hospitable, Cretans maintain a rich connection to their culture. They will often identify themselves as Cretans before they say they are Greek, and even within different parts of Crete people maintain strong regional identities. Exploring beyond major tourist centres, you'll meet Cretans speaking local dialects, creating regional delicacies, and combining the old world with the new.

Lifestyle & State of Mind

Centuries of battling foreign occupiers have left Cretans with a fiercely independent streak, residual mistrust of authority and little respect for the state. Personal freedom, regional pride and democratic rights are sacrosanct and there is a strong aversion to the Big Brother approach of highly regulated Western nations. National laws are routinely ignored. Guns, for example, are strictly regulated in Greece, yet the evidence suggests that Cretans are stashing an astounding arsenal. Several smoking bans (the last one was introduced in 2010) have also been widely flouted. When it comes to road rules, many visitors are surprised to learn that they even exist. Despite hefty fines, wearing a seatbelt is treated as an optional inconvenience; creative and inconsiderate parking is the norm; dangerous overtaking is rife; and you may well see people riding motorbikes helmetless as they chat on their mobile phones.

Harvard anthropologist Michael Herzfeld makes interesting observations of Cretans in *The Poetics of Manhood: Contest and Manhood in a Cretan Village*, while his *A Place in History* looks at life in and around Rethymno, including issues such as the Cretan vendetta.

These days, though, the resilience of Cretan culture and traditions is being tested by globalisation, market forces and social change. The Cretan lifestyle has changed dramatically in the past 40 years. As Cretan society has become increasingly urbanised, living standards have improved significantly; Cretans are conspicuously wealthier and the towns have more sophisticated restaurants, bars and clubs. In the shift from living a largely poor, agrarian existence to becoming increasingly urban dwellers, Cretans are also delicately balancing cultural and religious mores. The younger generation is highly educated and most speak at least some English.

As with most households in Greece, Cretans have felt the brunt of higher living costs since the introduction of the euro, while recent austerity measures to tackle the country's economic problems have taken some of the shine off their famously relaxed disposition. Still, Cretans have a work-to-live attitude and pride themselves on their capacity to enjoy life. They enjoy a rich social life, and you'll often see them dressed up and going out en masse for their *volta* (evening walk), and filling tavernas and cafes with family or their *parea* (group of friends). The Greek Orthodox Church, its rituals and celebrations are still deeply influential in Cretan society, including among the young and urban.

Unlike many Western cultures where people avoid eye contact with strangers, Cretans are unashamed about staring and blatantly commenting on the comings and goings of people around them. Few subjects are off limits, from your private life and why you don't have children to how much money you earn and how much you paid for your house or shoes. And they are likely to tell you of their woes and ailments rather than engage in polite small talk.

Cretans turn their heads downward to indicate yes *(nai)* and upward to signal no *(ohi)*. The latter is often accompanied by an upward eye roll and a tongue click.

Family Life

Cretan society is still relatively conservative and it is uncommon for Greeks to move out of home until they are married, apart from leaving temporarily to study or work. While this is slowly changing among professionals, lack of economic opportunities and low wages are also keeping young people at home.

Parents strive to provide homes for their children when they get married, with many families building apartments for each child above their own homes. Construction is often done in a haphazard fashion depending on cash flow, which accounts for the large number of unfinished houses you encounter throughout the island.

Extended families often play an important role in daily life, with parents preferring to entrust their offspring to the grandparents rather than hiring outside help.

Cretans who moved away to other parts of Greece or overseas maintain strong cultural and family links and return regularly to their ancestral land. Even the most remote mountain villages are bustling with family reunions and homecomings during national and religious holidays, and Cretan weddings and baptisms are huge affairs.

Greece has compulsory military service of nine months for the army and one year for the navy and air force for all males aged 19 to 45 years. Women are accepted into the Greek army, though they are not obliged to join and rarely do.

City Versus Countryside

Generational and rural/city divides are major features of modern Crete. In rural areas, you will see shepherds with their flocks, old women riding on donkeys, and men congregating in the *kafeneia* (coffee houses) after their afternoon siesta. Mountain villages are repositories of traditional culture and you'll still occasionally see older folk dressed in black *vraka* (baggy trousers) and leather boots.

In general terms, the major population centres of the north attract companies, industry and universities, whereas agriculture accounts for the bulk of economic activity in the less-populated interior and south. The mountainous southwest has some of the more traditional villages on the island.

But even pastoral life has changed. While people still live off the land – and provide for their families in the cities – subsistence farming has

KOMBOLOЇ

You can still see men – usually the older generations, and usually in the villages – stroking, fiddling and masterfully playing with the de-stressing worry beads called *komboloï*. An amalgam of the words *kombos* (knot) and *leo* (to say), *komboloïa* (plural) may look like prayer beads, but they have no religious purpose and are only used for fun and relaxation. There just seems to be something soothing about flicking and flipping those beads – some people also use them to help them stop smoking.

Komboloïa were traditionally made from amber, but coral, handmade beads, semi-precious stones and synthetic resin are also widely used. No exact number is prescribed but most *komboloïa* have between 19 and 23 beads strung up on a loop. There's a fixed bead that is held between the fingers, a shield that separates the two sides of the loop, and a tassel.

The vast majority of what you see in souvenir shops is plastic but there are also prized rare and old *komboloïa* that can be worth thousands of euros and are considered highly collectable.

mostly given way to commercial production. Well-to-do farmers drive pick-up trucks and shepherds can often be seen tending to their flocks while chatting away on their mobile phones. In the fields, foreign workers are also a major part of accomplishing the grunt work.

No matter where you are, though, you'll find that a pride in and connection to food and local produce, from mountain herbs and honey to regional dishes and cheeses made uniquely in each village, are vital to Cretan daily life.

The word *xenos* means both 'stranger' and 'guest', and Greeks see *filoxenia* (hospitality, welcome, shelter) almost as a duty and a matter of personal pride and honour.

Hospitality & Tourism

The Cretan people have a well-justified reputation for hospitality and for treating strangers as honoured guests. They pride themselves on their *filotimo* (dignity and sense of honour) and *filoxenia* (hospitality, welcome, shelter). If you wander into mountain villages you may well be invited into someone's home for a coffee or even a meal. In a cafe or taverna it is customary for people to treat another group of friends or strangers to a round of drinks (however, be mindful that it is not the done thing to treat them straight back – in theory, you will do the honours another time).

Surprisingly, this hospitality and generosity diminish in the public sphere, where customer service is not a widely lauded concept. The notion of the greater good can play second fiddle to personal interests, and there is little sense of collective responsibility in relation to issues such as the environment, though that is starting to change with the younger generation.

Crete takes in more than 3.5 million visitors annually, which has an impact on both the environment and the economy: the majority of tourists come on package trips and are sequestered in northern-coast all-inclusive hotels. The overdevelopment of much of northern-coast Crete has left hotel owners susceptible to larger trends in the travel world, whereas smaller places elsewhere on the island experience less volatile swings as the economy waxes and wanes. New EU grants have been given to promote green tourism and restore historic buildings and traditional settlements, and there is a growing awareness that sustainable, ecofriendly tourism will pay dividends as the tastes of foreign visitors change.

Cretans often deal with the seasonal invasion of foreign tourists by largely operating in a different space-time continuum to their guests. They will often tell you a particular place is 'only for tourists', and that's normally their hint to you to avoid it. From April to around October, many Cretans live in the hurly-burly of the coastal resorts and beaches –

TRIGGER-HAPPY

Cretans have a reputation for their fierce fighting ability (they have battled with invaders for centuries, after all) and for having Greece's most notable gun culture. Estimates have indicated that one in two Cretans owns a gun, while others suggest there could be over one million weapons in Crete – more than the island's population.

At Cretan weddings and celebrations volleys of gunshots occasionally punctuate events. Some musicians refuse to play in certain areas unless they get an assurance that there won't be any guns. At one time, acclaimed composer Mikis Theodorakis led a campaign trying to change the island's gun culture. But, today, road signs riddled with bullet holes are the first inkling that you are entering the mountain country that was historically a stronghold for Crete's resistance fighters, particularly around Sfakia in Hania and Mylopotamos province in Rethymno. Sfakiots are aware of their reputation, though, and you'll find T-shirts in their souvenir shops with images of the bullet-riddled signs.

Top *Kafeneio* (coffee house)

Bottom *Kandylakia* (roadside shrine)

ARTEM KNIAZ/SHUTTERSTOCK ©

running shops, pensions or tavernas – and then return to their life in the hills for the autumn olive and grape harvests, or in the cities.

While many tourists eat early in the evening (by Greek standards, at least) in restaurants along a harbour or beach, Cretans drive out to village tavernas or frequent local favourites, for a dinner that begins as late as 10pm. Nightlife goes equally late.

For a useful but by no means exhaustive list of books about Crete, with reviews, visit www.hellenicbookservice.com.

Multiculturalism

After the exodus of Crete's Turkish community in the population exchange of 1923, the island became essentially homogeneous and its population virtually all Greek Orthodox. In recent years, though, Crete has become an increasingly multicultural society, with migrants from the Balkans and Eastern Europe, especially Albania, Bulgaria and Russia, filling labour shortages in the fields of agriculture, construction and tourism. The total foreign population is now about 11%.

Since 2015 Crete has taken in some 50,000 refugees and migrants, mostly from Afghanistan, Syria and Iraq. Economic migrants are a relatively new phenomenon for Crete, which, like most of Greece, is struggling to come to terms with the new reality and concepts of multiculturalism. While there are tensions and mistrust, immigrants appear to have fared better in Crete than in many other parts of Greece.

A small group of English, German and northern European expats has also settled and bought property in Crete, though they live on the more affluent fringes, and there are some foreigners married to Cretans.

Religion

The New Testament was written beginning around AD 50 in Koine Greek, which was the day-to-day language in the eastern part of the Roman Empire at the time.

The Orthodox faith is the official and prevailing religion of Crete and a key element of local identity and culture. While younger generations are not necessarily as devout as their elders, nor do they attend church regularly, most still observe the rituals and consider the faith integral to their identity. Between 94% and 97% of the Cretan population belongs at least nominally to the Greek Orthodox Church.

The Orthodox religion held Cretan culture, language and traditions together during the many centuries of foreign occupation and repression, despite numerous efforts by the Venetians and Turks to turn locals towards Roman Catholicism or Islam. Under Ottoman rule, religion was the most important criterion in defining a Greek.

Despite growing secularism, the Church still exerts significant social, political and economic influence. The year is centred on the saints' days and festivals of the religious calendar. Easter is bigger than Christmas. Most people are named after a saint, as are boats, suburbs and train stations. Name days (celebrating your namesake saint) are more important than birthdays, and baptisms are an important rite. If you're invited to

ROADSIDE SHRINES

Buzzing around Crete's winding country roads, you'll see them everywhere: doll's-house-sized chapels on metal pedestals by the roadside. Called *kandylakia,* they come in all shapes and sizes, some simple, some elaborate, some weathered, some shiny and new. A votive candle may flicker behind tiny dust-encrusted windows, faintly illuminating the picture of a saint. They are especially prevalent in hairpin corners, blind bends and on the edges of precipitous slopes, and though they have often been put there by the families of those who died in an accident on this very spot, some are also set up in gratitude by those who miraculously survived such accidents or to honour a particular saint. As you're driving, recognize these symbols of both tragedy and happy endings as a reflection of those things important to Cretans: family, faith and tradition.

a name-day celebration, it's a good idea to bring a present, but don't be surprised if it won't be opened until you've left; any meal or offering of food, sweets or drink is usually paid for by the celebrant.

Hundreds of privately built small chapels dot the countryside, while the miniature roadside *kandylakia* are either shrines to road-accident victims or dedications to saints.

The Greek year revolves around saints' days and festivals of the Orthodox Church calendar. Easter is bigger than Christmas, and name days (celebrating your namesake saint) are more important than birthdays. Most people are named after a saint, as are boats, suburbs and train stations.

Women in Society

The role of women in Cretan society has been complex and shifting since Greek women first gained universal suffrage in 1952. While traditional gender roles are prevalent in rural areas and among the older generation, the situation is much more relaxed for younger women in cities and large towns. Entrenched attitudes towards the 'proper role' for women are changing fast as more women are educated and entering the workforce. Still, although some 40% of Greek women are in the workforce, they struggle when it comes to even finding the career ladder or earning the same as their male counterparts. There are few public programs to help them balance careers and motherhood.

Paradoxically, despite the machismo, Cretan society is essentially matriarchal. Men love to give the impression that they rule the roost and take a front seat in public life, but it's often the women who run the show, both at home and in family businesses.

In villages, men and women still tend to occupy different spheres. When not tending livestock or olive trees, Cretan men can usually be found in a *kafeneio* (coffee house), playing *tavli* (Greek backgammon), gossiping and drinking coffee or raki. Although exceptions are made for foreign women, the *kafeneio* is a stronghold of male chauvinism and generally off limits to Cretan women.

The older generation of Cretan women is house-proud and, especially in villages, spends time cultivating culinary skills. Most men rarely participate in domestic duties (or certainly don't own up to it).

Minoan Art & Culture

The Minoans' palaces were lavishly decorated with art, and the surviving paintings, sculptures, mosaics, pottery and jewellery at archaeological sites and museums across Crete demonstrate the Minoans' extraordinary artistry. Minoan painting is virtually the only form of Greek painting to have survived through the ages; large-scale sculptures having disappeared in natural disasters like the great tsunami that swept over from Thira (Santorini) in 1450 BC. Minoan art inspired the invading Mycenaeans and its influence spread to Santorini and beyond.

Minoan Society

Mystery shrouds the Minoans: we don't even know what they called themselves, 'Minoan' being the term given by archaeologist Sir Arthur Evans, in honour of the mythical King Minos. They are thought to have been possibly related to the pre-Greek, Pelasgian people of western Anatolia and the Greek mainland, and to have spoken a unique language unrelated to the Indo-European ones.

Minotaur: Sir Arthur Evans and the Archaeology of the Minoan Myth by Joseph Alexander MacGillivray is a fascinating portrait of the British archaeologist who excavated the Palace of Knossos.

Evidence uncovered in the island's grand palaces indicates they were a peaceful, sophisticated, well-organised and prosperous civilisation with robust international trade, splendid architecture and art, and seemingly equal status for men and women. The Minoans had highly developed agriculture, extensive irrigation systems and advanced hydraulic sewerage systems. The accounts and records left behind suggest that their society was organised as an efficient and bureaucratic commercial enterprise.

Although the evidence for a matriarchal society is scant, women apparently enjoyed a great degree of freedom and autonomy. Minoan art shows women participating in games, hunting and all public and religious festivals. They also served as priestesses, administrators and participated in trade.

Pottery

Pottery techniques advanced in the Early Minoan years. Spirals and curvilinear motifs in white were painted on dark vases and several distinct styles emerged. Pyrgos pottery was characterised by black, grey or brown colours, while the later Vasiliki pottery (made near Ierapetra) was polychrome. In the Middle to Late Minoan period, the style shifted to a dark-on-light colour technique.

Highly advanced levels of artisanship developed in the workshops of the first palaces at Knossos and Phaestos. Kamares pottery, named after the cave where the pottery was first found, was colourful, elegant and beautifully crafted and decorated with geometric, floral, plant and animal motifs. Human forms were rarely depicted. During the entire Middle Minoan period, Kamares vases were used for barter and were exported to Cyprus, Egypt and the Levant.

With the invention of the potter's wheel, cups, spouted jars and *pithoi* (large Minoan storage jars) could be produced quickly and there was a new crispness to the designs. The most striking were the 'eggshell' vases with their extremely thin walls.

In the late Neopalatial era, marine and floral themes in darker colours reigned. After 1500 BC, vases sprouted three handles and were frequently shaped as animal heads. The decline of Minoan culture saw the lively pottery of previous centuries degenerate into dull rigidity.

Jewellery & Sculpture

Jewellery making and sculpture in various media reached an exceptional degree of artisanship in the Protopalatial period. The exquisite bee pendant found at Malia displays extraordinary delicacy and imagination. Another Minoan masterpiece is a 15th century BC gold signet ring found in a tomb at Isopata, near Knossos, which shows women in an ecstatic ritual dance in a meadow with lilies, while a goddess descends from the sky.

Minoan sculptors created fine miniatures, including idols in faience (quartz-glazed earthenware), gold, ivory, bronze and stone. One of the most outstanding examples is the bare-breasted serpent goddess with raised arms wielding writhing snakes above an elaborately carved skirt.

KING MINOS & DAEDALUS

Minos, the legendary ruler of Crete, was the son of Zeus and Europa and attained the Cretan throne, aided by Poseidon. Homer describes him and his land in the 'Odyssey': 'Out on the dark blue sea there lies a rich and lovely land called Crete that is densely populated and boasts 90 cities... One of the 90 cities is called Knossos and there for nine years, King Minos ruled and enjoyed the friendship of the mighty.'

Whatever his character might have been, his fate was ultimately interwoven with an Athenian master craftsman named Daedalus, who, having fled from Athens for murdering his nephew (for being more inventive), sought sanctuary in Crete. Minos was quick to utilise his skills, commissioning the inventor to design the legendary Palace of Knossos. It is said that Daedalus' statues were so lifelike that they had to be chained down to stop them moving. However, the inventor's talents were sometimes used to dark ends, as when Minos' Queen Pasiphae, who had fallen in love with the white bull of Poseidon, urged Daedalus to make a hollow wooden bull that she might satisfy her enflamed desire with it. Meanwhile, with Knossos as his base, Minos gained control over the whole Aegean basin, colonising many of the islands and ridding the seas of pirates. Again his naval success was often attributed to the ingeniousness of Daedalus, whose successes included designing the prow of the modern boat.

Then, as with many great partnerships, the relationship soured when the infamous half-bull, half-human Minotaur was birthed by Queen Pasiphae as a punishment from the gods. Daedalus was called upon to create a prison strong enough to contain the monster which possessed the strength of an army. The inventor's answer was to construct the labyrinth, an endless maze of tunnels, where the creature was fed with seven boys and seven girls from Athens every year.

When Daedalus and Icarus left Crete without permission, Minos was enraged. In their escape the inventor lost his son Icarus who famously flew too near the sun, his waxened feathers melting. Minos pursued him to the city of Kamikos, baiting the inventor with a challenge: a reward to anyone who could pass a thread through a shell. Overtaken by hubris, Daedalus solved the problem, but it was Minos who came to a nasty end not the wily inventor, who was under the protection of King Kokalios. After Minos threatened a war if the legendary father of flight did not turn up, the Sicilian king tricked the Cretan into bathing with his daughters – who promptly killed him with a device Daedalus had designed, a pipe that poured boiling water over his head. After his death the Cretan king became a dread judge in Hades' realm, the Underworld.

As to whether King Minos actually existed and reigned, however, is open to debate. The Homeric reference *enneaoros* used to describe Minos could mean 'for nine years' or 'from the age of nine years'. Was Minos able to create an empire in nine short years, or was he a long-reigning monarch who started his kingly career as a boy?

Phaistos disc, Heraklion Archaeological Museum (p170)

Another incredible piece is the small rock-crystal *rhyton* from the Palace of Zakros. All of the above are displayed at the Heraklion Archaeological Museum.

The art of seal-stone carving also advanced in the palace workshops. Using semiprecious stones and clay, artisans made miniature masterpieces that sometimes contained hieroglyphic letters. Goats, lions, griffins, and dance scenes were rendered in minute detail. Arthur Evans spent much of his first trip to Crete collecting these seals.

In the Postpalatial period, the production of jewellery and seal-stones was replaced by the production of weaponry, reflecting the influence of the warlike Mycenaeans.

The Famous Frescoes

Minoan frescoes are renowned for their vibrant colours and the vivid naturalism in which they portray landscapes rich with animals and birds, marine scenes teeming with fish and octopuses, and banquets,

NO BULL

The bull was a potent symbol in Minoan times, featuring prominently in Minoan art. The peculiar Minoan sport of bull-leaping, where acrobatic thrill-seekers seize the charging bull's horns and leap over its back, is depicted in several frescoes, pottery and sculptures. Scantily clad men and women are shown participating in the sport, which may have had religious significance. One of the most stunning examples is the Middle Minoan bull-leaping fresco found at the Palace of Knossos, which shows a man leaping over the back of a bull with a female figure on each side. Another prized bull is the carved stone *rhyton* (libation vessel) in the shape of a bull's head, with rock-crystal eyes and gilded wooden horns.

DECIPHERING THE MYSTERIES OF LINEAR B

The methodical decipherment of the Linear B script by English architect and part-time linguist Michael Ventris in 1952 provided the first tangible evidence that the Greek language had a recorded history longer than any scholar had previously believed. The language was an archaic form of Greek 500 years older than the Ionic Greek used by Homer.

Linear B was written on clay tablets that lay undisturbed for centuries until they were unearthed at Knossos in Crete. Further tablets were unearthed later on the mainland at Mycenae, Tiryns and Pylos in the Peloponnese and at Thebes in Boeotia in central Greece.

The clay tablets, found to be mainly inventories and records of commercial transactions, consist of about 90 different signs, and date from the 14th to the 13th centuries BC. Little of the social and political life of these times can be deduced from the tablets, although there is enough to give a glimpse of a fairly complex and well-organised commercial structure.

Importantly, what is clear is that the language is undeniably Greek, thus giving the modern-day Greek language the second-longest recorded written history, after Chinese. Read Andrew Robinson's biography, *The Man Who Deciphered Linear B*, to learn more about the fascinating life and great genius of Michael Ventris.

games and rituals. Although fresco painting probably existed before 1700 BC, all remnants vanished in the cataclysm that destroyed Minoan palaces around that time. Knossos yielded the richest trove of frescoes from the Neopalatial period, most of which are on display in the Heraklion Archaeological Museum.

Only fragments of the frescoes survive but they have been very carefully (and controversially) restored and the technique of using plant and mineral dyes has kept the colours relatively fresh. Minoan fresco painters borrowed heavily from certain Egyptian conventions but the figures are far less rigid than most Egyptian wall paintings.

The Knossos frescoes suggest Minoan women were white-skinned with elaborately coiffured glossy black locks. Proud, graceful and uninhibited, these women had hourglass figures and were dressed in stylish gowns that exposed shapely breasts. The bronze-skinned men were tall, with tiny waists, narrow hips, broad shoulders and muscular thighs and biceps; the children were slim and lithe.

Many of the frescoes show action scenes, from boxing and wrestling to solemn processions, saffron gathering to bull-leaping.

The Minoans knew how to enjoy themselves – playing board games, boxing, wrestling and performing bold acrobatic feats including the sport of bull-leaping, while Minoan dancing was famous throughout Ancient Greece.

Religious Symbols

The Minoans were not given to building colossal temples or religious statuary. Caves and mountain peak sanctuaries appear to have been used for cult or religious activity, and were probably only visited once a year for a particular ritual (like the many tiny chapels you see dotted around Greece). Tables and jars found around these sites suggest agricultural produce was left as an offering. Minoan spiritual life was organised around the worship of a Mother Goddess. Often represented with snakes or lions, the Mother Goddess was both healer and the deity-in-chief, while the male gods were clearly subordinate.

The double-axe symbol that appears in frescoes and on the palace walls at Knossos was a sacred symbol for the Minoans. Other religious symbols that frequently appear in Minoan art include the mythical griffin and figures with a human body and an animal head. The Minoans appear to have worshipped the dead and believed in some form of afterlife, while evidence uncovered in Anemospilia suggests that human sacrifice may also have taken place.

MORE CRETAN MYTHS

Some of the key stories in the panoply of Greek *mythos* (myths) emanate from Crete.

Zeus & Cronus Before Zeus formed the pantheon of the gods, the earth was in the hands of his father Cronus and his monster Titans. When Cronus learned he was destined to be overthrown by one of his sons, he ate each of them – including Hades and Poseidon – upon their birth. When Zeus was born in the Dikteon Cave on Crete's Lasithi Plateau, his mother Rhea deceptively wrapped a stone in swaddling clothes and gave it to Cronus who promptly swallowed it. Zeus grew up, overthrew Cronus, freeing his brothers and sisters from his father's belly, and imprisoned the Titans in the underworld.

Theseus & the Minotaur Seven Athenian sons and daughters are annually fed to the monstrous half-bull half-man imprisoned in the labyrinth of King Minos' palace in Knossos. Among them is Prince Theseus, who volunteers for the task and, through the intervention of Aphrodite, is aided by Minos' daughter, Ariadne, who gives him a ball of thread to help him find his way out of the labyrinth. Theseus slays the beast and escapes Crete, taking Ariadne with him, but forgets to change the sails from black to white, a sign to King Aegeus of Athens of his safe return. Broken-hearted Aegeus throws himself from the cliffs into the waves and the Aegean Sea is born.

Writing & Language

The Minoan's inscrutable written hieroglyph system, Linear A, provides another indication of a culture that was very advanced. The Cretan hieroglyphic was the system of writing used in the Protopalatial period that later evolved into Linear A and B script. The most significant example of this writing is on the inscrutable 3600-year-old terracotta tablet known as the Phaestos Disk, which has been the object of much speculation since it was discovered at Phaestos in 1908. The disk, about 16cm in diameter, consists of an Early Minoan pictographic script made up of 242 'words' written in a continuous spiral from the outside of the disk to the inside (or the other way round). The repetition of sequences of words or sentences has led to speculation it may be a prayer. It has never been deciphered.

For photos and descriptions of more than 50 Minoan sites around Crete, see archaeology buff Ian Swindale's comprehensive website at www.minoancrete.com.

As far as the spoken language of the Minoans goes, this too remains unclear. While Mycenaean-era Linear B records something that is definitely an archaic form of Greek, Linear A may well be a script for something completely different. Scholars have speculated that it may have had connections with pre-Greek Mesopotamian tongues, but unless more samples are found, it will remain a mystery.

The Arts

Crete is a powerhouse for music, dance and the visual arts, going back millennia. From priceless Minoan sculptures to homegrown mountain musicians playing the *lyra* in tavernas, this massive island has developed its own ways of living, loving, lamenting and showing it all to the world through the arts. Prepare to browse museums, read local lit while you sunbathe, seek out frescoed chapels, or dance in the streets – this is Crete!

Music

Cretan music is the most dynamic and enduring form of traditional music in Greece today, and on the island it remains the most popular music, staving off mainstream Greek and Western pop. You'll hear it accompanying weddings, holidays, harvesting and any other celebration. Crete's thriving local music scene generates successive generations of folk musicians who perform regularly and produce new recordings of traditional songs, as well as contemporary styles based on Cretan tradition. You'll also find Cretan music on the world-music scene as a genre in its own right.

Greeks have been playing music for thousands of years. In fact, archaeologists have found ancient Greek vases decorated with depictions of an instrument very much resembling the *lyra* (lyre).

Instruments & Musical Styles

Cretan music has been influenced by many musical traditions over the centuries and resembles eastern modal music. The lead instrument is the *lyra,* a three-stringed instrument similar to a harp that is played resting on the knee. It is often accompanied by the eight-stringed *laouto* (lute), which keeps the rhythm for the *lyra*. Other traditional instruments include the *mandolino* (mandolin), the *askomandoura* (bagpipe), the *habioli* (wooden flute) and the *daoulaki* (drum). The bouzouki, so associated with Greek music, is not part of traditional Cretan music.

One of Crete's favourite forms of musical expression is the *mantinadha* (a style of traditional Cretan rhyming couplets), which expresses the timeless concerns of love, death and the vagaries of fate. Thousands of *mantinadhes* helped forge a sense of national identity during the long centuries of occupation. *Mantinadhes* rely on the decapentasyllabic (15-syllable) count of Byzantine vernacular literature going back at least to the 12th century. The best 'rhymers' at Cretan festivals would tailor their songs to the people present and try to outdo each other in skill and composition. These days, young Cretans continue the tradition, and *mantinadhes* are still part of the modern courtship ritual, albeit often via mobile-phone messages. The best-known piece of Cretan Renaissance literature, the 17th-century 'Erotokritos' by Vitsentzos Kornaros, consists of language and rhyme consistent with *mantinadhes*, and continues to inspire Crete's musicians today.

Another popular form of music is *rizitika*, which are centuries-old patriotic songs from western Crete, especially the Lefka Ori (White Mountains) region. They are thought to have derived from the songs of the border guards of the Byzantine Empire, though their roots may be even older. Many of the *rizitika* deal with historical or heroic themes. One of the most popular is the song of Daskalogiannis, the Sfakiot hero who

TPHOTOGRAPHY/SHUTTERSTOCK ©

Top Traditional instruments, including the Cretan *lyra* (on left).

Bottom Cretan folk dancing.

led the rebellion against the Turks in 1770; it has 1034 verses. The period of German occupation in WWII also produced a fertile crop of *rizitika*.

Prominent Musicians

Traditional folk music was shunned by the Greek bourgeoisie during the period after independence when they looked to Europe – and classical music and opera – rather than their eastern or 'peasant' roots. However, a new wave of *entehni mousiki* (artistic music) that emerged in Athens in the 1960s drew on urban folk instruments such as the bouzouki and created popular hits from the works of Greek poets.

Acclaimed composer Yiannis Markopoulos (from Ierapetra) upped the ante by introducing rural folk music into the mainstream. He's best known internationally for his composition for the TV series *Who Pays the Ferryman?* Markopoulos was also responsible for bringing the icon of Cretan music, the late Nikos Xylouris, to the fore. The latter's career was tragically cut short in 1980 when he died of a brain tumour at the age of 43. With his superb voice and talent on the *lyra,* he remains the biggest-selling and most revered Cretan musician. During the junta years, Xylouris' music became a leading voice of the resistance. He came from a great musical family in Anogia, a village that has spawned many musicians and which has a good museum today.

One of the oldest pieces of written music ever found is from 408 BC. The music was sung by a choir in the ancient Greek tragedy *Orestes* by Euripides.

Xylouris, Thanasis Skordalos and Kostas Mountakis are considered the great masters of Cretan music, and most current musicians follow one of their styles. The most prominent Cretan musician today is the legendary Psarantonis (Antonis Xylouris, brother of Nikos); he's known for his unique style of playing music and is instantly recognisable from his wild beard and mane of hair. Psarantonis still performs – everywhere from the smallest Cretan village to the clubs of Athens and the international festival circuit. In addition to the Xylouris family from Anogia, another famous musician from the village is Loudovikos Ton Anogion.

An intriguing figure of Crete's music scene is Ross Daly (of Irish descent), a master of the *lyra* and the creator of a high-calibre world-music workshop in Houdetsi.

The excellent sextet Haïnides is one of the more popular acts to emerge from Crete in recent years, playing its own brand of music and giving memorable live performances around Greece. Other leading figures include Mitsos and Vasilis Stavrakakis and contemporary musicians such as the band Palaïna, Nikos Zoidakis, Stelios Petrakis from Sitia, Papa Stefanis Nikas and Yiannis Haroulis. Other names to watch include Australian-born Sifis Tsourdalakis and Belgian-born Mihalis Tzouganakis.

Popular artists of Cretan origin playing mainstream Greek music include the talented Manos Pirovolakis with his rock-*lyra* sound. One of Greece's most famous international performers, Nana Mouskouri, was born in Hania, though her family moved to Athens when she was three years of age.

Dance

Dancing has been part of social life in Crete since the dawn of Hellenism. Some folk dances derive from the ritual dances performed in ancient Greek temples. Dancers are also depicted on ancient Greek vases and Homer lauded the ability of Cretan dancers.

Cretan dances are dynamic, fast and warlike, and many of them are danced by groups of men. Dances for women are traditionally related to wedding or courtship, and are more delicate and graceful. Like most Greek dances they are normally performed in a circle; in ancient times, dancers formed a circle to seal themselves off from evil influences. In times of occupation, dancing became an act of defiance and a way to keep fit under the noses of the enemy.

The most popular Cretan dances are the graceful and slow *syrtos* and the *pentozali*. The latter was originally danced by armed warriors and has a slow version and a faster one that builds into a frenzy, with the leader doing kicks, variations and fancy moves while the others follow with more mild steps. Another popular dance is the *sousta,* a bouncy courtship dance with small precise steps that is performed by couples. The *maleviziotiko* (also known as *kastrino* or *pidikto*) is a fast triumphant dance.

Dancing well is a matter of great personal pride, and most dancers will take their turn at the front to demonstrate their prowess. Be aware that cutting in on somebody's dance is absolutely bad form, as families have usually paid for the dance (this is how Cretan musicians often make their living).

The best place to see Cretan dancing is at festivals, weddings and baptisms. Folkloric shows are also put on for tourists in many areas. Although these are more contrived, they can still be a decent show.

Fine Arts

The artistry of the Minoans ranks with the best in human history. During a brief artistic renaissance on the island that lasted from the 8th to 7th centuries BC, a group of sculptors called the Daedalids perfected a new technique of making sculptures in hammered bronze, working in a style that combined Eastern and Greek aesthetics. Their influence spread to mainland Greece. Cretan culture went into decline at the end of the 7th century BC, though there was a brief revival under the Romans, a period notable for richly decorated mosaic floors and marble sculptures. Then came the paintings and frescoes that culminated in the renowned Cretan School of painting.

Byzantine Art

Greek painting came into its own during the Byzantine period, which lasted roughly from the 4th century BC until the fall of Constantinople in 1453. Much Byzantine art was destroyed in popular rebellions during the 13th and 14th centuries. In the 11th century, émigrés from Constantinople brought portable icons to Crete, but the only surviving example from this period is the icon of the Virgin at Mesopantitissa, now in Venice.

From the 13th to the early 16th centuries, churches around Crete were decorated with frescoes on a dark-blue background with a bust of Christ in the dome, the four Gospel writers in the corners, and the Virgin and Child in the apse. They also feature scenes from the life of Christ and figures of saints. Many fine frescoes can still be seen today, albeit moodily faded. The great icon painter of the 14th century was Ioannis Pagomenos, who worked in western Crete. Examples of his frescoes can be found in the churches of Agios Nikolaos in Maza, where he's also buried, and in Agios Georgios in Sfakia. The best-preserved Byzantine frescoes in Crete are in the Church of Panagia Kera (p234) at Kritsa in Lasithi province.

The Cretan School

With the fall of Constantinople in 1453, Crete became the centre of Greek art as many Byzantine artists fled to the island. At the same time, the Italian Renaissance was in full bloom and many Cretan artists studied in Italy. The result was the Cretan School of icon painting that combined technical brilliance and dramatic richness. Artists drew inspiration from both Western and Byzantine styles. In Iraklio alone there were more than 200 painters working from the mid-16th to mid-17th centuries.

The most famous and internationally successful of these artists was El Greco, who was heavily influenced by the great Iraklio-born Michael Damaskinos (1530–91). Damaskinos' long sojourn in Venice introduced

EL GRECO THE CRETAN

One of the geniuses of the Renaissance, El Greco ('The Greek' in Spanish), was a Cretan named Domenikos Theotokopoulos. He was born in the Cretan capital of Candia (present-day Iraklio) in 1541, during a time of great artistic activity, following the arrival of painters fleeing Ottoman-held Constantinople. These painters had a formative influence upon the young El Greco, giving him grounding in the traditions of late-Byzantine fresco painting.

El Greco went to Venice in his early twenties, joining the studio of Titian, but he came into his own as a painter after he moved to Spain in 1577, where his highly emotional style struck a chord with the Spanish. He lived in Toledo until his death in 1614. Many of his famous works, such as *The Burial of Count Orgaz* (1586), are in Toledo but his paintings are in museums around the world. *View of Mt Sinai and the Monastery of St Catherine* (1570), painted in Venice, hangs in Iraklio's Historical Museum of Crete (p167), next to the tiny *Baptism of Christ*. You can see *Concert of Angels* (1608) at the National Gallery in Athens.

A marble bust of the painter stands in Iraklio's Plateia El Greco, and there are streets, tavernas and hotels named after him throughout the island. A small museum (p183) dedicated to El Greco has been established in the village of Fodele, in a house he allegedly spent time in as a child. The 2007 biopic *El Greco* was partly shot in Iraklio.

him to new techniques of rendering perspective. The centrepieces of the collection of the Museum of Christian Art in Iraklio are six Damaskinos icons. The third star in the trio of Cretan top artists is Theophanes Strelitza (aka Theophanes the Cretan), who was a prominent mural painter of the day, though all of his frescoes are in mainland Greece.

Contemporary Arts

The fine arts have a relatively low profile in Crete today. Though contemporary artists and artisans work and exhibit on the island, many live and work in Athens and abroad. Rethymno's Museum of Contemporary Art (p121) is one of the island's leading galleries for local artists, as are the municipal galleries around Crete. Private art galleries can be found in Hania and Iraklio.

Literature

Crete has a rich literary tradition that sprang from the Cretan love of songs, verses and wordplay. In the late 16th and early 17th centuries, the island experienced a tremendous literary flowering under Venetian rule. The era's greatest masterpiece was undoubtedly the epic 'Erotokritos', written in Cretan dialect by Vitsentzos Kornaros of Sitia. More than 10,000 lines long, this poem of courtly love is full of nostalgia for the dying Venetian regime that was threatened by the rise in Turkish power. Revolving around the troubled love story between Erotokritos, an adviser to King Heracles, and the king's daughter, Aretousa, it is an intricate tale of love, honour, friendship and bravery. The poem was recited for centuries by illiterate peasants and professional singers alike, embodying the dreams of freedom that enabled Cretans to endure their many privations. Many of the verses were incorporated into Crete's beloved *mantinadhes* (a style of traditional Cretan rhyming couplets). It is considered the most important work of early modern Greek literature.

Literary Lions

Greece's best-known and most widely read author since Homer is Nikos Kazantzakis (1883–1957), born in Crete amid the last spasms of the island's struggle for independence from the Turks. His novels, all of which have been translated into English, are full of drama and larger-than-life characters such as the magnificent title character in *Zorba the Greek* (1946) and the tortured Captain Michalis in *Freedom and Death*

(1950), two of his finest works. Along with Zorba, *The Last Temptation* (1953) was also made into a film. *Zorba the Greek* takes place in Crete and provides a fascinating glimpse into the harsher side of Cretan culture. Kazantzakis had a chequered, and at times troubled, literary career, clashing frequently with the Orthodox Church for his professed atheism.

Kazantzakis may be Crete's most famous writer, but it was Odysseus Elytis (1911–96) who won the Nobel Prize in Literature in 1979. One of his main works is 'Axion Esti – It is Worthy' (1959), a complicated poem that deals with existentialist questions and the identity of the main character's country and people. It was set to music by Mikis Theodorakis and to this day is one of the best-known poems and songs in Greece.

A noted contemporary of Elytis was Rethymno-born Pandelis Prevelakis (1909–86). He was primarily known as a poet, but also wrote plays and novels. His best-known work is *The Tale of a Town,* a nostalgic look at his home town in the early 20th century.

Contemporary Writers

Contemporary Cretan writers include Rhea Galanaki (b 1947), whose prize-winning *The Life of Ismail Ferik Pasha* (1989) has been translated into six languages; it's a story about the clash of Christianity and Ottoman Islam in Crete.

Ioanna Karystiani (b 1952), who wrote the screenplay for the Greek film *Brides* (2004), received the Greek National Award for Literature for her novel *Mikra Anglia* ('Little England', published in English as *The Jasmine Isle,* 2006). Also made into a film, it describes the lives of a sailor's family on the island of Andros. Other Cretan writers include Minas Dimakis, Manolis Pratikakis, Yiorgis Manoussakis and Victoria Theodorou.

The most famous novel written by a non-Greek but set in Crete is *The Island* by Victoria Hislop. The historical novel set in the leper colony on Spinalonga Island was Newcomer of the Year at the 2007 British Book Awards. More recent fiction includes *The Girl Under The Olive Tree* (2013) by another Brit, Leah Fleming, which takes place in Crete during WWII.

NIKOS KAZANTZAKIS

Crete's most famous contemporary writer is Nikos Kazantzakis. Born in 1883 in Iraklio, the then Turkish-dominated capital, Kazantzakis spent his early childhood in the ferment of revolution and change. In 1897 the revolution against Turkish rule forced him to leave Crete for studies in Naxos, Athens and later Paris. It wasn't until he was 31 that he turned his hand to writing, by translating philosophical books into Greek. He travelled throughout Europe, thus laying the groundwork for travelogues in his later literary career.

Kazantzakis was a complex writer and his early work was heavily influenced by philosophical and spiritual thought, including the philosophies of Nietzsche. His relationship with religion was equally complex – his official stance being that of a nonbeliever, yet he studied and wrote about religion and religious figures.

Kazantzakis' self-professed greatest work is *The Odyssey: A Modern Sequel* (1938), an opus of 33,333 iambic verses, and a modern-day epic loosely based on the trials and travels of ancient hero Odysseus (Ulysses). It was only much later in his career, though, when Kazantzakis turned to novel writing, that his star shone brightest. Works such as *Christ Recrucified* (1948), *Kapetan Mihalis* (1950; now known as *Freedom and Death*) and *The Life and Adventures of Alexis Zorbas* (1946; later renamed *Zorba the Greek*) made him internationally known. Zorba gave rise to the image of the ultimate free-spirited Greek male, immortalised by Anthony Quinn in the 1964 movie.

Kazantzakis died of leukemia in Germany on 26 October 1957, while travelling. Despite resistance from the Orthodox Church, he was given a religious funeral and buried in the southern Martinengo Bastion of the old walls of Iraklio. There is a museum honouring him in Myrtia (p190).

Nature & Wildlife

Crete is an island of geographical contrasts, to say the least – you could swim in Vaï's palm-fringed bay and hike in the snow of the Lefka Ori (White Mountains) on the same day. As you pass through its myriad caves, gorges and plateaux, and up and down its stickleback mountains and vast coastline, Crete feels like many countries rolled into one. It's no surprise, then, that the island has a dizzying biodiversity of flora and fauna, from monk seals to golden eagles.

Animals

While Crete is known for its large population of sheep and goats, the island is also home to some endemic fauna, including hares, rabbits, weasels and its own subspecies of badger. You are unlikely to catch sight of the big-eared Cretan spiny mouse, but you never know. The island also has a large population of bats, insects, snails and invertebrates. Other local species include the tiny Cretan tree frog and the Cretan marsh frog.

Between May and September, female loggerhead sea turtles arrive to lay their eggs on sandy beaches, especially in the north. For more information, contact the Archelon Sea Turtle Protection Society of Greece (www.archelon.gr).

The southern coastline, with its steep underwater cliffs, is home to the Mediterranean Sea's most significant population of sperm whales, who gather, feed and possibly mate in the area year-round. It's also abundant with squid, on which the giants feed. Keep your eyes open while on boat trips. Groups of striped dolphins, Risso's dolphins and Cuvier's beaked whales frequent waters off the southern coast. Bottlenose dolphins are often spotted in the shallow waters off Paleohora between Gavdos and its tiny neighbouring islet of Gavdopoula.

The Cretan Sperm Whale Project, run by the Pelagos Cetacean Research Institute (www.pelagosinstitute.gr), monitors the whale population.

Hard-core birdwatchers should try to get their hands on a copy of the excellent but out-of-print *A Birdwatching Guide to Crete* by Stephanie Coghlan.

Bird Life

Crete flies high in the bird world. It lies on the main Africa–Europe migratory routes and well over 400 species have been recorded on the island, including both resident and migratory species. Along the coast you'll find birds of passage such as egrets and herons during spring and autumn migrations.

UNUSUAL ANIMALS OF CRETE

Although you might not spot them, Crete is home to a variety of unusual animals, among them the European rattlesnake (non-venomous), dice snake, cat snake and whip snake. There are also three kinds of scorpion. Arachnophobes should stop reading now, as there are black widow and Araneus spiders in Crete, though instances of people being bitten are scarce. Finally, about 30 different types of shark are found in the Mediterranean, some of which are seen in waters around the island.

ENDANGERED SPECIES

Crete's most famous animal is the *kri-kri or agrimi*, a distinctive wild goat with large horns, often depicted in Minoan art. Only a few survive in the wild, in and around Samaria Gorge and on the islands of Agioi Theodoroi off Hania and Dia off Iraklio.

You may spot a lammergeier (bearded vulture) – one of the rarest raptors in Europe, with a wingspan of nearly 3m – in Samaria Gorge or hovering above the Lasithi Plateau. A few golden eagles and Bonelli's eagles are also recorded in these areas and elsewhere, including the Kato Zakros region. Much good work has been carried out by various organisations in rehabilitating raptors such as bearded vultures and eagles and releasing them into the remoter areas of the Lefka Ori and other ranges.

Crete is battling to protect its population of loggerhead turtles, which have been nesting on island shores since the days of the dinosaurs. The island also has a small population of the rare and endangered Mediterranean monk seal, breeding in caves on the south coast.

The mountains host a wealth of interesting birds. Look for blue rock thrushes, buzzards and the huge griffon vulture. Other birds in the mountains include alpine swifts, stonechats, blackbirds and Sardinian warblers. The fields around Malia host tawny and red-throated pipits, stone curlews, fan-tailed warblers and short-toed larks. On the hillsides below Moni Preveli you may find subalpine and Ruppell's warblers. The Akrotiri Peninsula is good for birdwatching – around the monasteries of Agias Triadas and Gouvernetou you'll find collared and pied flycatchers, wrynecks, tawny pipits, black-eared wheatears, blue rock thrushes, stonechats, chukars and northern wheatears. Migrating species, including avocets and marsh sandpipers, can be spotted in wetland areas such as Elafonisi. The Kavalli Islands off Xerokambos in the southeast are an important breeding ground of the Eleonora's falcon.

There are more than 200 species of wild orchid in Crete, including 14 endemic varieties and the island's famous *Ophrys cretica*, which uses its insectlike appearance as a disguise to attract male insects.

Plants

Crete blooms in every sense of the word, with an estimated total of about 1750 plant species, of which around 170 are endemic. The island's gorges are mini botanical gardens and their isolation has helped preserve many species.

Along the coast, sea daffodils flower in August and September. In April and May, knapweeds are in flower on the western coast and their purple or violet petals provide pretty splashes of colour on sandy beaches. At the same time of year in eastern Crete, especially around Sitia, watch for crimson poppies on the borders of the beach. At the edge of sandy beaches, you'll find delicate pink bindweeds and jujube trees that flower from May to June and bear fruit in September and October. In the same habitat is the tamarisk tree, which flowers in spring.

If you come in summer, you won't be deprived of colour, since milky white and magenta oleanders bloom from June through to August.

On the hillsides look for cistus and brooms in early summer, and yellow chrysanthemums in the fields from March to May. The rare endemic blue flowers of *Anchusa caespitosa*, a type of bugloss, are only found in the high peaks of the Lefka Ori.

With an area of 8335 sq km, Crete is the largest island in the Greek archipelago. It's 250km long, about 60km at its widest point and 12km at its narrowest.

Survival Guide

Directory A–Z

Accessible Travel

If mobility is a problem, visiting Crete will present serious challenges. Most hotels, ferries, museums and sites are not wheelchair accessible, and narrow streets, steep curbs and parked cars make getting around difficult. Newly built hotels are required to be more accessible to people with disabilities by having lifts and rooms with extra-wide doors and spacious bathrooms. People who have visual or hearing impairments are rarely catered to. Assume nothing.

Of the bigger cities, Rethymno has the best accessibility rating. Many of its beaches are wheelchair accessible, as is much of the old quarter, the Venetian Harbour and the waterfront promenade.

For full trip planning, consider **Eria Travel** (www.eria-travel.gr), a travel agency for people with disabilities. Staff can help you find accommodation, adapted transportation and medical support, as well as arranging excursions and activities. The company also operates the **Eria Resort** (☎28210 62790; www.eria-resort.gr; Maleme; d incl half-board from €164; P❄📶🏊) in Maleme in western Crete, which is one of the few in Greece customised to the needs of travellers with disabilities.

For additional help, download Lonely Planet's free Accessible Travel guides from http://lptravel.to/AccessibleTravel.

Customs Regulations

There are no longer duty restrictions within the EU. Upon entering the Crete from outside the EU, customs inspection is usually cursory for foreign tourists and a verbal declaration is generally all that is required. Random searches are still occasionally made for drugs. Note that codeine is illegal in Greece, so if you take medication containing this substance, carry your prescription or a doctor's certificate in case you are questioned.

It is strictly forbidden in Greece to acquire and export antiquities without special permits issued by the Hellenic Ministry of Culture/General Directorate of Antiquities and Cultural Heritage (gda@culture.gr). Severe smuggling penalties might be incurred. It is an offence to remove even the smallest article from an archaeological site.

Cash in excess of €10,000 must be declared.

Duty-free allowances (for anyone over 17) arriving from *non-EU* countries:

- 200 cigarettes or 50 cigars or 250g of tobacco
- 1L spirits over 22% volume or 2L under 22% volume
- 4L wine
- 16L beer
- other goods up to the value of €430 (€150 for under 15 years)

Discount Cards

Camping Card International (www.campingcardinternational.com) Up to 25% savings on camping fees and third-party liability insurance while in the campground.

European Youth Card (www.europeanyouthcard.org) Available for anyone up to the age of 26 or 31, depending on your country; no need to be a student or European resident; discounts of up to 20% at sights, shops and for some transport. Available through the app and website for €14.

International Student Identity Card (www.isic.org) Entitles full-time students aged 12 to 30 to discounts on museum admissions, hostels, shopping, eating and entertainment (searchable online and via the app). Available online or from issuers in your home country. You need proof of your student status, a passport photo and the fee.

Electricity

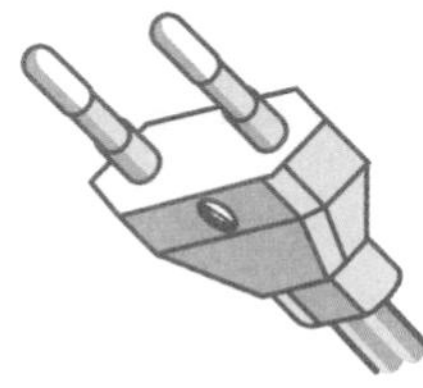

Type C
220V/50Hz

Type F
230V/50Hz

Food

Cretan food, which is distinct from Greek food in general, is some of the best to be found in the Mediterranean. This rustic but rich cuisine combines seasonal ingredients and balanced flavours that reflect the bounty of Crete's sun-blessed fertile land. See also Eat & Drink Like a Local (p47).

Health

Before You Go

HEALTH INSURANCE

If you're an EU citizen, a European Health Insurance Card (EHIC; formerly the E111) covers you for most medical care but not emergency repatriation home or non-emergencies. Citizens from other countries should find out if there is a reciprocal arrangement for free medical care between their country and Greece. If you do need health insurance, make sure you get a policy that covers you for the worst possible scenario, such as an accident requiring an emergency flight home. Find out in advance if your insurance plan will make payments directly to providers or reimburse you later.

RECOMMENDED VACCINATIONS

No vaccinations are required for travel to Crete, but the World Health Organization (WHO) recommends that all travellers be covered for diphtheria, tetanus, measles, mumps, rubella and polio.

MEDICAL CHECKLIST

➡ Bring your medications in original, clearly labelled containers.

➡ Get a signed and dated letter from your doctor describing your medical conditions and medications, including generic names. In Greece it is illegal to import codeine-based medication without a doctor's prescription or certificate.

In Crete

AVAILABILITY & COST OF HEALTHCARE

➡ If you need an ambulance call ☎166.

➡ For minor illnesses, pharmacies provide valuable advice, sell medication (often available only on prescription in the US and other European countries) and advise on whether to see a doctor.

➡ Medical training is of a high standard in Greece, but the health service is chronically underfunded. Public hospitals are often overcrowded, hygiene is not always what it should be, and relatives are expected to provide food for the patient. That said, Iraklio, Hania and Rethymno have modern public hospitals.

➡ Conditions and treatment are much better in private hospitals, but these are expensive. All this means that a good health-insurance policy is essential.

➡ Condoms are widely available but emergency contraception may not be.

TAP WATER

➡ Tap water is chlorinated and safe to drink.

➡ Bottled water in plastic bottles is widely available, but think about environmental considerations.

ENVIRONMENTAL HAZARDS

➡ Mosquitoes are annoying, but there is no danger of contracting malaria.

➡ The Asian tiger mosquito *(Aedes albopictus)*, which may be encountered in mountainous areas, can be a voracious daytime biter. It is known to carry several viruses, including the West Nile Virus and Eastern Equine Encephalitis, which can affect the central nervous system and cause severe complications and death.

➡ Electric mosquito-repellent devices are usually sufficient to keep the insects at bay at night. Choose accommodation that has flyscreens on the windows wherever possible.

EATING PRICE RANGES

The following price ranges refer to the average cost of a main course and are inclusive of tax and service charges.

€	less than €10
€€	€10–20
€€€	more than €20

Insurance

➡ Comprehensive travel insurance to cover theft, loss and medical problems is highly recommended.

➡ Some policies specifically exclude dangerous activities such as diving, motorcycling and even trekking; read the fine print.

➡ Check that the policy covers ambulances and an emergency flight home.

➡ Find out if your insurance plan makes payments directly to providers or reimburses you later.

➡ Paying for airline tickets or car hire with a credit card sometimes provides limited travel insurance – ask your credit-card company what it covers.

➡ Consider coverage for luggage theft or loss. If you have a home insurance policy, check it if also covers your possessions while travelling.

➡ Worldwide travel insurance is available at www.lonelyplanet.com/travel-insurance. You can buy, extend and claim online anytime – even if you're already on the road.

Internet Access

➡ Most cafes, bars, restaurants and hotels offer free wi-fi, although you may need to request a password.

➡ In some hotels, access may be limited to certain rooms and/or public areas.

➡ Some hotels have a business centre or internet corner with printer for their guests, often at no charge.

➡ There's free municipal wi-fi in numerous municipalities, including parts of Hania, Paleohora, Rethymno, Sitia, Iraklio and Agios Nikolaos.

Legal Matters

➡ It's a good idea to carry your passport with you at all times in case you're stopped by the police and questioned. Greek citizens are presumed to have identification on them and the police expect much the same from foreign visitors.

➡ The permissible blood-alcohol content for drivers is 0.05%.

➡ Greek drug laws are among the strictest in Europe. Possession of even a small amount of marijuana is likely to land you in jail.

➡ If you're arrested, insist on an interpreter (διερμηνέας; *the*-lo dhi-ermi-*nea*) and/or a lawyer (δικηγόρος; *the*-lo dhi-ki-*go*-ro). If you don't have a lawyer, contact your embassy for a referral.

EMBASSIES & CONSULATES

The UK is the only country with a consulate in Crete (in Iraklio). Other countries are represented by their embassies in Athens.

COUNTRY	TELEPHONE	WEBSITE
Australia	☎210 870 4000	www.greece.embassy.gov.au
Canada	☎210 727 3400	www.greece.gc.ca
France	☎210 339 1000	www.ambafrance-gr.org
Germany	☎210 728 5111	www.athen.diplo.de
Ireland	☎210 723 2771	www.embassyofireland.gr
Netherlands	☎210 725 4900	www.netherlandsandyou.nl
New Zealand	☎210 692 4136	www.mfat.govt.nz
Turkey	☎210 726 3000	http://athens.emb.mfa.gov.tr
UK	☎2810 224012	www.ukingreece.fco.gov.uk/en
USA	☎210 721 2951	https://gr.usembassy.gov

LGBT+ Travellers

Crete does not have much of an open LGBT+ scene. The church plays a prominent role in shaping Cretans' views and homosexuality is frowned upon by many locals, especially in rural areas and among the older generations. Overall, though, acceptance has increased in recent years, especially in bigger cities such as Iraklio and Hania. Still, the local LGBT+ community is discreet and it pays to follow its lead.

- Same-sex couples should not have trouble finding lodging. For leads on gay-friendly hotels, check www.travelbyinterest.com. Gay-owned Home Hotel (www.home-hotel.gr) near Hersonisos has a fine reputation among LGBT+ travellers.
- The website www.gaycrete.com has some useful information on gay beaches, gay-friendly bars and lodging.
- Despite the name, Villa Ralfa (www.villaralfa.com) is not a hotel but an LGBT+ information site, although much of it appears outdated.
- The Spartacus International Gay Guide (www.spartacusworld.com/en), published by Bruno Gmünder (Berlin), is widely regarded as the leading authority on gay travel.
- Popular international smartphone apps are also in use.

Maps

Google Maps works well for driving around and can be downloaded for offline use. However, if you're planning on doing extensive driving or hiking around Crete, a good printed map still has its uses. Printed maps are widely available online, in bookshops and in tourist shops, and cost around €8. Maps distributed by car-hire agencies and hotels are rarely useful and often inaccurate.

Anavasi (www.anavasi.gr) Publishes excellent digital and printed road and hiking maps, including three separate road maps covering Hania, Rethymno and Iraklio, and Lasithi at a scale of 1:100,000. Walking maps include the Lefka Ori (Sfakia and Pahnes), Samaria/Sougia, Mt Psiloritis and Zakros-Vaï at a scale of 1:25,000 or 1:35,000.

Michelin (www.michelin.com) Single-sheet map of the entire island at 1:140,000.

Terrain (www.terrainmaps.gr) Tops for waterproof and rip-proof hiking maps, with good labelled distances. Offers western Crete, central Crete and eastern Crete maps at 1:100,000. Maps are also available via the ViewRanger smartphone app.

Money

Currency in Crete is the euro (€), with seven notes (five, 10, 20, 50, 100, 200 and 500) and eight coins (one- and two-euro coins and one-, two-, five-, 10-, 20- and 50-cent coins).

ATMs

- The easiest, quickest and usually cheapest way to obtain cash is by using your debit (bank) card at an ATM linked to international networks such as Cirrus, Plus, Star and Maestro.
- There are ATMs in almost every town large enough to support a bank, and in tourist areas. In rural areas, only larger towns have ATMs, so plan ahead, especially in the southwest and southeast. It's best to carry some cash.

Credit Cards

- Big resorts and hotels accept credit cards, but family-owned properties often don't or don't like to. Ask. Likewise, upmarket shops and restaurants accept plastic, but village tavernas and small shops almost never do.
- The main credit cards – MasterCard and Visa – are widely accepted. American Express and Diners Club are common in tourist areas only.

Changing Money

- Post offices can exchange banknotes and charge less commission than banks.
- Travel agencies and hotels often change money at bank rates, but commission charges are higher.
- Automated foreign-exchange machines are sometimes available in major tourist areas. They take all the major European currencies, Australian and US dollars and Japanese yen, and are useful in an emergency, although they charge a hefty commission.

Opening Hours

- Museum and archaeological site opening hours depend on budgeting, ie if there's enough cash to hire afternoon staff. It's always wise to check ahead, especially for afternoon visits. Most sites are closed on Monday or Tuesday.
- *Periptera* (kiosks) open from early morning until late at night and sell everything from bus tickets and cigarettes to condoms.

Opening hours vary throughout the year. The following are high-season opening hours (July and August); hours are more limited in the shoulder seasons (April–June, September–October), and some places shut down completely during low season (November–March).

Banks 8am–2.30pm Monday to Thursday, 8am–2pm Friday

Bars 8pm–late

Cafes 10am–midnight

Clubs 10pm–late

Post Offices 7.30am–3pm Monday to Friday (rural); 7.30am–8pm Monday to Friday, 7.30am–2pm Saturday (urban)

PRACTICALITIES

Newspapers The daily English-language edition of Kathimerini (www.ekathimerini.com), published as part of the International New York Times, is handy for keeping tabs on Greek current affairs.

Smoking Antismoking legislation adopted in 2008 prohibits lighting up in all enclosed public spaces, including cafes, restaurants, nightclubs, offices, businesses and transport stations. Effectively, though, the law was never implemented and is widely ignored, both by smokers and local police.

Weights & Measures Greece uses the metric system.

Restaurants 11am–4pm and 7–11pm

Shops 9am–2pm Monday to Saturday and 5.30–8.30pm or 9pm Tuesday, Thursday and Friday; all day in summer in resorts

Photography

- Crete is a photographer's dream. *Lonely Planet's Guide to Travel Photography* is full of helpful photography tips.
- Never photograph a military installation.
- Flash photography is never allowed inside churches, and it's taboo to photograph the main altar.
- People generally don't seem to mind having their picture taken in the context of an overall scene, but if you want a close-up shot, ask first. Same goes for video.
- If a sign says no photography, honour it.
- At archaeological sites, you may be stopped from using a tripod, which marks you as a professional and thereby requires special permissions.

Postal Services

Postal service in Greece is provided by ELTA (Elliniki Tahydromia). Post offices *(tahydromia)* are easily identifiable by the yellow signs outside. Normal postboxes are also yellow, with red boxes for express mail. Check www.elta.gr (also in English) for up-to-date postage rates and locations of post offices.

- To mail abroad, use yellow postboxes labelled *exoteriko*.
- Some tourist shops also sell stamps.
- Don't wrap a parcel before sending it: post office staff may wish to inspect it.

Public Holidays

All banks, post offices, public services, museums and ancient sites close on public holidays. Small shops, especially in tourist towns, may be open. Greek national public holidays observed in Crete:

New Year's Day 1 January

Epiphany 6 January

First Sunday in Lent February

Greek Independence Day 25 March

Good Friday March/April

(Orthodox) Easter Sunday 19 April 2020, 2 May 2021, 24 April 2022

May Day (Protomagia) 1 May

Whit Monday (Agiou Pnevmatos) 50 days after Easter Sunday

Feast of the Assumption 15 August

Ohi Day 28 October

Christmas Day 25 December

St Stephen's Day 26 December

Telephone Services

The Greek telephone service is maintained by the public corporation OTE (pronounced o-teh; Organismos Tilepikoinonion Ellados). Public telephones are still quite common, although demand has dwindled with the proliferation of mobile phones. The phones are easy to operate, take phonecards, not coins, and can be used for local, long-distance and international calls. The 'i' at the top left of the push-button dialling panel brings up the operating instructions in English.

All phone numbers have 10 digits. Landline numbers start with '2', mobile numbers start with '6'.

Mobile Phones

- Mobile (cell) phones operate on GSM900/1800.
- In June 2017, the European Union implemented the 'roam like at home' rules. If your phone is registered in an EU country, you don't pay roaming charges when calling, texting (sending SMS), using data or receiving calls or texts while in another EU country (provided your tariff plan includes those services). If mobile services are provided via satellite, 'roam like at home' does not apply (eg on cruise ships).
- If you don't have a phone from an EU country, getting a local SIM card might work out cheaper than using your own network, provided you have an unlocked phone. US and Canadian phones need to be multi-band.
- SIM cards are sold by Greece's three mobile phone service providers – Vodafone, Cosmote and Wind. Top-up cards are available at supermarkets, kiosks and newsagents.
- Overall, Cosmote tends to have the best coverage, including in remote areas.

➡ Use of a mobile phone while driving is only allowed if you have a hands-free system.

Phone Codes

Calling Crete from abroad Dial your country's international access code, then 30 (Greece's country code) followed by the 10-digit local number.

Calling internationally from Crete Dial ☎00 (the international access code), the country code, and the local number.

Reverse-charge (collect) calls Dial the operator (domestic ☎129; international ☎139) to get the number in the country you wish to call.

Phonecards

➡ Public phones take OTE phonecards *(telekarta)*, not coins. These cards are sold at kiosks, corner shops and tourist shops.

➡ Don't remove your card before you are told to do so or you could wipe out the remaining credit.

➡ You can also buy a range of prepaid international calling cards *(hronokarta)* with good rates. Cards come with instructions in Greek and English. They involve dialling an access code, then punching in your card number.

Time

Clocks in Greece are set to Eastern European Time (GMT/UTC plus two hours). Daylight-saving time starts on the last Sunday in March and ends on the last Sunday in October.

Tipping

Bartenders An euro per round or round to the nearest euro.

Hotel porters or stewards on ferries Between €1 and €3 per bag.

Restaurants Generally included in the bill and a tip is not expected, but it is customary to round up the bill or add about 10% if the service was good.

Taxi drivers Round up the fare.

Toilets

➡ One peculiarity of the Greek plumbing system is that apparently it can't handle toilet paper as the pipes are too narrow and back up easily. Toilet paper, tampons etc should all be placed in the small bin provided.

➡ Very occasionally outside the big towns you might come across squat toilets in older houses, *kafeneia* (coffee houses) and public toilets.

➡ Public toilets are rare, except at airports and bus and train stations. Cafes are the best option, but you are expected to buy something for the privilege.

Tourist Information

Municipal tourist offices are rare outside the cities. Even then, most are only open on weekdays until the early afternoon and only have a smattering of free maps and brochures. Travel agencies often fill the void. The website of the **Greek National Tourist Organisation** (EOT; www.visitgreece.gr) has some information on Crete.

Visas

Greece is a Schengen Agreement nation and governed by those rules.

EU & Schengen countries No visa required.

Australia, Canada, Israel, Japan, New Zealand & USA Among the countries not requiring a visa for tourist visits of up to 90 days. For longer stays, contact your nearest Greek embassy or consulate and begin your application well in advance.

Other countries You need a Schengen Visa from the embassy or consulate of the country that is your primary destination. For details, check with a Greek mission in your country.

Volunteering

Lonely Planet does not endorse any organisation that it does not work with directly. Travellers should investigate any volunteering option thoroughly before committing to a project. Note that child welfare experts recommend against drop-in and short-term visits.

Crete for Life (www.creteforlife.com) Recuperative holiday camp for disadvantaged kids near Ierapetra.

Global Volunteers (www.globalvolunteers.org) Teach conversational English to children in Malevizi west of Iraklio.

Sea Turtle Protection Society of Greece (www.archelon.gr) Has monitoring programs in Hania, Rethymno and the Bay of Mesara.

Women Travellers

➡ Crete is remarkably safe for women to explore, even for solo travellers. Going alone to cafes and restaurants is perfectly acceptable. This does not mean you should be lulled into complacency; bag-snatching and sexual harassment do occur.

➡ On beaches and in bars and nightclubs, solo women are likely to attract attention from men. *Kamaki*, the Greek word for men on the hunt for foreign women, translates as 'fishing trident'.

➡ If you don't want company, most men will respect a firm 'no, thank you'. If you feel threatened, protesting loudly will often make the offender slink away or spur others to come to your defence.

Transport

GETTING THERE & AWAY

Crete is easy to reach by air or sea – particularly in summer when it opens its arms (and schedules) wide. In the off season, you will need to change planes in Athens. Flights, cars and tours can be booked online at lonelyplanet.com/bookings.

Entering Crete

Entering Crete is usually a very straightforward procedure. If arriving from any of the Schengen countries (ie EU member states plus Iceland, Norway and Switzerland), passports are rarely given more than a cursory glance, but customs and police might be interested in what you are carrying. EU citizens may also enter Greece on a national identity card. Visitors from outside the EU may require a visa (p295). This must be checked with consular authorities before you arrive.

Passport

Having stamps from certain countries (eg Israel, Cuba) in your passport does not automatically disqualify you from entry into Greece.

Air

Most travellers arrive in Crete by air, often with a change in Athens. Travellers from North America need to connect via a European gateway city such as Paris, Amsterdam or Frankfurt and sometimes again in Athens. To reach Crete by air from other Greek islands also requires a change in Athens, except for some flights operated by Crete-based airline **Sky Express** (☎21521 56510; www.skyexpress.gr).

Airports & Airlines

Iraklio's Nikos Kazantzakis Heraklion International Airport is Crete's busiest airport, although Hania is convenient for travellers heading to western Crete. The small airport in Sitia only receives a handful of domestic and summertime charter flights from northern Europe.

Between May and October, European low-cost carriers easyJet and Ryanair operate direct flights to Crete, mostly from the UK, Germany, Poland, Sweden and Italy. Ryanair also runs domestic flights to Iraklio from Athens and from Hania to Thessaloniki.

Nikos Kazantzakis Heraklion International Airport (HER;☎2810 397800; www.ypa.gr/en/our-airports/kratikos-aerolimenas-hrakleioy-n-kazantzakhs) About 5km east of the city centre, the airport has a bank, ATMs, duty-free shops and cafe-bars.

Hania International Airport (☎28210 83800; www.chania-airport.com) Hania's airport is 14km east of town on the Akrotiri Peninsula and is served year-round from Athens and seasonally from throughout Europe.

Sitia Municipal Airport (JSH;☎28430 24424) This small airport about 1km north of Sitia town centre handles domestic flights to Athens, Alexandroupoli, Iraklio, Kassos and Rhodes as well as seasonal charter flights from Germany and Scandinavia.

DOMESTIC CARRIERS

Aegean Airlines (☎210 626 1000; www.aegeanair.com) Greece's largest carrier has year-round flights between Athens and Iraklio, Hania and Sitia. From Iraklio it also flies to several other European destinations, including Paris, Berlin and Moscow (some seasonally). In 2013, Aegean merged with Olympic Air (www.olympicair.com), but flights operate under both brands.

Sky Express (☎21521 56510; www.skyexpress.gr) This Iraklio-based airline serves 32 destinations, mostly within Greece, including Athens, Corfu, Mytilini (Lesvos), Rhodes, Kos, Samos, Chios, Karpathos and Volos. From Sitia it flies to 10 destinations, including Alexandroupolis, Rhodes and Preveza.

Astra Airlines (☎23104 89391; www.astra-airlines.gr) This tiny Thessaloniki-based airline has flights from Thessaloniki to Iraklio and Sitia and seasonal services to Munich, Tel Aviv and Stockholm.

Land

Bus

Hardcore overlanders with plenty of time can cobble together a long-distance bus trip to Athens, which usually requires at least one change in an eastern European city, such as Bratislava, Budapest or Belgrade. From there, a ferry will take you to Crete. The journey takes at least two days and is usually more expensive than flying. A helpful website is www.rome2rio.com.

Car & Motorcycle

From most European countries, travelling to Crete by car takes several days and thus only makes sense for extended stays. The fastest way is to hop on a ferry from Italy. A high-speed ferry trip from Venice to Patra takes about 31 hours, or 16 hours from Bari. From Patra it's a further 200km drive south to Piraeus (near Athens), where you can catch another ferry to Iraklio, Sitia or Hania.

It's possible to drive to Athens via Slovenia, Croatia, Bulgaria and North Macedonia, but the savings are not huge and are far outweighed by the distance involved.

Train

A sample itinerary from London would see you catching the Eurostar to Paris, the TGV to Milan and, from there, a coastal train to Bari, where you can pick up an overnight ferry to Patra. From there, catch the train to Athens and hop on a ferry to Crete in Piraeus. Overland enthusiasts can also reach Athens on a fascinating rail route through the Balkan peninsula, passing through Croatia, Serbia and North Macedonia.

The excellent website www.seat61.com has comprehensive details.

Sea

Crete is well served by ferry, with at least one daily departure from Piraeus (near Athens) to Iraklio and Hania year-round and several per day in summer. There are also ports in Sita in the east and Kissamos in the west, which have slow-ferry routes. Timetables change from season to season and are not announced until just prior to the season, due to competition for route licences. Services are considerably curtailed from November to April. Ferries are subject to delays and cancellations at short notice due to bad weather, strikes or mechanical problems.

Ferry Routes to/from Crete

Ferries fan out across the Mediterranean from four ports in Crete, all on the north coast. The busiest is in Iraklio, from where **Anek Lines** (www.anek.gr) has daily boats to Piraeus and travels to Santorini, the Cycladic islands of Milos and Anafi as well as Kasos, Karpathos, Halki and Rhodes in the Dodecanese. **Golden Star** (www.goldenstarferries.gr) serves Santorini and Mykonos, while **Sea Jets** (www.seajets.gr) steers towards Mykonos, Paros, Naxos, Ios and Santorini. **Minoan Lines** (www.minoan.gr) runs a daily ferry from Iraklio to Piraeus, which is also served daily by Anek from Hania and weekly from Sitia. From the latter, Anek subsidiary **Aegeon Pelagos** (☎Hania 28210 24000; www.anek.gr) travels to various islands in the Cyclades and the Dodecanese. From Kissamos in the far west, there's direct service to Kythira and Gythio provided by **Triton Ferries** (☎28210 75444; www.tritonferries.gr).

All ferry companies adjust routes and services according to seasonal demand. For current routes, timetables and fares – and to book tickets – consult the companies' websites or go to www.gtp.gr, www.openseas.gr, www.ferries.gr or www.greekferries.gr.

DEPARTURE TAX

Departure tax is included in the price of a ticket.

CLIMATE CHANGE & TRAVEL

Every form of transport that relies on carbon-based fuel generates CO_2, the main cause of human-induced climate change. Modern travel is dependent on aeroplanes, which might use less fuel per kilometre per person than most cars but travel much greater distances. The altitude at which aircraft emit gases (including CO_2) and particles also contributes to their climate change impact. Many websites offer 'carbon calculators' that allow people to estimate the carbon emissions generated by their journey and, for those who wish to do so, to offset the impact of the greenhouse gases emitted with contributions to portfolios of climate-friendly initiatives throughout the world. Lonely Planet offsets the carbon footprint of all staff and author travel.

Ferries to Crete

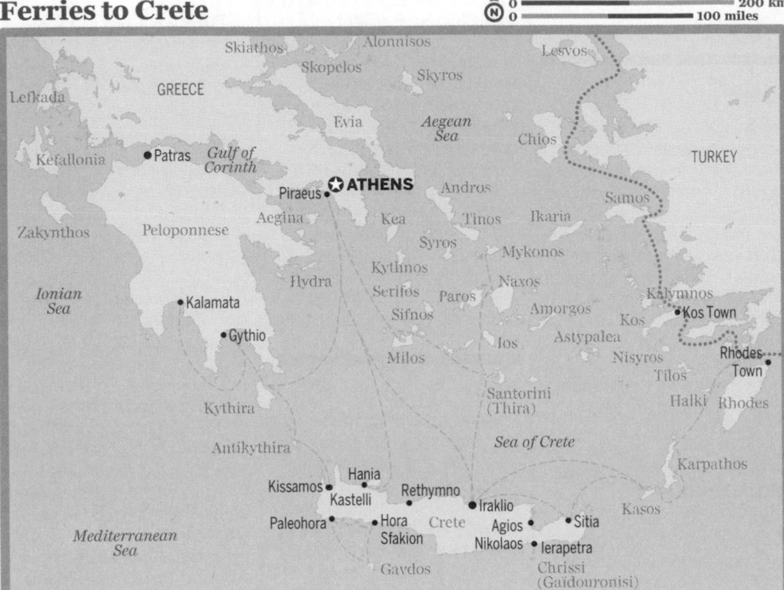

Ferry Companies

Anek Lines (www.anek.gr) Main ferry to/from Piraeus; ferries out of Sitia are operated by affiliated Aegeon Pelagos Sea Lines.

Golden Star (http://goldenstarferries.gr) Ferries to/from Cyclades.

Minoan Lines (www.minoan.gr) High-speed luxury ferries to/from Piraeus.

Sea Jets (www.seajets.gr) High-speed catamarans to/from Cyclades.

Triton Ferries (www.tritonferries.gr) Ferries linking Kissamos with Gythio and Kythira.

Tickets

➡ During high season, or if you're bringing a car, book well in advance, especially for overnight and high-speed catamaran services.

➡ Tickets are best purchased online, either directly from the ferry company or through a booking engine such as www.greekferries.gr or www.ferries.gr.

➡ If a service is cancelled, you can transfer your ticket to the next available service with that company.

➡ Prices are determined by the distance and the class, which ranges from deck class to double-berth outside cabins.

➡ Children, students and seniors usually qualify for discounts ranging from 10% to 50%. Children under the age of five often travel free.

Yacht

Although yachting is a popular way to explore the Greek islands, Crete is a long way from other islands and does not have a huge yachting industry. The sailing season lasts from April until October; however, between July and September the *meltemi* (dry northerly) winds can ground you regularly.

GETTING AROUND

Air

There are no commercial flights within Crete.

Bicycle

Cycling is becoming more common in Crete, but the often-hilly terrain means you need strong leg muscles and endurance if that's your preferred method of getting around. Dedicated bike lanes do not exist.

You can hire bikes in most tourist areas, with prices ranging from €10 to €30 per day, depending on the bike. Weekly hire tends to be a bit cheaper. Bicycles may be carried for free on ferries. For details, suggested routes and guided tours, see www.cyclingcreta.gr. Another good resource is www.bikemap.net.

Boat

Boats link the towns along Crete's southwestern coast in the Sfakia region of Hania. From May to October, **Anendyk** (☎8am-4pm Mon-Fri 28250 91221; www.anendyk.gr; New Harbour) operates daily boats between Paleohora, Sougia, Agia Roumeli, Loutro and Hora Sfakion, in both directions. Boats to Gavdos Island leave from Hora Sfakion and Paleohora, stopping in Sougia, Agia Roumeli or Loutro en route. Schedules change seasonally; always check ahead. Ferries get cancelled in bad weather.

Taxi boats operate in several southern coastal towns, including Agia Galini, Plakias, Sougia and Hora Sfakion. These are essentially small boats that transport people to places that are difficult to get to by land, such as secluded beaches. Some owners charge a set price for each person, and others charge a flat rate for the boat.

Local operators run excursions to offshore islands and nearby beaches, including Ierapetra to Chrissi Island (Gaïdouronisi or Hrysi), Agios Nikolaos to Spinalonga Island, Kissamos to the Gramvousa Peninsula (Balos beach), and Paleohora to Elafonisi.

Bus

Buses are the only form of public transport in Crete, but in most regions a fairly extensive network makes it relatively easy to travel between major towns and villages. Travel is safe and buses are quite comfortable. Fares are government regulated and quite reasonable by European standards. For the latest timetables, check http://e-ktel.com for western Crete and www.ktelherlas.gr for central and eastern Crete.

Car & Motorcycle

Having your own wheels is handy for getting around and necessary if you want to to explore Crete away from the coastal resorts. Although distances are often not that great, travelling on narrow and winding mountain roads will seriously slow you down, so factor that into your day's itinerary. In remote areas (particularly the south), you'll still come across unpaved roads that may require a 4WD.

Driving Licences

EU driving licences are valid in Crete. Hire companies require the corresponding driving licence for every vehicle class (for example, motorcycle/moped licence for motorbikes or mopeds). Greek law requires drivers from outside the EU to have an International Driving Permit (IDP). Hire companies will request it, as may local authorities if you're stopped. International Driving Permits can only be obtained in person and in the country where your driving licence was issued. Carry this alongside your regular licence.

Fuel

In the populated areas fuel is generally widely available, but petrol stations are quite rare in the mountain regions, so top up before setting out on a major road trip. Some service stations are closed on weekends and public holidays. Self-service pumps and credit-card pumps are not the norm. Some stations don't take plastic at all, so it is always advisable to carry some cash.

Hire

CAR

- The major international companies have branches at airports and in the bigger towns.
- Prices are often better if you prebook rentals through consolidators such as Auto Europe (www.autoeurope.com) and Holiday Autos (www.holidayautos.com). Rates from local companies can also be quite competitive and there's usually haggling room during the off season.
- The minimum driving age in Greece is 18 years, but most car-hire firms require you to be at least 21, or 23 for larger vehicles. In some cases, younger drivers may be able to hire (but they may have to pay extra).
- Most hire cars are manual, so book ahead if you need an automatic car as they are rare and usually more expensive.
- Always check what the insurance includes; there are often rough roads or dangerous routes that you can only tackle in a 4WD.

MOTORCYCLE

- Mopeds, motorcycles and scooters are available for hire wherever there are tourists who want to rent them. Most models are newish and in good condition. Nonetheless, check brakes before committing.
- You must produce a licence that shows proficiency to ride the category of bike you wish to hire; this applies to everything from 50cc up. British citizens must obtain a Category A1 licence from the Driver & Vehicle Licensing Agency (www.dft.gov.uk/dvla) in the UK (in most other EU countries separate licences are automatically issued).
- Rates start from about €20 per day for a moped or 50cc motorcycle, rising to €35 per day for a 250cc motorcycle, and drop considerably out of season.
- Most motorcycle hirers include third-party insurance in the price, but it's wise to check this. This insurance

ROAD HAZARDS

The main dangers in Crete lie in the local driving culture. Road rules are routinely ignored and there is barely any police presence. Cretan drivers are generally erratic: expect to be tailgated, honked at and aggressively and illegally overtaken if you move too slowly. Overtaking on bends and ignoring double lines and stop signs are also prevalent. Other dangers to keep in mind:

➡ Try to avoid night driving; drink-driving laws are barely enforced so roads are dangerous.

➡ Expect narrow roads, unprotected embankments and blind curves on mountain roads.

➡ Road surfaces can change unexpectedly when a section of road has succumbed to subsidence or weathering.

➡ In the mountains, expect to stop for herds of sheep or goats on the road.

➡ Not all falling-rock zones are signposted, nor hemmed with nets or tarps; always keep a keen eye out for loose rocks on the road.

will not include medical expenses.

➡ Helmets are compulsory and agencies are obliged to offer one as part of the hire deal.

Insurance

Greek law requires that all registered vehicles, including those brought in from abroad, carry third-party liability insurance. When hiring a vehicle, make sure your contract includes adequate liability insurance. Hire companies almost never include insurance that covers damage to the vehicle itself, called Collision Damage Waiver (CDW) or Loss Damage Waiver (LDW). It's optional, but driving without it is not recommended. Some credit-card companies cover CDW/LDW for a certain period if you charge the entire hire fee to your card (often with a deductible/excess). Always confirm with your card issuer ahead of time what coverage it provides in Greece.

Road Rules

➡ Driving is on the right side of the road and passing only on the left. On highways, slower drivers are expected to straddle the narrow service lane and let faster traffic pass.

➡ Outside built-up areas, unless signed otherwise, traffic on a main road has right of way at intersections. In towns, vehicles coming from the right have right of way. This includes roundabouts – even if you're in the roundabout, you must give way to drivers coming onto the roundabout to your right.

➡ Seatbelts must be worn in front seats, and in back seats if the car is fitted with them.

➡ Children under 12 years of age are not allowed in the front seat.

➡ It is compulsory to carry a first-aid kit, fire extinguisher and warning (hazard) triangle, and it is forbidden to carry cans of petrol.

➡ Helmets are compulsory for motorcyclists. Police will book you if you're caught without a helmet.

➡ The speed limit is 120km/h on highways, 90km/h on other roads and 50km/h in built-up areas. The speed limit for motorcycles is the same as cars. Drivers exceeding the speed limit will be fined. You will be told where to pay.

➡ A blood-alcohol content of over 0.05% can incur a fine and over 0.08% is a criminal offence.

➡ If you are involved in an accident and no one is hurt, the police will not be required to write a report, but it is advisable to go to a nearby police station and explain what happened. You may need a police report for insurance purposes. If an accident involves injury, a driver who does not stop and does not inform the police may face a prison sentence.

➡ Driving in the major cities and small towns is a nightmare of erratic one-way streets, double parking and irregularly enforced parking rules. Cars are not towed away but fines can be expensive.

➡ Designated parking for disabled drivers is a rarity.

➡ Using a mobile phone while driving is illegal.

Hitching

Hitchhiking is never entirely safe, and we don't recommend it. Travellers who hitch should understand that they are taking a small but potentially serious risk. If you decide to hitch, remember that it's safer to travel in pairs and be sure to inform someone of your intended destination. In Crete you don't hitch with your thumb up as in northern Europe, but with an outstretched hand, palm down to the road.

As elsewhere, getting out of cities tends to be hard work; hitching is much easier in rural areas. On country roads, it is not unknown for someone to stop and ask if you want a lift even if you haven't asked for one.

Local Transport

Bus

City buses operating in the larger towns, such as Iraklio, Rethymno, Hania, Agios Nikolaos and Ierapetra, serve mostly the residential suburbs and thus are rarely useful for visitors. Tickets are normally bought at *periptera* (kiosks). There may be a surcharge if buying from the driver.

Taxi

Taxis are widely available except in remote villages. Large towns have taxi stands that post a list of prices to outlying destinations, which removes anxiety about overcharging. Otherwise, in cities make sure the meter is used. Rural taxis often do not have meters, so you should always settle on a price before getting in.

Language

The Greek language is believed to be one of the oldest European languages, with an oral tradition of 4000 years and a written tradition of approximately 3000 years. Due to its centuries of influence, Greek constitutes the origin of a large part of the vocabulary of many Indo-European languages (including English), and many of the terms used in science.

Greek is the official language of Greece and co-official language of Cyprus, and is spoken by many emigrant communities throughout the world.

The Greek alphabet is explained on the next page, but if you read the blue pronunciation guides given with each phrase in this chapter as if they were English, you'll be understood. Note that dh is pronounced as 'th' in 'there'; gh is a softer, slightly throaty version of 'g'; and kh is a throaty sound like the 'ch' in the Scottish 'loch'. All Greek words of two or more syllables have an acute accent (΄), which indicates where the stress falls. In our pronunciation guides, stressed syllables are in italics.

In Greek, all nouns, articles and adjectives are either masculine, feminine or neuter – in this chapter these forms are included where necessary, separated with a slash and indicated with 'm/f/n'.

The Greek question mark is represented with the English equivalent of a semicolon (;).

BASICS

Hello.	Γειά σας. Γειά σου.	*ya*·sas (polite) *ya*·su (informal)

WANT MORE?

For in-depth language information and handy phrases, check out Lonely Planet's *Greek Phrasebook*. You'll find it at **shop.lonelyplanet.com**, or you can buy Lonely Planet's iPhone phrasebooks at the Apple App Store.

Good morning.	Καλημέρα.	ka·li·*me*·ra
Good evening.	Καλησπέρα.	ka·li·*spe*·ra
Goodbye.	Αντίο.	an·*di*·o
Yes./No.	Ναι./Οχι.	ne/*o*·hi
Please.	Παρακαλώ.	pa·ra·ka·*lo*
Thank you.	Ευχαριστώ.	ef·ha·ri·*sto*
That's fine./ You're welcome.	Παρακαλώ.	pa·ra·ka·*lo*
Sorry.	Συγγνώμη.	sigh·*no*·mi

What's your name?
Πώς σας λένε; — pos sas *le*·ne

My name is ...
Με λένε … — me *le*·ne ...

Do you speak English?
Μιλάτε αγγλικά; — mi·*la*·te an·gli·*ka*

I (don't) understand.
(Δεν) καταλαβαίνω. — (dhen) ka·ta·la·*ve*·no

ACCOMMODATION

campsite	χώρος για κάμπινγκ	*kho*·ros yia *kam*·ping
hotel	ξενοδοχείο	kse·no·dho·*khi*·o
youth hostel	γιουθ χόστελ	yuth *kho*·stel

a ... room	ένα … δωμάτιο	e·na ... dho·*ma*·ti·o
single	μονόκλινο	mo·*no*·kli·no
double	δίκλινο	*dhi*·kli·no

How much is it ...?	Πόσο κάνει …;	*po*·so *ka*·ni ...
per night	τη βραδυά	ti·vra·*dhya*
per person	το άτομο	to *a*·to·mo

air-con	έρκοντίσιον	er·kon·*di*·si·on
bathroom	μπάνιο	*ba*·nio
fan	ανεμιστήρας	a·ne·mi·*sti*·ras
TV	τηλεόραση	ti·le·*o*·ra·si
window	παράθυρο	pa·*ra*·thi·ro

DIRECTIONS

Where is ...?
Πού είναι ...; — pu *i*·ne ...

What's the address?
Ποια είναι η διεύθυνση; — pia *i*·ne i dhi·*ef*·thin·si

Can you show me (on the map)?
Μπορείς να μου δείξεις (στο χάρτη); — bo·*ris* na mu *dhik*·sis (sto *khar*·ti)

Turn left.
Στρίψτε αριστερά. — *strips*·te a·ri·ste·*ra*

Turn right.
Στρίψτε δεξιά. — *strips*·te dhe·*ksia*

at the next corner
στην επόμενη γωνία — stin e·*po*·me·ni gho·*ni*·a

at the traffic lights
στα φώτα — sta *fo*·ta

behind	πίσω	*pi*·so
in front of	μπροστά	bro·*sta*
far	μακριά	ma·kri·*a*
near (to)	κοντά	kon·*da*
next to	δίπλα	*dhi*·pla
opposite	απέναντι	a·*pe*·nan·di
straight ahead	ολο ευθεία.	*o*·lo ef·*thi*·a

EATING & DRINKING

a table for ...	Ενα τραπέζι για ...	e·na tra·*pe*·zi ya ...
(two) people	(δύο) άτομα	(*dhi*·o) *a*·to·ma
(eight) o'clock	στις (οχτώ)	stis (okh·*to*)

I don't eat ...	Δεν τρώγω ...	dhen *tro*·gho ...
fish	ψάρι	*psa*·ri
(red) meat	(κόκκινο) κρέας	(*ko*·ki·no) *kre*·as
peanuts	φυστίκια	fi·*sti*·kia
poultry	πουλερικά	pu·le·ri·*ka*

GREEK ALPHABET

The Greek alphabet has 24 letters, shown below in their upper- and lower-case forms. Be aware that some letters look like English letters but are pronounced very differently, such as **B**, which is pronounced v; and **P**, pronounced r. As in English, how letters are pronounced is also influenced by the way they are combined, for example the **ου** combination is pronounced u as in 'put', and **οι** is pronounced ee as in 'feet'.

Α α	a	as in 'father'
Β β	v	as in 'vine'
Γ γ	gh	a softer, throaty 'g', or
	y	as in 'yes'
Δ δ	dh	as in 'there'
Ε ε	e	as in 'egg'
Ζ ζ	z	as in 'zoo'
Η η	i	as in 'feet'
Θ θ	th	as in 'throw'
Ι ι	i	as in 'feet'
Κ κ	k	as in 'kite'
Λ λ	l	as in 'leg'
Μ μ	m	as in 'man'
Ν ν	n	as in 'net'
Ξ ξ	x	as in 'ox'
Ο ο	o	as in 'hot'
Π π	p	as in 'pup'
Ρ ρ	r	as in 'road', slightly trilled
Σ σ, ς	s	as in 'sand'
Τ τ	t	as in 'tap'
Υ υ	i	as in 'feet'
Φ φ	f	as in 'find'
Χ χ	kh	as the 'ch' in the Scottish 'loch', or
	h	like a rough 'h'
Ψ ψ	ps	as in 'lapse'
Ω ω	o	as in 'hot'

Note that the letter **Σ** has two forms for the lower case – **σ** and **ς**. The second one is used at the end of words. The Greek **question mark** is represented with the English equivalent of a semicolon (;).

What would you recommend?
Τι θα συνιστούσες; ti tha si·ni·*stu*·ses

What's in that dish?
Τι περιέχει αυτό το φαγητό; ti pe·ri·*e*·hi af·*to* to fa·ghi·*to*

That was delicious.
Ηταν νοστιμότατο! *i*·tan no·sti·*mo*·ta·to

Cheers!
Εις υγείαν! is i·*yi*·an

Please bring the bill.
Το λογαριασμό, παρακαλώ. to lo·ghar·ya·*zmo* pa·ra·ka·*lo*

Key Words

appetisers	ορεκτικά	o·rek·ti·*ka*
bar	μπαρ	bar
beef	βοδινό	vo·dhi·*no*
beer	μπύρα	*bi*·ra
bottle	μπουκάλι	bu·*ka*·li
bowl	μπωλ	bol
bread	ψωμί	pso·*mi*
breakfast	πρόγευμα	*pro*·yev·ma
cafe	καφετέρια	ka·fe·*te*·ri·a
cheese	τυρί	ti·*ri*
chicken	κοτόπουλο	ko·*to*·pu·lo
coffee	καφές	ka·*fes*
cold	κρυωμένος	kri·o·*me*·nos
cream	κρέμα	*kre*·ma
delicatessen	ντελικατέσεν	de·li·ka·*te*·sen
desserts	επιδόρπια	e·pi·*dhor*·pi·a
dinner	δείπνο	*dhip*·no
egg	αυγό	av·*gho*
fish	ψάρι	*psa*·ri
food	φαγητό	fa·yi·*to*
fork	πιρούνι	pi·*ru*·ni
fruit	φρούτα	*fru*·ta
glass	ποτήρι	po·*ti*·ri
grocery store	οπωροπωλείο	o·po·ro·po·*li*·o
herb	βότανο	*vo*·ta·no
high chair	καρέκλα για μωρά	ka·*re*·kla yia mo·*ra*
hot	ζεστός	ze·*stos*
juice	χυμός	hi·*mos*
knife	μαχαίρι	ma·*he*·ri
lamb	αρνί	ar·*ni*
lunch	μεσημεριανό φαγητό	me·si·me·ria·*no* fa·yi·*to*
main courses	κύρια φαγητά	*ki*·ri·a fa·yi·*ta*
market	αγορά	a·gho·*ra*
menu	μενού	me·*nu*
milk	γάλα	*gha*·la
nut	καρύδι	ka·*ri*·dhi
oil	λάδι	*la*·dhi
pepper	πιπέρι	pi·*pe*·ri
plate	πιάτο	*pia*·to
pork	χοιρινό	hi·ri·*no*
restaurant	εστιατόριο	e·sti·a·*to*·ri·o
salt	αλάτι	a·*la*·ti
soft drink	αναψυκτικό	a·nap·psik·ti·*ko*
spoon	κουτάλι	ku·*ta*·li
sugar	ζάχαρη	*za*·kha·ri
tea	τσάι	*tsa*·i
vegetable	λαχανικά	la·kha·ni·*ka*
vegetarian	χορτοφάγος	khor·to·*fa*·ghos
vinegar	ξύδι	*ksi*·dhi
water	νερό	ne·*ro*
(red) wine	(κόκκινο) κρασί	(*ko*·ki·no) kra·*si*
(white) wine	(άσπρο) κρασί	(*a*·spro) kra·*si*
with/without	με/χωρίς	me/kho·*ris*

KEY PATTERNS

To get by in Greek, mix and match these simple patterns with words of your choice:

When's (the next bus)?
Πότε είναι (το επόμενο λεωφορείο); *po*·te *i*·ne (to e·*po*·me·no le·o·fo·*ri*·o)

Where's (the station)?
Πού είναι (ο σταθμός); pu *i*·ne (o stath·*mos*)

I'm looking for (Ampfilohos).
Ψάχνω για (το Αμφίλοχος). *psakh*·no yia (to am·*fi*·lo·khos)

Do you have (a local map)?
Εχετε οδικό (τοπικό χάρτη); *e*·he·te o·dhi·*ko* (to·pi·*ko khar*·ti)

Is there a (lift)?
Υπάρχει (ασανσέρ); i·*par*·hi (a·san·*ser*)

Can I (try it on)?
Μπορώ να (το προβάρω); bo·*ro* na (to pro·*va*·ro)

I have (a reservation).
Εχω (κλείσει δωμάτιο). *e*·kho (*kli*·si dho·*ma*·ti·o)

I'd like (to hire a car).
Θα ήθελα (να ενοικιάσω ένα αυτοκίνητο). tha *i*·the·la (na e·ni·ki·*a*·so *e*·na af·to·*ki*·ni·to)

EMERGENCIES

Help!	Βοήθεια!	vo·*i*·thya
Go away!	Φύγε!	*fi*·ye
I'm lost.	Εχω χαθεί.	e·kho kha·*thi*
There's been an accident.	Εγινε ατύχημα.	*ey*·i·ne a·*ti*·hi·ma
Call ...!	Φωνάξτε ...!	fo·*nak*·ste ...
a doctor	ένα γιατρό	e·na yi·a·*tro*
the police	την αστυνομία	tin a·sti·no·*mi*·a

I'm ill.

Είμαι άρρωστος.	*i*·me *a*·ro·stos (m)
Είμαι άρρωστη.	*i*·me *a*·ro·st (f)

It hurts here.
Πονάει εδώ. — po·*na*·i e·*dho*

I'm allergic to (antibiotics).
Είμαι αλλεργικός/ αλλεργική (στα αντιβιωτικά). — *i*·me a·ler·yi·*kos*/ a·ler·yi·*ki* (sta an·di·vi·o·ti·*ka*) (m/f)

NUMBERS

1	ένας/μία ένα	e·nas/ *mi*·a (m/f) *e*·na (n)
2	δύο	*dhi*·o
3	τρεις τρία	tris (m&f) *tri*·a (n)
4	τέσσερεις τέσσερα	*te*·se·ris (m&f) *te*·se·ra (n)
5	πέντε	*pen*·de
6	έξη	*e*·xi
7	επτά	ep·*ta*
8	οχτώ	oh·*to*
9	εννέα	e·*ne*·a
10	δέκα	*dhe*·ka
20	είκοσι	*ik*·o·si
30	τριάντα	tri·*an*·da
40	σαράντα	sa·*ran*·da
50	πενήντα	pe·*nin*·da
60	εξήντα	ek·*sin*·da
70	εβδομήντα	ev·dho·*min*·da
80	ογδόντα	ogh·*dhon*·da
90	ενενήντα	e·ne·*nin*·da
100	εκατό	e·ka·*to*
1000	χίλιοι/χίλιες χίλια	*hi*·li·i/*hi*·li·ez (m/f) *hi*·li·a (n)

SHOPPING & SERVICES

I'd like to buy ...
Θέλω ν' αγοράσω ... — *the*·lo na·gho·*ra*·so ...

Question Words

How?	Πώς;	pos
What?	Τι;	ti
When?	Πότε;	*po*·te
Where?	Πού;	pu
Who?	Ποιος; Ποια; Ποιο;	pi·*os* (m) pi·*a* (f) pi·*o* (n)
Why?	Γιατί;	yi·a·*ti*

I'm just looking.
Απλώς κοιτάζω. — ap·*los* ki·*ta*·zo

May I see it?
Μπορώ να το δω; — bo·*ro* na to dho

I don't like it.
Δεν μου αρέσει. — dhen mu a·*re*·si

How much is it?
Πόσο κάνει; — *po*·so *ka*·ni

It's too expensive.
Είναι πολύ ακριβό. — *i*·ne po·*li* a·kri·*vo*

Can you lower the price?
Μπορείς να κατεβάσεις την τιμή; — bo·*ris* na ka·te·*va*·sis tin ti·*mi*

ATM	αυτόματη μηχανή χρημάτων	af·*to*·ma·ti mi·kha·*ni* khri·*ma*·ton
bank	τράπεζα	*tra*·pe·za
credit card	πιστωτική κάρτα	pi·sto·ti·*ki* *kar*·ta
mobile phone	κινητό	ki·ni·*to*
post office	ταχυδρομείο	ta·hi·dhro·*mi*·o
toilet	τουαλέτα	tu·a·*le*·ta
tourist office	τουριστικό γραφείο	tu·ri·sti·*ko* ghra·*fi*·o
wi-fi password	wi-fi κωδικό	wi-fi ko·dhi·*ko*

TIME & DATES

What time is it?	Τι ώρα είναι;	ti o·ra *i*·ne
It's (2 o'clock).	είναι (δύο η ώρα).	*i*·ne (*dhi*·o i *o*·ra)
It's half past (10).	(Δέκα) και μισή.	(*dhe*·ka) ke mi·*si*

today	σήμερα	*si*·me·ra
tomorrow	αύριο	*av*·ri·o
yesterday	χθες	hthes
morning	πρωί	pro·*i*
(this) afternoon	(αυτό το) απόγευμα	(af·*to* to) a·*po*·yev·ma
evening	βράδυ	*vra*·dhi

Signs

ΕΙΣΟΔΟΣ	**Entry**
ΕΞΟΔΟΣ	**Exit**
ΠΛΗΡΟΦΟΡΙΕΣ	**Information**
ΑΝΟΙΧΤΟ	**Open**
ΚΛΕΙΣΤΟ	**Closed**
ΑΠΑΓΟΡΕΥΕΤΑΙ	**Prohibited**
ΑΣΤΥΝΟΜΙΑ	**Police**
ΑΣΤΥΝΟΜΙΚΟΣ ΣΤΑΘΜΟΣ	**Police Station**
ΓΥΝΑΙΚΩΝ	**Toilets (Women)**
ΑΝΔΡΩΝ	**Toilets (Men)**

Monday	Δευτέρα	dhef·*te*·ra
Tuesday	Τρίτη	*tri*·ti
Wednesday	Τετάρτη	te·*tar*·ti
Thursday	Πέμπτη	*pemp*·ti
Friday	Παρασκευή	pa·ras·ke·*vi*
Saturday	Σάββατο	*sa*·va·to
Sunday	Κυριακή	ky·ri·a·*ki*

January	Ιανουάριος	ia·nu·*ar*·i·os
February	Φεβρουάριος	fev·ru·*ar*·i·os
March	Μάρτιος	*mar*·ti·os
April	Απρίλιος	a·*pri*·li·os
May	Μάιος	*mai*·os
June	Ιούνιος	i·*u*·ni·os
July	Ιούλιος	i·*u*·li·os
August	Αύγουστος	*av*·ghus·tos
September	Σεπτέμβριος	sep·*tem*·vri·os
October	Οκτώβριος	ok·*to*·vri·os
November	Νοέμβριος	no·*em*·vri·os
December	Δεκέμβριος	dhe·*kem*·vri·os

TRANSPORT

Public Transport

boat	πλοίο	*pli*·o
city bus	αστικό	a·sti·*ko*
intercity bus	λεωφορείο	le·o·fo·*ri*·o
plane	αεροπλάνο	ae·ro·*pla*·no
train	τραίνο	*tre*·no

Where do I buy a ticket?
Πού αγοράζω εισιτήριο; pu a·gho·*ra*·zo i·si·*ti*·ri·o

I want to go to ...
Θέλω να πάω στο/στη ... *the*·lo na *pao* sto/sti...

What time does it leave?
Τι ώρα φεύγει; ti o·ra *fev*·yi

Does it stop at (Iraklio)?
Σταματάει στο (Ηράκλειο); sta·ma·*ta*·i sto (i·*ra*·kli·o)

I'd like to get off at (Iraklio).
Θα ήθελα να κατεβώ στο (Ηράκλειο). tha *i*·the·la na ka·te·*vo* sto (i·*ra*·kli·o)

I'd like (a) ...	Θα ήθελα (ένα) ...	tha *i*·the·la (*e*·na) ...
1st class	πρώτη θέση	*pro*·ti *the*·si
2nd class	δεύτερη θέση	*def*·te·ri *the*·si
one-way ticket	απλό εισιτήριο	a·*plo* i·si·*ti*·ri·o
return ticket	εισιτήριο με επιστροφή	i·si·*ti*·ri·o me e·pi·stro·*fi*
cancelled	ακυρώθηκε	a·ki·*ro*·thi·ke
delayed	καθυστέρησε	ka·thi·*ste*·ri·se
platform	πλατφόρμα	plat·*for*·ma
ticket office	εκδοτήριο εισιτηρίων	ek·dho·*ti*·ri·o i·si·ti·*ri*·on
timetable	δρομολόγιο	dhro·mo·*lo*·gio
train station	σταθμός τρένου	stath·*mos* *tre*·nu

Driving & Cycling

I'd like to hire a ...	Θα ήθελα να νοικιάσω ...	tha *i*·the·la na ni·ki·*a*·so ...
car	ένα αυτοκίνητο	e·na af·to·*ki*·ni·to
4WD	ένα τέσσερα επί τέσσερα	e·na *tes*·se·ra e·*pi* *tes*·se·ra
jeep	ένα τζιπ	e·na tzip
motorbike	μια μοτοσυκλέττα	*mya* mo·to·si·*klet*·ta
bicycle	ένα ποδήλατο	e·na po·*dhi*·la·to

Do I need a helmet?
Χρειάζομαι κράνος; khri·*a*·zo·me *kra*·nos

Is this the road to ...?
Αυτός είναι ο δρόμος για ... af·*tos* *i*·ne o *dhro*·mos ya ...

Can I park here?
Μπορώ να παρκάρω εδώ; bo·*ro* na par·*ka*·ro e·*dho*

The car/motorbike has broken down (at ...).
Το αυτοκίνητο/ η μοτοσυκλέττα χάλασε στο ... to af·to·*ki*·ni·to/ i mo·to·si·*klet*·ta *kha*·la·se sto ...

I have a flat tyre.
Επαθα λάστιχο. e·pa·tha *la*·sti·cho

I've run out of petrol.
Εμεινα από βενζίνη. e·mi·na a·*po* ven·*zi*·ni

GLOSSARY

For culinary terms, see Eat & Drink Like a Local (p47).

Achaean civilisation – see *Mycenaean civilisation*

acropolis – highest point of an ancient city

agia (f), agios (m), agii (pl) – saint(s)

agora – commercial area of an ancient city; shopping precinct in modern Greece

agrimi – endemic Cretan animal with large horns similar to a wild goat; also known as the *kri-kri*

amphora – large two-handled vase in which wine or oil was kept

basilica – early Christian church

bouzouki – stringed lute-like instrument associated with *rembetika* music

Byzantine Empire – characterised by the merging of Hellenistic culture and Christianity and named after Byzantium, the city on the Bosphorus that became the capital of the Roman Empire in AD 324; when the Roman Empire was formally divided in AD 395, Rome went into decline and the eastern capital, renamed Constantinople after Emperor Constantine I, flourished; the Byzantine Empire (324 BC–AD 1453) dissolved after the fall of Constantinople to the Turks in 1453

capital – top of a column

Classical period – era in which the Greek city-states reached the height of their wealth and power after the defeat of the Persians in the 5th century BC; the Classical period (480–323 BC) ended with the decline of the city-states as a result of the Peloponnesian Wars, and the expansionist aspirations of Philip II, King of Macedon (r 359–336 BC) and his son, Alexander the Great (r 336–323 BC)

Corinthian – order of Greek architecture recognisable by columns with bell-shaped capitals with sculpted elaborate ornaments based on acanthus leaves; see also *Doric* and *Ionic*

dark age (1200–800 BC) – period in which Greece was under Dorian rule

domatio (s), domatia (pl) – room, often in a private home; a cheap form of accommodation

Dorians – Hellenic warriors who invaded Greece around 1200 BC, demolishing the city-states and destroying the *Mycenaean civilisation*; heralded Greece's *dark age*, when the artistic and cultural advancements of the Mycenaean and *Minoan civilisations* were abandoned; the Dorians later developed into land-holding aristocrats, encouraging the resurgence of independent city-states led by wealthy aristocrats

Doric – order of Greek architecture characterised by a column that has no base, a fluted shaft and a relatively plain capital, when compared with the flourishes evident on *Ionic* and *Corinthian* capitals

Ellada or Ellas – see *Hellas*

ELPA – Elliniki Leschi Aftokinitou kai Periigiseon; Greek motoring and touring club

ELTA – Ellinika Tahydromia; Greek post office organisation

EOS – Ellinikos Orivatikos Syllogos; the association of Greek Mountaineering Clubs

EOT – Ellinikos Organismos Tourismou; main tourist office (has offices in most major towns), known abroad as *GNTO* (Greek National Tourist Organisation)

estiatorio – restaurant serving ready-made food as well as à la carte

Geometric period – the period (1200–800 BC) characterised by pottery decorated with geometric designs; sometimes referred to as Greece's *dark age*

GNTO – Greek National Tourist Organisation; see also *EOT*

Hellas – the Greek name for Greece; also known as Ellada or Ellas

Hellenistic period – prosperous, influential period (323–146 BC) of Greek civilisation ushered in by Alexander the Great's empire-building and lasting until the Roman sacking of Corinth

hora – main town, usually on an island

Ionic – order of Greek architecture characterised by a column with truncated flutes and capitals with ornaments resembling scrolls; see also *Doric* and *Corinthian*

kastro – walled-in town; also describes a fortress or castle

Koine – Greek language used in pre-Byzantine times; the language of the church liturgy

kouros – male statue of the Archaic period, characterised by a stiff body posture and enigmatic smile

kri-kri – endemic Cretan animal with large horns similar to a wild goat; also known as the *agrimi*

KTEL – Kino Tamio Eispraxeon Leoforion; national bus cooperative, which runs all long-distance bus services

leoforos – avenue

libation – in ancient Greece, wine or food that was offered to the gods

Linear A – Minoan script; so far undeciphered

Linear B – Mycenaean script; has been deciphered

lyra – small harp-like instrument or lyre, played on the knee; common in Cretan and Pontian music

mantinadha (s), mandinadhes (pl) – a style of traditional Cretan rhyming couplets

megaron – central room or quarters of a Mycenaean palace

meltemi – dry northerly wind that blows throughout much of Greece in the summer

mezedhopoleio – restaurant specialising in *mezedhes*

Minoan civilisation – Bronze Age (3000–1200 BC) culture of Crete named after the mythical King Minos, and characterised by pottery and metalwork of great beauty and artisanship; it had three periods: Protopalatial (3400–2100 BC), Neopalatial (2100–1580 BC) and Postpalatial (1580–1200 BC)

mitata – round stone shepherd's huts

moni – monastery or convent

Mycenaean civilisation – first great civilisation (1900–1100 BC) of the Greek mainland, characterised by powerful independent city-states ruled by kings; also known as the *Achaean civilisation*

New Democracy – Nea Dimodratia; conservative political party

necropolis – literally 'city of the dead'; ancient cemetery

nisi – island

nymphaeum – in ancient Greece, building containing a fountain and often dedicated to nymphs

odeion – ancient Greek indoor theatre

odos – street

OTE – Organismos Tilepikoinonion Ellados; Greece's major telephone carrier

ouzerie – place that serves ouzo and light snacks

Panagia – Mother of God or Virgin Mary; name frequently used for churches

paralia – waterfront

pediment – triangular section, often filled with sculpture above the columns, found at the front and back of a classical Greek temple

periptero (s), periptera (pl) – street kiosk

peristyle – columns surrounding a building, usually a temple or courtyard

pithos (s), pithoi (pl) – large Minoan storage jar or urn

plateia – square

propylon (s), propylaia (pl) – elaborately built main entrance to an ancient city or sanctuary; a *propylon* had one gateway and a *propylaia* more than one

prytaneion – the administrative centre of the city-state

rembetika – blues songs, commonly associated with the underworld of the 1920s

rhyton – another name for a *libation* vessel

rizitika – traditional, patriotic songs of western Crete

stoa – long colonnaded building, usually in an *agora*; used as a meeting place and shelter in ancient Greece

taverna – the most common type of traditional restaurant that serves food and wine

tholos – Mycenaean tomb shaped like a beehive

Behind the Scenes

SEND US YOUR FEEDBACK

We love to hear from travellers – your comments keep us on our toes and help make our books better. Our well-travelled team reads every word on what you loved or loathed about this book. Although we cannot reply individually to your submissions, we always guarantee that your feedback goes straight to the appropriate authors, in time for the next edition. Each person who sends us information is thanked in the next edition – the most useful submissions are rewarded with a selection of digital PDF chapters.

Visit **lonelyplanet.com/contact** to submit your updates and suggestions or to ask for help. Our award-winning website also features inspirational travel stories, news and discussions.

Note: We may edit, reproduce and incorporate your comments in Lonely Planet products such as guidebooks, websites and digital products, so let us know if you don't want your comments reproduced or your name acknowledged. For a copy of our privacy policy visit lonelyplanet.com/privacy.

OUR READERS

Many thanks to the travellers who used the last edition and wrote to us with helpful hints, useful advice and interesting anecdotes: Charilaos Akasiadis, Jack Bairner, Simon Berwick, Jan Bretschneider, Natasha Cole, Nicolas Combremont, Martin Dolheguy, Mark Healey, Chris Hudson, David Hyams, Kevin Johnson, Imke Lerner, Michael Linnard, Veronica Lopes van Balen, Andrew Payne, Thomas Pellier, Michael Poesen, Dan Rigby, Rob Ryder, Robert Schindler, Katja Schmahl, Sandra Steinhause, Ian Webber, Selena Whitehead, John Wickkiser, Rolf Wrelf, Cathy Wright

WRITER THANKS

Andrea Schulte-Peevers

Heartfelt thank yous to Kerstin Göllrich for her patience, curiosity, stamina and awesome driving skills; Johannes Bolz for literally going the extra mile for me in the Kritsa Gorge; Konstantinos and Natalie Zivas for wonderful insider tips on Elounda and the north coast, and father Vaggelis for his kitchen wizardry; Alaska Klaus for his insights into hiking the E4; Margarita Kurowska and Jutta Berger for keeping things under control on the home front; and David for being with me in spirit.

Trent Holden

First up, a huge thanks to the destination editor, Brana Vladisavljevic, not only for commissioning me on this title, but for all her work at Lonely Planet over the past 15 years. You will be missed! Also sending out my gratitude to the Cretan people who make this island so special with their humbling hospitality, good humour and willingness to help out at all times. Finally lots of love to my fiancé Kate Morgan, and to my family and friends.

Kate Morgan

Huge thanks to amazing destination editor Brana Vladisavljevic for commissioning me to work on Crete, Lonely Planet won't be the same without you. Thank you to Despina in Hania for all of your assistance, to the staff at the Hania tourist information office for your help and to all of the amazing Cretans I met along the way – your generosity and hospitality is unforgettable. And, as always, thank you to my fiancé Trent for being the best travel companion and driving me all over Hania.

Kevin Raub

Thanks to Brana Vladisavljevic and all my fellow partners in crime at Lonely Planet. Thanks also to those I met on the road: Kjetil Jikiun, Giorges Kteniadakis, Andria Mitsakis, Iossif Serafimidis, Dr Emmanuel Prokopkis and the nurses at Pagni, Lydia and Nikos, and the brews of Kykao and Solo.

ACKNOWLEDGEMENTS

Climate map data adapted from Peel MC, Finlayson BL & McMahon TA (2007) 'Updated World Map of the Köppen-Geiger Climate Classification', *Hydrology and Earth System Sciences*, 11, 1633–44.

Illustrated Highlight p180-1 by Javier Martinez Zarracina

Cover photograph: Agios Nikolaos, Vladimir Sklyarov/Getty Images©

THIS BOOK

This 7th edition of Lonely Planet's *Crete* guidebook was curated by Andrea Schulte-Peevers and researched and written by Andrea, Trent Holden, Kate Morgan and Kevin Raub. The previous two editions were written by Alexis Averbuck, Kate Armstrong, Korina Miller, Richard Waters, Andrea Schulte-Peevers, Chris Deliso and Des Hannigan. This guidebook was produced by the following:

Destination Editor Brana Vladisavljevic

Senior Product Editor Elizabeth Jones

Regional Senior Cartographer Anthony Phelan

Product Editor Ross Taylor

Book Designer Ania Bartoszek

Cartographer David Connolly

Assisting Editors Sarah Bailey, James Bainbridge, Judith Bamber, Janice Bird, Samantha Cook, Melanie Dankel, Victoria Harrison, Jennifer Hattam, Rosie Nicholson, Charlotte Orr, Monique Perrin, Christopher Pitts, Tamara Sheward

Cover Researcher Naomi Parker

Thanks to Jessica Rose, Georgia Tsarouhas

Index

Map Pages **000**
Photo Pages **000**

Map Pages **000**
Photo Pages **000**

Map Legend

Sights

- Beach
- Bird Sanctuary
- Buddhist
- Castle/Palace
- Christian
- Confucian
- Hindu
- Islamic
- Jain
- Jewish
- Monument
- Museum/Gallery/Historic Building
- Ruin
- Shinto
- Sikh
- Taoist
- Winery/Vineyard
- Zoo/Wildlife Sanctuary
- Other Sight

Activities, Courses & Tours

- Bodysurfing
- Diving
- Canoeing/Kayaking
- Course/Tour
- Sento Hot Baths/Onsen
- Skiing
- Snorkelling
- Surfing
- Swimming/Pool
- Walking
- Windsurfing
- Other Activity

Sleeping

- Sleeping
- Camping
- Hut/Shelter

Eating

- Eating

Drinking & Nightlife

- Drinking & Nightlife
- Cafe

Entertainment

- Entertainment

Shopping

- Shopping

Information

- Bank
- Embassy/Consulate
- Hospital/Medical
- Internet
- Police
- Post Office
- Telephone
- Toilet
- Tourist Information
- Other Information

Geographic

- Beach
- Gate
- Hut/Shelter
- Lighthouse
- Lookout
- Mountain/Volcano
- Oasis
- Park
- Pass
- Picnic Area
- Waterfall

Population

- Capital (National)
- Capital (State/Province)
- City/Large Town
- Town/Village

Transport

- Airport
- Border crossing
- Bus
- Cable car/Funicular
- Cycling
- Ferry
- Metro station
- Monorail
- Parking
- Petrol station
- S-Bahn/Subway station
- Taxi
- T-bane/Tunnelbana station
- Train station/Railway
- Tram
- U-Bahn/Underground station
- Other Transport

Routes

- Tollway
- Freeway
- Primary
- Secondary
- Tertiary
- Lane
- Unsealed road
- Road under construction
- Plaza/Mall
- Steps
- Tunnel
- Pedestrian overpass
- Walking Tour
- Walking Tour detour
- Path/Walking Trail

Boundaries

- International
- State/Province
- Disputed
- Regional/Suburb
- Marine Park
- Cliff
- Wall

Hydrography

- River, Creek
- Intermittent River
- Canal
- Water
- Dry/Salt/Intermittent Lake
- Reef

Areas

- Airport/Runway
- Beach/Desert
- Cemetery (Christian)
- Cemetery (Other)
- Glacier
- Mudflat
- Park/Forest
- Sight (Building)
- Sportsground
- Swamp/Mangrove

Note: Not all symbols displayed above appear on the maps in this book

OUR STORY

A beat-up old car, a few dollars in the pocket and a sense of adventure. In 1972 that's all Tony and Maureen Wheeler needed for the trip of a lifetime – across Europe and Asia overland to Australia. It took several months, and at the end – broke but inspired – they sat at their kitchen table writing and stapling together their first travel guide, *Across Asia on the Cheap*. Within a week they'd sold 1500 copies. Lonely Planet was born.

Today, Lonely Planet has offices in Franklin, London, Melbourne, Oakland, Dublin, Beijing and Delhi, with more than 600 staff and writers. We share Tony's belief that 'a great guidebook should do three things: inform, educate and amuse'.

OUR WRITERS

Andrea Schulte-Peevers

Lasithi Born and raised in Germany and educated in London and at UCLA, Andrea has travelled the distance to the moon and back in her visits to some 75 countries. She has earned her living as a professional travel writer for over two decades and authored or contributed to nearly 100 Lonely Planet titles as well as to newspapers, magazines and websites around the world. Andrea's destination expertise is especially strong when it comes to Germany, Dubai and the UAE, Crete and the Caribbean Islands. She makes her home in Berlin. Andrea also wrote the Plan, Understand and Survival Guide sections.

Trent Holden

Rethymno An Australian-based writer, Trent has worked for Lonely Planet since 2005. He's covered 30 plus guidebooks across Asia, Africa and Australia. With a penchant for megacities, Trent is in his element when assigned to cover a nation's capital – the more chaotic the better – to unearth cool bars, art, street food and underground subculture. On the flipside, he also writes books on idyllic tropical islands across Asia, in between going on safari to national parks in Africa and the subcontinent. When not travelling, Trent works as a freelance editor and reviewer, and spends all his money catching live gigs. You can catch him on Twitter @hombreholden

Kate Morgan

Hania Having worked for Lonely Planet for over a decade now, Kate has been fortunate enough to cover plenty of ground working as a travel writer on destinations such as Shanghai, Japan, India, Russia, Zimbabwe, the Philippines and Phuket. She has done stints living in London, Paris and Osaka, but these days is based in one of her favourite regions in the world – Victoria, Australia. In between travelling the world and writing about it, Kate enjoys spending time at home working as a freelance editor.

Kevin Raub

Iraklio An Atlanta native, Kevin started his career as a music journalist in New York, working for *Men's Journal* and *Rolling Stone* magazines. He ditched the rock 'n' roll lifestyle for travel writing and has contributed to more than 95 Lonely Planet guides, focused mainly on Brazil, Chile, Colombia, USA, India, the Caribbean and Portugal. Kevin also contributes to a variety of travel magazines in both the USA and UK. Along the way, the self-confessed hophead is in constant search of wildly high IBUs in local beers. Follow him on Twitter and Instagram @RaubOnTheRoad.

Published by Lonely Planet Global Limited
CRN 554153
7th edition – February 2020
ISBN 978 1 78657 579 1
© Lonely Planet 2020 Photographs © as indicated 2020
10 9 8 7 6 5 4 3 2 1
Printed in China

Although the authors and Lonely Planet have taken all reasonable care in preparing this book, we make no warranty about the accuracy or completeness of its content and, to the maximum extent permitted, disclaim all liability arising from its use.

All rights reserved. No part of this publication may be copied, stored in a retrieval system, or transmitted in any form by any means, electronic, mechanical, recording or otherwise, except brief extracts for the purpose of review, and no part of this publication may be sold or hired, without the written permission of the publisher. Lonely Planet and the Lonely Planet logo are trademarks of Lonely Planet and are registered in the US Patent and Trademark Office and in other countries. Lonely Planet does not allow its name or logo to be appropriated by commercial establishments, such as retailers, restaurants or hotels. Please let us know of any misuses: lonelyplanet.com/ip.